Lecture Notes in Computer Science 7830

Commenced Publication in 1973
Founding and Former Series Editors:
Gerhard Goos, Juris Hartmanis, and Jan van Leeuwen

Joerg Doerr   Andreas L. Opdahl (Eds.)

Requirements Engineering: Foundation for Software Quality

19th International Working Conference, REFSQ 2013
Essen, Germany, April 8-11, 2013
Proceedings

 Springer

Volume Editors

Joerg Doerr
Fraunhofer IESE
Information Systems Division
Fraunhofer-Platz 1
67663 Kaiserslautern, Germany
E-mail: joerg.doerr@iese.fraunhofer.de

Andreas L. Opdahl
University of Bergen
Department of Information Science
and Media Studies
Fosswinckelsgate 7
5020 Bergen, Norway
E-mail: andreas.opdahl@uib.no

ISSN 0302-9743   e-ISSN 1611-3349
ISBN 978-3-642-37421-0   e-ISBN 978-3-642-37422-7
DOI 10.1007/978-3-642-37422-7
Springer Heidelberg Dordrecht London New York

Library of Congress Control Number: Applied for

CR Subject Classification (1998): D.2, K.6.3-4, H.4, D.3, I.2.7

LNCS Sublibrary: SL 2 – Programming and Software Engineering

Typesetting: Camera-ready by author, data conversion by Scientific Publishing Services, Chennai, India

Printed on acid-free paper

Springer is part of Springer Science+Business Media (www.springer.com)

Preface

Requirements engineering (RE) is a central prerequisite for developing high-quality software systems and services. The REFSQ — Requirements Engineering: Foundation for Software Quality — working conference series is well established as one of the leading international fora for discussing RE and its many relations to quality. The first REFSQ took place in 1994 and, since 2010, it has been organized as a stand-alone event.

REFSQ conferences have a long tradition for being highly *structured and interactive*. Each session is organized to provoke discussion among the presenters of papers, pre-assigned discussants, and all the other participants. For each paper, time is allocated so that the discussion is at least as long as the presentation. The series also highlights *requirements engineering in practice* by bringing together researchers, users, and practitioners in order to develop a better understanding of the practice of RE, to contribute to improved RE practice, as well as to share knowledge and experiences.

This LNCS volume contains the papers that were accepted for presentation at *REFSQ 2013* — the 19th International Working Conference on Requirements Engineering: Foundation for Software Quality — that took place in Essen, Germany, during April 8–11, 2013. For REFSQ 2013, we chose *Interdisciplinary RE* as the special theme. In addition to general papers on RE and quality, we encouraged submissions that highlighted the interplay of RE with related disciplines such as software architecture, quality assurance, user interface design, project management, and agile software development.

The Call for Papers attracted 105 submissions from authors in both industry and academia in 29 different countries on all six inhabited continents. After eliminating bogus and clearly out-of-scope submissions, 82 papers were sent out for reviewing, of which 35 were marked as belonging to the special theme *Interdisciplinary RE*. Each of them was evaluated carefully by at least three reviewers, before the online discussion phase, in which senior Program Committee members acted as discussion drivers for the most critical papers. Eleven members and two co-chairs also attended the Program Committee meeting in Essen on January 11 to discuss the 45 most promising submissions in even greater detail. The Program Committee selected 28 high-quality papers to be presented at REFSQ 2013: 23 full papers and five short ones. Among the full papers, there were three industrial experience reports and 20 regular research papers. Of the short papers, one was a problem statement and four were research previews. The acceptance rate was thus 28% for long papers and 34% overall.

The resulting program from REFSQ'2013 was organized in the following thematic sessions: *RE & Architecture, Natural Language Requirements, RE & Quality, Traceability, RE & Business/Goals, RE & Software Development, RE in Practice,* and *Product Lines and Product Management*. It thereby reflects how RE encompasses human and organizational issues in addition to technical aspects when developing quality software systems and services.

The research program also featured a keynote by Jan Bosch, a professor at Chalmers University of Technology in Gothenburg, Sweden, with many years' experience from industry. The theme of his talk was customer experimentation and its relation to requirements engineering. The conference also followed-up the positive experiences from earlier REFSQ conferences with a variety of activities such as a practitioner/industrial track, an empirical track including a live experiment and an empirical fair, a doctoral symposium, and a poster forum with posters both from the doctoral symposium and presenting other new research. REFSQ 2013 was also associated with the following three workshops:

CreaRE — the Third Workshop on Creativity in Requirements Engineering, organized by Maya Daneva, Andrea Herrmann, Anne Hoffmann, and Kurt Schneider; *IWSPM13 — the 7th International Workshop on Software Product Management*, organized by Richard Berntsson Svensson, Inge van de Weerd, and Krzysztof Wnuk; and *RePriCo13 — the 4th International Workshop on Requirements Prioritization and Communication*, organized by Benedikt Krams and Sixten Schockert.

We thank the members of the international Program Committee and their sub-reviewers for carefully reviewing the submitted papers. We devote special thanks to those committe members who travelled to attend the Program Committee meeting in Essen. Your dedicated work was vital for putting together a high-quality working conference. We also thank the REFSQ Steering Committee, and the other REFSQ 2013 Chairs (listed on the next page) for all their useful input to the organization process. We also thank the organizers of the associated workshops (listed above).

Last, but not least, we would like to thank PALUNO at the University of Duisbug-Essen for organizing REFSQ 2013, in particular General Chair Klaus Pohl and Organizers Roxana Klippert and Tobias Kaufmann, who dealt with all practical matters quickly and efficiently, as well as Vanessa Stricker, who is no longer formally involved in the organization after several years of service, but who nevertheless provided prompt and useful advice whenever needed.

Along with the REFSQ 2013 organizers we also want to thank the conference sponsors, whose logos are shown on a later page!

February 2013

Joerg Doerr
Andreas L. Opdahl

Conference Organization

General Chair

Klaus Pohl — University of Duisburg-Essen, Germany

Program Co-chairs

Joerg Doerr — Fraunhofer IESE, Germany
Andreas L. Opdahl — University of Bergen, Norway

Organizing Team

Tobias Kaufmann — University of Duisburg-Essen, Germany
Stella Roxana Klippert — University of Duisburg-Essen, Germany

Industry Track Co-chairs

Kai Petersen — Blekinge Institute of Technology, Sweden
Thorsten Weyer — University of Duisburg-Essen, Germany

Workshop Co-chairs

Raul Mazo — University of Paris 1 — Sorbonne, France
Camille Salinesi — University of Paris 1 — Sorbonne, France

Doctoral Symposium Co-chairs

Oscar Pastor — Polytechnical University of Valencia, Spain
Roel Wieringa — University of Twente, The Netherlands

Empirical Track Co-chairs

Daniel M. Berry — University of Waterloo, Canada
Norbert Seyff — University of Zurich, Switzerland

Steering Committee

Patrick Heymans (Chair)	University of Namur, Belgium
Pete Sawyer (Vice Chair)	Lancaster University, UK
Daniel M. Berry	University of Waterloo, Canada
Daniela Damian	University of Victoria, Canada
Joerg Doerr	Fraunhofer IESE, Germany
Xavier Franch	University Politècnica de Catalunya, Spain
Martin Glinz	University of Zurich, Switzerland
Andreas L. Opdahl	University of Bergen, Norway
Barbara Paech	University of Heidelberg, Germany
Anne Persson	University of Skövde, Sweden
Bjorn Regnell	Lund University, Sweden
Camille Salinesi	University of Paris 1 — Sorbonne, France
Inge van de Weerd	Vrije Universiteit Amsterdam, The Netherlands
Roel Wieringa	University of Twente, The Netherlands

Program Committee

Aybuke Aurum	University of New South Wales, Australia
Brian Berenbach	Siemens Corporate Research, USA
Dan Berry	University of Waterloo, Canada
Sjaak Brinkkemper	Utrecht University, The Netherlands
David Callele	University of Saskatchewan, Canada
Jane Cleland-Huang	DePaul University, USA
Eric Dubois	CRP Henri Tudor, Luxembourg
Armin Eberlein	American University of Sharjah, UAE
Xavier Franch	University Politècnica de Catalunya, Spain
Samuel Fricker	Blekinge Institute of Technology, Sweden
Donald Gause	Binghamton University, USA
Vincenzo Gervasi	University of Pisa, Italy
Martin Glinz	University of Zurich, Switzerland
Tony Gorschek	Blekinge Institute of Technology, Sweden
Olly Gotel	Independent Researcher, USA
Paul Gruenbacher	Johannes Kepler University of Linz, Austria
Peter Haumer	IBM Rational, USA
Andrea Herrmann	Free Software Engineering Trainer, Germany
Patrick Heymans	University of Namur, Berlgium
Matthias Jarke	RWTH Aachen University, Germany
Natalia Juristo	University Politécnica de Madrid, Spain
Erik Kamsties	University of Applied Sciences and Arts Dortmund, Germany
Peter Karpati	Institute for Energy Technology, Norway
Marjo Kauppinen	Aalto University, Finland
Eric Knauss	University of Victoria, Canada

Kim Lauenroth   adesso AG, Germany
Soren Lauesen   IT University of Copenhagen, Denmark
Pericles Loucopoulos   Loughborough University, UK
Nazim Madhavji   University of Western Ontario, Canada
Raimundas Matulevicius   University of Tartu, Estonia
Raul Mazo   University Paris 1 Panthéon — Sorbonne,
                                      France
John Mylopoulos   University of Trento, Italy
Cornelius Ncube   Bournemouth University, UK
Bashar Nuseibeh   Open University, UK
Barbara Paech   University of Heidelberg, Germany
Oscar Pastor Lopez   University Politécnica de Valencia, Spain
Anne Persson   University of Skövde, Sweden
Kai Petersen   Blekinge Institute of Technology, Sweden
Jolita Ralyte   University of Geneva, Switzerland
Gil Regev   Ecole Polytechnique Fédérale de Lausanne,
                                      Switzerland
Bjorn Regnell   Lund University, Sweden
Colette Rolland   University Paris 1 Panthéon — Sorbonne,
                                      France
Camille Salinesi   University Paris 1 Panthéon — Sorbonne,
                                      France
Kristian Sandahl   Linköping University, Sweden
Pete Sawyer   Lancaster University, UK
Kurt Schneider   Leibniz Universität Hannover, Germany
Norbert Seyff   University of Zurich, Switzerland
Guttorm Sindre   Norwegian University of Science and
                                      Technology, Norway
Janis Stirna   Royal Institute of Technology, Sweden
Christer Thörn   Jönköping University, Sweden
Inge Van De Weerd   Vrije Universiteit Amsterdam, The Netherlands
Thorsten Weyer   University of Duisburg-Essen, Germany
Roel Wieringa   University of Twente, The Netherlands
Eric Yu   University of Toronto, Canada
Didar Zowghi   University of Technology, Sydney, Australia

Additional Reviewers

Ulrike Abelein   Pascal Van Eck
Beatrice Alenljung   Xavier Ferre
Muneera Bano   Anne Hess
Elizabeth Bjarnason   Tom-Michael Hesse
Markus Borg   Cédric Jeanneret
Eya Ben Charrada   Alejandrina Mara Aranda López King
Alexander Delater   Anne Koziolek

Sponsors

Platinum Level Sponsors

Gold Level Sponsors

Silver Level Sponsors

Do as I Say; Not as I Do?
From Requirement Engineering to
Experimenting with Customers
(Keynote)

Jan Bosch

Chalmers University of Technology
Gothenburg, Sweden

Abstract: Asking users what they would like to have built is probably the worst question in the history of software engineering. Users don't know what they want and it's the engineer's job to find this out. Answering this question requires a systematic approach to exploring a broad set of hypotheses about functionality that might add value for customers at different stages of development. The talk introduces the notion of Innovation Experiment Systems as a systematic method for optimizing the user experience of existing features, developing new features as well as developing new products. The method uses different techniques dependent on the stage of development, including pre-development, development and commercial deployment. In each stage, frequent customer involvement, both active and passive, is used to constantly establish and improve the user experience. The method is based on data from eight industrial cases and stresses the importance of speed and rapid iterations in development. The talk uses numerous examples from industry are used to illustrate the concepts.

Short Bio: Jan Bosch is professor of software engineering and director of the software research center at Chalmers University Technology in Gothenburg, Sweden. Earlier, he worked as Vice President Engineering Process at Intuit Inc where he also lead Intuit's Open Innovation efforts and headed the central mobile technologies team. Before Intuit, he was head of the Software and Application Technologies Laboratory at Nokia Research Center, Finland. Before joining Nokia, he headed the software engineering research group at the University of Groningen, The Netherlands, where he holds a professorship in software engineering. He received a MSc degree from the University of Twente, The Netherlands, and a PhD degree from Lund University, Sweden. His research activities include open innovation, innovation experiment systems, compositional software engineering, software ecosystems, software architecture, software product families and software variability management. He is the author of a book "Design and Use of Software Architectures: Adopting and Evolving a Product Line Approach" published by Pearson Education (Addison-Wesley & ACM Press), (co-)editor of several books and volumes in, among others, the Springer LNCS series and (co-)author of a significant number of research articles. He is editor for Science of Computer Programming, has been guest editor for journal issues, chaired several conferences as general and program chair, served on many program committees and organized numerous workshops.

In the startup space, Jan serves on the advisory board of Assia Inc. in Redwood City, CA, as well as the advisory board of Burt, in Gothenburg, Sweden. He is chairman of the board of Evisto, in Gothenburg, Sweden. Also, he acts as an external business advisor for the School of Entrepreneurship at Chalmers University of Technology, Gothenburg, Sweden.

As a consultant, as a professor and as an employee, Jan has worked with and for many companies on innovation and R&D efficiency including Philips, Thales Naval Netherlands, Robert Bosch GmbH, Siemens, Nokia, Ericsson, Grundfos, Tellabs, Avaya, Tieto Enator and Det Norska Veritas. More information about his background can be found at his website: www.janbosch.com.

When not working, Jan divides his time between his family, a spouse and three sons, reading science fiction and sports, preferably long distance running, swimming, biking and horseback riding..

Table of Contents

Traceability

RE and Business/Goals

RE and Software Development

RE in Practice

Product Lines and Product Management

Software Architects' Experiences of Quality Requirements: What We Know and What We Do Not Know?

Maya Daneva[1], Luigi Buglione[2], and Andrea Herrmann[3]

[1] University of Twente, The Netherlands
[2] Engineering IT SpA, Italy
[3] Hermann & Ehrlich, Germany
m.daneva@utwente.nl, luigi.buglione@eng.it,
herrmann@informatik.uni-heidelberg.de

Abstract. **[Context/motivation]** Quality requirements (QRs) are a concern of both requirement engineering (RE) specialists and software architects (SAs). However, the majority of empirical studies on QRs take the RE analysts'/clients' perspectives, and only recently very few included the SAs' perspective. As a result, (i) relatively little is known about SAs' involvement in QRs engineering and their coping strategies, and (ii) whatever is known mostly comes from small and midsized projects. **[Question/problem]** The question in this exploratory study is how SAs cope with QRs in the context of large and contract-based software system delivery projects. **[Principal ideas/results]** We executed an exploratory case study with 20 SAs in the context of interest. The key results indicate the role SAs play in QRs engineering, the type of requirements communication processes SAs are involved in, the ways QRs are discovered, documented, quantified, validated and negotiated. Our most important findings are that in contract-based contexts: (1) the QRs are approached with the same due diligence as the functional requirements and the architecture design demand, (2) the SAs act proactively and embrace responsibilities over the QRs, (3) willingness to pay and affordability seem as important QRs prioritization criteria as cost and benefits do, and (4) QRs engineering is perceived as a social activity and not as much as a tool and method centric activity. **[Contribution]** The main contributions of the paper are (i) the explication of the QRs process from SAs' perspective, and (ii) the comparison of our findings with previously published results.

Keywords: Quality requirements, Software architecture design, Exploratory case study, Contract-based software development, Empirical research method.

1   Introduction

In the past 15 years, quality requirements (QRs), also referred to as Non-functional requirements (NFRs), became a key sub-field in the Requirements Engineering (RE) discipline. Many approaches to QRs have been designed and a large number of empirical studies has been carried out to evaluate various aspects of these approaches. However, most of these studies have taken the RE perspective exclusively, be it the

J. Doerr and A.L. Opdahl (Eds.): REFSQ 2013, LNCS 7830, pp. 1–17, 2013.

one of RE researchers, of RE practitioners or of business users. Very few studies have included the perspectives of those stakeholders involved in downstream software development activities, e.g. software architects (SAs) and developers. Yet, there is a clear consensus in the RE community that including multiple stakeholders' perspectives is necessary for the field to advance [1]. In particular, the perspective of SAs has been deemed one of the most important given the growing popularity of approaches to joint RE and software architecture [1,2,3,4,5,6,7,8,9]. A 2010 systematic review by Svensson et al [7] identified 229 empirical studies on the various aspects of QRs engineering. However, its authors found only 18 studies being well-documented and stating explicitly the perspectives taken in the empirical research. Moreover, our review of these 18 studies indicated that none of them considered the SAs' perspective. More recently (2010-2012), RE research yielded five publications [6,8,9,10,11] dedicated specifically to the SAs' perceptions on QRs. These studies agree that the perspectives of SAs and RE specialists do differ in both interpreting the role of QRs in downstream software development activities and in reasoning about how QRs problems and solutions are framed, analysed and resolved. While these empirical analyses represent an important progress to narrow the gap in our understanding of how SAs cope with QRs, the experiences these studies report come mostly from small and midsized projects.

In the present paper, we complement these published results with findings from an exploratory study with 20 SAs working in large or very large contract-based projects. The key results of the paper indicate the roles SAs play in QRs engineering, the type of requirements processes SAs are involved in, the way QRs are discovered, documented, quantified, validated and negotiated. The results are compared with findings from prior studies and some implications are drawn for research and practice. In what follows, Sect. 2 is on background and related work and Sect. 3 – on the case study research design. Sect. 4 and Sect. 5 present the results and our discussion of them, respectively. Sect. 6 evaluates validity threats and Sect. 7 concludes.

2   The SAs' Perspective on QRs: Background and Related Work

RE research has generated an overwhelming amount of publications explaining why and how SAs' perspective on QRs is key to project success, e.g. [2,3,4,5,6,7,8]. QRs are deemed key to defining architecture design and many large organizations now organize their work processes on the premise that SAs need to understand the clients' QRs because only through this they can get fully aware of the consequences of their design decisions from clients' perspective (e.g. impacts on total cost of ownership [12]). A 2010 systematic review [13] on the topic of architectural descriptions found a range of QRs driving the final architecture descriptions of those systems reported in published empirical studies. A 2011 SAs' survey [9] stated that SAs are "the population to deal with NFR". These authors went on making the case that shared knowledge and good practices on how SAs address QRs can potentially benefit IT organizations in two tangible ways, (1) by giving them a fact-based ground for improving their SA practices and (2) by helping them devise approaches that make the chances of success more predictable.

As the Introduction mentioned, the SAs' perspective on QRs was the explicit focus of five studies [6,8,9,10,11]. In [9], a survey with one company's SAs uncovered the importance of QRs as perceived by SAs, the ways in which they dealt with QRs, and the impact this had on IT project success. This survey found that projects where modifiability is perceived to be of low business criticality "lead to consistently high customer satisfaction" [9]. Also, projects that used QRs verification techniques were more successful than those that did not. In [11], the authors explain the effect of contractual client-vendor relationship on the interaction of software architecture and quantification of QRs. The authors put forward that if information-sharing between parties is limited, this would significantly impede the quantification of QRs. In [6], QRs were deemed instrumental for the SA's reasoning process while 'architecting'. Next, a 2010 survey [10] and a follow-up 2012 exploratory interview-based study [8] with SAs in small and medium size projects in Spain, investigated how SAs dealt with QRs. In these project contexts, the findings revealed the state of the art practices regarding QRs elicitation, modelling, and tool support. The study indicated important gaps between the QRs themes currently researched in the RE community and the state-of-the art industry needs, which motivated the authors' call for more empirical research on QRs from SAs' perspective.

3   Goal, Research Questions and Empirical Research Design

The goal of this study is to understand how SAs cope with QRs in large and contract-based software system development projects. Specifically, we wanted to gain insights and answer the following research questions: (RQ1) How do the SAs understand their role? (RQ2) Do SAs and RE staff use different terminology for QRs? (RQ3) How do QRs get elicited? (RQ4) How do QRs get documented? (RQ5) How do QRs get prioritized? (RQ6) How do QRs get quantified, if at all? (RQ7) How do QRs get validated? (RQ8) How do QRs get negotiated? (RQ9) What role does the contract play in the way SAs cope with QRs?

We conducted an exploratory multiple-case study, applying Yin's guidelines [14] and using structured open-end in-depth interviews with practitioners from 20 software project organizations (Table 1). The application domains where the SAs developed software solutions represent a rich mix of fields, incl. telecom, real estate management, air transportation, entertainment (online gaming/video streaming) educational services, hospitality services, and ERP. Our study was performed in four steps: (1) Compose an interview guide following the guidelines in [15]; (2) Do a pilot interview to check the applicability of the guide to real-life context; (3) Carry out interviews with practitioners according to the finalized questionnaire; (4) Sample and follow-up with those participants that possess deeper knowledge or a specific perspective. The interview guide is receivable from the authors. Each interview lasted 35 to 45 minutes. Eight interviews took place face-to-face, and 12 on the phone. Each interviewee was informed on the research purpose and the research process by the first author, and provided with the list of interview questions at least a week before the interview date. All interviewees came prepared to the interview, which was instrumental to the effective use of the interview time slots.

Choosing the Participants: Our selection criterion for participation in the case study was the participant's exposure to the realm of large and contract-based systems delivery. We included 20 SAs from 14 companies in the Netherlands, Belgium, Finland, and Germany. At the time of the interviews, the companies were engaged in large contract-based [1] projects. More in detail, the SAs were selected because they (i) had professional backgrounds pertaining to our research questions and its context (i.e. contract-based), and (ii) had the potential to offer information-rich experiences. Also, they demonstrated an interest in exploring similar questions from their companies' perspectives. All 20 SAs had the following backgrounds:

(1) They all worked in large projects that were running in at least three different development locations in one country, and had clients in more than two countries.

(2) All SAs had at least 10 years of experience in large systems and were familiar with the interactions that happen between SAs and RE staff.

(3) All SAs worked in contract-based projects where contracts between parties were established in two steps [1]: first, a contract was agreed upon for the purpose to get the requirements documented in sufficient detail, so that a SA can use them to work on architecture design. Then, a second contract dealt with the system delivery itself. The pricing agreements varied across the participating companies. Some were fixed-price, others variable, and a third group included a combination between fixed-price and variable. Four SAs worked in outsourcing contracts, and 16 were employed on projects where software development sub-contractors were participating. All SAs deemed their contracts comprehensive and aligned with the spirit of their projects. (In other words, none suggested their organization had any issue with the contract).They also said that their projects were considered successful, by both parties in the contract. The SAs got to know the first author during various business and research conferences in the period of 2001-2012. Using purposive sampling [15], she chose the interviewees, based on her knowledge about their typicality. The number of participants was large enough to provide a broad variety of viewpoints. We planned the interviews to be 'structured' [15] with regard to the questions being asked during the session. This means, the interviewer was the one to control what topics would be discussed and in which order.

We note that interview-based exploratory case studies usually are intended to promote self-disclosure and that is what we were after in this work. We collected data via one-on-one interactions of a researcher with each of the interviewees that have various backgrounds but also common professional values and common roles in which they execute their professional duties. As in [15], interview studies are not used to provide statistically generalizable results applicable to all people similar to the practitioners in a specific study. The intention of the exploratory case study is not to infer, but to understand and not to generalize, but to determine a possible range of views. Therefore, in this study we will adopt, based on the recommendations in [15], the criterion of transferability as a useful measure of validity. Transferability asks for whether the results are presented in a way that allows other researchers and practitioners to evaluate if the findings apply to their contexts.

Table 1. Case study participants and organizations

ID	Business	System description	Team size (# of people)	Project duration (months)
P1.	Large IT Vendor	ERP package implementation (Oracle)	35	18
P2.	Large IT Vendor	ERP package implementation (SAP)	60	15
P3.	Large IT Vendor	ERP package implementation (SAP)	75	18
P4.	Large IT Vendor	ERP package implementation (SAP)	41	12
P5.	Large IT Vendor	ERP package implementation (SAP)	51	12
P6.	Large IT Vendor	ERP package implementation (Oracle)	45	12
P7.	IT Vendor	ERP package implementation (SAP)	40	18
P8.	Software Producer	Online learning environment	22	12
P9.	Software Producer	Sensor system for in-building navigation	35	12
P10.	Software Producer	Online ticket booking application	15	12
P11.	Oil & Gas	Logistics planning application	21	12
P12.	Insurance	Web application for client self-service	61	24
P13.	Insurance	Client claim management and reimbursement app	53	16
P14.	Real Estate	Web application for rental contract handling	42	18
P15.	Air Carrier	Web app for passengers' feedback processing	11	14
P16.	Video Streaming	Viewer recommendation management system	18	18
P17.	Video Streaming	Viewer complaint management system	45	9
P18.	Online bookstore	Order processing system	15	10
P19.	Online game producer	Gaming system	81	21
P20.	Online travel agency	Room deal identification system	45	12

Data Analysis Strategy: We were guided by the Grounded Theory (GT) method of Charmaz [16], which is a qualitative approach applied broadly in social sciences to construct general propositions (called a "theory" in this approach) from verbal data. GT is exploratory and well-fitting situations where the researcher does not want to use pre-conceived ideas, and instead is driven by the desire to capture all facets of the collected data and to allow the propositions to emerge from the data. In essence, this was a process of making analytic sense of the interview data by means of coding and constant comparison of pieces of data that were collected in the case study. Constant comparison means that the data from an interview is constantly compared to the data already collected from previously held interviews. We first read the interview transcripts and attached a coding word to a portion of the text – a phrase or a paragraph. The 'codes' were selected to reflect the meaning of the respective portion of the interview text to a specific research question. This could be a concept (e.g. 'willingness to pay'), or an activity (e.g. 'operationalization', 'quantification'). We clustered all pieces of text that relate to the same code in order to analyze it in a consistent and systematic way. The results of the data analysis are in Sect. 4 and the discussion on them – in Sect. 5.

4   Results

Our findings are presented as related to each research question. As it is usual in qualitative studies, we supplement the observations with interviewees' quotations.

4.1   RQ1: How Do the Software Architects Understand Their Role?

All interviewees indicated their companies had SAs' job descriptions that list their most important duties, skills competence levels, and job salary scales. As all the organizations were mature in terms of project management processes and process-oriented thinking, the roles of the SAs were established and they were clearly recognizable by their fellow team members. 13 out of the 20 SAs thought of their role as *'a bridge'* between QRs and the underlying technology that they were dealing with.

"You've got to translate what their clients want in terms of working solutions and technology choices" (participant P1), "You learn pretty quickly to stretch the technology so that it works for those who you call 'requirements engineers', I mean here our Business Analysts and their "patrons", the business unit directors" (participant P2),

"I have days when I do nothing but 'translating' the language of our millions of players into the features that are technologically implementable in the next release. All I do is walking through a list of "user experiences" that our requirements folk want to launch in the market, and I make sure that it all works well at implementation level, that features build upon each other, so that the overall gaming experience and enjoyability are never compromised. That's why I'm coming to work every day" (participant P19).

Other seven SAs thought of their roles as *'review gate keepers'* in light of the active roles in QRs reviews, contract compliance evaluation and sign off:

"If you are sick, on vacation, or on a conference, there is no way this can go unnoticed; they will need you and if there is no one to tell them that what they are doing is right [according to contract and project goals], I mean it pure architecturally; they are going to wait for me so that I give the architecture approval. Otherwise, we run a risk of screwing up things miserably" (participant P15).

How many SAs are enough for engineering QRs? All SAs experienced one or two SAs have been involved in their projects. In case of two SAs to be involved, our interviewees meant one SA from the vendor and the client side, each.

"You may work with many RE people for the different subject areas, but one architect must be there to aggregate their input and evaluate what it means for the underlying architecture" (participant P6).

4.2   RQ2: Do SAs and RE Staff Use Different Terminology for QRs?

All SAs considered the process of gaining communication clarity with RE staff a non-issue. They thought this was due to their long years' experience in their respective business sectors (all interviewees had 10+ years of experience as indicated in Sect 3). Even when working with less experienced RE specialists, they thought that their domain knowledge has been instrumental to spot missing or incomplete requirements. For example, a SA who worked on the development of an online system for processing an air carrier's clients' feedback said that in this application domain scalability is usually regarded as the QR of the highest priority. If a specification says nothing about it, he considers this a *'red flag'* and acts accordingly:

"If your RE person says nothing about it, you are absolutely sure there is something going wrong here. And you better pick up the phone and call them ASAP because they may be inexperienced and who knows what else could go wrong beyond this point. Not doing this is just too much risk to bear" (participant P15).

Those SAs working in ISO-certified organizations suggested that the knowledge of the ISO standards adopted in their company, the mandatory ISO-training that everyone in the IT department should go through, *'the habit of looking back to what the ISO-compliant Quality Manual says'* help tremendously both the SAs and RE-staff understand each other: *"We don't use the term QRs, not even non-functional requirements, we call them ISO aspects, because we are ISO-certified and our system must show compliance to the ISO standards. Also our requirements specialists have in their template a special section that contains these aspects. We enumerate them one after another. All relevant aspects must be there, security, maintainability, performance, you name it. It's more than 40 aspects [in the company's Quality Manual that is consulted on an on-going basis]. They [the RE staff] know them and we know them [because we went to the same training], so we have a common ground" (participant P11).*

An interesting observation was shared by those SAs delivering large SAP systems. They indicated, the SAP vendor's Product Quality Handbook included around 400 QRs which are implemented in the standard software package and which everyone on the development team is aware of (as these team member learnt about the Product Quality Handbook in their professional training). If there were QRs specific to the client and unaddressed in the Handbook, then those should be specified on top of the 400 that come in the SAP's package. (SAP is ISO 9001-certified).

4.3   RQ3: How Do QRs Get Elicited?

14 SAs used checklists. These were based on a variety of sources: (i) ISO standards (e.g. 25045-2010, 25010-2011, 25041-2012, 25060-2010), (ii) architecture frameworks, be they company-specific or sector-specific, (iii) internal standards (e.g. vendor/client-organization-specific), and (iv) stakeholder engagement standards, e.g. AA1000SES [17]. Regardless the source, the interviewees agreed that the checklist-supported process is always iterative, because not all QRs could get 100% clear at the same time. *"You've got to go at least 4-5 times until you get a spec that makes sense to me and my fellows" (participant P4).*

In their views, the fact that most QRs are not global to the system but act on specific pieces of functionalities, imposes an order in the elicitation activities: SAs do expect first the functional requirements to be elicited and then to use the resulting functional requirements specification as the ground for eliciting QRs.

"How otherwise will you know which attribute matters to what piece of functionality?" (participant P9).

Four SAs argued QRs are never elicited but detected, e.g. one SA was involved in experimental serious-game-based process specifically designed to "detect" QRs. Two others shared they had *"a bunch of pilot users who volunteer to play the role of guinea pigs; they are passionate about the system and would love to tell you where it fails to deliver up to their expectations in terms of performance, availability, and user experience" (participant P10).* Another SA had been using storytelling techniques to uncover QRs, together with his RE counterpart and his clients.

4.4   RQ4: How Do QRs Get Documented?

15 out of the 20 SAs specified QRs by using predefined templates. Some of them were vendor-specific, e.g. in SAP projects, SAs used SAP's standard diagram notation called Technical Architecture Modelling [18], as it has been part of the SAP Architecture Curriculum [12]. Others were derived based on (i) the ISO standard, (ii) the House of Quality (HoQ) of the Quality Function Deployment (QFD) methodology [19], (iii) the Planguage approach [20], and (iv) the INVEST grid approach [21].

The other 5 SAs were using plain natural language text that provides at least the definition of each QR, plus information on the end user to do the acceptance test on it and the ways to demonstrate that the system meets it. The amount of detail in these specifications varied based on what the SAs deemed important to be provided to them by the RE staff or the users. For example, one SA wanted to hear a story from a user on *"how the user will know the system is slow? A user can tell you "If I manage to get one of my phone calls done while waiting, this means to me it's very slow." (participant P12).* Other SAs said they write their QRs definitions next to the functional requirements, if these are specified in a process model or a data model. *"This way you will know which smallest pieces of functionality and information entities are affected by which QR" (participant P1).*

4.5   RQ5: How Do QRs Get Prioritized?

All SAs agreed that (i) they make QRs trade-offs as part of their daily job on projects, and (ii) the project's business case was the driver behind their trade-off decision making. The key prioritization criteria for making the QRs trade-offs were cost and benefits, evaluated mostly in qualitative terms but whenever possible also quantitatively, e.g. person-months spent to implement specific QRs. Perceived risk was identified as subsumed in the cost category, as SAs deemed a common practice the tendency to translate any risks to QRs, into costs to bear in a contractual agreement. However, next to perceived cost and benefits, 12 SAs put forward two other QRs prioritization criteria: *client's willingness to pay* and *affordability*. The first is about the flexibility of the value of a QR to the client. It is expressed as the level of readiness of client organizations to pay extra charges for some perceived benefit that could be brought by implementing a specific QR. Six SAs elaborated that this criterion alone is instrumental to split up the QRs in three groups: (i) essential, which includes those QRs that directly respond to the reason of why the client commissioned the system in the first place, e.g. in a hotel reservation system, it's absolutely essential that a secure payment processing method is provided; (ii) marginal, which includes those QRs that are needed yet clients are willing to spend little on them, e.g. a user interface feature that might be appreciated and would be perceived as a value to pay a few hundred euro, but not thousands of euro; and (iii) optional, which includes QRs that clients will find enjoyable to have but would not be willing to pay for, e.g. flashy animation effects in a game system that are fun, yet not truly a *'money-maker'*.

Next, affordability is about whether or not the cost estimation of a QR is in accord with (1) the resources specified in the contract and (2) with the long term contract spendings of the client organization. This criterion determines whether or not a QR is aligned with (short term) project goals and/or (long-term) organizational goals.

Furthermore, SAs' experiences differed regarding who ultimately decides on the QRs priorities. 13 SAs suggested that in their projects the prioritization has been linked to a business driver or a KPI in the project and it has been the project's steering committee to decide on the priorities. They deemed the prioritization process *'iterative'* and a *'learning experience'* in which the SAs learn about what QRs the drivers *'dictate and how desperately the company needs those QRs'* and the RE specialists and the business owners learn about the technical and cost limitations.

"It's through this mutually educational process that you arrive at the priorities. This takes a few iterations, starting always from the Steering Committee that tells us what's most important to them. We tell them what we can do and check against budget, timelines and people resources. If we cannot do it within our limits, then they must decide either to pour more money into the project, or to rethink what they could live without, so that we have a good enough solution for our circumstances". *(participant P11).*

In contrast to these 13 SAs, the other 7 considered themselves as the key decision-makers in setting the priorities:

"You can stretch a technology to a certain point. No matter what your client wants, once in a while you've got to say 'no' and push back decisively" (participant P11).

Concerning the use of requirements prioritization methods, 19 SAs suggested no explicit use of any specific method other than splitting up QRs in categories of importance, namely 'essential', 'marginal', and 'optional'. SAs named these categories differently, yet they meant the same three. One SA named EasyWinWin [23] as the group support tool aiding the requirements prioritization and negotiation activities in a project. Three out of the 19 shared that nailing down the top 2-3 most important QR is a non-issue, because of the obviousness of these requirements to the client, e.g: *"If you develop a game, it's all about scalability and user experience. You have no way to make your fancy animation work if you cannot get scalable and if you jeopardize user experience" (participant P19).*

What is an issue is the prioritization of those QR that take less prominent place from user's perspective, e.g. maintainability, evolvability, e.g:

"These requirements matter to you, not to the client. Even you do a brilliant job on maintainability, nobody will pat you on the back and say thank-you for this. It's very difficult, I'd say, almost political, to prioritize this kind of QRs" (participant P13).

4.6   RQ6: How Do QRs Get Quantified, If at All?

All SAs agreed that expressing QRs quantitatively should not happen very early in a contract-based project. This was important in order to prevent early and not-well-thought-out commitments. Three SAs said they rarely use quantitative definitions of

QRs. Instead, they get on board an expert specialised in a specific QR (e.g. usability, or scalability) and let him/her *'do the quantification job'* for them. 10 other SAs used as a starting point the quantitative definitions that were pre-specified in the contract (e.g. a contract may state explicitly that the system should scale up to serve hundreds of thousands of subscribers). However, 8 of the 10 warned that more often than not contracts address design-level requirements [1], including (i) detailed feature specifications of how QRs are to be achieved (e.g. specifying a proprietary influence metric to be included in the ranking algorithms of the recommender system that is part of a larger online video streaming system), or (ii) a particular algorithm rather than required quality attribute value and criteria for verifying compliance (e.g coding a very specific search algorithm for finding hotel deals). Confusing QRs with design-level requirements was deemed a critical issue in industry; it points out to a mismatch in understanding what is really quantified and by using what kind of measures: design-level requirements are quantified by using product measures and not project measures which are those important for contract monitoring purposes. However, more often than not contracts use product and project measures incorrectly, the final effect being that a number of project tasks related to implementing QRs don't get 'visible' but 'implicit', and therefore no budget is previewed for them and, in turn, the client would not commit to pay.

Next, 7 SAs worked with a team of systems analysts on operationalizing QRs. In essence, it meant decomposing them until reaching the level of architecture design choices or of the smallest pieces of functional requirements. Once at this level, the practitioners felt comfortable starting quantifying the QRs, e.g. they used the operationalization specifications as input to a Function Points counting process, in order to 'size the QRs'. However, no common quantification method was observed to be used. Instead, the SA suggested the choice of a method should match the project goal (i.e. towards what end quantification was needed in the first place). E.g., if quantification of QRs is to serve project management and contract monitoring purposes, then it might be well possible that in the future those organizations experienced in Function-Points-based project estimation, would use the newly released IFPUG NFR Assessment standard [22], called SNAP (Software Non-functional Assessment Process).

4.7   RQ7: How Do QRs Get Validated?

All SAs were actively involved in QRs validation, 16 considered it part of their job, while four said that it's the job of the RE staff to ensure QRs are validated. These four SAs used the RE specialists as contact points on clarifying requirements. We make the note that for the purpose of this research, we call 'validation' the process that (a) ensures that QRs clearly describe the target solution, (b) confirms these QRs are technically implementable and the resulting architecture design satisfies the business requirements as per the contractual agreement.

14 SAs participated in requirements walkthroughs with clients led by a RE specialist where clients confirm the functionalities on which the QRs in question were supposed to act. The walkthroughs were deemed part of the client expectation

management process that the project manager established. The SAs considered them as the opportunity to inform the clients about those QRs that could not be implemented in the system or could not be implemented in the way the client originally thought: *"You've got to educate them on what your technology can and cannot do for them and the walkthroughs is how this happens relatively easily."(participant P1).*

Three SAs used the HoQ [19] to demonstrate the strength of the relationship between a QR-statement and its operationalization in terms of either functional requirements or architecture design choices. Two SAs validated QRs against internal architecture standards. Should they identify deviations from the standards, they escalate this to both managers and RE-staff. In extreme cases, when QRs are grossly misaligned with the architecture standards, this should be brought to the attention of the steering committee, the program director, and the architecture office manager responsible for the project. *"You have to inform them immediately that things have no way to work as planned, so they get back to negotiation and revise the concept" (participant P8).*

RQ8: How Do QRs Get Negotiated?

Ten SAs used their project's business cases as the vehicle to negotiate requirements. They considered this a common practice in enterprise systems projects. *"You need to express yourself in money terms, that they [the clients] can understand very well". (participant P20).*

Three SAs who worked on projects where user experience was the most important QR, said their goal in QRs negotiation is to prevent the most important QR from becoming suboptimal, if other QRs take more resources and attention. These SAs did not use their business cases, but considered effort and budget allocation as important inputs to negotiation meetings.

Five other SAs thought of themselves as *'information providers and mentors'* to the team, but not *'truly negotiators on QRs'* and that it's the project manager's responsibility to lead in the negotiation:

"It's his job to sell it to the other parties. I'm just an internal consultant; what they do with my information is their business" (participant P10).

Other three SAs used the HoQ, EasyWinWin [23], and the Six-Thinking-Hats method [24] to reason about QRs in negotiation meeting, respectively. We note that the Six-Thinking-Hats is a general approach to resolving complex issues and companies use it for any negotiation situation, be it QRs related or not. The approach was well-received and internalized in the company and people *'had fun using it as it takes pressure off them in this kind of difficult conversations' (participant P16).*

RQ9: What Role Does the Contract Play in the Way SAs Cope with QRs?

Did SAs have to refer to the contract, enforce it, or use it in any way in their projects so far? In the SAs' experiences, there were three ways in which the contract influenced how they coped with QRs: (1) the contract enforced the cost-consciousness of the SAs and was used to evaluate the cost associated with achieving the various QRs; (2) the contract stipulated QRs levels, e.g. in the Service Level Agreement (SLA) part, that were targeted and subjected to discussions with the stakeholders; and (3) the contract in fact pre-defined the priorities for some small but very important set of QRs. 17 SAs indicated that the contract was used on an on-going basis to stay focused on what counts most in the project. To these SAs, the contact was the vehicle to ensure the system indeed includes *'the right things'*, *'those that they needed in the first place, and that we are billing them for'*.

12 SAs shared that a contract-based context is conductive to understanding QRs as a way to maintain control. In their views, every comprehensive contract usually comes with SLA specifications, key performance indicators (KPI) and measurement plans that address multiple perspectives (clients/vendors), e.g., the Balancing Multiple Perspectives technique [25] is a way to help all involved parties in understanding and validating the right amount of things to do in a contract-based project.

In contrast to this, three SAs thought the contract was not that important. They said, it was just *'the beginning of their conversation'* on QRs and not as the reference guide to consult on an on-going basis. They thought it's the people who make the contract work. In their view, it has always been the RE-staff and project managers who work with the contract and who usually communicate to everyone else if the project efforts get misaligned with the clauses of the contract.

5   Discussion

This section compares and contrasts our finding to those in previously published studies on QRs from SAs' perspective. Our discussion is organized according to our research questions.

RQ1: How do the SAs understand their role? Our results suggest that in contract-based and large projects, the SAs define their role as "a bridge" that connects clients QRs to the architecture design. This contrasts to the results in [8] where the SAs had indicated a broad diversity of roles and tasks they took on (e.g. coding). We think the contrast is because our SAs came from regulated environments where terminology, roles and processes are determined, well communicated, and lived up to. Our findings agree with [11] on the importance that SAs place on gaining as deep as possible understanding of the QRs and using it to deliver a good quality architecture design. Regarding how many SAs are enough for engineering QRs, we note that this question has not been yet researched in RE studies. In our interviewees' experiences, it's usually one or two SAs that operate together in a large contract-based project. This is in line with Brooks' most recent reasoning on "the design of design" of large systems [26] where he explains that a 2-person team can be particularly effective where larger teams are inefficient (other than for design reviews where the participation of a large number of reviewers is essential).

RQ2: Do SAs and RE staff use different terminology for QRs? Our results did not indicate this as the issue that preoccupied the SAs. This contrasts [8] where Spanish SAs collectively indicated a broad terminological gap between SAs and RE staff. The authors of [8] made observations that the absence of shared glossary of QRs types was part of the problem. We think the difference between our findings and those in [8] may well be due to the fact that our case study projects were happening in regulated organizations where standards defined terminologies that all project team members adopted (including SAs) and assumed ownership over their use. We found that SAs implicitly referred to at least two main streams of standards: (i) management systems as e.g. 9001-27001-20000, and (ii) 'technical standards' (as 14143-x, 9126-x, etc.), where (i) are about 'requirements' to be accomplished and (ii) are about processes and/or solutions about 'how to' do things. However, terms from both streams were used interchangeably and it was not clear which QR followed the terminology of which stream. This made us think that contract-based development would greatly benefit if a common and shared glossary of ISO terms existed (and help make explicit the difference between the two steams of ISO standards).

RQ3: How do QRs get elicited? Our study revealed all SAs were actively involved in elicitation. This agrees with [9] and is in contrast to [8]. Our assumption is that the sense of ownership over the QRs that the SAs shared could be the possible reason for their proactiveness and involvement. Also, we found checklist-based techniques as the predominant approach in contract-based project context.

RQ4: How do QRs get documented? We found that standardized forms/templates plus natural language were used most. This is in contrast with [8] where the SAs could not agree on one specific systematic way to document QRs and natural language was the only common practice being used. Why this difference occurs? We assume that it's because of the regulated nature of the contract-based environments and of the use of standards. We think it's realistic to expect that in such contexts, a contract is monitored on an on-going basis (e.g. all relevant SLAs are well specified and how they would be measured is explicitly defined) and its use forces IT professionals to adopt a sound template-based documentation flow throughout the project [27].

RQ5: How do QRs get prioritized? Two 'new' prioritization criteria crystalized in this study: client's willingness to pay and affordability. These complement the well-known criteria of cost, benefits and risk (as stated e.g. in [28]). We assume that the choice of these criteria could be traced back to the contract-based nature of the projects in our study where both vendors and clients had to get clear as early as possible on, scope, project duration and the way they organize their work processes and its impact on each party.

RQ6: How do QRs get quantified, if at all? Our results agree with [11] on the importance of QRs quantification in practice. However, unlike [4], our SAs did not indicate that searching for new or better quantification techniques was their prime concern. Similarly to [11], they warned about the pitfalls of premature quantification, meaning that early QRs quantification may be based on too many assumptions about the solution. As in [11], our SAs thought that if those assumptions turn out unrealistic, a vendor may find itself in the precarious situation of having committed resources to unachievable QRs. Regarding how quantification happens, the SAs suggest that either using a standard (e.g. 22]) or engaging an expert in specific type of QRs (e.g. security, scalability). While the first ensures that all tasks of implementing QRs are explicitly accounted for in a project, the second allows for deeper analysis on a single quality attribute and its interplay with others.

RQ7: How do QRs get validated? No SA witnessed a contract that stated an automated (model-checking) tool be used for validating QRs. Instead, our results suggest that common sense practices dominate the state-of-the-art:e.g. using requirements walkthroughs, documentation reviews, building up communication processes around the artefact-development activity (e.g. escalation if a QR is not timely clarified) are simple, yet powerful ways to ensure QRs are aligned with client's expectations and SLAs. This contrasts the QRs literature [4,7] where much accent is placed on tools and methods. One could assume that the active and persuasive behaviour of the SAs regarding QRs validation could be due to the explicit contractual agreements (e.g. SLA), controls and project monitoring procedures (e.g. KPI).

RQ8: How do QRs get negotiated? The business case turned out to be the most important vehicle for SAs to support their negotiation positions in meetings with other stakeholders. In contrast to RE literature (e.g. [1]) that offers an abundance of negotiation methods, we found that only one (EasyWinWin) was mentioned (and it's by only one SA). SAs hinted to general purpose negotiation techniques, e.g. the Six-Thinking-Hats method as being sufficient to help with QRs negotiation. This suggests that it might be worthwhile exploring the kind of support that negotiation methods from other fields (management science, psychology) can offer to QRs negotiation.

RQ9: What role does the contract play in the way SAs cope with QRs? We found that the contract reinforced the SA's role in his/her project organization and redefined the inclusion of this role in QRs engineering. We observed, the SAs were well aware of the possible impacts of a contract on their professional behaviour, e.g. SAs assumed responsibility to clarify QRs priorities and escalated to project managers and/or RE staff if they suspected project goals threatened or contact clauses being violated. Because we could find no prior study that looked into how contracts shape the professional behaviour of RE professionals or of SAs with respect to how QRs are dealt with, we consider it an interesting line of future research.

6   Validity Threats

Our evaluation of the possible threats to validity of the observations and conclusions in this research, followed the checklist in [29]. As our research is exploratory, the key question to address when evaluating the validity of its results, is [15]: to what extent can the practitioners' experiences in coping with QRs could be considered representative for a broader range of projects, companies, application domains? Our case study projects are not representative for all the possible ways in which engineering of QRs is performed in large contract-based settings. Following [30], we think that it could be possible to observe similar experiences in projects and companies which have contexts similar to those in our study, e.g. where large and contract-based projects hire experienced SAs in teams with mature process-oriented thinking, and where standards define the terminology to use for QRs. As the authors of [30] suggest "if the forces within an organization that drove observed behaviour are likely to exist in other organizations, it is likely that those other organizations, too, will exhibit similar behaviour" (p.12). Moreover, we acknowledge that the application domain may have influenced the ways the SAs coped with QRs. We, therefore, think that more research is needed to understand the relationship between application domains and the way in which the QRs processes happen.

We also acknowledge the inherent weaknesses of interview techniques [15]. A threat is the extent to which the SAs answered our question truthfully. We took two steps to minimize this threat by (i) recruiting volunteers, under the assumption that if a practitioner would not be able to be honest, he/she could decline his/her participation at any stage of the research and (ii) that we ensured no identity-revealing data will be used in the study. Next, it's possible that an interviewee has not understood a question. However, we think that in our study, this threat was reduced, because the interviewer used follow-up questions, and asked about the same topic in a number of different ways. Next, we accounted for the possibility that the researcher might instil his/her bias in the data collection process. We followed Yin's recommendations [6] in this respect, by establishing a chain of findings: (i) we included participants with diverse backgrounds (i.e. industry sector, type of system being delivered), and this allowed the same phenomenon to be evaluated from diverse perspectives (data triangulation [15]); (ii) the interview answers were sent to each SA prior to data analysis to confirm the information he/she provided; and (iii) we had the draft case study report reviewed by the SAs (some of whom provided feedback, which however did not affect our conclusions).

7   Conclusion

The number of studies on the involvement of SAs in QRs engineering is growing and understanding the ways it works would give us a firmer ground for organizing eventually better RE processes that lead to better definitions of QRs, and in turn, architecture designs better aligned with them.

Our study clearly indicates that making SAs an integral part of the QRs processes has been commonplace in the investigated contract-based development contexts. Unlike prior research [8] that revealed important discrepancy between literature and practice as part of small and midsized projects, this study shed light into the perspective of SAs on QRs as treated in large and contract-based projects. Compared to literature, the overriding messages of this paper are that in contract-based projects:

- the QRs are approached with the same due diligence as the functional requirements and the architecture design demand,
- the relationship between RE staff/clients and SAs is actively managed whereby the contract means embracing responsibilities over QRs (and not abdicating thereof),
- client's willingness to pay and affordability seem as important prioritization criteria for QRs as cost and benefits are,
- both the prioritization decisions on QRs and the QRs trade-offs are aligned with the contract (specifically, with the SLA and KPIs),

- checklist-based elicitation is the most common technique for eliciting QRs,
- template-based documentation in natural language is most common approach to documentation,
- quantification of QRs is done with and by experts specialized in a specific QRs sub-field (e.g. performance, scalability)
- QRs validation and negotiation are considered more organizationally and in terms of social interactions with RE staff and clients, than in terms of tool-supported processes.

Our findings have the following implications: To SAs, this study suggests the conversation on QRs starts with the contract, and specifically with the SLA and the business case. To RE tool vendors, it suggests they are better off to think about how RE tools should be better embedded into social processes and broader social interaction context. To RE researchers, our study suggests that instead of solely focusing on QRs methods, tools and techniques, it makes good sense to extend existing research by including analysis of QRs processes as socially constructed ones. How a contract shapes the behaviour of RE staff and SAs is an interesting question demanding future research. One could think of borrowing theories from other disciplines (e.g. behaviour science) to explain why RE staff and SAs engineer QRs the way they do.

In our immediate future, we plan to use these results in follow-up studies, in other countries, specifically in USA, Canada, India, Israel, Brazil and Argentina. Comparing the present results with findings in locations outside Europe would benefit both outsourcing vendors and clients in informing them on the extent to which handling QRs depends on country-specific business culture concerning contractual agreements, industry sector, and levels of maturity.

References

1. Lauesen, S.: Software requirements: Styles and techniques. Addisson-Wesley (2002)
2. Sommerville, I.: Integrated Requirements Engineering. IEEE Software 22(1), 16–23 (2005)
3. Avgeriou, P., Grundy, J., Hall, J.G., Lago, P., Mistrík, I. (eds.): Relating Software Requirements and Architectures. Springer (2011)
4. Capilla, R., Babar, M.A., Pastor, O.: Quality requirements engineering for systems and software architecting: methods, approaches, and tools. Requir. Eng. 17(4), 255–258 (2012)
5. Bass, L., et al.: Software Architecture in Practice, 2nd edn. Addison-Wesley (2003)
6. van Heesch, U., Avgeriou, P.: Mature Architecting - A Survey about the Reasoning Process of Professional Architects. In: 9th WICSA, pp. 260–269
7. Bentsson-Svensson, R., Höst, M., Regnell, B.: Managing Quality Requirements: A Systematic Review. In: EUROMICRO-SEAA 2010, pp. 261–268 (2010)
8. Ameller, D., Ayala, C., Cabot, J., Franch, X.: How do software architects consider non-functional requirements: An exploratory study. In: RE 2012, pp. 41–50 (2012)
9. Poort, E.R., Martens, N., van de Weerd, I., van Vliet, H.: How Architects See Non-Functional Requirements: Beware of Modifiability. In: Regnell, B., Damian, D. (eds.) REFSQ 2011. LNCS, vol. 7195, pp. 37–51. Springer, Heidelberg (2012)

10. Ameller, D., Franch, X.: How Do Software Architects Consider Non-Functional Requirements: A Survey. In: Wieringa, R., Persson, A. (eds.) REFSQ 2010. LNCS, vol. 6182, pp. 276–277. Springer, Heidelberg (2010)
11. Poort, E.R., Key, A., de With, P.H.N., van Vliet, H.: Issues Dealing with Non-Functional Requirements across the Contractual Divide. In: WICSA/ECSA 2012, pp. 315–319 (2012)
12. Groene, B., et al.: Educating Architects in Industry - The SAP Architecture Curriculum. In: 17th IEEE Int. Conf. on Eng. of Computer Based Systems (ECBS), pp. 201–205.
13. Guessi, M., Nakagawa, E.Y., Oquendo, F., Maldonado, J.C.: Architectural description of embedded systems: a systematic review. In: ACM SIGSOFT ISARCS 2012, pp. 31–40 (2012)
14. Yin, R.K.: Case Study Research: Design and Methods. Sage, Thousand Oaks (2008)
15. King, N., Horrock, C.: Interviews in Qualitative Research. Sage, Thousand Oaks (2010)
16. Charmaz, K.: Constructing Grounded Theory. Sage, Thousand Oaks (2007)
17. Stakeholder Engagement Standard (AA1000SES), http://goo.gl/fRopv
18. Groene, B.: TAM – The SAP Way of Combining FCM and UML, http://goo.gl/FW1IA (last viewed on November 8, 2012)
19. Gilb, T.: Competitive Engineering: A Handbook For Systems Engineering, Requirements Engineering, and Software Engineering Using Planguage, Butterworth (2005)
20. Karlsson, J.: Managing software requirements using quality function deployment. SQJ 6(4), 311–326
21. Buglione, L.: Improving estimated by a four pieces puzzle, IFPUG Annual Conference (May 2012), http://goo.gl/bFwRB
22. IFPUG, Software Non-functional Assessment Process (SNAP) – Assessment Practice Manual (APM) Release 2.0 (January 22, 2013)
23. Boehm, B., Grunbacher, P., Briggs, R.O.: EasyWinWin: A Groupware-Supported Methodology for Requirement Negotiation. In: 9th ACM SIGSOFT FSE, pp. 320–321 (2001)
24. de Bono, E.: Six Thinking Hats. Little, Brown, & Co., Toronto (1985)
25. Buglione, L., Abran, A.: Improving Measurement Plans from multiple dimensions: Exercising with Balancing Multiple Dimensions - BMP. In: 1st Workshop on Methods for Learning Metrics, METRICS 2005 (2005)
26. Brooks, F.P.: The Design of Design: Essays from a Computer Scientist. Addison-Wesley (2010)
27. Nicholson, B., Sahay, S.: Embedded Knowledge and Offshore Software Development. Information and Organization 14(4), 329–365 (2004)
28. Herrmann, A., Daneva, M.: Requirements Prioritization Based on Benefit and Cost Prediction: An Agenda for Future Research. In: RE 2008, pp. 125–134 (2008)
29. Runeson, P., Höst, M.: Guidelines for conducting and reporting case study research in software engineering. Empirical Software Engineering 14(2), 131–164 (2009)
30. Seddon, P., Scheepers, P.: Towards the improved treatment of generalization of knowledge claims in IS research: drawing general conclusions from samples. EJIS, 1–16 (2011)

A Persona-Based Approach for Exploring Architecturally Significant Requirements in Agile Projects

Jane Cleland-Huang, Adam Czauderna, and Ed Keenan

DePaul University, Chicago, IL 60422, USA
jhuang@cs.depaul.edu, aczauderna@gmail.com, ekeenan2@cdm.depaul.edu

Abstract. [**Context and motivation**] Architecturally significant requirements (ASRs) drive and constrain many aspects of the architecture. It is therefore beneficial to elicit and analyze these requirements in early phases of a project so that they can be taken into consideration during the architectural design of the system. Unfortunately failure to invest upfront effort in exploring stakeholders quality concerns, can lead to the need for significant refactoring efforts to accommodate emerging requirements. This problem is particularly evident in agile projects which are inherently incremental. [**Question/Problem**] Existing techniques for early discovery of ASRs, such as Win-Win and i*, are typically rejected by agile development teams as being somewhat heavy-weight. A light-weight approach is therefore needed to help developers identify and explore critical architectural concerns early in the project. [**Principal ideas/results**] In this paper we present the use of Architecturally-Savvy Personas (ASP-Lite). The personas are used to emerge and analyze stakeholders' quality concerns and to drive and validate the architectural design. ASP-Lite emerged from our experiences working with the requirements and architectural design of the TraceLab project. The approach proved effective for discovering, analyzing, and managing architecturally significant requirements, and then for designing a high-level architectural solution which was designed to satisfy requirements despite significant interdependencies and tradeoffs. [**Contributions**] This paper presents the ASP-Lite approach and describes its support for architectural design in the US$2 Million TraceLab project.

Keywords: personas, architecture, requirements, architecturally significant requirements, tradeoffs.

1 Introduction

The overall quality of a software intensive system is measured according to whether the system meets its functional requirements and addresses the underlying quality concerns of its stakeholders. For example, a safety-critical avionics system must guarantee levels of safety through performance and dependability requirements, while a mobile phone service must provide reliable hand-over as

J. Doerr and A.L. Opdahl (Eds.): REFSQ 2013, LNCS 7830, pp. 18–33, 2013.

a subscriber moves across various towers, deliver high quality voice and data service, and also provide fast response times for placing calls and sending text messages [18].

The quality requirements for a system represent a special subset of Architecturally Significant Requirements (ASRs) that describe non-behavioral constraints on the system. Yu et al., identified over 100 different types of ASRs [9] including qualities such as reliability, maintainability, safety, usability, portability, and security [4, 12]. ASRs are quite varied in their impact on the system and in the way in which they must be specified. For example, a performance requirement might describe the response time or throughput requirements of a system, while an availability requirement might specify the need for a system to be available 24/7 or to have less than 1 hour of scheduled downtime a week.

ASRs play a strategic role in driving the architectural design of a software intensive system [5, 15] and are often used as a selection criteria for deciding between alternate architectural options [16]. Architects must therefore understand the stakeholders' quality concerns and then utilize technical knowledge to design an architectural solution which balances the potentially complex interdependencies and tradeoffs of the requirements. Techniques such as Architecture Driven Design (ADD) [5] assume a starting point of clearly specified quality concerns documented in the form of Quality Attribute Scenarios, while the Volere approach presents proactive techniques for eliciting and documenting quality concerns [24]. Cohen also describes an agile approach for specifying ASRs (i.e. constraints) in the form of user stories [10]. Despite these techniques many projects fail to adequately explore quality concerns. For example, Franch et al. conducted a survey of ASR elicitation techniques in 13 different software projects [3] and found that in many cases projects did not specify any such requirements. In one documented case, a customer assumed that a web page would take no more than two seconds to load but did not specify this as a requirement. Following deployment he complained that the page loaded too slowly. Identifying ASRs in advance can help to mitigate this type of problem.

1.1 Quality Concerns in Agile Development

The continuous move towards agile development practices highlights the importance of developing light-weight approaches for handling ASRs. Abrahammson et al. discuss the role of architecture in the agile process [1]. They conclude that "a healthy focus on architecture is not antithetic" to agility, and advocate for finding the architectural sweet spot for a given project so that the emphasis on architecture is customized to the needs of the particular project. Similarly Beck asserted that architecture is just as important in XP (eXtreme Programming) projects as it is in any other project [6]. In an interview conducted for IEEE Software's special edition on the Twin Peaks of Requirements and Architecture [8], Jan Bosch outlines the growing acceptance of designing and constructing a system incrementally, and allowing both functional and non-functional requirements to emerge as the project proceeds. This practice assumes that refactoring the architecture to accommodate newly discovered NFRs is an acceptable cost of doing business in an agile project, and contrasts with more traditional practices such as ADD [5] and WinWin [7]. In these approaches ASRs are rigorously elicited and analyzed in early phases of the project and then used to drive and evaluate candidate architectural designs. Scott Ambler proposes some kind of middle ground, in which architectures are *sketched* in early phases of the project [2]. Denne and Cleland-Huang describe the incremental funding method (IFM) in which architectures are planned upfront, but then delivered incrementally as needed to support the user-required functionality [13]. This approach has been shown to increase the financial return on investment of the project. Unfortunately the agile mantra of 'no big upfront design' is often used to justify a less than effective exploration of the quality requirements during early phases of the software development lifecycle, thereby increasing the likelihood of later costly refactoring efforts.

In this paper we propose a novel approach for capturing and evaluating architecturally significant requirements in agile projects, and then using them to drive and evaluate the architectural design. Our approach, which we call ASP-Lite (Architecturally Savvy Personas - Lite), utilizes HCI personas to express quality concerns in the form of user stories, written from the perspective of specific user groups. While personas have traditionally been used to explore the way individual user groups will interact with a system, ASP-Lite focuses primarily on quality concerns and constraints of the system, and is used to design and evaluate the architectural design. Our approach supports incremental delivery of the architecture, reducing the risk of designing an architecture which requires excessive refactoring.

1.2   Our Proposed Approach

ASP-Lite emerged from our own experiences in the TraceLab project [17], a US$2 Million endeavor funded by the US National Science Foundation and developed by researchers at DePaul university, the College of William and Mary, Kent State University, and the University of Kentucky. The core part of the project involved developing an experimental environment in which researchers can design experiments using a library of pre-existing and user-defined components, execute their experiments, and then comparatively evaluate results against existing benchmarks.

Early in the project it became apparent that there were some challenging and conflicting quality goals that would impact both the time-to-market and the long-term adoption of the system. To fully explore and understand the impact of early architectural decisions, we developed a set of personas that represented distinct sets of users' needs, especially those needs which impacted major architectural decisions. The personas were initially developed through a series of brainstorming activities by the core project team. They were presented to collaborators from all participating universities during an initial project launch meeting and refined until all meeting participants were satisfied that the personas provided a realistic and relatively complete representation of TraceLab users' quality concerns. The personas were then used throughout the remainder of the project to guide and critically evaluate architectural design decisions.

1.3   Paper Structure

Section 2 of this paper introduces the concept of Architecturally-Savvy personas. Section 3 describes the overall process model integrated into the SCRUM framework. Section 4 describes the personas that we created for the TraceLab project, and then section 5 describes the way in which the personas support the architectural design process. Finally, Section 6 describes the benefits of our approach and reports on our initial findings.

2   Architecturally-Savvy Personas

HCI personas were first introduced by Cooper as a means for integrating user goals and perspectives into the design process [11]. A persona provides a realistic and engaging representation of a specific user group, and is typically depicted through a picture and personal description that portrays something about the pysche, background, emotions and attitudes, and personal traits of the fictitious person [21, 22]. The task of creating a persona usually involves surveying and interviewing users, identifying optimal ways for slicing users into categories, collecting data to demonstrate that the proposed slices create distinguishable user groups, discovering patterns within the user groups, constructing personas for each group, and then creating scenarios describing how the persona might interact with the system under development. A project will typically have from about 5-8 personas.

While personas are typically used for purposes of User-Interaction design, there are a few examples in which they have been used as part of the requirements elicitation process. Dotan et al. evaluated the use of personas to communicate users' goals and preferences to project members as part of a two-day design workshop for the APOSDLE project [14]. Similarly, Robertson et al. also discussed the use of personas for gathering requirements when actual stakeholders are not available [24]. In both cases, the focus was on eliciting a general set of requirements and/or goals.

In contrast, ASP-Lite focuses on architecturally significant requirements. This emphasis impacts the way we slice (or categorize) groups of users in order to create a set of personas whose needs represent distinct sets of quality concerns. In the TraceLab project, many of these competing concerns emerged as a result of an initial Joint Application Design (JAD) session and a series of subsequent brainstorming meetings. As a result, researchers, developers, and architects worked collaboratively to create a small and distinct set of personas and to write a series of architecturally significant user stories for each of them. These user stories focused on qualities such as performance (i.e how fast?), reliability (i.e. how reliable?), and portability etc.

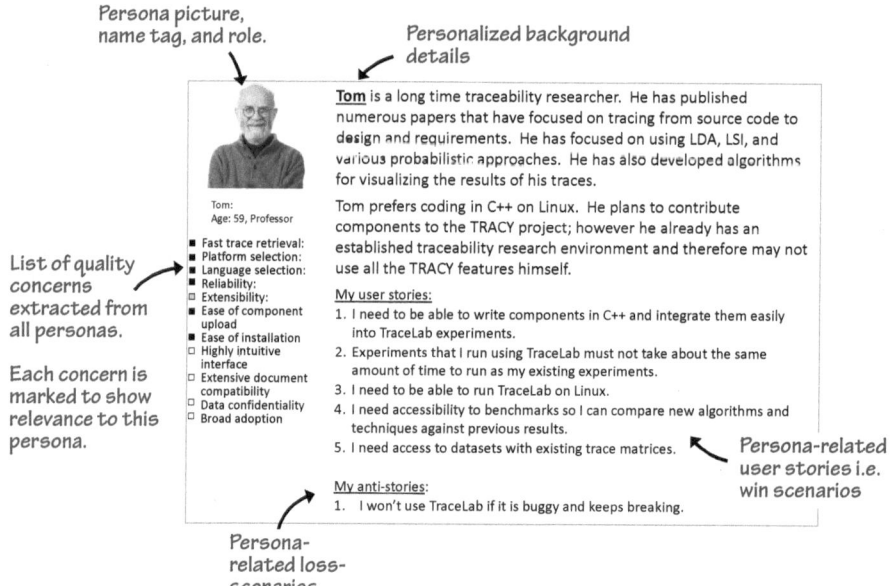

Fig. 1. Light-weight personas used as part of the agile development process to highlight quality concerns (i.e. Non-functional requirements). Personas are used to drive architectural design and to evaluate and validate candidate design solutions.

Once ASR-related user stories were identified for each persona in the project, they were compiled into a project-wide list containing quality concerns from all the personas, and then summarized in a succinct format as shown in the left hand side of Figure 1. A simple classification process was then used to mark each quality concern as *high* (black), *medium* (gray), or *low* (white) importance to each of the personas.

For example, Fig. 1 depicts Tom as a seasoned traceability researcher who has already established an effective research environment on the Linux/C++ platform. His particular concerns include (1) the ability to create components in C++ as this is the language of choice in his research group, (2) the need to run TraceLab on Linux, (3) the need to be able to easily compare results from existing experiments against benchmarks, (4) the ability to retrieve and rerun previously conducted experiments, and finally (5) the need for publicly available data sets. A deeper analysis of his functional requirements leads to the identification of several quality concerns related to language selection, platform selection, and ease of sharing experiments and components across research group boundaries.

3   Architecturally Savvy Personas and SCRUM

ASP-Lite can be used in any development environment; however we describe it within the context of the SCRUM process framework which was the primary project management process adopted in our project [23]. SCRUM is anchored around the concept of a *sprint*, which typically represents about 2-4 weeks of work, and also daily scrum meetings at which team members meet to assess progress, identify roadblocks, and plan next steps. At the start of each sprint, a set of features are selected from the prioritized list of features in the product backlog and placed into a sprint backlog. Each sprint produces potentially shippable code. In prior work, Madison [19] augmented the SCRUM process by injecting architectural concerns into the backlog so that architectural issues could be addressed incrementally throughout the development process.

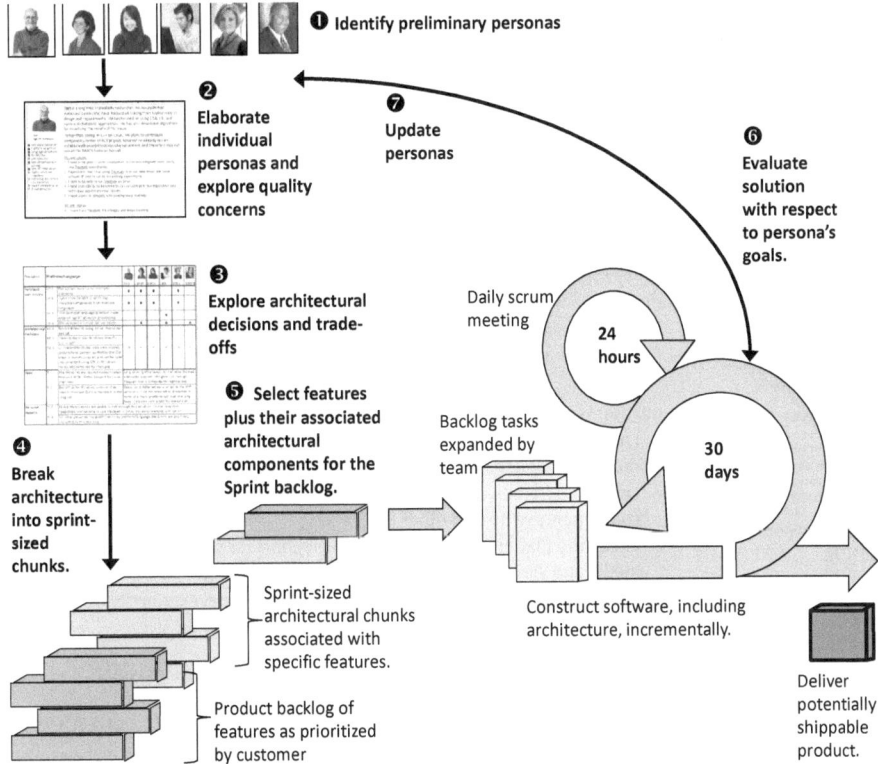

Fig. 2. Personas capturing role-specific quality concerns are used to augment the basic SCRUM life-cycle model in agile projects

ASP-Lite also augments the Scrum process in several important ways, depicted in the steps of Figure 2. First, ① a set of personas are identified and ② fleshed out. They are then used to ③ drive the architectural design and analysis process and then ④ the produced architecture is broken into sprint-sized chunks [20]. The product backlog is then populated with both functional features and architectural elements. ⑤ At the beginning of each sprint, the customer chooses features to implement, and the developers identify the architectural elements

Karly
Age: 26, PhD Student

☑ Fast trace retrieval:
☐ Platform selection:
☐ Language selection:
☑ Reliability:
☐ Extensibility:
☑ Ease of component upload
■ Ease of installation
■ Highly intuitive interface
☐ Extensive document
  compatibility
☐ Data confidentiality
  Broad adoption

Karly is a new PhD student. She is interested in tracing requirements to software architecture.

She has contacts with a local company who will allow her to access their data for her experiments; however this data is proprietary (i.e. protected by a NDA) and so she cannot share it with anyone else.

She predicts that it will take her about 6 months to set up her traceability environment, but then she discovers TRACY. Karly is quite a good programmer, but is much more interested in the process side of her research.

My user stories:

1. I need to be able to easily combine existing components to create an end-to-end tracing environment. The only programming I want to do is GUI programming in order to create new tracing interfaces.
2. I need to be able to develop my GUIs in C#
3. I need the GUIs to display quickly to the user during the experiment.
4. I need the installation process to be straight forward.

Jack, 34
Architect

☐ Fast trace retrieval:
■ Platform selection:
■ Language selection:
☐ Reliability:
☐ Extensibility:
☐ Ease of component upload
☐ Ease of installation
☐ Highly intuitive interface
☐ Extensive document
  compatibility
☐ Data confidentiality
  Broad adoption

Jack is married and has two young children. He has recently been hired by the TRACY project into the role of Software Architect/Developer. He has 6 years of experience as a software developer and 2 years as a lead architect in a successful gaming company. He has taken the job on the TRACY project because he is excited by the challenge of working in a research oriented project.

Jack is very motivated to build a high quality product. Jack has never worked in an academic research setting before. He is very collaborative and is looking forward to working with the other developers, academics, and students on the project.

My user stories:

1. I need to develop the TraceLab framework in a language which supports rapid prototyping.
2. I need the framework language to easily interface with, and call, components written in other languages.
3. I need the platform to provide natural support for the separation of model and view components.
4. I need libraries to be available for supporting GUI development.

Fig. 3. Two additional personas identified for the TraceLab project

that are needed to implement them. ⑥ Throughout the sprint, the system under development is evaluated with respect to the identified personas and when necessary, i.e. if new functionality is introduced, and further clarification is needed, ⑦ the personas are re-evaluated and modified accordingly.

4   Persona Creation and Use in the TraceLab Project

We created six personas for the TraceLab project. These included "Tom" previously presented in Fig. 1, and five additional personas discussed below:

• **Janet** has a PhD in Human Computer Interaction. She is interested in studying the ways users interact with traceability tools. Her research group develops GUI prototypes in C#. As Janet does not consider herself a programming whizz, she needs to be able to easily replace or modify one or more GUI screens in an existing tracing workflow so that she can capture user feedback on traces. Furthermore she is likely to abandon TraceLab if she is not able to download, install, and use it with minimal effort.

• **Karly** is a new PhD student. She is interested in tracing requirements to software architecture. Karly has contacts with a local company who will allow her to access their data for her experiments; however this data is proprietary (i.e. protected by a non-disclosure agreement) and so she cannot share it with anyone else. Maintaining full control and confidentiality over her data is essential, and so she is only able to use TraceLab if she can keep the data on her own desktop. Before she discovered TraceLab she had predicted that it would take at least 6 months to set up her traceability environment. Karly is quite a good programmer, but is much more interested in the process side of her research. Karly is depicted in Figure 3.

• **Jack** has recently been hired by the TraceLab project into the role of Software Architect/Developer. He has 6 years of experience as a software developer and 2 years as a lead architect in a successful gaming company. He has taken the job on the project because he is excited by the challenge of working in a research oriented project. Jack is very motivated to build a high quality product. It is critical to Jack that the selected platform and language support rapid prototyping and that libraries are available for developing GUI elements of the design. Jack is also depicted in Figure 3.

• **Mary** is a program director of the funding agency supporting TraceLab. She wants to see a return-on-investment through broad buy-in of TraceLab from the traceability community, reduced investment costs for new traceability research, enabling productivity much earlier in the research cycle, and evidence of broad-ranging support for the most critical areas of Traceability research.

• **Wayne** is the technical manager for a large industrial systems engineering project. He could be described as an early adopter, as he prides himself in keeping an eye out for good ideas that could help his organization. Wayne is concerned that current traceability practices in his organization are costly and inefficient. He has heard about the TraceLab project, and is interested in trying it out, but is concerned about investing time and effort in what appears to be an academic project. He has decided to use TraceLab in a small pilot study to see if it can meet his needs. In particular he needs TraceLab to be installable behind his firewall, configurable to work with his data, almost entirely bug-free, and to provide a professional standard GUI that his workers can use intuitively.

While there is no guarantee that these six personas are complete, they represent a solid starting point for reasoning about the quality concerns of TraceLab's end users.

5   From Personas to Architectural Design

An analysis of the personas' user stories revealed a set of architecturally significant requirements (ASRs) and also some potential conflicts. Specific issues

Decision:	Platform/Language		Tom	Janet	Karly	Jack	Mary	Wayne
Pertinent user stories:	US 1.	The system must run on multiple platforms	●	●	●		●	
	US 2.	Users must be able to write and integrate components from multiple languages	●	●	●		●	
	US 3.	The source language of each component must be invisible at runtime				●		
	US 4.	The selected language/platform must support rapid framework prototyping				●		
	US 5.	The selected GUI must deliver 'razzle dazzle'		●		●		●
Architectural Decisions	AD 1.	Build framework using Visual Studio.net and C#.						
	AD 2.	Develop the initial Windows-specific GUI in WPF.						
	AD 3.	Utilize MVVM (model view view model) architectural pattern, so that (a) the GUI View is loosely coupled and can be later implemented using GTK or Windows Forms and compiled for multiple platforms, and (b) the TraceLab engine can be compiled using Mono for porting to Linux and Mac environments.	½	✓	✓	✓	½	✓
Risks	R 1.	The Mono library may not support latest features of C#. Better support for Linux than Mac.	Long running OS project. Initial tests showed adequate support. Mitigate risk through frequent Mono compiles throughout the project.					
	R 2.	Build first for Windows solution may lead to multiple GUIs to maintain in the long run.	Decision is deferred as to whether the WPF version will be maintained or discarded in favor of a multi-platform GUI over the long term.					
Personal Impacts	PI 1.	Tom & Mary's needs are partially met through this solution. In the long-term researchers will be able to use TraceLab in Linux, but early releases will run on Windows only.						
	PI 2.	All other personas impacted directly by platform/language decisions are positively impacted by this decision.						

Fig. 4. Architecturally significant user stories related to the Platform/Language issue. Subsequent architectural decisions and their impact upon the personas are shown.

related to platform portability, programming language of the framework and components, and the plug-and-play ability of TraceLab were identified. In this section we explore these issues as part of the architectural design process. Our approach loosely follows SEI's Attribute Driven Design (ADD) process [5] which is an incremental scenario-driven approach to design that involves identifying quality attribute scenarios, and then proposing and evaluating candidate architectural solutions. ASP-List captures relevant user stories, architectural decisions, specific risks, and the impact of various decisions upon persona roles in an

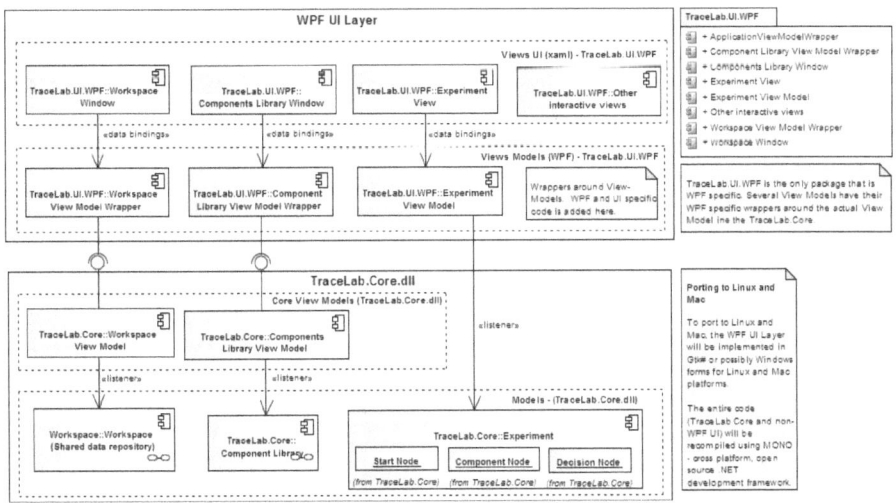

Fig. 5. TraceLab high level architectural design using the MVVM architectural pattern. This architectural diagram captures design decisions related to the platform/language issues that emerged through analyzing persona needs.

architectural issue template, illustrated in Fig. 4. Two examples of architectural issues are provided in the following discussion.

5.1   Architectural Issue # 1: Platform Language Portability

The personas' user stories highlighted the need for TraceLab to run on multiple platforms and to allow components to be developed in a variety of languages and then incorporated into TraceLab's plug-and-play environment at runtime. The following user stories, depicted in Fig. 4, were found to be particularly relevant:

1. The system must run on multiple platforms *(Tom, Janet, Karly, Mary)*
2. Users must be able to integrate components written in a wide variety of languages *(Tom, Janet, Karly, Mary)*
3. The source language of each component should be invisible at runtime *(Jack)*
4. The selected language and platform must support rapid prototyping (Rationale: As a research project we need the freedom to explore variations and to backtrack if and when necessary) *(Jack)*
5. Razzle dazzle (our metaphor for a GUI development environment which provides a high quality presentation to the user) *(Janet,Jack, Wayne)*

Team members met over a period of 2-3 weeks to brainstorm potential architectural solutions for addressing these quality concerns. The extended discussion period was needed to accommodate a series of architectural spikes in which proposed solutions were prototyped and evaluated. Serious consideration was given to three different framework languages: C++ (as this was the preferred language of at least one of our developers, Java (which would be intrinsically portable), and C# (which from the perspective and experience of the overall development team was the easiest language for development). C++ was discarded due to the learning curve needed by most of the developers and its anticipated lower productivity.

A series of architectural spikes were created to test the benefits of using a C# framework versus a java framework to support the integration of components from multiple source languages. The results from this phase showed that it was far simpler to make calls from C# to components written in other languages, than vice versa, which suggested developing the TraceLab framework in C# and then later compiling it to Mono so that it could run on other platforms. Future portability issues were addressed through a series of architectural decisions. For example, the VisualStudio.net environment provides intrinsic support for the MVVM (model view view model) architectural pattern and integrates closely with WPF. WPF supports rapid prototyping of professional GUIs, while the use of MVVM provides a clear separation between view and model and facilitates future reimplementation in GTK# or Windows Forms for porting to Linux and Mac platforms. Our design also separated out the WPF code in the views layer (which would need to be rewritten for porting purposes) from the non-WPF code which could be compiled using Mono.

The Architectural Issues Template shown in Fig. 6 also documents specific risks and their mitigations. For example, the decision to defer porting to the Linux/Mac environments is potentially impacted by the ability of Mono to compile framework code correctly. This risk was partially mitigated through testing Mono on a variety of projects, and through frequent compiles of the growing TraceLab framework into Mono.

Finally, the proposed architectural decisions were evaluated against the ability of the delivered architecture to meet each of the persona goals. In this case, four of the personas would be fully satisfied with the solution, while Tom and Mary would need to wait until later in the project for the port to Linux and Mac environments. However, this solution was determined to be an acceptable trade-off in light of the tight delivery constraints of the project, the need to build rapid prototypes in order to address the difficulty of potentially changing requirements in such a novel research instrumentation project, and the ease by which C# code was able to invoke components written in other languages.

5.2   Architectural Issue #2: Experimental Workflow

A second major architectural decision pertained to the requirements and design of the TraceLab experiments themselves. These experiments are composed from a series of pre-defined and/or user defined components, and therefore the Trace-Lab architecture needs to support communication between components and to control their execution. Relevant user stories included the following:

1. Experiments that I run using TraceLab must take about the same amount of time to run as my existing experiments. *(Tom, Janet, Karly)*
2. The TraceLab environment must incorporate plug-and-play. *(Tom, Janet, Karly, Wayne)*

Decision:		Workflow Architecture	 Tom	Janet	Karly	Jack	Mary	Wayne
Pertinent user stories:	US 1.	The TraceLab environment must support plug and play.	●	●	●			●
	US 2.	The performance penalty of using TraceLab must be low (i.e. close to runtime of non-TraceLab experiments).	●	●	●			●
	US 3.	Components should be reusable across research groups and experiments.	●				●	
Architectural Decisions	AD 1.	Utilize a blackboard architecture.						
	AD 2.	Create standard data types for exchanging data between components.						
	AD 3.	Construct the experiment around the concept of a workflow.	½	✓	✓			✓
	AD 4.	Support concurrent execution of components.						
	AD 5.	Trust the TraceLab users to create a viable workflow. Provide basic type checking only.						
Risks	R 1.	Performance may suffer as data is exchanged between components via shared memory.	Keep the data cache in the same App space as the experiment to avoid excessive data marshalling . Stream only critical data not entire data structure class.					
	R 2.	If TraceLab users proliferate the creation of data types, then plug-and-play ability will be lost.	Use community governance to increase the likelihood of shared use of data types.					
Personal Impacts	PI 1.	All personas are satisfied with the plug-and-play solution.						
	PI 2.	The performance penalty will be felt more by Tom, as he already has a functioning tracing environment. For other researchers the benefits of the plug-and-play environment and the use of previously defined tracing components far outweighs the slight performance penalty.						

Fig. 6. A second architecturally significant issue related to the way in which components should be built into an experimental workflow

3. Components should be reusable across experiments and research groups. *(Mary, Tom)*
4. Components should run concurrently whenever feasible. *(Tom)*

These user stories and associated architectural decisions are documented in Figure 6. Three different high-level architectural patterns were considered for connecting components in an experiment. A service oriented approach was proposed by an early consultant to the project based on his industrial experience as a SOA architect. However, this option was ruled out because we anticipated that some individual experiments might include over 50 fine-grained components (a supposition which has since proven to be correct). The overhead of calling so many services in a SOA environment was deemed to be prohibitively expensive. The second somewhat intuitive candidate architecture was the pipe-and-filter architectural pattern [5]. However, while this approach seemed to initially fit the concept of data flowing through the experiment, an initial analysis demonstrated that many filters (i.e. components) would in fact be assigned responsibility for the task of transferring data that they did not actually use. While this problem could be partially mitigated by having all components accept a composite message (containing self-describing datasets), this approach has the known flaw of

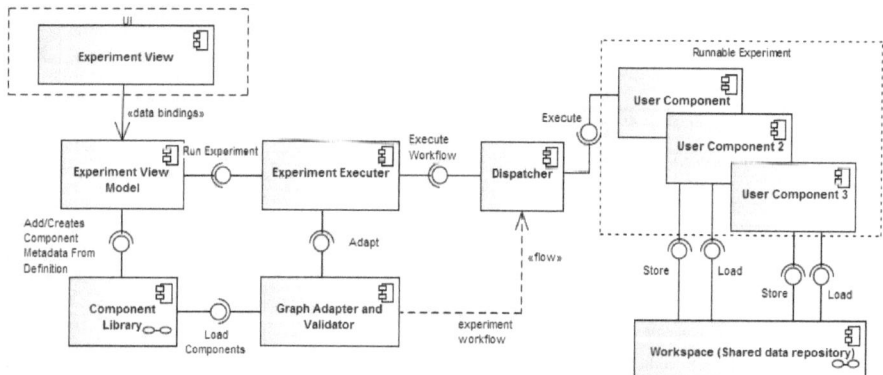

Fig. 7. The Architecture for the TraceLab workflow engine showing the execution control of components and the exchange of data through the blackboard workspace

creating ambiguous interfaces which cannot be understood without looking at the inner workings of the code. Furthermore, this approach would pass on the complexity of handling data typing to the component builders and could result in relatively large amounts of data being passed from one component to another. For these reasons, the pipe-and-filter approach was rejected.

The final architectural pattern we considered, and adopted, was the blackboard architecture. In this approach all data is transferred in standard datatypes, representing domain specific concepts such as trace matrices, artifact collections, and/or metric containers. Each component retrieves a copy of the data from a shared memory space (i.e. the blackboard), processes the data, and then returns the results in standard data formats back to the blackboard for use by other components. The TraceLab experimental graph represents a precedence graph, and the blackboard controller is responsible for dispatching components as soon as their precedence nodes in the graph complete execution. This design supports parallel computation and therefore also addresses performance concerns. In fact, once deployed we found that performance was still below expectations, but were able to modify the data marshaling functions to achieve Tom's performance goals. Some of the architectural decisions that contributed to satisfying the workflow requirements are shown in Figure 7.

6   Effectiveness of Our Approach

The ASR-aware personas we have created, and the supporting process in which they are deployed, brings several unique contributions to the current state of the art and practice in handling ASRs in agile projects. First, it has shown how personas can be used to capture quality concerns from the perspective of different user groups. Secondly, unlike the previous use of personas which have focused on interaction design and/or requirements elicitation, our approach is designed to drive and evaluate architectural design. Third, our approach introduces a light-weight approach to handling ASRs, which is particularly appropriate in an agile development process. Not as time-consuming as existing approaches such as Win-Win [7], ADD [5], or i* [26] techniques, our use of personas facilitates a meaningful exploration of the quality concerns of related stakeholder groups. Finally, the *architecture issues template* provides a useful means of exploring architectural options within the context of persona goals, and then of visualizing and documenting the extent to which a set of architectural decisions meets the quality requirements of the system. Like ADD [5], our approach is somewhat 'greedy' in nature, as it addresses one set of architectural issues at a time, and then accepts the constraints of that decision upon future decisions. This greedy approach is somewhat softened by the ability to backtrack whenever necessary. This introduces an enormous benefit to the agile process, because it allows backtracking to be performed during the design stage instead of relying upon more expensive backtracking (i.e. refactoring) following deployment.

In comparison to alternate techniques such as Win-Win [7] and i* [26], ASP-Lite facilitates the careful deliberation of competing quality concerns without introducing unnecessary upfront modeling activities. Using either win-win or a modeling approach such as i* would have slowed the project pace in a way that was unacceptable to the project team. In contrast, ASP-Lite fit seamlessly into the adopted agile process, and was perceived by all participants to deliver value to the project.

Formally evaluating a process such as ASP-Lite can be difficult and costly, and can effectively only be accomplished through examining the impact of the new process on practice [25]. For example, our approach could be evaluated by measuring the impact of the process upon the reduction in refactoring costs in a greenfield or even a long-lived project, and through making statistical comparisons between projects that use the approach versus those that do not. However this is an extensive process which can best be performed once a process is adopted in an industrial setting.

On the other hand, the purpose of this experience report is to describe a process which we found anecdotally to be effective in our own development project. The architectural decisions in the TraceLab project were made carefully in light of the persona user stories, and two and a half years into the project, the architectural decisions have all proven to be basically sound. For example, the decision to build first for Windows and then later to port to Linux and Mac environments allowed us to get TraceLab into the hands of our users much faster than would otherwise have been possible. Furthermore, the architectural decisions that were made to separate out WPF code are now paying dividends as we have already compiled TraceLab to run on multiple platforms and are in the process of completing a new multi-platform GUI in GTK#. Similarly, the decision to adopt a blackboard architecture has also proven successful, and early adopters have no problem creating components in multiple languages, integrating them into TraceLab's plug-and-play environment, and reusing them across experiments.

To evaluate whether ASP-Lite could be generalized to a broader set of systems, we also applied it as a reverse-engineering exercise against an enterprise level Mechatronics traceability project we conducted with a major Systems

Engineering Company. Five distinct personas were identified. Related user stories were written and analyzed which ultimately led to the identification of several architecturally significant requirements pertinent to the design of the system. Interestingly, the ASRs that were identified were significantly different from those discovered for the TraceLab project and focused more upon access control and confidentiality of data as well as usability and performance issues, suggesting that our approach is effective for identifying project-specific quality concerns. Based on this very initial analysis of our approach across an entirely different system, we conclude that it is applicable to a range of projects in which quality concerns need to be explored in a more incremental and agile environment.

7   Conclusions and Future Work

This paper presents an experience report of utilizing architecturally-aware personas within an agile project environment. As such, it provides a viable light-weight solution for addressing quality concerns in agile projects and for potentially reducing the need to refactor later in the project. Based on our initial experiences with ASP-Lite we are currently developing a tool which will make the process more accessible to practitioners.

Acknowledgments. This work was supported by National Science Foundation grants CCF-0959924 and CCF-1265178.

References

1. Abrahamsson, P., Babar, M., Kruchten, P.: Agility and architecture: Can they coexist? IEEE Software 27(2), 16–22 (2010)
2. Ambler, S.W.: Agile modeling: A brief overview. In: pUML, pp. 7–11 (2001)
3. Ameller, D., Ayala, C.P., Cabot, J., Franch, X.: How do software architects consider non-functional requirements: An exploratory study. In: RE, pp. 41–50 (2012)
4. Anton, A.: Goal Identification and Refinement in the Specification of Software-Based Information Systems. Georgia Institute of Technology, Atlanta (1997)
5. Bass, L., Clements, P., Kazman, R.: Software Architecture in Practice. Adison Wesley (2003)
6. Beck, K.: Extreme Programming Explained: Embrace Change. Addison-Wesley (2000)
7. Boehm, B.W., Egyed, A., Port, D., Shah, A., Kwan, J., Madachy, R.J.: A stakeholder win-win approach to software engineering education. Ann. Software Eng. 6, 295–321 (1998)
8. Bosch, J., Dvorak, D.: Traversing the twin peaks. IEEE Software (2012)
9. Chung, L.: Non-functional Requirements in Software Engineering. Kluwer Academic Publishers, Norwell (2000)
10. Cohen, M.: Non-functional requirements as user stories. Mountain Goat Software, mountaingoatsoftware.com
11. Cooper, A.: The inmates are running the asylum. Software-Ergonomie, 17 (1999)
12. Davis, A.: Software Requirements - Objects, Functions, and States. Prentice Hall, Englewood Cliffs (1993)

13. Denne, M., Cleland-Huang, J.: The incremental funding method: Data-driven software development. IEEE Software 21(3), 39–47 (2004)
14. Dotan, A., Maiden, N., Lichtner, V., Germanovich, L.: Designing with only four people in mind? – a case study of using personas to redesign a work-integrated learning support system. In: Gross, T., Gulliksen, J., Kotzé, P., Oestreicher, L., Palanque, P., Prates, R.O., Winckler, M. (eds.) INTERACT 2009. LNCS, vol. 5727, pp. 497–509. Springer, Heidelberg (2009)
15. Jansen, A., Bosch, J.: Software architecture as a set of architectural design decisions. In: Proceedings of the 5th Working IEEE/IFIP Conference on Software Architecture, pp. 109–120. IEEE Computer Society Press, Washington, DC (2005)
16. Kazman, R., Klein, M., Clements, P.: Atam: A method for architecture evaluation. Software Engineering Institute (2000)
17. Keenan, E., Czauderna, A., Leach, G., Cleland-Huang, J., Shin, Y., Moritz, E., Gethers, M., Poshyvanyk, D., Maletic, J.I., Hayes, J.H., Dekhtyar, A., Manukian, D., Hossein, S., Hearn, D.: Tracelab: An experimental workbench for equipping researchers to innovate, synthesize, and comparatively evaluate traceability solutions. In: ICSE, pp. 1375–1378 (2012)
18. Mirakhorli, M., Cleland-Huang, J.: Tracing Non-Functional Requirements. In: Zisman, A., Cleland-Huang, J., Gotel, O. (eds.) Software and Systems Traceability. Springer, Heidelberg (2011)
19. Madison, J.: Agile architecture interactions. IEEE Software 27(2), 41–48 (2010)
20. Madison, J.: Agile architecture interactions. IEEE Software 27(2), 41–48 (2010)
21. Nielsen, L.: Personas - User Focused Design. Human-Computer Interaction Series, vol. 15. Springer (2013)
22. Putnam, C., Kolko, B.E., Wood, S.: Communicating about users in ICTD: leveraging hci personas. In: ICTD, pp. 338–349 (2012)
23. Rising, L., Janoff, N.S.: The scrum software development process for small teams. IEEE Software 17(4), 26–32 (2000)
24. Robertson, S., Robertson, J.: Mastering the Requirements Process. Adison Wesley (2006)
25. Unterkalmsteiner, M., Gorschek, T., Islam, A.K.M.M., Cheng, C.K., Permadi, R.B., Feldt, R.: Evaluation and measurement of software process improvement - a systematic literature review. IEEE Trans. Software Eng. 38(2), 398–424 (2012)
26. Yu, E.S.K.: Social modeling and i*. In: Conceptual Modeling: Foundations and Applications, pp. 99–121 (2009)

Using Clustering to Improve the Structure of Natural Language Requirements Documents

Alessio Ferrari[1], Stefania Gnesi[1], and Gabriele Tolomei[2]

[1] ISTI-CNR, Pisa, Italy
{alessio.ferrari,stefania.gnesi}@isti.cnr.it
[2] DAIS, Università Ca' Foscari Venezia, Italy
gabriele.tolomei@unive.it

Abstract. [**Context and motivation**] System requirements are normally provided in the form of natural language documents. Such documents need to be properly structured, in order to ease the overall uptake of the requirements by the readers of the document. A structure that allows a proper understanding of a requirements document shall satisfy two main quality attributes: (i) *requirements relatedness*: each requirement is conceptually connected with the requirements in the same section; (ii) *sections independence*: each section is conceptually separated from the others. [**Question/Problem**] Automatically identifying the parts of the document that lack requirements relatedness and sections independence may help improve the document structure. [**Principal idea/results**] To this end, we define a novel clustering algorithm named Sliding Head-Tail Component (S-HTC). The algorithm groups together similar requirements that are contiguous in the requirements document. We claim that such algorithm allows discovering the structure of the document in the way it is perceived by the reader. If the structure originally provided by the document does not match the structure discovered by the algorithm, hints are given to identify the parts of the document that lack requirements relatedness and sections independence. [**Contribution**] We evaluate the effectiveness of the algorithm with a pilot test on a requirements standard of the railway domain (583 requirements).

Keywords: Requirements analysis, requirements documents structure, requirements quality, similarity-based clustering, lexical clustering.

1 Introduction

The quality of a natural language requirements document strongly depends on its *structure* [16,10]. A proper document structuring enables a better *understanding* of the requirements, and eases the modifiability of the overall requirements specification [20]. Even though many templates and recommendations are available to guide the structuring of a requirements document [10,14,3], few automatic approaches exist to evaluate the quality of the document structure *after* the document has been written. The current work presents a novel automated analysis method along this little-explored research path.

J. Doerr and A.L. Opdahl (Eds.): REFSQ 2013, LNCS 7830, pp. 34–49, 2013.
© Springer-Verlag Berlin Heidelberg 2013

Several factors affect the structure of a requirements document. The length of the sections, the number of nested paragraphs in each section, the clarity of the titles and the number of cross-references are only a limited list of those structural aspects that can make a requirements document completely clear or completely unintelligible. In this paper, we focus on two structural quality attributes that we consider relevant to facilitate the understanding of a requirements document, namely the *requirements relatedness* and the *sections independence.*

A requirements document provides proper requirements relatedness if each requirement is conceptually connected with the previous and following requirements of the same section. Furthermore, a requirements document provides proper sections independence when each section is conceptually separated from the others.

In principle, quantitative indexes of the two quality attributes defined above may be derived from a similarity-based lexical analysis of the document. Requirements relatedness could be mapped to an index of *cohesion* among requirements, while sections independence could be mapped to an index of *separation* among sections [18]. However, we argue that such indexes might be hardly usable to improve the structure of the document. Indeed, once we know that a requirements document has a low value of cohesion or separation – even assuming that we are able to define what is a low/high value for these indexes – we do not have any guidance to actually enhance the structure of such document.

Therefore, in our approach, we do not associate quantitative indexes to the quality attributes under analysis. Instead, we define a clustering-based approach that identifies the structure of the document in the way it might be perceived by the reader. Intuitively, if a lexical change occurs in the requirements document, the reader assumes that the discussed concepts are different, and she expects a new section. The document structure is supposed to reflect such conceptual changes.

The clustering algorithm employed in our approach, named Sliding Head-Tail Component (S-HTC), detects the conceptual changes in the requirements, and identifies the *hidden structure* of the document in terms of such changes. In the hidden structure, requirements are grouped according to their lexical relatedness, and sections are partitioned according to their lexical independence. Therefore, requirements relatedness and sections independence for the original document are evaluated in comparison to the hidden structure discovered by the algorithm. If the structure of the original document does not adhere to the hidden structure, hints are given to re-arrange the requirements document.

We present the results of a pilot test on the functional requirements document of the EIRENE (European Integrated Railway radio Enhanced NEtwork) system, a digital radio standard for railways [19] (583 requirements in total).

The paper is structured as follows. In Sect. 2, we present the overview of the method. In Sect. 3, we describe the approach in detail. In Sect. 4, the pilot test is discussed. In Sect. 5, we summarize the most relevant related work. In Sect. 6, we draw conclusions and we discuss the possible evolution of the approach.

2   Overview of the Method

An overview of the method is presented in Fig.1. The method is based on a clustering algorithm, named Sliding Head-Tail Component (S-HTC), which is described in Sect. 3. The input of the algorithm is the ordered list of the requirements (**Requirements List**) in the **Original Document**, without any information about the document structure (i.e., no sections, no indexes).

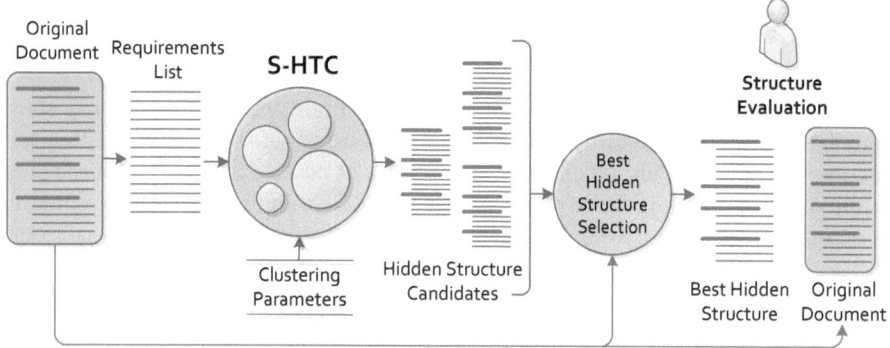

Fig. 1. Method Overview

The **S-HTC** algorithm is able to identify possible *hidden structures* of the requirements document. A hidden structure is a partitioning of the document into possible sections of requirements. The partitioning is performed according to the similarity among neighbouring requirements in the document. The algorithm produces hidden structures where requirements are grouped according to their lexical relatedness, and sections are partitioned according to their lexical independence.

The algorithm is executed several times, varying different clustering parameters that influence its behaviour. The output of each execution is a **Hidden Structure Candidate**. Intuitively, a hidden structure candidate represents the structure of the document perceived by a possible reader, who reads the document without having the original structure information (i.e., the document is made of a single, long sequence of requirements without sections).

Among the hidden structure candidates, we select the one that more closely matches the structure originally provided by the document (**Best Hidden Structure Selection**). We call this structure candidate the **Best Hidden Structure**. Intuitively, the best hidden structure is the structure of the document perceived by a reader who is provided with the original structure information. The assumption here is that the original structure is reasonable, but might require some improvements.

To this end, we finally observe the differences between the best hidden structure and the original structure (**Structure Evaluation**). The detected differences allows identifying the defects in the original structure related to: (1) requirements that are not sufficiently related with the other requirements of the same section; (2) sections that are not sufficiently independent from the others.

3   Requirements Clustering

The core of our method is the Sliding Head-Tail Component (S-HTC) clustering algorithm. The algorithm is a variant of the Head-Tail Component (HTC) algorithm defined by the third author for retrieving groups of task-related queries in Web-search engine query logs [12].

The S-HTC algorithm groups together those requirements that are lexically related, and that are contiguous in the document. The goal of this clustering approach is emulating the process of reading a requirements document: if two contiguous requirements are lexically related, they are likely to speak about the same content. Therefore, we assume that the reader is likely to interpret them as part of the same conceptual unit of the document. If there is a change in the lexical content (i.e., the reader reads a requirement that is not lexically related to the previous ones), the requirement is likely to speak about other concepts, and is likely to be part of another conceptual unit.

The S-HTC algorithm is designed to identify such conceptual units. From the ordered list of requirements in a document, the algorithm derives a *sequence* of clusters (i.e., ordered groups of requirements), each one representing a conceptual unit of the document. We call this sequence of clusters the *hidden structure* of the document. More formally, given the list of requirements in a document, i.e., $D = \langle R_1, R_2, \ldots, R_m \rangle$, the hidden structure is a ordered partitioning of D, i.e., $\pi(D)$, into a non-empty disjoint sequence of clusters C^i that completely cover D, namely $\pi(D) = \langle C^1, C^2, \ldots, C^{|\pi(D)|} \rangle$ [1].

3.1   Requirements Representation

In order for the requirements to be processed by the clustering algorithm, a proper representation is required that describes the lexical content of the requirement. To this end, we choose a representation of a requirement R_j that takes into account the set of lexical terms, which it is composed of.

In order to focus only on the *relevant* lexical aspects of a requirement, it is recommended to remove from its representation all those terms that are common in the language, which the requirements are written in. These common terms, such as articles and pronouns, are known as *stop-words*.

Furthermore, it is useful to reduce the remaining terms to their morphological root (e.g., the terms "equipment" and "equipped" are both reduced to "equip"). This procedure is called *stemming*.

---

[1] It should be $|\pi(D)| \ll m$ in order for the partitioning to be effective.

More formally, let $T = \{t_1, t_2, \ldots, t_n\}$ be the set of unique terms in D, i.e., the *vocabulary* of terms. Therefore, R_j may be represented as a subset of distinct terms, i.e., $\hat{R}_j \subseteq T$. Let $\overline{T} = T \setminus S$, where S is the set of stop-words. Moreover, let M be the set morphological roots, and let $\phi : T \to M$ be the stemming function that maps each term into its morphological root. Therefore, R_j may be represented as a set of distinct morphological roots of those terms that are not stop-words, i.e., $R'_j = \{\phi(t_j) \mid t_j \in \hat{R}_j \cap \overline{T}\}$.

Consider, for example, the requirement 5.4.6 extracted from the EIRENE dataset [19]: $R =$ *"The driver shall be able to adjust the contrast of the display"*. Its lexical representation is the set $R' = \{$driv, abl, adjust, contrast, display$\}$.

3.2   Similarity Metrics

In order to establish the degree of relationship among requirements, the clustering algorithm requires the definition of a similarity metric. Since requirements are natural language sentences, typical string similarity metrics can be used to establish the degree of relationship between pairs of requirements [1].

If we consider the lexical representation described in Sect. 3.1, an immediate way to compute the text similarity between two requirements R_i, R_j is to consider their corresponding term-set representations, i.e., R'_i and R'_j, respectively. An interesting measure is given by the *Jaccard index*, also known as *Jaccard similarity metric*, which is defined as follows:

$$\sigma_{jac}(R_i, R_j) = \frac{|R'_i \cap R'_j|}{|R'_i \cup R'_j|}. \tag{1}$$

This similarity metric measures the proportion of terms that two text strings have in common. It assumes that the greater is the number of shared terms the higher is the chance of the two strings to be similar.

Another popular lexical-based similarity metric is the *edit distance*, which counts the number of edit operations required to transform one text string into another. There are several different ways to define an edit distance, depending on which edit operations are allowed, e.g., *replace*, *delete*, *insert*, *transpose*, etc. In this work, we resort to using one of the most common metric for measuring the edit distance between two strings, namely the *Levenshtein distance* [11], which we properly transform in a similarity metric σ_{lev} normalized between 0 and 1. The Levenshtein distance allows capturing the character-level similarity among the sentences, while the Jaccard metric captures the term-level similarity.

Finally, we consider another similarity metric, which is obtained by a convex combination between σ_{jac} and σ_{lev} as follows:

$$\sigma_{jac-lev}(R_i, R_j) = \alpha \cdot \sigma_{jac}(R_i, R_j) + \beta \cdot \sigma_{lev}(R_i, R_j). \tag{2}$$

In our experiments, which are described in Section 4, we set $\alpha = \beta = 0.5$. This choice equally balances the impact of the two metrics, namely $\sigma_{jac}(R_i, R_j)$ and $\sigma_{lev}(R_i, R_j)$, in the computation of the final measure.

3.3   S-HTC Clustering Algorithm

The S-HTC algorithm comprises two steps. In the first step a preliminary list of clusters is built. In the second step, similar clusters are merged to create the hidden structure.

First Step: Preliminary List of Clusters. The first step aims at creating an approximate fine-grained clustering of the given requirement document D, represented as a *sequence*, i.e., $D = \langle R_1, R_2, \ldots, R_m \rangle$. S-HTC exploits the sequentiality of contract-style requirement lists, and tries to detect sequential clusters of requirements, denoted with $\tilde{C}^i$, namely groups of requirements that occur in a row in the document. Each requirement in the same sequential cluster is similar enough to the immediate next one. The behaviour of the algorithm relies on a threshold parameter τ, which defines how much similar two requirements are supposed to be, in order to be placed in the same cluster.

Each requirement is compared to the following one through a similarity function $\sigma : D \times D \longmapsto [0, 1]$. The similarity function can be computed in terms of σ_{jac}, σ_{lev}, or $\sigma_{jac-lev}$.

The first preliminary cluster $\tilde{C}^1$ is initialized with the requirement R_1. If $\sigma(R_1, R_2) > \tau$, R_2 is added to the $\tilde{C}^1$ cluster. Otherwise, a new cluster $\tilde{C}^2$ is created, and R_2 is added to this cluster. Then, R_2 is compared with R_3. If $\sigma(R_2, R_3) > \tau$, R_3 is added to the cluster where R_2 resides, otherwise a new cluster is created. The algorithm iterates this procedure until no more requirements are left.

At the end of the first step we have a sequence of preliminary clusters, namely $\tilde{\pi}(D) = \langle \tilde{C}^1 \ldots \tilde{C}^{|\tilde{\pi}(D)|} \rangle$.

Second Step: Hidden Structure. In this step we build the possible conceptual units of the document as they might be perceived by the reader, i.e., we identify a possible *hidden structure* of the document. To this end, we merge together related preliminary clusters.

The rationale of this step is as follows. In a requirements document, we might have a requirement that, though not being similar to the exact previous one, is similar to one of the requirements occurring slightly before in the document. For example, take the case of the three following requirements for a generic radio communication system for trains (adtapted from [19]):

- R_1 : *If the driver receives an incoming call, the system shall enable the loudspeaker.*
- R_2 : *If the driver receives an incoming call, the system shall visualize the identity of the caller through the driver visual interface.*
- R_3 : *If the loudspeaker is enabled, an audible indication shall be provided to the driver.*

A reader would naturally interpret these requirements as part of the same conceptual unit. We notice that R_1 and R_2 are lexically similar. Hence, after the first step of the algorithm, we expect to have a cluster $\tilde{C}^1 = \langle R_1, R_2 \rangle$. On the other hand, R_2 is not lexically similar to R_3. Therefore, we would have a separate cluster for R_3, i.e., a cluster $\tilde{C}^2 = \langle R_3 \rangle$. Nevertheless, we notice that R_3 is similar to R_1, and it is natural to interpret R_3 in relation to R_1. Therefore, in the final hidden structure we want a cluster to include all the three requirements.

The second step of the algorithm aims at systematically resolving situations such as the one described above. To this end, clusters are merged if the last requirements of a cluster (*tail*) are sufficiently similar to the first requirements (*head*) of a following cluster.

More formally, given a *window size* parameter $w \in \mathbb{N}$, we define the head of a cluster as the set of its first w requirements, while we define the tail of a cluster as the set of its last w requirements. If a preliminary cluster $\tilde{C}$ is composed by $|\tilde{C}|$ requirements $R_0 \ldots R_{|\tilde{C}|-1}$, its head is: $h(\tilde{C}) = \{R_i \in \tilde{C} : 0 \leq i < w\}$, while its tail is: $t(\tilde{C}) = \{R_i \in \tilde{C} : 0 < |\tilde{C}| - w \leq i \leq |\tilde{C}| - 1\}$.

The comparison among two preliminary clusters $\tilde{C}^i$, $\tilde{C}^j$ (with $i < j$) is performed considering the tail of $\tilde{C}^i$ and the head of $\tilde{C}^j$ according to the following similarity function:

$$s(\tilde{C}^i, \tilde{C}^j) = \max_{\substack{R' \in \{t(\tilde{C}^i)\} \\ R'' \in \{h(\tilde{C}^j)\}}} \sigma(R', R'').$$

Again, σ may be computed in terms of σ_{jac}, σ_{lev}, or $\sigma_{jac-lev}$.

In order to merge preliminary clusters, we compare head and tail of each cluster $\tilde{C}^i$ with the l following ones, from $\tilde{C}^{i+1}$ to $\tilde{C}^{i+l}$. The parameter l defines how many subsequent clusters shall be compared with $\tilde{C}^i$. We call this parameter *lookahead*. Clusters are merged if their similarity is higher than the previously defined threshold τ (i.e., if $s(\tilde{C}^i, \tilde{C}^j) > \tau$).

The goal of this comparison with the l clusters that follow $\tilde{C}^i$ – and not solely with $\tilde{C}^{i+1}$ – is to isolate requirements, or group of requirements, that are not sufficiently related with the neighbouring ones. Consider for example the following requirement, R_u : "*The system shall support recovery from loss of communication*".

Let us now consider again the requirements R_1, R_2, R_3. If we have an original requirement document such as $D = \langle R_1, R_2, R_u, R_3 \rangle$, requirement R_u might look misplaced. Indeed, it is related to the recovery part of the system, while the other requirements are speaking about procedural aspects. Therefore, we would like the hidden structure to include a $\langle R_1, R_2, R_3 \rangle$ cluster, and isolate R_u in a separate cluster. This goal is addressed by comparing the cluster $\tilde{C}^1 = \langle R_1, R_2 \rangle$ with both the cluster $\tilde{C}^2 = \langle R_u \rangle$ and $\tilde{C}^3 = \langle R_3 \rangle$. Since $\tilde{C}^1$ is similar to $\tilde{C}^3$, these will be merged, and $\tilde{C}^2 = \langle R_u \rangle$ will appear as an isolate cluster.

Summarizing, the final hidden structure $\pi(D)$ is computed as follows. The first cluster C^1 is initialized with the first preliminary cluster $\tilde{C}^1$. Then, C^1 is compared with with any other following preliminary cluster $\tilde{C}^j$, with $j = 2 \ldots 1 + l$, by computing the similarity $s(C^1, \tilde{C}^j)$. If $s(C^1, \tilde{C}^j) > \tau$, then $\tilde{C}^j$ is merged into C^1, the *head* and *tail* requirements of C^1 are updated consequently, and $\tilde{C}^j$ is removed from the set of preliminary clusters. The algorithm continues comparing the new cluster C^1 with the remaining preliminary clusters until

$j = 1 + l$. When all the remaining preliminary clusters within the lookahead interval have been considered, the oldest preliminary cluster available is used to build a new cluster C^2. The algorithm iterates this procedure until no more preliminary clusters are left.

The final output of the algorithm is the sequence of clusters that represents the *hidden structure*, namely $\pi(D) = \langle C^1 \dots C^{|\pi(D)|} \rangle$.

3.4   Best Hidden Structure

The output of the algorithm depends on the similarity function σ adopted, and on three parameters, namely, the similarity threshold τ, the window size w, and the lookahead l. By executing the algorithm with different similarity functions and different combinations of values for the parameters, different hidden structures are generated. We call these structures *hidden structure candidates*. These structures represent possible partitioning of the document perceived by a reader who reads the document without having the original structure information. Intuitively, the variation of the parameters allows the identification of possible variants in the interpretation of the document structure.

Given the hidden structure candidates, we select the one that more closely matches the structure originally provided by the document. We call this candidate the *best hidden structure*. In our view, the best hidden structure represents the structure that is the closest to the conceptual partitioning that might be perceived by a reader who is provided with the original structure information. The reasonable assumption here is that the original structure is not completely flawed, but has been defined with the purpose of providing a useful guidance for the reader.

The comparison among the hidden structure candidates and the original structure is performed according to the three following indexes: (1) *number of clusters*, (2) *average* number of requirements per cluster, and (3) *standard deviation* of the number of requirements per cluster. This last index is useful to discard hidden structures that, for example, have regular clusters, while in the original document the sections largely vary in length.

The hidden structure candidate that more closely matches the original structure according to these indexes is chosen as the best hidden structure.

Finally, the best hidden structure is analysed and compared with the original structure by a human operator to assess the differences, and identify parts of the document that lack *requirements relatedness*, and *sections independence*. Possible cases are the following:

- If there is a section in the document that includes several lexically independent sub-parts (i.e., a section corresponds different clusters of the best hidden structure), there is probably a lack of section independence. Such section should be probably partitioned into more sections.
- If two separate sections of the document are lexically related (i.e., the sections appears in a single cluster of the best hidden structure), there is too much dependency among sections. It should be probably preferable to merge the two sections into a single one.

– If some requirements are not lexically related to the neighbouring requirements, like in the case of R_u of the example in Sect. 3.3, there is likely to be a lack of requirements relatedness. The requirement should be placed in another section.

4   Pilot Test: EIRENE

We evaluate the effectiveness of our proposed method on a publicly available requirements document of the railway domain, namely the *UIC EIRENE Functional Requirements Specification version 7* [19], issued in 2006. The requirements specified by the document refer to the EIRENE (European Integrated Railway radio Enhanced NEtwork) system, which is the digital radio standard for the European railways. The standard gives prescriptions concerning the network services that are required to support communications that involve trains, stations and railway personnel. Furthermore, requirements are given also concerning the interface of the system with the driver of the train.

The document comprises 583 requirements partitioned into 14 sections. The introductory section of the document is not considered in our dataset. Other relevant statistics on the document content are reported in Table 1.

Table 1. The EIRENE dataset

Requirements	
Number of requirements	583
Total number of distinct terms (stemmed and without stop-words)	879
Average number of terms per requirement	16
Standard deviation of the number of terms per requirement	14
Sections	
Number of sections	14
Average number of requirements per section	42
Standard deviation of the number of requirements per section	46

The document has been processed through the S-HTC algorithm to produce the hidden structure candidates. Each run of the algorithm, and therefore each produced candidate, depends on the similarity metric adopted, and on the specific values of τ, w and l. The similarity metrics are the σ_{jac}, σ_{lev} and $\sigma_{jac-lev}$. Different combination of values of the parameters τ, w, and l have been used. In particular, the threshold τ varies between 0 and 1, with increasing steps of 0.1. For each value of τ, we vary both w and l. The window size is $w \in \{1, 2\}$, which implies that we consider the head/tail of a preliminary cluster as a single requirement, or two requirements. The lookahead is $l \in \{1, 2, 3\}$. Therefore, at most three preliminary clusters are compared each time with the current cluster, to evaluate possible merge operations in the second step of the S-HTC algorithm. In the context of the document under analysis, we considered that a maximum lookahead of three was sufficient to isolate misplaced requirements according to the rationale discussed in Sect. 3.3. Larger ranges could be used to properly discover misplaced requirements in documents with different writing styles.

Considering all the combinations of the parameters for each one of the similarity metric, we derive 198 hidden structure candidates in total (66 for each similarity metric). Fig. 2 gives a comparative view of the number of clusters produced with the different similarity metrics. In the x axis we order the hidden structure candidates considering increasing values of τ, and increasing variation of w and l within their ranges.

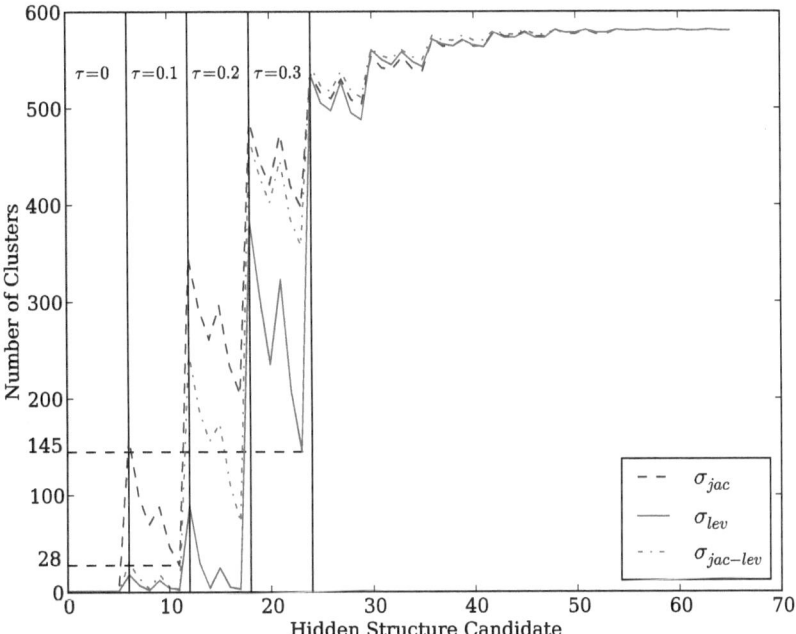

Fig. 2. Number of clusters for each hidden structure candidate

Hidden Structure Candidates. We notice that, regardless of the similarity metric considered, the number of clusters of the hidden structure candidates rapidly increases towards values that are not comparable with the number of sections of the original document. Indeed, already with $\tau = 0.3$ (hidden structure candidates from 18 to 23, according to the numbering of the x axis), the minimum number of clusters is 145, obtained for $\sigma = \sigma_{lev}$, $\tau = 0.3$, $w = 1$, $l = 3$.

We also notice that, for values of $\tau \leq 0.3$, the number of clusters produced with the σ_{jac} similarity metric is always higher than the number of clusters produced with σ_{lev} and $\sigma_{jac-lev}$. In particular, the minimum number of clusters produced with σ_{jac} is 28 (obtained for $\tau = 0.1$, $w = 2$, $l = 3$), exactly twice the number of sections in the original document[2]. Therefore, we argue that the σ_{jac}

---

[2] We do not consider the cases when $\tau = 0$, for which the algorithm produces always one cluster, regardless of the similarity metric employed.

similarity metric is basically not representative in the context of the requirements document under analysis.

According to these observations, the only candidates that can be reasonably evaluated to select the best hidden structure are those generated with $\sigma \in \{\sigma_{lev}, \sigma_{jac-lev}\}$, and $\tau \in [0, 0.2]$. Fig 3 reports an excerpt of the previous plot, centred on these hidden structure candidates.

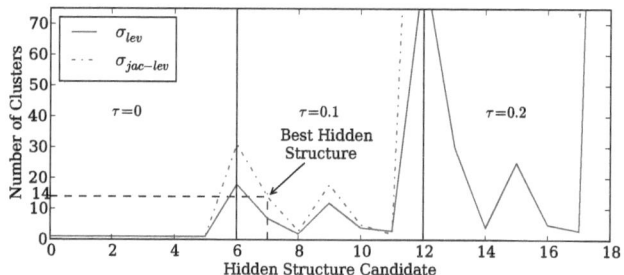

Fig. 3. Number of clusters produced when $\tau \in [0, 0.2]$

Best Hidden Structure. The best hidden structure, highlighted in Fig 3, is found for $\sigma_{jac-lev}$, $\tau = 0.1$, $w = 1$ and $l = 2$. In Table 2 we list the best candidates, together with the values for the indexes that have been used to select the best hidden structure (highlighted in bold).

Table 2. Best hidden structure candidates

σ	τ	w	l	Clusters	Average	Std Deviation
$\sigma_{jac-lev}$	0.1	1	2	**14**	**42**	**35**
σ_{lev}	0.1	2	1	12	49	58
$\sigma_{jac-lev}$	0.1	2	1	18	32	47
σ_{lev}	0.1	1	1	18	32	37
Expected				14	42	46

In the last row of the table we recall the expected values for such indexes, namely the number of sections of the original document, and the average and standard deviation of the number of requirements per section. More accurate approaches for the evaluation of clusterings could be employed (see, for instance, the similarity-oriented measures of cluster validity in [18]). However, in the presented experiment, the indexes adopted resulted sufficient to identify the best hidden structure.

We evaluate the original structure of the document and we compare it with the best hidden structure selected. Furthermore, we consider the most recent version of the requirements document (version 7.3, issued in 2012). The updates found in such document are used to give hints to evaluate the effectiveness of the approach.

Table 3. Comparison among the *original structure* and the *best hidden structure*

Section	Title	Cluster
2	Network Requirements	C^1
3	Network Configuration	C^2
4	Mobile equipment core specification	C^2
5	Cab radio	C^3, C^4, C^5
6	General purpose radio	C^6, C^7
7	Operational radio	C^8
8	Controller equipment specifications	C^9
9	Numbering plan	C^9
10	Subscriber management	C^{10}
11	Functional numbering and location dependent addressing	C^{10}
12	Text messaging	C^{11}
13	Railway emergency calls	C^{11}
14	Shunting mode	C^{11}
15	Direct mode	C^{12}
-	-	C^{13}, C^{14}

Table 3 compares the section of the original document with the clusters of the best hidden structure. In general, we observe that clusters in the hidden structure can be mapped to corresponding sections, or groups of sections. The two clusters that cannot be mapped (C^{13} and C^{14}) include requirements that are deleted from the specification, and which, in the original document, are formed solely by the term "deleted". These are basically clusters of noisy items.

Let us give a closer look to Table 3. The first section after the introduction, named "Network Requirements", has a corresponding cluster in the hidden structure that includes all its requirements. We conclude that such section is sufficiently independent from the others. The same observation holds for sections 7 and 15, named "Operational Radio" and "Direct Mode", respectively.

Different conclusion can be drawn from the evaluation of the other clusters. Most of the requirements of Sections 3 ("Network Configuration") and 4 ("Mobile equipment core specification") are included in the same cluster. Looking at the content, we see that the reason why the two sections are merged into the same cluster are the last requirements of section 3, namely requirements 3.5.7 and 3.5.8. The requirements are as follows:

- 3.5.7: *Cab Radios configured for reception of a call to all drivers in the same area entering an area where a call to all drivers in the same area is ongoing shall automatically join this call unless involved in a higher priority call or involved in a call of the same priority.*
- 3.5.8: *Requirement 3.5.7 needs further technical specification changes before field implementation can be achieved.*

The first requirement is evidently unreadable, and, most of all, anticipates some content discussed in section 4. This is the reason why the two sections appear in the same cluster, and it is an evident lack of *sections independence*. Instead, the second requirement is included in another cluster, since it is not lexically related with the previous one. The relation with the previous requirement is given by the cross-reference, and our algorithm is not thought to deal with such semantic issues.

It is worth noticing that, in the most recent version of the specification, both the requirements have been deleted.

Section 5, named "Cab Radio", is partitioned into 3 different clusters, which is an indicator of a lack of *section independence*. This section is the longest of the document (188 requirements in total, 32% of the entire document), and could be rearranged into smaller sections. In particular, there are requirements that are contiguous in the document, but that are not strictly related (i.e., there is a lack of *requirements relatedness*). Consider the following requirements:

- 5.4.3: *All call related functions shall be possible with the handset on or off the hook.*
- 5.4.4: *Note: there is no requirement for hands free operation.*
- 5.4.5: *The driver shall be able to adjust the brightness of buttons, indicator lights and displays according to the ambient lighting in the cab.*
- 5.4.6: *The driver shall be able to adjust the contrast of the display.*

In the best hidden structure, requirements 5.4.5 and 5.4.6, which concern the interface of the system with the driver of the train, are not clustered with requirements 5.4.3 and 5.4.4. Instead, they are clustered with other requirements that give prescriptions concerning the system-driver interface (5.2.3.18-19). The re-arrangement suggested by the best hidden structure is as follows:

- 5.2.3.18 *It shall be possible for the driver to increase and decrease the loudspeaker volume within the adjustment range selected.*
- 5.2.3.19: *When the handset is picked up, the loudspeaker shall continue to operate, but at a reduced volume level.*
- 5.4.5: *The driver shall be able to adjust the brightness of buttons, indicator lights and displays according to the ambient lighting in the cab.*
- 5.4.6: *The driver shall be able to adjust the contrast of the display.*

The best hidden structure suggests to group together requirements related to the audio interface with those related to the visual interface, which is a reasonable solution. Furthermore, we notice that requirement 5.4.4, which is evidently vague, has been largely modified in the most recent version of the document. We argue that such modification is an indicator that the part of the document considered lacked proper requirements relatedness, as pointed out by our algorithm.

Similar observations can be drawn from the analysis of the rest of the best hidden structure. We find that section 6 is partitioned into two clusters, revealing a lack of sections independence. Furthermore, the other remaining sections tend to be grouped together. In particular, we find three clusters that group sections 8-9, 10-11, and 12-13-14, respectively. This is a witness of dependency among sections. However, we have noticed that such dependency is not actually evident while reading the sections grouped in the same clusters. In these cases, the section partitioning given by the original document is probably preferable to the one suggested by the best hidden structure.

5 Related Work

The structure of the requirements document is considered as a central element to evaluate the quality of a requirements specification [20,2,8]. Several international standards provide templates to enforce a proper structuring of the requirements. The main reference in software engineering is the IEEE Standard 830-1998 [10], which defines eight possible templates, each one focused on a different approach for organizing the document (e.g., by functional hierarchy, by feature, etc.). Each template lists the sections and the content that a software requirements speci-fication is supposed to provide. A similar approach is adopted in the MIL 498 standard [14], where the template is tailored for requirements document of the defense sector. In the railway domain, the CENELEC EN 50128 standard [3] does not provide a specific template. Instead, guidelines are given to provide a proper structuring of the requirements document. In this case, companies nor-mally provide internal templates that are used across different projects.

Several studies exist that are focused on the automatic analysis of the struc-ture of a *generic* natural language document. Mao *et al.* [13] provides a com-prehensive survey of the different approaches available in the literature. Most of the works rely on a set of rules or templates that enable the automatic identifi-cation of the different logical parts of the document, such as titles, abstract and sections. To our knowledge, the only work on automatic structure analysis that is specifically concerned with requirements documents has been recently pro-posed by Rauf *et al.* [17]. In that paper, a framework is presented to retrieve the logical structure of requirements documents. The logical structure items (e.g., functional requirements or use cases) that the framework is supposed to identify are defined in the form of templates. The framework retrieves instances of such items from the document according to the templates.

Compared to the other works, the main novelty of the current paper is the auto-matic evaluation of the structure of a requirements document *without* a reference template. On the other hand, the technologies that we have employed, in particular the text similarity metrics, have been widely used in natural language requirements analysis. Such related works use technologies similar to ours to achieve different goals. Besides our previous contribution [7], where a clustering-based approach is used to identify requirements flaws, it is worth citing the comprehensive study of Falessi *et al.* [6]. Here, the authors experiment different similarity metrics to identify equivalent requirements. Other relevant contribution are those of Natt och Dag *et al.* [5], focused on the identification of conceptual links between newly-arrived and previously stored customer requirements, and Park *et al.* [15], where text similarity metrics are employed to support the requirements analyst in finding inconsistencies between high-level and low-level requirements.

Textual similarity analysis has been widely used also for automated require-ments tracing. The main reference works have been published, among others, by Hayes (see, e.g., [9]) and Cleland-Huang (see, e.g., [4]). However, in the trace-ability domain, the majority of the works employs information retrieval and statistical machine learning methods, while, in our work, a clustering-based ap-proach is adopted.

6 Conclusions

In this paper, a clustering-based approach to evaluate the structure of a natural language requirements document is presented. We focus on the identification of those parts of the document that lack proper requirements relatedness and proper sections independence. The approach identifies the *hidden structure* of the document (i.e., the structure possibly perceived by the reader) and compares it with the original document structure to assess inconsistencies.

The method has been employed to evaluate a requirements document standard of the railway domain. To fully evaluate the approach, further experiments on other documents, and with the support of domain experts, are required. Nevertheless, our pilot study has shown that the proposed algorithm is effective in identifying parts of the documents with poor structuring, sections that shall be re-arranged, and requirements that are misplaced.

On the other hand, the algorithm behaviour shall be tuned to better deal with issues related to sections dependency. We have seen that, in some cases, the algorithm reveals dependency among sections that, from a reader's perspective, are not actual conceptual dependencies. We argue that taking into account also semantic aspects when performing requirements clustering might resolve these situations. To this end, we plan to explore latent semantic analysis and term frequency analysis approaches, as well as exploiting external knowledge sources (e.g., Word-Net[3], Wikipedia[4]) for capturing the semantic relatedness between requirement pairs.

References

1. Achananuparp, P., Hu, X., Shen, X.: The evaluation of sentence similarity measures. In: Song, I.-Y., Eder, J., Nguyen, T.M. (eds.) DaWaK 2008. LNCS, vol. 5182, pp. 305–316. Springer, Heidelberg (2008)
2. Berry, D.M., Bucchiarone, A., Gnesi, S., Lami, G., Trentanni, G.: A new quality model for natural language requirements specifications. In: Proc. of REFSQ 2006, pp. 115–128 (2006)
3. CENELEC: EN 50128, Railway applications - Communications, signalling and processing systems - Software for railway control and protection systems (2011)
4. Cleland-Huang, J., Czauderna, A., Gibiec, M., Emenecker, J.: A machine learning approach for tracing regulatory codes to product specific requirements. In: Proc. of ICSE 2010, vol. 1, pp. 155–164. ACM, New York (2010)
5. Natt och Dag, J., Gervasi, V., Brinkkemper, S., Regnell, B.: A linguistic-engineering approach to large-scale requirements management. IEEE Software 22, 32–39 (2005)
6. Falessi, D., Cantone, G., Canfora, G.: Empirical principles and an industrial case study in retrieving equivalent requirements via natural language processing techniques. IEEE Transactions on Software Engineering PP(99) (2011)
7. Ferrari, A., Gnesi, S., Tolomei, G.: A clustering-based approach for discovering flaws in requirements specifications. In: Proceedings of ACM SAC 2012, pp. 1043–1050 (2012)

---

[3] http://wordnet.princeton.edu/
[4] http://www.wikipedia.org

8. Gervasi, V., Nuseibeh, B.: Lightweight validation of natural language requirements. Software: Practice and Experience 32(2), 113–133 (2002)
9. Hayes, J.H., Dekhtyar, A., Sundaram, S.K.: Advancing candidate link generation for requirements tracing: The study of methods. IEEE Trans. Software Eng. 32(1), 4–19 (2006)
10. IEEE: Std 830-1998 - Recommended Practice for Software Requirements Specifications (1998)
11. Levenshtein, V.I.: Binary codes capable of correcting deletions, insertions, and reversals. Soviet Physics Doklady 10(8), 707–710 (1966)
12. Lucchese, C., Orlando, S., Perego, R., Silvestri, F., Tolomei, G.: Identifying task-based sessions in search engine query logs. In: Proc. of WSDM 2011, pp. 277–286. ACM, New York City (2011)
13. Mao, S., Rosenfeld, A., Kanungo, T.: Document structure analysis algorithms: a literature survey. In: Proc. of DRR 2003, pp. 197–207 (2003)
14. MIL: Std 498 - Software Development and Documentation (1994)
15. Park, S., Kim, H., Ko, Y., Seo, J.: Implementation of an efficient requirements-analysis supporting system using similarity measure techniques. IST 42, 429–438 (2000)
16. Pohl, K.: Requirements Engineering: Fundamentals, Principles, and Techniques. Springer (2010)
17. Rauf, R., Antkiewicz, M., Czarnecki, K.: Logical structure extraction from software requirements documents. In: Proc. of IEEE RE 2011, pp. 101–110. IEEE Computer Society, Washington, DC (2011)
18. Tan, P., Steinbach, M., Kumar, V.: Introduction to Data Mining. Addison-Wesley, Boston (2005)
19. UIC - International Union of Railways: EIRENE Functional Requirements Specification v.7 (2006), http://www.uic.org/IMG/pdf/EIRENE_FRS_v7.pdf
20. Wilson, W.M., Rosenberg, L.H., Hyatt, L.E.: Automated analysis of requirement specifications. In: Proc. of ICSE 1997, pp. 161–171. ACM Press, New York (1997)

Automatic Requirement Categorization of Large Natural Language Specifications at Mercedes-Benz for Review Improvements

Daniel Ott

Research and Development
Daimler AG
P.O. Box 2360, 89013 Ulm, Germany
daniel.ott@daimler.com

Abstract. Context and motivation: Today's industry specifications, in particular those of the automotive industry, are complex and voluminous. At Mercedes-Benz, a specification and its referenced documents often sums up to 3,000 pages. **Question/problem:** A common way to ensure the quality in such natural language specifications is technical review. Given such large specifications, reviewers have major problems in finding defects, especially consistency or completeness defects, between requirements with related information, spread over the various documents. **Principal ideas/results:** In this paper, we investigate two specifications from Mercedes-Benz, whether requirements with related information spread over many sections of many documents can be automatically classified and extracted using text classification algorithms to support reviewers with their work. We further research enhancements to improve these classifiers. The results of this work demonstrate that an automatic classification of requirements for multiple aspects is feasible with high accuracy. **Contribution:** In this paper, we show how an automatic classification of requirements can be used to improve the review process. We discuss the limitations and potentials of using this approach.

Keywords: experimental software engineering, review, topic, topic landscape, classified requirements, inspection.

1 Introduction

Today, requirements of industry specifications need to be categorized based upon their aspects and stakeholder intent for many reasons.

Song and Hwong [6] state, for example, the need of a categorization of requirements for the following purposes: The need to identify requirements of different kinds (e.g. technical requirements), to have specific guidelines for developing and analyzing these requirement types. Especially, the identification of non-functional requirements is important for architectural decisions and to identify the needed equipment, its quantity and permitted suppliers. Another reason is the identification of dependencies among requirements, especially to detect risks and for scheduling needs during the project.

J. Doerr and A.L. Opdahl (Eds.): REFSQ 2013, LNCS 7830, pp. 50–64, 2013.
© Springer-Verlag Berlin Heidelberg 2013

Knauss et al.[2] also report the importance for many specifications nowadays, to classify the security-related requirements early in the project, to prevent substantial security problems later.

In addition to the above reasons, we at Mercedes-Benz are most interested in the aspect of categorizing requirements containing related information to improve our review activities in detecting consistency and completeness defects. Current specifications at Mercedes-Benz, and their referenced supplementary specifications, often have more than 3,000 pages [1]. Supplementary specifications can be, for example, internal or external standards. A typical specification at Mercedes-Benz is written in natural language (NL) and refers to 30-300 of these documents [1]. The information related to one requirement can be spread across many documents. This makes it difficult or nearly impossible for a reviewer to find consistency and completeness defects in the specification and between the specification and referenced supplementary specifications, as reported in a recent analysis of the defect distribution in current Mercedes-Benz specifications [4].

Considering the huge amount of requirements, it is obvious that the identification of topics and the classification of requirements to these topics must be done automatically to be of practical use. In this paper, we present a tool-supported approach to automatically classify and extract requirements with related information and to visualize the resulting requirement classes. The categorization is done by applying text classification algorithms like Multinomial Naive Bayes or Support Vector Machines, which use experience from previously classified requirement documents. We later evaluate this approach using two German specifications of Mercedes-Benz and investigate how the results of the classifiers can be improved with enhancements (for example pre-processing).

Section 2 provides an overview of the approach of collecting requirements of related information into classes, we call this concept "topic landscape". We also present the tool ReCaRe (**Re**view with **Ca**tegorized **Re**quirements), which realizes the topic landscape, and its concepts e.g. the classification algorithms. Section 3 presents the results of the evaluation of ReCaRe on the Mercedes-Benz specifications. These results are discussed in Section 4. In Section 5 we discuss related work and finally, in Section 6 we conclude with a summary of the contents of this work and describe our planned next steps.

2   The Topic Landscape Approach

The topic landscape aims at supporting the review process by classifying the requirements of the inspected specification and its additional documents into topics. A topic is defined by one or more key words. For instance, the topic "temperature" is defined by key words like "hot", "cold", "heat", "°C", "Kelvin" or the word "temperature" itself.

All requirements classified in a particular topic can be grouped for a specific review session. Due to this separation of the specification and its additional documents into smaller parts with content related requirements, a human inspector can more easily check these requirements for content quality criteria like consistency or completeness, without searching every single relevant document.

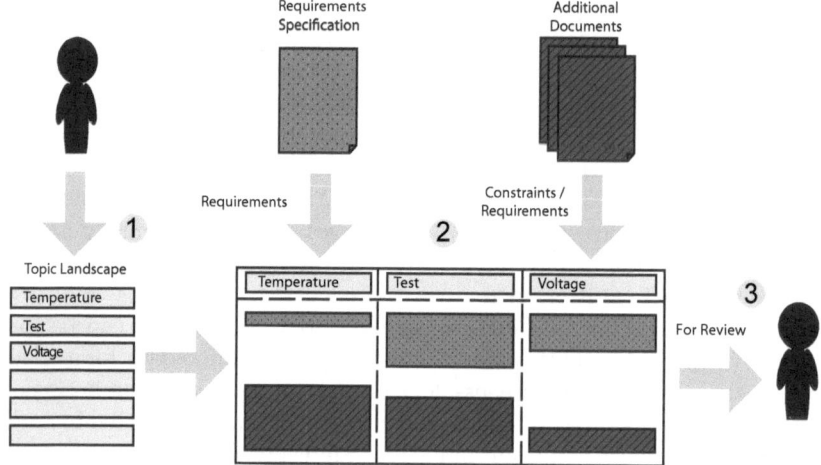

Fig. 1. Illustration of the Topic Landscape

Figure 1 illustrates the individual steps in order to use the topic landscape:

1. The user/author creates the topic landscape as a container of relevant topics for this particular specification. Each topic is described by one or more keywords.
2. Each requirement of the specification and the requirements/constraints of the additional documents are classified into individual topics.
3. The inspector chooses one topic from the topic landscape and checks all requirements assigned to the chosen topic for defects.

In this work, we research the performance of classifiers to automatically perform Step 2. Step 1 could also be performed semi-automatically by a sophisticated algorithm, but this remains future work.

The content of a topic may not be considered disjoint from other topics since a requirement normally includes information on different topics and thus will be assigned to several of them. For instance, the requirement "The vehicle doors must be unlocked when the accident detection system is not available." highlights many topics including, but not limited to, accident detection, accident, detection, availability, locking, vehicle door, door, security, door control, and functionality.

2.1   ReCaRe

The tool ReCaRe (**Re**view with **Ca**tegorized **Re**quirements) is the realization of the topic landscape. ReCaRe was implemented by the author based on eclipse[1] with a data connection to IBM Rational DOORS[2], because most of the requirement specifications at Mercedes Benz are stored there. Since ReCaRe is still

---

[1] www.eclipse.org
[2] www.ibm.com/software/awdtools/doors/

a prototype, we focused it on the basic use case of classifying text. Currently, ReCaRe cannot extract information from figures or tables. Our Mercedes-Benz specifications contain some requirements, which only consist of figures or tables, so these requirements cannot be classified correctly with the current version of ReCaRe.

Figure 2 shows the individual processing steps of ReCaRe. The pre-processing and classification steps should be read as parallel alternatives and we will investigate in later sections, which combination returns the best results.

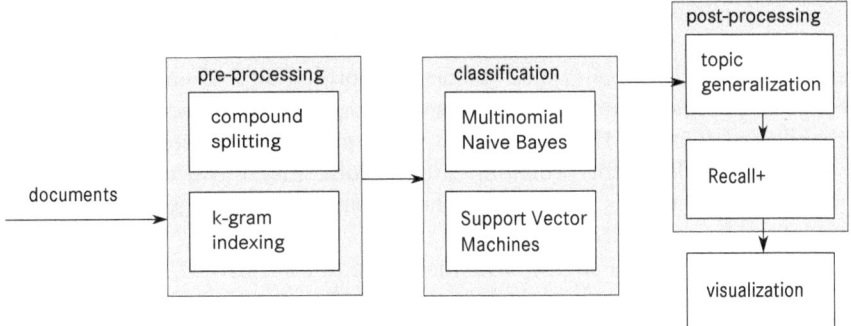

Fig. 2. Processing Steps in ReCaRe

In ReCaRe we assume that a requirement can be classified to multiple topics. Therefore, we train a binary classifier for each topic, which decides if a requirement is relevant or not for a certain topic. The classification algorithms are described in Section 2.2 and 2.3. Both classifiers are based on the work of Witten et al. [7] and more details to the classifiers can be found there. We choose Support Vector Machines and Multinomial Naive Bayes as classification algorithms because they are well known in literature (e.g. [7], [18]) for their exemplary performance in text classification tasks. Furthermore, initial tests with alternative classification algorithms like decision trees or rule based approaches returned poor results in comparison.

In Section 2.4, we describe, why we choose the illustrated selection of pre-processing steps. We also list alternative pre-processing steps and their short comings there. Finally in Section 2.4, we explain the unfamiliar post-processing steps "topic generalization" and "Recall+".

2.2   Multinomial Naive Bayes (MNB)

In our current work, the Naive Bayesian Classifier computes the probability that a requirement is relevant to a certain topic with the help of statistic methods.

The probability that a requirement R is relevant to a topic top is calculated with the Bayesian rule as follows [7], [23]:

$$P(top_R|W) = \frac{P(W|top_R) * P(top_R)}{P(W)}$$

W is the set of all words from the training data. For each word $w_i \in W$ the probability is calculated that the word is evident for being topic relevant. This is done, by using the number of topic relevant requirements containing w_i normalized with the total number of topic relevant requirements. To calculate $P(W|top_R)$ the name giving, naive assumption is made that the different words in the requirement are topic-conditional independent. Therefore $P(W|top_R)$ can be calculated with the following equation using the training data:

$$P(W|top_R) = \prod_{i=1}^{n} P(w_i|top_R)$$

The probability $P(top_R)$, which defines the probability of encountering topic relevant requirements in real-world specifications, is assumed to be the same probability as found in the training data as suggested by Witten et al. [7]. This probability is called prior probability. The probability P(W) disappears in the final normalization step, which sums the probabilities of the requirement being topic relevant or topic irrelevant to 1.

In this work we use a slightly modified form of the Naive Bayes called Multinomial Naive Bayes, which also considers the frequency of the words in a requirement and not only whether the word is appearing in the requirement. The details of this modification are described by Witten et al. [7].

2.3   Support Vector Machines (SVM)

The support vector machine approach works in ReCaRe as follows (based on Witten et al. [7] and Han et al. [23]) : A nonlinear mapping is used to transform the training data into a higher dimension. Within this new dimension, the classifier searches for the optimal separating hyperplane, which separates the class of topic relevant and topic irrelevant requirements. If a sufficiently high dimension is used, data from two classes can always be separated by a hyperplane. The SVM finds the maximum-margin hyperplane using support vectors and margins. The maximum-margin hyperplane is the one with the greatest separation between the two classes.

The maximum-margin hyperplane can be written as [7]:

$$x = b + \sum_{i \text{ is support vector}} \alpha_i * y_i * a(i) \cdot a$$

Here, y_i is the class value of training instance $a(i)$, while b and α_i are numeric parameters that have to be determined by the SVM. $a(i)$ and a are vectors. The vector a represents a test instance, which shall be classified by the SVM.

2.4   Domain and Review Specific Enhancements

As shown in Figure 2, we consider the following pre- and post-processing enhancements to improve the classification results:

The first part is the text pre-processing before the actual classification. Known pre-processing steps are removal of stopwords, stemming or lemmatization, decomposing of compounds, and the more recently used k-gram indexing. These steps are described in detail, for example, by Hollink et al. [19]. Because the Mercedes-Benz specifications are mainly in German, we focus on pre-processing steps, which have benefits in this language. Besides explaining the processing steps, Hollink et al. [19] show also that stemming and lemmatization result in almost no improvements for German texts. Leuser [20] confirms this for a large Mercedes-Benz specification. Removing stopwords using the well-known stopword list from snowball.tartarus.org has only improved the classification speed but not the results in our initial analyses. On the other hand, Hollink et al. [19] report that compound splitting and k-gram indexing improved the results for German texts significantly. Therefore, we analyse the benefits of both in Section 3. In k-gram indexing, each word of the requirement is separated in each ongoing combination of k letters and the classifier is then trained with these indexes instead of the whole words. For example, a k-gram indexing with k = 4 separates the word "require" to "requ", "equi", "quir", "uire". In compound splitting, compound words, like the German word "Eisenbahn" (English: railway), can be split in "Eisen" (English: iron) and "Bahn" (English: train).

The first post-processing step called "topic generalization" takes the structure of Mercedes-Benz specifications into account. All specifications at our company are written using a template, which provides a generic structure and general requirements, and are later filled with system specific contents. Because of this structure, we assume that if a heading was assigned to a topic, we can also assign each requirement and subheading under the heading to this topic. Furthermore, this is the only way, besides the thereafter following "Recall+" approach, to correctly assign requirements to topics, which only consist of a figure or a table, because ReCaRe has currently no potential to get information out of figures or tables.

Finally, there is also a possible review or ReCaRe specific enhancement: Because of the visualisation of the topics, we need to provide the ReCaRe-user with the context around of each requirement in each topic, so that the reviewer understands where in the document the specific requirement comes from. This is done by linking the requirement of the topic to the full document. So the reader has an awareness of the surrounding requirements during the review. Because of this, we assume that, if in a later stage of the analyses an unclassified requirement is within a certain structural distance to correctly classified requirements, we can also count this requirement as classified. We call this assumption "Recall+" because it only influences this specific measure later in the evaluation. Until now, Recall+ is not proven in experiments with ReCaRe-users. But we still want to share the idea of this concept in this work.

The benefits of all presented enhancements are analysed in Section 3.

3 Evaluation of the Automatic Requirements Classification

In this section, we automatically classify requirements of two German specifications by Mercedes-Benz to topics. We define our evaluation goals for this classification in Section 3.1. Further, we describe specification characteristics and the general evaluation process in Section 3.2. Finally, we show the results of each evaluation goal in the remaining Sections 3.3 and 3.4.

3.1 Evaluation Goals

To evaluate the automatic requirements classification to topics, we define the following evaluation goals:

- (G1) Evaluate accuracy of automatic classifiers at large automotive specifications.
- (G2) Evaluate improvements of the accuracy of automatic classifiers by domain and review specific enhancements.
- (G3) Evaluate the transferability of a trained classifier of a specification to an other specification in the same system domain.
- (G4) Evaluate the benefit of the topic landscape by review activities.

At Mercedes-Benz, we are mostly interested in G3 because the main problem in practical usage of such classifiers is getting the required training data: Our developers do not have the time to manually classify major parts of the requirements. Because of this, we want to use the advantage that most specifications do not have completely new contents. So, we can take previous specifications from older car series about the same system or system parts to train the classifiers for the new specification.

For Goal (G4), a first experiment utilizing the idea of using a categorization of requirements to topics in order to improve the review process was done in a previous work [3]. Unfortunately, this previous experiment showed how difficult it is to simulate reviews with industrial specification in external environments like universities. But, we cannot risk doing a pilot study with an unproven new approach at Mercedes-Benz, yet. Thus, the evaluation of (G4) remains future work. Then, we will do an replication of the mentioned experiment, but this time with the support of the ReCaRe-Framework.

3.2 Evaluation Strategy

The evaluation of the classifiers' accuracy is done with two German automotive specifications. The first specification is a published document [8], which originates from real specifications of the Mercedes-Benz passenger car development. It describes similar functionality and interfaces as the original data, but it contains dummy parameters and values, as we were not allowed to use the original data sets due to confidentiality aspects. This specification describes the functional and non-functional requirements of a Doors Closure Module (DCU). The second specification is a real Mercedes-Benz specification of an actual DCU. In the following, we call the first specification "public" and the second "confidential" DCU.

These specifications were chosen for two reasons: First, we can partly share the resulting data of our analyses for other research with the public DCU and still have actual, complex data with the confidential DCU. The second reason is goal G3. Although, the specifications describe the same content, they are not really similar: There are different authors, different structures, the public DCU describes the functional part in more detail whereas the confidential DCU has a huge testing part, and so on. Besides the first reason, we could also have chosen two actual DCU specifications from different car series, but they would be far more similar because they have mainly the same authors. With the public and confidential DCU, we can instead analyse sort of the worst case for G3 and therefore can assume better results with more similar specifications about the same system.

Table 1 shows the number of objects in each specification, how many objects of the documents were manually classified to topics and how many assignments of objects to topics were done for each specification. An object can be a requirement or a heading (or sometimes both) and one requirement typically consists of one to four sentences. The ratio between headings and requirements and the average word size is also stated in Table 1. The manual classification of requirements to topics was done by separating the data into parts of 150 objects. Each of these parts was then manually and independently classified by two persons and then synchronized in a review session using Cohen's Kappa [21] as an aid. Cohen's Kappa is a statistical measure to calculate the inter-rater agreement between two raters who each classify n items to x categories. The previous identification of topics was done the same way in one review session. We identified 141 topics.

The last two lines "figures and tables" and "influenced topic assignments" in Table 1 show the number of objects, which only contain figures or tables and how many assignments of objects to topics are influenced by them. There only is a chance to classify these objects by the classifiers with Recall+ or topic generalization, because the basic classifiers in ReCaRe cannot extract information of figures or tables (see also Section 2).

To measure the quality of the machine learning algorithm we used the k-fold cross validation, which is a well known validation technique in data mining research [2], [7], [18], [23]: The specifications are randomly sorted and then split into k parts of equal size. k-1 of the parts are concatenated and used for training. The trained classifier is then run on the remaining part for evaluation. This procedure is carried out iteratively k times with a different part being held back for classification. Then, this whole process is again repeated k times. The classification performance averaged over all k parts in k iterations characterizes the classifier. As shown by Witten et al. [7], using k = 10 is common in research

Table 1. Requirements Documents Statistics

document	Public DCU	Confidential DCU
objects	1223	3004
classified objects	1201	2916
topic assignments	8163	18031
requirements	1087	2385
words / requirement	10.0	14.8
headings	138	618
words / heading	1.9	2.6
figures and tables	29	145
influenced topic assignments	443	1406

about the benefits of machine learning algorithm, so we used this number in the current work, too.

To measure the performance of the classifiers, we use the standard metrics from data mining and information retrieval: recall and precision [7], [23], [22]. In this context, a perfect precision score of 1.0 means that every requirement that a classifier labeled as belonging to a topic does indeed belong to this topic. A perfect recall score of 1.0 means that every requirement belonging to a topic was classified to it.

3.3   Accuracy of Normal and Improved Classifiers: G1, G2

Table 2 shows the recall and precision results of Multinomial Naive Bayes (MNB) and Support Vector Machines (SVM) for the public and confidential DCU specifications. The first line contains the results of the basic algorithms, followed by the basic algorithms and splitting of compounds, the basic algorithms and the use of 4-gram indexing, and the basic algorithms and topic generalization. Thereafter, we show the results of the combination of the best enhancements as best practices (BP), namely 4-gram indexing and topic generalization. The k-gram indexing was tested with a range of numbers for k, but we got the best results using k = 4 for the two specifications.

Table 2. G1 and G2 Analyses Results

	public DCU				confidential DCU			
	SVM		MNB		SVM		MNB	
algorithm	recall	prec.	recall	prec.	recall	prec.	recall	prec.
basic	0.63	0.86	0.56	0.81	0.49	0.82	0.56	0.67
compound split	0.65	0.86	0.63	0.76	0.53	0.82	0.65	0.59
4-gram indexing	0.69	0.85	0.80	0.44	0.56	0.80	0.74	0.38
topic generalization	0.73	0.70	0.70	0.64	0.69	0.75	0.80	0.48
best practices	0.83	0.66	0.94	0.16	0.80	0.64	0.93	0.17

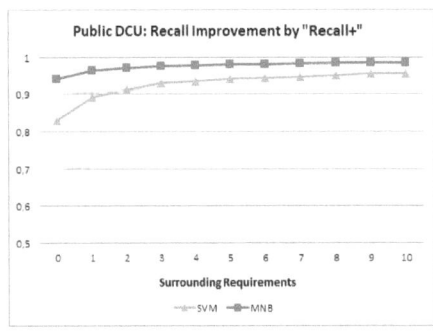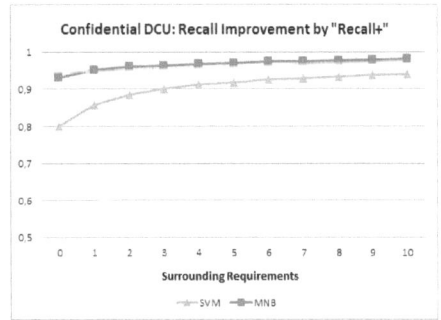

Fig. 3. Combination of Recall+ and Best Practices

Figure 3 shows the combination of best practices and the Recall+ approach. The horizontal axis **Surrounding requirements** gives the number of requirements, which are considered around already classified requirements.

We also analysed, whether there are requirements, which are incorrectly classified in each of the k iterations. For these requirements, we manually checked if the classifiers are correct and if we have overlooked something during the manual classification. This way, we improved the manual classification further.

3.4   Transferability of Trained Classifier over Specifications: G3

Table 3 shows the recall and precision results of Multinomial Naive Bayes (MNB) and Support Vector Machines (SVM) for the confidential DCU specification (C. DCU), trained by the public DCU specification (P. DCU) and vice versa. In the first four columns are the results for the basic MNB and SVM showed, followed up by the results for the classifiers and best practices as introduced in Section 3.3.

Table 3. G3 Analyses Results

	SVM		MNB		SVM+BP		MNB+BP	
training - test	recall	prec.	recall	prec.	recall	prec.	recall	prec.
P. DCU - C. DCU	0.12	0.48	0.15	0.45	0.41	0.51	0.77	0.13
C. DCU - P. DCU	0.16	0.56	0.23	0.50	0.48	0.54	0.79	0.16

4   Discussion

In this Section, we interpret the results to G1, G2 and G3 and discuss the applicability of these results in industrial practice. Thereafter, we investigate threats to validity in our research.

4.1   Interpretation of Results

The results from Section 3.3 showed that using the in G2 investigated improvements of the classifiers, we can get recommendable results with the well known validation technique k-fold cross validation with our two large and complex automotive specifications. Especially the results from SVM improved by the presented best practices with recall over 0.8 and precision over 0.6 are considered as sufficient in similar research (e.g. Knauss et al. [2]). Considering that the assumption of the Recall+ enhancement is correct, even if we only take into account a small number of requirements (see Figure 3), the SVM classifies almost every requirement to the right topic. As already stated, exceptions only are the requirements containing just figures or tables. MNB with best practices reaches even better recall but unfortunately with too much precision loss. We conclude that given enough training data, a sufficient classification of requirements to topics is possible.

4.2   Applicability in Industrial Practice

The problem in industrial practice is getting sufficient training data: At Mercedes-Benz, the developer cannot manually classify a great part of each current specification to topics. Instead, it would be possible to only classify an older specification once for a system and use this training data for newer specifications. Then we would only need to update the training data from time to time for new functionality in the system. The results in Section 3.4 showed that this is possible while still leaving room for improvements. Considering the above values for a sufficient classification, recall over 0.4 is not enough, same goes for a precision over 0.5. But we are still surprised of this result due to the already stated distance between the two used specifications. We assume that using two confidential DCU from different car series would have led to closer results to a sufficient classification. Because of this, we believe that this approach can be used in industrial practice under the condition that we can further improve the process of getting enough training data.

We will research this in future work, for example, under the aspect of using ontologies to improve the classification process or the idea of Ko et al. [11], which is described in detail in the related works.

4.3   Threats to Validity

In this section, the threats to validity are discussed. For that, we use the classification of validity aspects from Runeson et al. [12] on construction validity, internal validity, external validity and reliability.

Construction Validity. One obvious threat is the manual classification. It is questionable - there is no unique classification and it is reviewer dependent - which requirements must be considered as belonging to a topic. Another question is, whether there are no better algorithms for our text classification tasks, but the results show that we have at least chosen promising candidates.

Internal Validity. In data mining literature (e.g. [7]), stratified k-fold cross validation seems a slightly better validation technique, than the unstratified version used in this work. That means, instead of a random choice of requirements for the k parts, the requirements are selected in a way that positive and negative training examples are stratified in the k-parts. Unfortunately that would only be possible by using a time consuming evaluation for each individual topic, instead of evaluating all topics for one set of folds.

External Validity. First, there are limitations in the transferability of our results on German, natural language specifications drawn from the Mercedes-Benz passenger car development to specifications from other companies in the automotive industry or even to specifications from other industries because of different specification structures, the content and complexity of the specifications, and other company specific factors. Second, because of the German language, we may have advantages with certain pre-processing steps compared to other languages. On the other hand, some well known pre-proccessing steps, for example stemming, do not work on our data sets as shown during this work.

Reliability. The topic landscape and the manual classification is person dependent. But that should not be influencing the evaluation of the classifiers. Regarding the specifications, unfortunately, we cannot publish the confidential DCU or the analysis of it, but the analyses results of the public DCU and its manual classification is available for further research.

5   Related Work

In this section, we discuss research on reviews and approaches to support or improve the review process. Afterwards, we present existing research on the classification of requirements and talk about the different use cases and benefits to do these classifications.

The initial work about reviews was done by Fagan [13]. Since then, there have been many further developments of the review process. Aurum et al. [15] give an overview of the progress in the review process from Fagan's work until 2002. Gilb and Graham [14] provide a thorough discussion about reviews, including case studies from organizations using reviews in practice.

As stated before, the benefit of the review of natural language specifications becomes limited because of the increasing size and complexity of the documents to be checked. To overcome these obstacles, a lot of research has been done to automatically search for special kinds of defects in the natural language specification or to support the review process with preliminary analyses. Some examples are listed below:

The ARM tool by Wilson et al. [16] automatically measures and analyzes indicators to predict the quality of the documents. These indicators are separated in categories for individual specification statements (e.g. imperatives, directives, weak phrases) and categories for the entire specification (e.g. size, readability, specification depth).

The tool QuARS by Gnesi et al. [9] automatically detects linguistic defects like ambiguities, using an initial parsing of the requirements.

The tool CARL from Gervasi and Zowghi [17] automatically identifies and analyzes inconsistencies of specifications in controlled natural language. This is done by automatic parsing of natural language sentences into propositional logic formulae. The approach is limited by the controlled language and the set of defined consistency rules.

Similar to Gervasi and Zowghi, Moser et al. [10] automatically inspect requirements with rule-based checks for inconsistencies. Unfortunately, in their approach the specifications must be written in controlled natural language.

The following research focuses on the classification of requirements for multiple purposes:

Moser et al. [10] are using a classification of requirements as an intermediate step during the check of requirements with regard to inconsistencies.

Gnesi et al. [9] create a categorization of requirements to topics as a byproduct during the detection of linguistic defects.

Hussain et al. [5] developed the tool LASR that supports users in annotation tasks. To do this, LASR automatically classifies requirements to certain annotations and presents the candidates to the user for the final decision.

Knauss et al. [2] automatically classify security relevant requirements in specifications with Naive Bayesian Classifiers. Compared to our work, they only classified the requirements to one topic and used small specifications to evaluate the effectiveness of their approach. Nevertheless, they got similar results: Using the same specification as training and testing with the x-fold cross validation leads to satisfying results. The problem is getting sufficient training data for a new specification from other/older specifications in order to get useful results in practice.

One probably feasible way to get sufficient training data is the approach of Ko et al. [11]. They use Naive Bayesian Classifiers to automatically classify requirements to topics, but they also automatically create the training data to do that. The idea is to define each topic with a few keywords and then use a cluster algorithm for each topic to get resulting requirements, which are then used to train the classifiers. The evaluation results of this approach are promising, but the evaluation was only done by small English and Korean specifications (less than 200 sentences).

6   Conclusion and Future Work

In this paper, we addressed the problem that reviewers have major problems in finding defects, especially consistency or completeness defects, between requirements with related information, spread over various documents. This is a common case in today's industry specifications, for example, Mercedes-Benz has this problem. There, a specification and its referenced documents often sums up to 3,000 pages.

We presented the concept topic landscape implemented in the tool ReCaRe. ReCaRe automatically classifies and extracts requirements with related information spread over many sections over many documents with text classification algorithms to support reviewers with their work.

We evaluated two promising text classification algorithms, Multinomial Naive Bayes (MNB) and Support Vector Machines (SVM), using two automotive specifications from Mercedes-Benz. We also investigated enhancements, e.g. preprocessing steps, to further improve the results of these classifiers. The validation was positive: Especially the SVM reliably identifies the majority of topic relevant requirements (recall > 0.8) with a small enough amount of false positives (precision > 0.6).

The problem is getting sufficient training data in industrial practice: Further investigation showed that using training data from old specifications about the same system to classify the requirements of actual specifications is a promising solution, but the results are still not good enough. Future work must be done to enhance the acquisition of enough training data, but we believe that the approach of classifying information related requirements with text classification requirements is usable in practice.

This work contributes to the understanding of problems developers have to face in practice ensuring the quality in natural language specifications and presents a possible approach to mitigate some of these problems. Additionally, this work will support researchers and practitioners in software engineering:

For researchers, this work shows that it is possible to automatically classify current large and complex industry specifications with up to 3,000 requirements with positive results. We believe that this approach can be also used for categorization purposes besides the review improvement, for example, for security relevant aspects or for project planning as motivated in the introduction.

This work also presents researchers and practitioners a possible approach to improve a deficit of technical reviews to ensure the quality in industrial specifications.

Based on our work, there are a few further research directions. First, we are going to research how to get sufficient training data with minimal manual work. Another point is the (semi-)automatic identification of the topics itself and last, but not least, we will investigate the actual benefit of the topic landscape approach for technical reviews.

References

1. Houdek, F.: Challenges in Automotive Requirements Engineering. In: Industrial Presentations by Requirements Engineering: Foundation for Software Quality, Essen (2010)
2. Knauss, E., Houmb, S., Schneider, K., Islam, S., Jürjens, J.: Supporting Requirements Engineers in Recognising Security Issues. In: Berry, D., Franch, X. (eds.) REFSQ 2011. LNCS, vol. 6606, pp. 4–18. Springer, Heidelberg (2011)
3. Ott, D., Raschke, A.: Review Improvement by Requirements Classification at Mercedes-Benz: Limits of Empirical Studies in Educational Environments. In: International Workshop on Empirical Requirements Engineering (EMPIRE), Chicago (2012)
4. Ott, D.: Defects in Natural Language Requirement Specifications at Mercedes-Benz: An Investigation Using a Combination of Legacy Data and Expert Opinion. In: International Requirements Engineering Conference, Chicago (2012)

5. Hussain, I., Ormandjieva, O., Kosseim, L.: LASR: A Tool for Large Scale Annotation of Software Requirements. In: International Workshop on Empirical Requirements Engineering (EMPIRE), Chicago (2012)
6. Song, X., Hwong, B.: Categorizing Requirements for a Contract-Based System Integration Project. In: International Requirements Engineering Conference, Chicago (2012)
7. Witten, I.H., Frank, E., Hall, M.A.: Data Mining: Practical Machine Learning Tools and Techniques: Practical Machine Learning Tools and Techniques. The Morgan Kaufmann Series in Data Management Systems. Elsevier Science (2011)
8. Houdek, F., Peach, B.: Das Tuersteuergeraet – eine Beispielspezifikation (engl.: The doors closure module – an example specification), Fraunhofer IESE (2002)
9. Gnesi, S., Lami, G., Trentanni, G., Fabbrini, F., Fusani, M.: An automatic tool for the analysis of natural language requirements. International Journal of Computer Systems Science & Engineering 20, 53–62 (2005)
10. Moser, T., Winkler, D., Heindl, M., Biffl, S.: Requirements management with semantic technology: An empirical study on automated requirements categorization and conflict analysis. In: Mouratidis, H., Rolland, C. (eds.) CAiSE 2011. LNCS, vol. 6741, pp. 3–17. Springer, Heidelberg (2011)
11. Ko, Y., Park, S., Seo, J., Choi, S.: Using classification techniques for informal requirements in the requirements analysis-supporting system. Information and Software Technology 49, 1128–1140 (2007)
12. Runeson, P., Hoest, M.: Guidelines for conducting and reporting case study research in software engineering. Empirical Software Engineering 14, 131–164 (2009)
13. Fagan, M.: Design and code inspections to reduce errors in program development. IBM Journal of Research and Development 15(3), 182 (1976)
14. Gilb, T., Graham, D.: Software Inspection. In: Finzi, S. (ed.), Addison-Wesley (1994)
15. Aurum, A., Petersson, H., Wohlin, C.: State-of-the-art: Software Inspections after 25 Years. Software Testing, Verification and Reliability 12(3), 133–154 (2002)
16. Wilson, W., Rosenberg, L., Hyatt, L.: Automated analysis of requirement specifications. In: Proceedings of the 19th International Conference on Software Engineering (ICSE 1997), pp. 161–171. IEEE (1997)
17. Gervasi, V., Zowghi, D.: Reasoning about inconsistencies in natural language requirements. ACM Trans. Softw. Eng. Methodol. 14(3), 277–330 (2005)
18. Wang, S., Manning, C.D.: Baselines and Bigrams: Simple, Good Sentiment and Topic Classification. In: ACL vol. (2), pp. 90–94 (2012)
19. Hollink, V., Kamps, J., Monz, C., De Rijke, M.: Monolingual document retrieval for European languages. Information retrieval 7(1), 33–52 (2004)
20. Leuser, J.: Herausforderungen für halbautomatische Traceability-Erkennung (Challenges for Semi-automatic Trace Recovery). In: Systems Engineering Infrastructure Conference (2009)
21. Carletta, J.: Squips and Discussions Assessing agreement on classification tasks: The kappa statistic. Computional Linguistics 22(2), 249–254 (1996)
22. Baeza-Yates, R., Ribeiro-Neto, B.: Modern Information Retrieval. ACM Press, Addison Wesley
23. Han, J., Kamber, M., Pei, J.: Data Mining: Concepts and Techniques, 3rd edn. Morgan Kaufmann, Waltham (2012)

Requirement Ambiguity Not as Important as Expected — Results of an Empirical Evaluation

Erik Jan Philippo[1], Werner Heijstek[1,2], Bas Kruiswijk[3],
Michel R.V. Chaudron[1,4], and Daniel M. Berry[5]

[1] Leiden Institute of Advanced Computer Science, Leiden University
P.O. Box 9512, 2300 RA Leiden, The Netherlands
philippo@ejonline.nl
[2] Software Improvement Group, P.O. Box 94914
1090 GX Amsterdam, The Netherlands
w.heijstek@sig.eu
[3] Twynstra Gudde, P.O. Box 907, 3800 AX Amersfoort, The Netherlands
bkr@tg.nl
[4] Joint Computer Science and Engineering Department of Chalmers University of
Technology and University of Gothenburg, SE-412 96 Göteborg, Sweden
chaudron@chalmers.se
[5] Cheriton School of Computer Science, University of Waterloo
200 University Ave. West, Waterloo, ON N2L 3G1, Canada
dberry@uwaterloo.ca

Abstract. **[Context and motivation]** Requirement ambiguity is seen as an important factor for project success. However, empirical data about this relation are limited. **[Question/problem]** We analyze how ambiguous requirements relate to the success of software projects. **[Principal ideas/results]** Three methods are used to study the relation between requirement ambiguity and project success. First, data about requirements and project outcome were collected for 40 industrial projects. We find that, based on a correlation analysis, that the level of ambiguity in the requirements for a project does not correlate with the project's success. Second, using a root-cause analysis, we observe that ambiguity does not cause more defects during the test phase. Third, expert interviews were conducted to validate these results. This resulted in a framework that outlines factors influencing requirement-ambiguity risk. **[Contribution]** Empirical data are presented about the relationship between requirement ambiguity and project success. A framework is created to describe nine factors that increase or mitigate requirement-ambiguity risk.

Keywords: Requirements engineering, Empirical study, Software project risks, Requirement ambiguity, Natural language analysis.

1 Introduction

Written requirements are expected to be unambiguous [1]. However, in practice requirements are mostly written in natural language. Therefore, writing unambiguous requirements is practically impossible [2]. Nonetheless, academics and practioners regard

J. Doerr and A.L. Opdahl (Eds.): REFSQ 2013, LNCS 7830, pp. 65–79, 2013.
© Springer-Verlag Berlin Heidelberg 2013

requirement ambiguity as a serious threat to project success [3–6], especially in global software development [7]. Nevertheless, evidence about how requirement ambiguity relates to project success is limited. Different techniques exist to minimize the ambiguity in requirements (e.g. [8–10]). These techniques can be applied during the elicitation, specification and validation of requirements. However, decreasing the level of ambiguity in requirements is a labor-intensive activity, and it remains unclear whether investing effort is worthwhile. Recent research indicates that requirement ambiguity might not be as problematic as previously thought [11]. As a result, for software project managers it is unclear when requirement ambiguity becomes a threat for project success and thus, at which point they should take measures.

In this study, we analyze whether requirement ambiguity is a threat for software projects and which projects are really in danger. We therefore formulate the following research question:

How do ambiguous requirements relate to software project success?

In the rest of the paper, Section 2 introduces concepts and definitions. Section 3 describes the three research methods: interviews, correlation analysis, and root-cause analysis. Section 4 gives the raw results of the three methods. Section 5 discusses the individual results and relates the results of the three research methods. Section 6 details threats to the validity of the results, and Section 7 delivers the final conclusions.

2   Conceptual Framework

We use the IEEE definition of ambiguity: "A [software requirement specification] is unambiguous if, and only if, every requirement stated therein has only one interpretation" [1]. Berry et al. [8] divide ambiguity into four categories: *lexical ambiguity* (single word with several meanings), *syntactic ambiguity* (sentence with several parses), *semantic ambiguity* (sentence with several meanings but no lexical or syntactic ambiguity) and *pragmatic ambiguity* (sentence with several context-dependent meanings). Natural languages are highly flexible, especially in multi-cultural environments. Natural Language Processing (NLP) tools exist to detect the level of ambiguity in natural language requirements. Some are specifically focused on software requirement specification, e.g. QuARS [12] and RequirementsAssistant [13]. RequirementsAssistant is able to recognize lexical, syntactic, semantic, and pragmatic ambiguity. For all the ambiguity categories, there are rules defined to detect their instances.

This paper studies the relation between the ambiguity of a project's requirements and the project's success. Various indicators for project success exist. For instance, project success can be measured by lack of budget overrun, lack of time overrun, complete requirement coverage, high customer satisfaction, or high system quality. It is often important that a project stay within budget and that it be delivered on time, because management is typically rewarded for its good budgetary performance. Also, in many business domains, time-to-market is an important factor. For our study, we had a pragmatic constraint in that we are limited by the data that are available per project. Therefore, the lack of budget overrun was chosen to measure project success. Budget overrun for a project is defined as the difference between its actual cost and its estimated cost. This research regarded a project with a zero or negative budget overrun as successful.

Also the level of ambiguity in requirements is hard to measure. A requirement can contain one or more words that cause ambiguity. For example, the word "all" can cause ambiguous requirements when "all" is not defined. During any inspection, manual or automated, of requirements, the inspector, human or software, can be asked to add a remark to any word that the inspector believes might cause ambiguity. A possible measure of requirement ambiguity of a requirements document is simply the number of remarks the document earned. However, then the measure is affected inappropriately by the size of the requirements document. To control the effect of requirements document size, this study uses the number of remarks per some unit of requirement size as its measure of the level of ambiguity in a requirements document. In the earlier analyses, the unit was the individual requirement. However, later, we realized that a long, complicated requirement counted the same as a short, simple requirement, even though the former is more likely than the latter to suffer ambiguity. So, in the remaining analyses, the unit was changed to be the character.

3   Research Design and Environment

This study used three complementary methods to study the main research question. In the first method, experts from a software project were interviewed to analyze and understand requirement ambiguity and the associated project risks. In the second method, we collected requirements text and project information from 40 projects. Based on this information, we performed a correlation analysis to understand the relation between requirement ambiguity as measured by inspection remarks per character and project success as measured by lack of budget overrun. In the third method, a root-cause analysis was performed on a random selection of a project's defects to analyze the relation between the defects and requirement ambiguity. The project for this third study was different from that of the others and had its own set of requirements. All data were collected from a large financial institution in the Netherlands. Data used for the correlation analysis were collected from a specific department in the institution. This institution operates in more than 30 countries and serves millions of customers. In part because of these characteristics, we believe that this institution is a reliable source for data. For all the methods, a broad definition of ambiguity was used, including lexical, syntactic, semantic, and pragmatic ambiguity.

3.1   Interviews — Understanding the Requirement Ambiguity Risk

In order to better understand the ambiguity risk for software projects, we conducted four semi-structured interviews with experts in which we confronted them with our study. The roles of the four experts are project portfolio manager, business analyst, requirements engineer, and software architect. Except for the software architect, each worked within the financial institution. The main objective of these interviews was to understand the factors involved in the relation between requirement ambiguity and project success. The research question was:

Question 1. How does requirement ambiguity influence software projects?

All interviewees were asked similar questions. The concept of ambiguity was explained to the interviewees on a high level. We did not discuss the categories such as lexical ambiguity or pragmatic ambiguity. Rather, we explained ambiguity through examples. For each interview, a transcript was generated and then analyzed.

3.2   Correlation Analysis — Requirement Ambiguity and Project Success

The second research method was an analysis of quantitative data gathered from a single department's projects. We analyzed whether each project's requirement ambiguity as measured by inspection remarks, first, per requirement and later, per character, correlates with the project's success as measured by lack of budget overrun. The associated research question was:

Question 2. Do ambiguous requirements have an impact on project budget overrun?

Initially, requirements documents were collected for 112 software projects. These data were collected from a requirements management tool called Borland Caliber[1]. Data to calculate project success was extracted from the project administration tool CA Clarity[2]. The most relevant variables of this dataset for this calculation for a project are: start date, end date, estimated cost, and actual cost. A project's requirement data and the project's success data were linked by the project's unique identifier in the Clarity dataset as well as the name of the project. However, this link could be established for only 40, out of the 112, projects.

The RequirementsAssistant tool was used to automatically inspect the English natural language requirements. For any input text, the tool generates remarks which represent possible problems in the requirements. For example, for the requirement "Appropriate system standards shall be used where necessary." The tool will, e.g., mark the words "Appropriate" and "where necessary" as possible ambiguities. The number of remarks found in any run of the tool depends on the current configuration of the tool. The tool is not able to inpsect diagrams, and thus, diagrams are therefore not part of this analysis. A manual inspection of the requirements documents showed that none of the projects was using diagrams.

Three different configurations of RequirementsAssistant were used: (1) one generating all possible remarks regarding requirement quality; (2) one generating only those remarks pertaining specifically to requirement ambiguity; and (3) an improved ambiguity-detecting configuration, created in collaboration with the developer of RequirementsAssistant, that is able to find more ambiguous words. When the first configuration was created, the main author was not completely familiar with the tool.

To arrive at a measure of a project's requirement ambiguity, we divided the total number of remarks attributed to the project's requirements, first, by the number of requirements in the project's requirements specification and later, by the total number of characters in the project's requirement specification. These measures allowed comparing the requirement ambiguity of projects whose requirements differ in size.

---

[1] http://www.borland.com/products/caliber/
[2] http://www.ca.com/us/project-portfolio-management.aspx

The dataset was split into two groups, projects with and projects without budget overruns. For each group, the average *remarks per character* was calculated. The Mann-Whitney-Wilcoxon test was applied to determine whether there is a significant difference between the two groups.

3.3 Root-Cause Analysis — Defects Caused by Ambiguity

We performed a case study of one software development project and based the study's design on that of a very similar study by De Bruijn and Dekkers [11]. The software project we studied was to introduce and customize a document management system. Using the project's requirements specification, we performed a root-cause analysis of the defects detected during the project's testing phase. The research question for root-case analysis was:

Question 3. Do ambiguous requirements cause defects?

First, the level of ambiguity of the project's requirements was determined by a run of RequirementsAssistant on the requirements and by a manual inspection of the same by a review panel consisting of two persons. The review panel, operating as a unit, analyzed each of the project's 205 requirements using the following steps: (1) read the requirement, (2) check whether the requirement is understood, (3) discuss the interpretations and ambiguities found, and (4) provide possible explanations of any found ambiguities. Second, for each of a randomly selected sample of 100 out of 389 reported defects, we attempted to trace the cause of the defect back to the requirements. As in De Bruijn and Dekkers study, the four rules shown in Table 1 were used to determine whether a defect was caused by an ambiguity.

Table 1. Root-Cause Conditions

label	condition
RCC1	The implementation satisfies the requirement.
RCC2	The test team rejects this because of a different but also valid interpretation of the requirement.
RCC3	Test team respects the design space of the contractor
RCC4	Disambiguation of the requirement would have prevented these differences in interpretation

4 Analysis

This section reports the results of each of the three research methods.

4.1 Ambiguous Requirements

This section shows the determination of the level of ambiguity in the requirements. Both the correlation analysis and the root-cause analysis required determining the level

Table 2. Remarks Generated by RequirementsAssistant for the Correlation Analysis

	Ambiguity Config. 1	Ambiguity Config. 2	Ambiguity Config. 3
Unambiguous reqs.	-	-	361
Single ambiguity reqs.	-	-	734
Multiple ambiguity reqs.	61, 394	8, 422	14, 455
Average remarks per req.	12.66	1.73	2.98

Table 3. Remarks for the Root-Cause Analysis

	Panel	Tool
Unambiguous reqs.	78	0
Single ambiguity reqs.	19	51
Multiple ambiguity reqs.	31	45
Average remarks per req.	0.77	1.37

of ambiguity in the requirements using the RequirementsAssistant tool. For the root-cause analysis, a second method was used, an inspection by a two-student review panel that tallied the ambiguity remarks per requirement manually.

Tables 2 and 3 show the ambiguities found and the calculated average number of remarks per requirement. We established the threshold of 0.5 as the minimum average number of remarks per requirement for a set of requirements to be considered ambiguous. All methods of generating ambiguity remarks for both the correlation analysis and the root-cause analysis yielded average numbers of remarks per requirements greater than 0.5. For the root-cause analysis, although the review panel found fewer remarks than RequirementsAssistant, and the review panel gave no remarks to many requirements, the review panel concluded that the requirements are ambiguous. RequirementsAssistant found 96 remarks for the requirements of the root-cause analysis, resulting in 1.37 remarks for each requirement. Since each methods calculated an average greater than 0.5, the set of requirements collected for this study is considered ambiguous.

4.2   Interviews — Understanding the Requirement Ambiguity Risk

This section describes the results of the interviews conducted with experts. Four interviews were conducted with people in different roles within the software engineering process, namely a software architect, a requirements engineer, a business analyst, and a project manager. The requirements engineer is a requirement consultant and is well read on the subject. This person is clearly an expert, while the business analyst knows what requirements are, but learned the topic on the job. The requirement engineer has ten years of experience with requirements engineering.

The duration of each interview was approximately one hour, and it was divided into two sections. First, we asked the interviewee about his or her experience with requirement ambiguity and about the consequences of it. Second, we revealed the results of the correlation and root-cause analyses and asked for an explanation.

Examination of the interview transcripts led to the identification of four categories for classifying the sentences: (1) requirements properties, (2) consequences of insufficient requirements engineering, (3) the influence of requirement ambiguity, and (4) techniques for preventing ambiguity. Three interviewees explicitly noted that they perceived requirement ambiguity as a problem. The business analyst regarded requirement ambiguity as a minor issue that can be "circumvented easily". The interviewees mentioned eight quality properties for requirements: consistent, complete, feasible, manageable, unambiguous, verifiable, non-volatile, and traceable. These properties are largely in line with the quality properties defined by the IEEE [1].

The five consequences of requirement ambiguity mentioned by the experts are (1) improper solutions, (2) less efficient software development, (3) incorrect estimations, (4) conflicts between projects and (5) delayed software projects. The consequence of improper solution was mentioned by two interviewees, the architect and the business analyst. Each of the other consequences was mentioned by only one interviewee.

4.3 Correlation Analysis Results — Requirement Ambiguity and Project Success

This section explains the results of the correlation analysis that was done for 40 projects. As described in Section 3.2, two different datasets were merged into the dataset that was used for the analysis. By rigorously cleaning the data, we made sure that the combined dataset contains no false positives. Merging the datasets resulted in three subsets according to the variable or variables (project name, project code, or both) that correspond. Independently, RequirementsAssistant was configured in three different ways. The three different data subsets and the three configurations of RequirementsAssistant resulted in nine samples.

For each of the nine samples, the level of ambiguity was determined via the number of ambiguity remarks per character. In one sample, the projects that were on budget had 0.021 remarks per character, and the projects that were off budget had 0.018 remarks per character. Thus, projects that were on budget have more ambiguity. This result is consistent with those of the other eight samples. To see whether a difference exists in the levels of ambiguity for on-budget and off-budget projects, a Mann-Whitney test was applied. In a Mann-Whitney test, a P-value above 0.05 means that there is no significant difference between the two groups. The computed P-value for the test was 0.331, which means that there is no significant difference. We, therefore, have to conclude that projects that are on budget have a higher number of ambiguity remarks per character and thus have more ambiguous requirements. The results are counter intuitive, since we expected fewer ambiguous requirements for the on-budget projects.

4.4   Root-Cause Analysis Results — Defects Caused by Ambiguity

The project used in the root-cause analysis was to implement a document management system. The goal of the system was to store customer documents such as agreements in a reliable manner. During the project, the software was continually tested, and all defects were logged in a defect management system. The defect information was quite complete and consistent and included information regarding the reason for the closure and the cause of each defect. At the end of the project, 389 defects had been logged. We randomly selected a sample of 100 defects to be analyzed with the method defined by De Bruijn [11]. Only three of these 100 defects were determined to be caused by ambiguity in the requirements.

Table 4 shows the log for one of the defects that was found to have been caused by an ambiguous requirement. This requirement is about generating PDF files from other proprietary file formats such as Microsoft Word .DOC files or Microsoft Excel .XLSX files. In the requirements document, each requirement has a unique code. For this defect, the related requirement is *RDA4*, which is part of the group *Requirements Document Archiving*. The content of the requirement is: "The system should support the creation of a searchable rendition (PDF) of a native format." Using the root-cause conditions listed in Table 1, we can determine if any defect was caused by ambiguity. The first root-cause condition, RCC1, is that the implementation satisfies the requirement. This is the case, since the software is able to create a PDF from a Word file. However, the tester was expecting that *any* document would be transformed to a PDF file, another valid interpretation of the requirement. This is according to RCC2, "The test team rejects this because of a different but also valid interpretation of the requirement". RCC3 says to respect that the decision to support certain files is not part of the design space of the contractor. RCC4 says that additional information about the supported file formats should have prevented the defect. Therefore, we conclude that this defect is a direct result of a requirement ambiguity.

Although the requirements are considered ambiguous, the ambiguities caused only 3 out of 100 defects. Our root-cause analysis leads us to conclude that requirement ambiguity did not cause a significant number of defects. While the cost of fixing any defect might be very high, particularly in the later stages of a project, we estimated that the cost to fix the three defects we did find to be caused by ambiguity is quite small. This finding is consistent with those of De Bruijn and Dekkers who found only a small number of defects caused by ambiguity. They had observed that 1 out of 40 defects were caused by ambiguity.

5   Discussion

This section discusses the results from the previous sections and relates the three study methods' results with each other.

5.1   Influence of Requirement Ambiguity on Project Success

In our research, we analyzed the ambiguity of requirements for software development projects with an automated tool, RequirementsAssistant. A subset of these requirements

Table 4. An Anonymized Example Defect that Was Caused by Ambiguity

variable	value
Title	No PDF Rendition is made for a native Document
Description	Steps:
	Import a native document
	Actual result:
	Document is present, but pdf rendition isn't created
	Expected:
	pdf rendition is created automatic during the import proces
	Conform RDA4: The system should support the creation
	of searchable rendition (PDF) of a native format
Developer comments	Eddard Stark, 17/02/2009: PDF is made only for Word
	documents (.doc). Excel, Powerpoint or Text documents
	are not rendered.
	Eddard Stark 31/03/2009: PDF is made for Word, Excel,
	Powerpoint. Text or Outlook (.msg) is not rendered
	Robert Baratheon 26-5-2009: According to Peter
	the manual should be adjusted with the addition: Non-
	Office documents will not be rendered.
	John Snow 26-8-2009: This has been
	incorporated in User manual V1.2
Detected on	16-1-2009
Status	Closed
Type	Defect
Priority	High

was inspected also manually. The RequirementsAssistant tool and the manual inspection reported many potential ambiguities in the requirements. For each project, at least 50% of the requirements earned ambiguity remarks. For many projects, the percentage is even higher. We used 50% as the threshold to determine whether the requirements for a project are ambiguous.

Correlation analysis and root-cause analysis were used to check whether a high level of requirement ambiguity is visible in project outcomes. The first anlysis showed no correlation between a project's requirement ambiguity as measured by ambiguity remarks per requirement or per character and the project's success as measured by lack of budget overrun. This is not evidence of the absence of *any* relationship, but we reasoned that other factors such as project planning, control, and in-project discussions seem to diminish the influence of any ambiguity. These practices may inhibit requirement ambiguity from affecting project outcomes.

The root-cause analysis tried to determine the influence of a project's requirement ambiguity on the defects of the project. Automated and manual inspection of the requirements of a single project yielded similar conclusions that there was a large amount of ambiguity in the project's requirements. A root-cause analysis was performed on each of a random sample of 100 defects. Only three of these 100 defects were determined to be caused by ambiguous requirements. The three defects appeared to be uncomplicated and not difficult to fix. Thus, the costs of fixing these ambiguous requirements were probably not very high. However, the costs of finding these defects are difficult to determine in hindsight. A defect that is found after deployment is harder to fix than a defect that is found during pre-deployment testing. Nevertheless, there is no particular reason to believe that finding the particular defects was expensive. After all, since they were logged, they *were* found. Therefore, we concluded that the ambiguity in the project's requirement documents does not did not really affect the project's defects. Just as for the correlation analysis, it appears that the presence of many ambiguities in a project's requirements has no effect on the outcome of the project.

The relations we studied are depicted in Figure 1. When looking at a standard software development process, the following phases are included: requirements engineering, design, implementation, testing, and maintenance. The upper lines in the figure represent the relationships between requirement ambiguity on one hand and budget overrun or defects on the other hand, relationships for which we found no evidence. From this model, we deduce that somewhere between the requirement engineering and testing phases, during design and implementation, a majority of the ambiguity problem is solved. Therefore, even though the requirements may have been full of ambiguities, the design and implementation end up resolving most of the ambiguities.

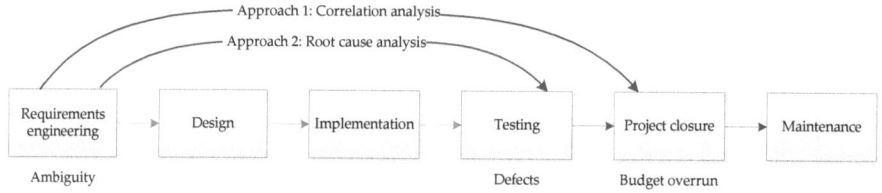

Fig. 1. Although the requirements contain many ambiguities, their consequences do not show up in the testing and project closure phases

5.2   Factors That Influence the Importance of Ambiguity

The reasons that prevent ambiguity from being a serious problem to a project are not completely clear. They may be different for different projects and dependent, e.g., on the software development method used in the project and on the balance of custom and off-the-shelf software used for the project. According to Alexander [14], "[i]nformal text, scribbled diagrams, conversations, and phone calls are excellent ways of removing ambiguity." This indicates that informal contact *can* solve the problem. Alexander states only that informal contact can remove ambiguity, but his quote does not necessarily mean that informal contact is the main reason preventing ambiguity from being a problem in the project we researched.

In order to better understand the reasons behind our findings, we conducted interviews with experts within the institution owning the project. The goal of the interviews was to specifically identify factors that aggravate the risk of requirement ambiguity and to learn how to solve the ambiguity problem. The interviews exposed different aspects of projects and institutions that can influence the consequence of ambiguity. These aspects are summarized in Figure 2.

Each non-central box is a factor that influences ambiguity risk. Each non-central box has an labeled arrow that points to the "Software project ambiguity risk" box and whose label indicates the direction of the box's factor on software project ambiguity risk. For example, when there are many locations, the ambiguity-related risk increases. Also time pressure can increase ambiguity risk. Many feedback loops, such as frequent meetings, can reduce ambiguity risk. Similarly, skilled teams can neutralize a high level of ambiguity in requirements documents. Each of remaining paragraphs in this section discuss one box.

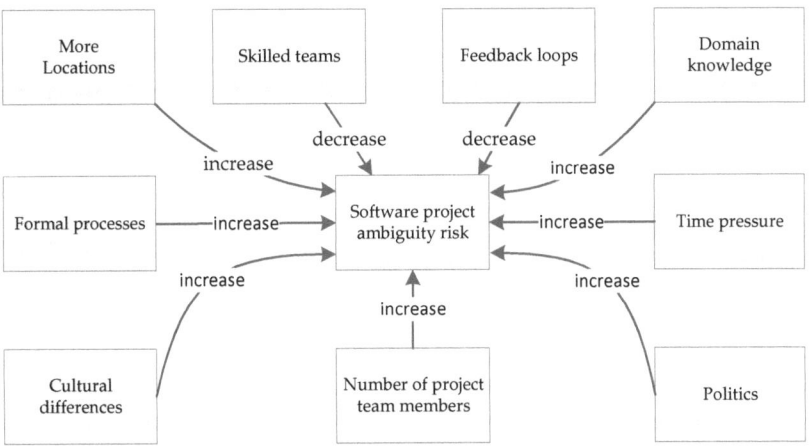

Fig. 2. Framework with Factors that Influence the Ambiguity Risk of Software Projects

The more skills project members have, the smaller the chances for ambiguity, especially when the skills include techniques to write less ambiguous requirements specifications. When the author of a requirements document understands how to write with less ambiguity, many ambiguity problems are avoided. For example, if he or she is aware that the term "all" can cause unclear requirements, he or she can use more precise terminology.

Frequent feedback loops reduce the risk of ambiguity. A feedback loop is the personal communication among the developers and the customer. Examples of this communication include informal chit-chat during breaks and small talk in the office. This communication enables developers and customers to discuss the work, to create a shared mental model [15, 16], and to understand the requirements better. When a developer does not need to move far from his or her desk to ask a question about requirements, ambiguities get resolved painlessly. When informal communication is not common in an organization, ambiguity resolution is thwarted.

Deep domain knowledge reduces ambiguity risk. When a software developer does not understand the organization's business and does not understand its terminology, then chances for lexical ambiguity increase. Understanding an organization's business is hard and time consuming. The more complicated the domain, the bigger the chances for ambiguity.

Under schedule pressure, priorities change. Predefined processes become less important, and employees will start to work around them. The outcome of a project becomes more important than its process. This effect also influences the requirement-ambiguity risk. When something is unclear, people will more quickly make assumptions to resolve incompleteness and ambiguities. When developers do not experience time pressure and stress, the requirement-ambiguity risk is reduced since they have the time to ask questions.

Different stakeholders often have different interests, resulting in requirements conflicts and negotiations. During a project, different stakeholders begin to develop a preference for particular decisions, and they start to support them. Often, an ambiguous requirement can be interpreted to the advantage of one of the stakeholders. This type of ambiguity is perpetrated on purpose and increases requirement problems.

The number of persons that work on a project influences the risk of ambiguity. When a single engineer develops an application for another person, the risks for unclear requirements and misunderstandings is relatively low because all converstations about the project that take place take place between only them. When a project consists of fifty employees, the ambiguity risk increases, because there are more people who need to understand the requirements documents, and there are more chances for misunderstanding. In a large project, not all project members will have read the requirements documents, and not all project members will speak with each other. The chances of misunderstanding increase with the number of project members. Larger projects try to reduce the risk of misunderstanding by, e.g., introducing walkthroughs and peer reviews.

Requirements depend on their context for their meaning. When a requirement can be interpreted in different ways due to different contexts, the requirement suffers pragmatic ambiguity. Culture defines the context for a requirement. The more cultures are involved in a project, the larger the chances for different interpretations.

The degree of formality in organizations influences the importance of ambiguity as well. When there is a lot formality, when two parties agree on a certain document, they stick to it. For example, when an external contractor is hired for software development, both parties agree on a contract and specifications. Because everything is stored in a formal document, people start to rely more on it, and the requirement specifications become more important. People communicate via documents and work less together. Due to the flexibility of the English language, it is virtually impossible to write an unambiguous requirements specification. The more people rely on documents, the bigger the chances that any ambiguity manifests itself. Within an organization, this phenomenon can happen, because people work within their own department and feel responsible for only their own jobs. This phenomenon was reported by the requirements engineer during the interviews.

The more locations involved in a project, the more problems its people face with communication. Although information technology improves the sharing of information, having many locations still hinders informal communication and prevents people from getting to know each other [17].

5.3   Requirement Ambiguity and Scrum

Scrum [18] is becoming increasingly popular in many organizations, including, to some extent, the institution providing data for this study. Simply put, Figure 2 shows effectively that many of Scrum's practices are those that appear to help prevent requirement ambiguity from becoming a problem. According to the framework, small teams reduce the requirement-ambiguity risk, and the Scrum method recommends teams with a maximum of five to nine members. Frequent feedback loops are encouraged in Scrum's so-called daily scrum and its on-site customer. The daily scrum is a ten-minute meeting during which the progress of the project is discussed. Scrum's allowing a team to create its own planning and Scrum's encouragement of realistic schedules reduce the risks associated with time pressure. The influence of personal preferences is minimized by having a product backlog, a list of requirements that should be implemented in upcoming sprints. By defining the backlog, all stakeholders are forced to agree on the requirements. Team members continue to learn and obtain additional skills by performing a sprint retrospective. Another recommendation of Scrum is that teams sit together, thus reducing the location risk. By sitting together, a team learns about different cultures faster, and their context converges faster. The formalities of Scrum processes are reduced by the team's collaborating closely with the on-site customer. The only factor from the framework of Figure 2 that does not have an associated best practice in Scrum is domain knowledge.

As Scrum specifically addresses a majority of what appear to be causes of requirement ambiguity, we hypothesize that projects that adopt Scrum are less likely to suffer budget overrun due to requirement ambiguity. This hypothesis should be tested in future work.

6   Threats to the Validity of the Results

Any research with empirical findings needs be understood bearing in mind the strengths and limitations of the research method. This section discusses three types of validity: internal, external and construct.

Internal validity in this study is the extent to which a correlation exists between requirement ambiguity and project success. A large dataset was available for the root-cause analysis and the correlation analysis. By rigorously cleaning the data, it was possible to obtain a clean dataset for analysis.

External validity is the extent to which the findings can be generalized to other organizations. We believe that dataset we used is representative of many organizations due to the institution's use of mostly the waterfall method, its project teams having fewer than 30 members, and its being a large organization operating worldwide.

Construct validity of a study refers to the extent to which the study's measures actually measure what they purport to. For this study, construct validity is that the measures for requirement ambiguity and project success are correct. The reader is reminded of the discussion in Section 2 about choosing the measures. For each property measured, there are clearly factors not captured by the chosen measure, and it measures factors other than the property as well. Nevertheless, most factors for each property are highly subjective and are labor-intensive to determine. The chosen measures are at least very objective and are easily calculated from existing project data with the help of existing software tools. Had we chosen more precise, subjective, and labor-intensive measures, we would not have been able to compute the correlation for as many projects as we did, and some statistical strength would be lost. Of course, each reader will have to judge for him or herself, the validity of the conclusions based on the chosen measures.

RequirementsAssistant is a tool to detect mistakes in requirements. No tool can detect ambiguity perfectly, and this is a limitation of the study. A project can be influenced by ambiguity in two ways: noticed and unnoticed ambiguity. There are probably many ambiguities that are missed by both RequirementsAssistant and the manual inspection. However, the inspecting review panel appeared to have overlooked many ambiguities which RequirementsAssistant did find. Moreover, NASA did a study on automatic requirement analysis tools and concluded that RequirementsAssistant is the best tool available for detecting quality issues in requirements [19]. For this research, a wide definition of ambiguity was used. The NLP tool will detect vague words like "all" or "real-time", but it cannot detect all contextual ambiguities such as those caused by cultural differences. RequirementsAssistant is able to detect many kinds of ambiguities in requirement documents, such as at least all of the types defined by Berry [8].

7 Conclusion

This study has addressed the relation between requirement ambiguity and project success. We performed a correlation analysis on the requirements of 40 industrial projects and concluded that a software development project's requirement ambiguity has no particular relation to the project's success. We performed a root-cause analysis of the defects reported in a single project and confirmed an earlier finding that requirement ambiguity did not cause many defects, and the few that it did cause were not very serious. Finally, we conducted interviews with project experts to confirm our findings. From these conclusions, we constructed a framework that explains factors that increase requirement-ambiguity risks. We ended up concluding that the institution under study is quite good at dealing with requirement ambiguity.

Generalizing beyond the research environment, this research helps project managers to decide whether they should invest resources in resolving ambiguous requirements and to decide when the risk of requirement ambiguity is low. For the RE research community, the findings from this study both give rise to doubt and put into perspective the risks that requirement ambiguity carry for the lack of success of software development projects.

References

1. Tripp, L.: IEEE Recommended Practice for Software Requirements Specifications, ANSI/IEEE Standard 830-1993. Institute of Electrical and Electronics Engineering, New York (1993)
2. Berry, D.M.: Ambiguity in natural language requirements documents. In: Martell, C. (ed.) Monterey Workshop 2007. LNCS, vol. 5320, pp. 1–7. Springer, Heidelberg (2008)
3. Han, W.M., Huang, S.J.: An empirical analysis of risk components and performance on software projects. Journal of Systems and Software 80(1), 42–50 (2007)

4. Keil, M., Cule, P.E., Lyytinen, K., Schmidt, R.C.: A framework for identifying software project risks. Communications of the ACM 41(11), 76–83 (1998)
5. Fabbrini, F., Fusani, M., Gervasi, V., Gnesi, S., Ruggieri, S.: Achieving quality in natural language requirements. In: Proceedings of the 11th International Software Quality Week (1998)
6. Hull, E., Jackson, K., Dick, J.: Requirements Engineering. Springer, London (2010)
7. Cheng, B.H.C., Atlee, J.M.: Current and future research directions in requirements engineering. In: Lyytinen, K., Loucopoulos, P., Mylopoulos, J., Robinson, B. (eds.) Design Requirements Workshop. LNBIP, vol. 14, pp. 11–43. Springer, Heidelberg (2009)
8. Berry, D.M., Kamsties, E., Krieger, M.M.: From contract drafting to software specification: Linguistic sources of ambiguity. Technical report, University of Waterloo (2003), http://se.uwaterloo.ca/~dberry/handbook/ambiguityHandbook.pdf
9. Gervasi, V., Zowghi, D.: On the role of ambiguity in RE. In: Wieringa, R., Persson, A. (eds.) REFSQ 2010. LNCS, vol. 6182, pp. 248–254. Springer, Heidelberg (2010)
10. Robertson, S., Robertson, J.: Mastering the Requirements Process. Addison-Wesley, Harlow (2006)
11. de Bruijn, F., Dekkers, H.L.: Ambiguity in natural language software requirements: A case study. In: Wieringa, R., Persson, A. (eds.) REFSQ 2010. LNCS, vol. 6182, pp. 233–247. Springer, Heidelberg (2010)
12. Bucchiarone, A., Gnesi, S., Lami, G., Trentanni, G., Fantechi, A.: Quars express — a tool demonstration. In: Proceedings of the 23rd IEEE/ACM International Conference on Automated Software Engineering, pp. 473–474 (2008)
13. Driessen, H.: Requirements Assistant (2012), http://www.requirementsassistant.nl/
14. Alexander, I.F., Stevens, R.: Writing Better Requirements. Pearson Education, Harlow (2002)
15. Mathieu, J.E., Heffner, T.S., Goodwin, G.F., Salas, E., Cannon-Bowers, J.A.: The influence of shared mental models on team process and performance. Journal of Applied Psychology 85(2), 273 (2000)
16. Levesque, L.L., Wilson, J.M., Wholey, D.R.: Cognitive divergence and shared mental models in software development project teams. Journal of Organizational Behavior 22, 135–144 (2001)
17. Herbsleb, J.D., Mockus, A., Finholt, T.A., Grinter, R.E.: An empirical study of global software development: Distance and speed. In: Proceedings of the 23rd International Conference on Software Engineering, pp. 81–90 (2001)
18. Schwaber, K., Beedle, M.: Agile Software Development with Scrum, 1st edn. Prentice Hall PTR, Upper Saddle River (2001)
19. Jones, V., Murray, J.: Evaluation of current requirements analysis tools capabilities for IV&V in the requirements analysis phase (2007), http://www.slideserve.com/shlomo/evaluation-of-current-requirements-analysis-tools-capabilities-for-ivv-in-the-requirements-analysis-phase

The Design of SREE — A Prototype Potential Ambiguity Finder for Requirements Specifications and Lessons Learned

Sri Fatimah Tjong[1] and Daniel M. Berry[2]

[1] University of Nottingham Malaysia Campus
Jalan Broga, 43500 Semenyih, Selangor Darul Ehsan, Malaysia
nien34@gmail.com
[2] Cheriton School of Computer Science
University of Waterloo
Waterloo, ON, Canada N2L 3G1
dberry@uwaterloo.ca

Abstract. **[Context and Motivation]** Many a tool for finding ambiguities in natural language (NL) requirements specifications (RSs) is based on a parser and a parts-of-speech identifier, which are inherently imperfect on real NL text. Therefore, any such tool inherently has less than 100% recall. Consequently, running such a tool on a NL RS for a highly critical system does not eliminate the need for a complete manual search for ambiguity in the RS. **[Question/Problem]** Can an ambiguity-finding tool (AFT) be built that has 100% recall on the types of ambiguities that are in the AFT's scope such that a manual search in an RS for ambiguities outside the AFT's scope is significantly easier than a manual search of the RS for *all* ambiguities? **[Principal Ideas/Results]** This paper presents the design of a prototype AFT, SREE (Systemized Requirements Engineering Environment), whose goal is achieving a 100% recall rate for the ambiguities in its scope, even at the cost of a precision rate of less than 100%. The ambiguities that SREE searches for by lexical analysis are the ones whose keyword indicators are found in SREE's ambiguity-indicator corpus that was constructed based on studies of several industrial strength RSs. SREE was run on two of these industrial strength RSs, and the time to do a completely manual search of these RSs is compared to the time to reject the false positives in SREE's output *plus* the time to do a manual search of these RSs for only ambiguities not in SREE's scope. **[Contribution]** SREE does not achieve its goals. However, the time comparison shows that the approach to divide ambiguity finding between an AFT with 100% recall for some types of ambiguity and a manual search for only the other types of ambiguity is promising enough to justify more work to improve the implementation of the approach. Some specific improvement suggestions are offered.

1 Introduction

This paper describes the engineering and design of a prototype ambiguity finding tool (AFT) called SREE for helping mainly requirements analysts (and anyone else with a stake in avoiding ambiguity) to find ambiguities in natural language (NL) requirements specifications (RSs). Berry, Gacitua, Sawyer, and Tjong suggest that to be really useful

J. Doerr and A.L. Opdahl (Eds.): REFSQ 2013, LNCS 7830, pp. 80–95, 2013.

for application to an RS for a critical system, an AFT must have 100% recall even at the expense of low precision. In order that this high imprecision be manageable, the AFT must produce output that is significantly smaller than the original RS submitted to the AFT, so that searching for false positives in the output is significantly easier than manually searching the whole RS for the same ambiguities [1]. They suggest dividing the process of finding ambiguities in a NL RS into two parts that must be easily distinguished:

1. the algorithmic part that can be done with 100% recall by a tool, the dumb tool, and
2. the nonalgorithmic part that is smaller than manually searching the entire RS and which requires the intelligence of a smart human.

As explained in Section 4.1, by "easily distinguished" is meant that for any *type of ambiguity*, the user knows for sure, in advance, in which part all of the type's instances will be found. While, in the end, SREE did not quite achieve this goal, a description of SREE's design and of the process by which it was designed and evaluated against the goals, are useful for informing any future research done according to Berry *et al*'s research agenda.

1.1   Background

Ambiguity in natural language (NL) is a major problem in many scientific disciplines [2, 3], including in requirements engineering (RE) [4] during which requirements specifications (RSs) for computer-based systems (CBSs) are written. Ambiguity in a requirement statement (RStat) occurs when the RStat has more than one meaning. The overwhelming majority of RSs are written in NL [5], although often amplified by information in other notations, such as formulae and diagrams. Despite NL's inherent ambiguity and informality, NL is still preferred for writing RSs simply because all stakeholders are able to read it and participate in writing it.

For a summary of the types of ambiguities that appear in requirements documents, please consult the tutorial titled "Ambiguity in Requirements Specification" [6]. Linguists consider ambiguity, imprecision, indeterminacy, and vagueness to be different phenomena. Nevertheless, the work described in this paper collapses all of these phenomena into one term "ambiguity", because all the phenomena have the same effect on RSs, making them interpretable differently by different developers. An ambiguous RStat can have hazardous consequences for a software development project as a whole, in which wrongly implemented requirements cause high costs for rework and delayed product releases [2–4].

In understanding a RStat, a requirements analyst often is not even aware of any ambiguity and instinctively employs immediate *subconscious disambiguation* [4]. In subconscious disambiguation, the listener or reader of an utterance, not even aware of the existence of ambiguity in the utterance, accepts as the only meaning of the utterance, the first meaning he thought of, a meaning that may not be that intended by the speaker of the utterance.

An AFT's *recall* is the percentage of the instances of ambiguity that the AFT actually finds. The AFT's *precision* is the percentage of the ambiguities that the AFT finds that are truly ambiguous. It is easy to achieve 100% recall if one does not care about precision: just identify everything as ambiguous. Conversely, it is easy to achieve 100% precision if one does not care about recall: just identify nothing as ambiguous. Neither of these ways of achieving perfection in one goal is useful. Thus, recall and precision are usually traded off. Nevertheless, in any tradeoff for the design of an AFT, recall is more important than precision for the AFT, because it is much harder to know what is missing than to know what is a false positive among the AFT's output.

1.2   This Paper

This work is derived from Tjong's Ph.D. thesis [7], and it describes the design and development of a prototype AFT, SREE (Systemized Requirements Engineering Environment), that helps detect the occurrence of instances of ambiguity in RSs. The performance goal for SREE, reflected in its design, is that it has 100% recall of the ambiguities in its scope even at the cost of it having less than 100% precision. For any type of ambiguity in SREE's scope, SREE searches in its input for all instances of that type in its goal of achieving 100% recall, and it reports all instances it finds. If, however, SREE has less than 100% precision for the type, then among the findings are false positives that the human user must weed out in a manual examination of the findings. Thus, what SREE actually finds are *potential ambiguities*. Therefore, SREE assists and does not replace an analyst in identifying instances of ambiguity in RSs. A *user* of SREE must decide whether or not any potential ambiguity detected by SREE is truly ambiguous.

Section 2 of this paper reviews past work about AFTs and finds all deficient in recall. Section 3 explains why 100% recall is essential for an AFT. Section 4 describes the goals of SREE. Section 5 describes the design and implementation of SREE according to these goals. Section 6 evaluates SREE with respect to its goals and the user's performance in dealing with imprecision, and it reports lessons learned about the functionality of AFTs. Section 7 summarizes the paper and suggests future work.

Quoted text from any RStat or other example is typeset in a sans serif typeface, and this text may end with punctuation, which is to be distinguished from any immediately following punctuation belonging to the sentence containing the quoted text, which is typeset in the background serifed typeface[1].

2   Past Work on Ambiguity Finding Methods and Tools

Research to resolve ambiguity started as early as the late 1980s, at which time ambiguity was said to be an impediment to elucidating a project's real design requirements [4]. This section focuses particularly on tool-assisted ambiguity detection and disambiguation.

Ambriola and Gervasi [8] achieved a high-quality NL RS through successive transformations that are applied to an early NL RS in order to obtain concrete and rendered views of models extracted from the NL RS. The transformations are automated in a tool named CIRCE (Cooperative Interactive Requirement-Centric Environment).

Wilson et al. [9] defined general quality criteria for RSs and developed an analysis tool ARM (Automated Requirements Management) to assess the structure of a given

---

[1] A good magnifying glass shows the difference in the typefaces of the two consecutive items of punctuation! :-).

RS, the structure of the RS's RStats, the vocabulary used to write the RS, and thus to determine if the RS meets the quality criteria.

Fabbrini ct al. [10, 11] distinguished between RStat quality and RS quality, and they identified a number of indicators of each kind of quality. They developed QuARS (Quality Analyser of Requirements Specifications) that evaluates any given RS against these indicators of RStat quality and RS quality.

Kasser [12] developed TIGER Pro, a tool that assists its user in writing a good RS by pointing out any instances of five types of defects it finds in the input RS. The five types of defects are 1) multiple requirements in a paragraph, 2) unverifiable requirements, 3) use of will or must instead of shall, 4) use of a wrong word, and 5) use of any user-defined so-called poor word.

Willis, Chantree, and De Roeck [13] defined a *nocuous ambiguity* as ambiguous text that is interpreted differently by different readers, as opposed to an innocuous ambiguity, which in spite of the ambiguity, is interpreted the same by all readers. Generally, domain knowledge or context allowing disambiguation of an ambiguity renders an ambiguity innocuous. Willis *et al.* developed and evaluated a tool using a heuristic method to automatically predict which sentences are likely to be interpreted differently by different readers. After determining which sentences *are* ambiguous with a parser, the heuristic, which is trained against a corpus in which all nocuous ambiguities have been marked, determines which ambiguous sentences are likely to be nocuously ambiguous.

Kiyavitskaya, Zeni, Mich, and Berry [14] did some case studies with prototypes of a proposed tool for identifying ambiguities in NL RSs in an effort to identify requirements for such tools. Their approach was to apply ambiguity measures to sentences identified by a parser based tool to try to increase the precision of the tool with respect to reporting genuine ambiguities. The measures are based on using lexical and syntactic proxies for semantic criteria and the WordNet thesaurus [15]. The case studies found that many of what the tool thought was ambiguous were not problematic given the normal knowledge that the analyst user would have about the domain of the specification and that the tool failed to find many of what one analyst who was particularly attuned to finding ambiguities found manually.

Gleich, Creighton, and Kof [16] built an automated AFT that has been measured to be about four times as effective as an average human analyst in finding genuine ambiguities. They have designed the AFT to automate the finding of ambiguities in requirements specifications, to make plausible to the user that the ambiguities it has found are genuine, and to teach the analyst by explaining the sources of the ambiguities it has found. The AFT first does part-of-speech (POS) tagging of its input and then uses a combination of techniques including simple keyword matching, regular expressions, and regular expressions matching POS tags to find instances of the ambiguities that are in its domain.

Some of the AFTs focus specifically on coordination ambiguity, that involving the coordinators, such as and and or. For example, Agarwal and Boggess [17] developed a tool that identifies a coordinator by matching the POS and semantic tags of the words modified by the coordinator. Resnik [18] proposed a semantic-similarity approach to disambiguate coordinators that involves nominal compounds. Goldberg [19] developed a tool that applies a co-occurrence-based probabilistic model to determine the attach-ments of ambiguous coordinators in phrases, using unsupervised learning.

Chantree, Willis, Kilgarriff, and De Roeck [20], in work predating that by Willis *et al.*, developed a binary classifier for coordination ambiguity. The classifier is based on a set of ambiguous phrases from a corpus of requirements specifications and a collec-tion of associated human judgements on their interpretations. The classifier uses word distribution information obtained from the British National Corpus (BNC).

The common drawback of many of these AFTs is that the recall of each is less than 100%, even for the ambiguities it claims to be detecting. Certainly, any AFT that depends on an auxiliary parser to find sentences with multiple parses or that depends on an auxiliary POS tagger to identify the POS of any word is going to have a recall of less than 100%, for no other reason than that no version of any of these auxiliary tools is perfect. Each parser or POS is easily fooled by anomalous sentences and words that can be in more than one POS, e.g., a word that is both a noun and a verb. The next section explains why an AFT's having less than 100% recall is a serious drawback.

On the other hand, each of ARM, QuARS, and TIGER Pro attempts to identify only specific types, namely those in its published scope. Its scope is designed to be some classes of ambiguities which can be recognized completely from keywords.

3   Why AFTs Applied to RSs of Critical Systems Need 100% Recall

Suppose that the CBS that is being built whose RS is being examined for ambiguities is a life-, safety-, or security-critical system. Then it is essential to find *all* ambiguities in the RS in order to resolve them. An AFT that does not find all ambiguities in the RS, because of inherent limitations, provides no real benefit to its user who must search the entire RS manually anyway to find the missing ambiguities. Use of the AFT is then a waste of time, and it may make the user less diligent in her search[2].

The fact that an AFT finds, say, even 90% of the ambiguities is of no particular help, because the user has no idea which 90% the AFT found and cannot just focus on finding the missing 10%, which are nevertheless critical to find. The missing 10% are not in any geographically identifiable parts of the RS; the missing 10% are not of any specifically identifiable types of ambiguity. The missing 10% arise from the fact that the underlying parser, POS tagger, or both are not perfect in unpredictable ways on actual input[3].

It is clear that some types of ambiguities are easier to find algorithmically than others. For example, a coordination ambiguity can occur only in a sentence with at least two occurrences of and or or and is thus easier to find than any semantic ambiguity. The approach taken in the work reported in this paper is to partition ambiguities by type into those that can be found algorithmically and those that cannot. Then an AFT would

---

[2] Of course, if the AFT is used *after* the human has made a serious attempt to find all ambiguities, then the AFT's output can be used to complement the human's findings. However, we would have to guard against the human's getting sloppy in her search in anticipation of the AFT's later use.

[3] Actually, it can be argued that an AFT needs to be only as good as a human ambiguity finder, who is, in the end, incapable of finding 100% of the ambiguities.

be built with 100% recall for the algorithmically findable types of ambiguities. In fact, even coordination ambiguities cannot be found with complete accuracy, i.e., with 100% recall *and* 100% precision. Some sentences with at least two occurrences of and or or are not coordination ambiguous. If the human user can tolerate imprecision, then identifying coordination ambiguity can be made to have 100% recall by presenting to the user every sentence with at least two occurrences of and or or. Then the user has to look at each presented sentence to decide if indeed it is coordination ambiguous or even ambiguous in some other way. The tradeoffs here are (1) recall versus precision and (2) imprecision versus burden to the user. The set of ambiguity types found by an AFT with 100% recall will be selected by careful consideration of these tradeoffs. This selection is a major focus of the research reported in this paper.

A type of ambiguity is in an AFT's scope if and only if the AFT can achieve 100% recall of instances of the type. The user knows that she can focus on finding instances of only those types of ambiguity outside the AFT's scope with the full confidence that the AFT will find and present as a potential ambiguity every instance of each type of ambiguity in the AFT's scope. It is, therefore, necessary to determine what types of ambiguities are detectable with 100% recall and tolerable imprecision and are, therefore, in the AFT's scope.

A type of ambiguity depends on a keyword if the keyword must be present in every instance of the type of ambiguity. For example, every instance of the only ambiguity must contain the word only. It is possible to have 100% recall of the only ambiguity simply by identifying every sentence with the word only. Of course, not every sentence with only is ambiguous. Therefore, simply identifying every sentence with the word only suffers from less than 100% precision for the only ambiguity. Being more precise about the only ambiguity requires being able to identify any sentence in which its only directly precedes the main verb of the sentence.[4] Doing this identification requires being able to identify the main verb of a sentence, which in turn requires parsing sentences and tagging each word with its POS. We know that parsing and POS tagging cannot be done by software with 100% accuracy. Therefore, achieving greater precision in recognizing instances of the only ambiguity costs a reduction in recall and may still not achieve 100% precision.

The goal of the research reported in this paper is to design an AFT that has 100% recall for all ambiguity types selected to be in its scope even if the 100% recall costs less than 100% precision. The AFT, as software, cannot have the intelligence necessary to determine if a potential ambiguity is a true ambiguity, but a human user has the intelligence. Therefore, the determination whether a potential ambiguity is ambiguous is left to the AFT's user. This division of labor and relaxation of the goal of 100% precision means that the AFT can afford to be less than precise in its goal to identify all possible potential ambiguities. However, if the AFT's imprecision is too high to the point that the user feels that using the AFT is burdensome, the AFT may end up not being used at all.

---

[4] The only ambiguity stems from the English convention of putting a sentence's only immediately before the sentence's main verb, regardless of what word or phrase is limited by the only. Thus, an only that precedes other than its sentence's main verb is probably not ambiguous.

Any AFT needs to be compared *in the way it is intended to be used* against a fully manual search for the same ambiguities. That is, if an AFT is intended to be used in conjunction with some manual work then that manual work must be considered in the comparison of the AFT with a fully manual search. The recall of the AFT-plus-its-required-manual work is to be compared with the recall of the fully manual search. The same must be done for time-required-for-using and for precision.

4   SREE

The main purpose for designing SREE was to experiment with the particular decomposition of the ambiguity identification task that meets the goals described in Section 3 for an AFT. The version of SREE described in this paper is in fact the third attempt, after two attempts [21–23] using more traditional parser-based designs failed to produce an AFT that was significantly better than the existing AFTs.

4.1   Use Lexical Analyzer Instead of Syntactic Analyzer for AFTs

The syntax analyzer that the Tjong developed in her early work [24] achieved only an 80% recall rate of correctly tagged words without any POS tagging algorithm. With more work, the parser could have been improved with a deep-search-and-match heuristic [25] and with machine learning [26]. However, as mentioned at the end of Section 2, achieving 100% accuracy in parsing and POS tagging is impossible. A SREE based on a parser would not be able to achieve 100% recall of any ambiguity whose recognition depends on having a correct parse or a correct POS assignment.

On the other hand, using a pure lexical (in the sense of compilation) strategy would allow SREE to achieve 100% recall of any potential ambiguity for which *all* of its indicators are specific words, i.e., a type of potential ambiguity that would be in SREE's scope.

We decided that SREE would do only lexical searches for potential ambiguities. Therefore, from a user's viewpoint, there are two types of potential ambiguities:

1. those in the scope of SREE, because they are lexically identifiable with 100% recall and
2. those not in the scope of SREE, because they cannot be identified lexically with 100% recall.

As mentioned, the user knows that SREE searches for only potential ambiguities in its scope. The user knows that she must decide for any potential ambiguity whether it *is* an ambiguity. The user knows that she must search manually for any kind of ambiguity not in SREE's scope. She can do this search while ignoring those types of ambiguities that are in SREE's scope, thus allowing her to focus on what she must find manually. This ability to focus on fewer types of ambiguities may increase her effectiveness in finding instances of the types of ambiguities she is focusing on.

4.2   Research and Design Method

To start the development of SREE in 2007, Tjong gathered a set of industrial-strength RSs [7]. In these RSs, she found all the instances of ambiguity she could. Each instance became the indicator of some potential ambiguity for SREE.

The set of RSs consists of the RSs from two case studies [27] and seven industrial strength RSs [28–34]. Each RS in the set contains both functional RStats and nonfunctional RStats. Tjong then studied each RStat in the RSs and identified all ambiguities she could find in the RStat. She used the ARM and QuARS indicators to help her find ambiguities. Each ambiguity was classified by its ambiguity type, such as coordination ambiguity, weak auxiliary, vagueness, etc.

For each type of potential ambiguity, a list of indicators was built in the hopes of finding an exhaustive list of indicators for the type. For some types of potential ambiguities, e.g., coordination and misplaced only, constructing an exhaustive list seems possible. For others, e.g., plural, it is probably impossible. For each type of potential ambiguity, part of the research is to determine if the type can be part of the scope of SREE, i.e., all of its indicators can be found and be used to build a lexical analyzer for the potential ambiguity with 100% recall. The game to be played is to see if the list of the indicators for a type of potential ambiguity stabilizes, i.e., no new elements for the list are found after some reasonable number of uses of SREE in a domain.

5   Architecture and Construction of SREE

This section describes the architecture and construction of SREE, which permit SREE to be modular, easy to change[5], extensible, and easy to use. Basically, SREE has two main components, the AIC and the lexical analyzer.

5.1   Ambiguity Indicator Corpus (AIC)

The AIC contains the corpus of indicators of potential ambiguity. Because of the vast richness of NL, it is simply not possible to have an AIC that contains an indicator of every possible potential ambiguity. Therefore, SREE allows its user to add new indicators to its AIC. There are two AICs in SREE, the original indicator corpus (OIC) and the customized indicator corpus (CIC). The OIC contains ten subcorpora, each in a separate file, each with its own list of indicators, and each named for the nature of the potential ambiguities indicated by elements of its contents. The indicators in these subcorpora are:

- *Continuance*: contains indicators: as follows, below, following, in addition, in particular, listed, meantime, meanwhile, on one hand, on the other hand, and whereas.
- *Coordinator*: contains the indicators: and, and/or, and or.
- *Directive*: contains the indicators: e.g., etc., figure, for example, i.e., note, and table.
- *Incomplete*: contains the indicators: TBA, TBC, TBD, TBE, TBS, TBR, as a minimum, as defined, as specified, in addition, is defined, no practical limit, not defined, not determined, but not limited to, to be advised, to be defined, to be completed, to be determined, to be resolved, and to be specified.

---

[5] The prototype's being easy to change is critical when one is continually subjecting the prototype to changes as new requirements are discovered.

- *Optional*: contains the indicators: as desired, at last, either, eventually, if appropriate, if desired, in case of, if necessary, if needed, neither, nor, optionally, otherwise, possibly, probably, and whether.
- *Plural*: contains a list of 11,287 plural nouns, each ending in "s". We differentiate the terms "Pluralnoun" and "plural noun". The former is what is detected by SREE as a result of its use of the Plural corpus. The latter is the collection of nouns, which are of plural types. SREE has 100% recall of Pluralnouns, but not of plural nouns.
- *Pronoun*: contains the indicators: anyone, anybody, anything, everyone, everybody, everything, he, her, hers, herself, him, himself, his, i, it, its, itself, me, mine, most, my, myself, nobody, none, no one, nothing, our, ours, ourselves, she, someone, somebody, something, that, their, theirs, them, themselves, these, they, this, those, us, we, what, whatever, which, whichever, who, whoever, whom, whomever, whose, whosever, you, your, yours, yourself, and yourselves.
- *Quantifier*: contains the indicators: all, any, few, little, many, much, several, and some.
- *Vague*: contains the indicators: /, < >, ( ), [ ], , ;, ?, !, adaptability, additionally, adequate, aggregate, also, ancillary, arbitrary, appropriate, as appropriate, available, as far as, at last, as few as possible, as little as possible, as many as possible, as much as possible, as required, as well as, bad, both, but, but also, but not limited to, capable of, capable to, capability of, capability, common, correctly, consistent, contemporary, convenient, credible, custom, customary, default, definable, easily, easy, effective, efficient, episodic, equitable, equitably, eventually, exist, exists, expeditiously, fast, fair, fairly, finally, frequently, full, general, generic, good, high-level, impartially, infrequently, insignificant, intermediate, interactive, in terms of, less, lightweight, logical, low-level, maximum, minimum, more, mutually-agreed, mutually-exclusive, mutually-inclusive, near, necessary, neutral, not only, only, on the fly, particular, physical, powerful, practical, prompt, provided, quickly, random, recent, regardless of, relevant, respective, robust, routine, sufficiently, sequential, significant, simple, specific, strong, there, there is, transient, transparent, timely, undefinable, understandable, unless, unnecessary, useful, various, and varying.
- *Weak*: contains the indicators: can, could, may, might, ought to, preferred, should, will, and would.

SREE automatically loads these corpora into the AIC each time a user starts up SREE. Note that the indicators for the only ambiguity are already listed among the indicators for vagueness.

The user of SREE is not allowed to modify or delete any of the original corpora in the OIC. He may add to the CIC any indicator of potential ambiguity that he may find that is not in the AIC. He may also remove from the CIC indicators that have proved less than helpful.

5.2   Lexical Analyzer

SREE's lexical analyzer scans a RS, RStat by RStat, and scans each RStat, token by token, for any occurrence of any indicator in the AIC. During the scan, the lexical analyzer of SREE reads tokens from its input RS and compares each token with each indicator in the AIC. If SREE finds a match, it reports the token and its containing RStat as a potentially ambiguous Rstat.

6 Evaluation of Design and Acceptability of Imprecision Amounts

The question that needs to be answered for SREE as an AFT is, "Which costs a user more, her searching for ambiguities with SREE or her searching for ambiguities totally manually?" To answer this question, we will need to know

- how much time is spent searching for any ambiguity in a totally manual search,
- the amount of time spent in rejecting a false positive, and
- whether knowing the scope of SREE really allows the user to ignore the types of ambiguities in SREE's scope.

This section uses this information to do an estimated evaluation of the times to use the AFT and to do a manual search to find all ambiguities in the same RS.

The evaluation in this section is not intended to be and is not an empirically sound validation of the effectiveness of SREE as an AFT. Because of the weaknesses reported in Section 7, empirically evaluating the reported version of SREE would be a waste of effort. The sole purpose of the estimation-based evaluation of this section is to determine if it is worth proceeding with the research to design an AFT with the stated goals.

6.1 Time Comparison

When Tjong was doing the research reported herein, she had to do a completely manual examination of each RS that was used in the research and experiments in order to determine which of its Rstats were ambiguous according to the list of ambiguity types that she had built. The New Adelaide Airport RS, with 63 Rstats, required 1.5 hours for its examination, i.e., about 86 seconds per Rstat to determine which of its Rstats were ambiguous. The MCSS RS, with 246 Rstats, required 6 hours, in 2 3-hour sittings, i.e., about 88 seconds per Rstat to make the same determination. The average of these inspection times per Rstat is about 87 seconds.

On the other hand, after she had run SREE on the 22 random Rstats, she spent 3 minutes and 45 seconds or about 10 seconds per Rstat to determine which of the 20 that were marked as potentially ambiguous were truly ambiguous[6]. This determination was essentially instinctive and did not require consulting any lists. That is, without looking at any lists, she could see very quickly what kind of potential ambiguity was present in each potentially ambiguous Rstat and was able to quickly decide if the potential ambiguity was actual. Of course, from her research, she was attuned to finding ambiguities, as would be any experienced ambiguity inspector.

When Tjong ran SREE on the 63 Rstats of the New Adelaide Airport RS [7, pp. A1–A37], SREE marked 42, or 66.66%, of them as potentially ambiguous. When she ran SREE on the 246 Rstats of the MCSS RS [7, pp. A38–A179], SREE marked 201,

---

[6] The first author had sent these 22 Rstats to others to have them identify the ambiguities they found. These included a PhC in knowledge management, two software engineers, and a marketing executive. None of them found anywhere near the number of ambiguities that the author had found. None of them but the PhC had background in RE and none was a specialist in ambiguity finding.

or 81.70% of them as potentially ambiguous. The weighted average fraction of the RStats that SREE marked as potentially ambiguous was 78.64%. This figure means that on average at about 80% of the Rstats an RS both lie within SREE's scope and are potentially ambiguous. Tjong's running of SREE against the RSs was about a year and a half after she had finished the manual examination of the RSs, enough time that she could not remember the details of what she had done previously, and which sentences were ambiguous.

Once SREE had produced its output from the RSs, Tjong had to examine each marked potentially ambiguous Rstat to determine if it is truly ambiguous. The examination of the 42 marked Rstats of the New Adelaide Airport RS required about 17 minutes, or about 24 seconds per Rstat. The examination of the 201 marked Rstats of the MCSS RS required about 43 minutes, or about 13 seconds per Rstat. The weighted average examination per potentially ambiguous Rstat is about 15 seconds.

So, the choices are:

1. **Completely Manual Inspection:** Manually inspect an entire RS of n Rstats for all types of ambiguities, having to continually consult a list of the types of ambiguities to ensure that none are overlooked, spending about 87 seconds per Rstat, for a total of $87 \times n$ seconds.

2. **Using SREE for the Ambiguities in its Scope and Manual Inspection for the Rest of the Ambiguities:** Run SREE on the RS to obtain a list of potentially ambiguous Rstats, spending about 15 seconds per Rstat to decide which potentially ambiguous Rstat is truly ambiguous. Then manually inspect the entire RS for only the types of ambiguities not in SREE's scope.

   If, as estimated, about 80% of the Rstats of a RS both lie within SREE's scope and are potentially ambiguous, then SREE will mark $.8 \times n$ Rstats as potentially ambiguous and the user will have to spend about 15 seconds to examine each of them, for a total of $12 \times n$ seconds. Then, the user will have to examine the full RS for ambiguities not in SREE's scope. Since at least 80% of the Rstats lie in SREE's scope, a lower bound of the fraction of the Rstats containing potential ambiguities not in SREE's scope is 20%. Of course, there will probably be some Rstats that have a potential ambiguity in SREE's scope and a potential ambiguity not in SREE's scope. So the actual fraction of Rstats containing potential ambiguities not in SREE's scope is more than 20%. We estimate that at worst, about 50% of the Rstats have potential ambiguities not in SREE's scope.

   On the assumption that the user of SREE is very familiar, from lots of practice, with the scope of SREE, we estimate that the examination of the entire RS for potentially ambiguous Rstats outside of the scope of SREE to be about $1.25 \times 87 \times .5 \times n = 54.4 \times n$ seconds, with about 25% more time spent per Rstat than in the normal manual examination of the Rstat to account for having to skip over potential ambiguities in SREE's scope.

Which is larger?

- $87 \times n$ or
- $12 \times n + 54.4 \times n = 66.4 \times n$?

Clearly, the former is larger, and it is about about 23% higher. Thus, the estimated time spent for each Rstat in the mixed-SREE-and-manual-inspection choice is about 75% of the estimated time spent per Rstat in the totally-manual-inspection choice.

As mentioned, this calculated estimated difference depends on the SREE user's having learned to ignore potential ambiguities in SREE's scope to focus her search on finding ambiguities not in SREE's scope. From our experience using other tools and having learned what they do and do not do, we believe that this assumption is reasonable.

The estimated advantage of using SREE in the proper manner over a completely manual search is not very large. In any case, 50% was used as the estimate of the percentage of Rstats that have potential ambiguities not in SREE's scope in order that the comparison be pessimistic on SREE's side. Part of the future work will surely be case studies with careful measurements of the values required for the comparison. Nevertheless, the estimated values are good enough to justify further research to find a better decomposition of the ambiguity finding task that allows an AFT that truly meets SREE's goals.

6.2   Evaluation of Imprecision

The analysis of the SREE runs on the New Adelaide Airport RS shows that there were 58 false positives among the 180 potential ambiguities that SREE found in the RS, for a precision of 68%. The analysis of the SREE runs on the MCSS RS shows that there were 247 false positives among the 723 potential ambiguities that SREE found in the RS, for a precision of 66%. Neither of these precisions is as close to 100% as we had hoped. In retrospect, however, when the AFT does no analysis of what it finds, it is to be expected that a large percentage of what it finds are false positives. Nevertheless, even with this high imprecision, the mixed-SREE-and-manual-inspection time is less than the totally-manual-inspection time. So, it is possible that SREE's imprecision will not be considered burdensome.

6.3   SREE's Weaknesses

SREE's weaknesses that can be observed from our findings are:

- the fact that SREE's scope includes only Pluralnouns and not plural nouns. As explained, Pluralnouns are those tokens recognized as potentially ambiguous by SREE as a result of the Plural corpus, whereas plural nouns is the actual set of nouns that are plural. SREE has 100% recall of Pluralnouns, but not of plural nouns. It may be better to report as potentially plural any word that ends in s and to put into the AIC a list of only irregular plural nouns that do not end in s. A complete enough list of irregular plural nouns that do not end in s is probably smaller than the current list of 11,287 Pluralnouns and is probably easier to make complete enough than a list of all plural nouns. Alternatively, the user is responsible for continuing to add more and more plural nouns to the list of Pluralnouns in the AIC until Pluralnouns has converged on all plural nouns that ever show up in the specifications that the user encounters. This convergence may never really happen due to the inherent and surprising richness of NL. In the end, if too many plural nouns are outside SREE's scope, then perhaps not even the 11,287 plural nouns in the Plural corpus should be in SREE's scope.

- the fact that the AIC is not complete, as evidenced by the continual, relentless discovery of new indicators to add to the AIC during the research to develop SREE. An outstanding question is whether this AIC will converge for a language or even a domain. We do expect that at some point, the rate of addition of new indicators for other than Pluralnouns will drop considerably, just because we will eventually begin not to find new types of ambiguities. Thus, this work is complementary to all other research work cited in Section 2 that attempts to find systematic ways of detecting or avoiding ambiguities.
- the fact that the SREE's measured precision rate is lower than the goal of not too much less than 100%, particularly because a singular verb that happens to look like an element of Pluralnouns is reported as potentially ambiguous and because a non-subject plural noun matching an element of Pluralnoun is reported as potentially ambiguous (Recall that a plural noun is ambiguous only when it is the subject of a sentence). Despite the low precision, the authors believe that the use of SREE with its 100% recall of potential ambiguities in its scope is better for the user than to have to have to find these potential ambiguities manually in close, error-prone readings of the RS.

7 Conclusion and Future Work

This paper has described the prototyping of SREE, which was designed to be the algorithmic AFT in a decomposition of a process for finding ambiguities in a NL RS into two easily distinguished parts:

1. the algorithmic part that can be done with 100% recall by a tool, the dumb tool, and
2. the nonalgorithmic part that is smaller than manually searching the entire RS and which requires the intelligence of a smart human.

While SREE does not meet all of its its goals, we have learned a lot that can be used in the next attempt to build an AFT according to the suggested decomposition.

The trials showed several weaknesses of SREE and, thus, opportunities for improvement,

- in determining if the list of indicators for the AIC will stabilize for any language or domain, and
- dealing with plural nouns.

The high number of false positives among the potential ambiguities matching indicators in the Plural corpus raises concerns about the usefulness of the chosen method to deal with the plural noun ambiguity. Perhaps, a larger list of plural nouns, including irregulars is needed in the AIC. Alternatively, it may be even better to have SREE's lexical analyzer recognize

1. all words ending in s, es, ae, aux, and other common plural noun endings, and
2. all words in a new Plural corpus consisting of as many irregular plural nouns as possible as potential plural nouns.

While this new method will probably find more potentially ambiguous plural nouns than the current method, the new method will probably have higher imprecision than the current method. Ultimately, the issue is which is worse: to have to manually search for plural nouns not currently in SREE's scope or to have more imprecision?

With this method of dealing with plural nouns, there is yet another tradeoff for an AFT designed with the goal of 100% recall as suggested by this paper. If the AFT has a smaller scope then it is easier to reach the goal of 100% recall. However, then the manual search that accompanies the AFT use would have more to do. So it pays to try to find a way to include more potential ambiguities in the scope of any AFT.

Finally, if ever a prototype AFT is developed that passes muster in an informal evaluation like that described in this paper, the AFT must be subjected to a proper, unbiased empirical evaluation, with several users using the AFT applied to several industrial-strength RSs.

Acknowledgements. The authors thank Michael Hartley, Jack, Shindy, and Inn Fang for their comments on all the research reported in this paper. Daniel Berry's work was supported in parts by a Canadian NSERC grant NSERC-RGPIN227055-00 and by a Canadian NSERC–Scotia Bank Industrial Research Chair NSERC-IRCPJ365473-05.

References

1. Berry, D.M., Gacitua, R., Sawyer, P., Tjong, S.F.: The case for dumb requirements engineering tools. In: Regnell, B., Damian, D. (eds.) REFSQ 2011. LNCS, vol. 7195, pp. 211–217. Springer, Heidelberg (2012)
2. van Rossum, W.: The implementation of technologies in intensive care units: Ambiguity, uncertainty and organizational reactions. Technical Report Research Report 97B51, Research Institute SOM (Systems, Organisations and Management), University of Groningen (1997), http://irs.ub.rug.nl/ppn/165660821
3. Sussman, S.W., Guinan, P.J.: Antidotes for high complexity and ambiguity in software development. Information and Management 36, 23–35 (1999)
4. Gause, D.C., Weinberg, G.M.: Exploring Requirements: Quality Before Design. Dorset House, New York (1989)
5. Mich, L., Franch, M., Inverardi, P.N.: Market research for requirements analysis using linguistic tools. Requirements Engineering Journal 9(1), 40–56, 9(2), 15 (2004); has full article with inverted names, No. 2 has correction of names and reference to full article in No. 1.
6. Berry, D.M., Kamsties, E.: Ambiguity in requirements specification. In: Leite, J., Doorn, J. (eds.) Perspectives on Requirements Engineering, pp. 7–44. Kluwer, Boston (2004)
7. Tjong, S.F.: Avoiding Ambiguity in Requirements Specifications. PhD thesis, Faculty of Engineering & Computer Science, University of Nottingham, Malaysia Campus, Semenyih, Selangor Darul Ehsan, Malaysia (2008), https://cs.uwaterloo.ca/~dberry/FTP_SITE/tech.reports/TjongThesis.pdf
8. Ambriola, V., Gervasi, V.: On the systematic analysis of natural language requirements with CIRCE. Automated Software Engineering 13, 107–167 (2006)
9. Wilson, W.M., Rosenberg, L.H., Hyatt, L.E.: Automated analysis of requirement specifications. In: Proceedings of the Nineteenth International Conference on Software Engineering (ICSE 1997), pp. 161–171 (1997)

10. Fabbrini, F., Fusani, M., Gnesi, S., Lami, G.: Quality evaluation of software requirement specifications. In: Proceedings of the Software and Internet Quality Week 2000 Conference, pp. 1–18 (2000)
11. Fabbrini, F., Fusani, M., Gnesi, S., Lami, G.: The linguistic approach to the natural language requirements, quality: Benefits of the use of an automatic tool. In: Proceedings of the Twenty-Sixth Annual IEEE Computer Society – NASA GSFC Software Engineering Workshop, pp. 97–105 (2001)
12. Kasser, J.: Tiger pro manual. Technical report, University of South Australia (2006), http://users.chariot.net.au/~g3zcz/TigerPro/tigerPro.pdf
13. Willis, A., Chantree, F., de Roeck, A.: Automatic identification of nocuous ambiguity. Research on Language and Computation 6, 355–374 (2008)
14. Kiyavitskaya, N., Zeni, N., Mich, L., Berry, D.M.: Requirements for tools for ambiguity identification and measurement in natural language requirements specifications. Requirements Engineering Journal 13, 207–239 (2008)
15. Miller, G.A., Felbaum, C., et al.: WordNet Web Site. Princeton University, Princeton, http://wordnet.princeton.edu/ (accessed March 12, 2006)
16. Gleich, B., Creighton, O., Kof, L.: Ambiguity detection: Towards a tool explaining ambiguity sources. In: Wieringa, R., Persson, A. (eds.) REFSQ 2010. LNCS, vol. 6182, pp. 218–232. Springer, Heidelberg (2010)
17. Agarwal, R., Boggess, L.: A simple but useful approach to conjunct identification. In: Proceedings of the Thirtieth Annual Meeting of the Association for Computational Linguistics (ACL 1992), pp. 15–21 (1992)
18. Resnik, P.: Semantic similarity in a taxonomy: An information-based measure and its application to problems of ambiguity in natural language. Journal of Artificial Intelligence Research 11, 95–130 (1999)
19. Goldberg, M.: An unsupervised model for statistically determining coordinate phrase attachment. In: Proceedings of the Thirty-Seventh Annual Meeting of the Association for Computational Linguistics on Computational Linguistics (ACL 1999), pp. 610–614 (1999)
20. Chantree, F., Willis, A., Kilgarriff, A., de Roeck, A.: Detecting dangerous coordination ambiguities using word distribution. In: Recent Advances in Natural Language Processing: Current Issues in Linguistic Theory, vol. 4 (292), pp. 287–296. John Benjamins (2007)
21. Tjong, S.F., Hallam, N., Hartley, M.: Improving the quality of natural language requirements specifications through natural language requirements patterns. In: Proceedings of the Sixth IEEE International Conference on Computer and Information Technology (CIT 2006), pp. 199–206 (2006), https://cs.uwaterloo.ca/~dberry/FTP_SITE/ reprints.journals.conferences/TjongHallamHartley2006A.pdf
22. Tjong, S.F.: Natural language patterns for requirements specifications. Technical report, Faculty of Engineering & Computer Science, University of Nottingham, Malaysia Campus (2006), https://cs.uwaterloo.ca/~dberry/FTP_SITE/ tech.reports/TjongTR-02_2006.pdf
23. Tjong, S.F., Hartley, M., Berry, D.M.: Extended disambiguation rules for requirements specifications. In: Proceedings of the Tenth Workshop on Requirements Engineering a.k.a. Workshop em Engenharia de Requisitos (WER 2007), pp. 97–106 (2007), http://wer.inf.puc-rio.br/WERpapers/ artigos/artigos_WER07/Lwer07-tjong1.pdf
24. Tjong, S.F., Hallam, N., Hartley, M.: An adaptive parsing technique for prorules grammar. In: Proceedings of the Computer Science and Mathematics Symposium (CSMS) (2006), https://cs.uwaterloo.ca/~dberry/FTP_SITE/ reprints.journals.conferences/TjongHallamHartley2006B.pdf

25. Collins, M., Duffy, N.: New ranking algorithms for parsing and tagging: Kernels over discrete structures, and the voted perceptron. In: Proceedings of the Fortieth Annual Meeting of the Association for Computational Linguistics (ACL 2002), pp. 263–270 (2002)
26. Hammerton, J., Osborne, M., Armstrong, S., Daelemans, W.: Introduction to special issue on machine learning approaches to shallow parsing. Journal of Machine Learning Research 2, 551–558 (2002)
27. Bray, I.K.: An Introduction to Requirements Engineering. Addison-Wesley, Harlow (2002)
28. Eng, C.S.: Batch poster system, detailed business requirements. Technical report, EDS MySC (2005)
29. EPRI: Cask loader software, general requirements document draft. Technical Report, Electric Power Research Institute Inc. (1999),
    http://www.epri.com/eprisoftware/
    processguide/docs/srdexdoc.doc
30. Nelbach, F.: Software requirements document for the data cycle system (DCS). Technical Report, Universities Space Research Association, UCLA (2002),
    http://www.astro.ucla.edu/~shuping/
    SOFIA/Documents/DCS_SRD_Rev1.pdf
31. Moeser, R., Perley, P.: Expanded very large array (EVLA) operations interface software requirements. Technical Report EVLA-SW-003, National Radio Astronomy Observatory (2003),
    http://www.aoc.nrao.edu/evla/techdocs/
    computer/workdocs/array-sw-rqmts.pdf
32. Dubois, R.: Large area telescope (LAT) science analysis software specification. Technical Report GE-0000X-DO, SLAC National Accelerator Laboratory (2000),
    http://www.last.slac.stanford.edu/
    IntegrationTest/DataHandling/docs/LA%T-SS-00020-6.pdf
33. George, S.: PESA high-level trigger selection software requirements. Technical Report, Centre for Particle Physics at Royal Holloway University (2001),
    http://www.pp.rhul.ac.uk/atlas/newsw/requirements/1.0.2/
34. Stevenson, M., Hartley, M., Iacovou, H., Tan, A., Phan, L.: Software requirements specification for sort algorithm demonstration program. Technical report, SDPM (2005)

Factors Influencing User Feedback on Predicted Satisfaction with Software Systems

Rumyana Proynova and Barbara Paech

Software Engineering Group, Institute for Computer Science,
University of Heidelberg, Germany
{proynova,paech}@informatik.uni-heidelberg.de

Abstract. Requirements engineers need feedback from users on planned system features. The simplest way is to present feature descriptions to the users and ask for their opinion. [Problem/question] The feedback users can give in such a situation is not always accurate. The mechanisms which cause a mismatch between actual and predicted user satisfaction are currently not well understood. [Method/results] We used the results from a previous study we conducted, together with insights on consumer satisfaction from marketing, to create a working model of predicted user satisfaction. We validated the model with a new, more extensive empirical study. [Contribution] We present a model of predicted user satisfaction. Unlike the existing models of user satisfaction for software systems, it can be used for gathering feedback before a user has had experience with a software system. Our study shows that measuring predicted satisfaction can deliver a good approximation of actual satisfaction, although there is some prediction discrepancy which could be reduced by choosing the right combination of influence factors.

1 Introduction

It is not feasible to involve users in requirements elicitation in all projects, even though this could lead to higher quality requirements. Factors like the unavailability of users (for example in global software development projects or off-the-shelf software products with no designated users) or limited budget and resources, as well as company culture, can dictate that the requirements for the software are derived from other sources. In order to ensure that these requirements are aligned with the needs of the users, the requirements engineers can let the users validate the requirements.

The constraints which preclude resource-intensive elicitation techniques are likely to also preclude similarly resource-intensive validation techniques. A technique which produces adequate results but requires a comparably low level of effort can enable early validation in projects where currently users are not involved until the very late stages of the project such as testing or even roll-out of a completed product. Our research focuses on defining such a technique, based on a questionnaire which asks the users to indicate their future satisfaction with a list of software features.

J. Doerr and A.L. Opdahl (Eds.): REFSQ 2013, LNCS 7830, pp. 96–111, 2013.
© Springer-Verlag Berlin Heidelberg 2013

While preparing a study conducted in a medicine information systems context, we designed a simple questionnaire using an ad-hoc approach to measuring satisfaction: users got a list of features and had to indicate their liking for the features and evaluate their usefulness. As they did not have experience with the actual system described, the questionnaire measured not the actual satisfaction, but rather the users' prediction of their future satisfaction once they will work with the system, which we call *predicted satisfaction*. During the study, we became aware of two difficulties with the ad-hoc approach to measuring predicted satisfaction:

Misunderstanding of features. We were not sure that the users understood the feature descriptions well enough to predict their satisfaction. It is possible that they were not able to form a clear conception of the feature based on its description only. Alternatively, they could have built a wrong conception and predicted their satisfaction based on this wrong conception.

Inaccurate prediction. We were not sure that predicted satisfaction will result in actual satisfaction, and we found no evidence either for or against this phenomenon in literature.

The current article describes our efforts to create a model of predicted user satisfaction, which is based on knowledge about individual features, as opposed to the need for the user to have experience with the entire system. We plan to use this model to create a questionnaire for measuring predicted satisfaction such that the discrepancy between actual satisfaction and the satisfaction predicted with our questionnaire is minimized.

In the next section, we give an overview of existing models for measuring satisfaction and the extent to which they apply to our problem. Section 3 describes the method we used to arrive at a working model of predicted user satisfaction. In Section 4 we present an empirical study validating our model. After a discussion of our results in Section 5 , we give an outlook of our future research in the last section.

2   Related Work

2.1   Consumer Satisfaction in Marketing

Our intention is to measure user satisfaction with a software product which does not yet exist, by asking users to predict their satisfaction based on a requirements specification. These methods are common in marketing, where prospective consumers are asked to predict their satisfaction based on planned product features.

Overview. Research in marketing and psychology has lead to the creation of elaborate theoretical models for consumer satisfaction [15] which can be used to create better methods for measuring satisfaction in specific contexts. Early theories assumed that satisfaction is proportional to *product performance*. Each product has attributes specific to its product category - for example, a soft drink has attributes like fizziness and sweetness, and a vehicle has attributes like gas mileage and number of seats. Performance is measured on appropriate scales, and it is assumed that high performance on attributes important to the customer automatically leads to high satisfaction. This model is known as importance-performance analysis [12]. A more modern model descended from importance-performance analysis is the Kano model [18], which can also be used to evaluate features of software systems [17]. This type of model can measure either predicted or actual satisfaction, depending on whether the consumer has experience with the product or is only presented with a description.

Empirical evidence suggests that direct product performance measurements are only weakly correlated with satisfaction [15]. This has led to the development of new models of satisfaction, some of which are context specific (e.g. SERVQUAL [2], which is constrained to services only), while others are universal. The model which predicts satisfaction best is that of *expectation disconfirmation* [14]. In this model, customers have expectations about the performance of the product they wish to buy. The expectation itself can be positive or negative, e.g. a consumer expects good print contrast when buying extra-bright office paper and bad contrast when buying recycled office paper. There is usually a discrepancy between expected and actual product performance, which results in positive or negative *disconfirmation* (The product turns out to be better/worse than expected). The combined effects of expectation and disconfirmation create the final level of satisfaction.

Applicability. The theoretical models of customer satisfaction used in marketing are very elaborate and include many variables not easily measured in a simple questionnaire. Indeed, we could not find an instrument combining all the known variables for measuring a single satisfaction score; even popular instruments such as the ACSI (American consumer satisfaction index) [8] only use a few of these variables. These models do not consider the specific problems which can occur in the situation of a user having to validate the requirements for a software product. Therefore, they are useful as a basis for our research, but do not offer an instrument which can be applied directly for measuring predicted user satisfaction.

2.2   User Satisfaction with Software Systems

We searched for user satisfaction in software engineering literature and found that there are several widely used methods for measuring satisfaction with existing systems, but their theoretical background has not been studied as extensively as the marketing models. We did not find publications on measuring predicted satisfaction in a software engineering context.

Overview. We found three approaches for measuring satisfaction with software systems. Numerous studies use ad-hoc measurements of satisfaction (such as Likert scales directly labeled with "high" and "low" satisfaction, e.g. in [13]).

There is a number of general models for measuring user satisfaction. An early instrument created by Bailey and Pearson [1] was validated and refined by many other researchers, finally resulting in the revised model of information system success by DeLone and McLean [6]. Another model used for measuring user satisfaction is the TAM (Technology Acceptance Model) first published in 1989 [5] and its descendant UTAUT (Unified theory of acceptance and use of technology) [19]. In the field of human-computer interaction, the QUIS instrument [3] (Questionnaire for user interaction satisfaction) is frequently used.

There are also specialized approaches which work with a very narrow model of satisfaction limited to a certain domain. Examples are the use of quality of service parameters as a proxy to user satisfaction (used for example in [9], [21]) employed when measuring user satisfaction with network products, and the PARADISE model [20] which is specific for measuring satisfaction with dialogue systems.

Applicability. The models of user satisfaction listed above are created for evaluating implemented systems in their entirety. Not all of the variables measured can be used on individual features. They also assume that the user has experience with the system. For example, they include variables for measuring the frequency of system use, or the quality of user support. Therefore, they can not be directly used for measuring predicted satisfaction based on a list of features only. Instead, we can create a model specifically intended for measuring predicted satisfaction, based on the parts of those models which have relevance for individual feature descriptions.

3   Towards a Model of Predicted User Satisfaction

Our long-term research goal is to construct an instrument for measuring predicted satisfaction and confirm that it delivers reliable results not distorted by misunderstanding of features or inaccurate prediction. In order to create a preliminary model of user satisfaction, we started with a list of variables describing the two effects mentioned above: *perceived understanding* and *actual understanding*, intended to measure the misunderstanding of features, and *satisfaction prediction error*, intended to measure inaccurate prediction. We also conjectured that the degree of understanding is influenced by the choice of *feature representation format*.

We conducted a first live study investigating the connection between these variables during RefsQ 2012. We then used our findings to create a more complete model of user satisfaction which we describe in Section 3.2 . We validated these findings in a new study, described in Section 4 . Raw data from both studies can be downloaded from www.varemed.org.

3.1   First Empirical Study

A detailed account of this study can be found in an earlier publication [16]. Here, we summarize those aspects of the design and the findings which are relevant for the understanding of the rest of the present publication.

Study Design. For the study, we created a requirements specification for a simple expense management system. The specification consisted of 16 features and was available in two different formats, as user tasks [10] and user stories [4]. We also implemented a prototype of the software specified by the features, which was capable of convincingly simulating the finished software with a prepared set of test data. We then recorded screen casts demonstrating the use of the features from the specification, including a narrated explanation of the software functionality. Each demonstration explained two to five features, resulting in a total of 5 recordings.

The 56 participants were self-selected requirements specialists playing the role of users. They were about equally divided between academic and industry background, with experience in requirements engineering varying from a few months to several decades. They were randomly assigned to one of two groups of equal size, the user tasks group and the user stories group. They were given time to read the requirements specification. Then they were asked to answer questions about each feature, measuring *perceived understanding* and *predicted satisfaction*. After they had completed this part, they were shown the recorded demonstrations. After each demonstration, they were asked to answer new questions about each feature, which measured the *actual satisfaction* and the *actual understanding* with the implemented features. The questionnaire also included space for free-text descriptions of the difference between the imagined and actual implementation of each feature, as well as space for suggestions and feedback. The exact wording of the questions was the same as in the second study, and is described in more detail in Section 4.

Findings. We evaluated the data from the experiment and found that *actual understanding* has a positive correlation with *perceived understanding* and *predicted satisfaction*. The correlation coefficient with *actual satisfaction* was 0.08 and not significant at a 5% confidence. We also calculated the variable *satisfaction prediction discrepancy* as the absolute difference between actual and predicted satisfaction. It had a negative correlation with actual understanding ($r = -0.23$, significant at $\alpha = 0.05$), meaning that better understanding results in more accurate satisfaction prediction. All of these effects appeared independently of the feature representation format used.

We were able to gain further insights based on the free-text answers. Participants suggested that their evaluations of the main variables were influenced by previous experience with the same feature in the context of a different software product (such as printing a document), by not being able to imagine a good use for the feature, and by having no emotional attachment to the software product.

Prediction discrepancy is a good way to describe the accuracy of our questionnaire. In our study, we found that the mean prediction discrepancy was 0.9, with standard deviation of 1.07 units (measured on a scale from 1 to 5). Based on these results, we feel that while our questionnaire delivers usable results of predicted satisfaction, its accuracy can be much improved.

3.2   A Preliminary Model of Predicted User Satisfaction

After our first study, we created a working version of our model of predicted user satisfaction. Figure 1 shows a graphical representation of the model. Bubbles represent variables, arrows denote influence of one variable on another. Variables which can only be measured after users have had experience with the implemented system have a grey background.

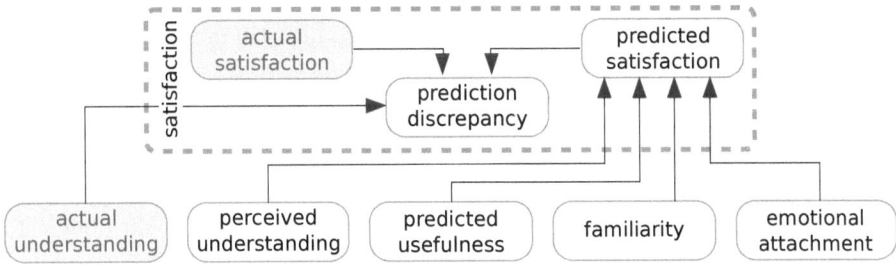

Fig. 1. Our working model of user satisfaction

We do not claim this model to be exhaustive. It is possible that there are more variables influencing predicted satisfaction, or that there are cross-links between the variables listed here. Our study provides only a first validation of the model. Still, even in its incomplete form, it can be useful for gaining insight in user satisfaction.

Actual satisfaction. This is the user's response to the implemented feature. It cannot be measured before the implementation exists.

Predicted satisfaction. This is a self-reported forecast of what the future satisfaction with a feature's implementation will be. Users can make these forecasts based on a feature description.

Prediction discrepancy. Predicting satisfaction is a form of affective forecasting [11]. It can never be completely precise, as humans do not exactly know what their emotional state will be in the future. We use the term *prediction discrepancy* in the context of a single prediction to denote the absolute difference between predicted and actual satisfaction. Thus, if user X predicted satisfaction with feature Y as 3, but later evaluated her actual satisfaction as a 5, the prediction discrepancy will be $|5 - 3| = 2$.

Our aim is to create an instrument for validating requirements. We are interested in minimizing the prediction discrepancies in the data gathered with it, thus obtaining more precise results. Therefore we consider prediction discrepancy to be our main goal variable.

Actual understanding. The users have to create an accurate mental model of the future implementation of a feature before they can predict their satisfaction. We use the term *actual understanding* to refer to the accuracy of the mental model. It can only be measured after users have been confronted with the implementation.

If the mental model of the user is inaccurate, his or her predicted satisfaction will not measure the response to the real feature, resulting in a larger prediction error. Therefore, our model contains a negative link between *actual understanding* and *prediction error*.

Perceived understanding. Users can judge the clarity of their mental model of a feature. If the model is vague, then they are aware that they did not understand the feature well. If their mental model is clear, they can report that they have understood the feature. This is not the same as actual understanding, as the mental model can be clear, but still inaccurate or wrong (we had examples for this in the first study, where some users answered an open-ended question with a request to change the feature so that it does something already shown in the demonstration). We measure this clarity of the mental model in a separate variable, *perceived understanding*.

We conjecture that *perceived understanding* has two major effects on the satisfaction variables. First, a low *perceived understanding* will obviously lead to a larger *prediction discrepancy*, as a user with hazy understanding does not have enough information to make a good prediction. Second, users dislike complexity and feel frustrated by concepts they do not understand, so perceived understanding should have a positive connection with *predicted satisfaction*.

Familiarity. We included this variable based on the feedback from the first study. While our participants had not used a software product of this type before, they had encountered some of its functionality in other contexts, and some of them noted that this had an influence on their answers. This can be easily explained by the expectation disconfirmation theory of satisfaction discussed in Section 2.1. Previous experience with a product attribute contributes to the consumer building a strong expectation for this attribute in other products of its class [15]. In a software context, previous experience with a software feature will help the user build a strong expectation of a feature providing the same functionality in a different product–for example, if a user has often encountered systems which offer a print preview before sending a document to the printer, he or she will expect a new software system to offer a preview too.

One of the likely effects of familiarity is to increase *perceived understanding*. Users who have past experience with a feature will use it as an example to imagine the implementation of the feature in the new system.

The effect of familiarity on the satisfaction variables is hard to predict. Different levels of expectation and disconfirmation can result in either a net positive or a net negative effect. Previous exposure to a well implemented feature is likely to result in a positive expectation and thus higher predicted satisfaction, which can then result in an even higher *actual satisfaction* if the feature is better than expected (positive disconfirmation), or lower *actual satisfaction* if the feature is implemented worse than expected (negative disconfirmation). Similarly, exposure to a low-quality implementation is likely to reduce *predicted satisfaction*, and the following disconfirmation has an effect on *actual satisfaction*. There is also a second-grade effect possible, where *familiarity* increases *perceived understanding*, which in turn increases *predicted satisfaction*.

Predicted usefulness. This variable was also included in the model after the first study. Some form of usefulness or adequacy for the task on hand is already considered in models for satisfaction with software systems, for example the variable *perceived usefulness* in TAM [5], or the item *adequate power* in QUIS [3]. We did not include usefulness in the first questionnaire, as we felt that it cannot be measured in our experiment setting, where the users do not try to complete a real task and do not have first-hand experience of the software. When we evaluated the open-ended questions, we noticed that usefulness of the features was salient for many users, and they obviously thought about it before forming a prediction for their satisfaction. Therefore, we included the variable *predicted usefulness* in our model. We expect that it has positive influence on *predicted satisfaction*.

Emotional attachment. Consumers can sometimes assign emotional value to a brand or to a specific product, which increases their satisfaction [15]. We had not planned to include this effect in our model, as we did not think that we will see a consistent effect of functionality-describing features on emotions. But the feedback on our first study uncovered that emotion still has an influence on our measurement approach. A participant who found the software "boring" wrote that he or she could not give any evaluation on their future satisfaction, and his or her answers were always the middle choice on the Likert scale, which was labeled with "indifferent" on the satisfaction scales. As predicting satisfaction is a form of affective forecasting, we can expect that users who are indifferent towards the software as a whole may expect to not have any emotions towards its individual features once it is implemented, and consistently choose a neutral option for all features. This will distort the final results. We decided to measure *emotional attachment* in our future studies so we can account for this effect. Our assumption is that positive emotions towards the software will also be correlated with positive predictions about the individual features and vice versa, hence we included a positive link between *emotional attachment* and *predicted satisfaction* in our model.

4   Empirical Study

We conducted a second study in May 2012. The general design was the same as in the previous study. We used the same requirements specification (translated to German) and software prototype. The demonstrations were re-recorded, this time with explanations in German. The participants read the feature descriptions first, answered the questions measuring the pre-exposure variables based on the descriptions. Then they were shown the recorded demonstrations and answered the questions measuring the post-exposure variables based on the implementation. However, the new study differed from the old one in several important points:

- The old study did not measure all the variables needed for our model. The new study allows us to make new evaluations and gain information needed for creating a more precise measuring approach.
- A limitation of the old study was that the participants were requirements engineers and therefore accustomed to evaluating software features. This is not a good representation of a population of generic software users. The participants of the new study were university students, and the demographic part of the questionnaire revealed that they have varied background, with their fields spread widely accros different branches of engineering, humanities and natural science. They constitute a much better, though still imperfect, representation of the sample population.
- We added a third format of feature representation in the new study, using *sentence templates* ("The system shall...") [17].

We measured the variables of our model using the questions listed in Table 1. It shows the variable, measuring phase, question text (translated from the original German) and labeling of the Likert scale. We used five-point scales, but only the first, third and fifth position were labeled. When calculating the numeric results, we assigned a 5 to the leftmost point and 1 to the rightmost point, so that for example a *predicted satisfaction* of 5 corresponds to the answer "like".

4.1 Research Goals

The purpose of the study was mainly confirmation of the model we described in Section 3.2. We also expected to confirm our previous finding that predicted satisfaction is independent of the format in which the features are presented. The study also included open-ended questions intended for explorative research.

Model Confirmation. Our model has a compound goal variable consisting of three satisfaction variables and five independent variables. Based on our model, we formulated a hypothesis for the effect of each independent variable on one of the satisfaction variables.

Hypothesis 1. Perceived understanding is positively linked with predicted satisfaction.

Hypothesis 2. Actual understanding is negatively linked with prediction error.

Hypothesis 3. Participants with high familiarity will have different predicted satisfaction than participants with low familiarity.

Table 1. Variables measured in the study. Variables marked with an asterisk were not measured in the previous study.

Variable	Measured	Question	Scale labels
perceived understanding	pre-exposure	I can imagine what the feature will look like in the finished software	clearly – vaguely – not at all
predicted satisfaction	pre-exposure	When the feature is implemented, I will have the following attitude	like – indifferent – dislike
predicted usefulness*	pre-exposure	I can imagine ... why the feature is needed and what I will use it for.	clearly – vaguely – not at all
actual satisfaction	post-exposure	My attitude to the feature as implemented is ...	like – indifferent – dislike
actual understanding	post-exposure	The implementation of this feature corresponds to my earlier concept	well – a bit – not at all
familiarity*	post-exposure	I have already used a similar feature in a different software product	yes, very similar – yes, somewhat similar – not at all
emotional attachment*	post-exposure	I found the idea of using this software product	great – boring – makes no sense

Hypothesis 4. Emotional attachment is positively linked with predicted satisfaction.

Hypothesis 5. Predicted usefulness is positively linked with predicted satisfaction.

Feature Representation Format. Our earlier study suggested that the variables we measured were independent of the format used for representing the feature descriptions in the requirements specification. To confirm this, we defined the hypothesis

Hypothesis 6. The answers to the model variables do not differ between participants from the user task group, user story group and sentence template group.

Open-Ended Questions. We did not use statistical evaluation on the answers to the open-ended questions. We read the answers expecting to find insights about following topics:

- Are there mentionings of new mechanisms influencing one or more of the three satisfaction variables?
- How detailed are participants' mental models of the features, can they tell the difference between their imagined implementation and the actual implementation they saw in the recordings?
- Are there any complaints about and/or improvement suggestions for the questionnaire?

4.2   Results

Before we tested our hypotheses, we ran some descriptive evaluations on the data. Figure 2 gives an overview of the absolute frequency distributions of all variables. It also shows the effect of the non-goal variables on the main goal variable, *prediction discrepancy*, expressed with a Spearman correlation coefficient. As we are not interested in the differences between individual features, the evaluations were calculated by combining the data over all participants and all features within a single study. This increases the data points available in each study to 16 per participant, improving the significance of our results. It also lists the same values for the old study, where available.

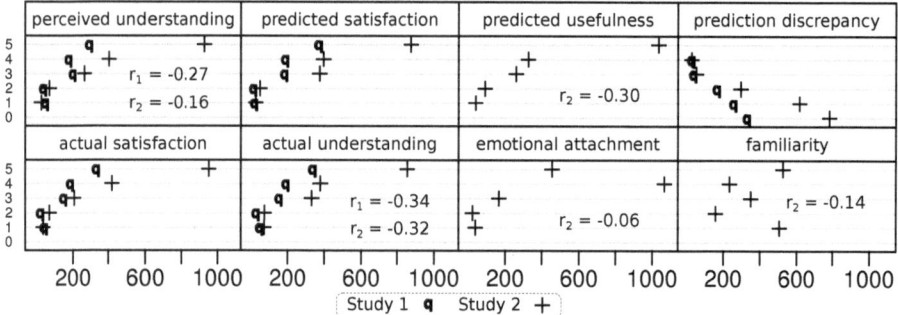

Fig. 2. Absolute frequency distributions for all variables and Spearman correlation with the variable *prediction error* for non-goal variables. All correlation coefficients are significant at $\alpha = 0.05$.

All measured variables except *familiarity* exhibit an obvious ceiling effect. All independent variables have a negative link with prediction discrepancy, which means that the prediction discrepancy diminishes with higher values of those variables. The correlation with each individual variable is not very strong, meaning that none of the effects can be used alone to achieve good precision.

Model Confirmation. We were able to confirm all hypotheses evaluated for this research goal. For hypotheses 1, 2, 4and 5 we calculated a Spearman correlation coefficient between the two variables in the hypothesis, combining the values over all participants and all features. Our findings are summarized in Table 2. All resulting coefficients had the sign our model predicts. The correlation strength is medium to good, except for *emotional attachment*. It is possible that the effect in this case is more complex than a straightforward correlation, for example there could be a minimal level of emotional attachment which creates enough motivation for giving differentiated answers, but there is no difference in answer quality above this level.

For hypothesis 3, we built a list of all data points where a participant had evaluated his/her familiarity with a feature with a 5, and another list with familiarity evaluated with a 1. Each of the two resulting smaller data sets still had a distribution of predicted satisfaction spanning all 5 possible Likert-scale values. We applied a Kolmogorov-Smirnov test which rejected the hypothesis that both data sets have the same distribution of predicted satisfaction (significance level

Table 2. Hypotheses confirmed by correlation. All correlation coefficients are significant for $\alpha = 0.05$.

Hyp. number	Variables	Cor. co-efficient	Result
1	Perceived understanding, Predicted satisfaction	0.57	Confirmed
2	Actual understanding, Prediction discrepancy (negative)	-0.32	Confirmed
4	Emotional attachment, Predicted satisfaction	0.11	Partly confirmed
5	Predicted usefulness, Predicted satisfaction	0.67	Confirmed

$\alpha = 0.05$). Our conclusion is that familiarity does have an effect on predicted satisfaction, and hypothesis 3 is confirmed.

Additionally to testing our hypotheses, we also calculated the correlation coefficients between all pairs of dependent variables in order to find out possible cross-relationships in our model. Beside the pairs mentioned in our hypotheses, we found medium or better correlation between *actual understanding* and *familiarity* ($r = 0.36$) and *perceived understanding* and *predicted usefulness* ($r = 0.64$), which was significant for $\alpha = 0.05$. We plan to work on finding a theoretical explanation and further confirmation for these effects before we include them in our model.

Feature Representation Format. For Hypothesis 6, we divided the data in three sets–the user stories group, the user tasks group, and the sentence template group–and calculated the arithmetic means of each variable as well as the Spearman correlation coefficient between each independent variable and *prediction discrepancy*. There were no significant differences between the results from each group and the results of the same calculation when applied to all data. We conclude that the variables in our model do not depend on the representation format of features.

Open-Ended Questions. The questionnaire contained three open questions. 1) In the post-exposure part, we asked the users to answer for each feature "My previous conception differs from the implementation in following ways". 2) At the end of the questionnaire, we also asked what the users think could have improved their understanding of the software. 3) Also at the end, we asked for feedback about the software itself and the study in general.

Out of the 112 participants, 108 answered at least one of the open quesitons. We read the answers without doing statistical evaluations. We subjectively judged the importance of the suggestions left by the users. Our criteria included the frequency with which some variation of a suggestion appeared in the feedback, as well as the reach of consequences we think it will have for our model, future versions of our questionnaires, or for our measuring approach as a whole. We list the five most important suggestions, as well a comment on how we view these suggestions.

– Users demanded examples or longer descriptions. They complained that some features were too abstract to be understood. We feel that including examples could be helpful for the less clear features, but it would be unnecessary overhead for familiar features like printing.

- Users demanded better integration with their existing workflows. Some of them requested export to common office suite formats. Others asked for the software to be implemented as a smartphone app.
- Users asked for visual aids in the requirements specification such as screenshots or mockups. While we are convinced that this will increase both actual and perceived understandability, we intend our approach to be used at an early stage in the development process, when mockups are not yet available.
- Users indicated difficulties with specific terms. Some of these terms were software engineering related, such as "feature". Others were abstract terms used in a very specific way in the context of the system, such as "tag". We are considering the inclusion of a short glossary for our measurement approach.
- Users asked for the rationale behind the software, an introduction explaining why the users need it and who is the target group. We consider adding both a short description for the whole software and using rationales for the more difficult features along with or instead of examples as discussed in the first point.

We also noticed that many participants had been able to construct detailed mental models based on just the feature descriptions. They were able to not only articulate what they exactly like or dislike in a feature, but also to offer alternatives which would presumably lead to higher satisfaction. This type of feedback is difficult to get even in a richer communication channel such as an interview [17], and we were glad to find out that a questionnaire with open-ended questions is sufficient for it. While many suggestions were not desirable or not possible to implement, others were obviously good ideas which would have resulted in improved software quality.

5   Discussion

5.1   Intended Use for Our Findings

The results of our study confirmed that our model is a good representation of some important mechanisms influencing predicted user satisfaction. They also show that our independent variables all have a medium strong negative link to *prediction discrepancy*.

As we intend to create a questionnaire with higher precision, we can use these findings to improve the questionnaire. For example, enhancing the feature descriptions with examples or rationale statements [7] could increase perceived and actual understanding and thus reduce the prediction discrepancy.

We are aware that our model of predicted user satisfaction is not complete, as there are many additional factors which can influence satisfaction. We are still searching for new factors which we can change in a questionnaire in order to improve precision. The open-ended questions gave us some insights about further factors, such as *integration*. We will examine their possible inclusion in our model.

Validating requirements with a questionnaire has more problems than just low precision of the satisfaction predictions. It restricts the communication considerably, especially by limiting the possibilities for users to receive clarifications from the requirements engineer and to give feedback beyond simple satisfaction evaluations. The results of our study show that a well-designed questionnaire still permits this important communication to take place. Users have both the ability and motivation to give high-quality feedback, including own ideas for alternative ways to implement a feature. We will consider these findings when constructing a finalized version of our questionnaire.

5.2 Threats to Validity

Conclusion Validity. We identified two possible threats to conclusion validity. First, we are not aware of any objective measures for the variables we measured, so we had to rely on self-reporting. Second, we evaluated several hypotheses on the same data set. Under some study designs, this can lead to false positives. This danger is mitigated by two factors. First, some variables were elicited in two different studies, and the results were very similar. Second, we did not evaluate all possible connections, picking the significant ones as "confirmed"; rather, we started the second study from a model which delivers theoretical explanation for each connection we expected to find.

Internal Validity. The quality of the instruments we used for our experiment can also have compromised our experiment validity. First, users may have misunderstood questions due to ambiguity. We tried to counter this by presenting the questionnaires to coworkers not involved in the project and asking them whether they understood the questions the way we intended them. Second, we used screen casts of the software. The users' true judgement of features may have been incomplete, because they did not work with the software themselves. We did not formally evaluate the internal validity of our questionnaire, but as its two versions delivered very similar results in two separate studies, we take this as an indication that its internal validity is adequate.

Also, we chose to use five-item scales. While this leads to somewhat reduced precision in our results, it is sufficient for recognizing trends in distributions and also places less cognitive burden on the study participants, allowing us to gather data on more features.

Construct Validity. The questions we asked may not be best suited to measure the concepts of understanding and liking. We used a bottom-up approach where we defined the variables used in our model based on empirical data gathered from the first study. As they are not derived from an existing theory, we could not use ready-made validated psychometric constructs for measuring them (such constructs are developed for existing theories). We had to rely on our own constructs, and we chose to keep them as simple one-item constructs. Sophisticated multi-item constructs would have offered more precision, but as each variable is measured once per feature (as opposed to once per questionnaire), the use of such constructs would have made the questionnaire prohibitively long. Also, the development of precise psychometric constructs is not central to our research, so we could not allocate the resources needed for an undertaking of this size. The downside of this decision is reduced construct validity due to the simple approach to variable measuring. We feel that the reduction is acceptable for the purposes of this study.

External Validity. The situation we used in the experiment was not perfectly realistic. Our participants were students who volunteered for the study. They had neither interest in buying a finished version of our software nor the obligation to use it. Actual users would have a task they intend to solve with the software.

6   Conclusions and Future Work

We are working on a questionnaire suitable for measuring predicted user satisfaction based on feature descriptions. It can be used for validating a requirements specification with low effort for the requirements specialist. In an earlier study, we gathered first information on the mechanisms influencing predicted satisfaction. In this paper, we present a working model of predicted user satisfaction. We conducted an empirical study which confirmed the effects predicted by our model. Further, it confirmed that the effects occur independently of the format used for representing the features. It also uncovered other possible mechanisms for influencing predicted user satisfaction.

In our future work, we plan to use the now confirmed model to decide what questions must be included in a questionnaire suitable for reliably measuring future satisfaction. In order to gain higher precision, we also intend to create a better measuring strategy, for example by discarding the results of participants whose perceived understanding is at the lowest point. We will also try to confirm or reject the newly discovered possible links within our model as well as links to new variables such as workflow integration.

References

1. Bailey, J.E., Pearson, S.W.: Development of a tool for measuring and analyzing computer user satisfaction. Management Science 29(5), 530–545 (1983)
2. Buttle, F.: SERVQUAL: review, critique, research agenda. European Journal of Marketing 30(1), 8–32 (1996)
3. Chin, J.P., Diehl, V.A., Norman, K.L.: Development of an instrument measuring user satisfaction of the human-computer interface. In: Proceedings of the SIGCHI Conference on Human Factors in Computing Systems, pp. 213–218 (1988)
4. Cohn, M.: User stories applied. Addison-Wesley Professional (2004)
5. Davis, F.: Perceived usefulness, perceived ease of use, and user acceptance of information technology. MIS Quarterly 13(3), 319–340 (1989)

6. Delone, W., McLean, E.: Information systems success revisited. In: Proceedings of the 35th Annual Hawaii International Conference on System Sciences, pp. 1–11 (2002)
7. Dutoit, A., McCall, R., Mistrik, I., Paech, B.: Rationale management in software engineering, pp. 1–29 (2006)
8. Fornell, C., Johnson, M., Anderson, E.: The American customer satisfaction index: nature, purpose, and findings. The Journal of Marketing 60(4), 7–18 (1996)
9. Joumblatt, D., Teixeira, R.: ConnectionWatch: Passive monitoring of round-trip times at end-hosts. In: Proceedings of the 2008 ACM CoNEXT Conference, p. 52 (2008)
10. Lauesen, S.: User Interface Design - A software engineering perspective. Pearson education limited, Harlow (2005)
11. Lopez, S.: Encyclopedia of positive psychology. Wiley-Blackwell (2011)
12. Martilla, J., James, J.: Importance-performance analysis. The Journal of Marketing 41(1), 77–79 (1977)
13. Moshkina, L., Endo, Y., Arkin, R.C.: Usability evaluation of an automated mission repair mechanism for mobile robot mission specification. In: Proceeding of the 1st ACM SIGCHI/SIGART Conference on Human-Robot Interaction, HRI 2006, p. 57. ACM Press, New York (2006)
14. Oliver, R.: A cognitive model of the antecedents and consequences of satisfaction decisions. Journal of Marketing Research 17(4), 460–469 (1980)
15. Oliver, R.: Satisfaction: A behavioral perspective on the customer. M.E. Sharpe (2010)
16. Proynova, R., Paech, B.: Do Stakeholders Understand Feature Descriptions? A Live Experiment. In: REFSQ 2012 Workshop Proceedings, pp. 265–280 (2012)
17. Rupp, C.: Requirements-Engineering und -Management. Hanser (2009)
18. Sauerwein, E., Bailom, F., Matzler, K., Hinterhuber, H.H.: The Kano model: How to delight your customers. In: International Working Seminar on Production Economics, pp. 313–327 (1996)
19. Venkatesh, V., Morris, M., Davis, G., Davis, F.: User acceptance of information technology: Toward a unified view. MIS Quarterly 27(3), 425–478 (2003)
20. Walker, M.A., Litman, D.J., Kamm, C.A., Abella, A.: PARADISE: A Framework for Evaluating Spoken Dialogue Agents. In: Proceedings of the Eighth Conference on European Chapter of the Association for Computational Linguistics, pp. 271–280 (1997)
21. Yamazaki, T., Miyoshi, T., Eguchi, M., Yamori, K.: A service quality coordination model bridging QoS and QoE. In: 2012 IEEE 20th International Workshop on Quality of Service, pp. 1–4 (2012)

reqT.org – Towards a Semi-Formal, Open and Scalable Requirements Modeling Tool

Björn Regnell

Dept. of Computer Science, Lund University, Sweden
bjorn.regnell@cs.lth.se

Abstract. [**Context and motivation**] This research preview presents ongoing work on a free software requirements modeling tool called reqT that is developed in an educational context. [**Question/problem**] The work aims to engage computer science students in Requirements Engineering (RE) through a tool that captures essential RE concepts in executable code. [**Principal ideas**] Requirements are modeled using an internal DSL in the Scala programming language that blends natural language strings with a graph-oriented formalism. [**Contribution**] The metamodel of reqT and its main features are presented and modeling examples are provided together with a discussion on initial experiences from student projects, limitations and directions of further research.

Keywords: requirements engineering, requirements modeling, software engineering, CASE tool, requirements metamodel, requirements engineering education, internal DSL, embedded DSL, Scala programming language.

1 Introduction

There are many challenges in teaching Requirements Engineering (RE) [6, 9], including conveying requirements modeling skills [1]. Given a wide-spread attention on agile methods with less emphasis on extra-code artifacts [8], it may be particularly challenging to motivate coding-focused engineering students (and software practitioners) to spend serious effort on requirements modeling. One way to inspire software engineers to learn more about and do more RE may be to offer an interesting software tool. There are nowadays numerous commercial RE tools available, but many are expensive, complex and not sufficiently open [2].

This paper presents on-going work on a tool named reqT that aims to provide a small but scalable, semi-formal and free software package for an educational setting that (hopefully) can inspire code lovers to learn more about requirements modeling. A long-term goal of reqT is to offer an open platform for RE research prototypes, e.g. for feature modeling and release planning research. The tool development started in 2011 at Lund University, where reqT is used in RE teaching at MSc level in the Computer Science & Engineering program. In 2012 reqT was rebuilt from scratch based on student feedback. The tool can be downloaded from: http://reqT.org

The paper is organized as follows. Section 2 states the objectives and motivates the design strategy of reqT. Section 3 presents the metamodel of reqT and some example reqT models. Section 4 discusses limitations and some initial experiences from using reqT in teaching and concludes the paper with a sketch of future research directions.

J. Doerr and A.L. Opdahl (Eds.): REFSQ 2013, LNCS 7830, pp. 112–118, 2013.
© Springer-Verlag Berlin Heidelberg 2013

2   Goals, Design Strategy and Rationale

The main objective behind reqT is to establish a set of essential RE concepts and capture them in an expressive, extensible and executable language appealing to computer science students (and eventually practitioners). This general objective is accompanied by the following main goals and associated design strategies:

1. **Semi-formal.** *Goal:* Provide a semi-formal representation of typical requirements modeling constructs that can illustrate a flexible combination of expressive natural language-style requirements with type-safe formalisms allowing static checks. *Design:* Use graph structures based on typed nodes representing typical requirement entities and attributes, and typed edges representing typical requirements relations, and implement the graph as an associative array (map). *Why?* Graphs are well-known to many CS students. Maps are efficient from an implementation perspective and may be less complex to master compared to e.g. SQL databases.

2. **Open.** *Goal:* Provide a platform-independent requirements tool that is free of charge. *Design:* Use Java Virtual Machine technology and release the code under an open source license. Use tab-separated, tabular text-files for import and export. Use HTML for document generation. *Why?* There are many free libraries available that runs on a JVM. Tab-sep and HTML support interoperability.

3. **Scalable.** *Goal:* Provide an extensible requirements modeling language that can scale from small, concise models to large families of models with thousands of requirements entities and relations. *Design:* Implement reqT as an internal DSL (Domain-Specific Language) in the Scala programming language [7]. Use Map and Set from Scala collections to represent requirements graphs. *Why?* Scala is a modern, statically typed language with an efficient collections library. Scala offers scripting abilities that provide general extensibility without re-compilation. Integrated development environments [11], as well as interactive scripting tools are available [3].

These goals, design strategies and rationale are directing the on-going work, and it remains to be investigated to what extent the main objective and goals can be met. A critical issue is how to interpret what are "essential" RE concepts and "typical" modeling constructs. The reqT tool is used in a course based on a specific text book [4] and a specific student project concept [5], and the concepts of the reqT requirements metamodel (see Fig. 2) reflect that context. However, the reqT architecture is prepared for extensions of new concepts in the metamodel to cater for different educational contexts.

3   Modeling Requirements with reqT

A reqT model includes sequences of graph parts `<Entity><Edge><NodeSet>` separated by comma and wrapped inside a `Model( )` construct. A small reqT Model with three `Feature` entities and one `Stakeholder` entity is shown below:

```
Model(
  Feature("f1") has (Spec("A good spec."), Status(SPECIFIED)),
  Feature("f1") requires (Feature("f2"), Feature("f3")),
  Stakeholder("s1") assigns(Prio(1)) to Feature("f2")
)
```

The corresponding graph implied by the above model is depicted in Fig. 1. The edges represent different relations between entities, in this case the requires and assigns relations. Nodes with outgoing edges are called *sources* and nodes with incoming edges are called *destinations*. There is a special edge called has that is used to attach attributes to entities. The different types of entities, relations and attributes of the reqT metamodel, depicted in Fig. 2 can be combined freely, although a has-edge can only link to attributes,

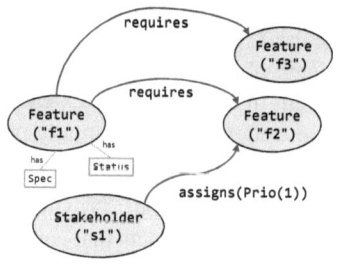

Fig. 1. A reqT model depicted as a graph

while a relation can only link to entities. In the metamodel of reqT in Fig. 2, abstract types are shown in italics and concrete types are shown in bold. All concrete types are Scala case classes [7]. All entities have a string-valued id for unique identification. Most attributes have string values that can be used to combine informal, natural-language expressions with formal graph-structures. The Status attribute can be associated to entities to reflect their degree of refinement in RE and down-stream processes by different Level values, as depicted in Fig. 3.

Domain-level task descriptions [4] can be modeled using the scenario-type requirement entity Task, as shown in the model below. This example[1] is modified from Lauesen [4], p. 93. The special relation owns is used to express hierarchical decomposition and reqT ensures that an entity only can be owned by one other entity.

```
var m = Model(
  Task("reception work") owns (Task("check in"), Task("booking")),
  Task("check in") has (
    Why("Give guest a room. Mark it as occupied. Start account."),
    Trigger("A guest arrives"),
    Frequency("Average 0.5 check-ins/room/day"),
    Critical("Group tour with 50 guests.")
  ),
  Task("check in") owns (
    Task("find room"), Task("record guest"), Task("deliver key")),
  Task("record guest") has Spec(
    "variants: a) Guest has booked in advance, b) No suitable room"
  )
)
```

There are a number of operators defined for reqT models including the aggregate, restrict and exclude operators denoted by double plus ++ and slash / and backslash \ respectively. The expression m1 ++ m2 results in a new aggregated model with m1 and m2 merged, with parts of m2 potentially overwriting overlapping parts of m1. The restrict and exclude operators produce new submodels including or excluding parts of a Model based on the right operand argument that can be of different Element types, as explained subsequently.

---

[1] For more examples on how to combine various entities and relations of reqT into different requirements modeling styles, see: http://reqT.org/

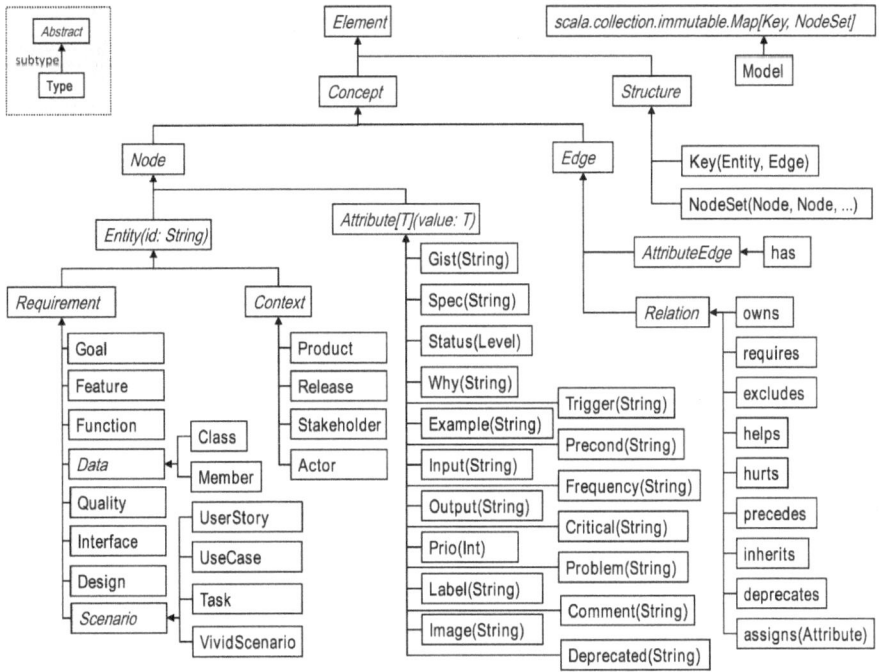

Fig. 2. The reqT version 2.2 metamodel

The expression m / Task("x") results in a new submodel that is restricted to all parts of m with Task("x") as source node, while the expression m \ Task results in a new submodel that excludes all Task sources. The expression

((m / e) ++ (m \ e) == m)

is always true.

A reqT Model has the methods up and down that promote or regress all its Status attributes according to the state machine in Fig. 3. By using / and \ for extracting submodels, levels can be selectively promoted, e.g. the expression

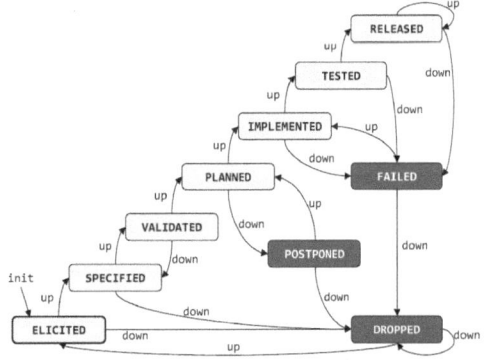

Fig. 3. Refinement levels of the Status attribute

m = (m / Feature("x")).up ++ (m \ Feature("x")) updates m to a new model where only Feature("x") is promoted to the next level. Several more operators and methods for create/read/update/delete of entities using Scala scripts are available in the Model case class, see further: http://reqT.org/

In our course projects [5] students shall produce requirements documents that can be validated by laymen. This is supported in reqT by an export operation on models called `toHtml` that generates files that can be shown in web browsers as illustrated in Fig. 4. The HTML generation is controlled by a DocumentTemplate case class that allows for specifying title, free form text paragraphs and optional numbers of Chapters containing optional Sections including specified parts of a reqT model in flexible ways using Scala function literals that can, e.g., apply restrict and exclude operators to models. In Fig. 4 the Scala function literal `m => m / Context` restricts the contents of a chapter to only `Context` type source entities. Fig 4 also shows `toTable` export to spreadsheet programs via tab-separated text files. The code in Fig. 4 can be executed e.g. as a script using the interactive Scala Read-Evaluate-Print-Loop (REPL) from the command line, or in a scripting environment such as Kojo [3], or inside the Scala Eclipse IDE [11].

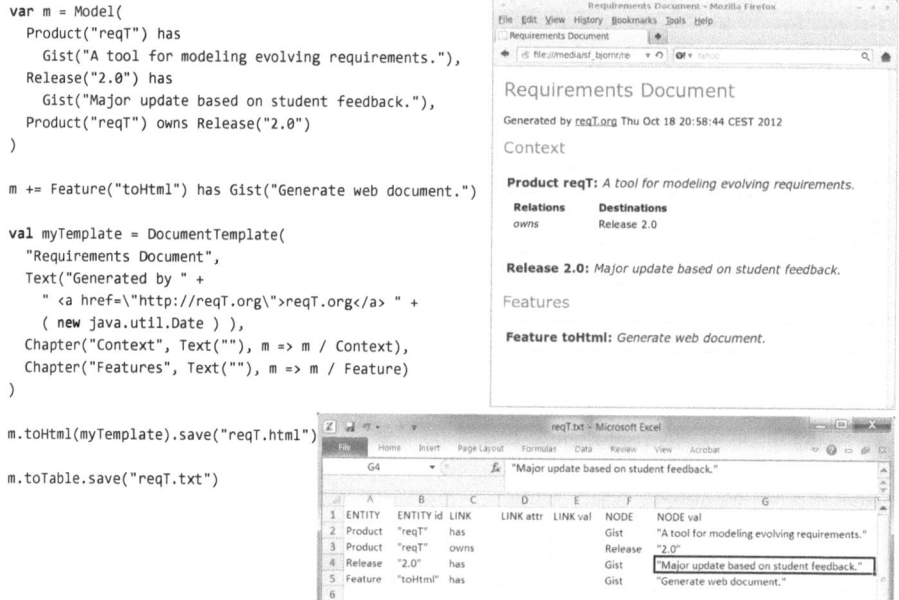

Fig. 4. Example of template-based export to HTML and tab-separated table export

4   Discussion and Conclusion

The results of the on-going work with reqT remains to be further investigated and a validation of reqT as a RE learning tool and research experimentation platform is subject to future work. This section discusses some preliminary experiences, limitations, relation to state-of-the-art and future research directions.

Preliminary Proof-of-concept. The first version of reqT was tried on a voluntary basis by 12 students working in groups of 6 students each during fall 2011. Statements from course evaluations indicate that the students found reqT useful in their learning. One group used a configuration management tool for reqT models to manage their parallel work, while one group used a cloud service and tab-sep export/import to collaborate over the Internet. The group with the largest requirements model produced 64 features, 18 tasks, 12 functions, 30 data requirements and 33 quality requirements, in total 157 requirements entities.

Several students appreciated that reqT can mix informal text with a graph-oriented formalism, but some requested more elaborated functionality for document generation, as well as linking to external images. Some students also requested more modeling examples that show how the text book techniques could be transferred to reqT models.

Based on student feedback, reqT was rebuilt from scratch during 2012 with a new architecture and a new version of the meta model (see Fig. 2), as well as a revised Scala-internal DSL. The template-controlled HTML generation was implemented based on student suggestions. The teaching material was complemented with more example models directly related to the textbook. The second version of reqT is currently tested by students in a new course instance and a post-course evaluation of reqT is planned in spring 2013.

Our preliminary experiences from applying reqT in teaching suggest that reqT, if used in a suitable teaching context, may encourage students with a code-focused mind set to learn and practice RE in the following ways: (1) A free and platform-independent software tool that is implemented using a modern programming language with interactive scripting facilities can attracts the interest of code-focused students. (2) Requirements can be processed, queried, transformed or exported using Scala scripts, and the open-ended nature of reqT that allows students to code their own scripts to both manage requirements models and to adapt reqT to fit their RE needs in the course project was appreciated by several coding-literate students. (3) By turning requirements models into executable code, students can use programming tools such as a console command line interpreter (the Scala REPL) as well as a source code version control system (e.g. git-scm.com) to branch and merge their collaborative work on requirements in ways they are used to from their previous collaborative software implementation courses, including issue tracking systems and code review support.

Relation to State-of-the-Art. To the best of our knowledge there is no other RE tool that allows semi-formal requirement models to become executable programs through an internal Scala DSL, and thus letting coding, testing and requirements engineering share the same media. In the RE tool survey by Carrillo de Gea et al. [2] it is pointed out that "many expensive tools aren't sufficiently open". The reqT technology aims to be completely free and open to facilitate academic usage, collaborative evolution and incorporation of new RE concepts in different teaching and research contexts. Many of the existing tools have proprietary representations [2], while users of reqT can extend the reqT metamodel with new entities and attributes simply by adding case classes with a few lines of code. However, reqT cannot compete with versatile commercial RE tools [2] in terms of e.g. features completeness and graphical user interface.

Limitations. In its current version, reqT has a number of limitations: (1) As the user interface is text based and depends on the command line interface of the Scala REPL or a script editor environment [3, 11], students that only are prepared to use graphical user interfaces may be discouraged. Some of our students preferred to work in a GUI spreadsheet application using tab-separated exports from reqT that was generated by other team members assigned by the student group to be reqT experts. (2) It requires some knowledge of Scala to tailor reqT exports and there is a need for a more comprehensive API for adaptable document generation. (3) The embedded DSL requires some learning efforts and it remains to be investigated if the effort is justified by the knowledge gained. (4) To support scalability to large families of reqT models there is a need for modularization concepts and overview visualizations. (5) The explicit typing of entities with keywords such Feature and Stakeholder can be perceived as verbose compared to more concise but potentially cryptic abbreviations (e.g. Fe, Sh). This may be addressed by DSL-specific editor support, such as code-completion, code folding and code templates.

Future Work. Further directions of research include (1) incorporation of constraints on models for support of prioritization and release planning [10], (2) more elaborate semantic checks to better guide requirements modelers, and (3) graphical visualization of requirements graph models. (4) Natural Language Processing technology including e.g. ambiguity risk detection may be interesting to combine with reqT. (5) It is also important to further investigate the pedagogic advantages and limitations of the approach.

A major objective of this research preview paper is to expose the latest version of reqT to the community of RE scholars and to invite discussions and contributions.

Acknowledgments. This work is partly funded by VINNOVA within the EASE project.

References

1. Callele, D., Makaroff, D.: Teaching requirements engineering to an unsuspecting audience. In: Proceedings of the 37th SIGCSE Technical Symposium on Computer Science Education, SIGCSE 2006, pp. 433–437 (2006)
2. Carrillo de Gea, J., Nicolas, J., Aleman, J., Toval, A., Ebert, C., Vizcaino, A.: Requirements engineering tools. IEEE Software 28(4), 86–91 (2011)
3. Kogics: Kojo, http://www.kogics.net/kojo (visited November 2012)
4. Lauesen, S.: Software Requirements - Styles and Techniques. Addison-Wesley (2002)
5. Lund University: http://cs.lth.se/ets170 (visited November 2012)
6. Memon, R.N., Ahmad, R., Salim, S.S.: Problems in requirements engineering education: a survey. In: Proceedings of the 8th International Conference on Frontiers of Information Technology, FIT 2010, pp. 5:1–5:6. ACM (2010)
7. Odersky, M.: et al.: An overview of the Scala programming language. Tech. rep (2004), http://lampwww.epfl.ch/~odersky/papers/ScalaOverview.html
8. Ramesh, B., Lan, C., Baskerville, R.: Agile requirements engineering practices and challenges: an empirical study. Information Systems Journal 20(5), 449–480 (2010)
9. Regev, G., Gause, D.C., Wegmann, A.: Experiential learning approach for requirements engineering education. Requirements Engineering 14(4), 269–287 (2009)
10. Regnell, B., Kuchcinski, K.: Exploring software product management decision problems with constraint solving - opportunities for prioritization and release planning. In: 2011 Fifth International Workshop on Software Product Management, IWSPM, pp. 47–56 (2011)
11. Scala Eclipse IDE: http://scala-ide.org/ (visited November 2012)

Maps of Lessons Learnt in Requirements Engineering: A Research Preview

Ibtehal Noorwali and Nazim H. Madhavji

University of Western Ontario, London, Canada
inoorwal@uwo.ca, madhavji@gmail.com

Abstract. [**Context and Motivation**] "Those who cannot remember the past are condemned to repeat it" -- George Santayana. From the survey we conducted of requirements engineering (RE) practitioners, over 70% seldom use RE lessons in the RE process, though 85% of these would use such lessons if readily available. Our observation, however, is that, RE lessons are scattered, mainly implicitly, in the literature and practice, which, obviously, does not help the situation. [**Problem/Question**] Approximately 90% of the survey participants stated that not utilising RE lessons has significant negative impact on product quality, productivity, project delays and cost overruns. [**Principal Ideas**] We propose "maps" (or profiles) of RE lessons which, once populated, would highlight weak (dark) and strong (bright) areas of RE (and hence RE theories). Such maps would thus be: (a) a driver for research to "light up" the darker areas of RE and (b) a guide for practice to benefit from the brighter areas. [**Contribution**] The key contribution of this work is the concept of "maps" of RE lessons.

Keywords: requirements engineering, lesson maps, lessons learnt, software quality, empirical study.

1   Introduction

The importance of learning from past experiences has been stressed upon in the literature [1, 5]. Yet, in a survey we conducted of 50 RE practitioners [12], 70% of the respondents indicated that they seldom use RE lessons; 85% of these would use such lessons if readily available; and 90% of them stated that not utilising RE lessons can have significant negative impact on product quality, productivity, project delays and cost overruns. This motivated us to investigate further on the topic of RE lessons.

An important goal of our research is to determine the state of lessons learnt (LL) in RE. LLs can exist in various sources (e.g. literature, project documents, researchers and practitioners, etc.). In attempting to achieve the aforementioned goal, we propose, in this research preview paper, the concept of "*lesson maps[1]*" which, when populated

---

[1] By "map" we mean "a diagram or collection of data showing the spatial arrangement or distribution of something over an area" (New Oxford American Dictionary). It is not a road map.

J. Doerr and A.L. Opdahl (Eds.): REFSQ 2013, LNCS 7830, pp. 119–124, 2013.

with lessons elicited from the literature and practice, would expose weaker (darker) and stronger (brighter) areas of RE. In this paper, we describe the proof of concept of lesson maps with example lessons identified from published literature. The paper does not depict fully populated maps, which is part of our ongoing research. The populated maps are anticipated to promulgate research in the weaker areas and improve practice in the brighter areas of RE.

Section 2 discusses related work. Section 3 describes the concept of lesson maps in requirement engineering. Section 4, gives an example of a sample map. Section 5, discusses the implications of the lesson maps and threats to validity. Section 6 concludes the paper and describes future work.

2   Related Work

Though LL are known in non-software disciplines (such as management [11], education [4], medicine [13], and others), in this section we first touch upon LL in software engineering (SE) followed by LL in RE.

The literature on lessons learnt in SE can be roughly categorized into (i) discovering and sharing lessons learnt and (ii) process and software technologies to support lessons learnt. Examples of the former category include the experience gained at NASA's Software Engineering Laboratory (see Basili et al. [2]) and the experience described by Boehm [5]. Examples of the latter category include: Abdel-Hamid and Madnick's [1] post mortem diagnostic tool to learn from project failures; the approximate reasoning-based approach [15]; Case-Based Reasoning (CBR) approach [14]; and the Experience Factory Framework [3]. The process and software technologies are used in organizational settings.

Unfortunately, in RE not much attention has been paid to lessons learnt. While some literature discusses lessons learnt explicitly [6, 7], much of it is implicit [8] making it difficult to utilise lessons in practice.

3   The Concept of a Map of RE Lessons

In an attempt to create a discipline surrounding lessons learnt in RE, we propose the concept of a *map* of lessons learnt in RE. With reference to the definition of a map in section 1, a map of RE lessons is based on two types of elements: (i) the content (i.e. the lessons) and (ii) the context (i.e. specific attributes selected by the user). Example context attributes are: RE practice, RE phase, process type, application domain, project size, rationale, source, and others. In principle, therefore, it is possible to produce many permutations of lesson maps, e.g.: RE practices; RE practices X RE phases; RE practices X RE phases X application domains; project size X RE phases X sources; application domain X process type; etc. The actual rendering of a map in various permutations is a matter of technological support, which is outside the scope of this concept paper.

After populating a map with some lessons learnt, it can be indicative of the 'state' of lessons learnt in RE (in a project, organisation, body of knowledge, etc.) identified by scarce (dark) and abundant (bright) areas of the map (see Table 1).

Table 1. An example map with context attributes X and Y

Let us assume that context attributes X and Y (selected by the user) are process activities and practices in RE, respectively, where, they are depicted here as a table but could be depicted in another form (e.g. hierarchically). LL1, LL2, etc., are the lessons learnt relating to specific process activities and practices. Examples of dark areas are: X3Y2 and X4Y2 and of bright areas are: X1Y1and X2Y3.

	X1	X2	X3	X4	....
Y1	LL1	LL7	LL13	LL6	
	LL2	LL8			
	LL3				
Y2	LL16	LL4			
		LL5			
Y3	LL17	LL9	LL14	LL6	
	LL18	LL10	LL15		
		LL11	LL6		
		LL12			

4 Example

With reference to Table 2, we can see three lessons spread along RE phases (e.g. elicitation, analysis, etc.): LL1, LL2, LL3.

LL1 [6]: *Lesson:* "Systematically validate and verify requirements by documenting the rationale for requirements." *Related RE phase:* Requirements validation. *Related RE practice:* documentation. *Domain:* enterprise resource planning systems. *Expression:* explicit. *Type:* negative. *Rationale:* Doing so let 39 out of our 67 teams eliminate as much as 43 percent of the stated requirements.

LL2 [6]: *Lesson:* "use prototypes for validation only if you also do process walk-throughs." *Related RE phase:* Requirements validation. *Related RE practice:* prototyping. *Domain:* enterprise resource planning systems. *Expression:* explicit. *Type:* negative. *Rationale:* "In three subprojects, we observed a tendency to rely exclusively on prototypes to negotiate requirements, which led to prototyping spirals in which the teams never built the actual solution."

LL3 [9]: *Lesson:* "use the adjustable requirements reuse approach where requirements can be adjusted without independently creating and storing the different variants of the requirement." *Related RE phase:* elicitation. *Related RE practice:* reuse. *Domain:* Fluid control equipment, pump, seal & valve manufacturing. *Expression:* implicit. *Type:* negative. *Rationale:* "quality and readability of each requirement is improved since it is not split up to a general and a variable part. Since it is not required to document every variation in a separate node it keeps the structure of the requirements much more simple."

With reference to LL1, *Lesson* denotes the content of the lesson. Context attributes are such items as: Related RE phase, Related RE practice, Domain, etc. Expression indicates whether a lesson was explicitly expressed as a lesson learnt in the literature, or the context and surrounding literature had to be analysed to elicit the lesson. Type can mean a positive lesson (one learnt from a successful past experience) or a negative lesson (one learnt from an unsuccessful past experience). There are some other context attributes not included in the lessons here because these are either not known to the creator of the lesson or are empty. Examples are: related lessons involved in solving a particular problem such as hazard analysis in a safety critical system; contradictory lessons; specialization and generalization relationships, etc. LL2 and LL3 have similar structure and attributes.

Assuming the user chooses 'RE phases' from the full set of context attributes, the resultant map would be as shown in Figure 1. With the choice of additional context attributes, the resultant map would contain corresponding entries of lessons. Table 2 shows the map with context attributes 'RE phases' and 'RE practices'.

Upon analysing the map in Table 2, we note that in the elicitation phase, most of the lessons learnt are positive; whereas, in the validation phase, most of the lessons learnt are negative. This could be helpful in the practice of RE. Positive experience, for example, would exude higher confidence in the way elicitation is carried out from descriptive experiences of the RE community; whereas, negative experience would suggest caution in the way requirements are validated. Also, if the lessons identified in the map are found useful in a particular process type (e.g. iterative process), this could lead to savings in costs, time and product quality in other projects in similar process contexts. Caution is in order where process contexts differ (e.g. agile process).

Elicitation	Analysis	Specification	Validation
LL3			LL1
			LL2

Fig. 1. An example of a map of RE lessons with context attribute 'RE phases'

Table 2. An example of a map of RE lessons with context attributes 'RE phases' and 'RE practices'

	Elicitation	Analysis	Specification	Validation
Documentation				LL1
Prototyping				LL2
Using checklists				
Reuse	LL3			

5   Discussion

Implications of this research are anticipated for both practice and research. In industry, use of lesson maps could be felt on project costs, time, and quality. In research, the maps could help in generating new RE theories by identifying weak and strong areas of LL across RE sub-processes and practices. Because patterns and anti-patterns are built upon recurring events, situations, problems, etc., they seem to be good candidates to be associated with lessons learnt in RE.

We identify two threats to validity that may be relevant when building lesson maps: internal (researcher bias) and external validity. Researcher bias can be present during elicitation of lessons learnt from archival sources and practice. External validity can be threatened if the lessons are not generalised enough for use in other contexts. These threats can be mitigated to some degree by obtaining feedback from researchers and practitioners to validate the maps and elicited lessons and by identifying and analyzing the context of each lesson.

6   Conclusion and Future Work

In this research preview, we introduce the concept of *maps* for lessons learnt in requirements engineering. A map consists of actual lessons and the context of these lessons (e.g., RE phases, RE practices, application domains, implicit/explicit lessons, etc.) – see section 3. In section 4, we give an illustrative example of a map (with several lessons [6,9]) that is anticipated to be of benefit to both practitioners and researchers in RE. Based on the concept of the map and the example (described in sections 3 and 4), we conclude that it is a promising stepping-stone towards defining the state of lessons learnt in the field of RE. As next steps in this research, we intend to further explore the concept of the map and subsequently elicit lessons learnt, from various sources in order to gain an understanding of the state of lessons learnt in RE. Further, we have begun to build technological support to operationalise lesson maps for use in RE projects.

References

1. Abdel-Hamid, T.K., Madnick, S.E.: The Elusive Silver Lining: How we Fail to Learn from Software Development Failures. J. MIT Sloan Management Review 32(1), 39–48 (1990)
2. Basili, V.R., McGarry, F.E., Pajerski, R., Zelkowitz, M.V.: Lessons Learned from 25 Years of Process Improvement: The Rise and Fall of the NASA Software Engineering Laboratory. In: International Conference on Software Engineering, pp. 69–79. ACM, Orlando (2002)
3. Basili, V.R., Tesoriero, R., Costa, P., Lindvall, M., Rus, I., Shull, F., Zelkowitz, M.: Building an Experience Base for Software Engineering: A report on the first CeBASE eWorkshop. In: Product-Focused Software Process Improvement, Kaiserslautern, pp. 110–125 (2001)

4. Bodycott, P., Walker, A.: Teaching Abroad: Lessons Learned about Inter-Cultural Understanding for Teachers in Higher Education. J. Teaching in Higher Education 5(1), 79–94 (2000)
5. Boehm, B.: A View of 20th and 21st Century Software Engineering. In: International Conference on Software Engineering, pp. 12–29. ACM, Shanghai (2006)
6. Damian, D.: Stakeholders in Global Requirements Engineering: Lessons Learned from Practice. IEEE Software 24(2), 21–27 (2007)
7. Daneva, M.: ERP Requirements Engineering Practice: Lessons Learned. IEEE Software Journal 21(2), 26–33 (2004)
8. Ebert, C.: Understanding the Product Life Cycle: Four Key Requirements Engineering Techniques. IEEE Software Journal 23(3), 19–25 (2006)
9. Hauksdottir, D., Vermehren, A., Savolainen, J.: Requirements Reuse at Danfoss. In: 20th IEEE Requirements Engineering Conference, pp. 309–314. IEEE, Chicago (2012)
10. Kotonya, G., Sommerville, I.: Requirements Engineering: Processes and Techniques. John Wiley, New York (1998)
11. Lee, M.: Making Lessons Learned a Worthwhile Investment. J. PM World Today 5(7) (2008)
12. Noorwali, I., Madhavji, N.H.: A Survey of Lessons Learnt in Requirements Engineering. Technical Report No. 750, Dept. of Computer Science, University of Western Ontario (2012)
13. Rogers, D.A., Elstein, A.S., Bordage, G.: Improving Continuing Medical Education for Surgical Techniques: Applying the Lessons Learned in the First Decade of Minimal Access Surgery. J. Annals of Surgery 233(2), 159–166 (2001)
14. Sary, C., Mackey, W.: A Case-Based Reasoning Approach for the Access and Reuse of Lessons Learned. In: Fifth Annual Symposium of the National Council on Systems Engineering, St. Louis, pp. 249–256 (1995)
15. Vandeville, J.V., Shaikh, M.A.: A Structured Approximate Reasoning-Based Approach for Gathering "Lessons Learned" Information from System Development Projects. J. Systems Engineering 2(4), 242–247 (1999)
16. Weber, R., Aha, D.W., Becerra-Fernandez, I.: Intelligent Lessons Learned Systems. J. Expert Systems with Applications 20(1), 17–34 (2001)
17. Wellman, J.: Lessons Learned about Lessons Learned. J. Organization Development 25(3), 65–72 (2007)

Requirements Traceability across Organizational Boundaries - A Survey and Taxonomy

Patrick Rempel, Patrick Mäder, Tobias Kuschke, and Ilka Philippow

Department of Software Systems, Ilmenau Technical University
{patrick.rempel,patrick.maeder,tobias.kuschke,
ilka.philippow}@tu-ilmenau.de

Abstract. **[Context and motivation]** Outsourcing of software development is an attractive business model. Companies expect cost reduction, enhanced efficiency, and exploited external resources. However, this paradigmatic shift also introduces challenges as stakeholders are spread across distinct organizations. **[Question/problem]** Requirements traceability supports stakeholders in satisfying information needs about developments and could be a viable way of addressing the challenges of inter-organizational development. While requirements traceability has been the subject of significant research efforts, its application across organizational boundaries is a largely unexplored area. **[Principal ideas/results]** We followed a qualitative research approach. First, we developed a taxonomy identifying the needs of inter-organizational traceability. Second, we conducted semi-structured interviews with informants from 17 companies. Eventually, we applied qualitative content analysis to extract findings that supported and evolved our taxonomy. **[Contribution]** Practitioners planning and managing inter-organizational relationships can use our findings as a conceptual baseline to effectively leverage traceability in those settings. Effective traceability supports projects in accomplishing their primary goal of maximizing business value.

1 Introduction

Requirements traceability has been commonly recognized by researchers and practitioners alike as critical element of a rigorous software development process[1]. Gotel and Finkelstein defined requirements traceability as the ability to describe and follow the life of requirements, in both a forwards and backwards direction (i.e., from its origins, through its development and specification, to its subsequent deployment and use, and through all periods of on-going refinement and iteration in any of these phases) [1]. Software process initiatives, such as CMMI, formulated the goal of maintaining bidirectional traceability of requirements. Requirements traceability supports a stakeholder in satisfying information needs within a software development process. The applicability of this concept has been studied for ordinary software development projects. However, as

---

[1] http://www.coest.org/index.php/what-is-traceability (accessed: October, 2012).

J. Doerr and A.L. Opdahl (Eds.): REFSQ 2013, LNCS 7830, pp. 125–140, 2013.
© Springer-Verlag Berlin Heidelberg 2013

software projects become bigger and bigger there is a tendency to outsource parts of the software development process [2].

In IT outsourcing the software development process is distributed across two types of actors – clients and suppliers. In a simplified view, a client produces a requirements specification. A supplier implements the software product according to the client's requirements specification. This form of IT outsourcing offers advantages like leveraging external IT assets [3] and capitalizing the global resource pool [2]. Due to these advantages, outsourcing is a commonly applied IT strategy pattern. However, beside these advantages the organizational border between two or more cooperating actors produces a distance. This distance leads to complexity risks in the software development process that need to be bridged [4]. Traceability could be viable way of bridging inter-organizational distance.

Only little empirical knowledge is available on the impact of IT outsourcing on requirements traceability. We followed a qualitative research approach to close that gap. First, we developed a taxonomy to identify actors and their interactions in inter-organizational projects. Second, we conducted semi-structured interviews with informants from 17 companies to understand the impact of inter-organizational software projects on requirements traceability. Eventually, we applied qualitative content analysis to extract findings that supported and evolved our taxonomy. We discussed needs for requirements traceability from the perspectives of actors in inter-organizational projects.

Our paper is organized as follows. Section 2 reviews related work in the area of requirements traceability and inter-organizational software projects. In Section 3, we propose a taxonomy of actors and interactions in inter-organizational outsourcing projects based on a literature study. This conceptual framework was used to plan and conduct the interview study, which is described in Section 4. In Section 5 we discuss the results of our study, which we extracted via qualitative content analysis from the captured interview minutes and field notes. Section 6 discusses possible threats to the validity of our work and how we mitigated them. Finally, Section 7 concludes our work and outlines future research directions.

2   Related Work

Several studies examined the general application of requirements traceability in software development projects. Gotel and Finkelstein [1] studied requirements traceability practices and highlighted especially the demand for supporting pre-requirements traceability. Ramesh and Jarke [5] conducted intensive interview studies with practitioners. As a conclusion they proposed two traceability reference models. Arkley and Riddle [6] conducted a survey and explored the so-called traceability benefit problem. This problem arises as trace recorder and user are typically different stakeholders. We also conducted a survey on how requirements traceability activities are embedded into company processes [7]. We identified problems that need to be addressed to make traceability more beneficial for software practitioners. An important finding of that study was that practitioners struggle to implement inter-organizational traceability workflows.

The interviewed practitioners demanded for guidance on how to enable the usage of traceability across organizational boundaries. Similarly to our findings, other researchers stated that outsourcing complicates requirements traceability [8,4]. Although, the problem of inter-organizational traceability was recognized by these researchers, none of them studied it or provided possible solutions.

Lormans et al. [9] conducted an industrial case study with a single international company to understand how requirements traceability is impacted by the outsourcing context. The authors specified requirements for a requirements management system in the context of inter-organizational development. They used these requirements to customize a commercial requirements engineering tool to the needs of their industrial partner. The proposed approach is valuable for the studied case. However, the authors did not focus on a more general understanding of inter-organizational projects as well as the application of requirements traceability in that context. Damian and Chisan [10] studied inter-organizational project relationships in general and identified mistrust and power struggles as critical issues. The authors mentioned requirements traceability as a possible solution to overcome these issues. Alvare et al. [11] studied factors that shape client-supplier relationships and their impact on food traceability. Similar to our approach, the authors propose a conceptual framework of relationships between actors in a distributed production environment.

As a result of our review of related work we can conclude that IT outsourcing is a commonly applied strategy pattern and of high relevance to the software industry. Further, various researchers recognized that inter-organizational specifics need to be carefully considered when applying requirements traceability in the outsourcing context. Beside the small case study on requirements traceability within an international company by Lormans et al. [9], there are no empirical studies that examined the specific challenges of leverage requirements traceability in inter-organizational projects. To close this gap in this relevant area of software development, we found that a systematic study of this problem is necessary.

3   A Taxonomy of Inter-organizational Software Projects

Over the past years, several studies reported a general shift of paradigm from static functional organizations to organizations composed of rapidly changing temporary projects, often referred to as "projectification" [12]. The following rationales for advancing this paradigmatic change emerged as most important. (I) Flexible project organizations allow task-specific resource allocation and avoid long-term resource commitments [13]. (II) Well informed consumers in globalized markets are demanding genuinely innovative products with reasonable pricing and quality that satisfy varying needs [12].

In parallel with projectification, many companies concerned with software development followed IT outsourcing strategies, which we call inter-organizational projectification. The following rationales for this inter-organizational projectification were identified. The fact that well educated people are scarce resources led to high labor costs or even worse to the inability to develop the software product. Outsourcing provided the ability to capitalize a globalized resource pool and to address the scarce resource issue [2]. DiRomualdo and Gurbaxani [3] synthesized the more general strategic intent of IT outsourcing to leverage external IT assets such as applications, operations, infrastructure, and know how.

We decided to study this problem in more detail due to the practical relevance of IT outsourcing on the one hand ("inter-organizational projectification") and the limited empirical knowledge on how to deal with requirements traceability in outsourcing scenarios on the other hand. Our research is motivated by the following research questions:

Q1: Who are key actors in inter-organizational projects?
Q2: How do actors interact in inter-organizational projects?
Q3: What goals do interacting parties have in inter-organizational projects?
Q4: How can traceability be leveraged to accomplish Q3's objectives?

Guided by our research questions, we developed a taxonomy that conceptualizes relationships of actors in inter-organizational projects. These actors were characterized by their goals (see Section 3.1). Different interactions between these actors were then described in detail (see Section 3.2).

3.1   Actors and Their Perspectives

According to the definition of Jones and Lichtenstein [14] *inter-organizational projects involve two or more organizational actors from distinct organizations working jointly to create a tangible product/service in a limited period of time. These actors minimally refer to a client and a contractor.* Based on this definition, we identified two types of actors: **client** and **supplier**.

Both, client and supplier simultaneously cooperate in temporary projects and are embedded in their own organizational context [15] as illustrated in Figure 1-a. That means that every actor in an inter-organizational project has an organizational and a project perspective. As both perspectives need to be satisfied, each actor pursue two types of goals, a strategic and a tactical goal. *Strategic goals* describe objectives from an organizational perspective. *Tactical goals* describe objectives from a project perspective (see Figure 1-b). On the one hand, this implies that project team members of client and supplier share the common tactical project goal to develop a certain software product within distinct time and budget [15]. On the other hand, client and supplier organizations also have their individual strategic goals. With strategic goals we mean business goals such as efficiency, innovation, and risk management [16] that are pursued by companies to ensure competitiveness and profitability.

3.2   Interactions

Interactions between client and supplier as well as organization and project are required to align various goals [17]. Based on these often conflicting goals, actors

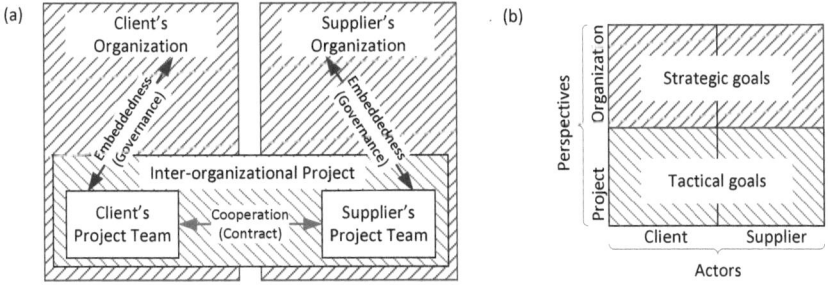

Fig. 1. Actors and their perspectives in inter-organizational projects

need to interact inter- and intra-organizationally. Figure 2 summarizes these interactions as a taxonomy.

Inter-organizational interactions emerge from the cooperation relation between client and supplier. A client-supplier relationship is grounded on contracts. Contracts between client and supplier define exchanges of service and/or products, financial matters, service enforcement and monitoring methods, and communication and/or information exchanges[17,18]. Thus, we distinguish four different inter-organizational interactions (see Figure 2-a) within our taxonomy: (I) transfer product & service, (II) monetary compensation (III) enforce & monitor quality & progress, and (IV) communicate with project partner.

Intra-organizational interactions emerge from the embeddedness of projects in an organizational context. This embeddedness relation is determined by the fact that tactical project goals need to be aligned with strategic organizational goals. The concept of organizational alignment is known as IT governance. As outlined in Figure 2-b, IT governance can be divided into three types of intra-organizational interactions: (V) compliance verification, (VI) strategic alignment, and (VII) operational excellence [19].

In the next section (see Section 4), we are using the developed taxonomy as a framework to conduct an interview study. We interviewed software development experts from various companies for this study. The findings of our study are then structured according to the developed taxonomy (see Section 5).

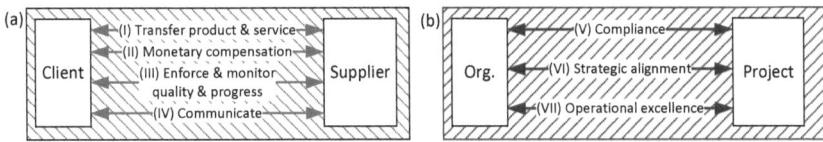

Fig. 2. Overview of (a) inter-organizational and (b) intra-organizational interactions within distributed projects

4   Interview Study

The objective of our study was to gain a better understanding of traceability workflows across organizational boundaries. Thus, we conducted interviews with informants from 17 different companies. Every informant was interviewed in an individual session to prevent that different informant's opinions interfered with each other during the interview. We chose this qualitative research approach for the following reasons. Workflows in inter-organizational projects are complex and multi-faceted. Thus, it would be difficult to define specific context variables required for a quantitative research methodology. In addition, our qualitative interview approach ensured that we were close to the studied software projects and its participants. This proximity helped us to gained an in-depth understanding of the mechanics behind the observed phenomena and avoided misinterpretations during the qualitative content analysis.

4.1   Sampling Cases for the Study

We assembled a list of potential companies from the membership list of the association of friends of the Technical University Ilmenau. This list was extended by contacts we made at a practitioners forum on requirements engineering. We considered every company in the resulting list of 85 companies as a potential case for our study. In order to prioritize this list, we collected general information about each company and identified contact persons from the internet. We then developed a case sampling strategy in order to select the most suitable companies and informants for our study. Following the framework of Curtis et al. [20], we defined and used the following sampling criteria:

- How relevant are general case characteristics to our taxonomy?
- What potential to generate rich information provides the case?
- How generalizable are findings from this particular case?
- What resources (e.g., money and time) are required to study this case?
- Does any ethical issues force us to exclude this case from our list?

After prioritizing the list of potential cases, the contact persons of highest prioritized cases were contacted in order to arrange an interview. Provided that the sampled company agreed, we conducted either one or multiple interviews with key informants of this company. Every informant was interviewed in an individual interview session to avoid influences between informants.

4.2   Data Collection

We decided to employ a semi-structured interview technique with closed-ended and open-ended questions. This approach aimed to guarantee that our investigations are guided by theory, while keeping the flexibility to explore unforeseen information. As described in Section 3, we synthesized our taxonomy from literature. While developing our interview questionnaire, this taxonomy served us as theoretical guidance. The questionnaire consisted of three parts:

1. **General company and project characteristics:** we collected background information about the key informant and the company. Then we asked the informant to describe the software development project she or he is currently involved or has recently finished.
2. **Software development process:** we asked for important process elements such as activities, tasks, roles, stakeholders, artifacts, and tools. Thereby, we aimed to generate a holistic view on the software development process from the beginning to the end.
3. **Inter-organizational traceability workflows:** we asked the informant to provide us with her or his definition of requirements traceability. The answer to that introductory question enabled us to subsequently verify that informants from different cases shared a common understanding of that concept. We then collected characteristics of requirements traceability workflows across organizational boundaries. Hence, we asked for requirements traceability objectives and challenges.

We applied a two phased approach for conducting the interviews. (I) We selected a company in close proximity and performed a three hours lasting interview, which we considered as a pilot run. In result, we produced interview minutes and field notes. We analyzed the interview minutes in order to reveal and eliminate conceptual weaknesses from the questionnaire. We further conducted a retrospective review of our field notes to improve our interview tactics. Thereby, we realized the necessity to approach certain topics differently in order to avoid unwittingly influencing the informant. (II) The actual interviews were conducted with 20 informants from 17 different companies. All interviews were recorded in writing by a designated minute taker.

4.3 Data Analysis

To extract findings from the written interview minutes we applied qualitative content analysis [21]. Our taxonomy served as a qualitative description model. We derived a system of codes from our taxonomy. We classified informant's statements of all written interview minutes and field notes using the defined codes and the qualitative analysis tool MAXQDA10[2].

4.4 Data Demographics

In our study a single case referred to a distinct company concerned with software development. Table 1 outlines that our study contains *small* (less than 100 employees), *medium* (100 to 1,000 employees), *large* (1,001 to 10,000 employees), and *huge* (more than 10,000 employees) companies. It can be seen that small and medium companies mainly conduct *small* (less than 5 project member) or *medium* (5 to 9 project member) projects, while large and huge companies mainly conduct *large* (10 to 100 project members) or *huge* (more than 100

---

[2] http://www.maxqda.com

project members) projects. Most companies (15) are headquartered in Germany. The remaining companies two headquarters are USA and Austria. All projects were spread across multiple locations, often across multiple countries such as Germany, USA, India, Bulgaria, Czech Republic, Austria, France, and Croatia. The studied companies are active in various domains (Avionic, Finance, Insurance, Logistics, Retail, Security, Transportation) and produce different offerings (Software Product, Hardware Product, Software Development Services). The captured projects represented various types of software development projects, namely New-development, Maintenance, and Migration.

Table 2 outlines characteristics of the interviewed informants. To provide more context to the reader, the table relates every informant to the case she/he belongs to. The table shows that our data covers both actors (Client and Supplier) and both perspectives (Project and Organization). Informant's primary roles are spread across all phases of the software development process (Project Management, Requirements Analysis, Implementation, and Verification).

Table 1. Characteristics of studied companies and their projects

Project size	Company size	Case	Project type	Offering	Domain
< 5	< 100	**I**	New-development	Service	Public service
		IV	New-development	SW Product	Retail
		VI	Maintenance	HW Product	Robotic
	100..1,000	**VIII**	Maintenance	SW Product	Finance
5..9	< 100	**II**	Maintenance	Service	Insurance
		XI	Maintenance	Service	Insurance
	100..1,000	**VII**	Maintenance	Service	Finance
		XIII	New-development	Service	Finance
	> 10,000	**X**	New-development	Service	Insurance
		XII	Maintenance	Service	Retail
10..100	< 100	**XVI**	Maintenance	SW Product	RE
	1,001..10,000	**IX**	Maintenance	SW Product	IT Security
	> 10,000	**XIV**	New-development	HW Product	Avionic
> 100	100..1,000	**XVII**	Maintenance	HW Product	Telecommunic.
		V	Maintenance	SW Product	Retail
	1,001..10,000	**III**	Migration	Service	Finance
	> 10,000	**XV**	Migration	Service	Logistic

5 Study Results

This Section provides insights on the results that we extracted from the interview minutes and field notes. Following our taxonomy, we present our extracted findings from different viewpoints. We discuss the client's viewpoint in Section 5.1,

Table 2. Inter-organizational perspective and primary role of interviewed informants

Actor	Perspective	Case	Informant	Informant's primary role
Client	Project	III	Inf-III-1	Project manager
		XV	Inf-XV-1	Business analyst
	Organization	X	Inf-X-1	Process manager
		XII	Inf-XII-1	Portfolio manager
Supplier	Project	I	Inf-I-1	Developer
		I	Inf-I-2	Project manager
		II	Inf-II-1	Project manager
		IV	Inf-IV-1	Development lead
		V	Inf-V-1	Development lead
		VI	Inf-VI-1	Development lead
		VII	Inf-VII-1	Specification manager
		VIII	Inf-VIII-1	Project manager
		IX	Inf-IX-1	Development lead
		X	Inf-X-2	Release & Configuration manager
		XI	Inf-XI-1	Development lead
		XII	Inf-XII-2	Test manager
		XIV	Inf-XIV-1	Tester
		XVI	Inf-XVI-1	Development lead
	Organization	XIII	Inf-XIII-1	GRC manager
		XVII	Inf-XVII-1	Process manager

supplier's viewpoint in Section 5.2, and the organizational viewpoint in Section 5.3 on requirements traceability in inter-organizational outsourcing projects.

5.1   Client's Viewpoint

In this section we report findings that are specific to the client of an inter-organizational relationship. These findings are structured according to the inter-action types of our taxonomy.

Transfer Product and/or Service: The quality of the delivered end-product was mentioned as most important by all informants. *The supplier hands over a fully verified roll-out baseline to us [Inf-III-1], we insist on a proof of full requirements coverage from the supplier [Inf-XV-1].* Due to contractual obligations, the client demanded a proof of quality via traceability from the supplier that can be objectively assessed. Especially, clients in strictly regulated environments referred to requirements traceability as a must. Though, traceability appeared to be of great support to objectively assess product quality, two main issues were reported by clients. (I) First, differences in tooling, methodology, and processes between client and supplier made it difficult to efficiently leverage requirements traceability. Main reason for this gap is the fact that technology and processes of each organization were primarily aligned to the organizational goal. That implies that traceability can typically only be used efficiently if this gap is bridged. (II) Second, the existence of one common project goal and two independent organizational goals implied a natural conflict. As a result, traceability information could not or only partially be used across organizational boundaries as its complete disclosure would contradict with supplier's organizational goals.

Monetary Compensation: *Change and executive board of the client formally accept and release the roll-out baseline. The final payment is made when this critical milestone is reached [Inf-III-1].* Clients typically defined quality gates that needed to be passed before any kind of payment was executed to the supplier. The assessment of whether or not a quality gate had been passed is a very difficult task for the client. Typically, the client had no direct access to resources at the supplier's side that would be able to provide required input for this assessment. In this case, traceability was the only source that could be used by clients for assessment. Client informants highlighted the issue that traceability information must be reliable due to its high financial impact.

Enforcement and Monitoring: *Traceability is used by the client's project managers to control the supplier's progress and quality [Inf-XV-1, Inf-XII-1].* Primary task of the client's project managers was to continuously monitor whether or not the project can still be finished in time and budget and with the expected result. As the client's project managers had typically no direct access to all resources at supplier's side, they required access to reliable traceability information that could be used to measure project progress properly. *All test cases created by the supplier must be accepted and released by the client side before any test execution activity can be started [Inf-III-1].* For a complex scenario with multiple suppliers, the client's project manager pointed out that all supplier activities were synchronized with the help of traceability.

Communication: *Traceability information prepared by the supplier provides valuable input for our further release planning [Inf-XV-1].* Due to the fact that the supplier developed the software, product specific knowledge was generated by the supplier's team members. This product specific knowledge provided valuable input for the client's product manager. The limited access to the supplier's resources forced the client's product manager to gain product specific knowledge indirectly via traceability information. Nevertheless, the supplier's organizational goal of keeping technical or functional knowledge confidential often contradicted the goals of the client's product manager.

5.2 Supplier's Viewpoint

In this section we report findings that are specific to the supplier of an inter-organizational relationship. These findings are structured according to the interaction types of our taxonomy.

Transfer Product and/or Service: *We use traceability to proof the completeness of our implementation to the client [Inf-XIV-1].* The supplier needed to proof the quality and completeness of the implementation in order to avoid expensive disputes. Client and supplier often contractually agreed upon penalties for the case that the delivery of a product with a certain quality was missed. *Our client issues a bug in the application. In case of a false alarm (no bug present) we leverage traceability to proof that the system works as specified by the client [Inf-I-1, Inf-VII-1].* Usually, repairing software defects is covered by the supplier's warranty. Many suppliers reported on the common scenario that a client raised a bug by mistake even though the software was working as specified by the client. Due to warranty obligations, the supplier had either to proof that the product is working properly or to fix the bug. Without traceability between client's requirements and supplier's implementation/verification artifacts the proof of correctness was almost impossible.

Monetary Compensation: *When disputing with our clients about product reliability, we use traceability to proof that we did not act with gross negligence in order to avoid paying punitive damages [Inf-XVII-1].* Software errors may have extraordinary impact. In such cases the supplier must be able to proof that she or he did not act with gross negligence. Otherwise, the client may demand compensation, which could even threaten the supplier's existence.

Enforcement and Monitoring: *We leverage traceability to monitor our progress and communicate reliable release dates to our clients [Inf-IX-1].* The supplier's project manager used traceability to track the project progress. This information was important to estimate and communicate reliable release dates. Additionally, the project could be monitored to predict project delay. *We must have traceability information to successfully pass quality audits, which are periodically operated by our clients [Inf-XVII-1].* Two informants reported on the fact that they were forced by the client to provide traceability. Otherwise, the client would not even consider entering into a contractual relationship with the supplier. The client regularly verified traceability by supplier audits. Especially, informants working in highly regulated domains highlighted this issue.

Communication: *Our product serves the needs of three different client types. When writing technical product specifications, we typically trace back to the origin of requirements in order to really understand the specific need [Inf-V-1].* Technical project team members at the supplier's side such as designers, architects, developers, or testers directly or indirectly depended on a proper understanding what software was supposed to be built. To gain this understanding a direct communication with the client's requirements engineers was required. Though, direct communication was limited due to organizational boundaries. Thus, traceability was used to reduce the necessity for direct communication.

5.3 Organization's Viewpoint

The following findings were extracted from interviews with informants that represents the organizational perspective.

Compliance: *Internal auditors reproduce executed software development processes of critical projects [Inf-XVII-1].* Suppliers that developed software for regulated markets were obligated by legal regulation. Thus, compliance with legal regulation was a strategic company goal. Retrospective audits of the software process were supposed to verify whether or not project execution conformed with regulation. Traceability was required to reproduce the process.

Strategic Alignment: *We monitor aggregated traceability information from all projects across the company to identify bug hot spots [Inf-XIII-1].* The purpose of identifying bug hot spots with traceability is twofold. First, the risk of delivering low quality products had to be reduced for the company. Second, bug hot spots indicated that the used technology or architecture in this area was insufficient.

Operational Excellence: *We use requirements traceability information to establish an early warning system for predicting project crashes [Inf-XVII-1].* Traceability information of running projects could be compared with traceability information of previous projects. By this comparison, critical project evolution could be identified and counter-measures were taken.

5.4 A Practicioner's Checklist

As a conclusion of our previously discussed findings, we derived three success criteria for requirements traceability in inter-organizational projects. We substantiated each success criteria with a list of questions that can be used by practitioners as a checklist.

Criteria I: Ensure availability and reliability of traceability

- What traceability information is required from our project partner?
- Do we rely on traceability information provided by the project partner?
- Is the provision of traceability information contractually specified?
- How can we assess our project partner's trace recording process?
- What are our traceability information quality gates?

Criteria II: Identify and mitigate conflicting objectives

- Do we understand our project partner's organization sufficiently to identify conflicting objectives?
- Are there any conflicting objectives that discourage our project partner from providing necessary traceability information?

- How to establish trust between client and supplier to mitigate conflicting goals?
- Do we need measures to mediate conflicting objectives (e.g. signing non-disclosure agreement)?

Criteria III: Bridge the technological gap between client and supplier

- How does our project partner provide traceability information?
- Are we able to effectively use provided traceability information?

While the above checklist provides guidance for practitioners planning inter-organizational projects towards addressing potential traceability problems, further research effort must be devoted to the question how to address each of the discovered and discussed problems (see Sections 5.1, 5.2, and 5.3). We found that due to the organizational boundary and often contradicting organizational strategies, applying requirements traceability becomes more complicated. We would like to encourage the research community to seek for appropriate traceability solutions for inter-organizational project setups.

6 Threats to Validity

When planning and conducting our study we carefully considered validity concerns. This section discusses how we mitigated threats to the validity.

6.1 External Validity

Due to their nature, interview studies cannot be replicated as identical interview circumstances cannot be recreated. Qualitative studies are primarily concerned with describing and understanding existing phenomena. We described such observed phenomena from our interviews. In an attempt to make these findings usable to other practitioners, we developed a list of critical success factors for requirements traceability in distributed project (see Section 5.4). The fact that our cases diverge across multiple domains, locations, and sizes contributes to the applicability of our findings. However, we are aware of the fact that this kind of study is not generalizable.

6.2 Internal Validity

The instrumentation threat was addressed by applying qualitative content analysis [21], which must be guided by theory from the beginning. We derived a taxonomy from literature as described below. Activities of our study, like creating the questionnaire, conducting the interviews, and extracting the findings were all guided by this taxonomy. We mitigated the threat of case selection bias by defining the selection scheme described in advance (see Section 4.2).

6.3 Construct Validity

Our study is grounded on a taxonomy that conceptualizes inter-organizational software development projects. Thus, we describe and justify how our taxonomy was constructed. To determine the number of potentially relevant studies, we conducted a preliminary search for existing meta-studies on our topic. Then, we extracted primary (P: *inter-organizational*) and secondary (S: *software project*) search term categories from our research questions. Then, we extracted synonym keywords for both categories from labels (headlines, captions) of the evaluated meta-studies as additional search terms (see Table 3). The cross product of both search term categories ($P \times S$) defines our super set of 16 combined search terms. Searching with all these 16 terms produced a list of 9157 unique hits. We narrowed this list to 76 hits by applying the following inclusion criteria: (i) a publication's title must contain a primary search term (ii) a publication's abstract must contain a secondary search term. We carefully read and compared the abstracts of the remaining publications. Additionally, we studied the abstracts of their referencing and referred publications. Following this procedure, we found publications that present definitions on inter-organizational projects as well as typical client/supplier interactions. We then created a taxonomy that is synthesized from overlapping information across these publications. We consider the created taxonomy a reasonable framework for our study as the process for selecting publications followed in principle the accepted Kitchenham method and the publications that we built upon are well referenced by other researchers.

Table 3. Categorized search terms for the literature study

Primary terms (P)	Secondary terms (S)
inter-organizational	*software project*
cross-organizational	*software development project*
outsourcing	*software process*
	software development process
	software workflow
	software development workflow

6.4 Conclusion Validity

As described in Section 4.2 we employed a preliminary prototypical interview under realistic conditions to improve our questionnaire and our questioning technique. Thereby we emphasized on eliminating influencing information from questions or questioning behavior. All interviews of our study were conducted with one informant in a single session without break. We offered no room for distractions and interruptions during the interview in order to avoid influences on subjects' answers.

7   Conclusions and Future Work

In this paper we focused on the characteristics of inter-organizational software development projects. In particular, we were interested in whether requirements traceability can help to overcome challenges that a distributed development inherits. We identified three problem areas as most challenging for practitioners.

Different **organizational background** from client and supplier pose the challenge that different technology and methodology is used, e.g., for requirements engineering and software development. This gap needs to be bridged in order to provide sufficient requirements traceability. Although, adapters and tool chains are implemented to handle that issue, practitioners repeatedly reported on their struggle with this technological gap. Inter-organizational outsourcing projects are of temporary nature and client-supplier relationship are manifold. Thus, requirements traceabiliy must be customized for every project. Requirements traceability should therefore be defined as a strategic goal.

Due to **organizational boundaries** between client and supplier the access to artifacts created by the project partner is typically restricted. Negotiated contracts specify artifacts to be delivered either by the client or the supplier. These deliverables are typically only a very small subset of all artifacts created during the requirements engineering and software development of a system. This reduced set of deliverables is often not sufficient to accomplish comprehensive requirements traceability. That implies that requirements traceability needs to be planned very carefully in advance and access to the necessary artifacts guaranteed via contract.

Conflicting objectives exist in two dimensions. The first dimension of conflict is client vs. supplier objectives. The second dimension of conflict is organizational vs. project objectives. Resolving a conflict in one dimension may negatively impact the other dimension. Therefore, a traceability strategy should address all conflicting objectives. If the demand for certain requirements traceability information is contradicting an objective then this traceability information will likely not be provided by the project partner. Eventually, the challenge is to reach a trade-off mediating all four objectives.

Though, we conducted a broad interview study with cases from various domains, more empirical knowledge is required for a generalizable theory. We plan to extend our study and to iteratively evolve the provided practitioner guidelines on requirements traceability in inter-organizational projects. Additionally, further research on supporting tools and approaches is required to provide solutions in the three problem areas identified above.

Acknowledgment. The authors would like to thank all practitioners participating in the interview study. We are supported by the German Research Foundation (DFG): Ph49/8-1 and the German Ministry of Education and Research (BMBF): Grant No. 16V0116.

References

1. Gotel, O.C.Z., Finkelstein, A.C.W.: An analysis of the requirements traceability problem. In: IEEE Proc. of the First Int. Conf. on RE, pp. 94–101 (1994)
2. Herbsleb, J., Moitra, D.: Global software development. IEEE Software 18(2), 16–20 (2001)
3. DiRomualdo, A., Gurbaxani, V.: Strategic intent for it outsourcing. Sloan Management Review 39(4), 67–80 (1998)
4. Cleland-Huang, J., Settimi, R., Romanova, E., Berenbach, B., Clark, S.: Best practices for automated traceability. Computer 40(6), 27–35 (2007)
5. Ramesh, B., Powers, T., Stubbs, C., Edwards, M.: Implementing requirements traceability: a case study. In: IEEE 2nd Int. Symposium on RE, pp. 89–95 (1995)
6. Arkley, P., Riddle, S.: Overcoming the traceability benefit problem. In: Proc. 13th IEEE Int'l Conf. on Requirements Engineering, pp. 385–389 (2005)
7. Mäder, P., Gotel, O., Philippow, I.: Motivation matters in the traceability trenches. In: Proc. of 17th Int'l Requirements Engineering Conference, RE 2009 (2009)
8. Gotel, O.: Contribution Structures for Requirements Traceability. PhD thesis, Imperial Collage of Science, Technology and Medicine, University of London (1995)
9. Lormans, M., van Dijk, H., Van Deursen, A., Nocker, E., de Zeeuw, A.: Managing evolving requirements in an outsourcing context: an industrial experience report. In: 7th Int'l Workshop on Principles of Software Evolution, pp. 149–158 (2004)
10. Damian, D., Chisan, J.: An empirical study of the complex relationships between requirements engineering processes and other processes that lead to payoffs in productivity, quality, and risk management. IEEE TSE 32(7), 433–453 (2006)
11. Rábade, L., Alfaro, J.: Buyer–supplier relationship's influence on traceability implementation in the vegetable industry. PSM 12(1), 39–50 (2006)
12. Midler, C.: "projectification" of the firm: the renault case. Scandinavian Journal of Management 11(4), 363–375 (1995)
13. Grabher, G.: Temporary architectures of learning: knowledge governance in project ecologies. Organization studies 25(9), 1491–1514 (2004)
14. Jones, C., Lichtenstein, B.: Temporary inter-organizational projects: How temporal and social embeddedness enhance coordination and manage uncertainty. In: The Oxford Handbook of Inter-Organizational Relations, pp. 231–255 (2008)
15. Bakker, R., Knoben, J., De Vries, N., Oerlemans, L.: The nature and prevalence of inter-organizational project ventures: Evidence from a large scale field study in the netherlands 2006–2009. IJPM 29(6), 781–794 (2011)
16. Von Krogh, G., Nonaka, I., Aben, M.: Making the most of your company's knowledge: a strategic framework. Long Range Planning 34(4), 421–439 (2001)
17. Kern, T., Willcocks, L.: Exploring information technology outsourcing relationships: theory and practice. JSIS 9(4), 321–350 (2000)
18. Halvey, J., Melby, B.: Information technology outsourcing transactions: process, strategies, and contracts. Wiley (2005)
19. Van Grembergen, W., De Haes, S., Guldentops, E.: Structures, processes and relational mechanisms for it governance. SITG 2004, 1–36 (2004)
20. Curtis, S., Gesler, W., Smith, G., Washburn, S.: Approaches to sampling and case selection in qualitative research: examples in the geography of health. Social Science & Medicine 50(7), 1001–1014 (2000)
21. Mayring, P.: Qualitative content analysis. In: Forum Qualitative Sozialforschung/-Forum: Qualitative Social Research, vol. 1 (2000)

Regulatory Requirements Traceability and Analysis Using Semi-formal Specifications

Travis D. Breaux[1] and David G. Gordon[2]

[1] Institute for Software Research, Carnegie Mellon University, Pittsburgh, PA, USA
breaux@cs.cmu.edu
[2] Engineering and Public Policy, Carnegie Mellon University, Pittsburgh, PA, USA
dggordon@andrew.cmu.edu

Abstract. Information systems are increasingly distributed and pervasive, enabling organizations to deliver remote services and share personal information, worldwide. However, developers face significant challenges in managing the many laws that govern their systems in this multi-jurisdictional environment. In this paper, we report on a computational requirements document expressible using a legal requirements specification language (LRSL). The purpose is to make legal requirements open and available to policy makers, business analysts and software developers, alike. We show how requirements engineers can codify policy and law using the LRSL and design, debug, analyze, trace, and visualize relationships among regulatory requirements. The LRSL provides new constructs for expressing distributed constraints, making regulatory specification patterns visually salient, and enabling metrics to quantitatively measure different styles for writing legal and policy documents. We discovered and validated the LRSL using thirteen U.S. state data breach notification laws.

Keywords: requirements specification, traceability, domain specific languages, legal requirements.

1 Introduction

Increasingly, new government laws and regulations are being introduced to address new challenges posed by emerging information systems (IS). For software developers, this emergence of IS-related laws places constraints on what systems must do (the matter of requirements) and whether system requirements documents include all the right requirements (the matter of validation). In the United States, a prominent example includes the recent surge in state data breach notification laws, which have been empirically observed to reduce identity theft [27]. Collectively, these laws combine the act of notification to various stakeholders with technical security controls (e.g., encryption, data destruction, etc.) targeted at different information types, business practices and consumers. These laws require the development of a new, interstate information system that most businesses in the U.S. must participate in by modifying their organizational practices and software systems to account for data breaches and to deliver notices under specifically governed situations. Many of the legally imposed security requirements follow conventional security design wisdom; however, the legally

J. Doerr and A.L. Opdahl (Eds.): REFSQ 2013, LNCS 7830, pp. 141–157, 2013.

mandated parameters in these requirements vary across jurisdiction. For example, using encryption or disposing of unnecessary data is a security best practice; however, the required type of encryption and length of data retention does vary across state and national boundaries. The challenge for developers, especially in small businesses, is to distill these regulations into actionable requirements that are traceable across their business practices. Simply skimming a regulation for keywords or phrases exposes software developers and users to the risk of missing subtle constraints and relationships. Example relationships affect who is covered, under what circumstances, and to what extent. Finally, a systematic, traceable and comprehensive account of existing legal requirements can facilitate the integration with industry standards to further articulate how businesses comply with government laws [28].

We believe existing approaches to governance, which consists of independently published, paper-based laws and policies, can no longer scale with rate of technology innovation. Furthermore, if an honest expectation of compliance is to be preserved in this new environment, regulations must be made accessible to policy makers, business analysts and software developers, alike. We propose that regulators and industry can reach a coordinated solution wherein regulations become a computational software artifact that are dynamically linked across jurisdictions and that enable tool-based requirements analysis. These computational artifacts can integrate with industry standards to become more easily comparable and addressable in a manner that reflects the jurisdiction of the computer's memory state, users' location, and the rate of technological change. To this end, we report our efforts to develop a legal requirements specification language (LRSL), derived from grounded analysis of conflicting regulations from multiple jurisdictions. By translating requirements into the LRSL, document authors can design and debug their requirements documents using improved tracing, patterns and metrics that we discuss in this paper.

The remainder of the paper is organized as follows: in Section 2, we discuss related work; in Section 3, we introduce the LRSL by example; in Section 4, we present our research methodology to discover and validate the LRSL; in Section 5, we summarize our research findings, including techniques for navigating and cross-linking legal requirements; and in Section 6, we conclude with our discussion and summary.

2   Related Work

Related work includes research on requirements languages, extract requirements from laws, prioritize requirements, and model legal documents and their legal effects.

Requirements specification languages (RSLs), including requirements modeling languages (RMLs), have a rich history in requirements and software engineering [20]. RSLs include informal, natural language descriptions to provide readers with context and elaboration, and formal descriptions, such as mathematical logic, to test assumptions across requirements using logical implications [13]. Goal-oriented languages, such as i* [36] and KAOS [11], and object-oriented notations, such as ADORA [17], include graphical notations to view relationships between entities, such as actors, actions and objects. Because of computational intractability and undecidability of using highly expressive logics [16], RSLs often formalize only a select class of requirements phenomena, e.g., using description logic [5] and various temporal logics, such as interval [26], real-time [11] or linear [14] temporal logic. Consequently, RSLs and RMLs may struggle with the balance between expressivity and readability [13]. Unlike i*, KAOS and ADORA, the LRSL proposed herein is designed for the law and policy domain by integrating formal expressions of document structure using regular expressions with semi-formal expressions of rights, permissions and obligations using text-based predicates and annotations. Unlike frame-based approaches that seek to classify phrases by logical roles [7], our LRSL simulates how policies are written by formalizing the cross-links among requirements in ways originally specified by regulators, and preserving traceability to the original legal document references. The aforementioned notations do not account for this integration of requirements and original sources in policy and law.

Approaches to formalize laws in requirements engineering have focused on *prescriptions*, called rights, permissions and obligations [6], ownership and delegation [15], and production rule systems [22]. In addition, cross-references within and among laws have been shown to coordinate definitions, exceptions and refinement and must be addressed in a comprehensive legal requirements management strategy [8]. Recent analysis of external cross-references emanating from the Health Information Portability and Accountability Act (HIPAA) shows the potential for conflicts between HIPAA and other laws [23]. Recently, Siena et al. describe the *Nómos 2* framework to model norms, which they claim can be used to determine compliance with law [31]. We believe the LRSL could be combined with the inference layer provided by *Nómos 2* to reason about legal requirements coverage.

Research in artificial intelligence (AI) and law has long sought to encode regulations into formal models. Among many others, this includes work by Biagoli et al. [2] and Sergot et al. [29] to express statutes as logic programs. Allen and Saxon describe the A-Hohfeld language [1] based on Hohfeld's legal concepts [18]. The language is used to reason about legal powers, rights, and duties. More recently, Sergot describes a theory of normative positions based on the Kanger-Lindahl theory [30]. The aim of this work was to develop automated legal reasoning tools. Because regulatory documents were not intended to be formalized and often contain ambiguities, our approach has been to develop methods to express a normative semi-formal semantics [9] that yield "islands of formality" while preserving legal ambiguity for later analysis by an appropriate legal analyst. Stamper argues this approach provides an "economy of expression" in regulatory requirements analysis [32], which is a commonly held view of domain specific languages, in general [25]. Thus, our approach is concerned with repeatable, semi-formalization that strictly deals with issues of ambiguity and document structure. Approaches to formalize judicial legal arguments, such as LegalXML, concern a different problem. Judicial reasoning can be used to refine one's interpretation of regulations, which aim to explore in future work.

Within the limited scope of our paper, Bourcier and Mazzega propose a vision to represent legal documents using networks, wherein legal articles are nodes connected by edges that represent either "legal influences" or quotations, called "legal selection" [3]. They advocate for content-based measures that account for legal effects produced by normative statements [3]. Massey and Antón propose several metrics for measuring regulation dependency and complexity [21]. Our LRSL addresses these needs in three respective ways: 1) by codifying legal influences in typed, priority-based relations (including exemptions, pre-emptions and waivers) that cross-link between portions of regulatory documents; 2) by assigning types to cross-references between individual requirements (a much finer level of detail than Bourcier and Mazzega) that encodes certain legal effects, such as refinement, exception and pre- and post-conditions; and 3) by measuring these relations to quantify complexity exhibited in legal writing styles.

2.1   Writing Legal Requirements Specifications

The Legal Requirements Specification Language (LRSL) makes several assumptions about the domain of legal requirements. These assumptions were first observed in our case study and thus incorporated into the LRSL syntax and semantics described here. As we discuss later, they support what we believe are good requirements specification practices. In addition to these assumptions, the analyst who translates a law into the LRSL uses several techniques that we have previously identified [4, 6]: phrase heuristics to identify modal verbs corresponding to rights, obligations and prohibitions; re-topicalization shifts the subject of a requirement to a principal actor; case-splitting to separate one compound requirement into separate requirements; and balancing rights and obligations to identify inferred requirements.

In the discussion that follows, we use the following excerpt in Figure 1 that was acquired from Arkansas Title 4, §110.105 to present the LRSL.

4-110-105. Disclosure of security breaches.

(a)(1) Any person or business that acquires, owns, or licenses computerized data that includes personal information shall disclose any breach of the security of the system… to any resident of Arkansas…

(2)   The disclosure shall be made in the most expedient time and manner possible and without unreasonable delay, consistent with the legitimate needs of law enforcement as provided in subsection (c) of this section

---

Fig. 1. Excerpt from the Arkansas (AR) Title 4, §110.105 of the Personal Information Protection Act

The analyst converts statements and phrases from the original text into expressions in the LRSL. Figure 2 shows the excerpt from Figure 1 expressed in the LRSL: reserved keywords, special operators, and line numbers along the left side appear in bold. The DOCUMENT keyword (on line 1) assigns a unique index to the specification. The SCHEMA keyword (on line 2) precedes an expression consisting of *components* in curly brackets. Each component corresponds to a different reference level within the document model, beginning with the topmost level, in this case the title and chapter. References within the specification are parsed by the automated parser using this schema. Line comments are denoted by the "//" operator. We use the ellipsis "…" to denote omissions from the specification to simplify presentation in this paper.

The document model consists of sections and nested paragraphs, expressed in the LRSL by the SECTION and PAR keywords, respectively. These keywords are followed by a reference and an optional title: line 5 shows the section reference

4-110-105 followed by the title from Figure 1; sub-paragraphs (a) and (1) follow on lines 6-7.

Requirements consist of roles, pre-conditions and prescriptive clauses, organized into first-order logic expressions using operators "|" for logical-or (see line 9, Figure 2), and "&" for logical-and. Roles are noun phrases that describe the actors or objects to whom the requirements apply. Next follows the *clause*, preceded by a ":" and starting with a verb. Modal verbs indicate requirements, such as "shall" to indicate an obligation (see lines 13 and 16); otherwise, the clause is a pre-condition that is often assumed to be an implied permission (see line 10). Finally, analysts can link categories to requirements using the keyword ANNOTATE (see lines 11 and 17).

```
1    DOCUMENT US-AR-4-110
2    SCHEMA {title:4}-{chapter:110}-{section:\d+}{par:\([a-z]\)}{par:\(\d+\)} //...
3    TITLE 4-110 Personal Information Protection Act
4
5    SECTION 4-110-105 Disclosure of security breaches
6    PAR (a)
7    PAR (1)
8    person
9      | business
10     : acquires, owns, or licenses computerized data that includes personal
         information
11     ANNOTATION implied-permission
12     PRECEDES (a) #2 // comment: a pre-condition
13     : shall disclose a breach of the security of the system to any resident
14   PAR (2)
15   disclosure
16     : shall be made in the most expedient time and manner possible and without
         unreasonable delay
17     ANNOTATE timing-requirements
18     REFINES (1) #2
19     EXCEPT (c)(1) #1
```

Fig. 2. Excerpt from Arkansas 4-110-105 expressed in the LRSL

Cross-references serve to coordinate requirements and constraints expressed in different regions of a regulatory text. In some regulations, cross-references are coarse-grained, meaning they refer to whole paragraphs; in which case, the analyst must determine which specific requirements in that paragraph are intended. The LRSL allows analysts to express coarse references with the added ability to distinguish which requirements they deem as applicable; preserving their interpretation for later review by other analysts and legal counsel.

We discovered three types of cross-references in our case study (see Section 5):

- REFINES, with the inverse relation REFINED-BY, indicates that this requirement is a sub-process or quality attribute that describes how another requirement is fulfilled.
- EXCEPT, with the inverse relation EXCEPT-TO, indicates that this requirement has an exception (another requirement). If the pre-conditions of the exception are satisfied, then this requirement does not apply (it becomes an exclusion, e.g., *is not required*).
- FOLLOWS, with the inverse PRECEDES, indicates that this requirement is a *post-condition* to another requirement, e.g., this requirement is permitted, required, or prohibited after the other requirement is fulfilled.

In Figure 2, the command keyword REFINES (line 18) establishes a refinement relation from the preceding requirement (line 16) to the second requirement (line 13) in paragraph (1). The refinement on line 16 is a quality attribute, because it elaborates when the "disclose" action must occur: "expediently, without delay." Generally, quality attributes refine another requirement's action or object in the LRSL.

Section and paragraph references are either absolute or relative: absolute references begin from the top-level component in the schema and walk each component to the paragraph that contains the target requirement; relative references are matched by the nearest ancestor in the hierarchical schema, beginning with the parent paragraph. References in the LRSL can be expressed as a single paragraph, such as "(1)" or a paragraph range, such as "(1)--(3)". Other operators exist to refer to the last paragraph and all sub-paragraphs (i.e., the transitive closure). Rule selection is done in three ways: a) by default, references select all rules within the referenced paragraphs; b) singular paragraph references followed by the ordinality operator "#" and a number n will identify the nth rule in that paragraph (see lines 12, 18, or 19); and c) references followed by a comma-separated list of annotations will find rules that share those annotations (e.g., all "permissions" or all "timing-requirements"). Finally, multiple references can be joined in logical expressions using simple Boolean logic operators: "&" for logical-and, and "|" for logical-or, and parentheses for associativity.

Definitions describe the actors and objects in the system. In Figure 3, paragraph (a) on lines 4-8 contains a definition for *data storage device*, indicated by the "=" operator. Definitions are expressed using the Boolean logical operators for logical-and and logical-or, in addition to the inclusion operator "<", which means "includes" and precedes examples or sub-classes (see line 7), and the exclusion operator "~", which means "excludes" (see line 13). By default, definitions apply to the paragraph in which they occur, unless instructed otherwise using the INCLUDE keyword, followed by two references: the source paragraph containing the definitions, and the target section or paragraph to which the definitions will apply. The instruction in Figure 3, line 2 tells the parser to apply all the definitions from paragraph (5) and all sub-paragraphs (indicated by the "*") to §215. In contrast, the INCLUDE EXTERNAL instruction on line 15 instructs the parser to lookup the definition "payment card" by finding a regulatory specification indexed by NV-205.602, and to apply this definition to §215. This second usage enables reuse of definitions from and across multiple regulations. In other words, the LRSL supports tracing dependencies from one or more definitions to other definitions and requirements across multiple specifications.

```
1    PAR 5.
2    INCLUDE 603A.215.5* 603A.215*
3    PAR (a)
4    data storage device
5      = device
6      & stores information or data from any electronic or optical medium
7      < computers
8        | cellular telephones
9    // ...
10   PAR (c)
11   facsimile
12     = electronic transmission between two dedicated fax machines using Group 3
         or Group 4 digital formats...
13     ~ onward transmission to a third device after protocol conversion,
         including, but not limited to, any data storage device
14   PAR (d)
15   INCLUDE EXTERNAL NV-205.602 603A.215* "payment card"
```

Fig. 3. Excerpt from Nevada 603A.215(5)(c) expressed in the LRSL

2.2   Tool Support and Generated Artifacts

The LRSL is complemented by an automated parsing tool, which checks the language for syntax errors, such as malformed or unassociated logical expressions, and semantic errors, such as incorrect references, empty relations that refer to no rules, unreferenced definitions, and cycles among relations of the same type, e.g., REFINES, EXCEPT, FOLLOWS. The parser applies Deontic annotations to requirements based on established phrase heuristics [6], and the model created by the parser can then be used to find requirements as needed, e.g., find all the obligatory timing requirements. The parser-constructed model is exportable to other formats, such as the HyperText Markup Language (HTML), the Graph Markup Language (GraphML), and the eXtensible Markup Language (XML). Each format offers a different perspective: the HTML allows users to browse the specification by clicking hyperlinks, viewing definitions and referenced rules *in context* of a single rule; the GraphML allows users to visualize relationships across multiple requirements and identify regulatory patterns, which we discuss in Section 4.2; and the XML enables data inter-operability, which may eventually include exporting the model to the Requirements Interchange Format (RIF) and the User Requirements Notation (URN). Figure 4 shows a graph generated from the LRSL example in Figure 2: text labels include a unique requirement identifier (e.g., AR-7), followed by the requirement clause (abbreviated in this figure). Nodes are colored by whether they are permissions (green), obligations (yellow), and prohibitions (red) based on annotations generated by the phrase heuristics. Directed edges represent relations and point to referenced rules as follows: solid edges are REFINES, dashed edges are EXCEPT, and dotted edges are FOLLOWS relations. This support addresses previously identified limitations in analysis tools, including the need to reference requirements at the statement-level [19, 24] and the need to add types to cross-references [34].

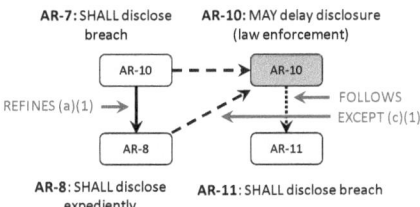

Fig. 4. Excerpt from Arkansas §110.105 expressed in GraphML

3   Research Methodology

Our study aims to describe variation in regulations across multiple jurisdictions. In preparation to achieve this goal, we focus on developing a method to extract and encode these regulations. We selected a single theme (data breach notification) to illustrate dependencies between functional system requirements and personnel responsibilities. In the United States, this theme represents the recent enactment of 46 state and territorial laws from 2002-2011, each governing personal information about state residents. For distributed and pervasive systems, variations in these laws require businesses to reconcile different legally required practices for customers of different states. The laws we selected are as follows:

- **AK**: *Personal Information Protection Act*, Alaska Chapter 45.48, enacted 2009.
- **AR**: *Personal Information Protection Act*, Arkansas Chapter 14.110, enacted 2005.
- **CT**: *Breach of Security Regarding Computerized Data Containing Personal Information*, Connecticut General Statute 36a-701b, enacted 2006.
- **MA**: *Security Breaches*, Massachusetts Chapter 93H, enacted 2007.
- **MA-S**: *Standards for the Protection of Personal Information of Residents of the Commonwealth*, Massachusetts Chapter 17, enacted Sep. 19, 2008.
- **MD**: *Personal Information Protection Act*, Maryland Subtitle 14-35, enacted 2008.
- **MS**: *(no title given)* Mississippi House Bill 583. Enacted 2011.
- **NV**: *Security of Personal Information*, Nevada Chapter 603A, enacted 2006.
- **NY**: *Notification of Unauthorized Acquisition of Personal Information*, New York General Business Law 899-aa, enacted 2005.
- **OR**: *Oregon Consumer Identity Theft Protection Act*, Oregon Chapter 646A, enacted 2008.
- **UT**: *Protection of Personal Information Act*, Chapter 44, enacted 2006.
- **VT**: *Protection of Personal Information*, Vermont Chapter 26, enacted 2007.
- **WI**: *Notice of Unauthorized Access to Personal Information*, Wisconsin Chapter 134.98, enacted 2006.

We down-selected from 46 to 13 laws as follows: first, we surveyed legal expert with seven years of privacy and security law expertise to highlight industrial challenges, resulting in AR, MA-S, MA, MD, and NV; and second, we selected three laws with the largest number of pages, resulting in AK, OR, and VT. The remaining laws had noteworthy, uncharacteristic features: unique (WI) or broad (NY) definitions, the most recent law to expose evolution (MS), interfaces to external agencies (CT), and severe penalties (UT). In addition, we constructed document schemas for 49 data breach laws to validate the construction of SCHEMA expressions across a larger dataset.

Two investigators (the authors) separately translated each statement in each law using the LRSL. The translation includes a general classification of each statement, as a definition, requirement, exemption, etc., and writing an expression in the language to characterize the statement. Definitions were identified by key phrases, such as "*x* means *y*", where a term *x* has the logical definition *y*. Requirements and exemptions were identified using phrase heuristics identified by Breaux et al. [6]. Comments were used in the translation to capture questions, issues and other discrepancies. We maintained a *caveats list* of translation strategies that reflect unusual cases and how the parser should treat such cases, and a *proposed changes list* of requirements with examples for new language constructs. For each new construct, we reviewed each law to update the translation to ensure consistency across the entire dataset. Corbin and Strauss state, "The essential element of theory is that categories are interrelated into a larger theoretical scheme" and a theory represents an "abstract rendition of that raw data" [10]. In this regard, the LRSL is an expression of a grounded theory in a context-free grammar that explains how legal requirements are expressed. The theory extends prior theoretical findings [8] and consists of concepts (rights, obligations, permissions, etc.) and cross-reference relationships (refinements, exceptions and pre- and post-conditions) that link these concepts together and explains how to trace legal definitions and requirements across a legal text. Our analysis checked for internal consistency, and if the language covers variations across all cases that we studied.

Grounded theories are limited to studied cases and new cases may invalidate the theory.

4   Research Findings

The translation of thirteen laws by two investigators (the authors) yielded 808 statements, required an average of 2.26 minutes per statement with the longest document consisting of 148 statements and requiring an average of 5.5 hours. Each investigator spent an average total of 30.5 hours to encode the thirteen laws. Figures 5 and 6 present summary statistics for the units of analysis encoded in the LRSL. Recall these laws cover the same theme (data breach notification). We observed the number of definitions did not vary greatly and that the number of exemptions was a matter of writing style; neither definitions nor exemptions are proportional to the number of requirements in this dataset.

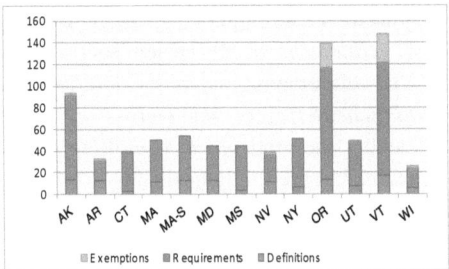
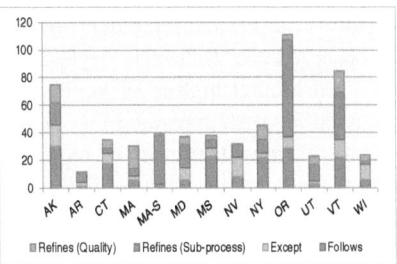

Fig. 5. Summary Units of Analysis– Statements   **Fig. 6.** Summary Units of Analysis – Reference

The references reported in Figure 6 originate from multiple origins, including: *anaphora*, which is indicated by determiners (e.g., such) and pronouns (e.g., this); *case-splitting*, which is indicated by English conjunctions (and, or) separating verb clauses that follow a modal phrase (e.g., must, may, shall); and direct references to sections and paragraph that may be anaphoric (*this* section, *this* paragraph) or indexed by paragraph number, such as "paragraph (a)." Table 1 presents summary statistics for each of these observed origins. For direct references, we present the number of corresponding rules identified by the original reference for each regulation, called *direct literal* (dL), and the number of corresponding rules indexed by the operationalized reference using the LRSL language construct, called *direct indexed* (dI). Because the operationalized references are more precise, we can calculate the ambiguity loss, which is the proportion of false positives referenced by an ambiguous cross-reference and which we express as (dL – dI) / dL. The operationalized references expressed in the LRSL, which allow analysts to link requirements to only true positives, reduce reference ambiguity by 50-93%.

Table 1. Cross-Reference Origins and Ambiguity

State Law	Anaphora	Case Split	Direct	Direct Literal	Direct Indexed	Ambiguity Reduction
AR	2	4	5	24	7	0.708
AK	16	19	35	143	36	0.748
CT	8	3	3	14	5	0.642
MA	20	1	3	45	3	0.933
MA-S	4	34	1	2	1	0.500
MD	4	12	21	62	23	0.629
MS	7	4	6	19	6	0.684
NV	7	3	13	83	14	0.831
NY	16	6	8	41	17	0.585
OR	29	15	24	190	24	0.874
UT	3	12	17	136	40	0.706
VT	36	10	25	269	32	0.881
WI	6	0	18	78	20	0.744

We developed metrics to measure stylistic properties that affect the extent to which an analyst must make inferences to resolve requirements ambiguity. Using the metrics, we observed the following styles: *cascading refinement* occurs when sections are organized around high-level goals in which goal-refinements and post-conditions are expressed in nested paragraphs; *reference uniqueness* occurs when cross-references refer to the fewest number of requirements, ideally one; and *block formatting* occurs when the paragraphs contains multiple requirements, but are rarely nested.

We now discuss other observations from this case study.

4.1   Shaping Conditionality and Coverage

Conditionality is the extent to which a legal requirement is conditioned by *who stakeholders are* and *what events have occurred*, which we call pre-conditions. Definitions and exemptions shape conditionality by relaxing or tightening the meaning of terms and thus scaling the number of possible situations those terms cover. We discuss two ways that these effects are observed through the LRSL: (1) cross-linking of terms-of-art to paragraphs and to pre-conditions, requirement clauses and other definitions; and (2), cross-linking of exemptions to modify pre-conditions and clauses.

The LRSL parser automatically cross-links definitions to requirements by matching terms-of-art in definitions with phrases in. Recall from Figure 3 the definitions for terms *data storage device* (line 4) and *facsimile* (line 11) and the imported term payment card (line 15) from another law, NV §205.602. The instructions INCLUDE (lines 2 and 15) orchestrate these definitions by applying them to all sub-paragraphs in §603A.215. This includes linking to other definitions, such as the phrase on line 13 that excludes "data storage device" from the onward transmission of a facsimile. Figure 7 illustrates this linking to requirements in paragraphs §603A.215(1) and (2): the underlined phrases match the terms-of-art from Figure 3 as determined by the parser. Both *when to apply* a prescription and *the extent of* the prescription can be computationally adjusted by relaxing or tightening definitions using the includes "<" and excludes "~" operators, respectively.

```
1    SECTION 603A.215
2    PAR 1.
3    data collector
4      : does business in this State
5      : accepts a payment card in connection with a sale of goods or services
6      : shall comply with the current version of the Payment Card Industry (PCI)
             Data Security Standard...
7      FOLLOWS #1 & #2
8    PAR 2.
9    data collector
10     : does business in this State
11     EXCEPT 1.
12   PAR (a)
13     : does not use encryption to ensure the security of electronic transmission
14     : shall not transfer any personal information through an electronic, non-
             voice transmission other than a facsimile to a person outside of the
             secure system of the data collector
15     FOLLOWS 2. #1 & 2.(a) #1
16   PAR (b)
17     : does not use encryption to ensure the security of the information
18     : shall not move any data storage device containing personal information
             beyond the logical or physical controls of the data collector or its data
             storage contractor
19     FOLLOWS 2. #1 & 2.(b) #1
```

Fig. 7. Excerpt from Nevada §603A.215(1) and (2)

For example, if we redefine *payment card* to exclude *gift card*, then the scope of when to apply the requirement to comply with the PCI DSS standard (on line 8, Figure 10) would be further restricted to omit the case of gift cards. Alternatively, if *data storage device* were redefined to include *USB drives*, then the extent of the prohibition on moving such devices (on line 18, Figure 7) would be extended to include this interpretation. The ability to shape *when to apply* and *the extent of prescriptions* using the LRSL can enable regulators and businesses to evolve conditionality as new technologies emerge over time.

Whereas definitions shape terms used in pre-conditions and requirements clauses, exemptions fine-tune what is excluded from pre-conditions and clauses. Figure 8 shows a description of the role "telecommunications provider" with a role constraint on line 4. The EXEMPT keyword instructs the parser to exclude this role and constraint from all rules in §215 and all sub-paragraphs therein. While such an exemption could be stated in a definition using the excludes operator "~", exemptions provide a mechanism to tighten meanings across a document cross-section, unbounded by a single term-of-art or definition.

```
1    PAR 4.
2    PAR (a)
3    telecommunications provider
4      : acts solely in the role of conveying the communications of other persons,
             regardless of the mode of conveyance used...
5      EXEMPT 603A.215 *
```

Fig. 8. Excerpt from Nevada §603A.215(4)(a) expressed in LRSL

Figure 9 illustrates how constraints, expressed as definitions and exemptions, are traced by the parser through parser instructions. The INCLUDE EXTERNAL instruction imports (in purple) the *payment card* definition from another regulation, NV 205.602, into NV 603A.215(5)(d). The INCLUDE instruction maps (in blue) the definitions from 603A.215(5), including any imported definitions, onto 603A.215; this mapping includes the inner link from *data storage device* to *facsimile*, and the outer links to requirements in 603A.215(1) and (2). Last, the exemption 603A.215(4)(a) is mapped (in red) onto requirements 603A.215 to exclude interpretations implied by definitions.

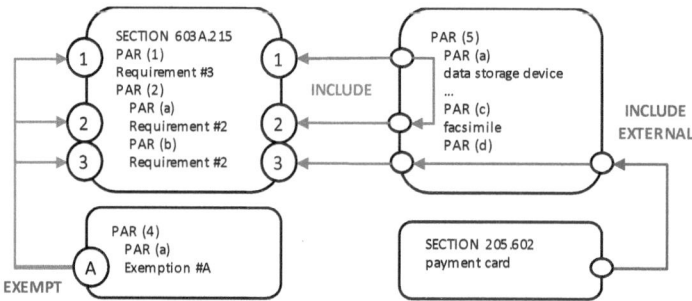

Fig. 9. Summarizing the Effects of Conditionality

4.2   Regulatory Specification Patterns

When visualized graphically, the LRSL-encoded regulations reveal several regulatory specification patterns. Visual specifications have been hypothesized to improve requirements comprehension [12]. These patterns describe legal mechanisms for prescribing the behavior of personnel and systems in the environment. In Figure 4, we presented the first pattern, called a *suspension*, in which a permission (AR-10) is an exception to an obligation (AR-7) and satisfying the pre-conditions of the permission causes the obligation to be suspended. We now discuss three other patterns: system design alternatives and scaling restrictions; standards and indemnification; and limited exceptions for legacy systems. We believe these patterns can be re-used in writing new regulations and standards or for identifying similar dependencies among requirements.

Figure 10 shows three system design options for sending written (MD-15), electronic (MD-16) and telephonic (MD-17) notices as means for notifying individuals, data owners and data licensees of a security breach under MD §14.3504(e); note the arc indicating the "or" relationship between these options means only one option is necessary to discharge the obligations MD-10 and MD-7. These alternatives are intended to allow businesses to leverage a diverse set of contact options based on the level of technological sophistication of the business. In addition, the exception MD-18 permits a substitute notice via statewide media and other broadcast mechanisms, when the cost of notification becomes too prohibitive. This type of scaling mechanism (a permitted exception conditioned on measurable limits of effect size, in this case a finite number of notices or monetary value) can be used to control regulatory system costs across an entire industry.

Figure 11 shows the combined uses of deference to external standards with indemnification from NV §603A.215. The Payment Card Industry Data Security Standard (PCI-DSS), cited in NV-5, prescribes several technical security requirements for businesses that handle payment cards. In Figure 11, a business is prohibited (in red) from transferring data (NV-6) or moving data storage devices (NV-7), excluding facsimiles. However, complying with the PCI-DSS standard (in yellow, NV-5) is an exception that permits transferring data and moving devices. Whether a business chooses to accept the more prohibitive restrictions or to comply with the exception, NV §603A.215 prohibits the business from being liable for data breach damages. This prohibition is an example of a *safe harbor*, which is a regulatory mechanism designed to encourage industry to act against uncertainty (the uncertain costs of data breach damages vs. the more certain and predictable costs of PCI-DSS compliance).

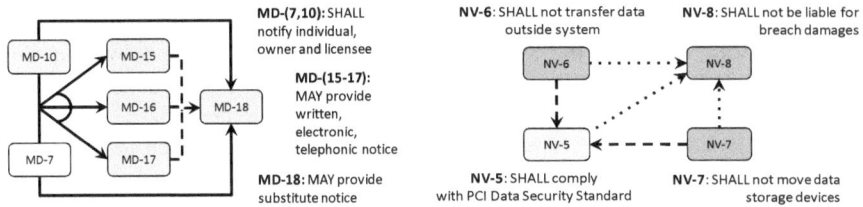

Fig. 10. System Design Alternatives and Scaling **Fig. 11.** External Standards and Indemnification Restrictions

In Figure 12, the State of Vermont describes a set of prohibitions (in red, VT-40 through VT-43) on the use of Social Security Numbers (SSNs) of Vermont residents. In the United States, SSNs are issued by the government for tracking government-sponsored pensions, but have over time been used to track individuals for other purposes, such as health benefits and credit-based services, including cellular telephones, utilities, loans and credit cards. Because of the prevalent and historic use of SSNs to authenticate and identify individuals, VT §62.2440(c)(8)(A) includes an exception, which permits (in green) continuous use of SSNs to accommodate legacy systems. Continuous use includes the follow-on obligations (in yellow) to notify residents about such use (VT-48) and provide the option to halt such use (VT-49). Such exceptions provide businesses with the ability to scale their business practices to a new standard of care based on individual consumer preferences over time.

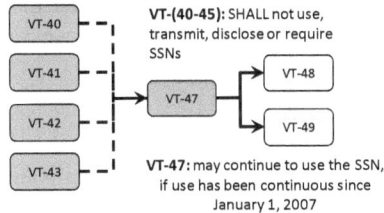

Fig. 12. Limited Exceptions for Legacy Systems

As technology evolves, we foresee increasingly design-invasive regulations that can potentially limit the range of solutions available to a designer. Thus, we believe patterns such as these should be part of the requirements nomenclature, to aid businesses in understanding the scope and implication of regulations on system design.

5   Threats to Validity

In grounded analysis, multiple analysts derive theoretical constructs from a dataset to describe or explain the data; these insights only generalize to that dataset [10]. Because we selected a single theme (data breach notification), our theory may not be externally valid in other domains, such as medical devices or aviation. However, we did validate the schema notation and document model by systematically inspecting data breach notification laws in all 46 U.S. states and territories, two U.S. Federal regulations (HIPAA Privacy Rule and the Section 508 Access Standards), the European Union Directive 95/46/EC and a Canadian privacy law (PIPEDA). We found the schema sufficiently robust to model these documents and their cross-references.

Construct validity is the correctness of operational measures used to collect data, build theory and report findings [35]. To improve construct validity, we maintained a *caveats list* of translation strategies that reflect unusual cases and how the parser should treat such cases, and a *proposed changes list* of requirements with examples for new language constructs. As new constructs were introduced, we reviewed each previously encoded law to update the translation to reflect the new construct to ensure consistency across the translated datasets. In addition, we developed analytic tools using the parser and a research database to collect all the statistics reported, here.

Internal validity is the extent to which measured variables cause observable effects within the data [35]. Our results show that writing styles can positively or negatively impact reference ambiguity and ambiguity loss, as measured by our LRSL translation presented in Table 1. New research is needed to evaluate if these styles affect an analyst's ability to resolve cross-references and locate relevant requirements.

External validity describes the extent to which a theory generalizes. While two investigators have applied the LRSL in 13 cases, further evaluation is needed to know to what extent others can apply the language with the same effects and to what extent the language is complete.

Reliability describes the consistency of the theory to describe or explain environmental phenomena over repeated observations [35]. To improve reliability, both investigators (the authors) separately translated the datasets into the LRSL and compared their results to identify alternate modes of expression and language caveats.

6   Discussion and Summary

In this paper, we introduce a legal requirements specification language (LRSL) for codifying legal requirements with typed cross-references. In Section 4, we show how the LRSL can be used to shape conditionality of regulatory coverage, which is enabled by the tool-supported ability to trace definitions across a single regulation, or across multiple regulations as definitions are shared across laws. Reusing technical terminology improves requirements engineering practices, as it avoids misconceptions among stakeholders and competing viewpoints that introduce inconsistency into design specifications [33]. Zave and Jackson have noted the importance of grounding terminology in the reality of the environment to which a machine will be built [37]. Increasingly, this includes the *legal reality* as software systems contribute to social and environmental hazards and regulators attempt to shape the outcome of automation by defining legal boundaries that limit the behavior of information systems and software-supported practices. By systematically tracing and encoding legal terms, constraints and requirements, we believe the LRSL can aide engineers at design time to manage this changing reality, while also supporting users who are responsible for deployment and maintenance. The work to write better software requirements and realize how software satisfies a particular legal constraint, however, is still outside our findings.

In addition, we discovered several regulatory requirements patterns that become visually salient and enable measuring different styles of regulatory document construction. These patterns, described in Section 4.3, include strategies for pairing permitted refinements to the obligations that they refine to create design alternatives that allow organizations to scale their information practices over time. A similar pattern invokes prohibitions with limited exceptions to accommodate legacy systems: this pattern effectively expires the legacy system as the exceptions are discharged over the life of the new system. Finally, a third pattern uses indemnification to encourage design changes to accommodate increased security. We envision requirements analysts using these patterns in several ways. First, analysts may be trained to identify these and similar patterns from the LRSL-generated graph. Identifying these patterns can help analysts see higher-order constructs, such as temporary suspensions of duties and legal indemnification. Second, these patterns can be used to compare and contrast regulatory mechanisms across regulations: indemnification is an incentive to reduce legal liability, whereas design alternatives are a legal means to accommodate variation in practices. Because we only observed these patterns in a few cases, however, further evidence must be collected to understand the extent to which regulators reproduce these patterns. That said, the LRSL's ability to transform the encoded regulatory specifications into corresponding graphs enables visualizing this higher-order information and provides analysts with access to this regulatory information described in the regulation.

The LRSL only begins to address a small part of the larger problem, however. Laws include statutes that govern regulatory agencies, regulations created by those agencies to govern industry, and informal agency guidance intended to help companies interpret laws. In addition, court proceedings describe judicial interpretations of regulations. While the LRSL is not a legal document, it provides an intermediary artifact that legal and requirements analysts can use to engage in discussing compliance strategies. These discussions may link legal opinion and context to the LRSL-generated artifacts as a means to preserve rationale and enable traceability.

We further envision the LRSL capabilities as enabling document authors to design and debug specifications, to remove ambiguity and organize requirements around central themes. The LRSL's ability to reuse and extend definitions and link to regulatory rules across multiple regulations supports our vision of requirements as open, dynamically evolving systems, wherein the discovery of conflicts becomes increasingly critical to creating regulatory harmony. Finally, the LRSL parser supports several features that can be used to "debug" regulatory specifications, by identifying cycles in cross-references, definitions for terms not used in the regulation, and possible conflicts or contradictions through visual inspection of the generated graphs. We believe these techniques can benefit both regulators who write regulations as well as requirements engineers and software designers who seek to understand the regulation and seek guidance from their corporate legal compliance office. We found the time required to translate the regulations into the LRSL well worth the ability to debug and analyze the relations using the LRSL-generated model.

Acknowledgment. This research was supported by the U.S. Department of Homeland Security (Award #2006-CS-001-000001), Hewlett-Packard Labs (Award #CW267287) and ONR Award #N00244-12-1-0014.

References

[1] Allen, L.E., Saxon, C.S.: Better language, better thought, better communication: the a-hohfeld language for legal analysis. In: 5th Int'l Conf. AI & Law, pp. 219–228 (1995)

[2] Biagioli, C., Mariani, P., Tiscornia, D.: ESPLEX: A rule and conceptual model for representing statutes. In: Proc. 1st Int'l Conf. AI & Law, pp. 240–251 (1987)

[3] Bourcier, D., Mazzega, P.: Toward measures of complexity in legal systems. In: Int'l Conf. AI & Law, pp. 211–215 (2007)

[4] Breaux, T.D., Antón, A.I.: Analyzing Regulatory Rules for Privacy and Security Requirements. IEEE Transactions on Software Engineering 34(1), 5–20 (2008)

[5] Breaux, T.D., Antón, A.I., Doyle, J.: Semantic parameterization: a process for modeling domain descriptions. ACM Trans. Soft. Engr. Method. 18(2), 5 (2008)

[6] Breaux, T.D., Vail, M.W., Antón, A.I.: Towards compliance: extracting rights and obligations to align requirements with regulations. In: 14th IEEE Int'l Req'ts Engr. Conf., pp. 49–58 (2006)

[7] Breaux, T.D.: Exercising due diligence in legal requirements acquisition: a tool-supported, frame-based approach. In: IEEE 17th Int'l Req'ts Engr. Conf., pp. 225–230 (2009)

[8] Breaux, T.D.: Legal requirements acquisition for the specification of legally compliance informaiton systems, North Carolina State Univ. Ph.D. thesis (2009)

[9] Bench-Capon, T.J.M.: Deep models, normative reasoning and legal expert systems. In: Proc. 2nd International Conference on Artificial Intelligence and Law, Vancouver, British Columbia, Canada, pp. 37–45 (1989)

[10] Corbin, J., Strauss, A.: Basics of Qualitative Research, 3rd edn. Sage Pubs (2008)

[11] Dardenne, A., Fickas, S., van Lamsweerde, A.: Goal–directed requirements acquisition. Sci. Comp. Prog. 20, 3–50 (1993)

[12] Dulac, N., Viguier, T., Leveson, N., Storey, M.-A.: On the use of visualization in formal requirements specification. In: IEEE Joint Int'l Conf. Req'ts Engr., pp. 71–80 (2002)

[13] Fraser, M.D., Kumar, K., Vaishnavi, V.K.: Informal and formal requirements specification languages: bridging the gap. IEEE Trans. Soft. Engr. 17(5), 454–466 (1991)

[14] Fuxman, A., Liu, L., Mylopoulos, J., Pistore, M., Roveri, M., Traverso, P.: Specifying and analyzing early requirements in Tropos. Req'ts Engr. Journal 9(2), 132–150 (2004)

[15] Giorgini, P., Massacci, F., Mylopoulos, J., Zannone, N.: Modeling security requirements through ownership, permissions and delegation. In: IEEE 13th Int'l Req'ts Engr. Conf., pp. 167–176 (2005)

[16] Greenspan, S., Mylopoulos, J., Borgida, A.: On Formal Requirements Modeling Languages: RML Revisited. In: 6th IEEE Int'l Soft. Engr. Conf., pp. 1–13 (1994)

[17] Glinz, M., Berner, S., Joos, S.: Object-oriented modeling with ADORA. Info. Sys. 27, 425–444 (2002)

[18] Hohfeld, W.N.: Some fundamental legal conceptions as applied in judicial reasoning. The Yale Law Journal 23(1), 16–59 (1913)

[19] Lauritsen, M., Gordon, T.F.: Toward a general theory of document modeling. In: Int'l Conf. AI & Law, pp. 202–211 (2009)

[20] Levene, A.A., Mullery, G.P.: An investigation of requirement specification languages: theory and practice. IEEE Computer 15(5), 50–59 (1982)

[21] Massey, A.K., Anton, A.I.: Triage for legal requirements. NCSU Technical Report #TR-2010-22 (October 11, 2010)

[22] Maxwell, J., Anton, A.I.: Developing production rule models to aid in acquiring requirements from legal texts. In: IEEE 17th Int'l Req'ts Engr. Conf., pp. 101–110 (2009)

[23] Maxwell, J., Anton, A.I., Swire, P.: A legal cross-references taxonomy for identifying conflicting software requirements. In: IEEE 19th Int'l Req'ts Engr. Conf., pp. 197–206 (2011)

[24] Martinek, J., Cybulka, J.: Dynamics of legal provisions and its representation. In: Int'l Conf. AI & Law, pp. 20–24 (2005)

[25] Mernik, M., Heering, J., Sloane, A.M.: When and how to develop domain-specific languages. ACM Computing Surveys 37(4), 316–344 (2005)

[26] Mylopoulos, J., Borgida, A., Jarke, M., Koubarakis, M.: Telos: representing knowledge about information systems. ACM Trans. on Info. Sys. 8(4), 325–362 (1990)

[27] Romanosky, S., Telang, R., Acquisti, A.: Do data breach disclosure laws reduce identity theft? In: W'shp Econ. of Info. Sec. (WEIS), June 25-28 (2008)

[28] Rubinstein, I.: Privacy and Regulatory Innovation: Moving Beyond Voluntary Codes. I/S: A Journal of Law and Policy for the Information Society (April 2011) (in press)

[29] Sergot, M.J., Sadri, F., Kowalski, R.A., Kriwaczek, F., Hammond, P., Cory, H.T.: The British Nationality Act as a logic program. Communications of the ACM 29(5), 370–386 (1986)

[30] Sergot, M.: A computational theory of normative positions. ACM Transactions of Computational Logic 2(4), 581–622 (2001)

[31] Siena, A., Jureta, I., Ingolfo, S., Susi, A., Perini, A., Mylopoulos, J.: Capturing variability of law with Nomós 2. In: 31st Int'l Conf. Conc. Mod., pp. 383–396 (2012)

[32] Stamper, R.K.: LEGOL: Modelling legal rules by computer. In: Proc. Advanced Workshop on Computer Science and Law, pp. 45–71 (September 1979)

[33] Wasson, K.S.: A case study in systematic improvement of language for requirements. In: Proc. IEEE 14th Int'l Req'ts Engr. Conf., pp. 6–15 (2006)

[34] Winkels, R., Boer, A., de Maat, E., van Engers, T., Breebaart, M., Melger, H.: Constructing a semantic network for legal content. In: Int'l Conf. AI & Law, pp. 125–132 (2005)

[35] Yin, R.K.: Case study research, 4th edn. Applied Social Research Methods Series, vol. 5. Sage Publications (2008)

[36] Yu, E.: Modeling organizations for information systems requirements engineering. In: Int'l Symp. Req'ts Engr., pp. 34–41 (1993)

[37] Zave, P., Jackson, M.: Four dark corners of requirements engineering. ACM Trans. Soft. Engr. & Method. 6(1), 1–30 (1997)

A Survey on Usage Scenarios for Requirements Traceability in Practice

Elke Bouillon, Patrick Mäder, and Ilka Philippow

Department of Software Systems, Ilmenau Technical University
Ilmenau, Germany
{elke.bouillon,patrick.maeder,ilka.philippow}@tu-ilmenau.de

Abstract. **[Context and motivation]** Requirements traceability is known as an important part of development projects. Studies showed that traceability is applied in practice, but insufficient tool- and method-support hinders its practical use. **[Question/problem]** We conducted a survey to understand which traceability usage scenarios are most relevant for practitioners. Gaining this information is a required step for providing better traceability support to practitioners. **[Principal ideas/results]** We identified a list of 29 regularly cited usage scenarios and asked practitioners to assess the frequency of use for each in a typical development project. Our analysis is restricted to those 56 participants that were actively using traceability in order to ensure comparable results. Subjects held various roles in the development and reported about diverse projects. **[Contribution]** This study provides not only an initial catalog of usage scenarios and their relevance, but also provides insights on practitioner's traceability practices. In result, we found all scenarios to be used by practitioners. Participants use traceability especially for: finding origin and rationale of requirements, documenting a requirement's history, and tracking requirement or task implementation state. Furthermore, we highlight topics for ongoing evaluation and better method and tool support in the area of requirements traceability.

Keywords: requirements traceability, traceability usage, usage scenario.

1 Introduction

Requirements traceability is an important part of a software development process and defined as the "ability to follow the life of a requirement in both a backward and forward direction" [8]. Traceability influences the quality of software products positively, supports changes throughout the development life cycle and eases reuse of software assets [7, 19, 21]. The importance of traceability is also demonstrated, as it is a precondition for the development of safety-critical systems in various domains, e.g., in aerospace (ISO12207, DO-178B), and in railways (EN50128). In addition, traceability is required for a certified development process according to process standards like CMMI, SPICE and the telecom TL9000. Nevertheless, numerous authors also point out that the practical use of traceability is often hindered by problems in its implementation and application, [2, 8 16, 17]. There are five main problems: (1) high

J. Doerr and A.L. Opdahl (Eds.): REFSQ 2013, LNCS 7830, pp. 158–173, 2013.

manual effort for up-to-date traceability links, (2) ad-hoc traceability without strategy, (3) insufficient tool support, (4) creator and user of links are often not identical, and (5) distributed development projects require traceability across organizational boundaries.

The community of traceability researchers agrees on the fact that project-specific traceability strategies are required for a successful traceability implementation [6, 10, 21]. However, that does not mean that each traceability strategy and their parts are unique. Our hypothesis is that parts of a strategy are reusable across different projects.

Currently, very little is known about how practitioners use traceability and what they demand from it [17]. We agree with Winkler and von Pilgrim that it is an important research task to study traceability practices in order to propose and develop traceability support that suits practical needs [21]. With traceability practice, we mean the way in which traceability is used by practitioners. As a way to overcome this problem, we propose the identification, the analysis and the definition of practical usage scenarios for requirements traceability. This paper focuses especially on the first step, the identification of usage scenarios. By usage scenario, we are referring to recurring situations in which requirements traceability is used for supporting a development activity. Throughout the paper, we are using the terms usage scenario, scenario, and activity interchangeably. We consider the following information relevant for capturing a traceability usage scenario:

- The development activity that is supported or enabled by the use of traceability
- The goal of traceability in this scenario
- Participating development artifacts
- Required traceability links, their granularity, and their properties
- Stakeholder roles participating in the scenario
- A scenario flow involving links, artifacts, and roles
- A creation and update strategy for required traces
- Relevance and usage intensity of the scenario

While part of that information is invariant across different projects, other parts are dependent on project specifics like size, domain, or applied development process. The goal is to abstract from such variations where possible and to capture alternatives where required. As a result, we propose to create a catalog of traceability usage scenarios. That catalog will help users, tool vendors, and researchers to develop better traceability practices, tailored automations and training material for practitioners. In this paper, we are reporting about a survey with focus on the identification of scenarios, their usage intensity, and their relation to characteristics of the project.

This paper is structured as follows. Section 2, summarizes key prior traceability studies. Section 3 states our research questions, describes the designed survey and profiles the subjects and projects involved in our study. Our findings are reported in Section 4. Section 5 discusses the results of the survey and its limitations are considered in Section 6. We draw conclusions in Section 7 and discuss future work.

2   Related Work

In the past, two larger traceability studies were conducted, analyzing the use of requirements traceability in practice.

Gotel and Finkelstein [8] reported in 1992 about a study with the aim of finding an explanation for the weak application of requirements traceability in practice, despite its numerous scientifically cited benefits. Major findings were that support for pre-requirements traceability should be improved and that problems existed especially with the process and its stakeholder. They found multiple perspectives on what traceability was expected to enable and on the problems experienced, conflicts particularly evident between those parties responsible for establishing traceability and those parties using it (not always identical people). Further, they found that pre-requirements traceability, referring back to the origin or the source of a requirement was in need of more attention, so the need to integrate a wider variety of data in traceability, such as source material and the people involved in the project.

Ramesh and Jarke [15] carried out a several year study at the end of the 1990s. The authors investigated especially the impact of individual factors, such as employee motivation or organizational and technical support on the use of traceability. Within this study two reference models for requirements traceability were developed. These models meet the needs of high-end and low-end traceability users at the time of the study and show the activities that the participants wanted to be supported.

Furthermore, several smaller studies focused on the state of practice in traceability [1, 4, 11, 12]. These studies aimed to identify reasons for rare use of requirements traceability in practice and derived relevant research questions. As a result, all studies recognize a discrepancy between the extensive research in the field and its current practical application. However, recent studies confirm that traceability is a topic of large interest in development projects and that it is implemented in projects to some extend [12]. Nonetheless, authors also found that traceability is rarely used. None of the discussed studies focused on concrete usage scenarios, but instead evaluated traceability in general. We found across all studies examples of possible traceability usage scenarios and incorporated them in our survey. Additionally, von Knethen and Paech [20] discuss particular interests of individual stakeholders in traceability. Spanoudakis and Zisman [19] refer to a number of possible usage scenarios for traceability. Finally, Winkler and Pilgrim [21] also collected possible usage scenarios for traceability.

Despite of all these efforts, little is still known about the practical use of traceability in development projects [17]. In order to provide better project-specific support for requirements traceability, we need to answer the following research questions: (RQ1) What are practical applications of requirements traceability? (RQ2) How important is each usage scenario and how often is it applied?

3   Set-Up of the Survey

We intended that study to be an initial attempt in identifying traceability usage scenarios and in assessing their importance. A number of empirical research methods is suitable for software engineering problems and offers different benefits and drawbacks [13, 18]. We decided to perform a survey as it facilitates high numbers of participants and allows for the recognition of trends [18]. Subjects invest only a limited amount of time and can schedule the participation according to their needs.

3.1   Objective of the Survey

Our study had the goal of understanding the current state of practice in traceability usage. Specifically, we were interested in finding relevant usage scenarios and in quantitative data about how regular scenarios are applied in development projects.

3.2   Collecting Scenario Candidates

In order to create a comprehensive list of usage scenario candidates, we started to gather information from the three main literature surveys previously conducted on requirements traceability: Spanoudakis and Zisman [19], von Knethen and Paech [20], and Winkler and Pilgrim [21]. All provide lists of development activities supported by traceability (see Section 2). Furthermore, we analyzed a number of publications on requirements traceability and selected those that referred to applications of traceability. We found the studies discussed in the related work section very useful and also the following publications [9, 10]. We also analyzed websites, forums e.g. [3] and studied tool documentations.

We removed redundancies and consolidated similar activities where appropriate. Eventually, we identified a list of 29 activities that were mentioned as being supported by requirements traceability. We grouped these usage scenario candidates into six groups referring to typical facets of development processes: requirements engineering and management, project management, compliance demonstration, design and implementation, testing, and maintenance and evolution. We presented grouped scenarios together in order to support subjects in understanding the context of scenarios.

1) Requirements Engineering and Management	Source
a) Finding origin and rationale of requirements, i.e., pre-requirements traceability to regulatory and other source of a requirement	[1, 8, 9, 10, 11, 19, 21]
b) Refinement and detailing requirements	[10, 11, 15, 19]
c) Documenting a requirement's history, i.e., to be able to trace to previous versions of a requirement in order to find out about changes	[15, 19]
d) Identifying stakeholders for the ongoing development of the requirements	[1, 8, 11, 15]
e) Quality- and maturity-analysis of requirements	[10, 11, 15, 20]
f) Impact analysis, which other stakeholders are important by a change to a requirement	[19]
2) Project Management	
a) Tracking the state of requirement or task implementation in detail	[9, 11, 12, 20, 21]
b) Initial Release planning	[10, 21]
c) Progress assessment on project or subproject level for getting an overview of already implemented requirements	[9, 10, 20]
d) Task assignment to stakeholders, e.g., assignment of a requirement to a developer for implementation	Tool documentation
e) Notification of stakeholders about changes, e.g., after a change to a requirement all owners of dependent artifacts are automatically informed	Tool documentation
f) Adjusting project and release plan, e.g., in case of time limit exceeding	Suggested by pretester

3) Compliance Demonstration	
a) Analyzing requirements coverage in source code, e.g., for the customer	[9, 10, 12, 15, 19, 20, 21]
b) Traceability documentation for certification purposes	[9, 10, 11, 15, 21]
c) Justification of all written code based on specification for certification purposes	[10, 20, 21]
4) Design and Implementation	
a) Navigation between specification, design, test, and code via traces	[12, 21]
b) Navigation within artifacts of the same type, e.g., within source code	[12]
c) Design assessment based on traceability metrics, e.g., to find components that contain too much functionality and should be split	[19, 21]
d) Understanding of software artifacts, e.g., project familiarization of development team members	[15, 20]
5) Testing	
a) Development of test cases based on requirements	[1, 10, 11, 15, 20, 21]
b) Defect location within the source code for failed test cases	[11, 21]
c) Discovering regression tests to be executed after code change	[10, 15, 20]
d) Test coverage analysis of specification and code	[1, 10, 11, 15, 21]
e) Stakeholder identification for understanding behavior and solving complicated problems	[21]
6) Maintenance and Evolution	
a) Change impact analysis to determine artifacts impacted by a feature extension	[9, 10, 11, 12, 15, 19, 20, 21]
b) Change effort estimation for feature extensions	[9, 19, 20, 21]
c) Feature location and support during change implementation via use of traces	[12]
d) Reuse of specification and code components, e.g., a feature with all its implementation	[19, 21]
e) Knowledge transfer to the maintenance team, e.g., in cases where a team performs maintenance that does not include any of to original team members	[11, 12, 15, 21]

3.3   Implementation of the Survey

We aimed to address and attract participants with a variety of different roles and scopes in a typical development process. Therefore, we focused on a clear structure and generally understandable language within the questionnaire. The number of questions was reduced to a minimum in order to not annoy participants. Where appropriate, questions were complemented with a text field for capturing feedback and for capturing usage scenarios not covered in our list. The survey was implemented with Unipark EFS Survey. The language of the questionnaire was German [5].

The main part of the questionnaire referred to the 29 identified usage scenario candidates and evaluated their frequency of application within the whole project a subject reported about. Evaluating the concrete frequency in which traceability is used to support a certain development activity is difficult. Projects, developments procedures and the perception of participants vary a lot. Activities may be performed daily, others only when certain milestones are reached. Accordingly, we asked subjects to estimate the frequency in which a particular scenario is used to support a given development activity as one of the three categories: regularly, occasionally, or never. We explained that regularly should be chosen, if traceability is applied more than half of the times that an activity is performed and occasionally otherwise.

3.4   Pretest

We performed a two-stage pretest to improve questionnaire quality. First, we asked five colleagues, familiar with the topic, to complete the questionnaire and to give suggestions for improvements. Their feedback helped us in getting a coherent structure, in correcting errors, and in improving linguistic accuracy. Second, we asked five members of the target group to complete the questionnaire and to give feedback on problems they encountered. This feedback was used in creating the final version of the questionnaire. Pretest data was not used for the actual analysis.

3.5 Participants

We defined our target group as traceability-applying stakeholders of software development projects. In order to attract participants, we advertised the study at workshops and meetings of practitioner communities focused on requirements engineering and software quality. Moreover, we used social networks and forums to advertise the study in virtual practitioner groups, relevant to the focus of the study. We asked subjects to only participate, if they had an almost complete overview of the traceability usage within the project they reported about, ensuring high-quality results. As incentive for participating in the study, we offered a report with the study's results.

Over a period of 6 weeks (October – December 2011), 369 subjects visited the initial page of the survey. 117 out of these subjects responded to one or more questions. We assume that subjects that do not use traceability often just did not respond at all. Our survey does not allow us to reason about how many participants adopt traceability in practice. However, that was not the goal of our study. We decided not to use partly answered questionnaires in order to ensure high data quality and to be able to compare usage rates of traceability scenarios between another. The resulting list includes 56 participants that filled in the questionnaire completely and that also use traceability in the project they were reporting about.

We asked participants about their role in the project they reported about. We allowed multiple answers as especially in small projects people often work in more than one role. Our participants covered the following roles: project manager (41%), requirements engineer (39%), quality manager (38%), architect (25%), developer (25%), test manager (14%), and CEO (11%). This broad range of participants with different focus on the development process allowed us to capture a variety of positions and opinions on the usage of requirements traceability.

3.6 Projects

We asked subjects to answer questions with respect to a project they typically work on and to preferably refer to their current project. Furthermore, we asked them to classify this project according to three criteria: project size in terms of team members, project duration and distribution of development sites. 23% of the participants were reporting about a small-scale project with 1 to 6 team members. 45% of the participants reported about a medium-scale project with 7 to 50 team members. Finally, 32% of our subjects were reporting about a large-scale project with more than 50 team members. Subjects could classify the duration of their project as a short-term project that runs for less than one year (24%), as a medium-term project that runs for one to three years (46%), or as a long-term project that runs for more than three years (30%).

One subject told in a verbal comment that her or his current project was under continuous development for 20 years. Furthermore, we asked subjects whether the project they were reporting about is being developed at one local site (49%), at multiple national sites (25%), or at multiple international sites (27%).

4   Results

In the first three parts of this section, we analyze general questions about the traceability in a subject's project. The fourth subsection discusses particular usage scenarios applied in these projects.

4.1   Reasons for Applying Requirements Traceability

We asked subjects about reasons for the application of traceability. Fig. 1 shows the possible reasons that we offered and the percentages of subjects that selected each. For space reasons, we cannot show all results in figures, the following text contains additional results not visualized.

A majority of 80% of the participants applies requirements traceability because of expected benefits. Given that only 2% of the subjects responded not to know the reasons for applying traceability, there is a remaining group of 18% of the participants that performs traceability because they are forced to by regulations, management orders, or the development environment. Only 36% of all participants are applying traceability purely for expected benefits. Association of given replies with another shows that around one fifth of the subjects that apply traceability because of regulations (17%), management requests (18%), or development process preconditions (23%) do not expect benefits.

We associated the reasons for applying traceability in a particular project with the size of that project and found no considerable differences (85% small-scale, 76% medium-scale, and 83% large-scale projects). Considerably more subjects reporting about large-scale projects report to perform traceability because of regulations (15% small-scale, 12% medium-scale, and 39% large-scale projects). The percentages of participants that reported to perform traceability because of management requests or development process preconditions grow with the project size (management request: 15% small-scale, 32% medium-scale projects, and 39% large-scale; development process preconditions: 23% small-scale, 36% medium-scale, and 56% large-scale).

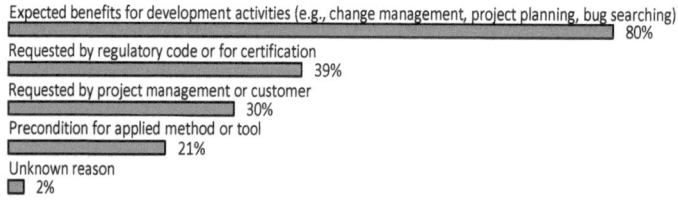

Fig. 1. Overview of replies to the question: "Why is traceability applied in your project?" (Multiple selections allowed)

4.2   General Assessment of Requirements Traceability

We asked participants to rate five statements about requirements traceability as true, partly true, or false given a subject's experience of applying traceability in the project she/he was reporting about. We allowed to rate statements as partly true in order to get an understanding of how sure subjects were in their responses. Fig. 2 summarizes responses to those questions. The figure shows that the majority of participants (63% true, 32% partly true) consider traceability as an important basis for the development process (see statement a). Also the majority of participants (48% true, 39% partly true) state that traceability should be used more actively (statement b). Nonetheless, almost the same percentage of respondents (50% true, 34% partly true) found statement c already true within their projects that the experienced benefits outweigh the cost of traceability. The cross test (statement e) supports this statement (4% true, 21% partly true). Statement d aimed to evaluate whether all development team members are involved in the traceability process, know the objectives of traceability, and also know their own role in the traceability process. Only 29% of the subjects fully agreed with that statement, 52% partly agreed. An association of those replies with project size showed that 44% of the subjects reporting about large-scale projects fully agreed with that statement, while 39% of those partly agreed. Only 20% of the subjects working in medium-scale projects fully agree with that statement, 60% partly agree. Subjects working in small-scale projects fully agree to 23% and partly agreed to 54%.

We also allowed participants to comment and report about issues in their traceability practice. More than a quarter of the participants gave such comments. The majority of those statements refer to benefits and especially costs of requirements traceability. Several subjects mention positive effects for their work or project due to traceability, but always in relation to high costs. Other subjects simply complain about too high costs and that they do not think that traceability can be applied cost efficiently in small- and medium-scale projects. Other issues that are mentioned multiple times across these comments are better tooling and better training and motivation of team members. We knew all these statements from introduction sections of research papers, but it was very enlightening to see them mentioned by practitioners struggling with the implementation and application of requirements traceability.

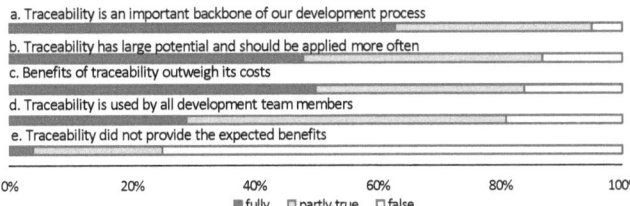

Fig. 2. Replies to the question: "Which of the following statements do you consider true, partly true, or false based on the experiences with requirements traceability in your project?"

4.3   Instrumentation of Requirements Traceability

A wide variety of general-purpose and development tools is used to instrument requirements traceability in practice. We asked our respondents about their tooling for
implementing requirements traceability. We found that general-purpose applications
(e.g., office, spreadsheet, and wiki) and configuration management tools were the
most reported tools (both 64%). Almost equally often, subjects report about the use of
integrated development environments (61%) and requirements engineering tools
(57%). Only about one fourth of the subjects (27%) are using project planning and
management tools for implementing traceability (see Fig. 3). A customized tooling
solution is used in 39% of the projects, involving several tools that realize requirements traceability in their projects. An interesting observation is that subjects with
customized solution in their project are more often fully agreeing to the statement that
the benefits of traceability supersede its costs (see Fig. 2 statement c).

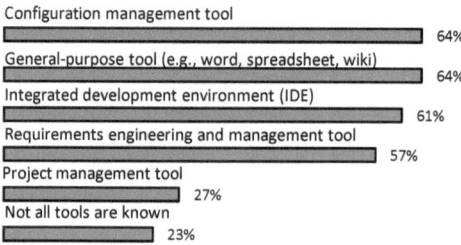

Fig. 3. Replies to the question: "Which tools for implementing and using requirements traceability are applied in your project?"

4.4   Application of Usage Scenarios

We found that the 56 traceability-using subjects in our study apply 42% of the 29
assessed usage scenarios regularly (standard deviation (sd) 22%). These subjects apply another 29% of the usage scenarios occasionally (sd 15%). The percentage of
regularly used scenarios is clearly higher in large-scale projects (53%) than in medium-scale projects (36%) and small-scale projects (37%). Occasionally applied
usage scenarios are less dependent on the project size (small-scale project 25%, medium-scale project 31%, and large-scale project 30%).

Table 1 list from top to bottom all 29 usage scenarios that were assessed by the
subjects. The second to fourth column show for each scenario, the percentage of subjects that is performing the scenario regularly (R), occasionally (O), and never (N).
The following four groups of columns evaluate the influence of project size, project
duration and kind of development sites on each usage scenario. Per subgroup (e.g.,
small projects) we computed average usage rates and compared those against a
weighted mean of all subgroups (i.e., small-, medium-, and large-scale projects). We
decided for that way of comparison, as the weighted mean is independent of the number of samples per subgroup. In order to avoid a large table with figures and in order
to emphasize on the interesting associations, we defined two thresholds for

divergences to appear in the table. Major divergences, above 20% and below -20% of the weighted group mean, are visualized by vertical arrows (↑ and ↓), while minor divergences, in the range (10%, 20%] and (-10%, -20%], are visualized as diagonal arrows (↗ and ↘). We do not consider differences smaller or equal to 10%. They are represented as blank cells in the table. For space reasons, we only show differences for regular and occasional usage per subgroup. Differences in the percentage of subjects that never uses a scenario follow implicitly from differences in the regular and occasional usage. When reading the table, it is important to focus on the pair of R and O column per subgroup in relation with each other. For example, the arrows for the combination: scenario 1.c)–medium project are meaning that this scenario is applied 10-20% less regularly, but 10-20% more occasionally in medium projects than in the weighted mean of all projects. In the following paragraphs, we are discussing all six groups of usage scenarios and refer to the introduced percentages and influences.

1. Requirements engineering and management. All usage scenarios in this area are used in at least 70% of the reported projects either regularly or occasionally. The most regular used scenarios in this group are "traceability for finding origin and rationale of requirements" (64%) and "traceability for detailing requirements" (63%), which are even more often used in larger and longer projects. The use of traceability for "impact analysis" is with 70% combined regular and occasional usage also well established, but the low value of 25% regular use raises questions about problems in the application of traceability. We identify here a need for further detailed evaluation.

Regarding development sites, we found a high usage of traceability especially in international distributed projects. The scenarios 1.a) and 1.c) are used in all international distributed projects either regularly (67%) or occasionally (33%). We also associated the use of the scenarios in this group with the application of a specific requirements management tool. We found that the scenarios 1.a), 1.b), and 1.c) are used about 20% more regularly, if the subject was reporting that such a tool is used in the project.

2. Project management. Similar to requirements engineering and management, project management is also a popular area for the application of requirements traceability. All assessed scenarios in the group are performed in 72% of the reported projects, either regularly or occasionally. With 75%, the "tracking of requirements or task implementation progress" is the most regular performed scenario of all 29 assessed scenarios. The regular usage of traceability for this activity is even higher in national and international distributed projects.

Four out of the six scenarios in this group are less regularly used in medium-scale projects. This raises a question about differences in the project management of medium-scale projects with 7 to 50 team members. We will further investigate that issue in an ongoing study. We could not find any influence of the applied tools on the use of traceability in this area. We also studied whether participants having a role in the project management of a project would favor these scenarios over others, but could not find relevant differences.

Table 1. Average usage of all assessed usage scenarios across the projects that subjects reported about (R – regularly used, O – occasionally used, N – never used)

Usage scenario	Average usage rate [%]			Project size						Project duration						Dev. sites					
				Small		Med.		Large		Short		Med.		Long		Local		Nat'l		Int'l	
	R	O	N	R	O	R	O	R	O	R	O	R	O	R	O	R	O	R	O	R	O
1. Requirements Engineering and Management																					
a) Finding origin and rationale of req´s	64	27	9					↗		↘				↗	↘						
b) Detailing requirements	63	18	19			↘	↗														
c) Documenting a requirement's history	54	36	10		↘	↗	↗	↘												↗	
d) Identifying stakeholders	46	32	22	↘				↗										↗	↘		
e) Quality- and maturity-analysis of req´s	45	34	21							↘	↗	↘									
f) Impact analysis	25	45	30					↗													
2. Project Management																					
a) Tracking requirement/task implementation state	75	16	9			↘				↘	↗			↘				↗	↘	↗	
b) Release planning	63	20	17			↘				↗	↘	↘	↗					↗	↘	↗	
c) Progress assessment on project or subproject level	43	38	19	↘	↓	↑	↗	↘						↘		↘		↗			
d) Task assignment	43	29	28	↓		↗								↘				↗		↘	↗
e) Notification of stakeholders about changes	39	34	27	↘	↗			↗	↘	↓	↑	↗	↘	↘	↗	↗		↗	↘		
f) Adjusting project and release plan	34	38	28			↘				↗	↘	↗	↘					↗		↗	
3. Compliance Demonstration																					
a) Analyzing requirements coverage in source code	64	25	11	↗		↘				↗				↘							
b) Pure traceability documentation	43	13	44	↘		↘	↗	↑	↘	↘										↗	
c) Justification of all written code based on specification	29	27	44	↘				↗		↘								↗		↘	
4. Design and Implementation																					
a) Navigation between specification, design, test, and code artifacts	43	32	25			↘		↗								↘		↗			
b) Navigation within artifacts of the same type	25	34	41	↘				↑		↘		↗	↗			↘		↗	↗		↘
c) Design assessment based on traceability metrics	14	45	41													↘					
d) Project familiarization of development team members	13	36	51	↘	↘	↘		↑		↘	↗										
5. Testing																					
a) Development of test cases based on req´s	61	14	25	↘				↗		↘				↗	↘	↘					
b) Defect location for failed tests	50	16	34	↘	↗			↑		↓	↗	↗	↘					↗			↘
c) Discovering regression tests	41	29	30	↘				↗		↘			↘	↘	↗						
d) Test coverage analysis of specification and code	41	25	34					↗		↓		↗							↘		
e) Stakeholder identification	36	36	28	↘				↘		↗	↘							↗			
6. Maintenance and Evolution																					
a) Change impact analysis	48	23	29											↗	↘			↗		↘	
b) Change effort estimation	39	38	23	↘	↘	↗	↗									↘				↗	
c) Feature location and support during change implementation	38	30	32	↘	↘	↑	↗	↘		↘						↘					
d) Reuse of specification and code components	16	43	41	↘												↘		↘			
e) Project familiarization of maintenance team members	11	25	64													↗					

3. Compliance demonstration. Compliance demonstration is not a traditional part of a development process, but rather a major cited benefit of requirements traceability. We decided to create a separate group for scenarios with this purpose. The "demonstration of requirements coverage in code" is among the most used scenarios of all the 29 assessed. This scenario is regularly applied by 64% of the participants. In total 89% of the participants use this scenario at least occasionally. An interesting observation is that this scenario is even more regularly applied in small projects (77%).

As expected, we found strong associations between the usages of the scenarios in this group and whether one reason for applying traceability in the reported project was certification (see Section 3.1). Interestingly, the scenario focusing on the reverse activity "justifying written code based on the specification" seems far less important to the subjects. In only 29% of the reported projects this scenario is performed regularly and in another 27% occasionally. Nonetheless, we found a strong association between the regular use of this scenario and subjects mentioning certification as one reason for doing traceability in the reported project. Furthermore, we found that subjects performing this scenario also perform a large number of other scenarios in the areas of requirements engineering and management, compliance demonstration, and testing.

4. Design and Implementation. We asked subjects to assess four scenarios that are related to design and implementation of a development. These scenarios refer to navigation between artifacts, to evaluating the design of a system based on traceability, and to familiarizing the development team with the project by using traceability. The "navigation between different artifacts" is with 43% regular usage the most used scenario of this group (32% occasional usage). Only 25% of the participants use traceability regularly for navigating between artifacts of the same type (e.g. within code or within the design). We found that both navigation scenarios are more often used by larger, longer and more distributed projects. The other two scenarios seem to be less important to the subjects. Only 14% of the projects use traceability regularly for design assessment (45% occasionally) and 13% of the projects apply traceability regularly for familiarizing new team members (36% occasionally).

5. Testing. In our literature study (see Section 2) we found testing regularly cited as a software development area that is supposed to greatly benefit from established requirements traceability. The "development of test cases based on requirements" is the most regularly used scenario in this group (61%).

We found that the application of traceability for testing activities is associated with the size and the duration of the project. Smaller and shorter projects apply all scenarios less frequently, while larger and longer project apply them more frequently. A reason for this finding might be differences in the overall testing procedures in smaller and shorter projects as compared to larger and longer.

6. Maintenance and evolution. Our participants also had to assess four scenarios that were considered maintenance and evolution activities. Out of these scenarios, "change impact analysis" was the most regularly used one (48%). Overall, the three scenarios (6.a-6.c) that deal with change implementation are used in around 70% of the reported projects, but their regular usage is behind the popular scenarios supporting requirements engineering and management, project management, and compliance demonstration activities. This finding is interesting, as one should assume that traceability is especially helpful when it comes to changes and reevaluating decisions made in the past. The analysis of why practitioners often chose not to apply traceability for change related tasks is an issue for our ongoing study.

Additionally proposed scenarios. Participants had the chance to leave comments about their traceability usage and to propose scenarios that they found not covered in our list. 13 subjects used this opportunity and left comments about their traceability usage. Within these comments we found candidates for additional scenarios. Several comments referred to the application of traceability for demonstration purposes. For example, subjects want to demonstrate project progress and success to other stakeholders; they want to give rationale for why certain changes were required; and they want to demonstrate that the development followed a requested methodology. Other suggested usage scenarios are the creation of a knowledge database of project-specific decisions and issues, impact analysis of errors, and the use of traceability during release planning.

5   Discussion

Regarding our research goal (see Section 3.1), we found that usage scenarios known from literature are in fact relevant in practice and that practitioners use them. However, we also found that on average only a selection of 42% of all scenarios is applied per project. This selection usually focusses on groups of related scenarios, like requirements management or test.

Regarding the areas in which requirements traceability is most applied, we found requirements engineering, project management and compliance demonstration to be the groups with the heaviest used scenarios. We found that the most common usages for requirements traceability are: "Finding origin and rationale of requirements" (1.a), "Documenting a requirement's history" (1.c), "Tracking requirement or task implementation state" (2.a), and "Analyzing requirements coverage in source code" (3.a). These four scenarios are used in around 90% of all projects either regularly or occasionally.

Traceability is used across all types of projects, but we found that for many scenarios its usage increases with project size, project duration, and the distribution of development sites. The differences in usage that we observed are not dramatically, but clearly visible. To identify reasons for this observation, further investigation has to be done. Even more interesting are the cases, which do not follow this pattern. For example, "Analyzing requirements coverage in source code" (3.a) is more regularly used in short-term than in long-term projects.

Our results show that the usage of requirements traceability is less common in the areas design and implementation as well as in maintenance and evolution. We identify two reasons for this situation, which we aim to further explore in ongoing studies. First, later development stages deal with larger numbers of artifacts and accordingly with high numbers of traceability links to create and maintain. Second, most of the scenarios in these areas refer to tool-supported navigation between heterogeneous artifacts or build upon this ability in order to perform analyses. Our hypothesis is that more efficient and more specific tool support could make requirements traceability more attractive to stakeholders working in these areas.

The tools most used in the projects of our subjects for implementing requirements traceability were configuration management tool (64%) and general-purpose tool (64%). Along with the fact that a large number of verbal comments (50%) given by participants refer to the bad cost-benefit ratio of traceability in their projects, we hypothesize that tool-support that is better aligned to the actual usage scenarios could help in reducing cost and raising benefit of traceability. Supporting this hypothesis, we found that subjects with customized tooling perceive traceability to be more beneficial (see Section 4.3).

6   Threats to Validity

Construct validity. By conducting a questionnaire-based survey, we tried to eliminate the influence of the experimenter on the subject as far as possible. We aimed for a simple and precise language for our questions. We assigned questions assessing the usage of scenarios randomly, but grouped into phases, removing the order of questions as possible bias. A two-tier pretest was performed to gain feedback on the understandability of questions, the structure of the questionnaire, and on ambiguous or missing information in the questionnaire. The positive feedback from practitioners doing the pretest and from subjects as part of their comments suggests success in this regard. Nonetheless, due to the diverse background of our participants we cannot fully exclude misunderstandings. Our result might be biased (i.e., too positive) as participants assessed traceability usage on their own project. However, this is a general problem of online surveys and there was no incentive for them to do so. We explained in Section 3 that we decided for that research method as it allowed us to reach a larger number of possible participants.

Internal validity. A problematic issue in performing a survey is finding a representative group of participants. In order to mitigate this problem, we decided to perform an online survey, which offered the opportunity for a wide population of subjects to easily participate. An often-cited barrier of online surveys, which are said to favor more technically affine subjects, seems irrelevant for a study focusing on subjects performing software engineering. We advertised our study across newsgroups and social networks. This form of advertising bared the risk of only inviting subjects that are very active and interested in the topic of requirements traceability [14]. In order to at least partly mitigate that threat, we also took great efforts to advertise our study on workshops, meetings and through personal contacts. Nonetheless, we have to acknowledge that our study mainly involved subjects that were already interested in the topic of requirements traceability.

External validity. We had a relatively high number of 117 subjects that at least partly responded to our questions. Out of those we selected 56 that had fully answered the questionnaire and that applied traceability in the project they were reporting about. We were able to attract participants with a large number of roles in a project's development process (see Sections 3.5 and 3.6). This fact suggests that our data covers a variety of perspectives on the application of requirements traceability in practice. However, all our subjects were working in German-speaking companies and had mostly experiences in national and European projects. We understand our results as a trend showing the application frequency of usage scenarios within our study group. In order to gain generalizable results, more and larger studies are required.

7   Conclusions and Future Work

In this paper we reported about a survey designed to get information on how practitioners use requirements traceability in development projects. Based on a literature study, we collected 29 regularly cited usage scenarios of requirements traceability. We found that those 56 participants of our study that actually applied requirements traceability in practice use 42% of the 29 scenarios regularly. We analyzed the usage of all scenarios and found that requirements engineering and management, project management, and compliance demonstration are the areas in which traceability is heavily applied. We found that the usage of requirements traceability during design and implementation as well as during software maintenance and evolution is less common. In verbal comments, practitioners reported that they struggle with the bad cost-benefit ratio for their traceability. This problem could be addressed by more integrated method and tool support. Based on these observations, we derive two general goals for future work in the area of requirements traceability. First, goal-oriented application of traceability according to required project-specific usage scenarios. Second, developing traceability methods and tools that are adaptable to usage scenarios. For both goals it is important to understand the identified usage scenarios in more detail. We see an important task in analyzing the discovered traceability usage scenarios in practical settings in order to find out, which artifacts participate in a scenarios and what traces are required to optimally support a scenario. We are currently working on a study with a selected number of participants from this survey. In this ongoing work, we are elaborating the major traceability usage scenarios identified in this study.

Acknowledgements. We thank all participants for their help. We are funded by the German Research Foundation (DFG): Ph49/8-1.

References

1. Ahmad, A., Ghazali, M.A.: Documenting requirements traceability information for small projects. In: IEEE International Multitopic Conference, INMIC 2007, pp. 1–5 (2007)
2. Aizenbud-Reshef, N., Nolan, B.T., Rubin, J., Shaham-Gafni, Y.: Model traceability. IBM Systems Jounal 45(3), 515–526 (2006)
3. Appleton, B.: The trouble with tracing (2005),
   http://www.cmcrossroads.com/agile-scm/
   6685-the-trouble-with-tracing-traceability-dissected

4. Arkley, P., Mason, P., Riddle, S.: Enabling traceability. In: Proceedings of 1st International Workshop on Traceability in Emerging Forms of Software Engineering, pp. 61–65 (2002)
5. Bouillon, E.: Fragebogen: Nutzerszenarien für den Einsatz von Traceability, http://www.tu-ilmenau.de/fileadmin/media/sspi/Forschung/UmfrageFormatiert.pdf
6. Cleland-Huang, J.: Just enough requirements traceability. In: Computer Software and Applications Conference, COMPSAC 2006, vol. 1, pp. 41–42 (2006)
7. Cleland-Huang, J., Gotel, O., Zisman, A.: Software and Systems Traceability. Springer (2012)
8. Gotel, O., Finkelstein, A.C.W.: An analysis of the requirements traceability problem. In: Proceedings of the First International Conference on Requirements Engineering, pp. 94–101. IEEE Computer Society Press, Colorado Springs (1994)
9. Kannenberg, A., Saiedian, H.: Why Software Requirements Traceability Remains a Challenge. CrossTalk - Journal of Defense Software Engineering, 14–19 (July/August 2009)
10. Kirova, V., Kirby, N., Kothari, D., Childres, G.: Effective requirements traceability: Models, tools, and practices. Bell Labs Technical Journal 12(4), 143–157 (2008)
11. Klimpke, L., Hildenbrand, T.: Towards end-to-end traceability: Insights and implications from five case studies. In: Fourth International Conference on Software Engineering Advances, ICSEA 2009, pp. 465–470 (2009)
12. Mäder, P., Gotel, O., Philippow, I.: Motivation matters in the traceability trenches. In: Proceedings of 17th International Requirements Engineering Conference, pp. 143–148 (2009)
13. Padberg, F., Tichy, W.F.: Empirische Methodik in der Softwaretechnik im Allgemeinen und bei der Software-Visualisierung im Besonderen. In: Gesellschaft für Informatik, Software Engineering 2007 - Beiträge zu den Workshops, pp. 211–222 (2007)
14. Punter, T., Ciolkowski, M., Freimut, B., John, I.: Conducting on-line surveys in software engineering. In: Proceedings of the International Symposium on Empirical Software Engineering, ISESE 2003, pp. 80–88 (2003)
15. Ramesh, B., Jarke, M.: Toward reference models for requirements traceability. IEEE Trans. Softw. Eng. 27(1), 58–93 (2001)
16. Ramesh, B., Stubbs, C., Powers, T., Edwards, M.: Requirements traceability: Theory and practice. Annals of Software Engineering 3, 397–415 (1997)
17. Schwarz, H., Ebert, J., Winter, A.: Graph-based traceability: a comprehensive approach. Software and Systems Modeling 9(4), 473–492 (2009)
18. Singer, J., Sim, S.E., Lethbridge, T.: Software engineering data collection for field studies. In: Shull, F., Singer, J., Sjøberg, D. (eds.) Guide to Advanced Empirical Software Engineering, pp. 9–34. Springer, London (2008)
19. Spanoudakis, G., Zisman, A.: Software traceability: A roadmap. In: Chang, S.K. (ed.) Handbook of Software Engineering and Knowledge Engineering, vol. III, pp. 395–428. World Scientific Publishing Co, River Edge (2005)
20. von Knethen, A., Paech, B.: A survey on tracing approaches in practice and research. IESE-Report, Fraunhofer Inst. Experimentelle Software Engineering, Kaiserslautern (2002)
21. Winkler, S., von Pilgrim, J.: A survey of traceability in requirements engineering and model-driven development. Software and Systems Modeling 9(4), 529–565 (2010)

The Emergence of Mutual and Shared Understanding in the System Development Process

Axel Hoffmann[1], Eva Alice Christiane Bittner[1], and Jan Marco Leimeister[1,2]

[1] Information Systems, Kassel University, Pfannkuchstr. 1, 34121 Kassel, Germany
[2] Insitute of Information Management, University of St. Gallen, Mueller-Friedberg-Strasse 8, CH-9000 St. Gallen, Switzerland
`{axel.hoffmann,eva.bittner,leimeister}@uni-kassel.de`

Abstract. **[Context and motivation]** In interdisciplinary requirements engineering, stakeholders need to understand how other disciplines think and work (mutual understanding) and agree on the system they develop (shared understanding) in order to collaborate effectively. **[Question/problem]** In this paper we analyse extent and forms of (lacking) mutual understanding according to the periods in the process of conceptual change. **[Principal ideas/results]** We analyse the communication of a multidisciplinary team while developing a mobile application. Although the team tried to resolve differences in meaning early on by applying approaches for clarification, questions for consolidation, exploration and elaboration occurred at different points in time throughout the process. Even when artefacts were already agreed upon, the development team explored lack of mutual understanding to underlying concepts or relationships. A revised shared understanding led to adjustments of the artefacts and thus hampered the process. **[Contribution]** We therefore call for research that explores ways of systematically building mutual and shared understanding in the development process.

Keywords: Mutual Understanding, Shared Understanding, Requirements Engineering, System Development Process.

1 Introduction

It is widely acknowledged that mutual and shared understanding between stakeholders is important for successful development projects [1]. This is especially true for the requirement engineering activities [2-4]. Stakeholders need to understand what other stakeholders are able to understand and work with, and they need to deliver artefacts that can be used by others [5]. Further, the stakeholders need to agree on and determine the system that is built in subsequent activities.

When developing socio-technical systems many stakeholders from various backgrounds are involved in requirement engineering activities. This interdisciplinary development enhances the importance of a shared understanding of the system and the requirements. While the stakeholders involved usually do not need to be experts in all fields tackled by the development project, "they have to be able to integrate their

J. Doerr and A.L. Opdahl (Eds.): REFSQ 2013, LNCS 7830, pp. 174–189, 2013.
© Springer-Verlag Berlin Heidelberg 2013

knowledge bases in a sensible manner" [6]. Coming from different disciplines, actors might - without noticing - be using the same words for different concepts or different words for the same concepts [7]. They might be unaware of unshared individual knowledge crucial for completing the task successfully (lack of mutual understanding). Or even if they are aware of differences in knowledge and understanding, they might not agree on a shared perspective at an early stage (lack of shared understanding). This can lead to substantial losses in efficiency in collaboration processes and suboptimal outcomes [8-10]. Necessary late changes to requirements are likely to be followed by evitable rework and time-consuming changes to the whole system. Unfortunately, assessing whether a shared understanding of the system exists is not trivial. Various ideas and views only become evident in the course of the project, making a potential adjustment of the system and its requirements necessary.

As we identify shared understanding as a key success factor of interdisciplinary development projects and as a dynamic state that changes through interaction and communication, we aim to examine the interactive process of building shared understanding throughout a real world software development project. This paper explores in which stages of the development project a lack of mutual or shared understanding is discovered and how this is resolved. Different sources of disagreement require different strategies to resolve them [11], and an understanding of the causes of lacking shared understanding is also necessary. Therefore, we further investigate which different types of conflicts are discovered at which phases. Thus, we show particular types of understanding that should be improved by using additional effort. To achieve this, we examine the evolution of shared understanding on properties and requirements of a mobile application in an interdisciplinary development project by focusing on development artefacts and the correlating communication. We categorise questions and hints that are raised by stakeholders according to the process of conceptual change. Consolidation and exploration questions indicate effort to gain mutual understanding. Elaboration questions try to reconcile different understandings or resolve conflicts.

This paper has been structured in the following manner. First, a short explanation of what mutual and shared understanding will be presented, as well as how they can be achieved in development projects. Subsequently, the research design of the case study will be described, including the team, the development approach, data collection and data analysis. Further, we report and discuss the results. The paper closes with limitations and implications for further research.

2   Mutual and Shared Understanding in Development Projects

We define shared understanding as the ability of multiple agents within a group to coordinate behaviours towards common goals or objectives based on mutual knowledge, beliefs and assumptions on the task, as well as the group, the process or the tools and technologies used that may change throughout the course of the group work process and may impact group work processes and outcomes [12]. This definition implies a dynamic (process) view of shared understanding. Mohammed et al. [10] note, that "in order for a team to achieve a shared, organized understanding of knowledge about key elements in the relevant environment, changes in the knowledge and/or behavior of team members will most likely occur. Therefore, group learning plays a significant role in the development, modification, and reinforcement of mental models" [10]. The definition of shared understanding is furthermore based on a "meaning in use" point of view, which refers to coordinated action based on some resource being possessed jointly by several people. This means that it is a necessary but still insufficient prerequisite for each stakeholder to know how other disciplines think and work, and recognise where different understanding occurs (mutual understanding) in order to reach shared understanding.

However, mutual understanding does not yet mean that group members share a common viewpoint or are able to act in a coordinated manner. As our definition of shared understanding involves a "meaning in use" aspect, mutual agreement on one perspective is thus necessary to achieve shared understanding. For example, it is not enough to have a collection of requirements the different stakeholders hold, since in the course of development not only differences and conflicts among those requirements may hinder goal directed action but also different actors may prioritize and omit different requirements in their activities. The development team needs to negotiate and agree on a shared and non-conflicting mental model they want to follow.

Briggs et al. [13,11] and Kolfschoten et al. [11] distinguish between five potential sources of disagreement in collaborative requirements engineering. Three of these (differences of meaning, mental models and information) fall into the core of our concept of shared understanding, as they refer to a lack of mutual knowledge, beliefs or assumptions. They are mainly related to a certain proposal or proposal-outcome judgement [13,11]. "Differences of meaning occur when the same words or labels are used for different concepts or when different words or labels are used for the same concept" [11]. Differences of mental models occur on the level of cause and effect chains rather than on individual concepts. Both can be based on knowledge, beliefs and assumption, whereas differences of information are defined as conflicting knowledge or knowledge that not all of the stakeholders have.

When these sources of disagreement are revealed through asking clarification questions and communicating different views, mutual understanding evolves. If stakeholders agree on a common perspective on meaning, information and mental models, a shared understanding can be reached. The other two sources of disagreement are about conflicting goals or taste and might require other consensus building strategies that focus on negotiation rather than on clarification, as they exist due to differences in outcome-instrumentality judgments [13,11]. They do not result from differences in understanding, but mutually exclusive individual goals that hinder stakeholders from committing to a group goal or action.

A lot of effort has been spent on providing techniques to enhance shared understanding in the requirements engineering activities (see [14] for a discussion of the contribution of different representations to the RE activities). For example, goals [15], application scenarios [16-18] and requirements negotiation with EasyWinWin

[19,20] are proposed to support a shared understanding between stakeholders. We focus on the effectiveness and results of the combination of these three techniques to clarify the requirements in a multidisciplinary project team. There is some effort in the community to categorize and detect clarification events in written communication about requirements [21]. In our research, we distinguish between different types of clarification questions to get an idea if, and how, a mutual and shared understanding is reached, as well as which sources of disagreement are revealed.

3   Research Method

A case study to investigate the emergence of mutual and shared understanding in the system development process was performed in the research project VENUS. In this case study, a project was carried out in which a multidisciplinary team developed the mobile application Meet-U. This is depicted in the next section, followed by a description of the multidisciplinary project team. The development process including the approaches to fostering mutual and shared understanding is further shown. After the description of the case study, we describe the data collection and data analyses.

3.1   The Mobile Application Meet-U

In the case study the development of the mobile application Meet-U was attended. The idea for Meet-U had already been developed and realised in a technically oriented prototype [22]. The goal of Meet-U is to support users with regards to organising and arranging meetings with their own friends. Meet-U assists them in planning meetings or events on the way to the location or even at an actual meeting or event.

In greater detail, users can register for public events or create private meetings to which they can invite other people. Further, users can provide personal information about themselves or their interests in order to receive recommendations for events and other users with similar interests. If a user would like to attend a public event, Meet-U creates recommendations using the provided data and interests upon request. When creating private events, Meet-U recommends contacts upon request that are determined by using the settings for the event, as well as the personal interests listed by the users. Depending upon the current location of the users, they are reminded of the beginning time of the event. In addition, Meet-U provides navigation services. On-site, the event host can offer services that Meet-U recognises and integrates into the graphical user interface, such as ticket services or site plans.

3.2   The Multidisciplinary Development Team

For the development of Meet-U, socio-technical concerns and requirements [23] should be taken into account. They are related to legal conformance, usability and trust. Legal conformance refers to the inclusion of legal requirements. Usability wants to ensure that users can handle and interact with the application. Trust refers to the intention or willingness of users to be vulnerable to important actions of the system without the ability to monitor or control the system [24].

To consider the socio-technical requirements, a multidisciplinary development team consisting of four developers and three domain experts was formed; more precisely, a legal expert, an expert for perceived user trust and user acceptance, and a usability expert were involved. The most experienced developer was responsible for the management of the project. The first author functioned as an observer in the development team and attended the project meetings. The team members had known each other for at least one year due to the cooperation in the research project.

3.3   Development Approach

The development of Meet-U took place from October 2011 until April 2012 (there was a four week Christmas break). To assess the socio-technical requirements, the whole development was carried out by the multidisciplinary team: demand analysis, requirements engineering, conceptual design, software design, implementation and evaluation. Figure 1 illustrates the phases that are briefly summarised in the following sections (see Comes et al. [25] for details and a discussion of the results regarding the development approach). Due to the fact that the development was integrated in a research project, the requirements were repeatedly reflected upon and discussed anew by the development team until September 2012.

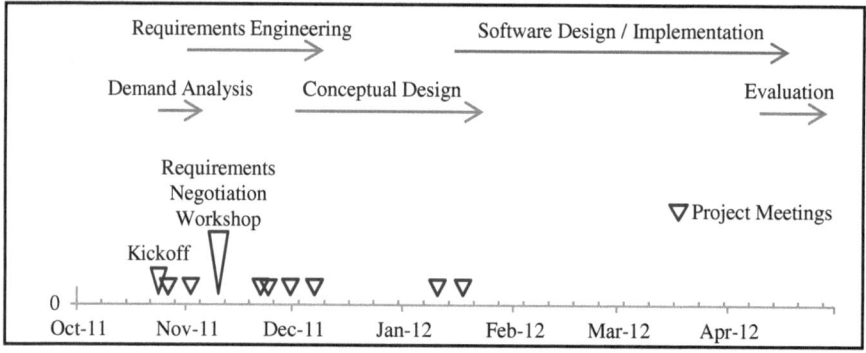

Fig. 1. Phases of the Development Project

In order to enable the collaboration of stakeholders in the first phase of development beginning with a kick-off on the 25th of October 2011, the team created goals [15] and application scenarios [16] to establish an interdisciplinary vision of the mobile application. Scenarios are a particular kind of design artefact intended to facilitate shared understanding of the target system, its interaction with users and subject domain, and its larger context [17]. Goals and scenarios are widely used in requirements engineering as a common basis for communication, and are well suited to resolve misunderstandings with stakeholders from different disciplines [26,18]. They also enforce interdisciplinary learning [18]. Therefore, the application goals were outlined from the perspective of users, after which they were refined for the application scenarios.

Further, persona were created as archetypical representatives of user groups in order to make the scenarios as realistic and comprehensible as possible for all involved stakeholders with specific, future users. In an additional activity, a business model was developed as an extension to the scenarios in order to assess the marketability. A validation of the extended scenarios was carried out with potential users to reveal incorrect assumptions about users and the application. Later, the scenarios were used as a reference by stakeholders during the development project in order to retain focus on the goals selected from the user perspective.

In requirements engineering, the stakeholders collected, analysed and documented the requirements. A computer assisted requirements negotiation workshop following EasyWinWin [19] was used to agree upon all requirements that were collected in advance. EasyWinWin "is based on the WinWin requirements negotiation model and helps a team of stakeholders to gain a better and more thorough understanding of the problem and supports co-operative learning about other's viewpoints" [20]. The workshop took place at the 10th and 11th of November 2011.

In a first step, the stakeholders evaluated the comprehensibility of the requirements, created a glossary of terms and definitions, and adjusted the requirements. The requirements deemed important by one stakeholder were transferred to a new list if all stakeholders agreed that they had understood the requirement (in order to avoid redundancies). In accordance with EasyWinWin, the requirements were then rated by the stakeholders in terms of importance and ease of realisation. In the next step, stakeholders could express concerns regarding certain requirements in the tool. In another round, proposals for solutions for the issues were collected, before a conjoint agreement was reached by means of a group discussion. After the requirements negotiation, the requirements were structured and added to the requirements documentation.

In the concept design, different kinds of design artefacts intended to facilitate shared understanding were used. First, use cases were developed. The multidisciplinary team verified the use cases in order to ensure a correct requirement transformation. In the second step, the data and functional elements of the application were described. Thus, all information provided for the user and every operation the user could make were identified. Flowcharts were employed to graphically illustrate the operation steps and the corresponding data and functional elements. Further, the structure of the user interface was depicted in a sitemap. The fourth step consisted of deriving a first graphical design with a functionless prototype of the user interface. All stakeholders received the produced artefacts and were asked to check if the requirements had been fulfilled.

The resulting artefacts, agreed upon in an interdisciplinary manner, functioned as a working basis for the developers in the implementation phase. The application concept was implemented in an iterative process. Next, the created prototypes were assessed by experts with regards to whether the previously defined requirements were taken into account during the realisation. This examination enabled changes to be made to the application concept that were integrated into the next iteration. In addition, the component functions developed in the process were evaluated from a user perspective.

The concluding evaluation of the usage aimed at assessing the functionality as well as the social compatibility of the system. It was experimentally tested with real users in as realistic application surroundings as possible in order to see whether the requirements had been fulfilled. See Söllner et al. [27] for more information concerning the realisation and selected evaluation results.

3.4   Data Collection

In order to analyse the communication in the development project, quantitative data collection and evaluation methods were selected. We conducted a document analysis for the collection of data. The objects of investigation were: the description of the application scenarios in six versions; the business model in three versions; the list of requirements in six versions; four versions of the use cases; the workflows and screens designs in four versions; as well as minutes of the ten project meetings. All documents as well as complementing communication were exchanged in 611 emails between members of the development team for the duration of the whole project using a project specific mailing list. These emails were the data basis for our assessment. The documents contained, apart from the actual content, distinguished changes of the pre-version, as well as comments and notes made by the involved stakeholders. The project language was German. During the collection of data, the first author functioned as an observer in the meetings of the development team.

3.5   Data Analysis

The evaluation of the documents was accomplished with the aid of a quantitative content analysis. To reduce the amount of data, the 611 emails were screened through, and relevant emails with development artefacts or textual contributions were extracted. The 183 resulting emails and documents were transformed to PDF files and stored in ATLAS.ti 6.2, providing support for manual qualitative coding. As we were interested in the emergence of mutual and shared understanding, we conducted the data analysis in three steps.

In the first step, 330 comments (one or more sentences from emails or annotations of the documents) were marked that contained questions, raised issues or indicated different understandings about a requirement. We refer to these comments as *questions* in the remainder of the text. One of the authors marked the questions in the ATLAS.ti by reading all emails twice.

In the second step, we analysed the questions of the team members. To distinguish the questions, we used the classification that was proposed by Watts et al. [28] to classify questions of understanding according to the periods in the process of conceptual change. Conceptual change occurs when participants either consolidate their current understanding, explore beyond their current knowledge to expand it or elaborate on it to challenge and test their framework of understanding [28]. Consolidation, exploration and elaboration are all indicative of changes in the current conceptual thinking of the person asking those questions. For elaboration question that reconcile different understandings or resolve conflicts, in the third step, we used subcategories containing the key sources of conflicts proposed by Briggs et al. [13] and Kolfschoten et al. [11]. The subcategories are differences of meaning, differences of mental models, differences in information, mutually exclusive individual goals and differences of taste (Table 1).

Table 1. Categories and subcategories used for coding

Category	Subcategory	Explanation
Consolidation	-	Confirm explanations and consolidate new ideas (mutual understanding)
Exploration	-	Seek to expand knowledge and test constructs (mutual understanding)
Elaboration		Reconcile different understandings, resolve conflicts (shared understanding)
	Differences of meaning	The same words are used for different concepts or different words are used for the same concept
	Differences of mental model	Different understandings of the means for achieving desired outcomes, or of sequences of cause and effect
	Differences in information	stakeholders do not have the same information, or one stakeholder has information that other stakeholders do not have
	Mutually exclusive individual goals	Difference of interests or values
	Differences of taste	There is no rational conflict of stakes or values but rather one of taste

Two graduate students coded the questions according the categories with ATLAS.ti. They were provided with explanations and examples and received 30 minutes of training. For the coding, one student needed 5 hours and 15 minutes and the other needed 5 hours and 30 minutes. The students could, and did, ask the first author if they faced difficulties. Questions that were not assigned to the same category by both students were discussed and assigned to a category by two of the authors.

4   Results

This section reports the number of questions assigned to the different categories and subcategories. We divided the development project into three stages that are important for mutual and shared understanding in requirements engineering: the stage before the requirement negotiation where the scenario is developed and the requirements are collected, the requirements negotiation workshop which is designed to reveal misunderstandings and reach an agreement about the system and its requirements, and the time after this agreement. In the next section, we first report the results of the assignment to the categories consolidation, exploration and elaboration. The elaboration questions are further analysed in the second subsection.

4.1   Questions for Consolidation, Exploration and Elaboration

To analyse the emergence of mutual and shared understanding, we categorised the questions and pointers in the documents according to the periods in the process of conceptual change. Questions for consolidation and exploration indicate a lack of mutual understanding; questions for elaboration indicate a lack of shared understanding.

Table 2. Questions before, during and after requirements negotiation (RN)

	Before RN	During RN	After RN	Total
Consolidation	20	24	74	118
Exploration	16	34	54	104
Elaboration	22	51	35	108
Total	58	109	163	330

Table 2 shows that there are a similar number of questions in each category and that one third of all questions were raised in the requirements negotiation workshop. Further, most conflicts could be elaborated upon before the end of the requirements negotiation, but there were more questions regarding the mutual understanding after requirements negotiation than there were in the combined before and during the requirements negotiation.

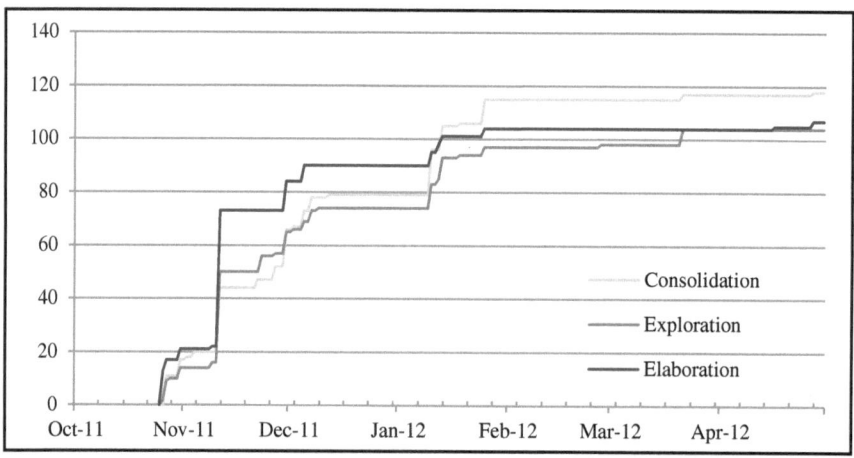

Fig. 2. Cumulative quantity of questions according to the process of conceptual change throughout the development project

Figure 2 shows the emergence of questions regarding mutual and shared understanding. Especially in late November, December and January, after requirements negotiation (including a four week Christmas break), team members raised questions for consolidation and exploration almost continuously.

This indicated that the stakeholders had the same goal but understood the requirement differently. This conflict was assigned to the category difference of mental model. The incidents of lacking shared understanding/differences in mental models concerning the requirements were especially critical, as system specification and development had already been executed at this point in time, based on the requirements, which had been agreed upon but had obviously not been fully understood.

4.2   Elaborated Conflicts

To analyse the conflicts that were revealed in the development project, we categorised the elaboration questions according to their key differences. We found that most conflicts during the whole development project dealt with different goals of stakeholders that, in most cases, were connected to their disciplinary background. For example, the legal expert wanted the user to agree on every function using personal data. In contrast, the usability expert did not want to interrupt the user while executing a task with the application. Almost the same quantity could be identified for the differences of mental models. Fewer conflicts belonged to differences of meaning, conflicting information and differences of taste (Table 3).

Table 3. Elaborated conflicts before, during and after requirements negotiation (RN)

	Before RN	During RN	After RN	Total
Differences of Meaning	5	3	4	12
Difference of Mental Model	12	8	17	37
Conflicting Information	1	5	2	8
Mutually Exclusive Individual Goals	3	33	8	44
Differences of Taste	1	2	4	7
Totals	22	51	35	108

Most conflicts regarding goals were elaborated in the requirements negotiation workshop, but differences of mental model were mostly revealed later in the project, which is critical, based on our assumption that revealing conflicts in the proposal-outcome judgement should be the basis for all further negotiation.

Figure 3 shows that differences of mental models were revealed throughout the project. Considering the differences of meaning, most conflicts were revealed before the requirements negotiation workshop; however, similar to the conflicting information and differences of taste, there were no peaks throughout the development project. Therefore, the number of conflicts remained at a low level, in contrast to the differences of mental models and individual goals.

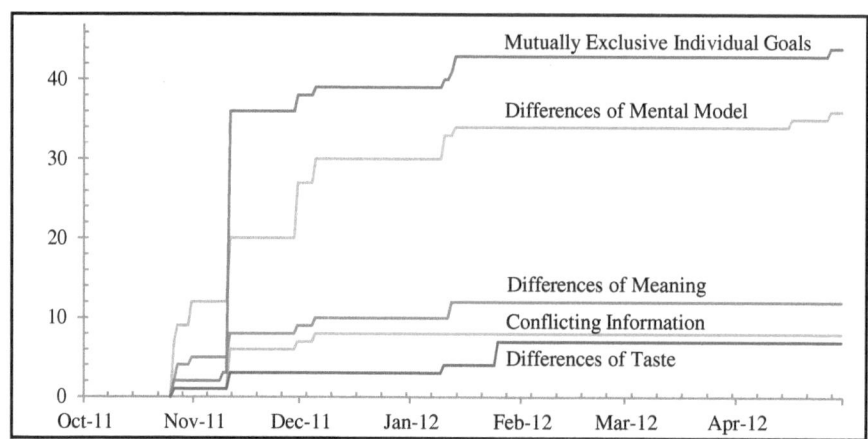

Fig. 3. Cumulative quantity of conflicts revealed throughout the development project

Summarizing, a revised shared understanding evolved late in the development phases. This led to adjustments of the artefacts and, thus, hampered the development process.

5   Discussion

The aim of our study was to analyse extent and forms of (lacking) mutual and shared understanding and how this understanding emerges in the system development process. Further, we wanted to examine which forms of conflicts occurred and in which stages of the development process they were revealed. This section discusses the results and provides suggestions for the improvement of mutual and shared understanding in development projects.

We first checked the questions according to the process of conceptual change. We could find an almost equal number of questions regarding consolidation, exploration and elaboration. As shown in the results section, the mutual and shared understanding emerged together. There were a lot of elaboration questions among the requirements negotiation workshop, but questions regarding mutual understanding emerged evenly distributed in the project. Due to the fact that a lack of shared understandings can only be detected effectively if a mutual understanding exists, there should be additional effort made in the beginning of the development project that would foster mutual understanding of the multidisciplinary team [3]. This could be done, e.g., by enforcing reflection and actively introducing techniques for construction and co-construction of meaning [29]. Bittner et al. [12] present a first attempt to develop reusable techniques for systematically building mutual and shared understanding.

To strengthen this stream of research and enlarge the set of available techniques, further research into understanding and designing mutual and shared understanding is thus necessary. In requirements engineering, natural language software requirement patterns [30-32] could help to foster a mutual understanding by using standardised, well defined and discipline independent terms and formulations. Further, the unambiguity could be fostered with a proven template that is provided by the requirement pattern.

The investigation of the elaboration questions indicated that all five types of conflicts occurred in the development project. This goes in line with Briggs et al. [13] and Kolfschoten et al. [11]. Further, we could quantify the different categories. Most conflicts belonged to the categories' mutually exclusive individual goals und difference of mental model. While the requirements negotiation workshop was good at revealing mutually exclusive individual goals, it was insufficient for revealing differences of the mental model. Over the time of the project the differences of the mental model emerged continuously, only fostered by repeated interactions of the stakeholders. Together with the observation that there was also no concentration of consolidation and exploration questions in the requirement negotiation workshop, we assume that EasyWinWin helps to deal with conflicting goals of the stakeholders, but other approaches are necessary to foster other problems in understanding.

These issues - important to address as artefacts in the development process - are highly interrelated and build on each other. Late changes of requirements due to differences in meaning or mental models, which should have been detected and clarified early in the process, might require new negotiation efforts on goals or taste when the system has already been agreed on. We assume that in an effective requirements negotiation process, differences of understanding should be discovered as early as possible, as mutual understanding is a prerequisite for shared understanding.

Based on mutual understanding, a shared perspective can be negotiated. Shifts in this process of detecting and resolving sources of disagreement might require unnecessary iterative loops and delays. Thus, collaboration techniques should be applied to shift those attempts from coincidence to a systematic and reusable process. For this purpose, group model building techniques can be used or analysts should search for conflicting assumptions behind the conflicting models [11]. A lack of shared understanding caused by differences of the mental model might also be addressed with software requirement patterns. Apart from the proven formulation of the requirement template, they can provide background information that helps other stakeholders understand the causes and estimate the effects of the requirement.

6   Limitations

This section summarises the threats to the validity of the work.

The internal validity of the case study could be threatened by the fact that we analysed only the written communication (including the annotated development artefacts) in the project and minutes that were taken in the meetings. The requirements negotiation workshops and the meetings were conducted in the presence of the observer but without recording of the oral communication. In the requirements negotiation workshop, the stakeholders were encouraged to write down their questions and issues through the use of the computer-based EasyWinWin. Thus, we could analyse them in detail. Although we did not prevent oral communication in the workshop or in other meetings, the focus on the written communication is a limitation of this study.

Coding the data analysis, the students reached agreement on most questions but were also faced with difficulties. Especially questions that were asked very politely to show (in subsequent discussion between the stakeholders) that there might be a conflict. These were partly assigned to consolidation or exploration. Also, they had some difficulties with questions that consolidated new ideas. If they read a question alone they had difficulty deciding if it was just a new idea or a conflict. To clarify this, the students could consult the first author that observed the development project and had attended the project meetings. All questions with such uncertainties were discussed by two of the authors before they were assigned to categories. Therefore, background knowledge of the development project was partly necessary to assign some of the questions.

Regarding external validity, the major concern is the generalizability of the results since we conducted only one case study. The case study with seven people is embedded in a research project that has distinct features such as the repeated discussion and reflection about requirements, which might have an impact on the emergence of the shared understanding. Due to the diversity of the development and requirement engineering approaches, we cannot claim that the results are representative for all development projects. Further, the team and stakeholders involved with their different backgrounds could have had an effect on the emergence of mutual and shared understanding. This study is a first step to analyse the emergence of mutual and shared understanding. To strengthen the results, other development teams with stakeholders from various disciplines should be analysed.

7   Conclusion

In this paper we analysed the emergence of mutual and shared understanding in the written communication of a multidisciplinary team that developed a mobile application. The team used application scenarios and an EasyWinWin requirement negotiation workshop to reveal and overcome a lack of understanding. We showed that the workshop helped to identify most conflicting goals of the stakeholders, but differences in the mental model were mostly identified in other stages of the process. Further, consolidation and elaboration questions belonging to mutual understanding were equally distributed in the process. Hence, we could not observe an effect by the requirement negotiation workshop. Even when artefacts were already agreed upon, the development team explored lack of mutual understanding to underlying concepts or relationships. If a shared understanding in the development team is important, there should be additional approaches used in requirement engineering activities.

This paper has several implications for research. We used a classification for mutual and shared understanding based on the process of conceptual change. This approach can differentiate the success of clarification techniques based on different types of understanding and can be used to get a deeper understanding of project communication. The results show that in our case study the requirements negotiation workshop worked well for most things but not for the crucial issue of different mental models. This indicates, on the one hand, the suitability of this requirements negotiation technique, but, on the other hand, calls for other techniques to build shared mental models. Future work should examine whether these observations can also be done in other settings.

In practice requirements, analysts should be aware that a lack of understanding can have different sources and that RE techniques are more or less suited to address the different types of mutual and shared understanding. If an agreement by stakeholders shall be reached, requirement analysts should spend effort to achieve a mutual understanding of the requirements and a shared mental model of the planned system before other kinds of conflicts are elaborated upon.

To foster mutual and shared understanding in interdisciplinary projects, we call for future research to analyse extent and forms of (lacking) mutual understanding in other development projects consisting of stakeholders from various backgrounds and using various development approaches. Further, we call for research that explores ways to systematically build upon this understanding.

References

1. Tan, M.: Establishing mutual understanding in systems design: An empirical study. Journal of Management Information Systems 10(4), 159–182 (1994)
2. Aranda, G., Vizcaíno, A., Piattini, M.: A framework to improve communication during the requirements elicitation process in GSD projects. Requirements Engineering 15(4), 397–417 (2010), doi:10.1007/s00766-010-0105-9
3. Corvera Charaf, M., Rosenkranz, C., Holten, R.: The emergence of shared understanding: applying functional pragmatics to study the requirements development process. Information Systems Journal 23(2), 115–135 (2012), doi:10.1111/j.1365-2575.2012.00408.x
4. Berkovich, M., Leimeister, J., Hoffmann, A., Krcmar, H.: A requirements data model for product service systems. Requirements Engineering (online first), 1–26 (2012), doi:10.1007/s00766-012-0164-1
5. Baxter, G., Sommerville, I.: Socio-technical systems: From design methods to systems engineering. Interacting with Computers 23(1), 4–17 (2011), doi:10.1016/j.intcom.2010.07.003
6. Kleinsmann, M., Buijs, J., Valkenburg, R.: Understanding the complexity of knowledge integration in collaborative new product development teams: A case study. Journal of Engineering and Technology Management 27(1-2), 20–32 (2010)
7. de Vreede, G.-J., Briggs, R.O., Massey, A.P.: Collaboration Engineering: Foundations and Opportunities. Journal of the Association of Information Systems 10(3), 121–137 (2009)
8. Valkenburg, R., Dorst, K.: The reflective practice of design teams. Design Studies 19(3), 249–271 (1998), doi:10.1016/s0142-694x(98)00011-8
9. Darch, P., Carusi, A., Jirotka, M.: Shared understanding of end-users' requirements in e-Science projects. In: 5th IEEE International Conference on E-Science, pp. 125–128 (2009)
10. Mohammed, S., Dumville, B.C.: Team mental models in a team knowledge framework: Expanding theory and measurement across disciplinary boundaries. Journal of Organizational Behavior 22(2), 89–106 (2001)

11. Kolfschoten, G., Briggs, R.O., de Vreede, G.J.: A Diagnostic to Identify and Resolve Different Sources of Disagreement in Collaborative Requirements Engineering. In: International Meeting on Group Decision and Negotiation (GDN), Toronto, Canada (2009)

12. Bittner, E.A.C., Leimeister, J.M.: Why Shared Understanding Matters - Engineering a Collaboration Process for Shared Understanding to Improve Collaboration Effectiveness in Heterogeneous Teams. In: 46th Hawaii International Conference on System Sciences (HICSS), Maui, Hawaii (2013)

13. Briggs, R.O., Kolfschoten, G.L., de Vreede, G.J.: Toward a theoretical model of consensus building. In: Americas Conference on Information Systems (AMCIS), Omaha, Nebraska, USA, p. 12 (2005)

14. Sutcliffe, A.: Collaborative Requirements Engineering: Bridging the Gulfs Between Worlds. In: Nurcan, S., Salinesi, C., Souveyet, C., Ralyté, J. (eds.) Intentional Perspectives on Information Systems Engineering, vol. 1, pp. 355–376. Springer, Heidelberg (2010)

15. Dardenne, A., Lamsweerde, A.V., Fickas, S.: Goal-directed requirements acquisition. Sci. Comput. Program. 20(1-2), 3–50 (1993), doi:
http://dx.doi.org/10.1016/0167-6423(93)90021-G

16. Haumer, P., Pohl, K., Weidenhaupt, K.: Requirements elicitation and validation with real world scenes. Transactions on Software Engineering 24(12), 1036–1054 (2002)

17. Jarke, M., Bui, X.T., Carroll, J.M.: Scenario management: An interdisciplinary approach. Requirements Engineering 3(3), 155–173 (1998)

18. Weidenhaupt, K., Pohl, K., Jarke, M., Haumer, P.: Scenarios in system development: current practice. IEEE Software 15(2), 34–35 (1998), doi:10.1109/52.663783

19. Gruenbacher, P.: Collaborative requirements negotiation with EasyWinWin. In: Database and Expert Systems Applications, London, pp. 954–958 (2000)

20. Briggs, R.O., Grünbacher, P.: EasyWinWin: Managing Complexity in Requirements Negotiation with GSS. In: 35th Hawaii International Conference on System Sciences, Hawaii (2002)

21. Knauss, E., Damian, D., Poo-Caamano, G., Cleland-Huang, J.: Detecting and classifying patterns of requirements clarifications. In: 20th IEEE International Requirements Engineering Conference (RE), pp. 251–260 (2012), doi:10.1109/re.2012.6345811

22. Comes, D., Evers, C., Geihs, K., Saur, D., Witsch, A., Zapf, M.: Adaptive Applications are Smart Applications. In: International Workshop on Smart Mobile Applications, San Francisco (2011)

23. Geihs, K., Leimeister, J.M., Roßnagel, A., Schmidt, L.: On Socio-technical Enablers for Ubiquitous Computing Applications. In: The 12th IEEE/IPSJ International Symposium on Applications and the Internet (SAINT), Izmir, Turkey (2012)

24. Lee, J.D., See, K.A.: Trust in Automation: Designing for Appropriate Reliance. Human Factors 46(1), 50–80 (2004)

25. Comes, D.E., Evers, C., Geihs, K., Hoffmann, A., Kniewel, R., Leimeister, J.M., Niemczyk, S., Roßnagel, A., Schmidt, L., Schulz, T., Söllner, M., Witsch, A.: Designing Socio-technical Applications for Ubiquitous Computing - Results from a Multidisciplinary Case Study. In: Göschka, K.M., Haridi, S. (eds.) DAIS 2012. LNCS, vol. 7272, pp. 194–201. Springer, Heidelberg (2012)

26. Pohl, K.: Requirements Engineering. dpunkt-Verls., Heidelberg (2008)

27. Söllner, M., Hoffmann, A., Hoffmann, H., Wacker, A., Leimeister, J.M.: Understanding the Formation of Trust in IT Artifacts. In: International Conference on Information Systems (ICIS), Orlando, Florida, USA (2012)

28. Watts, M., Gould, G., Alsop, S.: Questions of Understanding: Categorising Pupils' Questions in Science. School Science Review 79(286), 57–63 (1997)

29. Van den Bossche, P., Gijselaers, W., Segers, M., Woltjer, G., Kirschner, P.: Team learning: building shared mental models. Instructional Science 39(3), 283–301 (2011), doi:10.1007/s11251-010-9128-3
30. Hoffmann, A., Söllner, M., Hoffmann, H.: Twenty software requirement patterns to specify recommender systems that users will trust. In: 20th European Conference on Information Systems (ECIS), Barcelona, Spain (2012), paper 185
31. Withall, S.: Software Requirement Patterns. Microsoft Press, Redmont (2008)
32. Renault, S., Mendez-Bonilla, O., Franch, X., Quer, C.: A Pattern-based Method for building Requirements Documents in Call-for-tender Processes. International Journal of Computer Science and Applications 6(5), 175–202 (2009)

Highlighting Stakeholder Communities
to Support Requirements Decision-Making*

Zeina Azmeh, Isabelle Mirbel, and Pierre Crescenzo

I3S Laboratory, CNRS UMR 7271
University of Nice Sophia Antipolis, France
{firstname.lastname}@unice.fr

Abstract. [**Context & motivation**] Stakeholders participation is recognized as
a key issue in the development of useful and usable systems. The Web has given
rise to a growing number of collaborative working tools that facilitated the participation of stakeholders (and especially end-users). These tools create new opportunities of practice regarding requirement elicitation. [**Question/problem**] Nevertheless, they result in an information overload lacking structure and semantics.
Consequently, requirements analysis and selection becomes more challenging.
[**Principal ideas/results**] In this paper, we propose an approach based on semantic web languages as well as concept lattices to identify relevant groups of
stakeholders depending on their past participation. [**Contribution**] These groups
can be used to enable facilitated decision-making and handling of requirements.
We detail the different steps and the possible configurations, using an example
inspired by a collaborative software development environment.

Keywords: Stakeholder communities, concept lattices, requirements elicitation.

1   Introduction

Requirements engineering is an essential process of software engineering, during which,
the complete behavior of a software system can be defined. The success of this process
plays a crucial role in the success of the whole software project. A part of this success is achieved by the good selection of pertinent stakeholders, and by the proper understanding of their particular needs, in a core activity called requirements elicitation.
Stakeholders participation is thus recognized as a key issue in the development of useful
and usable systems, which can be hard to attain efficiently. The Web has given rise to
several platforms serving the purpose of collaborative software development [3]. These
online platforms enable the covering of a larger number of stakeholders that are able to
express their needs freely online. The problem lies in the large number of requirements
that need to be handled. Deciding on these requirements can not be done in a straightforward manner, especially with the poor stakeholder profiles that are not helpful for
evaluating neither the stakeholders nor their requirements. This in addition to the fact
that there is an overload of data generated by these stakeholders that is quite hard to
process or to share, since it lacks structure and semantics. There is a need for a mechanism able to facilitate the selection of requirements to be analyzed, by knowing the past
activity of stakeholders who are involved in them. Stakeholders who were previously

---

* This work was supported by the DreamIT Foundation - University of Nice Sophia Antipolis.

J. Doerr and A.L. Opdahl (Eds.): REFSQ 2013, LNCS 7830, pp. 190–205, 2013.

involved in accepted requirements, must be judged to have a higher priority over other stakeholders. They are intuitively more important than stakeholders who proposed only refused requirements, or proposed nothing at all.

We propose an approach for discovering communities of stakeholders to support requirements management (classification for instance) and decision-making (prioritization and potentiality of being accepted for instance). The approach works on deriving profiles for representing evaluated requirements, according to some values like priority and status. Then, it clusters stakeholders into communities according to their participation in requirements belonging to these profiles. This results in having a better overview of stakeholders and knowing in what profile of requirements they participated previously. Consequently, this helps to better evaluate their new requirements. The approach is based on semantic Web languages and concept lattices. We propose an ontology to represent the different actors and activities that are involved in collaborative software development environments. The objective of using semantic web languages is to annotate the user-generated data to enable a better understanding and sharing of knowledge [13], as well as the ability to reason about the data. Concept lattices are data structures that reveal the hidden relationships between the different entities of the contained data. They can be constructed using a method called Formal Concept Analysis (FCA) [10], which clusters a set of given objects into concepts, according to the attributes they share. The set of derived concepts are ordered into a lattice afterwards.

We explain our approach using an example inspired by a collaborative software development environment. We show how to analyze annotated data using concept lattices to extract stakeholder communities and we interpret the obtained results.

The paper is organized as follows: in the next section, we give an overview about concept lattices using Formal and Relational Concept Analysis (FCA, RCA). In Section 3, we present our approach and detail its different steps. In Section 4, we present a conducted experiment. In Section 5, we discuss the related work. Finally, in Section 6, we conclude the paper and describe our future work.

2   Background

In this section, we give the basic definitions of Formal and Relational Concept Analysis (FCA, RCA). We explain their use for the generation of concept lattices along with simple examples.

2.1   Formal Concept Analysis (FCA)

We base our approach on FCA [10] which is a classification method that permits the identification of groups of objects having common attributes. It takes a data set represented as an $n \times m$ table (formal context) with objects as rows and attributes as columns. A cross "$\times$" in this table means that the corresponding object has the corresponding attribute. An example of a formal context is shown in Table 1, for a set of objects O=$\{1,2,3,4,5,6,7,8,9,10\}$ and a set of attributes A=$\{$odd,even,prime, composite,square$\}$.

From a formal context, FCA extracts the set of all formal concepts. A formal concept is a maximal set of objects (called extent) sharing a maximal set of attributes (called intent). For example, in Table 1, a= ({4,6,8,10},{even, composite}) is a formal concept because the objects 4, 6, 8, and 10 share exactly the attributes *even* and composite (and vice-versa). On the other hand, ({6},{even, composite}) is not a formal concept because the extent {6} is not maximal: other objects share the same set of attributes.

Table 1. A formal context for objects O and attributes A

	odd	even	prime	composite	square
1	X				X
2		X	X		
3	X		X		
4		X		X	X
5	X		X		
6		X		X	
7	X		X		
8		X		X	
9	X			X	X
10		X		X	

FCA reveals the inheritance relations (super-concept and sub-concept) between the extracted concepts and organizes them into a partially ordered structure known as Galois lattice or concept lattice. The resulting concept lattice is illustrated in Fig. 1(L).

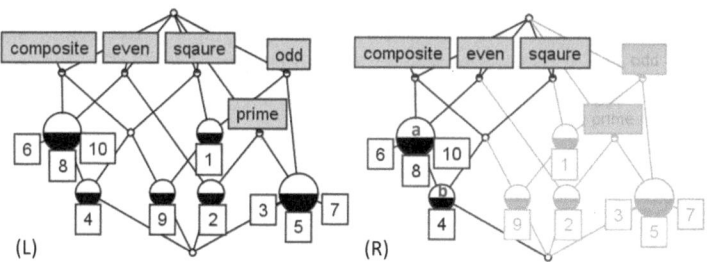

Fig. 1. Formal concept lattice[1] for the context in Table 1 (L); focus on the concept b (R)

This lattice reveals phenomena that may not be recognized intuitively. For example, in Fig. 1(R) appears the concept b= ({4},{composite,even,square}) as a subconcept of the concept a. It inherits a's attributes composite and even, and extends it by the square.

---

[1] Built using the Concept Explorer (ConExp) tool: http://conexp.sourceforge.net/users/index.html
In a lattice, a full node indicates that the concept introduces objects and attributes that weren't introduced before; a half-full node introduces either objects when the bottom half is full, or attributes when the upper half is full; and an empty node represents an intermediary concept, which does not introduce any objects or attributes.

2.2   Relational Concept Analysis (RCA)

RCA [14] is an extension of FCA that takes into consideration the relations between the objects. Thus, it takes as input two types of contexts: (non-relational) ones that are previously used with FCA to classify objects by attributes, and inter-context (relational) ones that represent the relations between the objects. RCA generates lattices similar to the ones generated by FCA, but enriched with the information about the relation between the objects. We take as an example two sets of numbers, $\{1,2,3,4,5\}$ and $\{11,12,13,14,15,16,17,18,19,20\}$. We build two non-relational contexts similar to the one in Table 1. We consider a relation called Divides between the first and second sets of numbers, and we build the relational context in Table 2.

Table 2. The relational context Divides

Divides	11	12	13	14	15	16	17	18	19	20
1	×	×	×	×	×	×	×	×	×	×
2		×		×		×		×		×
3		×			×			×		
4		×				×				×
5					×					×

RCA takes the two non-relational contexts (numbers × attributes), and the relational context Divides, then generates the two lattices in Fig. 2.

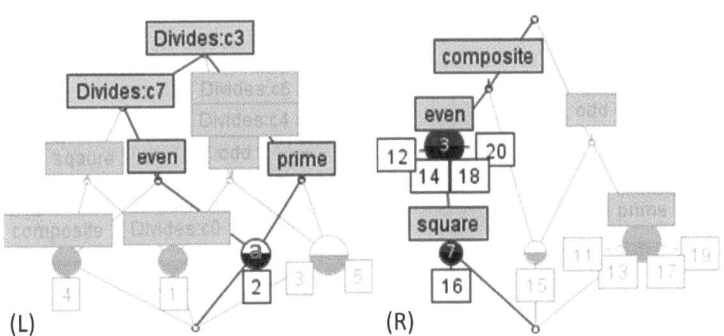

Fig. 2. The enriched lattices generated by RCA

These lattices are similar to FCA lattices, but one of them is enriched with the relation *Divides*. For example, by regarding the concept a= ({2}, {prime, even, Divides:c7, Divides:c3}) in lattice (L), we notice that the numbers in its extent can divide the numbers in the extents of the concepts 7 and 3 in lattice (R).

3   Highlighting Stakeholder Communities

The objective of our approach is to discover stakeholder communities, according to the requirements in which they participate. The approach is composed of two main steps: structuring the data of a project, by semantically annotating the different actors and artifacts, together with the possible interactions between them; and analyzing this annotated data, using concept lattices to discover stakeholder communities.

We explain our approach along with an example that is inspired by a collaborative software development platform, called Launchpad [2]. In such platforms, stakeholders are themselves involved in various activities of the software development life-cycle, which may not be necessarily the case in platforms devoted to requirements elicitation. The different tasks performed by stakeholders result in rich information that we can exploit to discover groups of requirements and groups of stakeholders. On the other hand, requirements captured through this kind of platforms are low level requirements.

Indeed, Launchpad enables stakeholders of proposing blueprints (new functionalities that they require) and reporting bugs (existing functionalities that need to be enhanced or repaired). Every project in this platform has a set of artifacts like: blueprints, bugs, and code branches, as well as a set of stakeholders participating in these artifacts. This platform provides the ability to track blueprints and bugs, as well as code branches. A large collection of projects are being managed through this platform, we mention some featured projects like: MySQL, Ubuntu, Mozilla, etc.

Let us consider the simplified example in Fig. 3. It presents a sample of data that can be obtained from this platform, involving a set of stakeholders and their different activities performed on a set of blueprints.

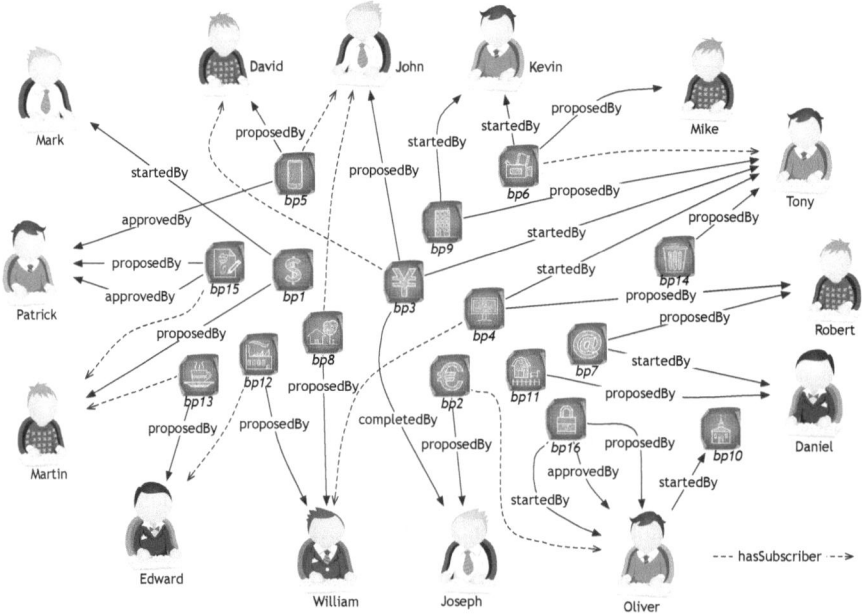

Fig. 3. An example of stakeholders performing different activities on a set of blueprints

The stakeholders contributing to a project are not necessarily members of this project. Their profile pages give an overview about their personal information, which is usually very poor and insufficient for determining stakeholders importance. We can also have access to the list of artifacts, in which they participate. The artifacts also have profiles, in which we can find different attributes related to them like: status, importance, .., and other attributes indicating the involved stakeholders with their different activities.

The problem in this kind of platforms lies in the large number of blueprints and bugs that we can find for each project. Deciding on these requirements can not be done in a straightforward manner, especially with the poor stakeholder profiles that are not helpful for evaluating neither the stakeholders nor their requirements.

We propose to annotate semantically data from such a platform, using an ontology that we define and explain hereafter. Then we process the annotated data with concept lattices, to highlight stakeholder communities.

3.1 Ontology for Collaborative Software Development

We propose the ontology in Fig. 4 for collaborative software development (CSD) [13]. The advantage of annotating data from CSD environments with the help of such an ontology is embodied in the ability to share data across platforms. This is in addition to the ability to reason about the data, by exploiting classes and properties at different levels of granularity.

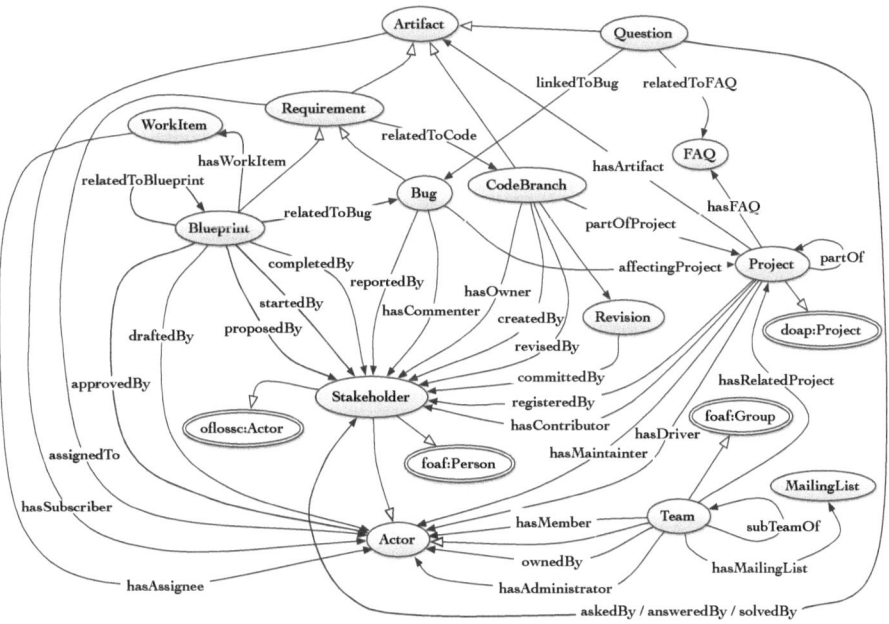

Fig. 4. An ontology for collaborative software development

In this ontology, we represent the different actors (stakeholders and teams) and their interactions with the different artifacts of a software project.

This ontology is described using the RDF Schema vocabulary [5]. It makes use of several other ontologies like the FOAF vocabulary (Friend of a Friend) to describe stakeholders and groups [6], and the DOAP vocabulary (Description of a Project) to describe a software project itself with its various resources [1]. It is also connected to an ontology called OFLOSSC [17] that annotates community members and resources for open source development.

Every software project is annotated by the class *doap:Project*. It has a set of actors and a set of artifacts. Actors can either be individuals (stakeholders) or teams of individuals. A stakeholder is annotated by the class *foaf:Person*, while a team is annotated by the class *foaf:Group*. Project artifacts can be blueprints, bugs, code branches, or questions. We consider blueprints and bugs to be two different kinds of requirements. As we mentioned before, a blueprint is a proposal of a new functionality, while a bug is a proposal of enhancement of an existing functionality.

Using this ontology, we can reason about the annotated data. For example, a requirement is a coarse-grained artifact that can be replaced by either a blueprint or a bug to get further relationships.

As the matter of fact, it can be used to annotate data retrieved from almost any collaborative software development platform. For example, we developed a crawler that harvests data from Launchpad pages, and represents them in an RDF graph [16], conforming to the defined ontology.

We explain below the use of concept lattices to analyze the annotated data.

3.2 Using Concept Lattices

We mentioned above in Section 2 that concept lattices are data structures that reveal the hidden relationships between the different entities of the contained data.

The objective of using concept lattices is to extract hidden profiles for the set of requirements of a certain project, then to use these profiles for extracting stakeholder communities. Therefore, we make use of two kinds of information: the set of attributes defined for each requirement, as well as, the different interactions (participation) between stakeholders and the considered requirements.

Let us take again the example in Fig. 3. In this example, we have profile information for each blueprint (requirement), as well as stakeholder participation information. This different information is retrieved using the Launchpad crawler and is annotated in an RDF format. We analyze this annotated data according to two steps: blueprints explicit profile information is used to build a lattice of blueprints, which enable us to discover implicit blueprint profiles, following their common attributes; then, the identified blueprint profiles are used to classify the stakeholders according to their participation in these blueprints.

In Launchpad, an explicit (provided by stakeholders) blueprint profile consists of several attributes. These attributes can be numerical (like: the number of involved stakeholders) or nominal (non-numerical). Nominal attributes can further be divided into two types: ordinal attributes that have sortable enumerated values, and categorical attributes that have enumerated values with no ordering.

We suppose that a requirement analyst can specify his configurations of the attributes to consider. This includes specifying what attribute values are considered to be equivalent, for example: a blueprint that has the status "new" or the status "under discussion" can be considered in the two cases to be "pending approval". An expert can also specify if the values of an attribute are ordinal or not, for example: the priority values of a blueprint can be specified as "low < medium < high".

In our running example, we consider values for priority and definition status only, for simplicity sake. These two attributes have sortable values: priority can take the values (undefined, low, medium, high), while definition status can take the values (unknown, approved, started, suspended, completed). In fact, we extract the information we need to analyze by querying the RDF data using the SPARQL query language [21].

Let us suppose having the formal context in Table 3, describing the set of blueprints by their values of priority and status. Since these attributes are ordinal, a blueprint in this formal context that has a high priority, covers also the other values of priority. This is also the case for the status values.

Table 3. Blueprints formal context

	Priority				Status				
	high	medium	low	undefined	completed	suspended	started	approved	unknown
bp1	×	×	×	×	×	×	×	×	×
bp2	×	×	×	×		×	×	×	×
bp3	×	×	×	×			×	×	×
bp4		×	×	×				×	×
bp5		×	×	×				×	×
bp6		×	×	×			×	×	×
bp7		×	×	×	×	×	×	×	×
bp8		×	×						×
bp9			×	×			×	×	×
bp10			×	×		×	×	×	×
bp11			×	×					×
bp12			×	×					×
bp13				×	×	×	×	×	×
bp14				×					×
bp15				×				×	×
bp16				×			×	×	×

FCA classifies the set of considered blueprints into the concept lattice in Fig. 5. This lattice reveals the blueprints that are more important than the others. These are the blueprints that appear in the lower part of the lattice, because they have more attributes than the others. This is the case for the blueprint *bp3*, appearing at the bottom, since it has the best values for the considered attributes (priority:high and status: completed).

In this lattice, several groups (profiles) of blueprints can be extracted. We consider for example, the four following profiles (appearing in Fig. 5): blueprints that are approved regardless of priority (includes all the blueprints except for *bp14*, *bp8*, and *bp12*); the ones that are completed regardless of priority (*bp13*, *bp11*, *bp7*, and *bp3*); the ones having medium priority at least and are approved at least (*bp5*, *bp4*, *bp6*, *bp1*, *bp2*, *bp7*, and *bp3*); and finally the ones having a high priority and that are started at least (*bp1*, *bp2*, and *bp3*).

We use these four blueprint profiles to construct a new formal context of stakeholders. We make use of RCA (expressing the relation between objects and the concepts of another lattice), as we can see in Table 4. In this formal context, we can determine if a stakeholder has a profile or not by fixing a minimal number of blueprints belonging to

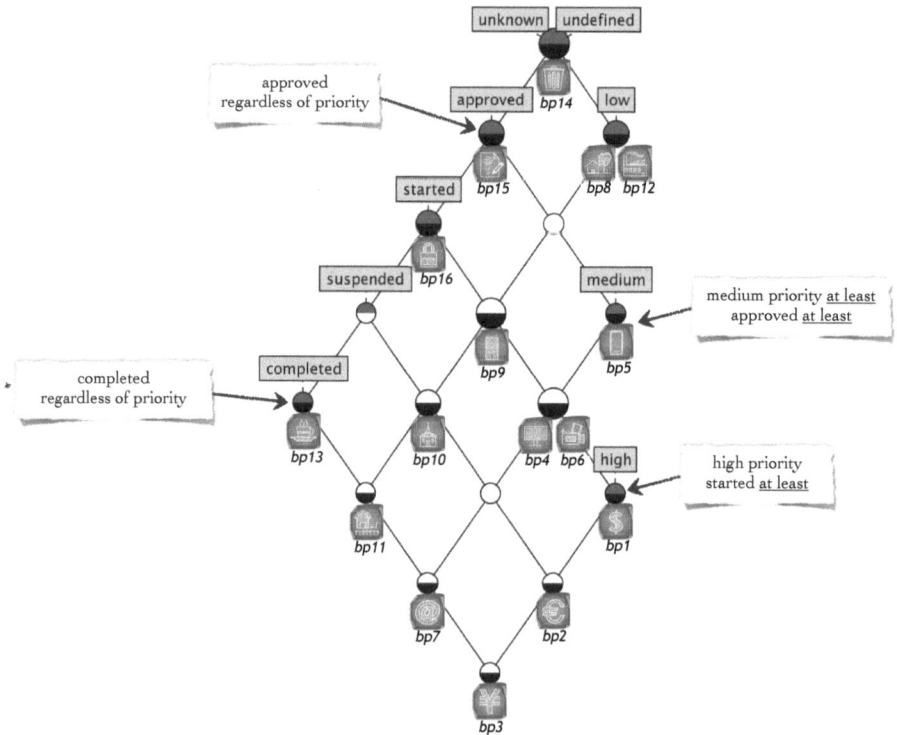

Fig. 5. Blueprints lattice revealing different profiles

this profile, in which the stakeholder participated. In this example, we considered this number to be one blueprint at least. We also considered stakeholder participation to be a coarse-grained relation that includes proposing, approving, starting, and completing a blueprint. This aggregation of relations and getting the corresponding data is obtained through a direct SPARQL query on the RDF data.

Table 4. Stakeholders formal context

	completed regardless of priority	high priority started at least	medium priority at least approved at least	approved regardless of priority
david		×	×	
john		×		
robert		×	×	
tony		×	×	×
oliver		×	×	×
mark		×		
joseph		×		
martin		×	×	
daniel	×			
kevin		×	×	×
mike		×	×	
william				
patrick		×	×	×
edward	×			

The stakeholder lattice that results from the context in Table 4, is shown in Fig. 6. In this lattice, we can notice the formation of four communities of stakeholders. Stakeholders inside each community share the fact that they participated in blueprints belonging to one of the four chosen profiles. We can notice that the stakeholder called *William* does not belong to any community. This is normal since we did not consider the blueprint profile (low priority and unknown status), in which he participates. We can notice also that these communities are overlapping. For example, the members of community $C4$ participate in blueprints of all profiles. While for example, the members of community $C1$ participate only in blueprints of a high priority and that are started at least.

Like this, stakeholder profiles can now be enriched with an additional information concerning their participation, obtained in a collective relative manner.

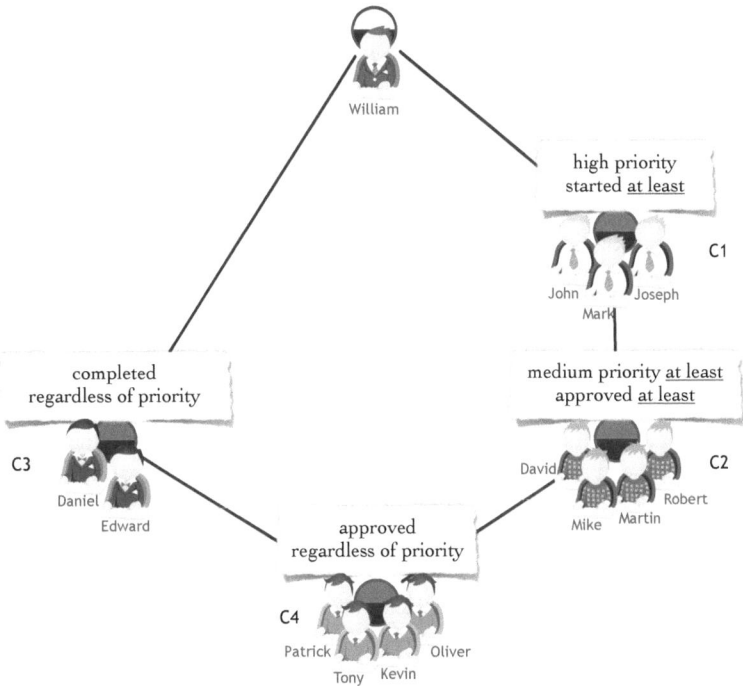

Fig. 6. Lattice of stakeholder communities

Possible Configurations: FCA and RCA tend to generate fairly large lattices when dealing with datasets of large sizes. Possible solution to such an issue is to use the notion of a Galois Sub-Hierarchy [12], which is a compressed representation of the lattice. It encodes in a non-redundant way all the information that is necessary for the recovery of the complete lattice [14]. Another possibility is to impose constraints on the number of requirements inside each profile, and the number of requirements a stakeholder must participate in to have a certain requirement profile.

4 Proof of Concept

In this section, we present one of our conducted experiments, the Inkscape project[2], and we show the obtained results.

The Inkscape project contains 3840 contributing stakeholders, and 227 blueprints. We choose to show how the approach processes the blueprints only, because of the limited paper space. The analyst configurations[3] that we choose for classifying the blueprints are the following:

- **definitionState**, takes the values: **pendingApproval** = {new, review, drafting, discussion}, **approved**, **discarded** = {obsolete, superseded};

- **priority**, takes the values: **undefined**, **not**, **low** < **medium** < **high** < **essential**;

- **relatedToBlueprint**, takes the value true if it is related to another blueprint;

- **relatedToBug**, takes the value true if it is related to a bug.

We also specify the relations that we want to take into consideration. We consider that stakeholders who **proposed** and **subscribed** to blueprints, have **participatedIn-Blueprint**. Running the approach on this data results in two lattices[4]: a lattice of blueprints, and a lattice that classifies stakeholders by the extracted blueprint profiles.

The blueprints lattice, shown in Fig. 7, gives us an overview of the blueprints, according to the considered attributes. It shows three main profiles: discarded, pendingApproval, and approved blueprints. The approved blueprints profile contains itself three other main sub profiles. We list these profiles in Table 5 together with the number of blueprints inside each one of them. Thereafter, we build the stakeholders lattice using the three main blueprint profiles. This lattice is shown in Fig. 8, it highlights six communities of stakeholders. The communities 1, 3, and 6 correspond to stakeholders participating in approved, pendingApproval, and discarded blueprints, respectively. *Community*1 for example, contains itself two other sub communities, with a total number of 80 stakeholders (63 of them participated in accepted blueprints only). Usually, stakeholders appearing closer to the bottom of a lattice tend to have more

Table 5. Extracted blueprint profiles

Blueprint profile	Description	# blueprints
blueprint-p1	discarded	41
blueprint-p2	pendingApproval	161
blueprint-p3	approved	25
blueprint-p3.1	approved-low	4
blueprint-p3.2	approved-medium	12
blueprint-p3.2.1	approved-medium-relatedToBug	10
blueprint-p3.3	approved-high	6
blueprint-p3.3.1	approved-high-relatedToBug	4
blueprint-p3.4	approved-essential	2

---

[2] Data retrieved on September 18, 2012, from `https://launchpad.net/inkscape`.

[3] The attributes and values are provided by Launchpad. We specify the values that we consider to be equivalent and also specify the ones that should be treated according to some order.

[4] Here, we show a compact version of the lattices. The complete lattices can be visualized on: `www-sop.inria.fr/members/Zeina.Azmeh/REFSQ13/`

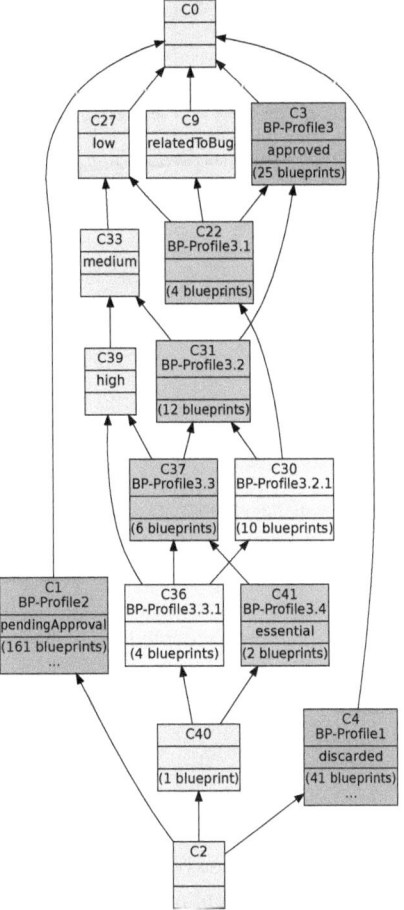

Fig. 7. The blueprints lattices

profiles. For example, the three stakeholders of $Community4$ have participated in blueprints belonging to the three blueprint profiles.

Lattices Utilization: The blueprints lattice gives us a better view on the blueprints according to their various attributes. It enables us to identify the different profiles, in addition to exploring a classification of these profiles. This is quite useful because if we consider for example the case of accepted blueprints, the next activity that may be applied to them might be selection for processing. Having such a blueprint classification (embodied in the lattice) enables us to identify the blueprints that have the best values for the chosen attributes. These blueprints are the ones appearing closer to the bottom of the lattice (because they cover more attribute values than the others).

Using the stakeholders lattice, we can discover stakeholders having specific profiles. In this experiment, we considered the main blueprint profiles only, but if we consider all the profiles in Table 5, we can then discover for example, the stakeholders who

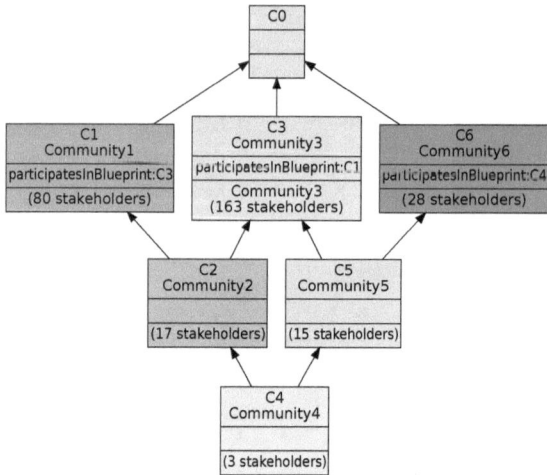

Fig. 8. Lattice of stakeholders of the Inkscape project

participated in approved blueprints with high to essential priority values (the profile *blueprint-p*3.3). Blueprints that may be proposed in the future by these stakeholders may have a higher probability of being accepted than the ones potentially proposed by stakeholders of *Community*6 (who participated in discarded blueprints only). We can also decide to prioritize stakeholders having the best blueprint profiles, and consequently prioritize their blueprints.

Threats to Validity: According to the experiments that we conducted, we noticed some limitations in our proposed approach. These limitations appear in three situations: when the contributing stakeholders are newbies with no previous participation in any blueprint or bug, when there is no sufficient number of evaluated blueprints or bugs to extract stakeholder communities, and when the retrieved dataset is fairly huge (the case for instance of the Ubuntu project having more than 290,000 bugs).

Since our approach has a learning aspect (evaluating stakeholders according to their evaluated artifacts), in the first two situations, the approach will fail to produce useful lattices. In such a case, stakeholders might get grouped into only one community; the community of stakeholders participating in requirements that are pendingApproval.

Having large datasets will also cause some inefficiency to the approach, regarding the ability to analyze the resulting lattices due to the added complexity.

Discussion: In this experiment, we considered the stakeholders' participation in blueprints only. Considering their participation in other artifacts (bugs or code branches) gives us more information about them that would help in better evaluating them. The advantage of using RCA is that we can choose to consider any other artifact to enrich the stakeholders lattice without affecting the approach. Especially with the use of the ontology that we are proposing, since we can choose the different levels of granularity that we wish to consider. Nevertheless, this may add more complexity to the resulting lattices, regarding their readability and understandability.

What should be noticed is that the approach can be totally configured regarding the chosen levels of granularity, even when deciding the blueprint profiles to consider. For example, the stakeholders lattice was generated considering a coarse granularity. Considering finer granularity would leads us to generate the stakeholders lattice using all of the extracted blueprint profiles.

5   Related Work

In this section, we list related work of two main categories: works dealing with requirements engineering using social network analysis (SNA), and works dealing with community detection. Social Network Analysis is the application of methods to understand the relationships among actors and on the patterns and implications of the relationships. A social network is a structure consisting of actors and the relations defined on them. It is often depicted as a graph. A community in a social network is a group of people that are gathered according to their common properties or approximating interests.

Social Network Analysis (SNA): In [15], Lim and Finkelstein propose a tool for the elicitation of pertinent highly wanted requirements in a software system. It is a semi-automatic approach that makes use of social network analysis for requirement engineering. Fitsilis et al. present in [8] the use of SNA for the management and prioritization of software requirements. In [20], Pagano lists the challenges, embodied in the fairly huge amount of unstructured data that may suffer of a low quality and possible conflicts. He also lists the current techniques aiming at facing each of these challenges, like SNA and collaborative filtering. In [18], Mulla and Girase proposed an approach that uses social networks and collaborative filtering for requirements prioritization.

Community Detection: Community detection and graph partitioning share the goal of separating a network into groups of nodes having few connections between them [19]. The difference is that in community detection, the objective is to find the naturally occurring groups regardless of their number or size. Another difference is that in graph theory, ideal partitioning results in disjointed groups, while in community detection, groups may be overlapping.

In [24], Veerappa and Letier propose an approach for stakeholders clustering based on their approximating ratings on requirements. The discovered stakeholders groups can be used afterwards for requirements decision-making. In [7], Cuvelier and Aufaure explain the notion of a community in the light of graph theory. They present the principle graph definitions and the different graph related measures that can be employed for social network analysis [23]. They list and detail the existing methods for community detection, categorized according to the used techniques.

In [25], Wang et al. models the interactions of users and information in a bipartite graph. They propose to manipulate the resulting graph by one-mode projections to capture the shared interests of users and the information similarity. In [9], Flake et al. propose an algorithm for detecting communities in graphs of Web pages connected by hyperlinks. In [4], Blondel et al. present a heuristic method for discovering communities based on modularity optimization. Modularity, which is detailed in [19], is a score for measuring the density of links inside and outside communities that helps in determining the belonging of a node to a certain community. Other works that we can find adopt divisive algorithms that work on splitting a network by deleting edges [22]. Additionally, others use agglomerative algorithms that work on adding nodes to groups until no individual node remains [11].

Discussion: To our knowledge, current techniques for SNA and community detection manipulate social graphs according to their topologies only. They do not consider the semantics conveyed by the network elements. Consequently, a lot of important information may get discarded (as we showed in Section 4). Moreover, in the presented works, communities are considered as disjointed groups of nodes that do not overlap. While using concept lattices, the communities overlap.

An advantage of using FCA and RCA lies in the fact that we can represent any social network with its complete set of data, without any loss of information. Then the derived concepts enable us to reveal groups of each type of nodes with inclusion relations between these groups.

6   Conclusion

In this paper, we presented an approach for discovering communities of stakeholders to support requirements handling and decision-making. The approach is based on semantic Web languages and concept lattices. It reveals stakeholder communities by analyzing their past participation in requirements. We considered as a study context a platform for collaborative software development, from which we retrieved datasets about projects and annotated them semantically. The use of concept lattices enabled us to analyze heterogeneous multi-relational social networks of stakeholders and artifacts.

There are diverse perspectives for this work. On top of these perspectives is to study the utilization of the approach for the purpose of prioritization as well as recommendation of requirements and/or stakeholders, in addition to introducing the notion of trust among stakeholder communities. Another point that we would like to work on is to connect data from several platforms to enrich user profiles. An important issue to be considered also, is the scalability of the approach, when considering fairly large datasets. This may imply the dynamic updating of the resulting concept lattices, using incremental lattice construction algorithms. We may also consider the use of Galois Sub-Hierarchies (GSH) [12] as compact alternatives for concept lattices.

References

1. DOAP vocabulary (description of a project),
   https://github.com/edumbill/doap/wiki
2. Launchpad, https://launchpad.net/
3. Begel, A., Herbsleb, J.D., Storey, M.A.: The future of collaborative software development. In: Proceedings of CSCW 2012, pp. 17–18. ACM, New York (2012)
4. Blondel, V., Guillaume, J., Lambiotte, R., Mech, E.: Fast unfolding of communities in large networks. J. Stat. Mech., P10008 (2008)

5. Brickley, D., Guha, R.V.: Rdf vocabulary description language 1.0: Rdf schema. Tech. rep. (February 2004),
   `http://www.w3.org/TR/2004/REC-rdf-schema-20040210/`
6. Brickley, D., Miller, L.: FOAF Vocabulary Specification 0.98. Namespace document (August 2010), `http://xmlns.com/foaf/spec/`
7. Cuvelier, E., Aufaure, M.-A.: Graph mining and communities detection. In: Aufaure, M.-A., Zimányi, E. (eds.) eBISS 2011. LNBIP, vol. 96, pp. 117–138. Springer, Heidelberg (2012)
8. Fitsilis, P., Gerogiannis, V., Anthopoulos, L., Savvas, I.K.: Supporting the requirements prioritization process using social network analysis techniques. In: Proceedings of WETICE 2010, pp. 110–115. IEEE CS, Washington, DC (2010)
9. Flake, G.W., Lawrence, S., Giles, C.L., Coetzee, F.M.: Self-organization and identification of web communities. Computer 35(3), 66–71 (2002)
10. Ganter, B., Wille, R.: Formal Concept Analysis: Mathematical Foundations. Springer, Heidelberg (1999)
11. Girvan, M., Newman, M.: Community structure in social and biological networks. Proceedings of the National Academy of Sciences 99(12), 7821–7826 (2002)
12. Godin, R., Mili, H.: Building and maintaining analysis-level class hierarchies using galois lattices. SIGPLAN Not. 28(10), 394–410 (1993)
13. Happel, H.-J., Maalej, W., Seedorf, S.: Applications of ontologies in collaborative software development. In: Mistrík, I., Grundy, J., Hoek, A., Whitehead, J. (eds.) Collaborative Software Engineering, pp. 109–129. Springer, Heidelberg (2010)
14. Huchard, M., Hacene, M.R., Roume, C., Valtchev, P.: Relational concept discovery in structured datasets. Ann. Math. Artif. Intell. 49(1-4), 39–76 (2007)
15. Lim, S.L., Finkelstein, A.: Stakerare: Using social networks and collaborative filtering for large-scale requirements elicitation. IEEE Trans. Softw. Eng. 38(3), 707–735 (2012)
16. Manola, F., Miller, E.: RDF primer. W3C Recommendation 10, 1–107 (2004),
   `http://www.w3.org/TR/rdf-primer/`
17. Mirbel, I.: OFLOSSC, an ontology for supporting open source development communities. In: Cordeiro, J., Filipe, J. (eds.) ICEIS (4), pp. 47–52 (2009)
18. Mulla, N., Girase, S.: A new approach to requirement elicitation based on stakeholder recommendation and collaborative filtering. IJSEA 3(3), 51–60 (2012)
19. Newman, M.: Modularity and community structure in networks. Proceedings of the National Academy of Sciences 103(23), 8577–8582 (2006)
20. Pagano, D.: Towards systematic analysis of continuous user input. In: Proceedings of the 4th International Workshop, SSE 2011, pp. 6–10. ACM, New York (2011)
21. Prud'hommeaux, E., Seaborne, A.: SPARQL query language for RDF. W3C Recommendation 4, 1–106 (2008), `http://www.w3.org/TR/rdf-sparql-query/`
22. Shen, Y., Pei, W., Wang, K., Li, T., Wang, S.: Recursive filtration method for detecting community structure in networks. Physica A: Statistical Mechanics and its Applications 387(26), 6663–6670 (2008)
23. Tang, L., Liu, H.: Graph mining applications to social network analysis. In: Aggarwal, C.C., Wang, H. (eds.) Managing and Mining Graph Data, Advances in Database Systems, vol. 40, pp. 487–513. Springer US (2010)
24. Veerappa, V., Letier, E.: Clustering stakeholders for requirements decision making. In: Berry, D. (ed.) REFSQ 2011. LNCS, vol. 6606, pp. 202–208. Springer, Heidelberg (2011)
25. Wang, F., Xu, K., Wang, H.: Discovering shared interests in online social networks. In: ICDCS Workshops, pp. 163–168. IEEE Computer Society (2012)

Choosing Compliance Solutions through Stakeholder Preferences

Silvia Ingolfo[1], Alberto Siena[1], Ivan Jureta[2],
Angelo Susi[3], Anna Perini[3], and John Mylopoulos[1]

[1] University of Trento, via Sommarive 14, Trento, Italy
{silvia.ingolfo,a.siena,jm}@unitn.it
[2] University of Namur, 8, rempart de la vierge, 5000 Namur, Belgium
ivan.jureta@fundp.ac.be
[3] FBK-Irst, via Sommarive 18, Trento, Italy
{susi,perini}@fbk.eu

Abstract. [**Context and motivation**] Compliance to relevant laws is increasingly recognized as a critical, but also expensive, quality for software requirements. [**Question/Problem**] Laws contain elements such as conditions and derogations that generate a space of possible compliance alternatives. During requirements engineering, an analyst has to select one of these compliance alternatives and ensure that the requirements specification she is putting together complies with that alternative. However, the space of such alternatives is often large. [**Principal ideas and results**] This paper extends Nòmos 2, a modeling framework for laws, to support modeling of and reasoning with stakeholder preferences and priorities. The problem of preferred regulatory compliance is then defined as a problem of finding a compliance alternative that matches best stakeholder preferences. [**Contribution**] The paper defines the concept of preference between situations and integrates it with the Nòmos 2 modeling language. It also presents a reasoning tool for preferences and illustrates its use with an extract from a use case concerning the Italian law on Electronic Health Record.

Keywords: Regulatory compliance, stakeholder preferences, models of law.

1 Introduction

We have entered an era where software quality is determined not only by the degree to which a software system meets its requirements (fitness-for-purpose), but also by the degree to which it complies with relevant norms (fitness-to-norms) [3]. There is now a rapidly growing number of laws and regulations world-wide that impacts on software systems, and requirements engineers are challenged to understand and analyze the various ways their systems can fulfill their requirements, while complying with all applicable laws.

Fitness-to-norms, or compliance, is usually understood as a binary criterion: either a system complies with a given law, or it is in violation. However, there can

J. Doerr and A.L. Opdahl (Eds.): REFSQ 2013, LNCS 7830, pp. 206–220, 2013.

be (and generally there are) multiple ways to comply with a given law because of variability elements contained in legal texts, such as conditions, exceptions, derogations, alternatives, cross-references, etc. Such elements allow alternative ways to comply, depending on which conditional elements apply for a system under design. This variability implies that there isn't a single compliance solution, but rather a space of compliance alternatives. While alternatives in law are equal to the legislator, they are not equal to stakeholders: some alternatives may fit better existing requirements, while others may cost less to comply with. In other words, if a software system has to comply with a given law, *how* it complies also defines how well stakeholder requirements are met. So the problem of ensuring regulatory compliance of requirements includes a search for the best way to comply. We define the Preferred Compliance Problem as the problem of finding the best compliance solution, given a law and a set of stakeholder preferences.

The main objective of this paper is to formulate and address the Preferred Compliance Problem. Our solution to the problem is based on the idea that stakeholder preferences drive the search in a space of compliant alternatives. Norms are modelled with Nòmos 2, a modelling framework tailored to law that supports reasoning about regulatory compliance of software requirements [22]. In this proposal, our norm models [22] are enriched with preferences between situations (partial states of the world) entailed by norms. Moreover, stakeholder assumptions can be expressed and included in the model as hard constraints. Models built in terms of such concepts are subsequently analyzed to find candidate compliance solutions. We acknowledge that the usefulness of the analysis of these models — like any engineering model — critically depends on its quality. Our proposal is illustrated through a small part of a real use case involving the Italian law on Electronic Health Record. A prototype tool is used to analyze Nòmos 2 models using disjunctive logic programming. Details about the tool are presented in a companion paper [10].

The rest of the paper is organized as follows. Section 2 recalls basic definitions of the Nòmos 2 conceptual modelling framework for laws, founded on the concepts of norm and situation. Section 3 provides a formulation of the Preferred Compliance Problem and defines the solution concept to this problem. An overview of a functioning prototype tool is presented in section 4, while section 5 illustrates our approach and the capabilities of the tool with a use case. Related work is discussed in section 6, while section 7 concludes the paper.

2   Modelling Law with Nòmos 2

Nòmos 2 is a modeling framework proposed in [22] that aims at capturing the variability of compliance alternatives for norms. Indeed, legal texts contain elements such as conditions, exceptions or derogations defining the *applicability* of alternative norms within a piece of law. In Nòmos 2 a Norm[1] is defined as

---

[1] 'Norm' refers to the concept, while lowercase 'norm' refers to an instance. Similarly with 'Situation'/'situation'.

a 5-tuple *(type, hol, ctrpart, ant, cons)*, where *type* is the type of the Norm (e.g., duty or right); *hol* is the *holder* of the Norm, the role having to satisfy the Norm, if that Norm applies; *ctrpart* is the *counterpart*, the role whose interests are helped if the Norm is satisfied;[2] *ant* is the *antecedent*, the conditions to satisfy for the Norm to apply; *cons* is the *consequent*, the conditions to satisfy for the Norm to be complied with.

The applicability and satisfaction of a norm depend on situations which are satisfied, the idea being that if some situations are satisfied, the norm will apply, and when other situations are satisfied, the norm will be satisfied. Situations and norms are partial states of the world that we may know to hold (meaning the situation or norm is satisfied), not hold, or neither (when we can't conclude satisfaction or denial).

In our model, situations are linked to norms in terms of four relations: two relations for applicability (activate, block), and two relations for satisfiability (sat, break). The relation *activate* (resp. *block*), from a situation to a norm, means that if the situation is satisfied the norm is applicable (resp. not applicable). The relation *satisfy* (resp. *break*), from a situation to a norm or another situation, means that if the situation is satisfied the norm or the other situation is satisfied (resp. not satisfied). On top of these four basic relations we have three composite relations for norms.[3] The relation *derogate*, means that complying with the first norm makes the second norm not applicable. The relation *endorse*, means that complying with the first norm makes the second norm applicable. The relation *imply*, means that satisfaction of the first norm entails satisfaction of the second norm.

Norm models are used to reason about compliance of requirements. Consistent sets of requirements satisfy one or more situations, and according to how situations are related to norms they make certain norms applicable or satisfied. Situations are labeled as ST (Satisfiability True) if there is evidence that they are satisfied; as SF (Satisfiability False) if there is evidence that they are not satisfied; as SU (Satisfiability Unknown) if there is no evidence or no decision is made. The relations of our model act as label-propagation channels that propagate labels from their source (situation or norm) to their target. Depending on the pair of labels associated to a norm (for applicability and satisfiability) the norm may be compliant, violated, tolerated or inconclusive. Anytime a norm is not applicable it is 'tolerated', when the applicability is not known it is 'inconclusive'. When a norm is applicable it can be either 'complied with', 'violated' or 'tolerated' depending on the satisfiability value and on the type of norm (duty/right).[4]

Use of the language. Nòmos 2 models allow us to represent fragments of laws or regulations by representing the different conditions and rules described by

---

[2] In the rest of the paper we use the term 'legal subject' to refer to the role holder and counterpart.

[3] These relations, *shortcuts* in [22], can be defined as a composition of the four basic relations.

[4] For more details see [22].

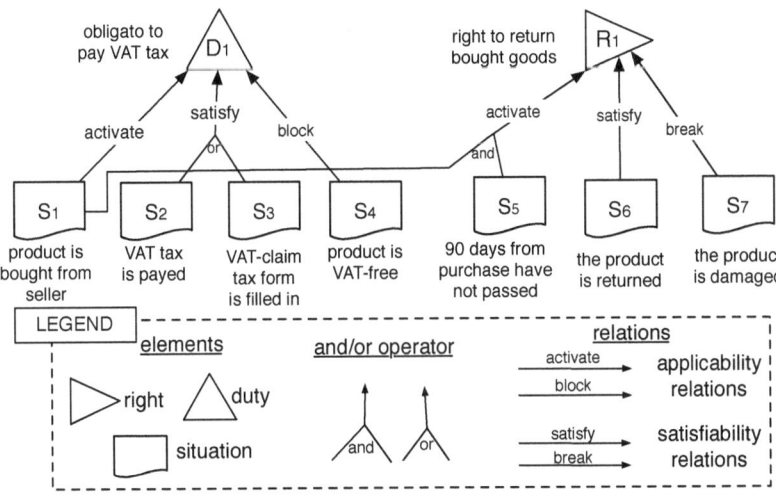

Fig. 1. An example of our modeling language and its graphical syntax

a law or regulation, and the alternative ways to comply with it. For example when the legal subject 'customer' is in the situation 'product is bought from seller', then several legal clauses regarding reimbursement, tax-payment and tax-declaration apply. We say that a legal subject *complies* with a clause if that clause applies to that legal subject and the subject satisfies that clause. If the customer pays the taxes on the product — i.e., the legal subject is in the situation 'VAT-tax on product is paid' — then the customer is *complying* with the clause about paying VAT taxes. Leveraging on applicability and satisfiability of the different situations that are holding, it is possible to identify how to comply with a law in different ways (e.g., by paying the VAT tax, by buying a VAT-free product, ...).

In figure 1 we show an example with the graphical syntax of our modeling language, applied to an hypothetical tax law. This simple example shows how, when a product is bought from a seller ($S_1 \xrightarrow{\text{activate}} D_1$), the duty to pay taxes is activated. You comply with this duty either by paying the taxes ($S_2 \xrightarrow{\text{satisfy}} D_1$) or by filling in the VAT-claim tax form ($S_3 \xrightarrow{\text{satisfy}} D_1$). This option is represented by an or-operator that satisfies the duty. VAT-free product are untaxed by definition, so if the product is VAT-free (i.e. S_4 is ST), the duty is no longer applicable ($S_4 \xrightarrow{\text{block}} D_1$). For purposes of this example, we consider that most stores have a return policy for which you have up to 90 days to return the product bought in that store. These two situations (S_1, S_5) activate the right to return the good, which in turn is complied with (*exercised*) when the product is returned ($S_6 \xrightarrow{\text{satisfy}} R_1$). However, if the product is damaged, then you can not exercise the right ($S_7 \xrightarrow{\text{break}} R_1$).

Notice that this simple model has different compliance solutions (for example, paying VAT tax, filling in the VAT-claim tax form, buying VAT-free products, etc.). To generalize, since in a norm model situations constitute free variables, and their possible labels (satisfied, not satisfied, undefined) determine the number of permutations on the model, the total amount of possible permutations is 3^s, where s = number of situations. The total number of compliance solutions is between 0 and 3^s, and depends on the topology of the model. In any case, since the number of possible permutations grows exponentially, the number of compliance alternatives also grows quickly. Given a large number of compliance alternatives, it becomes necessary to compare them, so as to help identify one that best responds to stakeholder expectations.

3 The Preferred Compliance Problem

This section defines the *Preferred Compliance Problem* (PCP hereafter), as the problem of identifying alternative ways to comply with applicable Norms, and comparing these alternatives on the basis of stakeholder preferences. Since there can be different criteria for comparison and as their relative importance can vary across stakeholders and systems engineering projects, PCP does not prescribe a specific procedure or rule for ranking alternatives.

Compliance can be understood as a relation between a design of a system-to-be, environment conditions in which the system-to-be will operate, the requirements it will satisfy, *and* a set of applicable Norms. To get to the PCP, we will start from the known Zave & Jackson [24] (Z&J) requirements problem formulation, which abstracts from the issue of compliance. We will suggest below how to extend Z&J requirements problem to the Compliance Problem (CP) using Nòmos 2, explain where variability is in the CP, define the preference relation needed to compare alternatives in the CP, which will finally lead us to state the PCP.

Z&J requirements problem is: Given domain assumptions D and requirements R, find a design of the system-to-be, such that its specification S is consistent with D and R, and together with D satisfies R, i.e., $D \cup S \vdash R$, where $\vdash$ is the consequence relation of classical (propositional or first-order) logic.

How does Z&J Relate to Situations and Norms? Applicable Norms, to which a system-to-be needs to comply, are a function of Situations that will occur in the environment in which the system-to-be will operate. In other words, which Norms apply depends on what the system does, and on the environment in which it does it. Since the system is designed to satisfy requirements within that environment, it follows that applicable Norms will depend on all three components of the Z&J requirements problem — the requirements R, the conditions in the environment D, and the design of the system-to-be S.

Given this dependency, we can write the function $\mathrm{Sit}(D, R, S)$ for the set of Situations that can occur if we choose the design S of the system-to-be, for the requirements R, and domain assumptions D. If we choose some different D_j, R_j, S_j, then $\mathrm{Sit}(D, R, S)$ is not necessarily same as $\mathrm{Sit}(D_j, R_j, S_j)$, i.e., different systems, environments, requirements result, quite expectedly, in different Situations.

We know from Nòmos 2 that whether a Norm applies depends on the Situation that occurs. Therefore, the set of applicable Norms, given all potentially applicable Norms N, is returned by $\text{App}(N, \text{Sit}(D, R, S))$. Now, we need to distinguish two kinds of Norms in $\text{App}(N, \text{Sit}(D, R, S))$:

- Norms which play a role analogous to domain assumptions in the Z&J requirements problem, in the sense that Situations should be not be in conflict (i.e., Nòmos 2 break or block relations) with these Norms. We denote these $\text{App}_1(N, \text{Sit}(D, R, S))$.
- Norms which have a role analogous to new requirements in the Z&J requirements problem, requiring us to ensure that we satisfy Situations in which these Norms are satisfied. We will denote them $\text{App}_2(N, \text{Sit}(D, R, S))$.

What is the Compliance Problem? Following the argument above, CP is: Given domain assumptions D, requirements R, and Norms N, find a design of the system-to-be, such that its specification S ensures the following conditions are satisfied:

1. $D \cup \text{App}_1(N, \text{Sit}(D, R, S)) \cup S$ is consistent;
2. $D \cup \text{App}_1(N, \text{Sit}(D, R, S)) \cup S \vdash R \cup \text{App}_2(N, \text{Sit}(D, R, S))$.

Since Situations depend on D, R, and S, we can reformulate the CP as follows: *Given a set of potentially satisfiable Situations $\mathcal{S}$, find a set of Situations $X \in \wp(\mathcal{S})$, such that X satisfies $App_1(N, Sit(D, R, S)) \cup App_2(N, Sit(D, R, S))$*, where $\wp(\mathcal{S})$ is the powerset of Situations.

The limitation of this CP is that, when there are alternative sets of Situations which satisfy the said conditions, the CP does not compare these alternatives. This is misleading, as it makes the alternatives, which we call below Candidate Compliance Solutions, appear equally desirable, yet they are not: some of them will be produced by systems that satisfy more desirable requirements than others.

What is a Candidate Compliance Solution? It seems, from the CP, that a solution to the CP is a set of Situations. We prefer, however, to keep also in that solution, the Norms satisfied by these Situations. This leads us to the following *Candidate Compliance Solution* concept: A Candidate Compliance Solution i, to a CP instance, is a pair (X_i, N_i), such that:

1. $X_i \in \wp(\mathcal{S})$ is a set of Situations,
2. $N_i = \text{App}_1(N, \text{Sit}(D, R, S)) \cup \text{App}_2(N, \text{Sit}(D, R, S))$,
3. X_i satisfies all Norms in N_i.

How to Compare Candidate Compliance Solutions? To capture the information that some Candidate Compliance Solutions are more desirable than others, we add to Nòmos 2 a set of binary reflexive, antisymmetric and transitive relations $\leq_C \in \mathcal{S} \times \mathcal{S}$, each $\leq_C$ defining a partial order on Situations. Informally, we call these relations *preference relations*, and we read $\phi \leq_C \psi$ as "ψ is at least as desirable as ϕ according to criterion C". We let $\phi =_C \psi$ abbreviate

"$\phi \leq_C \psi$ and $\psi \leq_C \phi$", so that $\phi <_C \psi$ abbreviates "$\phi \leq_C \psi$ and not $\phi =_C \psi$", and informally reads "ψ is strictly more desirable than ϕ according to criterion C". Each criterion C defines a partial order over Situations. Note that adding preference relations to Nòmos 2 does not influence the satisfaction values, and other features of that language.

Preference relations allow us to record relative desirability of stakeholders between Situations, according to different criteria for comparison. Let $\mathcal{C}$ denote the set of all criteria. We can further add relations between criteria, to help comparisons. We can define a hierarchy of domain-specific criteria for comparison, such as, for example: Criterion *Cost* is an aggregate of criteria *Production cost*, *Infrastructure cost*, *Transportation cost*, etc. Such a structuring can help define aggregation functions and/or procedures to automatically rank alternative sets of Situations.

We do not discuss how preferences are negotiated between stakeholders, since different stakeholders can have opposing preferences over the same criteria. Both the definition of aggregation functions of preferences over criteria, and the negotiation of conflicting preferences are outside the scope of this paper.

What is the Preferred Compliance Problem? The presence of two or more Candidate Compliance Solutions, to a given CP, and the availability of preferences leads to the Preferred Compliance Problem. In contrast to CP, where the aim is to identify a (or at least one) Candidate Compliance Solution, PCP requires that preference be used to select one Candidate Compliance Solution, as *the* Compliance Solution to the PCP. We state the PCP as follows.

> *Preferred Compliance Problem:* Given a set of potentially satisfiable Situations $\mathcal{S}$, find a set of Situations $X \in \wp(\mathcal{S})$, such that:
> 1. X satisfies $\text{App}_1(N, \text{Sit}(D, R, S)) \cup \text{App}_2(N, \text{Sit}(D, R, S))$,
> 2. there is no set of Situations X' such that the Candidate Compliance Solution (X', N) ranks higher than Candidate Compliance Solution (X, N), according to a given ranking function r, which returns a total order over all Candidate Compliance Solutions.

Informally, PCP requires us to compare Candidate Compliance Solutions according to preferences, and to select one of the Candidate Compliance Solutions. Above, we assume that there is a ranking function r, which establishes from a set of preferences over Situations, a total order over all Candidate Compliance Solutions. Note that r need not be given as a mathematical function, but can be defined as a process that results in a ranking (for example, the process of asking stakeholders to vote for Candidate Compliance Solutions).

4   Automated Reasoning

As the size of a reasoning problem grows, it becomes harder for humans to deal with its complexity. It is therefore important to support automated reasoning of large models in order to check for important and interesting properties, such as consistency. The overhead of building these kinds of model — which can be reduced with the support of automated tools such as [14] — is indeed compensated by the consistent and completeness of its automated analysis.

In order to support analysts to solve the PCP, we are developing a tool called NRTool.[5] It essentially performs bottom-up and and top-down analysis to search for a Nòmos 2 model for Candidate Compliance Solutions, and rank them according to the preference function r.

The space of situations to be analyzed in a Nòmos 2 model can become intractable (3^s, where s corresponds to the number of situations in the model), so in our implementation of the problem we give the analyst the possibility to specify *assumptions*: strong constraints on the satisfaction value of some specific situations in the model. The use of assumptions helps the tool cut down the space of possible solution, and allows the analyst specify known facts that must hold in every Candidate Compliance Solutions.

The NRTool works by translating the PCP into a disjunctive Datalog [1, 17] program. Disjunctive Datalog is a declarative logic language and a deductive system where facts and deduction rules are expressed in the logic language. Disjunctions may appear in the rule heads to allow multiple alternative consequences to be drawn from a rule. Situations and norms are mapped onto Datalog facts, while relations are mapped onto deduction rules. NRTool relies on DLV [2] as Datalog reasoning engine. DLV further extends disjunctive Datalog to also support weak constraints, priorities for their satisfaction, and costs for their violation. These extensions allow us to represent the *preferences* on the satisfaction value of pairs/group of situations (represented as weak constraints and priorities on them), and to have an evaluation of the costs to be payed for the set of violated preferences. Concerning the search techniques and heuristics used by DLV, it implements a back search similar to SAT algorithms and advanced pruning operators, (look-ahead and look-back techniques) for model generation, and innovative techniques for answer-set checking.

An important characteristic of DLV is the possibility to obtain the complete set of solutions (models) produced by a set of predicates and assignments to the variables or to prune the set of models depending on the preferences specified by the decision makers. We exploit these features indeed to generate and prune the alternatives that fits the preferences specified in the input compliance problem. With the specification of assumptions (fixed assignments to some situations of the model), we further help this pruning mechanism.

NRTool works as depicted in figure 2: using a custom input language, the analyst provides the description of the PCP to be solved: (i) a set of *preferences* between pairs or groups of situations, and (ii) a *query* about norms to be complied with. Additionally he can specify the value of some situations that are known or hypothesized to be true or false (*assumptions*). A Nòmos 2 model of the law is then added to this specification of the PCP problem, and it is then

---

[5] The tool is in a prototype development phase and can be made available upon request. As soon as a stable release will be ready, it will be published online.

converted by the tool into Datalog.[6] Finally, the tool parses the output of the reasoning engine and presents it to the user. The use of preferences is used to return the best solutions to the problem. In the next section we will see how the tool can help us find the best Candidate Compliance Solutions.

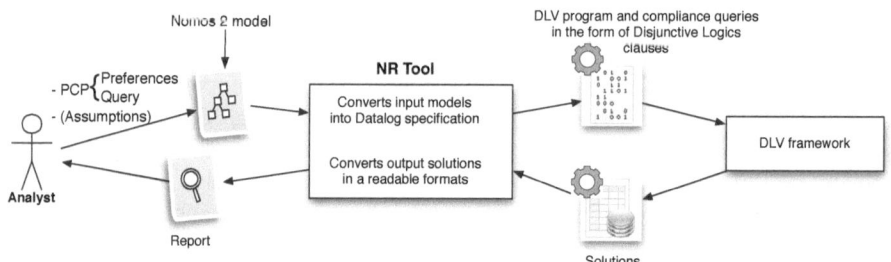

Fig. 2. NRTool transforms the input provided by the analyst (PCP and assumptions) into a disjunctive Datalog program, and reports the output of the Datalog engine back to the analyst

5 Use Case: The CSS Project and the Italian Law on Electronic Health Record

In a recent industrial case study [11], we have been involved in the analysis of the Italian law on Electronic Health Record (EHR).[7] The context of the study was that of an Italian organization involved in the design and development of a project called CSS (*Cartella Socio Sanitaria* — Electronic Social/Health Record) aimed at monitoring healthcare and social processes in Trentino, a region in northern Italy. The main goal of the CSS project was to support sharing the information of the patients among the different health care entities involved in the project (e.g., hospitals, family doctors, and other agencies for social, mental health and other medical services). The CSS system needed therefore to be designed and created in respect of the principles set forth by the Guidelines on EHR and the Italian Privacy Law.

During our study we have closely analyzed the problem of complying with section 3.10 and 3.11 of the law. In this section it is explained how a patient has the the right not to include some information in the EHR system, and also how the patient has the right to have some information removed from his record (called 'blanking' right). Moreover this section shapes an important duty for the EHR system which is forbidden to notify the event that some information has been blanked in a patient's record. In the context of CSS, the purpose of this EHR system was indeed to share the patient information among all authorized entities. To achieve this goal, it was envisaged for the system not to directly share

---

[6] We assume that a Nòmos 2 model of the law is given.

[7] http://www.garanteprivacy.it/garante/doc.jsp?ID=1634116

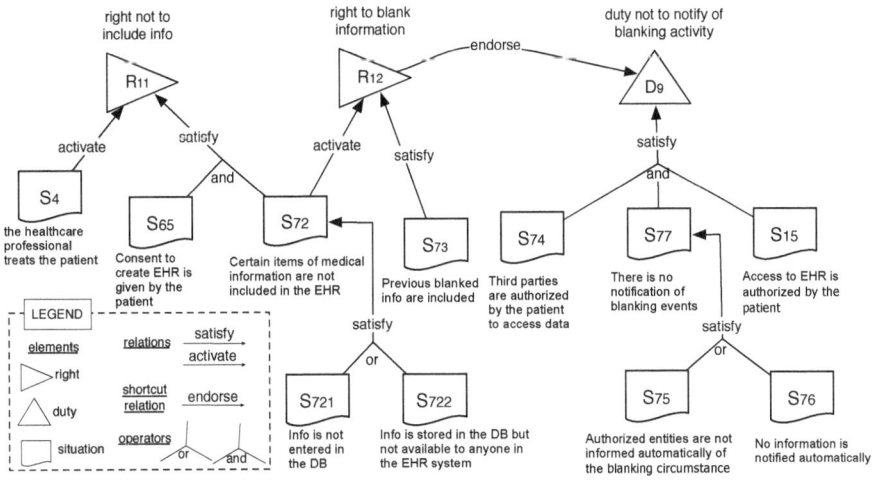

Fig. 3. Nòmos 2 model of section 3.10/3.11 of the Italian Law on EHR

the patient information using a centralized database, but rather to only share notifications regarding the metadata of the information. This way the original information would have remained stored in the database of the entity creating it. The need to comply with sections 3.10/3.11 of the Italian law was therefore opening the design possibilities.

In figure 3 we have represented the graphical model of sections 3.10/3.11 of the Italian Law on EHR that we are considering. This Nòmos 2 model shows how the three norms considered are activated ($S_4 \xrightarrow{\text{activate}} R_{11}$, $S_{72} \xrightarrow{\text{activate}} R_{12}$, $R_{11} \xrightarrow{\text{endorse}} D_9$),[8] how they can be satisfied through the satisfy relation, and how the and or-decomposition can help opening the possibilities for complying with the norms. Each of the 11 situations represented in the model of figure 3 can have three values (ST, SF, SU): we therefore have a total of $3^{11} = 177147$ possible models.[9] In the following paragraphs we will see how the tool can help us reduce this space of alternatives and find the best solutions to the PCP.

The main objective of the CSS project was indeed to manage information sharing among the entities involved. All the healthcare entities involved in the project provided some medical services to the patients, so one first assumption was that S_4 is satisfied (i.e., $\text{sat}(S_4) = \text{ST}$). Moreover, all entities responsible for collecting the patients' information were assumed to have the proper consent from the patient to create and access their info in the EHR ($\text{sat}(S_{65}) = \text{sat}(S_{15}) = \text{ST}$). Given these constraints, we have that one of the input to the tool is the assumption $a_1 = \{\text{sat}(S_4) = \text{ST}, \text{sat}(S_{65}) = \text{ST}, \text{sat}(S_{15}) = \text{ST}\}$. For example, only

---

[8] The endorse relation ($\text{Norm}_1 \xrightarrow{\text{endorse}} \text{Norm}_2$) is a shortcut relation meaning that when the first norm is activated and satisfied, the other one is activated.

[9] Depending on the topology of the model, some alternatives are not evaluated by the reasoner as they are not possible solutions (e.g., S_{72} is SF, while S_{721} is ST).

Table 1. The 4 Candidate Compliance Solutions solutions to the PCP problem that rank best for the example in figure 3. In the PCP problem all norms are asked to be tolerated or complied with, two preferences are expressed $(pref_1, pref_2)$, and some assumptions (a_1).

	$S_4, S_{65}, S_{73}, S_{74}, S_{75}, S_{15}, S_{722}$	S_{76}	S_{721}	R_{11}, R_{12}, D_9
1:		SU	SU	
2:	ST	SU	SF	com
3:		SF	SU	
4:		SF	SF	

with the specification of this assumption and asking the tool to return all possible model where the assumption holds, the space of alternatives drops to 619.[10]

In this scenario, when we *query* the model and ask for all three norms to be complied or at least tolerated (so, both *tol* and *com* value are acceptable) we obtain 25 possible models. In order to further reduce the space of alternatives and return only the best solutions, we introduce *preferences*. In the context of CSS, patient information was maintained in the database of the healthcare entity creating the data. These entities evaluated that S_{721} ("Information not entered in the Database") was a "more expensive" operation than S_{722}, as it would have implied the need of an dedicated operator to add the information in a second moment. Moreover, the possibility of not-notifying in automatic any information (S_{76}) was considered as it would have allowed each entity in the system to autonomously evaluate on a case-by-case basis when/which information to notify. This option though was also considered to have higher costs as it also would have relied on an extra-operator in the process, making it a less manageable and flexible approach. In this context one set of preferences can then be expressed as $pref_1 = \{S_{721} >_{cost} S_{722}\}$ and $pref_2 = \{S_{76} >_{cost} S_{75}\}$, indicating the preferences with respect to the cost criterion.

The specification of these preferences can then be included in the input to the NRTool together with the assumption (a_1) and the query with the compliance values (all norms *tol* or *com*) to reduce the space of alternatives. In table 1 we show the 4 Candidate Compliance Solutions to the PCP problem returned by the NRTool that rank best with respect to the specified preferences. All Candidate Compliance Solutions presented in table 1 rank best among the other possible solutions to the model: they all have the desired compliance value for the norms, they rank best with respect to the specified preferences, and they satisfy the assumption. For example we can see how in the first solution, the assumption are respected: the healthcare entities provide medical service to the patient, and the consent to create and access the EHR is given (S_4, S_{65}, and S_{15} are satisfied). To respect the indicated preferences, we have that there is no automatic notification of a blanking event (sat(S_{75}) = ST), and 'inaccessible' information is safely stored in the DB (sat(S_{722}) = ST). Thanks to the label propagation rules encoded in the input to the reasoner, the NRTool can evaluate

---

[10] So in this case the query is for model where the norms can have any value and no preferences are expressed.

that the three norms R_{11}, R_{12}, D_9 are activated and satisfied, ergo, they are complied with.

What lies behind these four best solutions, is how all the other assignments to the Nòmos 2 model in figure 3 are either (a) less desirable (w.r.t. $pref_1$ and $pref_2$), or (b) do not satisfy the query (all norms complied with or tolerated), or (c) they violate the assumption a_1. The tool uses this information to indeed prune and rank the space of alternative solutions to the Nòmos 2 model in order to find the best ones.

For example, a less desirable Candidate Compliance Solution would be one were the assumption are respected (S_4, S_{65}, and S_{15} are satisfied), also S_{72} and S_{677} are satisfied, while all other situations are unknown. The norms respect the query (they are evaluated as complied with), though the two most desired situations (S_{721} and S_{76}) are not satisfied, therefore making the solution less desirable.

Similarly there are assignment to the situations of the Nòmos 2 model that are desirable but that violate one of the norms. For example one could consider the model where the healthcare entities provide medical service to the patient, the consent to create and access the EHR is given (S_4, S_{65}, and S_{15} are satisfied), the info is stored in the database but not accessible (S_{722} is satisfied), and authorized entities are not automatically notified of the blanking right (S_{722}) is satisfied). However, the patient did not authorize third parties to access the data, therefore S_{74} is not satisfied ($sat(S_{74}) = SF$). In this possible model the preferred situations hold and the assumption are met, but the model violates the duty D_9.

Lastly, the specification of the assumptions from the analyst allows the tool to prune the solution space and return only candidate solutions that do not violate the values expressed in the assumption. For example, consider one of the four best solutions of table 1, where instead S_4 is not satisfied ($sat(S_4) = SF$). This scenario represents an assignment to the model that respects preferences and queried norm values (R_{11} is evaluated to tolerated), but it violates the assumption that the healthcare treat the patient, therefore making it a useless solution to the analyst.

We acknowledge as limitation and as part of our future work the challenge to collect these preferences in a bigger model/scenario. Also, the effectiveness of our method and its scalability are currently under investigation in our future work.

6   Related Work

In this work we have proposed an extension to the Nòmos 2 modeling framework [22], where we exploit the notion of stakeholder preference as an heuristic to select a minimal set of compliance alternatives for the design of a compliant requirement model. In requirement engineering the notion of preference and preference-based prioritization is generally used to characterize different decision making processes. In Techne [12] a stakeholder preference over two requirements is defined as a binary relationship between the two elements representing them. In this framework, preferences provide criteria for the comparison of candidate solutions to a requirements problem. In [15] the term stakeholder priority is instead used to refer to this notion, while the concept of preference is used to indicate a "nice-to-have" property. This formulation allows exploiting planning techniques to build solutions to requirements problems that satisfy mandatory requirements and the preferences to a different degree. Elicitation of stakeholder preferences to prioritize set of requirements for the purpose of release planning is a key issue, as discussed in [19], and calls for specific techniques to keep as lower as possible the preference elicitation effort by stakeholders, still resulting in an satisfactorily ranking of the candidate requirements.

The problem of regulatory compliance is being investigated for several years now in the requirement engineering community. A recent survey review [8] summarizes some of the main proposals concerning methods and techniques to address regulatory compliance with goal-oriented frameworks. In this context for example, Darimont and Lemoine have used KAOS to represent objectives extracted from regulation texts [6]. Ghanavati et al. [7] use URN (User Requirements Notation) to model goals and actions prescribed by laws. Likewise, Rifaut and Dubois use $i*$ to produce a goal model of the Basel II regulation [20]. Goal-oriented approaches are useful approaches for modeling norms when their complexity is small enough to be reduced to goal relations. However, when the notion of applicability is needed or the variability of the law becomes more prominent, goal-oriented techniques fail in capturing its effects on reasoning about alternatives [21]. Also recently Tawhid et al. [23] have proposed an new approach in dealing with the problem of compliance by enriching a GRL model of requirements with qualitative indicators.

Among the challenging problems these approaches need to cope with are the complexity, ambiguity, variability and evolvability of the law. In fact, as pointed out in a recent case study analysis in the transportation domain [18], these issues can indeed become particularly critical in complex application domains.

Focusing on the problem of complexity and ambiguity of regulatory code, recent works propose methodologies supporting the understanding of legal documents for the purpose of software requirements analysis. For instance in [4] it is described a systematic process called semantic parametrization, which consists of identifying in legal text restricted natural language statements (RNLSs) and then expressing them as semantic models of rights and obligations (along with auxiliary concepts such as actors and constraints). Heuristics are created to systematically convert unstructured legal texts into structured artifacts [14]. Artifacts are then combined into a frame-based method for manually acquiring legal requirements from regulations. Such approach has been used as a basis for tool-supporting the identification of requirements in legal documents. [5] focuses on supporting software developers while analyzing regulatory codes with the aim of identifying sections that are relevant to contractual and product level requirements. This task is formulated in terms of a traceability problem which is addressed exploiting machine-learning techniques, and combined with web-mining features to reconstruct the original trace query. The approach is illustrated using the HIPAA security rule. [13] proposes a framework that supports analyzing the compliance of legacy Information Systems, which rests on the alignment of a model of the transactions in the legacy system with an ontology of the laws that regulated the IS domain. This law ontology explicits the organizational roles, which correspond to the legal subjects of the laws governing the IS domain, with the domain artifacts and processes under their responsibility. Aligning and reconciling requirements from multiple jurisdictions is one of the problem that arises because of the variability of a law from country to country [9]. In this work the authors propose an approach to identify similarities and differences between pairs of requirements. This is achieved by comparing variants of norms — encoded in a specific legal requirements specification language — with respect to a suitable set of metrics. Moreover, the problem of regulatory evolution and its impact on compliance requirements has been recently investigated in [16], where the authors suggest a taxonomy of legal cross-reference of the HIPAA Privacy Rule that can be used to identify possibly conflicting requirements. As a result of the proposed strategies to solve these conflicts, software engineers are guided to build requirement-models towards the more stable sections of the rule, thus limiting the impact on the deployed software of possible changes in norms.

7   Conclusions

In this paper we have defined the Preferred Compliance Problem (PCP) for legal alternatives impacting software requirements. Stakeholder preferences are used to compare the desirability of possible solutions to a compliance problem. Apart from defining the problem, our contributions include a prototype tool for reasoning with preferences, as well as a use case where the tool is applied to model and analyze an Italian law on Electronic Health Records. Because of space limitations, only parts of the use case are presented herein. Ongoing work is devoted to the consolidation of the tool, as well as experimentally evaluating its scalability and effectiveness on larger models. We're working towards revising the requirement process in order to exploit the use of these variability models (see [11] for some preliminary results in this area).

References

1. Abiteboul, S., Hull, R., Vianu, V.: Foundations of Databases. Addison-Wesley (1995)
2. Alviano, M., Faber, W., Leone, N., Perri, S., Pfeifer, G., Terracina, G.: The disjunctive datalog system DLV. In: de Moor, O., Gottlob, G., Furche, T., Sellers, A. (eds.) Datalog 2010. LNCS, vol. 6702, pp. 282–301. Springer, Heidelberg (2011)
3. Bray, I.: An Introduction to Requirements Engineering. Addison-Wesley (2002)
4. Breaux, T., Antón, A.: Analyzing regulatory rules for privacy and security requirements. IEEE Trans. Softw. Eng. 34, 5–20 (2008)
5. Cleland-Huang, J., Czauderna, A., Gibiec, M., Emenecker, J.: A machine learning approach for tracing regulatory codes to product specific requirements. In: Kramer, J., Bishop, J., Devanbu, P.T., Uchitel, S. (eds.) ICSE (1), pp. 155–164. ACM (2010)

6. Darimont, R., Lemoine, M.: Goal-oriented analysis of regulations. In: ReMo2V, held at CAiSE 2006 (2006)
7. Ghanavati, S., Amyot, D., Peyton, L.: Towards a framework for tracking legal compliance in healthcare. In: Krogstie, J., Opdahl, A.L., Sindre, G. (eds.) CAiSE 2007. LNCS, vol. 4495, pp. 218–232. Springer, Heidelberg (2007)
8. Ghanavati, S., Amyot, D., Peyton, L.: A systematic review of goal-oriented requirements management frameworks for business process compliance. In: RELAW 2011, pp. 25–34. IEEE (2011)
9. Gordon, D.G., Breaux, T.D.: Reconciling Multi-jurisdictional Legal Requirements: A Case Study in Requirements Water Marking. In: RE 2012. IEEE (2012)
10. Ingolfo, S., Siena, A., Jureta, I., Susi, A., Perini, A., Mylopoulos, J.: Modeling and reasoning with stakeholder preferences among legal alternatives. Submitted to CAISE13 (2012)
11. Ingolfo, S., Siena, A., Mylopoulos, J., Susi, A., Perini, A.: Arguing regulatory compliance of software requirements. Accepted for publication in Data & Knowledge Engineering, DKE (2012), http://dx.doi.org/10.1016/j.datak.2012.12.004
12. Jureta, I., Borgida, A., Ernst, N.A., Mylopoulos, J.: Techne: Towards a new generation of requirements modeling languages with goals, preferences, and inconsistency handling. In: RE 2010, pp. 115–124. IEEE Computer Society (2010)
13. Khadraoui, A., Leonard, M., Thi, T.T.P., Helfert, M.: A Framework for Compliance of Legacy Information Systems with Legal Aspect. In: Gronau, N. (ed.) AIS Transactions on Enterprise Systems, vol. 1. GITO Publishing GmbH (2009) ISSN 1867-7134
14. Kiyavitskaya, N., Zeni, N., Breaux, T.D., Antón, A.I., Cordy, J.R., Mich, L., Mylopoulos, J.: Automating the extraction of rights and obligations for regulatory compliance. In: Li, Q., Spaccapietra, S., Yu, E., Olivé, A. (eds.) ER 2008. LNCS, vol. 5231, pp. 154–168. Springer, Heidelberg (2008)
15. Liaskos, S., McIlraith, S.A., Sohrabi, S., Mylopoulos, J.: Representing and reasoning about preferences in requirements engineering. Requir. Eng. 16(3), 227–249 (2011)
16. Maxwell, J.C., Antón, A.I., Swire, P.: Managing Changing Compliance Requirements by Predicting Regulatory Evolution: An Adaptability Framework. In: RE 2012. IEEE (2012)
17. Minker, J.: Overview of disjunctive logic programming. Ann. Math. Artif. Intell. 12(1-2), 1–24 (1994)
18. Nekvi, M.R.I., Madhavji, N.H., Ferrari, R., Berenbach, B.: Impediments to requirements-compliance. In: Regnell, B., Damian, D. (eds.) REFSQ 2011. LNCS, vol. 7195, pp. 30–36. Springer, Heidelberg (2012)
19. Perini, A., Susi, A., Avesani, P.: A Machine Learning Approach to Software Requirements Prioritization. IEEE Transactions on Software Engineering (2012) (to appear)
20. Rifaut, A., Dubois, E.: Using goal-oriented requirements engineering for improving the quality of iso/iec 15504 based compliance assessment frameworks. In: RE 2008, pp. 33–42 (2008)
21. Siena, A., Ingolfo, S., Susi, A., Jureta, I., Perini, A., Mylopoulos, J.: Requirements, intentions, goals and applicable norms. In: ER Workshops, pp. 195–200 (2012)
22. Siena, A., Jureta, I., Ingolfo, S., Susi, A., Perini, A., Mylopoulos, J.: Capturing variability of law with Nòmos 2. In: ER 2012 (2012)
23. Tawhid, R., et al.: Towards outcome-based regulatory compliance in aviation security. In: RE 2012, pp. 267–272 (2012)
24. Zave, P., Jackson, M.: Four dark corners of requirements engineering. ACM Trans. Softw. Eng. Methodol. 6(1), 1–30 (1997)

Supporting Decision-Making for Self-Adaptive Systems: From Goal Models to Dynamic Decision Networks

Nelly Bencomo and Amel Belaggoun

INRIA Paris - Rocquencourt, France
nelly@acm.org, amel.belaggoun@inria.fr

Abstract. [**Context/ Motivation**] Different modeling techniques have been used to model requirements and decision-making of self-adaptive systems (SASs). Specifically, goal models have been prolific in supporting decision-making depending on partial and total fulfilment of functional (goals) and non-functional requirements (softgoals). Different goal-realization strategies can have different effects on softgoals which are specified with weighted contribution-links. The final decision about what strategy to use is based, among other reasons, on a utility function that takes into account the weighted sum of the different effects on softgoals. [**Questions/Problems**] One of the main challenges about decision-making in self-adaptive systems is to deal with uncertainty during runtime. New techniques are needed to systematically revise the current model when empirical evidence becomes available from the deployment. [**Principal ideas/results**] In this paper we enrich the decision-making supported by goal models by using Dynamic Decision Networks (DDNs). Goal realization strategies and their impact on softgoals have a correspondence with decision alternatives and conditional probabilities and expected utilities in the DDNs respectively. Our novel approach allows the specification of preferences over the softgoals and supports reasoning about partial satisfaction of softgoals using probabilities. We report results of the application of the approach on two different cases. Our early results suggest the decision-making process of SASs can be improved by using DDNs.

Keywords: requirements, specification-methodologies, goal models, dynamic decision networks, bayesian decision theory.

1   Introduction

Goal models have been used to model requirements and decision-making of self-adaptive systems [8, 18, 12, 23]. Goal models support the reasoning about partial and total fulfillment of functional (or goals) and non-functional requirements (or softgoals). Measurement of softgoals fulfillment is difficult due to the vague or fuzzy nature of softgoals satisfaction. Softgoals may not be absolutely fulfilled, yet they can be labelled as sufficiently satisficed [4]. An area of limited study has been the use of probability on goal models [14]. Probability theory can

J. Doerr and A.L. Opdahl (Eds.): REFSQ 2013, LNCS 7830, pp. 221–236, 2013.
© Springer-Verlag Berlin Heidelberg 2013

also be used to describe the lack of crispness about the satisfiability nature of softgoals. Given a chosen goal realization strategy a probability of satisfaction of a softgoal can be associated with it. The higher this probability the better the satisfaction level associated with the softgoal. Information can be incorporated as new knowledge is acquired.

In this paper we present a mathematical model supported by Dynamic Decision Networks (DDNs) [21] that enriches the decision-making support provided by the goal-based approach and allows reasoning about partial satisfaction of softgoals (expressed with probabilities) and expected utilities.With DDNs, preferences among softgoals are specified using expected utilities with reward functions but expected utilities are also associated with penalty functions. In this paper we explore the usefulness of DDNs to support decision-making for self-adaptation and we also describe a translation method from goal models to DDNs. The resulting DDNs can then be used to trigger adaptation and automatically make the best decision in SASs.

The remainder of this paper is organized as follows: Section 2 presents background on DDNs and previous work using goal models. Section 3 presents how the requirements specification of requirements can be performed using DDNs. Section 4 reports results of experiments. Section 5 described related work. Finally, Section 6 concludes the paper and overviews future research directions.

2   Background

This section briefly overviews DDNs and goal models explaining their relevance for decision-making in SASs.

2.1   Dynamic Decision Networks

Dynamic decision networks (DDNs) extend decision networks, which in turn extend Bayesian networks. Bayesian networks [16] are composed of chance nodes with their associated conditional probabilities and influence arcs that collectively form a directed acyclic graph. Decision networks [10] extend Bayesian networks to provide a mechanism for making rational decisions by combining probability and utility theory. In decision networks, in addition to chance nodes, utility and decision nodes are also included. The decision nodes represent the choices of the decision-maker while utility nodes model the decision-maker's preferences.

DDNs [21] provide a principled approach to make rational decisions in the face of uncertainty within changing environments. To cope with time varying nodes, DDNs maintain a series of time slices to represent nodes at successive moments in time. An arc connecting a node in a previous time slice to a node in a later time slice encodes an influence on the node's value from the previous node value. DDNs provide a useful framework for modeling beliefs about the world, associating preferences with states of the world, and making decisions. Fig. 1 shows a DDN with its components and several time slices.

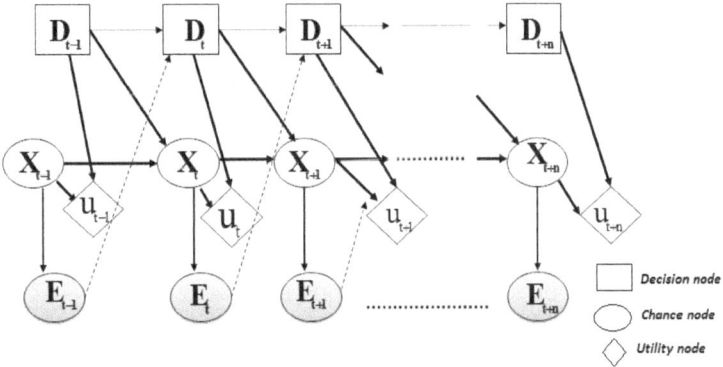

Fig. 1. The General structure of DDN

Why DDNS to Support Decision-making in Self-adaptive Systems.
Dynamic decision networks address the problem of decision-making with the
following characteristics:

- The environment for making decisions changes over time.
- Information is available to the DDN (as a decision maker) based on data
  provided by monitorables (i.e. entities in the environment and the system
  itself that can be monitored) and human-made reports.
- The DDN can be prompted to make a decision at specific times (known or
  unknown before the DDN is built).
- These decisions are best characterized as choices associated with meeting a
  goal.
- New decision alternatives can arise at unexpected times. Decision alternatives can also disappear (product of earlier decisions or by known/unknown
  causes) [5].

Crucially, the above are characteristics exposed by SASs. If we assume that the
DDNs can provide support for decision-making in a SAS, the decision process
of a DDN-based approach must do the following:

- Define the uncertainty associated with the current situation.
- Balance different conflicting softgoals according to given preferences.
- Maintain the definition of uncertainty over time as new information arrives
  in a consistent way with the past.
- Incorporate risk preferences (i.e., rewards and penalties) that properly ad-
  dress the current situation modeled.

The above are the basis of the approach presented in this paper and represent
the assumptions we have used. The rest of the paper shows our ideas on the use
of DDNs for the case of SASs. The incorporation of new decision alternatives
and preferences at runtime are not the focus of this paper, but is discussed as
future work.

2.2   Goal-Based Models to Support Decision-Making

In [8] and [23] goal-based approaches to reason under uncertainty have been presented. A goal can be satisfied by different goal realization strategies also called tasks. The set of alternative realization strategies that describe different ways how a goal g can be realized is called a variation point associated with goal g (VPg). Different realization strategies have different effects on softgoals. Authors of [23] show how the automatic selection of the best strategy is based on a utility function that sums the possible realization strategies' impacts on the softgoals and priorities of goals (see equation (1)).

The determination of the best realization (task) is as follows: Let the function *satisfices* represent the contribution value for a task, softgoal:

$$satisfices : T \times SG \to C$$

where T is a set of tasks, SG a set of softgoals and C is the set of possible contribution values *break, hurt, neutral, help, make*. These are interpreted as corresponding to the range of integer values -2,-1,0,1,2. Moreover i is an index in the set of tasks that represent alternative realizations of goals g, and t_{ig} is thus one of these tasks. The task selected as the realization strategy for goal g is the one with the greatest value of contribution link values for all of the softgoals it influences as presented in the following objective function:

$$max_i \sum_{sg \in SG} w_{sg} satisfices(t_{ig}, sg) \qquad (1)$$

Claims [4, 23] has been used to explicitly represent design assumptions made about the contexts that a system may encounter at runtime, and their affect on the realization of system goals. At runtime, such design assumptions can proof to be wrong or not valid anymore, i.e., *Claims* can be seen as markers of uncertainty that can be solved at runtime when more information in obtained. The authors in [23] have shown how *Claims* are useful during execution to maximize the satisficement of a system's softgoals by dynamically choosing between alternative goal realizations after the assumptions have proven to be not valid anymore. The verification of the validity of a *Claim* is done based on monitorables. At runtime and when the monitoring infrastructure notifies that a *Claim* does not hold anymore, system adaptations to an alternative goal realization can be triggered. In terms of the variation points (VPs), it means that a VP will be solved during runtime by the selection of new alternative configurations that will correspond to the realization strategies.

Example: The Vacuum Cleaner. As an example to show the mapping consider the fragment of a simple i* Strategic Rationale(SR) model of a robot vacuum cleaner for a domestic apartment in Fig.2. The vacuum cleaner has a goal to clean apartment (clean apartment) and two softgoals; to avoid causing danger to people within the house (avoid tripping hazard) and to be economical to run (minimize energy costs). The goal clean apartment can be satisfied by two different realization strategies; Clean at night or Clean when empty. These are represented by two alternatives tasks connected to clean apartment by means-end links. The expected effects of the two tasks on the two softgoals are represented by the contribution links between the tasks and the softgoals clean at night task

and the avoid tripping hazard softgoal. Cleaning at night partially denies tripping hazard avoidance but completely satisfies energy cost minimization, while
cleaning when empty partially denies energy cost minimization but completely
satisfies tripping hazard avoidance. Therefore, the decision of what is the best
goal operationalization is not clear as the sum of both tasks' effects on the softgoals is the same, *hurt + make*.

A Claim with the value *break* is attached to the contribution link with the
value *hurt* that connects the clean at night task and the avoid tripping hazard softgoal. According to the semantics of Claim propagation [23], this has the
effect of changing the contribution link value to *neutral*. This in turn has the
effect of favouring the task clean at night over the task cleaning when empty
because the former has a more positive net contribution to satisfaction of the
two softgoals; *neutral + make > hurt + make*. During runtime the goal models
are kept in memory to support reasoning. Let us suppose that during the execution and when the vacuum cleaner is cleaning the apartment, the monitoring
infrastructure may sense a person is at home. In this case, the Claim No tripping
hazard is falsified and the run-time reasoning engine (supported by the runtime
goal models) is able to evaluate the consequences and order an adaptation from
cleaning at night strategy to cleaning when empty. The focus of this paper is to
evaluate decisions supported by DDNs instead of the goal-based reasoning capabilities shown above, during both development time and runtime. DDNs are
briefly described in the next section.

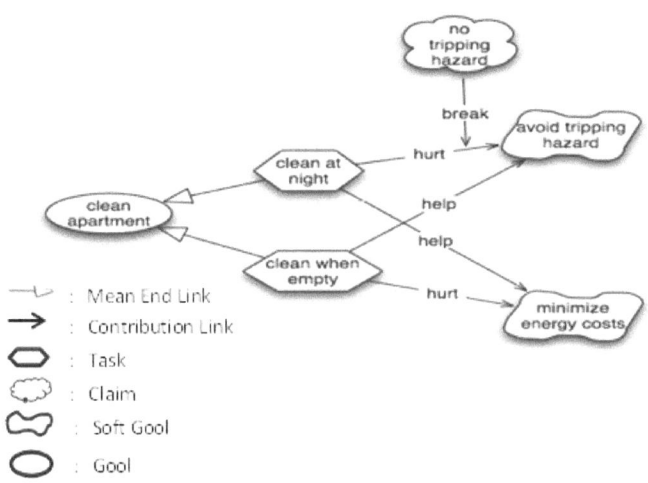

Fig. 2. A robot vacuum cleaner

3   Requirements Specifications of SASs Using Dynamic Decision Networks

In this section we describe and justify the process to map goal models, as
presented in Section 2.2, into DDN-based specifications of decision-making for

self-adaptive systems. A set of mapping rules are described and discussed in the context of the vacuum cleaner example.

3.1   Mapping from Goal Models into DDNs

To construct a DDN, we need to specify 5 kinds of information:

- Chance nodes (C_k) also called random variables. Each chance node is associated with a conditional distribution that is indexed by the state of the parent nodes (i.e., the decision node) [20].
- A set of decisions $D_1, ..., D_m$ related to the decision node D_t.
- Utility node and its utility function U.
- The evidence node (E_t)(also called observation node).
- The dependencies between the different nodes described above.

In the rest of this section we explain the mapping process from the goal model ($\mathcal{GM}$) to DDNs.

a) DDNs Correspond to Variation Points and their Subgraphs in Goal Models. We adopt a separate DDN for each goal and its required decision-making. Specifically, a DDN corresponds to the variation point of a given goal g and its subgraph (i.e., realization strategies, softgoals, and claims). In the running example of the vacuum cleaner the *VP* associated with the goal Clean apartment and its subgraph is mapped into a *DDN* (see Fig 3).

b) Decision Nodes and Goal Realization Strategies. Goal-realization strategies in the goal model represent the set of the possible design alternatives. In the context of DDNs, these strategies correspond to the set of possible decisions in the DDN. The following is the corresponding mapping rule:

Mapping Rule 1. Each goal-realization strategy $T_k \in \{T_1, ..., T_l\}$ in $\mathcal{GM}$ corresponds to a $D_k \in \{D_1, ..., D_m\}$, where D_k represents a value of the decision in the DDN.

c) Chance Nodes and Softgoals. The softgoals represent the non-functional requirements to be satisfied [4]. Different design decisions may have positive or negative effects, and in different proportions, towards meeting a softgoal. Different from goals, softgoals can hardly ever be labelled 100% satisfied or %100 unsatisfied in an unambiguous sense. Satisficement of a softgoal needs a decision-making strategy that attempts to meet an acceptability threshold rather than an absolute value [4]. In the case of goal models, like the one in Fig. 2, whether the softgoals are considered satisfied or not depends on the realization strategies and their effects on each softgoal (represented by the contribution links).

In the context of DDNs, each softgoal SG_j in the goal model is viewed as a chance node C_k whose values are dictated by some probability distribution.

Definition 1. *The probability distribution represents the probability of being satisficed given a decision (i.e., realization strategy).*

Therefore, each contribution link that departs from a realization strategy to a SG_j in the goal model is translated into a conditional probability distribution (CPD) associated with each softgoal SG_j. Given that the realization strategies are mutually exclusive, the Bayes theorem can be applied to calculate the probability of satisficement for each SG_j. Table 1 and Table 2 show examples of the conditional probabilities tables for the example of the vacuum cleaner. Given the above the following is the corresponding mapping rule:

Mapping Rule 2. Each softgoal $SG_j \in \{SG_1, ..., SG_n\}$ in $\mathcal{GM}$ corresponds to a chance node $C_k \in \{C_1, ..., C_n\}$ in the DDN.

Each contribution link $l_k(T_i, SG_j)$ that describes the effect of a T_i on a SG_j corresponds to a conditional probability $P(SG_j|T_i)$. A simple way to propose the values of these conditional probabilities is to make a direct map from the five point range of values $\{break, hurt, neutral, help, make\}$ to the probability values $\{0.0, 0.25, 0.5, 0.75, 1.0\}$. However, if more information is available a more sophisticated mapping can be performed.

In the case of the example of the vacuum cleaner, two realization strategies T_1, T_2 exist that affect the softgoal SG_1 (i.e., Avoid tripping hazard)and SG_2 (i.e., Minimize energy costs). The conditional probability tables associated to SG_1 and SG_2 are shown in Tables 1 and 2.

Table 1. CPT of the node Avoid Tripping Hazard

Avoid tripping hazard node (SG_1)		
T_i	$P(SG_1=F)$	$P(SG_1=T)$
Clean when empty	0.45	0.55
Clean at night	0.11	0.89

Table 2. CPT of the node Minimize energy Costs

Minimize energy Costs node (SG_2)		
T_i	$P(SG_2 = F)$	$P(SG_2 = T)$
Clean when empty	0.25	0.75
Clean at night	0.1	0.9

d) Preferences in the Utility Node and Softgoal Priorities. In decision theory, a utility function is a scalar that assigns a cardinal scale to each outcome and decision indicating its desirability [9].

Softgoals can have an associated priority, that indicates how important it is to satisfice that particular softgoal. The specification of the weights in the utility function (utility node in the DDN) can be based on the softgoals priorities.

Table 3 defines the utility table with all the possible combinations of effects on the softgoals (using the values *true* T and *false* F) given a cleaning strategy.

The weights are ranged from 0 until 200 in this case. The following is the corresponding mapping rule:

Table 3. Utility table (preferences)

Utility node			
Cleaning Strategy	Avoid tripping hazard	Minimize energy costs	**Weight**
1 Clean When empty	F	F	0
2 Clean When empty	F	T	15
3 Clean at night	F	F	0
4 Clean at night	F	T	30
5 Clean When empty	T	F	200
6 Clean When empty	T	T	90
7 Clean at night	T	F	150
8 Clean at night	T	T	90

Mapping Rule 3. For each goal realization T_i (i.e., decisions in DDNs) and each softgoal SG_j (i.e., the chance nodes in DDNs) we assign a weight w_{ji} that expresses the preferences which is set as a function $U(SG_j | T_i)$.

$$w_{ji} \colon \mathbf{T} \times \mathbf{SG} \to U(SG_j | T_i)$$

where SG is the set of softgoals, T is the set of goal realizations and w_{ji} represents the set of the priorities over the goal realizations. The domain expert sets the weights of the utility table. These weights are known as rewards or penalties. Table 3 shows an example of a possible set of weights that describes the domain expert preferences. The weight 0 in the 1st and 3rd rows means that the domain expert penalizes those combinations as they have negative effects on both softgoals (note the value *false* F related to both softgoals). Similarly, the 2nd and 4th row also have low weights (respectively 15 and 30) what means a low level of preference. The 5th and 7th rows, on the contrary, show high weights, 150 and 200 respectively. These highest weights mean that these combinations are considered by the expert as the most suitable. The domain expert has a preference on the strategy "Clean when empty" over the strategy "Clean at night". Furthermore, both combinations represent positive effects on the softgoal "Avoid tripping hazard" and negative effects on "Minimize energy costs" what means that for the expert it is more important to favor 'Avoid tripping hazard" than "Minimize energy costs" (see that 6th and 8th rows have lower weights, specifically 90).

e) Evidence Node and Claim Monitoring *Claim* monitoring offers the appropriate mechanism to support the observation model and provide the observations required by the DDNs.

An example of an Observation or Evidence can be the fact that a Claim has been falsified, e.g. the *Claim* No tripping hazard goes from True to False). This falsification could trigger the need to make a decision about what adaptation to realize, if any.

The observation model should include the possibility of failure, i.e., the possibility that the observation may not be 100% accurate due to problems and failures associated to monitorables. In terms of the observation of the falsification of a *Claim*, this refers to the fact that such a falsification may not be true.

In the running example, if we have consider an ideal world where failures do not exist (i.e., the monitorables are 100% reliable) when Evidence is observed the probability is believed to be P(E) = 1. Otherwise, if the monitorables are not 100% reliable, P(E) is less than 1. P(Obs | (no shock detected AND light level constant)) < 1. A graphic showing the mapping is depicted in Fig 3.

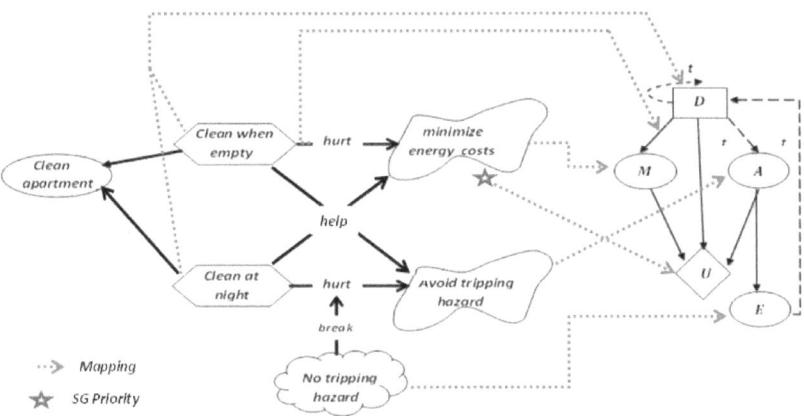

Fig. 3. The robot vacuum cleaner system's i* goal model mapped into a condensed form of DDN

3.2   Evaluating the DDN

A DDN is evaluated in order to make a decision based on the realization strategies with the highest utilities. The DDN is evaluated using the formula (2) for every realization realization strategy T_i to compute the probability-weighted average utility for that realization strategy, also known as the expected utility. The set of preferences over every softgoal is represented by $U(SG_j|T_i)$ and the conditional probability of each softgoal given the available evidence E is represented by $P(SG_j|E, T_i)$. The realization strategy with the highest expected utility is chosen.

$$EU(T_i|E) = \sum_j P(SG_j|E, T_i) \times U(SG_j|T_i) \tag{2}$$

Next, we present an application of DDNs to decision-making in SASs.

4   Experiments

This section describes experimental results for demonstrating the value of our approach using DDNs to support decision-making for self-adaptation. Section 4.1 describes the Remote Data Mirroring (RDM) example. Section 4.2 shows the application of our approach based on DDNs for the case of the RDM application.

4.1   Remote Data Mirroring

RDM [19] is a classic technique for tolerating failures by keeping copies of important data at physically isolated locations to protect data against inaccessibility, to reliability and provide resistance to data loss. An RDM system can be configured in terms of the topology of the network (e.g. using a minimum spanning tree algorithm) and also in terms of how data is distributed among data servers. There are two modes to configure data distribution: synchronous and asynchronous. The synchronous mode is the only mode in which non-catastrophic multiple failures will ever provoke the lose of data. In contrast, in the asynchronous remote mirroring mode, data that hasn't propagated to other sites can be lost at certain risk. Each configuration provides different levels of data protection, performance and costs. For example, the synchronous mode provides better data protection than the asynchronous mode, but it also incurs a network performance penalty as every change must be distributed across the network. The asynchronous mode provides better network performance, however it also provides weaker data protection.

Fig. 4 shows the i* SR goal models for the RDM application. The RDM application must achieve functional goals such as constructing a connected network and distributing data. These functional goals can be achieved through alternative goal realization strategies that includes constructing different network topologies, such as a Minimum Spanning Tree or Redundant Topology and Changing Propagation Parameters. The application has three softgoals Minimize Operational Expense, Maximize Data Reliability and Maximize Network Performance. A Claim Redundancy Prevent Network Partition has been attached to the goal model [19] to make explicit the uncertainty about the usefulness of the choice of Redundant Topology at any point at runtime. The Claim can become disproven at runtime for several reasons, for example it can be provoked due to simultaneous failures of two or more links. Monitorables and sensor allow the the system to check the validity of the Claim at any point during runtime.

4.2   Experiments

Netica [1], a tool for Decision and Bayesian networks, has been used for the experiments. A DDN to support the decision-making of the best topology to use has been associated with the the variation point Select Topology (see Fig. 4). The DDN constructed (with three unrolled time slices) is shown in Fig. 5 . D_{jt} represents the decision node with two possible decisions $D_1 and D_2$ which correspond with the realization strategies T_1:Use MST Topology and T_2:Use Redundant Topology respectively. The DDN also presents a set of three chance nodes MR_t, MP and MO used to model the softgoals Maximize Reliability, Maximize Performance and Minimize Operational Costs respectively. Notice that MR_t comes from a softgoal with a contribution link with a Claim attached. MR_t is therefore an observable chance node. MP and MO are modeled as static chance nodes. The evidence node E_t represents the event that the Claim Redundancy Prevents Network Partitions is changes is value True or False at time t.

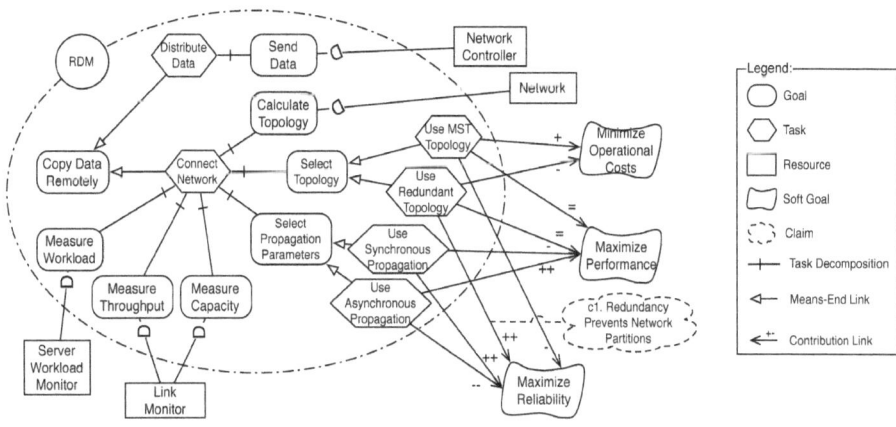

Fig. 4. i* SR goal model for the remote data mirroring application (RDM) (from [19])

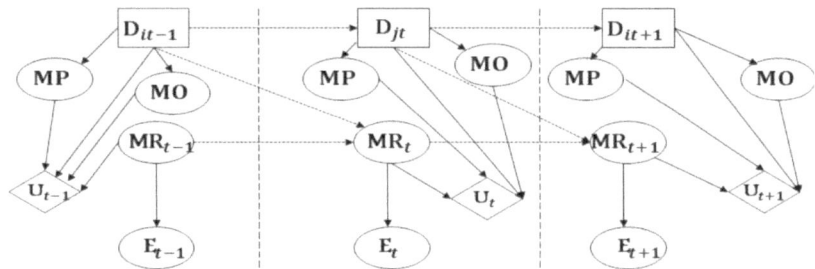

Fig. 5. DDN for the case of the RDM application (with three time-slices)

In order to evaluate the DDN we have considered the following probabilities:
$P(MR_t = true | \text{Mst Topology}) = 0.3$, $P(MR_t = true | \text{Redundant Topology}) = 0.9$,
$P(MP = true | \text{Mst Topology}) = 0.5$, $P(MP = true | \text{Redundant topology}) = 0.5$,
$P(MO = true | \text{Mst Topology}) = 0.75$, $P(MO = true | \text{Redundant topology}) = 0.3$.

The weights associated with the possible combination of nodes are given in
Table 4. Take note that these weights express the preferences that represent the
relative importance of each combination of effects of the topology used on the
softgoals. For example, the 3rd row in Table. 4 has the highest weight value (200)
in the utility table what means that the 3rd row is the most favored combination
as it encodes that the cost of using Redundant Topology has a positive effect on
the three softgoals Maximize Reliability, Minimize Operational Costs and Maximize
Performance(see the values T for the three softgoals). Note also the 2nd row has
a weight value that is much lower (i.e., 10) what means that even if we have the
same Redundant topology this time, it is not suitable as it has negative effects
on Maximize Reliability and Minimize Operational costs.

Fig. 6 shows the computation of the expected utility (EU) of the possible
topologies from time $t = 0$ to $t = 7$, based on the probability of Maximize
Reliability node, Maximize Performance node, Minimize Operational Costs and

Table 4. Utility table

Utility node				
Topology	MR	MP	MO	**Weight**
1 Use MST Topology	F	F	F	0
2 Use Redundant Topology	F	T	F	10
3 Use Redundant Topology	T	T	T	200
...	..	..	..	...
15 Use Redundant Topology	T	F	F	10
16 Use MST Topology	T	T	F	80

utility node predicted by each decision taken at the next time slice (as shown in Fig. 5 topology decisions have influence on the Maximize Reliability node on the next time slice).

At development time (i.e. at time slice 0), the designer selects Redundant Network Topology as the best decision to use with synchronous propagation as the initial configuration. This configuration is based on the validity of the assumption Redundancy Prevents Network Partitions that states that a redundant network topology prevents network link failures from partitioning the network (the reason why the *Claim c1* has been made to explicitly record that assumption). In terms of a DDN this mean that with no evidence about the fact that Redundancy Prevent Networks Partitions entered yet in the DDN the most likely decision is to use Redundant Topology as the expected utility EU(Redundant Topology)>the expected utility EU(MST Topology).

At some points during runtime (i.e., from time slice 1 to 7 in Fig. 6), however, new information is collected that concludes the *Claim c1* Redundancy Prevent Networks Partitions is false meaning that according to current environmental conditions, the Use of redundant Topology decision does not necessarily prevent network partitions anymore. EU(MST Topology) >EU(Redundant Topology) and therefore, the decision to use MST Topology is considered by the DDN as the best one. The DDN triggers an adaptation accordingly. Fig. 7 shows the case of the monitored falsification of the *Claim c1* at slice time 3 and the monitored value True of *Claim c1* at slice time 6; the DDN has correctly suggested the adaptations from the original design decision Redundant Topology to MST Topology after slice time 3 to go back to Redundant Topology after slice time 6.

The results appear to be consistent with the evidence (observations) that provoked the adaptations and furthermore, they agree with those presented in [19]. Our approach using DDNs has also been successfully applied on the case study of the sensor network GridStix [11] with results also compatible with those shown in [23]. The results of the evaluation of the DDN to the robot vacuum cleaner, RDM system, and GridStix, reported in [2], while somewhat preliminary, are positive as the DDNs allowed both (1) the analyst to make design decisions during development time and (2) the applications to make decisions to adapt to new situations at runtime.

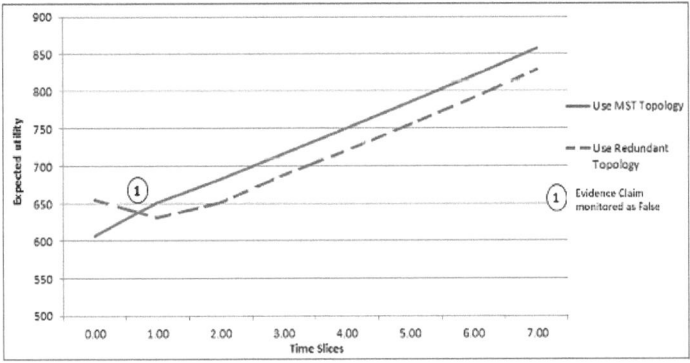

Fig. 6. Expected utilities during seven time slices

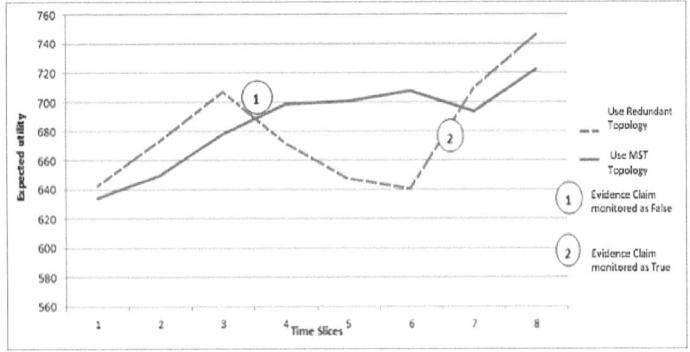

Fig. 7. Expected Utilities during eight time slices

5   Related Work

The related work described in this section is divided in two categories, work on uncertainty tackled using goal-based models for the case of SASs and decision-making using Bayesian theory.

Researchers have tackled uncertainty in SASs in different ways. As discussed by [3, 13], there is a dearth of applicable techniques for handling uncertainty in this setting. Welsh et al [23] introduced REAssuRE to use goal models and *Claims* for driving self-adaptation. In contrast to REAssuRE, in our case and when using DDNs, preferences among softgoals are specified using both expected utilities with reward functions and also penalty functions. Uncertainty in adaptive systems has also been tackled by RELAX [22], a requirements language that explicitly addresses uncertainty inherent in adaptive systems. While RELAX uses fuzzy logic to specify more flexible requirements within a goal model to handle the uncertainty, we use probabilities. Emmanuel et al. [14] specify partial degrees of goal satisfaction and quantify the impact of different system alternatives on high level goals that can be used to guide requirements elaboration and design decision-making. The degree of satisfaction of such goals is modeled by objective functions on quality variables. The non-functional goals are specified formally using a probabilistic model and interpreted in terms of application specific measures. Their approach is different from ours. They tackle decision about alternative system designs during requirements and design engineering. In our case we are concerned about decision-making between alternative decisions to meet a functional goal due to environmental changes what crucially includes also decision-making at runtime. The work of Giorgini et al. [7] deals with formal reasoning about goal models. They use a probabilistic model and label propagation to calculate the evidence for satisfiability and deniability of goals. Their approach deals with conflicts between softgoals, however, different from our work, they do not resolve conflicts but just tackle their identification. Instead of probability they use evidence which can be seen as less precise than calculating the exact probability. In this paper, we have not taken into account uncertainties about quality of observations, i.e. we have assumed no errors or noise introduced by the monitoring infrastructure and therefore we trust 100% the monitoring infrastructure. Hence, we have assumed the following values for the evidence node P(Observation|Redundant Prevents Network Partitions $=$ *true*)=0.0 and P(Observation|Redundant Prevents Network Partitions $=false$)= 1.0. However, different from our earlier research [23], the DDN approach can take into account those uncertainties what we leave for future work. As in the case of DDNs, the approach presented in [19] can tackle the uncertainty related to lack of confidence of sensor's reports.

Liaskos et al. [15] present a framework for specifying both mandatory and optional requirements, along with quantitative preferences over the optional requirements, within the context of a goal model. The goal tree and the specified preferences are translated into the Hierarchical Task Network (HTN) and Planning Domain Description Language (PDDL) planning formalisms, respectively; the HTNPlan-P planning tool is then used to obtain the most preferred design. Similar to our work, [15] focus on on modeling and reasoning about properties and alternative solutions and working on preferences-based exploration of alternatives requirements. However, they do not use probability theory.

Bayesian networks have been used to enable reasoning over probabilistic causal model and to make predictions about partially satisfied affirmation [6]. However the Bayesian paradigm does not provide any direct means for modelling dynamic systems [21]. In contrast to our model in which we combine Bayesian networks and decision networks to achieve a sophisticated architecture that could be used as a powerful decision-making tool for solving complex or real-time decision problems and to model a system that is dynamically changing or evolving over time such as SASs. A number of interesting and related research approaches using DDNs can be found in the area of AI, Portinale and Raiteri [17] have proposed a formal model for FDIR(Fault Detection, Identification and Recovery) analysis in autonomous systems based on a formal Fault Tree modeling language able to express stochastic dependencies and multi-state components which is called Extended Dynamic Fault Tree (EDFT). In their approach, a compilation process producing from EDFT an equivalent DDN on which to exploit standard DDN algorithms to perform the required FDIR analysis. Their approach is very relevant in our case because we are using similar model to trigger the adaptations needed by the systems however we have different focus.

6   Conclusion and Future Work

In this paper we have argued how decision analysis of a SAS can be defined as a formal quantitative technique based on Bayesian and decision theory to guide an informed decision making process under uncertainty. Using our approach the best choices to meet a goal are identified from a range of alternatives decisions (i.e., goal realization strategies). Satisficement of softgoals is modeled using conditional probabilities (probability of satisficement of SGj given that a goal realization strategy was chosen). Preferences are modeled using weights associated to pairs of alternative solutions and softgoals. A typical problem arising during the construction of the DDN model is the choice of this quantitative parameters (i.e., weights). More experience in this direction is expected in the near future. Further work is also required towards systematic techniques for studying the value of the probabilities, and even utility weights, that change over time (due to the machine learning process) an their impact on the evaluation of the alternative decisions.

We also want to take advantage of the dynamic structure of the DDNs. We are studying the suitability of DDNs for domains where requirements, goals, and their respective expected values change over time (i.e., during execution). Interesting issues for future research concern the possibility of the utilization of the model with imprecise evidences (e.g. low level of confidence of sensors) to study how the quality of the infrastructure monitoring affect the decisions made by a DDNs. Also the development of new tools to help the requirement engineer to design a DDNs would be certainly very helpful as the current tool support imposes limitations; there is not enough software that supports DDNs.

Acknowledgments. We thank Pete Sawyer and Valerie Issarny for their useful feedback. Also thanks to Andres Ramirez for the support on the use of the RDM case study. This research is partially supported by Marie Curie Fellowship "Requirements@run-time".

References

[1] Norsys software corporation. netica - user guide (1997)
[2] Belaggoun, A.: Exploring the Use of Dynamic Decision Networks for Self-Adaptive Systems. Master's thesis, Univ. de Versailles Saint-Quentin-En-Yvelines (2012)
[3] Cheng, B.H., de Lemos, R., Giese, H., Inverardi, P., Magee, J.: Software engineering for self-adaptive systems: A research roadmap. In: Cheng, B.H.C., de Lemos, R., Giese, H., Inverardi, P., Magee, J. (eds.) Software Engineering for Self-Adaptive Systems. LNCS, vol. 5525, pp. 1–26. Springer, Heidelberg (2009)
[4] Chung, L., Nixon, B.A., Yu, E., Mylopoulos, J.: Non-Functional Requirements in Software Engineering, vol. 5. Springer (1999)

[5] da Costa, P.C.G.: The Fighter Aircrafts Autodefense Management Problem: A Dynamic Decision Network Approach. Master's thesis, School of Information Technology and Engineering, George Mason University (1999)

[6] Fenton, N.E., Neil, M.: Making decisions: using bayesian nets and mcda. Knowl.-Based Syst. 14(7), 307–325 (2001)

[7] Giorgini, P., Mylopoulos, J., Nicchiarelli, E., Sebastiani, R.: Formal reasoning techniques for goal models. In: Spaccapietra, S., March, S., Aberer, K. (eds.) Journal on Data Semantics. LNCS, vol. 2800, pp. 1–20. Springer, Heidelberg (2003)

[8] Goldsby, H.J., Sawyer, P., Bencomo, N., Hughes, D., Cheng, B.H.: Goal-based modeling of dynamically adaptive system requirements. In: IEEE Int. Conference on the Engineering of Computer Based Systems, ECBS (2008)

[9] Horvitz, E.J., Breese, J.S., Henrion, M.: Decision theory in expert systems and artificial intelligence. Int. Journal of Approximate Reasoning 2, 247–302 (1988)

[10] Howard, R., Matheson., J.: Influence diagrams. In: Readings on the Principles and Readings on the Principles and Applications of Decision Analysis II. Strategic Decisions Group, Menlo Park (1984)

[11] Hughes, D., Greenwood, P., Coulson, G., Blair, G.: Gridstix: Supporting flood prediction using embedded hardware and next generation grid middleware. In: Proceedings of the 2006 International Symposium on on World of Wireless, Mobile and Multimedia Networks, pp. 621–626. IEEE Computer Society, USA (2006)

[12] Lapouchnian, A.: Exploiting Requirements Variability for Software Customization and Adaptation. Ph.D. thesis, University of Toronto (2011)

[13] de Lemos, R., Giese, H., Müller, H., Shaw, M.: Software Engineering for Self-Adpaptive Systems: A second Research Roadmap. In: Software Engineering for Self-Adaptive Systems. No. 10431 in Dagstuhl Seminar Proceedings, Schloss Dagstuhl, Germany (2011)

[14] Letier, E., van Lamsweerde, A.: Reasoning about partial goal satisfaction for requirements and design engineering. SIGSOFT Softw. Eng. Notes 26 (2004)

[15] Liaskos, S., McIlraith, S.A., Sohrabi, S., Mylopoulos, J.: Representing and reasoning about preferences in requirements engineering. Requir. Eng. 16(3), 227–249 (2011)

[16] Pearl, J.: Probabilistic reasoning in intelligent systems: networks of plausible inference. Morgan Kaufmann Publishers Inc., San Francisco (1988)

[17] Portinale, L., Raiteri, D.C.: Using dynamic decision networks and extended fault trees for autonomous fdir. In: ICTAI, pp. 480–484 (2011)

[18] Qureshi, N.A., Peini, A.: Engineering adaptive requirements. In: Workshop on Software Engineering for Adaptive and Self-Managing Systems, SEAMS 2009 (2009)

[19] Ramirez, A.J., Cheng, B.H.C., Bencomo, N., Sawyer, P.: Relaxing claims: Coping with uncertainty while evaluating assumptions at run time. In: France, R.B., Kazmeier, J., Breu, R., Atkinson, C. (eds.) MODELS 2012. LNCS, vol. 7590, pp. 53–69. Springer, Heidelberg (2012)

[20] Russell, S.J., Norvig, P.: Artificial intelligence - a modern approach: the intelligent agent book. Prentice Hall series in artificial intelligence. Prentice Hall (1995)

[21] Russell, S.J., Norvig, P.: Artificial intelligence: A modern approach, 2nd edn. Prentice Hall series in artificial intelligence. Prentice Hall (2003)

[22] Sawyer, P., Bencomo, N., Letier, E., Finkelstein, A.: Requirements-aware systems: A research agenda for re self-adaptive systems. In: Proc. of the 18th IEEE International Requirements Engineering Conference, pp. 95–103 (2010)

[23] Welsh, K., Sawyer, P., Bencomo, N.: Towards requirements aware systems: Runtime resolution of design-time assumptions. In: ASE, pp. 560–563 (2011)

Mapping i* within UML for Business Modeling

Yves Wautelet[1] and Manuel Kolp[2]

[1] Hogeschool-Universiteit Brussel, Belgium
yves.wautelet@hubrussel.be
[2] Université catholique de Louvain, Belgium
manuel.kolp@uclouvain.be

Abstract. [**Context and Motivation**] Business modeling is nowadays a common approach in huge enterprise software developments. It notably allows to align business processes and supporting IT solutions at best, to produce a documentation of the company's "savoir-faire" and to look for possible optimizations. The *business modeling* discipline of the *Rational Unified Process* (*RUP*) has enriched the semantic of the *Unified Modeling Language's* (*UML*) use case diagrams for the special purpose of representing the organization's processes with accurate elements. [**Question/Problem**] RUP/UML business use case scemantics are nevertheless only intended to further stereotype use case models and not to be used for reasoning. In parallel and in line with artificial intelligence concepts, researchers have developed the i* framework enabling the evaluation and decomposition of multiple design opportunities. RUP/UML business use case scemantics could be used more efficiently to integrate the latter benefits. [**Principal ideas/results**] Through a systematic mapping of elements from i* on the one side and of the RUP/UML business use case model on the other, we have set up a RUP/UML graphical notation for i* elements. Applicability has been shown on an illustrative example. [**Contribution**] The main contribution of the framework is allowing to model in an i* fashion using CASE-tools meant for RUP/UML and proposing an interface for forward engineering the produced model in a classical UML requirements model. Future work is required to fully validate the proposal, notably to measure the method's efficacy.

Keywords: i*, RUP/UML Business Use Case Model, Business Modeling.

1 Introduction

Business modeling provides guidance for the analyst on how to understand and represent an organization. It has now been recognized as an important analysis workflow within the information systems engineering process. Frameworks and models to support this engineering step exist today notably i* [20,18,19] for researchers and the RUP/UML business use case model[1] for practitioners. The

---

[1] We do not refer here to the use case model as defined by the OMG in [11] but to the refinement proposed in the business modeling discipline from the RUP (see [14,8,9,10]). That is why, in this paper, we refer to it as the RUP/UML business use case model.

J. Doerr and A.L. Opdahl (Eds.): REFSQ 2013, LNCS 7830, pp. 237–252, 2013.
© Springer-Verlag Berlin Heidelberg 2013

latter is indeed an extension of the *Unified Modeling Language* (*UML*) [11] use case model supported by the *Rational Unified Process* (*RUP*) [14,9] methodology and many case tools. i* is an early requirements framework founded on the notions of *actor*, *goal* and *social dependency*. It could be considered as an agent-oriented alternative to the use-case model used as the foundation of the Tropos agent methodology. Unfortunately, even if i* can provide the business analyst with richer qualitative semantics and reasoning, it is only supported by a few modeling prototypes not widely adopted in the industry.

The paper proposes to reinterpret the RUP/UML business-use-case model in order to fully capture the benefits of i*. In other words, the gain for business analysts will be to integrate the i* approach when still using RUP/UML business use case semantics and its associated case tools. Indeed, i* constitutes a more advanced reasoning technique for organizational modeling than what is simply proposed within the business modeling discipline of RUP/UML even if, as we will see later, all the semantical elements are available to do so. The use by business analysts of semantics they already know and CASE tools they already use should ease its integration process. We also point to a forward engineering method to determine software specifications (in the form of classical use case models). This is a major step for smooth integration.

The research method consisted in comparing each i* element with each UML business use case model elements as defined by the business modeling discipline of the RUP. The element with the highest alignment was systematically selected as counterpart. When multiple elements were possible, we have justified the choice among candidates. Then, we point to the use of i* tasks (represented by RUP/UML business use case realizations) for the interfacing with the next RUP/UML discipline (called *requirements*). This is in line with current RUP practice.

The paper is structured as follows. Section 2 summarizes the principles of the i* modeling framework, Section 3 studies the research approach, Section 4 presents the results of the mapping/matching study, Section 5 instantiates the proposed model onto an illustrative example and Section 6 studies the derivation of system specifications to align at best with the RUP. Section 7 overviews related work. Finally, Section 8 concludes the paper.

2   Background

In *i** (which stands for "distributed intentionality"), stakeholders are represented as (social) actors who depend on each other for goals to be achieved, tasks to be performed, and resources to be furnished [4]. The framework and its applications are described in detail in [20,18]; it includes:

- The Strategic Dependency Model (SD) that describes a network of dependency relationships among various actors in an organizational context. Actors are usually identified within the context of the model. This model shows who an actor is and who depends on the work of an actor. An SD consists of a set of nodes and links connecting actors. Nodes represent actors and

each link represents a dependency between two actors. The depending actor is called *Depender* and the actor who is depended upon is called the *Dependee*;
- The Strategic Rationale Model (SR) provides an intentional description of processes in terms of process elements and the rationale behind them. While the Strategic Dependency (SD) model maintains a level of abstraction by modeling only the external relationships among actors, the SR model forgoes that abstraction in order to allow a deeper understanding about strategic actors' reasoning about processes to be explicitly expressed. The SR model describes the intentional relationships that are "internal" to actors, such as means-ends relationships that relate process elements, providing explicit representation of "why" and "how" and alternatives. Rationales are at strategic level, so that the process alternatives being reasoned about are strategic relationships, i.e., SD configurations. Using knowledge represented in and organized by these modeling concepts, process alternatives can be systematically generated and explored to help actors to find new process designs that better address their interests, needs, and concerns. The SR model is a graph, with several types of nodes and links that work together to provide a representational structure for expressing the rationale behind processes.

3   Research Approach

The applied method firstly consisted in distinguishing groups of elements both within the ones defined by i* and the RUP/UML business use case model. The i*elements taken into account have been selected on the basis of the meta-models presented in [15][2]; further extensions of the framework have not been taken into account and are left for future work. Similarly, UML elements considered here are only the ones from the business use case model as defined in the business modeling discipline of the *RUP knowledge base* (see [10,9]) and provided into CASE tools like *Rational Rose* [12] or *Rational Software Architect* [13].

As presented in Table 1, three categories of elements have been distinguished within the i* ones: *Dependum Elements (DE)*, *Actor Elements (AE)* and *Links (iStarLink)*. Similarly, as presented in Table 2, three categories of elements have been distinguished within the RUP/UML business use-case model: *Inheriting from Use Case (IUC)*, *Inheriting from the Actor (IA)* and *Links (UMLLink)*.

In order to compare i* elements and find best matches with UML ones we have firstly compared the *DE* set with the *IUC* one, such as $DE \times IUC$ (i.e, the carthesian product). However, no satisfying match was found for the *Softgoal* element so that we have further compared this element with the set *IA*. After having found the best possible matches for each element of the *DE* set, we have proceeded to a comparison of *AE* with *IA*, such as $AE \times IA$. However, no satisfying match was found for the *Actor Boundary* so that we further compared this element with the *IA* set. Finally, when this was achieved and the best possible

---

[2] Except for the *plan* element called here *task* according to the original definition given by [18,19].

Table 1. i* Elements to be Mapped

Dependum Elements (DE)	Actor Elements (AE)	Links (iStarLink)
(Hard)goal	Actor	(Strategic) Dependency
Task	Position	Means-end
Resource	Agent	Decomposition
Softgoal	Role	Contribution
	Actor boundary	Actor association

Table 2. Target UML Elements

Inheriting from Use Case (IUC)	Inheriting from the Actor (IA)	Links (UMLLink)
Use Case	Actor	Unidirectional Association
Business Use Case (BUC)	Boundary	Dependency or Instanciates
BUC Realization	Business Actor	Generalization
Use Case Realization	Business Entity	Association
	Business Event	Aggregation
	Business Goal	Include
	Business Worker	Realize
	Control	Refine
	Domain	Extend
	Entity	Derive
	Interface	Package
	Table	
	View	

match was found for each element in the set *IA*, we have compared the *iStarLink* set with *UMLLink* like *iStarLink* × *UMLLink*. Complete results are presented in Section 4, while the rest of this section discusses choices made.

The reader should notice that matching those elements is often a matter of (best possible) compromise. Indeed, some elements from those paradigms are closely related within their definition but seldom entirely define the same reality since their conceptualization is different. It is thus impossible to find a perfect match for each i* element and it would also be nonsense since this would mean that i* and RUP/UML business use case models have exactly the same elements with another graphical notation and use. If the purpose was to translate a particular model from i* to the RUP/UML business use case model (or vice-versa), then some knowledge would typically be lost from the original model and other, new, knowledge would be required to be defined (manually) in the target model. This way both models could benefit since traceability between both analysis models is maintained. Also, additional advantage could come from the representation of the same problem using different modeling perspective. Nevertheless, for now our purpose is to directly integrate the i* approach (and thus its benefits) within a RUP/UML context so that the modeler will be provided the ability to (and is also expected to) model directly in an i* fashion while relying on the definition of elements (and their icon) he already knows. Then, he is expected to forward engineer the produced i* models into software specifications (see section 6) following its present habits. Further work is required to analyze the opportunity of both approaches using a common syntax and, in this perspective, comparing the elements from both for formalisms using the Unified Enterprise Modeling Language (UEML) framework [3] could be helpful to go beyond the purely syntax level and better understand the semantic implications. Beyond allowing to formally establish the better correspondence of each chosen element of our mapping model, it should also allow to study the respective benefits of each of the approaches evoked in this paragraph.

For lack of space and to keep the focus on contributions, the whole process of comparing i* and RUP/UML business-use-case elements will not be entirely presented. We only focus here on elements with multiple (or no) matchings and justify our choices.

3.1 (Hard)Goal

Definition: Following [21], *in a goal dependency, the depender depends on the dependee to bring about **a certain state of affairs in the world**.*

Selected Matching Elements in IUC: *Use Case, Business Use Case.*

Chosen Element: *Business Use Case.*

Rationale: The conflict here was that two UML elements could have been apropriate. Following the RUP knowledge base, *a Business Use Case (class) defines a set of business use-case instances in which each instance is a sequence of actions that a business performs that **yields an observable result of value** to a particular business actor* and *a use case defines a set of use-case instances, where each instance is a sequence of actions a system performs that **yields an observable result of value** to a particular actor.* The *Business Use Case (BUC)* element has been chosen because it is located at business (i.e., organizational) level such as the i* goal rather than at system level as the traditional use case.

3.2 Task

Definition: Following [21], *in a task dependency, the depender depends on the dependee to carry out an activity. The dependum names a task which specifies how the task is to be performed, but not why. The depender has already made decisions about how the task is to be performed.*

Selected Matching Elements in IUC: *Use Case, Use Case Realization, Business Use Case Realization, Business Goal.*

Chosen Element: *Business Use Case Realization.*

Rationale: Following the RUP knowledge base, *a Business Use-Case Realization describes* **how** *business workers, business entities, and business events collaborate* **to perform a particular business use case.** This corresponds to the purpose of the i* Task and is in line with the choice made for the (hard)goal element since we have selected the BUC at that stage.

3.3   Softgoal

Definition: Following [21], *in a softgoal dependency, a depender depends on the dependee to perform some task that meets a softgoal. A softgoal is similar to a goal except that the criteria of success are not sharply defined a priori. The meaning of the softgoal is elaborated in terms of the methods that are chosen in the course of pursuing the goal.*

Selected Matching Element in IUC: *None.*

Selected Matching Element in IA: *Business Goal.*

Chosen Element: *Business Goal.*

Rationale: Following the RUP knowledge base, *a Business Goal is a requirement that must be satisfied by the business. Business Goals describe the desired value of a particular measure at some future point in time and can therefore be used to plan and manage the activities of the business.* This definition corresponds to the purpose of the Softgoal.

3.4   The Actor Boundary

Definintion: Actor boundaries indicate intentional boundaries of a particular actor.

Selected Matching Element in IA: *None.*

Selected Matching Element in UMLLink: *Package.*

Chosen Element: *Package.*

Rationale: Following the RUP knowledge base, *a general purpose mechanism for organizing elements into groups. Packages may be nested within other packages.* Organizing elements into groups is precisely what we intend to do so we have selected this element for this purpose.

4   UML Profile for i* Modeling

The result of our study is summarized in Table 3 for the elements specific to the Strategic Dependency Model and Table 4 for the elements specific to the Strategic Rationale Model. Figure 1 gives the graphical representation of the i* elements with the RUP/UML business use case model.

The reader should note that the graphical representation of elements that we have used is the one from *Rational Rose*. If some graphical icons are not available within the particular case tool that the modeler is using, we suggest to just stereotype the element on its canonical form. For example, if no BUC realization element is available, it could use a traditional use case element with the stereotype <<*Business Use Case Realization*>> written between the use-case icon and the name; the stereotype is written guillemets (i.e., angle brackets).

Table 3. Strategic Dependency Model Mapping

i* element	Selected UML "rich" Use-Case Model Element
Goal	Business Use Case
Task	Business Use Case Realization
Resource	Business Entity
Softgoal	Business Goal
Actor	Business Actor
Position	Control
Agent	Actor
Role	Business Worker
Actor boundary	Package
(Strategic) Dependency	Dependency or Instanciates
Actor association	Generalization

5   Illustrative Example

This section illustrates the framework of Section 4 using the *Media Shop*[3] example. We nevertheless limit the study to showing the applicability of the framework on a case study previously modeled using i*. Within the RUP software development process flow, the i* analysis should take place within the *business modeling* discipline by simply replacing the business use case model (because it now uses the same semantics but with more powerful analytical abilities). It can easily be interfaced with the RUP *requirements* discipline (see Section 6).

---

[3] This illustrative example as well as the descriptions of the strategic dependancy and strategic rationale models are taken from [4].

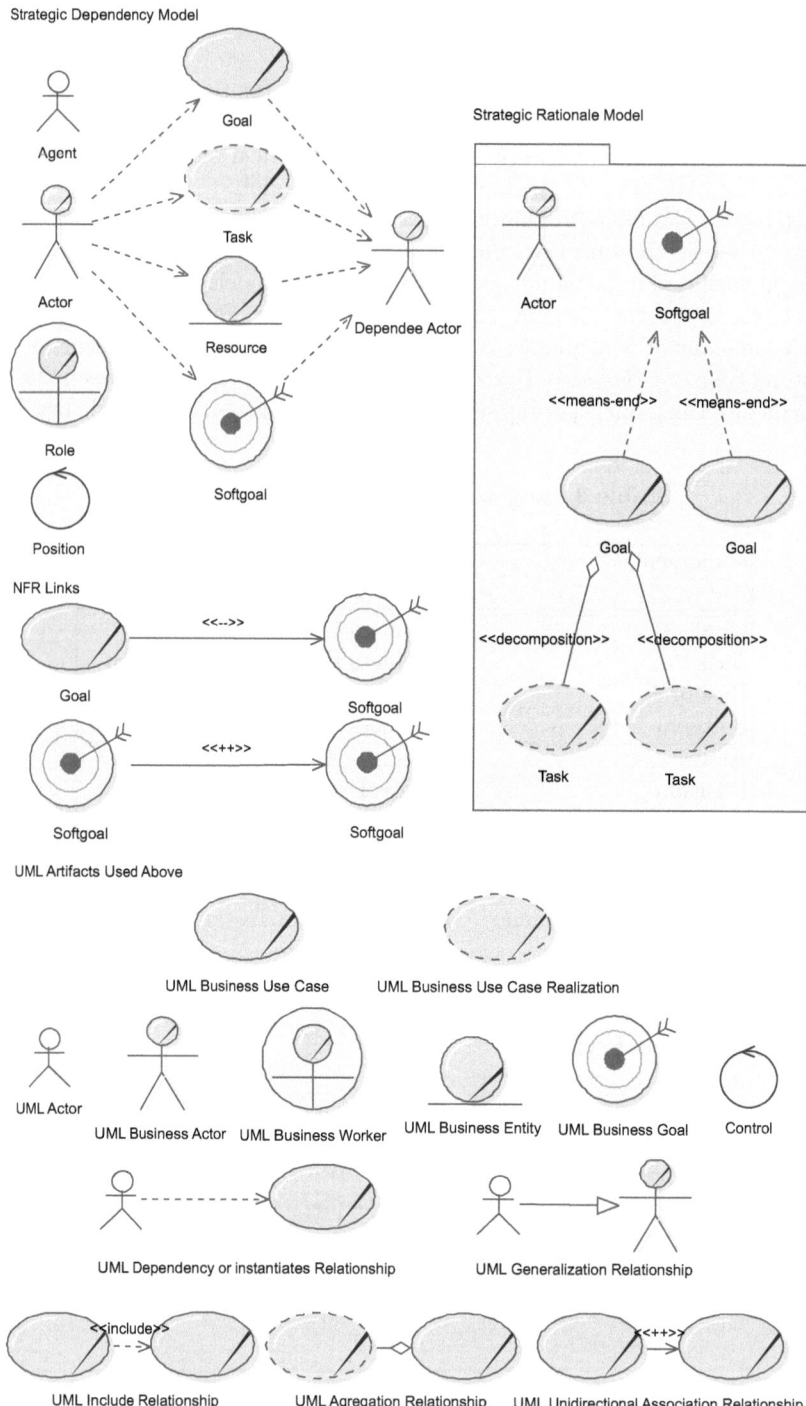

Fig. 1. UML Graphical Notation for i* Elements

Table 4. Strategic Rationale Model Mapping

i* element	Selected UML Element
Means-end	Include
Decomposition	Agregation
Contribution	Unidirectional Association

5.1   Context

Media Shop is a store selling and shipping different kinds of media items such as books, newspapers, magazines, audio CDs, videotapes, and the like. *Media Shop* customers (on-site or remote) can use a periodically updated catalogue describing available media items to specify their order. *Media Shop* is supplied with the latest releases and in-catalogue items by *Media Supplier*. To increase market share, *Media Shop* has decided to open up a B2C retail sales front on the internet. With the new setup, a customer can order Media Shop items in person, by phone, or through the internet. The system has been named *Medi@* and is available on the world-wide-web. It also uses financial services supplied by *Bank Cpy*, which specializes on on-line transactions.

5.2   Strategic Dependency Diagram

These elements are sufficient for producing a first model of an organizational environment. For instance, Figure 2 depicts an i* model of our *Medi@* example with the traditional syntax while Figure 3 represents the same diagram using the UML profile for i* modeling. The main actors are *Customer*, *MediaShop*, *Media-Supplier* and *MediaProducer*. *Customer* depends on *MediaShop* to fulfill her goal: *Buy Media Items*. Conversely, *MediaShop* depends on *Customer to increase mar-ket share* and make *"customers happy"*. Since the dependum *HappyCustomers* cannot be defined precisely, it is represented as a softgoal. The *Customer* also de-pends on *MediaShop* to *consult the catalogue* (task dependency). Furthermore, *MediaShop* depends on *MediaSupplier* to supply media items in a continuous way and get a *Media Item* (resource dependency) . The items are expected to be of good quality because, otherwise, the *Continuing Business* dependency would not be fulfilled. Finally, *MediaProducer* is expected to provide *MediaSupplier* with *Quality Packages*.

5.3   Strategic Rationale Diagram

The Strategic Rationale Diagram in Figure 4 focuses on one of the (soft)goal dependency identified for *Media Shop*, namely *Increase Market Share* using the traditional syntax while Figure 5 represents the same diagram using the UML profile for i* modeling.

To achieve that softgoal, the analysis postulates a goal *Run Shop* that can be fulfilled by means of a task *Run Shop*. Tasks are partially ordered sequences

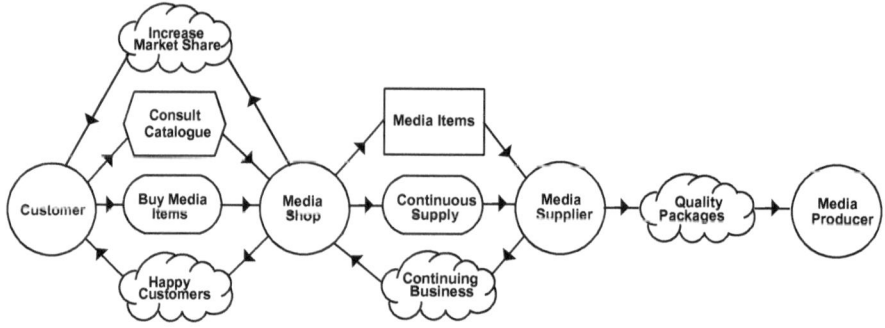

Fig. 2. Medi@: Strategic Dependency Diagram

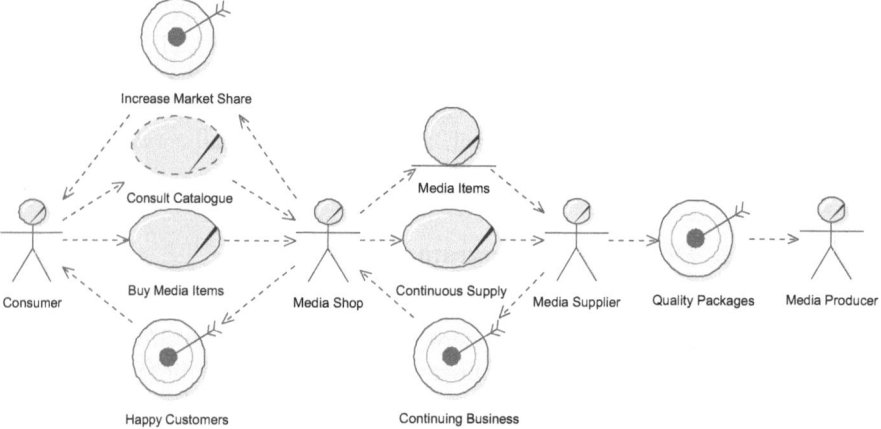

Fig. 3. Medi@: Strategic Dependency Diagram with RUP/UML Use Case Semantics

of steps intended to accomplish some (soft)goal. Tasks can be decomposed into goals and/or subtasks, whose collective fulfillment completes the task. In the figure, *Run Shop* is decomposed into goals *Handle Billing* and *Handle Customer Orders*, tasks *Manage Staff* and *Manage Inventory*, and softgoal *Improve Service* which together accomplish the top-level task. Sub-goals and subtasks can be specified more precisely through refinement. For instance, the goal *Handle Customer Orders* is fulfilled either through tasks *OrderByPhone*, *OrderInPerson* or *OrderByInternet* while the task Manage Staff would be collectively accomplished by tasks *Sell Stock* and *Enhance Catalogue*.

6   Producing System Specifications

Even if the discipline can take various names including *business modeling, organizational modeling, early requirements*, ..., modeling company's processes is

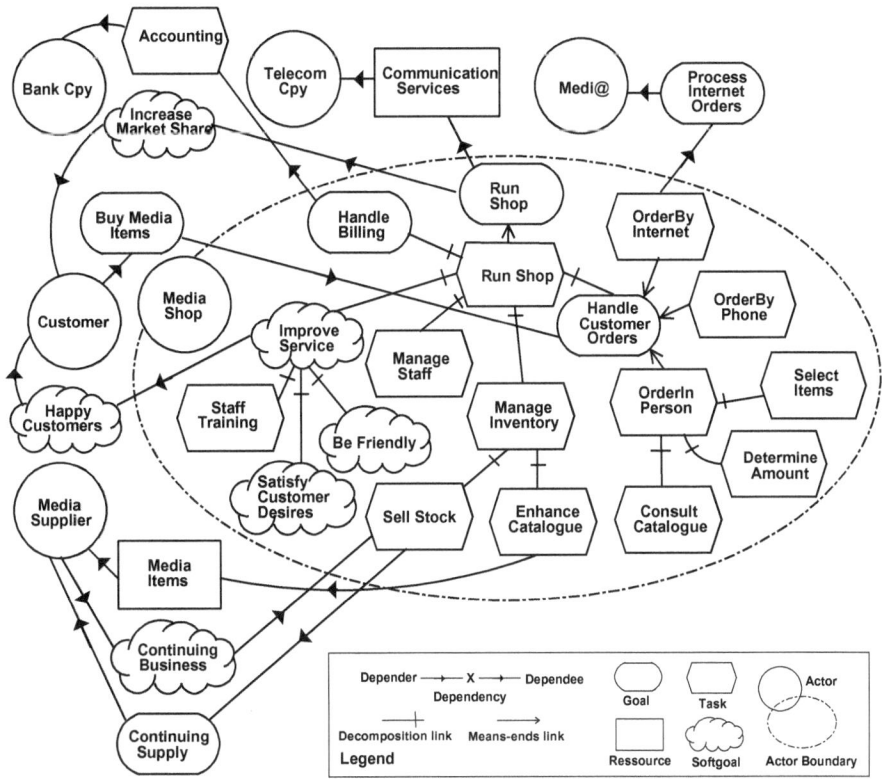

Fig. 4. Means-Ends Analysis for the Softgoal *Increase Market Share*

the first stage in software engineering methodologies like the RUP or Tropos. However, to produce a software architecture and develop an executable release, one needs a set of explicit requirements depicting how the system should behave to satisfy their needs so that the business process model (or organizational model) needs to be forward engineered to achieve this. Within a traditional[4] RUP project, once we have build a consistent business use case diagram into the business modeling discipline, we analyze business use-case realizations to build-up a system use-case model. The latter documents, in terms of coarse grained elements, the system to be build. Similarly, when applying the UML profile for i* modeling, the same business use-case realization elements (corresponding to i* tasks) constitute the functional output of the business analysis. We thus suggest to focus exclusively on the business use case realizations to determine the system use cases.

In line with this, we propose in Listing 1.1 an algorithm to convert business use case realizations (*BUCReal*) into system use cases (*UC*). As first precondition to this JAVA method, we need to dispose of an *ArrayList* containing the business

---

[4] *Traditional* means a RUP project that does not use the UML profile for i* modeling.

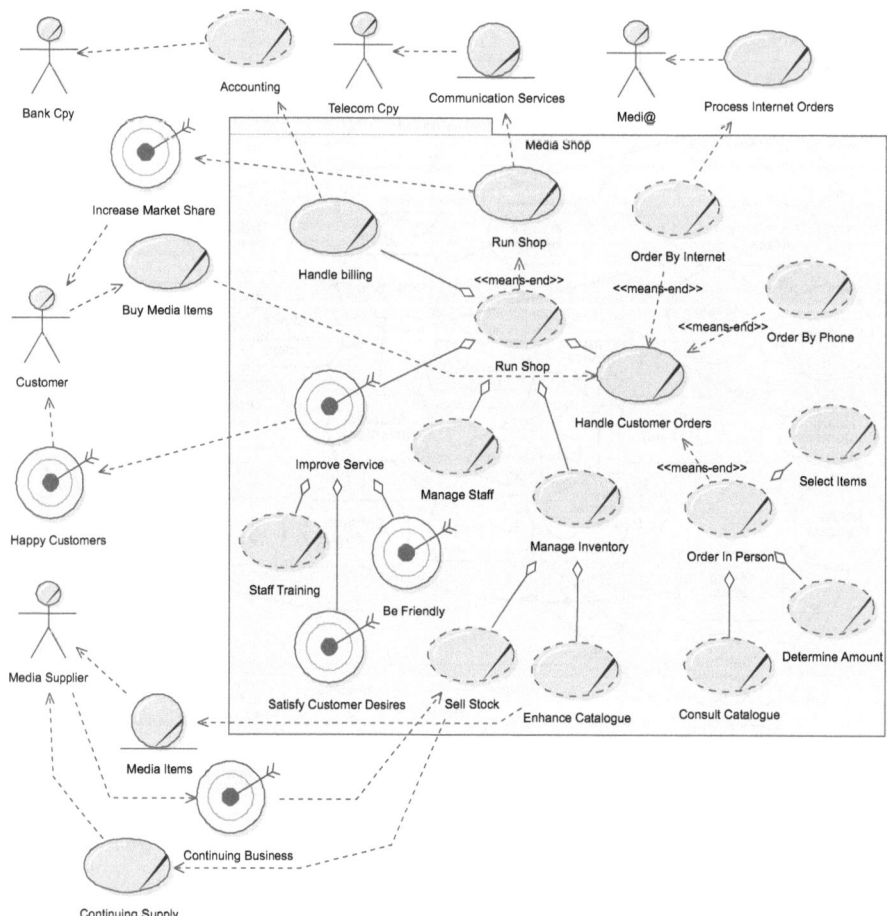

Fig. 5. Means-Ends Analysis for the Softgoal *Increase Market Share* with RUP/UML Use Case Semantics

use case realizations (BUCReal) resulting from an i* means-ends analysis with the RUP/UML profile from a particular project. As second precondition the BUCReal elements are stored in the *ArrayList* in a sequence corresponding to a preorder traversal. This *ArrayList* is used as input and the method is intended to return an *ArrayList* containing a set of use cases derived from the set of BUCReal elements. Indeed, for a given means-ends analysis, we isolate all of the BUCReal elements (thus corresponding to i* task elements) then evaluate the need for IT support for each of them. If IT support is required, the BUCReal element leads to the set up of a use case (UC) element that needs to be further specified in terms of system behavior (outside the scope of this algorithm). Also, if within the means-ends analysis a BUCReal element requiring IT support is the child (i.e. decomposition) of a BUCReal element also requiring IT support, we track this link within the UC elements using a UML <<*extend*>> link from the child to the parent UC element. The actor in charge of the UC can also be identified on the basis of the scope of which actor the BUCReal falls into.

The i* approach is thus no more complementary or parallel to UML analysis but fully integrated into the RUP. Indeed, deriving UC from BUCReal is a common technique in RUP projects and once a (system) use case model is available, the object-oriented software design (i.e. the system behavior) can be set-up.

```java
public static ArrayList<UC>
                     BUCReal2UC(ArrayList<BUCReal> mySRD)
{
    ArrayList<UC> myUCs = new ArrayList<UC>();

    for(int i=0; i<mySRD.size(); i++){
        BUCReal thisBUCReal = mySRD.get(i);
        if (thisBUCReal.requiresITsupport()) {
            UC thisUseCase = new UC(thisBUCReal.getName());

            if (thisBUCReal.hasParent()) {
                BUCReal parentBUC = thisBUCReal.getParent();
                    String ucName = parentBUC.getName();
                    UC parentUC;
                    for(int j=0; j<myUCs.size(); j++){
                        String temp = (myUCs.get(j)).getName();
                        if (ucName.compareTo(temp)==0)
                        {
                            parentUC = myUCs.get(j);
                            thisUseCase.setExtend(parentUC);
                        }
                    }
            }
            myUCs.add(thisUseCase);
        }
    }

    return myUCs;
}
```

Listing 1.1. From Business use case realizations to use cases algorithm

7   Related Work

The willingness to integrate both i* abilities within a software development methodology have firstly arisen into Tropos [4], it however consisted into an agent-oriented development method and only used a waterfall development life cycle. To address this last issue, evolutions of the method have been proposed, notably I-Tropos [16,17] which adapts the iterative lifecycle of the RUP in an i*-driven way; nevertheless, it remains an agent-development context.

A few papers address the problem of using i* as a first framework for business modeling (also called early requirements) into UML-based development:

- [5] proposes a set of traceability relations between i* organizational models and use-case and class models. They, however, do not furnish a systematic way of tracing elements but evaluate each of the possible overlaps on a case by case basis;
- In line with our proposition, [6] proposes to generate use cases from a business model. Their method is different since they suggest using the system as an actor and *if a goal dependency has not given rise to dependencies with the system actor, then it represents a manual activity in which there is no interaction between the user and the software system.* This is not the way we model into the RUP/UML business use model where we represent company's processes in an as-is situation. Within our proposal we nevertheless implicitly suggest to use i* as a framework to represent the business/organization only and to focus on business use case realizations to generate system use cases to be in line and integrated at best within the RUP;
- Finally, [1,2] propose to directly pass from i* models to UML design models (essentially the class diagram). Unfortunately, the proposal is not adapted for an integration into large scale projects as the ones targeted by RUP/UML.

Finally, the question of an alternative representation of i* elements has been envisaged in [7]. Their proposal is based on an empirical study of preferred icons; we point to the use of the ones that are already adopted in the industry by RUP/UML practitioners.

8   Conclusion

Business modeling as a first discipline in engineering software is a common best practice of the last fifteen years notably in methodologies based on or derived from RUP/UML or Tropos. For adequate business modeling, the i* framework provides reasoning techniques that are not present within the business use case model introduced within the RUP. The main difference between those two frameworks does however not lie into their semantics – since we have seen that we can find a fitting equivalent for each i* concept into RUP/UML business use case models – but into their use; i* indeed allows reasoning.

The first proposal of the paper has been to study whether the business use case model provides adequate semantics for modeling in an i* way. We have been able to find satisfying answers for each of them and we have shown within the illustrative example that modeling in an i* fashion with the RUP/UML business use case model semantics is possible. As a second proposal, by distinguishing a set of business use case realizations elements through the i* analysis we can study required IT support and generate a use-case diagram to forward engineer the project within the RUP. We have thus argued that this way of modeling can be perfectly integrated into RUP/UML projects without requiring changing habits for the IT professionals using it. They just have to integrate the i* way of modeling and can still use their CASE tools and their forward engineering habits while disposing of reasoning abilities at business level.

Future work include presenting the UML profile for i* modeling to software modelers familiar with RUP/UML, make them apply it on a case study and evaluate their opinion on the basis of a qualitative study.

Acknowledgements. The authors would like to thank the anonymous reviewers for their valuable comments and suggestions to improve the quality of the paper.

References

1. Alencar, F.M.R., Castro, J., Filho, G.A.C., Mylopoulos, J.: From early requirements modeled by the i* technique to later requirements modeled in precise uml. In: WER, pp. 92–108 (2000)
2. Alencar, F.M.R., Filho, G.A.C., Castro, J.: Support for structuring mechanism in the integration of organizational requirements and object orien. In: Pastor, O., Díaz, J.S. (eds.) WER, pp. 147–161 (2002)
3. Anaya, V., Berio, G., Harzallah, M., Heymans, P., Matulevicius, R., Opdahl, A.L., Panetto, H., Verdecho, M.J.: The unified enterprise modelling language - overview and further work. Computers in Industry 61(2), 99–111 (2010)
4. Castro, J., Kolp, M., Mylopoulos, J.: Towards requirements-driven information systems engineering: the tropos project. Inf. Syst. 27(6), 365–389 (2002)
5. Cysneiros, G.A.A., Andrea, F., Spanoudakis, Z.G.: A traceability approach for i* and uml models. In: Proceedings of 2nd International Workshop on Software Engineering for Large-Scale Multi-Agent Systems (SELMAS 2003) (2003)
6. Estrada, H., Martínez, A., Pastor, Ó.: Goal-based business modeling oriented towards late requirements generation. In: Song, I.-Y., Liddle, S.W., Ling, T.-W., Scheuermann, P. (eds.) ER 2003. LNCS, vol. 2813, pp. 277–290. Springer, Heidelberg (2003)
7. Genon, N., Caire, P., Toussaint, H., Heymans, P., Moody, D.: Towards a more semantically transparent i* visual syntax. In: Regnell, B., Damian, D. (eds.) REFSQ 2011. LNCS, vol. 7195, pp. 140–146. Springer, Heidelberg (2012)
8. Dennis Gibbs, R.: Project Management with the IBM®Rational Unified Process®: Lessons From The Trenches. IBM Press (2006)
9. Kruchten, P.: The rational unified process: An introduction. Longman (Wokingham). Addison-Wesley (December 2003)
10. Nailburg, E.J., Maksimchuk, R.A.: UML for Database Design. Addison-Wesley Longman Publishing Co., Inc., Boston (2001)
11. OMG. Omg unified modeling language (omg uml). version 2.4. Technical report, Object Management Group (2011)
12. Quatrani, T.: Visual Modeling with Rational Rose 2002 and UML, 3rd edn. Addison-Wesley Longman Publishing Co., Inc., Boston (2002)
13. Quatrani, T., Palistrant, J.: Visual Modeling with IBM Rational Software Architect and UML (The developerWorks Series). IBM Press (2006)
14. Shuja, A., Krebs, J.: Ibm®; rational unified process®; reference and certification guide: solution designer, 1st edn. IBM Press (2007)

15. Susi, A., Perini, A., Mylopoulos, J., Giorgini, P.: The tropos metamodel and its use. Informatica (Slovenia) 29(4), 401–408 (2005)
16. Wautelet, Y., Kolp, M.: Goal driven iterative software project management. In: Cuaresma, M.J.E., Shishkov, B., Cordeiro, J. (eds.) ICSOFT (2), pp. 44–53. SciTePress (2011)
17. Wautelet, Y., Kolp, M., Poelmans, S.: Requirements-driven iterative project planning. In: Escalona, M.J., Cordeiro, J., Shishkov, B. (eds.) ICSOFT 2011. CCIS, vol. 303, pp. 121–135. Springer, Heidelberg (2013)
18. Yu, E.: Modeling strategic relationships for process reengineering. PhD thesis, University of Toronto, Department of Computer Science, Canada (1995)
19. Yu, E.: Towards modeling and reasoning support for early-phase requirements engineering. In: Proceedings of the 3rd IEEE International Symposium on Requirements Engineering, RE 1997, p. 226 (1997)
20. Yu, E., Giorgini, P., Maiden, N., Mylopoulos, J.: Social Modeling for Requirements Engineering. MIT Press (2011)
21. Yu, E.: Agent-oriented modelling: Software versus the world. In: Wooldridge, M.J., Weiß, G., Ciancarini, P. (eds.) AOSE 2001. LNCS, vol. 2222, pp. 206–225. Springer, Heidelberg (2002)

Risk Identification at the Interface between Business Case and Requirements

David Callele[1], Birgit Penzenstadler[2], and Krzysztof Wnuk[3]

[1] University of Saskatchewan Saskatoon, Canada
callele@cs.usask.ca
[2] Software & Systems Engineering
Technische Universität München, Germany
penzenst@in.tum.de
[3] Software Engineering, Lund University, Sweden
Krzysztof.Wnuk@cs.lth.se

Abstract. [**Motivation:**] The requirements engineering (RE) research community is aware of the importance of performing feasibility studies before starting requirements elicitation. Unfortunately, projects still frequently fail to achieve commercial success, responsibility is often unknown, and requirements engineers may be deemed responsible for mistakes made by others. [**Problem:**] There is neither empirical evidence available from a post-mortem risk analysis for projects that performed adequate RE but commercially failed nor guidance for requirements engineers on validating a business case analysis to mitigate this risk. [**Principal idea:**] By performing a post-mortem analysis of software development projects that failed to achieve commercial success, we investigate the root causes for the failures and, in most cases, trace the causes back to business case issues. We identify risk areas and provide practical due diligence guidance to the practitioner. [**Contribution:**] This exploratory case study performs an in-depth review of a detailed post-mortem analysis of three software development projects performed over a 2.5 year period. Each of the analyzed projects failed to make the expected transition to commercialization despite using appropriate RE techniques and achieving satisfactory deliverables. The analysis identifies risk factors that the RE practitioner should consider and we provide a checklist for RE practitioners to use when checking for these risks in an antecedent business case as part of their due diligence. A low-cost commercial viability assessment technique, employing Fermi approximation, is provided to equip the RE practitioner with a risk mitigation tool in the absence of business analyst resources.

Keywords: Risk identification, risk mitigation, commercial risk, due diligence, commercialization, commercial success, success factors, business case, business analyst.

1 Introduction and Motivation

Many new product software development projects fail to achieve commercial success despite following established requirements engineering practices and

J. Doerr and A.L. Opdahl (Eds.): REFSQ 2013, LNCS 7830, pp. 253–268, 2013.

development methodologies. Unfortunately, iterative refinement (independent of the methodology) can leave critical requirements unknown at project inception or even until late in the development cycle. As observed by de Marco [1], this imperfect knowledge can lead to issues such as inadequate budgets, significant changes to timelines, missing key skills (personnel mismatch) and, in the worst case, even project failure. When the unknown requirements are exposed later in an iterative process it can be challenging to ensure that the requirements are consistent with the antecedent business case, especially if stakeholder engagement has waned.

Problem: It is generally accepted that development risk is inversely correlated with knowledge. While numerous project risk management techniques exist, to our knowledge this is the first work focused on identifying risks at the boundary between the business case and requirements engineering efforts. This work focuses on the boundary between these efforts because it is at this boundary that responsibility often passes between different individuals or teams – a transition that offers increased opportunity for problems to occur.

In this work, we review the results of a major postmortem analysis effort performed upon a new product development program at an industrial entity (referred to hereafter as CASECO). The review sought risk factors of potential concern to RE practitioners, asking the following research questions:

RQ1: What are the risk factors identified in the postmortem analysis effort that exist at the interface between the business case and the software requirements? (Section 5)

RQ2: Are there mitigation techniques already available at CASECO that could be used to mitigate one or more of the risk factors? (Section 6)

Identifying antecedent business case risks that can pose threats to subsequent requirements efforts provides the RE practitioner the opportunity to mitigate these risks in a context-appropriate manner. To a degree, this work builds upon the work of Boehm [2] wherein he explicitly includes business case analysis as one of the seven key elements in value-based software engineering and also builds upon the work of Aurum and Wohlin who promoted better alignment of technical decisions with business strategy [3]. Our in-depth analysis of the risks at the interface between BA and RE, supported by significant industry-grounded empirical evidence, provides evidence-based support of the need for business case analysis and alignment with business strategy.

Contribution: This work provides three principal contributions toward risk identification and mitigation in RE practice. First, we contribute a post-mortem analysis of the CASECO new product development program (composed of three in-depth reviews with internal and external stakeholders and 10 shallower reviews engaging internal stakeholders only). We provide evidence for necessitating that requirements engineers review the antecedent business case analysis upon which they should, in part, base their work.

Secondly, we provide support for due diligence efforts in the requirements process, at least in the context of new products and services, in the form of numerous questions that can be used as a basis for a risk identification checklist. The risks are grouped into eight categories and these categories have minimal overlap with those identified by [4], significantly extending the available practical guidance for risk management.

Thirdly, given that identifying the bounds on the commercial value of a given project is a critical element of the business opportunity assessment, we propose the use of Fermi[1] approximation techniques [5] as a low-cost approach to performing this assessment of commercial viability.

Outline: In Section 2 we discuss related work, in Section 3 we present the study description and in Section 4, the methodology followed. Our analysis and results are presented in Section 5 and risk mitigation via commercial viability assessment approximation is presented in Section 6. A short discussion is presented in Section 7 followed by the conclusions and directions for future work in Section 8.

2   Related Work

Several researchers have stressed the necessity for more interaction between business analysis and requirements engineering. Bubenko [6] states that most requirements problems can be traced to a lack of appreciation of their importance at the business management and IT management levels. Despite this rather early recognition (1995) of a strong link between requirements engineering and business management, the effects of a business case[2] on requirements engineering efforts seems to be under-represented in the literature. Among available studies, Gulla [8] discussed challenges of business modeling in re-engineering projects while Farbey [9] proposed a new design for a software supply chain, heavily influenced by the business perspective. Arao *et al.* [10] proposed a process where business requirements and system of software requirements are integrated in one information model and thus create a 'to-be' process. Lehtola *et al.* [11] proposed using roadmapping to link the business case to requirements engineering efforts while Monteiro *et al.* [12] proposed techniques for improved requirements sharing and requirements engineering collaboration, a possible solution to some of the communications challenges observed in this work.

---

[1] Fermi estimation is used to make high-quality estimations about the order of magnitude of a problem or, in the context of this paper, business opportunity. The technique enables surprisingly correct estimates, often within an order of magnitude of the exact answer, even for complex calculations with little available data.

[2] A business case captures the reasoning for initiating a project or task and should show how the decision will alter cash flows over a period of time, and how costs and revenue will change [7].

Gordijn *et al.* [13] proposed using goal-oriented requirements engineering methods to better understand business goals. Wegmann *et al.* [14] stressed that early phases of requirements engineering in an IT system should be aligned with the business imperatives of the organization. Karagiannis *et al.* [15] presented a business-process based solution that assists requirements reporting based on core business processes supporting our claim for the need for greater collaboration between business analysis and requirements engineering. Finally, Wever and Maiden [16] investigated the barriers that business analysts perceive as hindering effective requirements work in business-oriented projects finding that there are mismatches and disconnects in training, application and recognition of the critical nature of the business analysis and requirements efforts from upper management to the project team.

Ropponen and Lyytinen empirically confirmed that using risk management methods improves system development performance [17]. A literature review by Lyytinen and Hirschheim [18] derived twelve categories for the reasons for IS failures. Lyytinen *et al.* [19] presented a framework for managing software risks that combines behavioral and organizational models, suggesting that risk management should be the responsibility of all team members. Palmer and Evans [20] proposed a method for quantitative identification and extraction of requirements-based software risk metrics throughout the requirements engineering life cycle.

Collectively, these works analyze facets of the interaction between the business perspective and the production perspective. However, none of them have analyzed an industrial postmortem review of a significant number of projects for contributions to requirements engineering practices. Analyzing projects after they fail is an important contribution, providing evidence that some risk factors are realized when appropriate counter measures are not taken.

3   Study Context Description

The study was performed at CASECO, a 25-year-old Information and Communications Technology (ICT) sector company with locations in five different cities spread across three jurisdictions. Each location has permanent employees, contract employees and interns (both student and professional). The management structure is hierarchical on the organization chart but is relatively flat in practice – senior management and junior management interact in an informal manner.

CASECO was chosen for this study because: (1) they were performing their own in-depth post mortem study, (2) they were involved in a large number of related projects, undertaken with a diverse set of clients, and (3) the researchers were granted access to the internal information. The diversity of the clients improves the probability that the results can be generalized given that this is not a study of a single commercial entity. While CASECO is a common factor across all projects, they were a service provider and not the project driver.

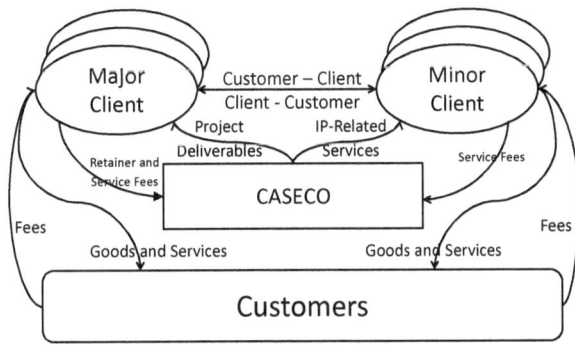

Fig. 1. CASECO operating environment

CASECO is a not-for-profit economic development organization whose goal is to accelerate the technological and business growth of Small and Medium sized Enterprises (SMEs) throughout the operating region. This growth is achieved by making in-kind investments of highly skilled manpower on specific projects done in partnership between CASECO and the client, appearing to a typical observer as some form of consulting service arrangement. Clients are of two types (see Figure 1). Major Clients pay a significant retainer fee to ensure access to CASECO services and to have a voice in determining the CASECO operating mandate. Minor Clients interact with CASECO on a fee-for-service basis wherein work performed for the Minor Client is subsidized as part of the not-for-profit economic development mandate. Both Major Clients and Minor Clients can have customer-client and client-customer relationships. Further, both classes of clients have customers to whom they provide goods and services in exchange for revenue. However, in the context of the current work the Minor Client can only access the Customer via the Major Client. Given CASECO's economic development mandate, each client project is expected to have clear commercialization objectives, set and controlled by the client, with responsibility and authority resident within the client organization.

A 2.5-year targeted R&D program was undertaken by CASECO in response to the complete replacement, with a new technology, of a fundamental platform used by the Major Clients to provide services to their Customers across a large, geographically dispersed serving area. During this period, approximately 10 person-years of effort (in total) were invested in three (relatively large) projects that were taken from product concept to the pre-production prototype stage. One of the three large projects had both Major Clients and a Minor Client while the remaining two large projects only had Major Clients. One of the three large projects was the design and implementation of a multi-jurisdictional development environment for the new fundamental platform. The development environment was commissioned under the assumption that the Minor Clients would use it to develop products and services that met the wants and needs of the Customers of the Major Clients. In addition, approximately two more person years of effort were invested in 10 relatively small projects where a product or service concept was taken to the early prototype (proof-of-concept) stage. All of the early prototypes were sufficiently advanced that they could be placed before the end customer for market-based feedback.

Several RE techniques such as elicitation sessions, triage, prioritization and negotiation were used to define the functional requirements for each project (large and small) and every technical deliverable (software or hardware artifact) was considered successful. However, none of the projects moved beyond the identified stages and into production or commercialization. As products, every project was a commercial failure despite meeting the technical requirements for the project (as prototype or proof-of-concept).

4   Research Methodology

This paper reports on a case study that investigates an authentic [21] and significant [22] topic heavily grounded in industrial practice. A case study strategy is necessary to study phenomena in their natural context such as software engineering processes [22], facilitating our understanding of the complexity of the analyzed problem rather than abstracting from it [23]. In the paper at hand, an explanatory, curiosity-driven approach [24] was taken, principally employing qualitative methods for data gathering, focusing on risk identification (rather than risk mitigation) under the assumption that mitigation can only follow after identification and comprehension.

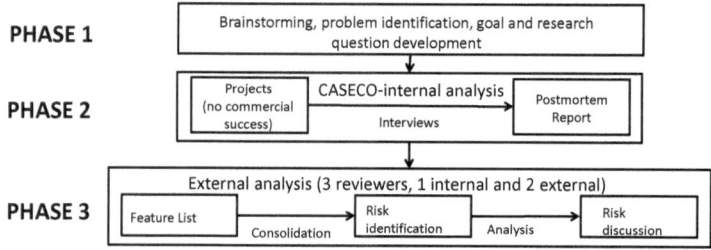

Fig. 2. Study Process

The case study was performed in three phases, see Figure 2. In the first phase, brainstorming and analysis of related work were applied in order to identify the scope and research focus of the study. Next, 13 projects were selected for analysis. Based on the results of the analysis, three projects were further analyzed during phase two interview sessions. In the third phase of the study, the results from previous steps were analyzed for specific evidence of the practices that RE practitioners could use to mitigate the observed risks or failures.

4.1   Phase 1: Problem Identification

The first phase of the study was triggered by the following phenomenon: all of the reviewed projects at CASECO failed to make the transition to commercialization despite using appropriate RE techniques and providing satisfactory deliverables. Motivated by this observation, the research team gathered and brainstormed about possible reasons for the phenomenon generating two research questions:

RQ1: What are the risk factors identified in the postmortem analysis effort that exist at the interface between the business case and the software requirements? (Section 5)

RQ2: Are there mitigation techniques already available at CASECO that could be used to mitigate one or more of the risk factors? (Section 6)

The research team decided to use multiple sources of evidence during the investigation by using interviews and analysis of work artifacts for data collection [25], both set within a pragmatic research stance [26].

4.2   Phase 2: Project Analyses

The set of 13 CASECO projects was reviewed by a post-mortem team composed of one executive, two business analysts, one combined business analyst and requirements engineer, two senior technology staff and one external consultant. The projects were selected for review based on their cost, complexity and importance to the internal and external stakeholders. Next, we performed both in-depth reviews within each project followed by a comparative review across the projects investigated for the post-mortem report to identify the risk factors to RE practice and their origins.

The review then focused on the three large projects (selected from the set of 13 projects), performing a series of interviews with developers and customer representatives. The interviews all followed the same format: a semi-structured interview consisting of an initial free-form discussion, followed by a structured interview session in which standardized questions were raised with the participants. The questions addressed issues of product definition, market requirements and shifting market forces, stakeholder identification and communication, product and project management and general feedback. After the initial responses were recorded, participants were asked to explicitly identify what went right and what went wrong in each of the question areas. Scribing services were provided by CASECO and meeting notes were provided to interviewees for review and corrections.[3]

The interview matrix is presented in Table 1. Each interview session has a unique identifier A through K. There are two types of CASECO interviews. The first set of interviews (G, H, J) were held with the CASECO team members directly responsible for the project. The second (shared) letter (K) denotes a

---

[3] The anonymized interview questions are available for download at
http://www4.in.tum.de/~penzenst/sources/caseco-interview.pdf

series of group interviews wherein all CASECO team members participated. In all interviews but (K), the interviewees always had direct experience with the subject of their specific interview. During the (K) interviews the CASECO team members were invited to provide feedback on challenges experienced by the 10 proof-of-concept projects – each of the projects had some, but not all, of the CASECO team members on the development teams. The analysis showed that the challenges experienced by the proof-of-concept projects were effectively the same as the challenges in the large projects. If this observation can be generalized beyond this study by further work then we have identified an important pattern: If challenges in proof-of-concept projects are highly similar to the challenges if large-scale projects then consistently performing a proof-of-concept project as a precursor to a large project could result in significant risk reduction for the large project. Further, if the business case analysis antecedent requirement generalizes beyond this study then RE practitioners have another significant risk mitigation tool available.

Table 1. Interview Matrix

	Project 1 Customer Product	Project 2 Client Product	Project 3 Ecosystem
Major Client 1	A		E
Major Client 2	B		E
Major Client 3		D	E
Minor Client 1	C		
Third Party			F
CASECO Proof-of-concepts	G K	H K	J K

4.3   Phase 3: External Analysis

After the interviews were completed, CASECO stakeholders were asked to formulate business rules and business policy guidance to be used to determine potentially viable commercialization paths for new products and services. The business models were generated and evaluated and conclusions presented to management.

Each of the three authors then independently performed a review of the material in the post-mortem report to extract the identified failure modes. These failure modes were translated into risks and the results are presented in the next section. In each instance, we can identify risks that occur outside of an RE practice that is focused on products and/or services – yet have the potential to have significant negative impacts upon RE and subsequent development efforts. In most instances, these risks are related to business case elements that should have been considered, either by the stakeholders or by the RE practitioner(s).

4.4   Pragmatic Reflection on Commercialization Failure

Due to commercial confidentiality constraints, we can only provide a high-level of our observations of specific details regarding the root causes for commercialization failure. The project proponents, particularly the Major Clients, expected that the technology platform shift would enable a diverse third-party application market much like that which has developed around smartphones. Unfortunately, numerous issues arose. First, the customer *willingness to pay* was not properly evaluated; the market segmentation analysis was weak and assumed that customer behavior on the prior platform would be an adequate predictor of customer behavior on the new platform. This issue was compounded by inadequate analysis of the commercial viability of Minor Clients developing third-party applications and subsequent analysis showed that the revenue streams for these applications were inadequate to sustain a commercially viable business in this market. As a result, those Minor Clients that did succeed in entering the market place were soon in financial difficulty because the customer uptake was smaller than anticipated. While all of the products could be interesting incremental revenue streams for an existing player (perhaps acting as market differentiators or barriers to competitive market entry), none of them were large enough to sustain a new business venture.

5   Analysis and Results: Identified Risks

We present here the eight identified cross-project risks (R1-R8) together with short questions formulated based on the reviewed evidence, abstracted to generic forms. These questions are consistent with those used in business case analysis [27] and can be used as the basis for a risk identification checklist supporting practitioner due diligence efforts. For example, we ask *'Is there a product champion?'* as a succinct alternative to *'A product champion advocates on behalf of the project and often assumes the role of the project leader. The lack of a clear product champion can lead to issues such as...'*

To be identified as a risk, the authors had to agree that there was evidence of that risk in at least two of the projects in the post-mortem report. The categories for the risks were determined by the authors using an affinity grouping technique and the fact that the risks are present in all projects may be because all of the projects were performed with CASECO as part of the team

R1 Motivation: Projects without strong motivation or strong champions have a significantly greater risk of failure.
Question checklist: Is there a product champion? A pain point that is motivating the stakeholder, *e.g.*, customer dissatisfaction? A pleasure point that is motivating the stakeholder, *e.g.* significant revenue? Is the project interesting or boring to upper management? Is the project a cost center or a revenue center? Is the motivation for pursuing the project emotional, *e.g.*, positive or negative, rational, *e.g.*, participate in standards efforts, or business or some combination thereof?

R2 Time and Schedule: Companies that operate on significantly different timelines, such as great disparities in the required time to take a product concept to commercialization, have difficulty working together.
Question checklist: Are all parties, vendor and customer, moving to the same timelines, toward the same product release schedule? Are the priorities relatively consistent for all parties? Can the Minor Client survive when working on the schedule of a Major Client?

R3 Constraints: Business constraints such as supplier qualifications, years in business, capitalization, etc. are often not apparent to the RE practitioner.
Question checklist: Are the non-functional, non-technical constraints clearly identified? Have the constraints been thoroughly investigated?

R4 Customer: Many entities, particularly startups, still operate under *beliefs* about their customer and target market rather than *facts*.
Question checklist: Is there evidence of willingness and ability to pay (at a price point that makes the project ROI attractive)? Can a sale be closed at the concept stage or does it require a proven product? Is the cost of access to and engagement with a customer known? Is the cost of sales and distribution known? What is the total number of possible customers for this project? What share of the market can this project reasonably acquire?

R5 Stakeholder (management): A strong primary stakeholder who is a firm supporter of a project (perhaps dominating meetings, *etc.*) can conceal a lack of general support from other stakeholders.
Question checklist: What is the confidence level that all significant stakeholders have been identified? Does the project rely upon proxy stakeholders rather than direct engagement with the real signing authorities? Are the levels of risk tolerance (or aversion) known for each stakeholder?

R6 Competition: Assessment of threats from alternative technology solutions that also meet the same market need is often outside of the competency of business analysts and is not typically the responsibility of the RE practitioner.
Question checklist: Are the stakeholders potential internal or external competitors? Are there hidden requirements, hidden agendas? (For example, projects with stakeholders from multiple organizations may not reveal their real requirements or may reveal only a subset of their requirements.) Is there a mechanism to force resolution of outstanding issues? Does the project have the ability (sufficient time and resources) to respond to competitive threats? Is the technology a commodity or are there non-trivial barriers to market entry? Is there a significant technology bypass threat?

R7 Value proposition: Scenarios where a Minor Client relies upon a Major Client to access the customer (*i.e.* a supply chain) have many potential levels of indirection. The RE practitioner should ensure these have been identified and resolved.

Question checklist: Are all stakeholders using consistent revenue, expense, and ROI models? Have these models been reviewed or validated? Do all shareholders share (approximately) consistent expectations regarding time-to-market and time-to-revenue?

R8 Communication: Significant size differences between parties can lead to communications challenges as they use the same domain specific terminology but in different contexts.

Question checklist: Do the project participants vary greatly in size? Is negotiation proceeding smoothly or does every point require significant discussion?

6   Risk Mitigation via Commercial Viability Assessment Approximation

Given the results of the postmortem review, we believe that there is substantial empirical industrial evidence that new product development efforts should have, as an antecedent, a sufficiently complete business case analysis before RE efforts begin. A prudent RE practitioner can mitigate risks by first checking for the existence of the business case and then performing a critical review of this information. If the project is an internal development effort that may not have a formal (or informal) business case, the RE practitioner can check to ensure that stakeholders, business goals and project authority (to start, stop and deem complete) have been properly identified. If there are concerns, the practitioner should be able to turn to the project authority for resolution.

However, appropriate resources may not always be available and the RE practitioner may have to extend themselves toward the role of the business analyst. We recognize that RE practitioners may not feel comfortable in this role and we would expect the project leader(s) (if they are not the RE practitioner) to assume this responsibility when necessary. We propose the use of Fermi approximation techniques [5] as a low-cost risk mitigation technique in this scenario. The technique can be applied by any team member and CASECO has successfully used Fermi estimation techniques in other projects *not* investigated in this paper. We demonstrate the application of this technique to commercial viability assessment in the rest of this section.

Commercial viability assessment is an investigation of project ROI. An estimate for (probable) upper revenue bounds for the initial stages of market introduction (*e.g.* one to three years) are combined with the estimated cost of market entry to determine whether the project should be pursued. Fermi approximation techniques (dimensional analysis – what factors dominate the results, bounds identification – how large or small can these factors be, and domain appropriate estimates of probable values within the bounds – using results from similar products) can be used to identify a reasonable upper bound on market value. If insufficient market value is identified then management can support a project cancellation order. However, a finding of sufficient market value does not necessarily mean that the project should proceed – further analysis of market share is required.

To use Fermi approximation techniques to determine commercial viability the practitioner needs to know (typically readily available) demographic information to determine the maximum number of possible customers. The total market size is then discounted to reflect realistic market penetration within the period of interest. The form of the market must then be determined (or assumed) to form the basis for estimating market share. We estimate the number of competitors in the market (n) – where the market is one of monopoly (100%), dominant oligopoly (50% + 50%/n), oligopoly (100%/n, n is small) and commodity (100%/n, n is large). Then, estimate customer willingness and ability to pay and perform a comparative analysis with like products to estimate product retail pricing. Finally, identify the elements of the distribution channel and apply industry standard margins to estimate gross unit revenues.

Given these estimates, the RE practitioner can calculate the gross revenues that the project can expect to generate over the first year to three years – CASECO experience with other projects indicates that the utility of the approximations is in the range of one to three years. Given that the team is about to embark upon building the product they should have reasonable quality estimates of the cost of development and the cost of production. (If the team does not, this is another danger sign with respect to due diligence). Given revenue and expenditure estimates, estimated ROI can be calculated in a straightforward manner and management should be able to determine project viability.

7   Discussion

The post-mortem analysis clearly identified the need to modify CASECO business processes to ensure the commercial viability of future projects. While it is easy for RE practitioners to say that the CASECO business process failures were obvious, and directly led to the project failures, the post mortem report leads us to ask whether RE practitioners have a responsibility to look beyond the technology artifact and consider the underlying business case. While we do not feel it is reasonable for management to hold RE responsible for errors in the business case perhaps there is a requirement for RE due diligence for validation of the business case for existence, accuracy and completeness. A due diligence effort by an RE practitioner (see Section 6) could have caught the business case issues and driven some form of project redefinition, perhaps even cancellation. It is possible that greater familiarity with project management [28] and business analysis [27] practices would provide greater practice scope for RE practitioners and may even improve practice reliability with knowledge of these domains.

Many of the risks presented in Section 5 are associated with a lack of valid information upon which to make an appropriate business decision. Further, these business decisions are often decisions as to whether to continue or cancel a project. For example, consider the scenario where the business case contains an inadequate investigation of the potential size of the market, failing to identify the portion of the market that the project may be reasonably expected to capture given the other elements of the business case. A due diligence process performed by the RE practitioner could include a check that the market investigation has been performed and that the validity of the market investigation has been assessed and agreed to by a second (or third) party. This due diligence effort could be used, for example, to justify stopping a development effort before significant resources are invested in developing a product for a market that may or may not exist. In this scenario, the requirements practitioner acts as a significant crosscheck for business process integrity.

In each project within the program review, this study can identify evidence that an appropriate commercial viability assessment was not performed. If the requirements effort had the performance of a commercial viability assessment, as a necessary precondition, the results might have been very different: the earliest projects undertaken would have identified the lack of commercial viability and the entire program might have been canceled much earlier (with the resulting savings to CASECO). Alternatively, if the RE practitioners had been familiar with the Fermi techniques described above they may have been able to perform the commercial viability assessment themselves.

While a rigorous determination of the root causes for the individual project failures is outside of the scope of this work, we emphasize that we found no evidence that the requirements engineering tasks within the analyzed projects were not performed as expected. Further work to strictly identify the root cause(s) for project failure is indicated.

Practitioners must be cognizant of the challenges and risks when performing a commercial viability bounds assessment on a project. Applying these economic constraints when exploring business systems, particularly at the early stages, can lead to projects being unnecessarily terminated if there is too much feedforward of existing business constraints. RE practitioners must remember that a business case is not a guarantee of commercial viability (or vice versa). For example, commercial viability assessment of dramatic innovations such as the smartphone is difficult and there may be significant disagreement regarding the probability of success. A checklist as we have proposed is useful in gathering evidence but is not a replacement for sound judgment.

Techniques that may be used to mitigate risks identified in this work include Fermi approximations for commercial viability assessment, more thorough identification of stakeholders and their roles (*e.g.* funding, adoption), expanded range of use-cases and scenarios, and mechanisms to help practitioners decide whether the RE phase of the project should even be undertaken.

Study Limitations and Threats to Validity: We discuss the limitations of the study based on the classification proposed by Yin [21]. To ensure *construct validity*, we used multiple sources of evidence while deriving presented risks. We confirmed subjective judgments from the interviews with the results from the project material reviews. The semi-structured form of interviews allowed investigators to ask follow up clarification questions. Finally, observer triangulation was used to minimize transcription and interpretation errors.

The exploratory nature of the study implies that threats to internal validity associated with causal relationships are not applicable in our case [21]. Further, the phenomena were observed in an unobtrusive way. The reviews were done by an independent, passive observer during the analysis phase. To ensure reliability [21] of the study we created a case study protocol and stored all documents associated with the study in a repository, ensuring that the results can be traced to the supporting empirical evidence.

With respect to *external validity*, we are aware that the study involves only one case company, raising concerns about our ability to generalize the results. Thus, the results should be interpreted with the case company context in mind. However, the CASECO company operates somewhat independently in three operating jurisdictions with significant client diversity by region, operations and size. Moreover, this case study is focusing on explaining or understanding a phenomenon in its natural setting. Thus, the attempt to generalize from the study is outside of the scope of this work [22].

8   Conclusions and Future Work

This paper provides an analytic review of a post-mortem analysis of the new product development program at an industrial partner. The post-mortem analysis was composed of three in-depth reviews with internal and external stakeholders (including interviews with developers and customer representatives) and 10 shallower reviews engaging internal stakeholders only. The analysis of the collected empirical evidence identified risks on the interface between RE and business analysis, particularly commercial viability assessment and competitive threat assessment.

Both research questions posed herein were answered in the affirmative with the results presented in Section 5 and Section 6. These results argue for more rigorous reviews of the business case by the requirements engineers when beginning their work on a project. The value-neutral perspective of many RE practices [3] can lead to a solution that meets the requirements but prioritizes aspects other than those present in the business case – especially if the requirements are derived without an antecedent business case. We have shown in this work there are many risks that can result, risks that can lead to commercial project failure. This study provides a checklist of questions in support of the business case review activities and we promote Fermi approximation as useful tool in support of these review activities.

This work demonstrates the need for a future investigation of the overlap between the role and responsibility of the business analyst and the requirements engineer, both in theory and in practice, to ensure that boundary risks are minimized. Further analysis of the costs of business case analysis compared to the risks of pursuing projects without due diligence is needed. How much analysis is "just enough?" We only mention the identification and exploration of potential business models as part of the post-mortem process. Our observations of these business models show intriguing results: including the elaboration of the business models as part of the requirements process could lead to serendipitous discovery of alternatives. Further investigation is indicated. CASECO will be revisited to determine whether they have been able to successfully modify their business processes in response to the postmortem report. If so, what have the modifications been? If not, what factors kept CASECO from making a successful transition?

Acknowledgements. The authors would like to thank Daniel Mendez for helpful feedback on an earlier version of this paper. This work is partly funded by the SYNERGIES project, Swedish National Science Foundation, grant 621-2012-5354.

References

1. de Marco, T.: All late projects are the same. IEEE Software, 102–103 (2012)
2. Boehm, B.: Value-based software engineering. ACM Software Engineering Notes 28, 1–12 (2003)
3. Aurum, A., Wohlin, C.: A value-based approach in requirements engineering: Explaining some of the fundamental concepts. In: Sawyer, P., Heymans, P. (eds.) REFSQ 2007. LNCS, vol. 4542, pp. 109–115. Springer, Heidelberg (2007)
4. Hughes, B., Cotterell, M.: Software Project Management. McGraw-Hill (2009)
5. Weinstein, L., Adam, J.A.: Guesstimation: Solving the World's Problems on the Back of a Cocktail Napkin. Princeton University Press (2008)
6. Bubenko, J.: Challenges in requirements engineering. In: Proc. Second IEEE Int. Symposium on Requirements Engineering, pp. 160–165. IEEE Press (1995)
7. WebFinance, Inc.: Definition by Business Dictionary: Business Case (2012) `http://www.businessdictionary.com/definition/business-case.html`
8. Atle Gulla, J., Brasethvik, T.: On the challenges of business modeling in large-scale reengineering projects. In: Proceedings of the 4th International Conference on Requirements Engineering, pp. 17–26 (2000)
9. Farbey, B., Finkelstein, A.: Software acquisition: a business strategy analysis. In: Proceedings of the Fifth IEEE International Symposium on Requirements Engineering, pp. 76–83 (2001)
10. Arao, T., Goto, E., Nagata, T.: "business process" oriented requirements engineering process. In: Proceedings of the 13th IEEE International Conference on Requirements Engineering, pp. 395–399 (2005)
11. Lehtola, L., Kauppinen, M., Kujala, S.: Linking the business view to requirements engineering: long-term product planning by roadmapping. In: Proceedings of the 13th IEEE Int. Conference on Requirements Engineering, pp. 439–443 (2005)
12. Monteiro, M., Ebert, C., Recknagel, M.: Improving the exchange of requirements and specifications between business partners. In: 17th IEEE International Conference on Requirements Engineering, RE 2009, pp. 253–260 (2009)
13. Gordijn, J., Petit, M., Wieringa, R.: Understanding business strategies of networked value constellations using goal- and value modeling. In: 14th IEEE International Conference on Requirements Engineering, pp. 129–138 (2006)
14. Wegmann, A., Julia, P., Regev, G., Perroud, O., Rychkova, I.: Early requirements and business-it alignment with seam for business. In: 15th IEEE International Conference on Requirements Engineering, RE 2007, pp. 111–114 (2007)

15. Karagiannis, D., Mylopoulos, J., Schwab, M.: Business process-based regulation compliance: The case of the sarbanes-oxley act. In: 15th IEEE International Conference on Requirements Engineering, RE 2007, pp. 315–321 (2007)
16. Wever, A., Maiden, N.: What are the day-to-day factors that are preventing business analysts from effective business analysis? In: 2011 19th IEEE International Requirements Engineering Conference (RE), pp. 293–298 (2011)
17. Ropponen, J., Lyytinen, K.: Can software risk management improve system development: an exploratory study. European Journal of Information Systems 6, 41–50 (1997)
18. Lyytinen, K., Hirschheim, R.: Oxford surveys in information technology, pp. 257–309. Oxford University Press, Inc., New York (1987)
19. Lyytinen, K., Mathiassen, L., Ropponen, J.: A framework for software risk management. Scandinavian Journal of Information Systems 8, 53–68 (1996)
20. Palmer, J., Evans, R.: Software risk management: requirements-based risk metrics. In: 1994 IEEE International Conference on Systems, Man, and Cybernetics, Humans, Information and Technology, vol. 1, pp. 836–841 (1994)
21. Yin, R.: Case study research: Design and methods. Sage Publications (2008)
22. Runeson, P., Host, M., Rainer, A., Regnell, B.: Case Study Research in Software Engineering: Guidelines and Examples. Wiley (2012)
23. Seaman, C.: Qualitative methods in empirical studies of software engineering. IEEE Transactions on Software Engineering 25, 557–572 (1999)
24. Robson, C.: Real World Research. Blackwell Publishing (2002)
25. Lethbridge, T., Sim, S., Singer, J.: Studying software engineers: Data collection techniques for software field studies. Empirical Software Engineering Journal 10, 311–341 (2005)
26. Easterbrook, S.M., Singer, J., Storey, M., Damian, D.: Selecting Empirical Methods for Software Engineering Research. In: Guide to Advanced Empirical Software Engineering, pp. 285–311. Springer (2007)
27. Brennan, K.: A Guide to the Business Analysis Body of Knowledge (Babok Guide). International Institute of Business Analysis (2009)
28. Project Management Institute: A Guide To The Project Management Body Of Knowledge (PMBOK Guides). Project Management Institute (2008)

Analyzing an Industrial Strategic Release Planning Process – A Case Study at Roche Diagnostics

Gabriele Zorn-Pauli[1], Barbara Paech[1], Tobias Beck[1],
Hannes Karey[2], and Guenther Ruhe[3]

[1] University of Heidelberg, Im Neuenheimer Feld 326, 69120 Heidelberg, Germany
{zorn-pauli,paech}@informatik.uni-heidelberg.de,
tobias.beck@stud.uni-heidelberg.de
[2] Roche Diagnostics GmbH, Sandhofer Strasse 116, 68305 Mannheim, Germany
hannes.karey@roche.com
[3] University of Calgary, AB T2N 1N4, Canada
ruhe@ucalgary.ca

Abstract. **[Context and motivation]** Strategic release planning (SRP) for a globally used information system is a challenging task. Changes to requirements on different abstraction levels are arriving continuously and have an impact on long-term selected features. **[Question/problem]** The major question is how to successfully do SRP to create competitive advantage. **[Principal ideas/results]** An exploratory case study in an industrial context was conducted (1) to get a deeper understanding of the as-is SRP process in practice, (2) to evaluate the suitability of a to-be SRP process, introducing the EVOLVE II method and corresponding ReleasePlanner tool and (3) to gather additional requirements for the to-be SRP process, with respect to feature generation and feature selection. **[Contribution]** In this paper we describe the case study and present lessons learned to improve and customize a SRP process in practice. In particular, we propose the Requirements Abstraction and Solution Model (RASM) to support feature generation.

Keywords: strategic release planning, product roadmapping, long-term feature selection, feature generation, requirement abstraction, decision-support.

1 Introduction

Software release planning focusses on the decision which features to assign to which consecutive future product releases. Strategic release planning (SRP), also called release roadmapping, is used to link business or organizational strategies and solution planning to support long-term product feature selection [11]. For this, SRP aims at long-term feature assignment to subsequent releases fulfilling technical, resource, risk and budget constraints [12]. Compared to SRP, operational release planning focuses only on the development of the next software release, planning the implementation of the identified features [1].

More and more demanding customer needs in a volatile and globally operating business environment require more agility with respect to strategic product planning [19].

J. Doerr and A.L. Opdahl (Eds.): REFSQ 2013, LNCS 7830, pp. 269–284, 2013.

Therefore, to be successful in the future an integrated approach for strategic decision-making, requirements management, and roadmapping processes is required [14]. SRP has to cope with unclear or high-level business requirements and continuously arriving changes to requirements on different abstraction levels that have an impact on existing release plans. Furthermore, competitive customer needs and varying implicit multiple feature selection criteria make SRP difficult. Additionally, the need of considering relevant changes faster increases the complexity of the SRP decision-making process. Since the feature concept is most often used for SRP purpose, the SRP process in practice is characterized by two major decision-makings: (a) *feature generation*, means bottom-up bundling of requirements on a lower abstraction level into features or top-down dividing business or organizational strategies into features, (b) *feature selection*, which means assigning features to subsequent releases based on multiple selection criteria.

In academia several SRP processes exist, where the planning item (e.g. feature) generation is neglected and planning item backlogs and corresponding requirement engineering tasks are taken for granted. Lethola et al. [12] states that the roadmap preparation process for release roadmaps consists of the following four steps: data collection, feature prioritization, release planning, and release roadmap validation, where the feature generation task is not addressed. Van de Weerd et al. [21] provide a reference framework for software product management, where release planning and requirements engineering are identified as separated key process areas. Therefore, product release planning starts with requirement prioritization. Svahnberg et al. [20] conducted a systematic literature review on strategic release planning processes, where all found processes focus on the requirement selection task. However, the feature generation task in practice is an essential part of the SRP process since features are generated in practice top-down and bottom-up. Further, due to the growing number of requirement changes and requirement volatility, which is reflected in the increasing adoption of agile software engineering methods in practice, the problem of overscoping, [4] arises. This requires the integration of strategic release re-planning decision-support to adequately adapt existing plans [9]. In particular, relevant changes to requirements on different abstraction levels have to be identified and aggregated in existing feature structures and validated against multiple business strategies. Currently, little is known about the application of SRP processes in practice [19]. Additionally, there is a need for further empirical validation of existing models in full-scale industry trials.

In this paper we report the results of an exploratory case study in industry and provide the following contributions: (1) a deeper understanding of the as-is SRP process in practice, with focus on the feature generation and feature selection decision-makings, (2) evaluation results on the suitability of a to-be SRP process, introducing the EVOLVE II method [15] and corresponding ReleasePlanner tool and (3) additionally gathered requirements for the to-be SRP process with respect to feature generation and feature selection decision support. The remainder of this paper is structured as follows: Section 2 presents related work. Section 3 describes the case study design and how we proceeded in the case study, while Section 4 presents the case study results. Section 5 discuss the results and presents lessons learned. Section 6 concludes the paper and gives an outlook on future work.

2   Related Work

The ability to successfully do SRP creates competitive advantage. *Selecting a subset of requirements for realisation in a certain release is as complex as it is important for the success of a software product* [5]. Suomalainen et al. [19] provide new empirical results about product roadmapping in volatile business environments, by defining main stakeholders and their roles and by proposing a product roadmapping process framework. The identified most problematic phases of the process are prioritizing features, managing changes and maintaining roadmaps. Through an interview study practitioners were asked about their feature capturing methods and sources. Market trends and standards were stated as the main feature source and the most commonly used method for capturing features was gathering ideas over time.

Bjarnason et al. [4] conducted an empirical interview study about the causes and effects of overscoping, setting a release scope that is too large to deliver in time, in a large-scale industrial setting. They identified six causes for overscoping, where for instance unclear business strategies for software development and continuously incoming requirements flow via multiple channels are stated. Danesh et al. [6] also conducted a qualitative study to increase the understanding of software release planning challenges in several software companies and states that unclear project objectives and frequent change of these objectives are key factors for release planning failures. The difficulties with linking business strategy to solution planning was reported by Komssi et al. [11] investigating the roadmapping process of two Finnish software product companies. An interesting suggestion was a focus shift away from low level software feature prioritization to the analysis of high level customers' business process activities. Komssi et al. see the benefit of discovering new service business opportunities and competitive advantage. Similar investigations according to linking product strategies are conducted by Khurum et al. [10] who developed a method for alignment evaluation of product strategies among stakeholders to ensure that strategies are the basis for planning and development of products.

In literature there are several strategic release planning processes proposed. Svahnberg et al. [20] provides a systematic literature review on 24 strategic release planning processes. The results show that more than 60 % of the presented academic papers belong to the EVOLVE family and most of them could be applied for market-driven and bespoke development. Svahnberg et al. also investigated the state of validation of the SRP processes and concludes that most of the processes are validated in industry with limited scale. An additional industrial proven release planning approach, that was not covered by the systematic literature review, is proposed by Fricker et al. [7]. The major idea is to simplify release planning by utilizing feature trees to structure requirements, instead of using flat requirements lists. The approach was also evaluated in an industrial case study with respect to feasibility.

3   Case Study Design

In this section we provide information about the two case study objects, describing the context of the company under consideration, the case project and the ReleasePlanner tool.

3.1   The Case Company

The case study was conducted in the context of a globally operating company in the health care domain that develops in-house a bespoke and globally used Customer Relationship Management (CRM) system. The case study aims at investigating the SRP process of a CRM subsystem called Global Deal Calculation (GDC), that implements parts of the Contract Life Management cycle. Agile software development methodologies and in particular the *Scrum* framework is used to incrementally develop the GDC subsystem by releasing two minor releases and several patches per year and a major release every three to four years. Due to the adoption of agile development methods the release cycles are partitioned into several iterations. That facilitates communication and negotiation possibilities with the stakeholders after every iteration to adapt existing release plans. An issue tracking system is used to submit requirements, such as bug, change or features requests to the development team. As the number of iterations is varying, the release duration also varies. The company is already in a transition to adapt agile software development practices such as Scrum and not all projects are done in an agile manner. Project management and release roll-outs are still conducted plan-driven, which causes a mix of agile and plan-driven elements. Additionally, not every release version is consumed by all company sites countries, because a roll-out project causes high testing and training effort.

The GDC system is used by different, geographically distributed company sites and corresponding country business units. Primarily, GDC is globally developed, providing standardized functionality, that is used by all countries, but is implemented locally by providing additionally country specific functionality. Since the number of GDC *consumer* countries is growing up to 17 countries in the future, the complexity of linking multiple country strategies to system solution planning requires a systematic SRP method. Some specific challenges of the company, like planning a bespoke and globally used information system considering multiple business strategies, have already been presented in [23].

Several stakeholder boards or teams on different management levels involve IT and business representatives for SRP. The *Change Advisory Board (CAB)* reviews and proposes the project portfolio and major release changes. CABs are also responsible for decisions and prioritization of changes that have been escalated by the Change Management Teams. The *Change Management Team (CMT)* is the global business process owner and prioritizes business requirements, reviews projects and budgets, makes trade-off decisions, discusses strategic and escalated operational issues. The *Iteration Review Group (IRG)* is responsible for the operational release planning by reviewing and approving planned iterations of the current release. The IRG involves also CMT members and the product owner who is primarily responsible for generating and managing release plan proposals. In general, strategic release plan relevant changes on corresponding feature sets are welcome to decrease reaction times on changing business or organizational needs to benefit from IT-enabled competitive advantages.

3.2 ReleasePlanner Tool

The ReleasePlanner[1] is a proprietary, web-based process and decision-support tool. We have chosen the ReleasePlanner, because the tool was proven successfully in about 25 industry and more than 250 academic and student projects (f.i. [16], [3], [18]). It allows prioritizing release objects by multiple stakeholders against multiple criteria and performing subsequent resource optimization to maximize the overall release value for a release period of typically more than just one release. The decision support process is based on an evolutionary problem solving approach called EVOLVE II [15], which is emphasizing the involvement of human experts. The approach comprises 13 different process steps, all of them supported by ReleasePlanner. At each iteration, five optimized and diversified planning alternatives are determined. The final decision is done based on additional aspects such as resource consumption profiles of the proposed alternatives. In addition, implicit concerns not being part of the explicitly formulated model are supposed to be included by the human expert in the selection process.

3.3 Research Methodology

An exploratory case study was planned and conducted based on the guidelines for case study research in Software Engineering by Runeson et al. [17]. The objective of the case study was threefold. (1) Understanding of the as-is SRP process in practice to identify problems and improvement capabilities for a to-be SRP process. (2) Providing a to-be SRP process proposal adopting the EVOLVE II method. (3) Evaluation of the to-be SRP process applying the ReleasePlanner, that implements EVOLVE II. Therefore, the following research questions are investigated with respect to the conducted industrial case study. *(RQ1) How is strategic release planning done in the company? (RQ2) How does the EVOLVE II method and corresponding ReleasePlanner cover/extend the as-is SRP process of the company? (RQ 3) What are additional requirements for the SRP to-be process?* To answer the research questions the case study provides results on qualitative and quantitative data. Table 1 shows the data collection strategy by illustrating which data was collected utilizing the respective data collection method.

3.4 Threats to Validity

Threats to the validity of empirical research have to be examined during all phases of the case study. To evaluate the validity of this case study, the validity perspectives proposed by Wohlin et al. [22] were considered and are analyzed in the following. The threats to *construct validity* are reduced by a cooperation with the industry partner over more than a year and by reviewing the research results by the practitioners in a focus group session and informal discussions to ensure that the studied parameters are relevant to the research questions. Further, the threats to *internal validity* are reduced by triangulation (see Table 1) over multiple empirical data sources and the combination of qualitative and quantitative data. For instance, reflecting the as-is SRP process by a retrospective data analysis helped to validate identified implicit feature selection criteria based on

---

[1] https://www.expertdecisions.com

Table 1. Data source collection strategy

Method	Data Source	Research Question
Archival Data Analysis (July-Aug 2012)	Feature backlogs; meeting notes and release notes of the last three GDC release versions	RQ 1
Observation of a requirements refinement and prioritization meeting (18.07.2012)	12 Participants: 9 country business representatives, product owner, Observer: first and third author	RQ1 RQ3
Focus Group Session (06.09.2012)	5 Participants: Product Owner, IT Consultant, IT Project Manager, Moderator: first author, Observer: third author	RQ 1 RQ 2 RQ 3
Simulation (Aug-Sep 2012)	Retrospective release planning (GDC 3.6 and 3.7) simulation using the ReleasePlanner	RQ 2 RQ 3

data analysis against feature selection criteria stated by the practitioners. Additionally, the data were collected by two researchers, which reduces the risk of being biased by one person. Finally, the threats to *external validity* are reduced by conducting the case study in a real-world industrial setting. However, the external validity might be still influenced by the studied specific context represented by the mixture of agile and plan-driven methods.

4 Results

In this section, the results of the case study are presented. First, in Subsection 4.1 the as-is SRP process is described thus to provide a deeper understanding of the as-is SRP process in practice (RQ1). Thereafter, Subsection 4.2 provides evaluation results on the suitability of the to-be SRP process, introducing the EVOLVE II and corresponding ReleasePlanner tool, are presented (RQ2). Additionally gathered requirements for the to-be SRP process with respect to feature generation and feature selection are described in Subsection 4.3 to answer RQ3. Finally, the developed Requirements Abstraction and Solution Model (RASM) is introduced in Subsection 4.4.

4.1 Understanding the As-Is Strategic Release Planning Process

To describe how SRP is done by the company (RQ1) in general, Figure 1 outlines the major identified SRP process elements. A *heterogenous requirement pool* comprises requirements on different abstraction levels, where requirements and changes to requirements continuously arrive during the SRP process. This requirement pool is the basis for *feature generation*, where this step also comprises the pre-selection of features to scope the *feature backlog*. After that, the features contained in the feature backlog are assigned to subsequent releases based on multiple *feature selection* criteria. The generated *release roadmap proposals* are basis for stakeholder negotiation and have to be *re-planned* after every release iteration cycle to accommodate intermediately occurring changes.

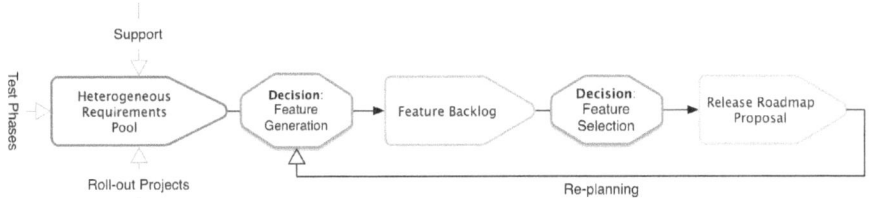

Fig. 1. Identified as-is strategic release planning process

Feature Generation. As mentioned above, the basis for SRP is a heterogeneous requirements pool that comprises all requirements related information used for release planning. We have used the Requirements Abstraction Model (RAM) provided by Gorschek et al. [8] to classify the requirements of the company that are available on different abstraction levels. The RAM was not used so far by the company for requirements engineering or release planning purpose. Table 2 shows sources of requirement relevant information, provides examples and classifies the requirements according to the RAM. The CAB is primary source for business and IT strategy concerns represented in business cases and corresponding IT roadmaps. The CMT assigns *main topics* to future releases, where main topics are used to communicate business strategies within release roadmaps. These main topics could be understood as features and are related to business case initiatives. The analysis of the archival release planning data showed, see Table 3, that release roadmaps for 3.6 comprised only low level requirements, where 3.7 comprised a combination of high level (main topics) and low level business requirements. Starting with 3.8 the feature concept, which groups low level business requirements, was adopted to reduce planning complexity. The requirement abstraction reduces communication and negotiation necessity, because only feature related changes were communicated (e.g. recently identified features). The IRG is responsible to review the release roadmaps after every release iteration duration (7 weeks) to discuss and negotiate changes. There are three different input channels, as shown in Figure 1, for requirements on a lower abstraction level. During (i) roll-out projects, (ii) support and (iii) test phases, requirements are gathered and submitted to the issue tracker system. Features are generated top-down, derived from business case initiatives and bottom-up by grouping low level delta requirements. Therefore, top-down features represent business strategies, whereas bottom-up features, addressing functionality enhancements, are bundled with respect to existing solutions.

Feature Selection. As mentioned above features are strongly connected to business case initiatives, where the initiative priority is based on different criteria, such as reducing costs, efficiency gains or customer impact. Any changes on these priorities directly affect existing release plans. The *pre-selection criteria* for scoping the release backlog are (a) *must* (b) *nice to have* and (c) *must not* considering business case initiative

Table 2. Source and classification of requirement relevant information

Source	Information Type	Examples	RAM [8]
CAB	Business Cases, IT Roadmaps (Business Case Initiatives)	Global Application Standardization	Organizational Strategies
		Provide multi-country system versions	Product Strategies
CMT, IRG	Release Roadmaps (main topics)	Handle several countries in one instance	Product Level (goal)
Roll-out Projects, Support, Test Phases	Business Requirements (Bug/Change/ Functionality Requests)	-	Feature Level (features)
		GDC shall enable multi-currency	Function Level (functions/actions)
		-	Component Level (details-consists of)

rankings and technical feasibility. Based on qualitative and quantitative data the following explicit and implicit SRP selection criteria were identified. Feature *priority* and *implementation risk* were stated by the practitioners as the determining feature selection criteria. The analysis of meeting notes, release notes and requirement documents showed that feature priority comprises additionally the following implicit feature selection criteria.

Requirement Issuer are those countries that rise a requirement, where countries have different priority primarily based on the revenue. In many cases requirements are suitable for all or most of the other countries and are classified as global features/requirements. It is a challenging task to decide which requirements are globally suitable and which of them should be only provided in local implementations.

Release Consumer Order For any new system release a pilot country is chosen to roll-out the new release as a first release consumer. Therefore, raised requirements of the pilot countries are preferred, in particular requirements that aim at assuring the roll-out of the system (e.g. interface or data migration requirements). Additionally, requirements of consumer countries of the next release are also preferred compared to requirements raised by countries that would not consume the current release. The results of the data analysis and observations surfaced the following implicit feature selection criteria:

Effort Estimation There are several stages for effort estimation during release planning. For SRP purpose in some cases it is required to estimate feature effort before solution concepts are developed. This is especially the case for top-down generated features. Assessing the number of touched software areas provides evidence on the expected implementation effort. If solution concepts are clear, the effort estimation is based on comparing the effort of one solution relative to that of another. Therefore, the feature effort includes the sum of all related solution efforts. Additionally, features with high effort estimations are implemented first, except technical constrains require another feature implementation order.

Requirement Volatility This selection criteria was primarily identified through the observation of planning meetings and the analysis of meetings notes. There are several risk factors for requirement volatility such as the involvement of new technology or unclear underlying business processes. Features with high volatility and middle business priority will be postponed, where features with high volatility and high stakeholder priority are assigned to the subsequent releases or release iterations to be able to accommodate intermediate requirement changes.

Table 3. Overview GDC Release Planning Data

	GDC 3.6	GDC 3.7	GDC 3.8
# planning items	89	51	14
# high level req.	0	3	14
# low level req.	89	48	0
# communicated changes	32	8	6

So far, the ad hoc strategic and operational release planning has worked well. However, the growing number of involved countries in the future and the demand to react faster on business change increases the complexity of strategic and operational release planning, which could not adequately be handled ad hoc any more. There are difficulties of utilizing the feature concept for SRP purpose at the company. A feature should be suitable to represent both, high level business requirements and software functionality abstraction at the same time. For operational release planning purpose low level requirements are assigned to 38 different software areas. In many cases a specific requirement is related to several areas and therefore these software areas are not suitable for bottom-up feature generation. Altogether, the GDC development is characterized both through project initiated requirements engineering (GDC roll-out projects) as well as through requirements initiated projects (global GDC development). Moreover, it is noteworthy that all requirements represent delta requirements by specifying enhancement proposals that are only understandable in relation with the existing system, which causes difficulties in relating them to business strategies.

4.2 Strategic Release Planning To-Be Process Proposal and Tool Evaluation

Along with the investigations of the as-is SRP process several issues and requirements for a to-be SRP process are gathered. The major improvement possibilities are seen by the practitioners in a systematic SRP process that integrates decision support for feature generation and feature selection. For that, the ad hoc as-is SRP process (see Figure 1) of the company was aligned to the 13 steps of the EVOLVE II method, as shown in Figure 2, to provide a SRP to-be process proposal (RQ2). To evaluate the suitability of the SRP process solution proposal, the ReleasePlanner was introduced at the company by retrospectively simulating the planning for GDC 3.6 and 3.7. In the following only SRP to-be process proposal gaps (additional requirements RQ3) are considered, which were identified and discussed together with the practitioners. These requirements primarily address decision support needs that are not or not sufficiently supported by the solution proposal.

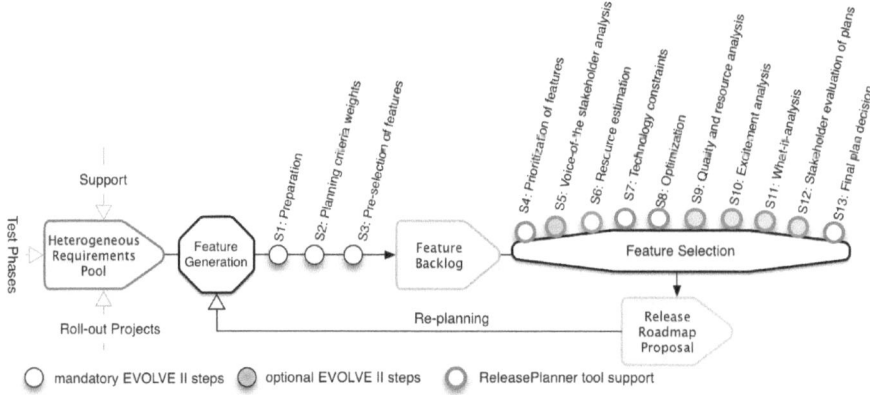

Fig. 2. Proposed to-be strategic release planning process

ReleasePlanner Simulation. Applying the tool at the company for release planning simulation creates some integration effort, where the effort depends strongly on the quality and availability of required planning data, the current SRP process and the utilized development tools. The most difficult task was to choose the selection criteria and selection criteria weights. Any adjustments on selection criteria or criteria weights caused significantly plan changes.

Simulation Setup The setup for the retrospective simulation of the release planning process for release 3.6 and 3.7 comprised *135 planning items*. These items probably do not represent the actual requirement backlog, because we cannot ensure that we have replicated the backlog completely. Requirement issuer and requirement volatility are used as selection criteria to represent stakeholder priority and implementation risk. To quantify requirements volatility the discrepancy rate of *best-case* and *worst-case* effort estimations are used. The higher the discrepancy the higher the requirement volatility risk. The selection criteria release consumer was considered by pre-assigning requirements of the pilot countries to the according release. The resource capacities are approximated through story points, where 160 story points for release 3.6 and 80 story points for release 3.7 were assumed.

Simulation Results The tool provides two measures, degree of optimality and stakeholder feature points, to evaluate the quality of the alternative plans. In Table 4 five optimized planning alternatives are compared with a manual baseline plan. Alternative 1 is the best possibility when relying on stakeholder features points, which measures the stakeholder satisfaction related to a specific plan. Compared to the manual plan it can be seen, that the tool computes a plan with which the stakeholder would be more satisfied than with the manual plan. Additionally, alternative 1 provides a plan with a better degree of optimality with respect to available resources, which could be also seen in the different number of assigned features. The discussion of the results with the practitioners yields the following conclusions: (a) the proper requirement selection criteria were identified for release planning, because the calculated plans are very similar to the manual plan. (b) it is difficult to assess, whether the quality of calculated plans is better than the manual plan, it depends strongly on the suitability of utilized planning data such as effort estimations and resource capacities.

Table 4. Comparison of ReleasePlanner computed plans against manual plan

	A 1	A 2	A 3	A 4	A 5	M. Plan
degree of optimality	99.7%	98.2%	97.6%	96.7%	95.7%	99.1%
stakeholder feature points	(566196)	(557325)	(553950)	(549044)	(543505)	(562520)
# features assigned 3.6	62	62	62	62	61	62
# features assigned 3.7	23	23	23	22	24	20

4.3   Additional Identified Strategic Release Planning Process Requirements

Feature Generation. The feature generation task is not addressed by the EVOLVE II method, because available feature sets are taken for granted. As a result the identified requirements (FGx) and corresponding rationals related to the feature generation task are gathered from and discussed with the practitioners.

(FG1) Support top-down and bottom-up feature generation Rationale: Features are used for strategic planning purpose. They are derived top-down from high level business strategies (business case initiatives) or they comprise a bundling of low level requirements that have arrived via different input channels.

(FG2) Support aggregation of relevant changes into existing release plans Rationale: Requirement relevant changes continuously arrive on different abstraction levels and have to be considered during re-planning. These changes for instance comprise priority change, intermediate identified requirements or changing effort estimations. Especially, the adaption of resource capacities or effort estimations are stated by the practitioners as a challenging task.

(FG3) Support delta requirements handling Rationale: Since GDC is developed incrementally over several years, the requirements, that are source for SRP, represent delta requirements. This causes major problems if these delta requirements cannot be linked to planned (to-be) and existing (as-is) system specifications. Due to the strategic (high level) planning purpose it is not clear which abstraction level is necessary to represent the system and how to link it with delta requirements.

FG4) Support feature classification and variability Rationale: Primarily, GDC is developed globally, developing functionality that is used by all countries. However, in some case specific functionality is not necessary (optional) since local business process are different and functionality (features) should be switched on/off for local GDC instances to reduce testing and maintaining costs. Additionally, the local instances of the GDC system require different configuration settings. Therefore, requirements should be classifiable into functional or configuration requirements.

Feature Selection. The feature selection task is well guided by the EVOLVE II method, and according tool, by supporting multiple selection criteria and comprehensive analysis capabilities. However, additional requirements (FSx) related to feature selection are identified and described in in the following.

(FS1) Support pre-selection (Scoping) Rationale: Because of continuously arriving changes overscoping arises. That requires iterative pre-selection and pre- selection support. This requirement is related to the FG2, because pre-selection is necessary after the aggregation of changes.

(FS2) Support multi-view selection criteria Rationale: The results on investigating the feature selection criteria of the as-is SRP have shown that implicitly business/technical and organizational views are reflected in the selection criteria. Providing decision-support for feature selection means to support the identification and solution of conflicts between the three different views, where selection criteria could be assigned to one of the three views.

(FS3) Support strategic analysis capabilities Rationale: A major challenge of developing a globally used software system is to balance multiple country specific business strategies to provide a system that satisfies all stakeholder adequately.

(FS4) Support the modeling of release dependencies Rationale: SRP focusses on long-term feature selection where features are assigned to subsequent releases. This rises the need of considering, besides feature dependencies also release dependencies. (e.g. dependencies to other projects or systems).

4.4   Requirement Abstraction and Solution Model

Based on the insights and requirements on feature generation (FGx) an extension of the RAM proposed by [8] was developed to support the mentioned problems and requirements. The requirement abstraction and solution model (RASM), illustrated in Figure 3, represents a preliminary solution proposal to address the elicited requirements. There are several reasons why the RAM [8] is not sufficient for the purpose of strategic release planning for the company. Most of the requirements are delta requirements, aiming at the change of existing software functionality. RAM provides the possibility of modeling low level requirements on component level, describing how something should be implemented instead of what. However, to handle delta requirements knowledge about the existing structure of software functionality is required. Therefore, the RAM is used to abstract business requirements and is extended by linking product strategies explicitly with software features. The linking on this specific level is necessary, because during SRP only high level requirements are available and the refinement of requirements on functional level happens later on. To overcome the dilemma that a feature should represent business requirements abstraction and software functionality abstraction at the same time, the model distinguishes explicitly between these two types of features to make SRP involved stakeholder also aware of it. We have learned from practice that features could be generated top-down, derived from business strategies, and bottom-up by bundling low level requirements. In some cases low level requirements do not address a specific business strategy, but have a high innovation character. A strictly business strategy oriented selection of requirements, as provided by Khurum et al. [10], could hamper innovation by neglecting requirements that provide innovative solution suggestions.

In the following the RASM elements, illustrated in Figure 3, are explained. A *system release* fulfills business features by implementing new features or by changing one or many existing software features. A *business feature* represents the refinement of business or organizational strategies or the bundling of low level business requirements. A constraint that was mentioned by the practitioners was that a business feature shall be implementable within a specific release and should be explicitly linked to software features. Business features represent the highest available level of business

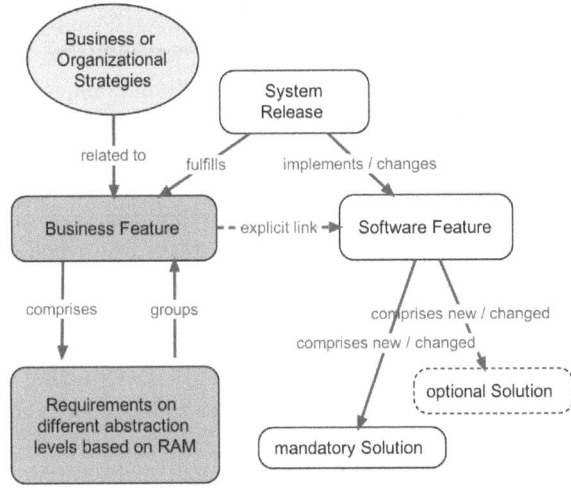

Fig. 3. Requirement and Solution Abstraction Model (RASM)

requirements according to RAM [8]. Referred to Table 2 business features could be mapped onto product strategy or product level and could be refined into one or many requirements on lower level. *Software features* represent the abstraction of planned and existing solutions, where solutions can be classified into optional/mandatory and functional/configurational solutions.

Utilizing RASM for feature generation the above mentioned requirements (FGx) are addressed as follows:

(FG1-Solution) The top-down feature generation decision is supported by the constrain of generating business features top-down only in relation to business strategies. Where as the bottom-up feature generation allows to use business and/or software features to bundle low level requirements.

(FG2-Solution) RASM enables the identification of release relevant change by bottom-up and top-down comparison of requirements change at different abstraction level to business strategies. Therefore, the aggregation of changes to requirements at any requirement abstraction level to business features is also possible.

(FG3-Solution) The linkage between business requirements and software features or corresponding solutions increase the understanding of delta requirements.

(FG4-Solution) The RASM provides a classification of solutions into optional or mandatory solutions that enables the modeling of solution variability.

5   Discussion

This section provides interpretations of the results in relation to existing work and a discussion of limitations. We interpret the SRP process of the company as an important task and the process has to be understood as a continuing activity. The results indicate that the introduction of the feature concept for SRP can provide two benefits. Firstly, through grouping of low level requirements into business features it reduces the complexity caused by huge flattened requirements lists. Secondly, the usage of high-level business features to better link them with business strategies improves the communication between the system stakeholders. Lethola et al. [12] recognized the latter as well in the context of market-driven development. Further, the ReleasePlanner evaluation results indicate that the ad hoc SRP process of the company works reasonably well. However, the systematic process provided by the tool ensures a sufficient degree of optimality and stakeholder satisfaction of release plans also when the complexity of release planning increases due to more involved countries and continuously changing criteria. Benestad et al. [2] also stated that the concern of evolving feature descriptions and design specifications are not well accounted for by release planning models and identified also the lack of handling continuous change. Determining the capabilities of an organizations release planning process was also addressed by Lindgren et al. [13]. They provide a capability model to identify areas for improvement.

As for every study there are limitations that should be discussed. In Section 3.4 we describe how we reduced threats to validity of the case study design, while in this section we discuss other limitations. There are two specific characteristics of the company that may have an impact on the SRP process and also influence the external validity of the results. *Mixture of plan-driven and agile software development elements.* Despite the adoption of agile software development methodologies by the company, there are only a few releases per year that are organized by plan-driven roll-out projects with fixed deadlines. This is necessary as long several depended projects have to be coordinated. In this study we have not analyzed which elements of the SRP process are plan-driven and which one agile or whether these two principles impede each other. To scale agile practices such as Scrum to larger projects and to coordinate several depended agile project releases without fixed deadlines is an open issue. *Mixture of customer- and market-driven development.* The information system is developed bespoke and used globally, where the end user and customers are known and provided functionality is strongly aligned with business processes to enable competitive advantage. However, there are some similarities to market-driven development, where the market is represented by the different globally distributed company sites. It is not always clear during planning and development time, which countries will finally consume which release version. This depends on whether the current system release provides features that are appropriate to satisfy country specific business strategies. The major intent of the company is to standardize the information system functionality to provide a customizable standard software *product* to all countries.

6   Conclusion and Future Work

In this paper, we reported on the results of an industrial case study that aims at the analysis of the SRP process of the company. We have analyzed qualitative and quantitative data to identify the as-is SRP process and developed based on the insights and results a to-be SRP process solution proposal. The major idea of the solution proposal was twofold. (1) The EVOLVE II method was adopted to the as-is process to provide a systematic method for release planning and (2) the RASM was developed to support requirements change on different abstraction level and to handle delta requirements by explicitly linking business strategies with solution planning and solution development. Finally, the SRP process solution proposal was evaluated by introducing the Release-Planner tool to the company. The evaluation results comprise additional requirements with respect to feature generation and feature selection decision-making support needs, that are not or not sufficiently supported by the tool.

Future work includes the implementation of the additional identified FGx and FSx requirements, listed in Section 4.3, where the RASM already addresses FGx requirements. In terms of requirement FG3, it has to be investigated whether a (software) feature-based representation of an existing system is sufficient to handle delta requirements, if solution specifications are rarely available. Moreover, the identified requirements FSx for the to-be SRP process can be used for tool functionality improvements. Finally, there is some effort required to integrate RASM and EVOLVE II to propose a SRP process that combines feature generation and feature selection.

Acknowledgements. The authors would like to thank Roche Diagnostics GmbH (Mannheim) for its financial support of this research. Many thanks are also due to the GDC project team for their participation and valuable discussions of the results.

References

1. Al-Emran, A., Pfahl, D.: Operational planning, re-planning and risk analysis for software releases. In: Münch, J., Abrahamsson, P. (eds.) PROFES 2007. LNCS, vol. 4589, pp. 315–329. Springer, Heidelberg (2007)
2. Benestad, H.C., Hannay, J.E.: A comparison of model-based and judgment-based release planning in incremental software projects. In: Proceeding of the 33rd International Conference on Software Engineering, ICSE 2011, vol. 1325, pp. 766–775. ACM Press, New York (2011)
3. Bhawnani, P., Ruhe, G., Kudorfer, F., Meyer, L.: Intelligent decision support for road mapping a technology transfer case study with seimens corporate technology. In: Proceedings of the 2006 International Workshop on Software Technology Transfer in Software Engineering, TT 2006, pp. 35–40. ACM Press, New York (2006)
4. Bjarnason, E., Wnuk, K., Regnell, B.: Are you biting off more than you can chew? A case study on causes and effects of overscoping in large-scale software engineering. Information and Software Technology 54(10), 1107–1124 (2012)
5. Carlshamre, P.: Release Planning in Market-Driven Software Product Development: Provoking an Understanding. Requirements Engineering 7(3), 139–151 (2002)
6. Danesh, A.S., Ahmad, R.: Software release planning challenges in software development: An empirical study. African Journal of Business Management 6(3), 956–970 (2012)
7. Fricker, S., Schumacher, S.: Release planning with feature trees: Industrial case. In: Regnell, B., Damian, D. (eds.) REFSQ 2011. LNCS, vol. 7195, pp. 288–305. Springer, Heidelberg (2012)
8. Gorschek, T., Wohlin, C.: Requirements Abstraction Model. Requirements Engineering 11(1), 79–101 (2005)
9. Jadallah, A., Galster, M., Moussavi, M., Ruhe, G.: Balancing value and modifiability when planning for the next release. In: 2009 IEEE International Conference on Software Maintenance, pp. 495–498 (September 2009)

10. Khurum, M., Gorschek, T.: A method for alignment evaluation of product strategies among stakeholders (MASS) in software intensive product development. Journal of Software Maintenance and Evolution: Research and Practice 23(7), 494–516 (2011)
11. Komssi, M., Kauppinen, M., Tohonen, H., Lehtola, L., Davis, A.M.: Integrating analysis of customers' processes into roadmapping: The value-creation perspective. In: 2011 IEEE 19th International Requirements Engineering Conference, pp. 57–66. IEEE (August 2011)
12. Lehtola, L., Kauppinen, M., Kujala, S.: Linking the business view to requirements engineering: long-term product planning by roadmapping. In: 13th IEEE International Conference on Requirements Engineering (RE 2005), pp. 439–443. IEEE (2005)
13. Lindgren, M., Land, R., Norström, C., Wall, A.: Towards a capability model for the software release planning process — based on a multiple industrial case study. In: Jedlitschka, A., Salo, O. (eds.) PROFES 2008. LNCS, vol. 5089, pp. 117–132. Springer, Heidelberg (2008)
14. Ngo-The, A., Ruhe, G.: Decision support in requirements engineering. In: Aurum, A., Wohlin, C. (eds.) Engineering and Managing Software Requirements, pp. 267–286. Springer (2005)
15. Ruhe, G.: Product Release Planning: Methods, Tools and Applications. CRC Press, Boca Raton (2010)
16. Amandeep, N.F.N.G., Ruhe, G., Stanford, M.: Intelligent support for software release planning. In: Bomarius, F., Iida, H. (eds.) PROFES 2004. LNCS, vol. 3009, pp. 248–262. Springer, Heidelberg (2004)
17. Runeson, P., Höst, M., Rainer, A., Regnell, B.: Case Study Research in Software Engineering. John Wiley & Sons, Inc., Hoboken (2012)
18. Bin Saleem, S., Yu, Y., Nuseibeh, B.: An Empirical Study of Security Requirements in Planning Bug Fixes for an Open Source Software Project. Tech. rep., Dep. of Computing, Faculty of Mathematics, Computing and Technology, The Open University (2012)
19. Suomalainen, T., Salo, O., Abrahamsson, P., Similä, J.: Software product roadmapping in a volatile business environment. Journal of Systems and Software 84(6), 958–975 (2011)
20. Svahnberg, M., Gorschek, T., Feldt, R., Torkar, R., Saleem, S.B., Shafique, M.U.: A systematic review on strategic release planning models. Information and Software Technology 52(3), 237–248 (2010)
21. van de Weerd, I., Brinkkemper, S., Nieuwenhuis, R., Versendaal, J., Bijlsma, L.: Towards a Reference Framework for Software Product Management. In: 14th IEEE International Requirements Engineering Conference (RE 2006), pp. 319–322 (September 2006)
22. Wohlin, C., Runeson, P., Höst, M., Ohlsson, M.C., Regnell, B., Wesslén, A.: Experimentation in software engineering: an introduction. Kluwer Academic Publishers, Norwell (2010)
23. Zorn-Pauli, G., Paech, B., Wittkopf, J.: Strategic Release Planning Challenges for Global Information Systems A Position Paper. In: International Workshop on Software Product Management (IWSPM), pp. 186–191. ICB-Research Report No. 52 (2012)

Redefinition of the Requirements Engineer Role in Mjølner's Software Development Process

Anders Bennett-Therkildsen, Jens Bæk Jørgensen, Kim Nørskov,
and Niels Mark Rubin

Mjølner Informatics A/S Finlandsgade 10, 8200 Aarhus N
{abt,jbj,kno,nmr}@mjolner.dk

Abstract. [Context and motivation] Our company's software development process describes seven roles, one of which is the requirements engineer. We want the work of the requirements engineer to give more benefit in our development projects than is currently the case.

[Question/problem] The requirements engineer works in an interdisciplinary setting closely together with the other roles, in particular with the user experience specialist, the software architect, and the project manager. We have found that these three roles are performing most of the actual RE work in our projects. As a consequence, the requirements engineer often only plays a minor role, which is also explained by the fact that the requirements engineer role is not given high organisational attention. With a few exceptions, the requirements engineer is appointed ad hoc, at project level. This poses a potential risk of neglecting important RE activities. The problem that we address is how to best distribute responsibilities between the requirements engineer role and the other roles in our organization.

[Principal ideas/results] We have surveyed a number of recent projects and have analysed to which extent RE has been carried out, by which roles, and with which techniques and tools.

[Contribution] Our contribution is to discuss our survey results and on this basis propose a redefinition of the requirements engineer role that respects that user experience, software architecture, and project management have a higher organisational priority.

Keywords: Software development process, requirements engineering in relation to other roles, relationship between RE theory and RE practice.

1 Introduction

Mjølner Informatics is a Danish software company, which develops custom-made software for customers like Terma, Danfoss, Velux, Big Dutchman, and Bankdata. We are around 80 employees; the majority has a master's degree in either computer science or software engineering. Many of our projects run for 6-12 months and have project teams with 6-10 employees.

Mjølner has a software development process, which is an iterative process that comprises seven roles: Architect, Developer, Infrastructure Manager, Project Manager

J. Doerr and A.L. Opdahl (Eds.): REFSQ 2013, LNCS 7830, pp. 285–291, 2013.

(PM), Requirements Engineer (RE), Test Manager, and User Experience (UX) Specialist. The roles should ensure a clear distribution of responsibilities during project execution. This very often works well, but improvements can be made as we discuss in this paper.

For each of the seven roles, a "process community" exists in our company. The process communities are the main drivers for the maintenance and improvement of the development process. Most employees are members of one or two communities. Focus in the communities is on sharing knowledge, experience and evaluating current practice to improve the development process and transfer knowledge between projects. To ensure a coordinated effort between the seven communities, the chairmen of the communities comprise a SPI coordination committee. For a more detailed description of our development process and SPI organization, please refer to [1].

Members in the RE process community in Mjølner have investigated how requirements work is done more specifically in practice in our projects. The overall goal of the investigation has been to redefine the requirements engineer role ("RE role") such that it provides a greater value in our projects. In this paper, we discuss this investigation. The paper is a Problem Statement in the sense that it describes a situation that we want to improve – but it also briefly outlines a possible solution.

The paper is structured as follows: In Section 2, we present our RE process, role, and the RE community at Mjølner. Section 3 describes results from the investigation of practice. In Section 4, we discuss considerations about a redefinition of the RE role and in Section 5 we state our proposal. In Section 6 we briefly discuss related work, and draw some conclusions.

2   RE Process, Role, and Community at Mjølner

The following figure outlines the RE process at Mjølner by describing the activities that must be carried out by the RE role, as prescribed by the development process.

This description is closely connected to the activities that are on the agenda in Mjølner's RE community. However, in this community, the work has mainly focused on how to improve the elicitation, specification and validation of requirements (the activities in the "Project startup" in the figure), and to a lesser extent on general requirement management and the other activities in the "Iterations" in the figure.

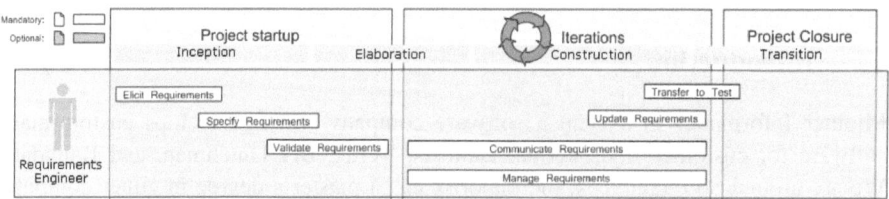

Fig. 1. Description of the RE role

The body of knowledge in Mjølner's RE community is manifested in a toolbox. This toolbox consists of a hands-on guide for doing RE, a software requirement specification template document, which includes many issues to take into account along with guiding descriptions, and an internal website, which contains supplementary material, including references to RE literature. We keep ourselves updated on the RE literature, e.g., by attending conferences such as the RE conference. As examples, we have read and found inspiration in the following books [2], [3], and [4]. Our template is to a large extent based on [2].

3   RE Practice at Mjølner

Members in Mjølner's RE community have interviewed project members from ongoing and past projects to identify how RE was performed and by whom in practice in our company. Different topics were covered during the interviews, e.g., the roles in the project, how requirements were elicited and by whom, the types of requirements, which methods were used, and how requirements were documented. The interviewers also asked if and how the knowledge from the RE Mjølner community came into play in the projects. We report on four projects below. The projects were quite different in many aspects, including RE. In none of those projects, the RE role was explicitly appointed to a team member. The interviews were therefore done with either the PM or the UX specialist.

In the first project, the customer came from the public sector. Requirements were already elicited by the customer and specified in a one thousand pages document. Despite the extensive document it was, according to the PM at Mjølner, a rather incomplete requirement specification and there was estimated only little time during the project to clarify the requirements and reach a satisfying level of detail. Requirements were written in use cases and managed by the PM along with a third party subcontractor. The project team at Mjølner did the design of the GUI as well, so some of the details of the requirements were brought to development by the UX specialist through screen mock-ups.

In the second project, Mjølner took over the project from another supplier and, consequently, inherited a way of cooperating with the customer. No requirement specification existed. Instead, requirements were inferred from screens of the system, which came from a third party. Rework became one of the challenges in this project. All the unknowns were dealt with at weekly meetings with customer stakeholders.

In the third project, the involvement of the team at Mjølner was initially to do the graphical layout of an already specified system. But as the UX specialist started asking questions about the system and the underlying requirements, the customer became convinced to do a complete redesign and let a team at Mjølner do the job. RE was done entirely by a UX specialist, who used methods and processes from a UX toolbox (different from the RE toolbox); in this case being flowcharts/sitemaps, wireframe mockups and scenarios. There is inherently a difference between UX and RE in process and approach to requirements – epitomised in the role of design [5].

In the fourth project, requirements were gathered as use cases by an internal product owner in a Word document and elicited through meetings with a few customer stakeholders – mainly a single representative. The document was revised, versioned and read together with a representative from the customer organization. The main challenge here was to ensure sufficient activity from other important customer stakeholders. Again, the RE role was not explicitly appointed to a team member, but was distributed between the product owner and the UX specialist.

4   Basis for Redefinition of the RE Role at Mjølner

In summary, the survey confirmed our conjecture that the RE role, if assigned in a project, only makes a minor contribution to the requirements management that is carried out in the project; the majority of the RE work is done by other roles. Moreover, none of the surveyed projects had benefitted much from artifacts from the RE body of knowledge in Mjølner. This fact confirmed that there is a gap between the issues on the agenda in Mjøner's RE community, and the RE work that is carried out in practice in the projects at Mjølner.

The conclusion from our survey has motivated us to take a closer look at how the RE role positions itself against the other roles in the projects at Mjølner.

To do this, and as a help to redefine the RE role, we (the authors) have created the grid shown in the figure below, which illustrates the RE activities (the horizontal bars), the education or skills of the project team participants at Mjølner (vertical bars), and the ellipses show the various roles in a project. It is a rough indication based on the assignments in several projects at Mjølner, in particular the projects we discussed in Section 3. Each ellipse illustrates a role and its horizontal extent shows the typical educational backgrounds of persons assigned to this role. The skills range from hardware-near computer engineer/technician skills to creative graphical design skills. The vertical extent of the ellipse shows various requirement activities to be done by the role - from highly technical requirement handling over interaction designs to more abstract business goals elicitation.

We plotted the roles in this grid as ellipses to see where the roles overlap each other. The picture was quite clear. The RE role is "squeezed" both in education/skills and RE activities in the projects at Mjølner, since a major part of the responsibility of the RE role is handled by the other roles, mainly the project manager, the architect, and the UX specialist.

There are a number of reasons for this. First of all, UX as a product is a selling point for Mjølner (RE is not). In a number of our projects, one or more UX specialists are allocated – catalyzed by our sales department and by agreement with the customer – as starting point.

Second, all the UX specialists that are assigned to the UX role are focused on and skilled in doing requirements elicitation because this is, obviously, necessary to ensure that the system being developed actually satisfies the needs of the users. The UX role does studies of users, field studies, and focus groups, often resulting in personas and scenarios, as well as workshops with stakeholders to elicit and specify requirements at different levels.

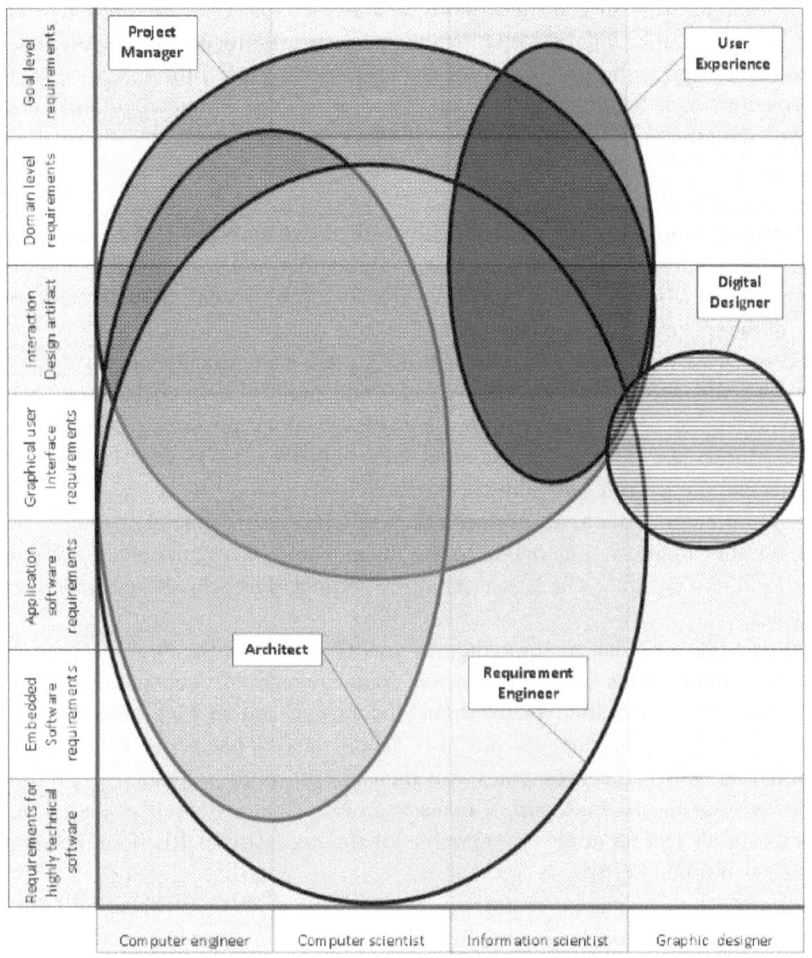

Fig. 2. Requirement activities, roles, and education

Third, in the initial phases of a project, the requirements specification document is often drafted and maintained by the project manager. When the implementation starts, this specification itself tends to become less relevant internally in the project; a Scrum-style backlog, along with references to deliveries from the architect and the UX specialist, serve the role as the requirements specification. In general, when the system is being implemented, often the software architect drives the RE process, because much requirements work assumes a detailed knowledge of the architectural details.

5   A Redefinition of the RE Role at Mjølner

The conclusion after the investigation was that we had the problem to redefine the RE role. Clearly, the RE role should focus more on activities that are "left" by the other roles with higher organisational priority. With a more specific focus, the RE role must make sure that the gaps that might appear between the architect, the UX specialist, and the project manager, in regard to requirements, are filled. Examples of areas that need the specific attention of the RE role, we believe, are data requirements, security requirements, quality requirements, and pure management, e.g. keeping track of requirements changes throughout a project.

Regarding data requirements, we specifically aim at two activities, which are often crucial for project success that should be given more attention by the RE role and the RE community at Mjølner; these activities are (1) development of dictionary or glossaries defining key domain terms, and (2) development of domain models, e.g. using ERD or ORM diagrams. This will help to visualise and document concepts of the domain in a way that our typical UX specialist and architect deliveries do not.

With respect to security requirements, for some of the systems we develop, it is critical that these are gathered, discussed and understood. This is a type of requirements that the RE role should be responsible for.

Quality requirements such as performance, reliability, and maintainability are important for the architect, but needs to be documented as requirements without getting into solution design - which is a risk if the architect has primary responsibility of these issues.

The last part that we wish to strengthen as an RE activity is the book-keeping of managing the requirements in our processes. Making sure that changes that arise during the project are specified in the right documents, and making sure that the "why" and "when" for the changes are also documented. This might just be in a meeting minutes, which the team roles can then discuss after workshops, or other encounters with the customer. A part of managing is also making sure that the proper level of traceability can be done. Discussions of the necessity of RE book-keeping activities are also found in [6].

This last activity of managing requirements is an activity that we expect will only become more important and bigger as projects done by our company grow in size. Our company's mission is to have projects at a larger scale and continuously moving up the value chain of the customers. This will mean a larger amount of requirements, but also a larger interface with the costumer, where customer stakeholder needs different parts of the requirements. Similar communication challenges are described in [7].

6   Related Work and Conclusions

Our findings and considerations presented above are done for our particular company and we do not have empirical evidence to make generalisations on a proper scientific basis. Other authors have done far more extensive investigations of related issues, e.g. [8]. An example of an investigation with similarities to ours is [6]. In both these cases – and many others that we have seen in the literature – the investigations and results are reported by researchers, i.e., by people who are external to the particular organisation being investigated and who, consequently, look at the situation from the outside. In contrast, we work for the company, whose situation we have discussed and described. An advantage of this is that it is likely that we have much more detailed and precise knowledge; a drawback may be that we are more involved and perhaps not able to be as objective as an outsider would be.

In spite of the remarks above, we believe that the issue that we have discussed in this paper is an instance of a very general problem: to position RE well in an interdisciplinary setting, properly coordinated with other roles in a software development process. We know companies, where (1) the RE role is under pressure, (2) where the role does not exist explicitly, or (3) where the role is near extinction – either because the activities, that are carried out by the requirements engineer are handled by other roles, or, worse, because the activities are not handled at all. In the latter case, there is a risk of leaving large gaps between, e.g., UX and architecture.

We have proposed a redefinition of the RE role in the software development process at Mjølner by narrowing its focus to activities not covered by other roles. In Mjølner's RE community we will prioritise these issues.

References

1. Jørgensen, J.B., Kjær, M.Y.: Mjølner's software process improvement: A discussion and strengthening using the SPI manifesto. In: Riel, A., O'Connor, R., Tichkiewitch, S., Messnarz, R. (eds.) EuroSPI 2010. CCIS, vol. 99, pp. 222–232. Springer, Heidelberg (2010)
2. Lauesen, S.: Software Requirements - Styles and Techniques. Addison-Wesley (2004)
3. Robertson, J., Robertson, S.: Mastering the Requirements Process. Addison-Wesley (2006)
4. Wieringa, R.J.: Design Methods for Reactive Systems. Morgan-Kaufmann (2003)
5. Sutcliffe, A.: Requirements Engineering From an HCI Perspective. In: Dam, R., Soegaard, M. (eds.) The Encyclopedia of Human-Computer Interaction (2011),
   http://www.interaction-design.org/encyclopedia/
   requirements_engineering.html
6. Sabaliauskaite, G., Loconsole, A., Engström, E., Unterkalmsteiner, M., Regnell, B., Runeson, P., Gorschek, T., Feldt, R.: Challenges in aligning requirements engineering and verification in a large-scale industrial context. In: Wieringa, R., Persson, A. (eds.) REFSQ 2010. LNCS, vol. 6182, pp. 128–142. Springer, Heidelberg (2010)
7. Hochmüller, E.: The Requirements Engineer as a Liaison Officer in Agile Software Development. In: AREW 201, 1st Workshop on Agile Requirements Engineering, Article No. 2, New York (2011)
8. Cao, L., Ramesh, B.: Agile Requirements: Engineering Practices: An Empirical Study. IEEE Software 25(1), 60–67 (2008)

Distances between Requirements Engineering and Later Software Development Activities: A Systematic Map

Elizabeth Bjarnason

Department of Computer Science, Lund University SE-221 00 Lund, Sweden
`elizabeth.bjarnason@cs.lth.se`

Abstract. **[Context and Motivation]** The main role of requirements engineering (RE) is to guide development projects towards implementing products that will appeal to customers. To effectively achieve this RE needs to be coordinated with and clearly communicated to the later software development activities. **[Question/Problem]** Communication gaps between RE and other development activities reduce coordination and alignment, and can lead to project delays and failure to meet customer needs. **[Principle ideas/results]** The main hypothesis is that coordination is enhanced by proximity to RE roles and artefacts, and that distances to later activities increase the effort needed to align requirements with other development work. Thirteen RE-related distances have been identified through a systematic map of existing research. **[Contribution]** Reported distances are mapped according to research type, RE activity and later software development activities. The results provide an overview of RE distances and can be used a basis for defining a theoretical framework.

Keywords: systematic map, distance, requirements, software development.

1   Introduction

Effective requirements engineering (RE) greatly depends upon successful coordination [12, 16] and communication of requirements with the downstream development activities [6, 24], e.g. design, implementation, and testing. Merely producing a perfect requirements specification is not sufficient. Rather it is vital to ensure that the requirements are clearly understood and agreed with implementation-near roles, and that sufficient requirements information is available for later development activities [14, 24]. Communication gaps between people may contribute to project delays, software quality issues and even failure to meet customer expectations [6].

Within global software development (GSD), project teams and members are globally distributed. These geographical distances between people have been found to negatively affect the communication and thereby also the coordination and success of the distributed development. In addition to geographical distance, socio-cultural and temporal distances have been found to be in play within GSD [1]. Agerfalk et al. have defined a theoretical framework of these different types of distances and how they affect communication, coordination and control [1]. However, coordination and

J. Doerr and A.L. Opdahl (Eds.): REFSQ 2013, LNCS 7830, pp. 292–307, 2013.

communication is also a challenge within non-distributed development, in particular for large development organizations and projects [6, 12].

Our main hypothesis is that distance plays an important role in development, whether distributed or not. In particular, the distances between RE and later software development activities may impact project effectiveness and efficiency. The systematic mapping study reported in this paper provides an overview of existing knowledge of RE-related distances within software engineering research.

Work related to the targeted area is described in Section 2. Section 3 outlines the research method while Section 4 presents the results, which are then discussed in Section 5. Finally, the paper is concluded in Section 6.

2   Software Development and RE

'Requirements are the basic building blocks gluing together [the] different ... activities needed to define, develop, implement, build, operate, service, and phase out a product and its related variants.' [16] However, in general most people focus mainly on one area of expertise: RE, project management, architecture, implementation, testing etc. Both in practice and in research, there is generally weak insight and knowledge into how to leverage software development by improving on the interaction and coordination of RE with later activities within software development.

In contrast, concurrent engineering [22] is an approach to product development where several engineering activities are carried out concurrently (at the same time by the same project team) with extensive feedback and iteration. The developers are to consider all aspects of the development cycle from requirements to cost and quality. Reported gains for this approach include increased efficiency, productivity and quality, and reduced waste and shortened lead times [22]. A concurrent approach is applied within agile software development by integrating the activities for requirements, architecture, implementation and testing, and the claimed gains are similar to those for concurrent engineering, including increased responsiveness to change.

Damian et al. found that improved RE practices within a more traditional plan-based development project may have an effect also on later software development activities. Effective RE can thereby support increased development effectiveness and augment the efficiency and productivity of the other development activities, and lead to improvements for a wide range of software development aspects, e.g. project planning, managing feature creep, testing, defects, rework, and product quality [14]. This indicates that RE can play a vital role for the total development effort, if RE is effective and well-coordinated with later development activities.

Requirements and Design Are Interdependent Activities. While design (either by architecture or directly during implementation) aims to realize the requirements, architectural and technical limitations, and new technical possibilities may affect the requirements and, thus, require requirements changes. For these reasons, it has been suggested that RE should be intertwined and performed in parallel with design [25, 29]. Nuseibeh et al. have designed a method that does this while still separating between problem and solution structure. The method is receptive to handling change in an efficient way, allows early exploration of the problem space, and enables engineers to identify requirements and match them to available components and products [25]. Similarly, Fricker et al. found that aligning requirements and architecture through a negotiation process between product management and architecture led to identifying missed requirements, and to a shared requirements understanding that mitigated problems related to missed requirements and requirements dependencies [17].

Coordination and Alignment of RE and Testing. We have previously reported on the situation of alignment between RE and testing in industry [5]. Two of the main challenges were found to be RE quality and the softer aspects of development, i.e. communication and collaboration [5]. Furthermore, a number of industrial practices for supporting alignment have been reported both by Bjarnason et al and by Uusitalo et al. These practices include traceability between requirements and test cases, and increased communication between roles [5, 31], e.g. by involving testers early in the project and in requirement reviews, and by establishing communication between testers and requirement owners [31]. Similarly, Marczak et al. found that in requirements-driven collaboration, close communication between requirements and testing depends on key roles which when absent cause disruptions within the development team [24].

3   Research Method

The systematic map reported in this paper was performed based on guidelines for systematic mapping [26] and insights for systematic literature reviews [7]. The steps taken in designing and performing the study are described below. The study protocol and full list of papers included in the study can be found on-line [4].

3.1   Research Questions

With the aim of locating research into RE distances within/between RE and later software development activities, the following research questions were formulated:

RQ1: Which RE-related distances are reported in peer-reviewed literature?
RQ2: To which extent is 'distance' used in GSD versus non-GSD papers?
RQ3: For which activities within RE has the concept of distance been researched?
RQ4: Towards which later development activities are RE distances investigated?

3.2   Search Strategy

The defined scope covers RE research and its intersection with later development activities. Papers focusing on non-RE topics were excluded, while general software development papers were included. Based on scope and research questions, search keywords were defined. The initial keywords were searched in well-known databases, e.g. IEEE Xplore, SciVerse. Based on search results, the keyword, scope and research questions were refined and search strings reformulated. The set of databases was expanded and re-searched for relevant papers.

3.3   Data Sources

Searches into the following databases are included in this mapping study:

1. IEEE Xplore (http://ieeexplore.ieee.org) covers computer science, electrical engineering, and electronic subject areas. Full-text and bibliographic access to almost 3 million of IEEE's publication including transactions, journals, magazines and conference proceedings published are provided.
2. Elsevier's SciVerse (http://sciencedirect.com) covers papers from more than 2,500 computer science and engineering journal.
3. ACM Digital Library (http://dl.acm.org) provides access to ACM journals, proceedings and transaction including ACM computing literature.
4. Inspec and Compendex provide access to huge amounts of scientific literature in many subjects including information technology, and are accessible via Engineering village's unified search interface (http://www.engineeringvillage2.org).

3.4   Data Retrieval

Search strings were constructed by combining the defined scope (software engineering OR software development OR requirements engineering) with the term 'distance'. The searches were limited to peer-reviewed material written in English. Material on 'distance learning' was excluded in the search to avoid a large number of irrelevant hits. The searches were limited to title, abstract and keywords.

3.5   Screening Process

The final searches yielded 2,427 papers (see Table 1). A title scan resulted in 161 relevant papers. The full references, abstract and search source of these papers were then stored in MS Excel (available on-line [4]). Duplicates were removed; 148 unique papers. These papers were then included or excluded based on the abstracts. The inclusion/exclusion decisions for both title and abstract were cautious, i.e. when in doubt the paper was included. When an abstract contained insufficient information, the introduction was reviewed. In total 53 papers were included in the final set.

3.6   Data Extraction, Classification and Synthesis

During data extraction and mapping, a classification scheme was developed according to guidelines provided by [26]. A set of keyword were identified through exploratory coding of the abstracts, and then clustered into the categories of the map. In a few cases, the abstract was insufficient and parts of the full text were reviewed to ensure a correct understanding. Two sets of categories were identified. One related to context and focus of the research (main development activity, specific RE activity, and organisational distribution) and the other related to distance type.

The initial set of keywords for distance types was refined through analysing parts of the full paper text. In some cases, *forwards snowballing* was applied to locate additional papers, which were consulted to ensure a correct understanding of the used terms. The coding of all included papers was then revised to match the final set of codes. The final coding of the included papers is available on-line [4].

Finally, a synthesis was performed on the included papers for each distance type to identify how the term is defined and applied, and if any causal relationships are reported for that term. In some cases, additional papers were located through forwards snowballing. For example, in GSD papers distances would typically be mentioned with a reference to previous work. In addition, for distances with only a few located papers supplementary searches on the specific distance type names were performed to identify additional papers. Parts of the full text was analysed for the synthesis, in particular introduction and conclusions sections, and all mentions of the term 'distance'.

Table 1. Number of papers in each step of the screening process

Source	Initial selection	Title review	Abstract review
SciVerse	51	7	2
IEEE Xplore	79	4	1
ACM Digital Library	1,951	52	33
Inspec	346	11	0
Compendex		74	17
TOTAL	**2,427**	**148**	**53**

4   Results

4.1   Demographics of Retrieved Literature (and RQ2)

The search and selection resulted in 53 individual peer-reviewed papers. The majority of these (42) were within GSD. The distribution of papers over time, split into GSD / non-GSD context, is shown in Figure 1. The maximum was in 2009 with 11 papers. It is worth noting that within GSD a framework for categorizing GSD challenges based on three types of distances was published in 2005 [1] and that the following 4 years (2006-2009) have the largest number of papers found in this study.

The research type for each paper was classified according to the scheme suggested by Wieringa et al. The following categories were considered in this study [33]:

1. *Evaluation research* investigates a problem or technique in practice and provides new knowledge of causal or logical relationships.
2. *Solution proposals* present a solution without a full-blown validation.
3. *Validation research* presents a solution proposal validated outside of industrial practice, e.g. experiments, prototyping, theoretical proof etc.
4. *Philosophical papers* sketch new theories or frameworks.
5. *Experience papers* describe the author's personal experience and may contain anecdotal evidence.

The distribution of the included papers according to research type and distribution context (GSD or non-GSD) is shown in Figure 2. The numbers indicate that, for the GSD context, more empirical evaluations and theoretical frameworks on the concept of distance have been researched than for the non-GSD context. For general development (non-GSD), the majority of included papers are in the form of validation research, indicating that more evaluation research is required into distances in the general software development context to establish foundations for more mature knowledge and for establishing theories based on empirical evidence.

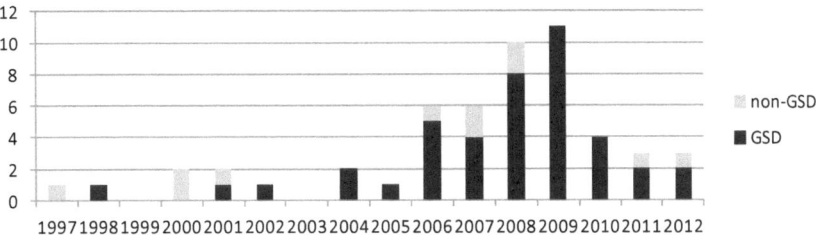

Fig. 1. Number of papers per year, categorised according to GSD or non-GSD context

4.2 Type of Distances (RQ1)

This study identifies thirteen distances. Eight of these, are distances between people, e.g. between roles, teams and organizations, while four address distances between artefacts. One distance concerns distance between an artefact (e.g. formal model) and reality. Unsurprisingly (since the majority of included papers address GSD), the most commonly referred distances are the ones defined within GSD, i.e. geographical, socio-cultural and temporal distances. Table 2 shows an overview of the number of papers for each distance. (The distances are described in Section 4.4.)

4.3 RE Activities (RQ3) and Later Software Development Activities (RQ4)

Distances were found in papers related to RE, project management, design, implementation, tools and processes. More than half of the papers (29 of 53) cover software development in general, while a third of the papers (17 of 53) cover RE, and a fourth (8 of 53) cover implementation. The numbers indicate that RE is acknowledged as an important activity for which distances are relevant to investigate. However, more research is needed to fully explore the field. In particular, research is needed on how RE distances relate to testing for which no papers were found, which is surprising considering that testing verifies that the requirements are fulfilled in the final product. A map of the number of papers per distance type and software development activity for which they were mentioned is shown in Table 2.

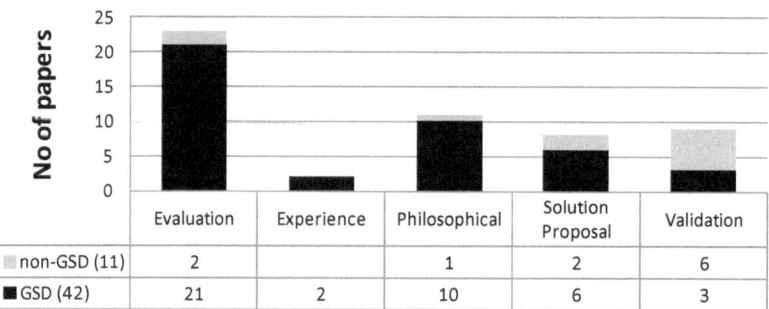

Fig. 2. The number of papers per research type and GSD vs. non-GSD context

Table 2. The number of papers per distance type and software development activity. The bar indicates relative amount. Papers covering several categories are counted for each category.

		TOTAL	General	RE	Impl	Tools	Prj mgmt	Design	Process
			29	17	8	7	6	1	1
PEOPLE	Geographical	41	27	7	6	6	3		
	Socio-cultural	25	17	3	4	1	2		
	Temporal	15	11	1	2	1	2		
	Power	3	3						
	Opinions	2		2		1			
	Psychological	2			2				
	Organisational	1		1					
	Cognitive	1		1					
ARTEFACTS	Similarity	3		3			3		
	Semantic	2	1	2					
	Syntactic	1		1					
	Impact	1		1				1	
OTHER	Adherence	2	1	1	1				1

Of the 17 RE-specific papers, 7 address negotiation and 4 cover RE in general, while for handling changes, elicitation, specification, validation and traceability only the odd papers was found for each RE activity. 7 of the RE-specific papers purely address RE, while the others also cover software development in general (3), project management (3), tools (3) and implementation (1). Table 3 shows a map of RE-specific papers per development activity and RE activity.

4.4   RE Distances in Context

The systematic map identifies 13 RE distances between people, artefacts, and other entities. This section describes each distance based on included papers.

Distance between People

Geographical distance denotes 'a directional measure of the effort required for one actor to visit another at the latter's home site [or home work place]' [1]. Even a geographical distance of 25 metres, i.e. within the same office building, has been found to reduce communication between engineers [2]. For off-shored projects where RE is geographically separated from other software development activities Dibbern et al. found that this distance can be a significant cost driver [15]. In particular, in cases where client-specific knowledge was crucial face-to-face collaboration was required for adequate knowledge transfer of domain knowledge and for requirements analysis and specification [15]. Tools for enhancing distributed group communication have been suggested for collaborative RE activities such as requirement negotiation and requirements traceability towards goals and design artefacts [18]. Calefato et al. found that computer-based communication provided better support for elicitation than for negotiation, and suggest that the general preference for face-to-face communication might be explained by this weakness of computer-based negotiations [9]. In contrast, Damian found that when using technology for negotiating requirements the group's overall performance was not decreased compared to when negotiating face-to-face, and could even be more effective in integrating multiple stakeholders' needs [13]. Similarly, Wolf et al. found no significant delays for geographical distance in a case study. This was believed to be due to practices applied to bridge these distances (collaborative tools, and processes and practices adapted to distributed software teams), but may also be explained by the fact that the delays were quantified as opposed to qualitatively measured as for most other studies [35].

Table 3. The number of RE-specific papers per RE activity and later activities. The bar indicates relative amount. Papers covering several categories are counted for each category.

	TOTAL	Negotiation	General RE	Specificaton	Analysis	Validation	Changes	Elicitation	Traceability
		7	4	3	3	2	1	1	1
Pure RE	7	4	1	1	1	1		1	1
General	3			2	2	1			
Project managmt	3		3						
Tools	3	3							
Design	1						1		
Implementation	0								
Process	0								

Temporal distance denotes 'a directional measure of the dislocation in time experienced by two actors wishing to interact' [1] due to different time zone, work shifts etc. In general, short temporal distances allow for timely synchronization between team members, while long temporal distances reduced the opportunities for synchronous communication and introduce delayed feedback [1]. Time zones and work shift schedules may work together to decrease temporal distance by adjusted office hours or utilized for working around the clock by passing on tasks between teams in different time zones [1]. Yousuf et al. suggest that when temporal distance is present certain requirements validation techniques which do not rely on synchronous communication are more suitable than others [36].

Socio-cultural distance denotes 'a directional measure of an actor's understanding of another actor's values and normative practices' [1] and includes organisational and national culture, language, individual motivations, work ethics, and politics.

In general, communication is improved by low socio-cultural distance thereby reducing risk, while long socio-cultural distances increase the risk of misunderstandings and may make coordination harder [1]. However, long distances also have a potential for increased learning and access to a richer skill set, and be stimulating for innovation [1].

In the context of RE for GSD, Dibbern et al. found that cultural distance can be a significant cost driver for a company with off-shored projects. Increased costs may be incurred for transfer of knowledge of domain, requirements etc., and additional specification effort to ensure accurate requirements [15]. Yousuf et al. mention socio-cultural distance as potentially influencing requirements validation though without specifically analysing how [36]. Real-time machine translation has been proposed for requirements negotiation among stakeholders separated by language barriers, and found to not disrupt real-time interaction in text-based chat [9].

Opinion distance denotes a measure of the difference of opinion on a certain aspect of an item between two actors. This distance has been investigated between decision makers and stakeholders in requirements negotiations with the aim of supporting group decision by measuring the differences in linguistic opinions of alternatives based on multiple criteria [10]. Chakraborty and Chakraborty propose using a fuzzy distance measure to measure the distance between fuzzy clusters of the opinions in order to improve 'accuracy' of the decision by identifying dissimilar opinions [10]. Similarly, Zhu and Hipel propose a method for dealing with multi-stage information, i.e. when information about alternatives evolves over time [38].

Organisational distance denotes a measure of one organisational unit's understanding of another unit's goals and perspectives, e.g. concerning priority of customer requirements relative cost of code design and quality. The organisational distance between people involved in RE was categorised in a study on pairing on RE tasks as *internal* or *external* depending on if they are part of the development team or not [37]. The study suggests that sharing RE tasks is more effective when there is a shorter organisational distance due to less delay in the (shorter) communication paths [37].

Psychological distance denotes a measure of the perceived psychological (subjective) effort of an actor to communicate with another actor [27]. This distance has been researched for software development in general, though not specifically for RE. Prikladnicki has defined a measurement for the perceived distance between people. This measurement relates to the social dimension of psychological distance that addresses the distance of a stimulus (social object or event) from the perceiver's self, e.g. my best friend or a person from another culture [23]. The measurement was evaluated in a project with development distributed between Brazil and India. The study shows that the psychological distance does not necessarily correspond to the geographical distance, but to a high degree depends upon trust and communication though the impact of these factors varied per country and per role [27]. For example, a project engineer in Brazil perceived the lowest distance while a project manager (also in Brazil) perceived the highest psychological distance [27].

Power distance denotes a measure of the degree to which unequal distribution of power is accepted within a society [19]. This distance has been researched for software development in general, though not specifically for RE. This distance is one of the dimensions of socio-cultural distance and has been found to affect relationships within distributed development and thereby also the success of distribution [34]. Winkler et al. found that difference in power distances may negatively affect communication. For example, in a culture with a large power distance saying no or voicing criticism is avoided, detailed specifications are preferred and instructions are preferred from superiors rather than from peers. All of these factors pose a risk of complicating collaboration with team members used to shorter power distances and more open communication [34]. Wende and Philip found communication via instant messaging improved communication and, thus, enabled bridging power distances [32].

Cognitive distance denotes a measure of the difference between two actors' cognition, e.g. what they each know and are aware of. Yu and Sharp observed this distance in a case study on pairing on RE tasks and identified that when one person fills many roles communication is immediate since the cognitive distance between the roles is zero, which is beneficial for communication and coordination [37].

Distance between Artefacts

Similarity distance denotes a measure of the similarity between an entity and another entity of the same type, e.g. project. This distance has been suggested as supporting the coordination between RE and project management, in particular for cost estimation of requirements. In analogy-based software effort estimation, the concept of similarity distance is used to identify completed projects with similar characteristics by measuring the Euclidian distance between project features [28], e.g. number of requirements, number of interfaces, project model etc. This approach has been validated using industrial data sets and the results confirm that this approach outperforms the usage of algorithmic models for effort estimation [28].

Several different approaches and variations have been proposed for measuring similarity distance. Chiu and Huang propose adjusting the estimations to take into account the re-use effect of the project identified as the most similar [11]. Azzeh et al. propose an approach that supports handling uncertainties and imprecision in project attributes by the use of fuzzy C-means clustering and fuzzy logic. With this approach, each attribute is represented with several fuzzy sets instead of by a single value. Furthermore, this approach clusters together the most similar projects and their values are represented in the same fuzzy set. The similarity between two projects is then measured by the similarity distance between the two sets to which they mostly belong [3].

Impact distance denotes a measure of the number of steps with which a change in one entity impacts another entity, e.g. through dependencies. This distance has been proposed by Briand et al. for addressing the issue of impact analysis, e.g. for requirements changes, in a UML modelling context. A measurement of the distance between a changed element and an impacted element is defined as the number of impact analysis rules, or steps, required to identify that the impacted element is affected by the change [8]. Initial empirical evaluations indicate that impacted elements at distance one lead to code changes, while those with a greater distance, in most cases, do not. However, further evaluations are required to determine at which maximum distance code changes for impacted elements should be considered [8].

Semantic distance denotes a directional measure of the amount of functionality of a specification that distinguishes it from another related specification. Semantic distance between requirements specifications and other artefacts may be used for supporting software re-use, e.g. to identify library components with a short semantic distance to the requirements. Jilani et al. pose a theoretical case that the use of semantic distance is applicable for decisions on black-box re-use and define a number of metrics for semantic distances. These include metrics for functional deficit that reflect how much functionality needs to be added to one specification in order to satisfy another, and metrics for functional excess that measure the amount of functional features of one specification that are irrelevant to another one [21].

Syntactic distance denotes a measure of dissimilarity of the design structure of two artefacts [21]. Syntactic distance between specifications has been suggested by Jilani et al. for supporting decisions on white-box reuse (where a component is modified). While providing theoretical arguments for applicability of this type of distance Jilani et al. also argues that it is unrealistic to define a measure for syntactic distances since this requires a uniform representation of specifications irrespective of abstraction level and a canonical scheme that supports the definition of a unique representation of specifications. Instead, semantic distances (for which measurements are defined) are suggested to be used as an approximation of syntactic distances [21].

Distance between Other Entities

Adherence distance denotes the size of the difference between a formal or theoretical model of a process or a phenomena and the actual enactment of it. Within software development this distance has been suggested for gauging the degree of adherence for models. For example, Huo et al. consider the distance between a formal process model and the actual work practices observed in a project [20], though no measurement of this distance is defined. Furthermore, a measure of the distance between a theoretical distribution and actual estimates is defined and evaluated by Thelin and Runeson in the context of assessing the accuracy of remaining faults in an inspected software artefact [30], which could be applied to validation of requirements specifications.

4.5   Limitations

Reliability of the results due to the risk of researcher bias in the inclusion process and the classification process remains an open issue since only one researcher was involved. However, for inclusions/exclusion a generous policy was used, and independent validation of both inclusion and classification is possible since the full set of papers, including the ones excluded through abstract review, is available on-line. Furthermore, there is a risk of incorrect classification when only performed on an abstract. This was addressed by reviewing the full text when the abstract was unclear. However, replication of the study may result in a slightly different set of papers, both in the initial search and in the inclusion/exclusion step.

Conclusion validity concerning the completeness of the results (e.g. number of distances) is one of the main limitations of this study. The search string was limited to 'distance' and did not include synonyms such as gap, proximity etc. This risk of missing relevant papers was partly addressed by broad searches for other aspects. For example, papers were collected from multiple sources incl. IEE and ACM, and wide search terms (software development, software engineering) were used for the scope aspect of the search. Furthermore, no limitation was set on publication year or type of publication (journal, conference etc.). These measures resulted in the study starting with a large set of papers (more than 2,000). However, extending the search to include synonyms would produce an even larger set of papers, and may uncover additional types of distances and applications of these. The main intention of this study was to act as a starting point and further research is planned to further explore the area.

5   Discussion

RE is a communication intense activity and the identified distances between people (see overview in Figure 3) may have an impact on the efficiency and effectiveness of communication and collaboration [1, 2, 13, 34, 35, 37] and can be a significant cost driver [15]. Within GSD, cases where communication is equally strong, or even improved, compared to co-located development have been reported [13, 35]. For example, computer-based group meetings were found to be more effective for requirements negotiation than face-to-face meetings [13]. Similarly, development environments with computer-based support for collaborative work in combination with best practices were found to contribute to reducing communication delays [35].

These contradicting results might be explained by the effect the applied practices have on the division between formal and informal communication. When (previously) informal information is re-routed to more formal communication channels the communication flow may be improved, resulting in reaching a wider audience. This correlates well with findings by Agerfeldt et al. Distance tends to affect informal communication in particular and leads to reduced trust, difficulty in conveying vision and strategy and lack of awareness [1]. Cases where formal communication including documentation is weak and the informal channels are important (e.g. for agile development) are likely to be very vulnerable to distances between people.

Some of the distances are subjective (e.g. geographical) while others are objective and based on people's perception [27], values and normative practices. The perceived (objective) distance can vary over team members and over time [27], and research has shown that quantifying this distance can support management and be beneficial for GSD practices [27]. All the objective people distances, i.e. organisational, power, opinions, cognitive and psychological, seem to be covered by the socio-cultural distance (see Figure 3). More research into these distances specifically for RE and for collocated development could potentially explain issues reported for RE communication and collaboration [6, 12, 24]. For example, several distances may be at play in co-located cross-functional teams with a product owner from a different organisational unit and with an RE background; short geographical, but long organisational and cognitive distances between the product owner and other team members. Awareness of distance and their impact could support management in optimising organisations [37], training efforts, and selected methods [36] and tools [9, 13, 18, 32, 35].

Temporal distance affects the possibly of synchronous communication and within GSD asynchronous communication is common [1, 36]. In addition, subjective distances caused by differences in culture, language etc. may make people reluctant to communicate directly, thus resulting in preferring to communicate via e-mail or through issue management systems. In general, the asynchronous communication that these distances may incur induce delays and increase lead times of RE and the entire development effort [36]. This may affect communication intense activities such as RE, in general, and elicitation and negotiation in particular.

Artefacts play an important role in communicating requirements to stakeholders and within a development project. The identified distances between artefacts have primarily been researched for cost estimation and re-use based on changes to, or different versions of, RE artefacts [8, 21, 28]. These distances may be used to characterise coverage and consistency between artefacts of different activities, e.g. as a measure of the alignment between RE and later development activities. For this reason, RE distances to artefacts of later development activities are an important area to research.

Adherence distance between an artefact and the actual enactment of it has been suggested for process improvement [20] and for estimating remaining fault content [30]. Additional interesting applications could be adherence between a requirement specification and the final product, as well as, the actual customer needs. Both of which are key factors for successful RE.

Finally, most of the identified distances are reported to be better the shorter they are, but there are some interesting exceptions. Within GSD, long socio-cultural distance may potentially increase learning by providing access to a richer skill set, and be stimulating for innovation [1]. Furthermore, organisational distance between testers and developers has been reported to improve alignment between testing and requirements by avoiding testing against developers' interpretation of the requirements [6]. Identifying and understanding additional cases where long distances result in positive effects can support defining a comprehensive theory of the impact of RE distances on software development.

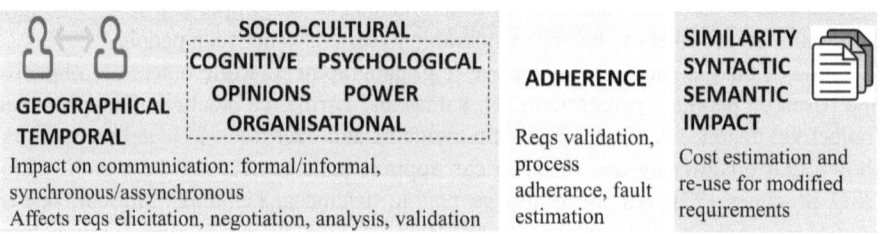

Fig. 3. Overview of interpretation of identified RE distances including relevant RE areas

6   Conclusions

Coordination and alignment of requirements with later activities is vital for enabling continuous development of successful products. Within global software engineering distances are reported as increasing risk and cost. Distances between RE and other development activities, e.g. in decision making and requirements communication, may hinder effective and efficient development of customer requirements.

In this systematic mapping study 13 RE-related distances were identified. Distances were mainly found between people (roles, teams etc.) and between artefacts (requirements and design specifications etc). Distance between people has primarily been researched within the context of GSD (geographic, socio-cultural and temporal), while distance between artefacts was found exclusively in non-GSD research.

GSD research on *distance between people* is fairly mature, though more empirical research is needed to understand the impact of these distances for non-distributed development, e.g. for large-scale development. Furthermore, no theory was found in the reviewed papers that could explain the contradicting findings of several studies concerning geographical distance. Further investigations are required to gain a deeper insight into relationship between different distances and the impact they have on division between formal and informal communication. Findings from other fields like psychology and cognitive science are relevant to consider when investigating these people-related distances in relation to RE activities.

Distance between artefacts has been suggested in the context of requirements change and traceability and is an interesting area for future RE research. Distance between RE artefacts and artefacts of later development activities, e.g. design and testing, could potentially be used to measure coverage and consistency between RE and other artefacts such as design and test specifications, and source code.

The systematic map reveals that RE distances in relationship to later development activities (e.g. design, implementation and testing) is largely un-researched. If distance is indeed an important factor in the coordination and communication of RE, research is much needed to address this gap. Examples of RE activities where distance may play an important role include elicitation, negotiation, specification, managing requirements changes and requirements traceability.

This study is a first step towards exploring and defining a theory for the role of RE distances in software development. Future work includes constructing a theoretical framework for RE distances in relationship to testing based on previous research and on empirical data.

Further empirical research into how RE distances, and combinations of these, affect later development activities may support constructing a theory that explains what mechanisms are at play in development projects, between people, artefacts and activities. Increased knowledge of such factors might enable optimization of RE methods and practices for eliciting, negotiating and communicating requirements. Furthermore, through researching new methods and practices for bridging or decreasing distances the effectiveness of RE in software development may be improved, ultimately resulting in more efficient development of better products.

Acknowledgement. This research was funded by EASE Industrial Excellence Centre for Embedded Applications Software Engineering (http://ease.cs.lth.se).

References

1. Agerfalk, P.J., Fitzgerald, B., Holmstrom Olsson, H., Lings, B., Lundell, B., Ó Conchúir, E.: A Framework for Considering Opportunities and Threats in Distributed Software Development. In: Proc. of Int. Works. on Distr. Softw. Eng., DiSD 2005, pp. 47–61 (2005)
2. Allen, T.: Managing the flow of technology. MIT Press, Cambridge (1977)
3. Azzeh, M., Neagu, D.C., Cowling, P.I.: Software project similarity measurement based on fuzzy C-means. In: Wang, Q., Pfahl, D., Raffo, D.M. (eds.) ICSP 2008. LNCS, vol. 5007, pp. 123–134. Springer, Heidelberg (2008)
4. Bjarnason, E.: Study material for RE distance study incl. list of all papers, http://serg.cs.lth.se/research/experiment_packages/distmap/ (latest access January 28, 2013)
5. Bjarnason, E., Runeson, P., Borg, M., et al.: Challenges and Practices in Aligning Requirements with Verification and Validation: A Case Study of Six Companies. Submitted to Empirical Software Engineering Journal (2013)
6. Bjarnason, E., Wnuk, K., Regnell, B.: Requirements are Slipping Through the Gaps – A Case Study on Cause & Effects of Communication Gaps in Large-Scale Software Development. In: Proc. of 19th IEEE Int Requirements Engineering Conf., pp. 37–46 (2011)
7. Brereton, P., Kitchenham, B.A., Budgen, D., et al.: Lessons from applying the systematic literature review process within the software engineering domain. Journal of Systems and Softw. 80(4), 571–583 (2007)
8. Briand, L.C., Labiche, Y., O'Sullivan, L., Sówka, M.M.: Automated impact analysis of UML models. Journal of Systems and Softw. 79(3), 339–352 (2006)
9. Calefato, F., Damian, D., Lanubile, F.: An Empirical Investigation on Text-Based Communication in Distributed Requirements Workshops. In: Proc. of Int. Conf. on Global Softw. Engineering (ICGSE 2007), pp. 3–11 (2007)
10. Chakraborty, C., Chakraborty, D.: A fuzzy clustering methodology for linguistic opinions in group decision making. J. of Applied Soft Computing 7(3), 858–869 (2007)
11. Chiu, N.H., Huang, S.J.: The adjusted analogy-based software effort estimation based on similarity distances. Journal of Systems and Softw. 80(4), 628–640 (2007)
12. Curtis, B., Krasner, H., Iscoe, N.: A Field Study of the Software Design Process for Large Systems. Commun. ACM, 1268–1287 (November 1988)
13. Damian, D.: An empirical study of requirements engineering in distributed software projects: Is distance negotiation more effective? In: Proc. of 8th Asia Pacific Softw. Engineering Conf., APSEC 2001, pp. 149–152 (2001)
14. Damian, D.: Chisan: An Empirical Study of the Complex Relationships between Requirements Engineering Processes and Other Processes that Lead to Payoffs in Productivity, Quality, and Risk Management. IEEE Trans. on Softw. Eng. 43(7), 433–453 (2006)
15. Dibbern, J., Winkler, J., Heinz, A.: Explaining variations in client extra costs between software projects offshored to India. MIS Quarterly: Management Information Systems 32(2), 333–366 (2008)
16. Ebert, C.: Understanding the product life cycle: four key requirements engineering techniques. IEEE Softw. 23(3), 19–25 (2006)
17. Fricker, S., Glinz, M.: Comparison of Requirements Hand-Off, Analysis, and Negotiation: Case Study. In: Proc. of 18th Int Requirements Engineering Conf., pp. 167–176 (2010)
18. Herlea, D., Greenberg, S.: Using a groupware space for distributed requirements engineering. In: Proc. of Workshop on Enabling Technologies: Infrastructure for Collaborative Enterprises, WET ICE, pp. 57–62 (1998)

19. Hofstede, G.: Cultural constraints in management theories. Academy of Management Executive 7(1), 81–94 (1993)
20. Huo, M., Zhang, H., Jeffery, R.: Detection of consistent patterns from process enactment data. In: Wang, Q., Pfahl, D., Raffo, D.M. (eds.) ICSP 2008. LNCS, vol. 5007, pp. 173–185. Springer, Heidelberg (2008)
21. Jilani, L.L., Desharnais, J., Mili, A.: Defining and Applying Measures of Distance Between Specifications. Journal IEEE Transactions on Softw. Eng. 27(8), 673–703 (2001)
22. Lawson, M., Karandikar, H.M.: A Survey of Concurrent Engineering. Concurrent Engineering 2(1) (1994)
23. Liberman, N., Trope, Y., Stephan, E.: Psychological Distance. In: Kruglanski, Higgins (eds.) "Social Psychology: Handbook of Basic Principles, 2nd edn., pp. 353–381. Guilford Press (2007)
24. Marczak, S., Damian, D.: How Interaction between Roles Shapes the Communication Structure in Requirements-Driven Collaboration. In: 19th IEEE Int. Req. Eng. Conf., pp. 47–56 (2011)
25. Nuseibeh, B.: Weaving together requirements and architectures. Computer 34(3), 115–119 (2001)
26. Petersen, K., Feldt, R., Mujtaba, S., et al.: Systematic Mapping Studies in Software Engineering. In: 12th Int. Conf. on Evaluation and Assessm. in Softw. Eng., pp. 71–80 (2008)
27. Prikladnicki, R.: Propinquity in global software engineering: Examining perceived distance in globally distributed project teams. Journal of Softw. Evolution and Process 24(2), 119–137 (2012)
28. Shepperd, M., Schofield, C.: Estimating Software Project Effort Using Analogies. IEEE Trans. on Softw. Eng. 23(11), 736–743 (1997)
29. Swartout, W., Balzer, R.: On the Inevitable Intertwining of Specification and Implementation. Comm. ACM 25(7), 438–440 (1982)
30. Thelin, T., Runeson, P.: Robust estimations of fault content with capture–recapture and detection profile estimators. Journal of Systems and Softw. 52(2-3), 139–148 (2000)
31. Uusitalo, E.J., Komssi, M., Kauppinen, M., et al.: Linking Requirements and Testing in Practice. In: 16th IEEE Int Requirements Engineering Conf., NJ, USA, pp. 265–270 (2008)
32. Wende, E., Philip, T.: Instant messenger in offshore outsourced software development projects: Experiences from a case study. In: Proc. of 44th Annual Hawaii Int. Conf. on System Sciences (2010)
33. Wieringa, R., Maiden, N., Mead, N., Rolland, C.: Requirements Engineering Paper Classification and Evaluation Criteria: a Proposal and a Discussion. Journal of Requir. Eng. 11(1), 102–107 (2006)
34. Winkler, J.K., Dibbern, J., Heinzl, A.: The impact of cultural differences in offshore outsourcing-Case study results from German-Indian application development projects. Inf. Systems Frontiers 10(2), 243–258 (2008)
35. Wolf, T., Nguyen, T., Damian, D.: Does distance still matter? Journal of Impr. and Practice of Softw. Process 13(6), 493–510 (2008)
36. Yousuf, F., Zaman, Z., Ikram, N.: Requirements validation techniques in GSD: A survey. In: Proc. 12th IEEE Int. Multitopic Conf. INMIC 2008, pp. 553–557 (2008)
37. Yu, Y., Sharp, H.: Analyzing requirements in a case study of pairing. In: Proc. of 1st Int. Workshop on Agile RE, Lancaster, UK (2011)
38. Zhu, J., Hipel, K.W.: Multiple stages grey target decision making method with incomplete weight based on multi-granularity linguistic label. Journal of Information Sciences 212, 15–32 (2012)

Analyzing the Tracing of Requirements and Source Code during Software Development
A Research Preview

Alexander Delater and Barbara Paech

Institute of Computer Science, University of Heidelberg
Im Neuenheimer Feld 326, 69120 Heidelberg, Germany
{delater,paech}@informatik.uni-heidelberg.de

Abstract. [**Context and motivation**] Traceability links between requirements and code are often created after development, which can, for example, lead to higher development effort. To address this weakness, we developed in previous work an approach that captures traceability links between requirements and code as the development progresses by using artifacts from project management called work items. [**Question/problem**] It is important to investigate empirically what is the best way to capture such links and how these links are used during development. [**Principal ideas/results**] In order to link requirements, work items and code during development, we extended our approach from previous work by defining three traceability link creation processes. We are applying these processes in practice in a software development project conducted with undergraduate students. The results indicate that our approach creates correct traceability links between requirements and code with high precision/recall during development, while developers mainly used the third process to link work items after implementation. Furthermore, the students used a subset of the created traceability links for navigating between requirements and code during the early phase of the development project. [**Contribution**] In this paper, we report on preliminary empirical results from applying our approach in practice.

Keywords: trace, requirement, work item, code, software development.

1 Introduction

Requirements-to-code traceability reflects the knowledge where requirements are implemented in the code. The capture of such links during development is the focus of recent research [6]. Asuncion & Taylor [1] presented an approach for capturing links between heterogenous artifacts, including requirements and code, by analyzing interactions of users while they create/generate or modify artifacts. Omoronyia et al. [8] capture links between requirements and code based on the operations carried out by developers creating code artifacts to realize requirements. In contrast to these approaches, we present an approach that captures traceability links between requirements and code using artifacts from project management called work items [3]. Practitioners have discussed the practice of

J. Doerr and A.L. Opdahl (Eds.): REFSQ 2013, LNCS 7830, pp. 308–314, 2013.

using work items to capture links between requirements and code, but to the best of our knowledge there has been no systematic study of this practice [2].

However, surprising little is known about the quality (precision/recall) and usage of requirements-to-code links during software development [6]. Asuncion & Taylor and Omoronyia et al. did not provide empirical work in which they showed the feasibility of their approaches in practice. Maeder & Egyed [5,6] report on the usage of such links during software maintenance. However, the authors did not investigate how these links are used during development, as software maintenance happens after development.

In this paper, we present preliminary research results from applying our approach [3] in practice. In order to do this, we extended our approach by defining three traceability link creation processes linking requirements, work items and code. We are applying these processes in practice in a software development project conducted with undergraduate students. Based on the gathered data, we are inferring direct traceability links between requirements and code using work items. We are investigating the precision/recall of the inferred traceability links between requirements and code as well as how often each process was executed by the students. Furthermore, we are analyzing whether the students actually use these direct links during the early phase of the development project for navigating between requirements and code.

The remainder of this paper is structured as follows: Section 2 presents the approach. Section 3 introduces the project context, while Section 4 reports on our research questions and preliminary results. Section 5 discusses threats to validity and Section 6 concludes the paper and discusses future work.

2   Approach

In [3], we defined a Traceability Information Model (TIM) consisting of artifacts from requirements engineering (features, functional requirements), project management (work items, sprints, developers) and code (code files, revisions) as well as the traceability links in between. A feature is realized in a sprint and is detailed in one or more functional requirements. Work items describe work to be done to realize functional requirements, are assigned to developers, have a completion status and a due date. A work item must have one or more linked functional requirements and is contained in a sprint. A feature can be related to a work item, e.g. during bug fixing. One work item can create one or more revisions. A revision contains one or more changed code files and is stored in a version control system (VCS).

We presume the following situation in a development project. First, a list of features and functional requirements exists. Second, a project manager has planned the implementation of the features in sprints and s/he has broken down the implementation schedule of the functional requirements into work items for the developers. Third, all work items are already assigned to developers. Below we use the term *requirement* to refer commonly to features and functional requirements.

Our approach uses work items to link requirements and code during development. As we presume that the implementation of the requirements is planned in work items, we need to capture links between the work item and the code that is created by its assigned developer. We identified three possibilities of developers to select a work item that is related to their implemented code. Developers can select a work item *before* they start the implementation of code (Process A), *during* implementation when they have created code but have not yet stored it in a VCS (Process B), or *after* implementation when they have created code that is already stored in a VCS (Process C). All three processes are depicted in Figure 1 and explained in the following.

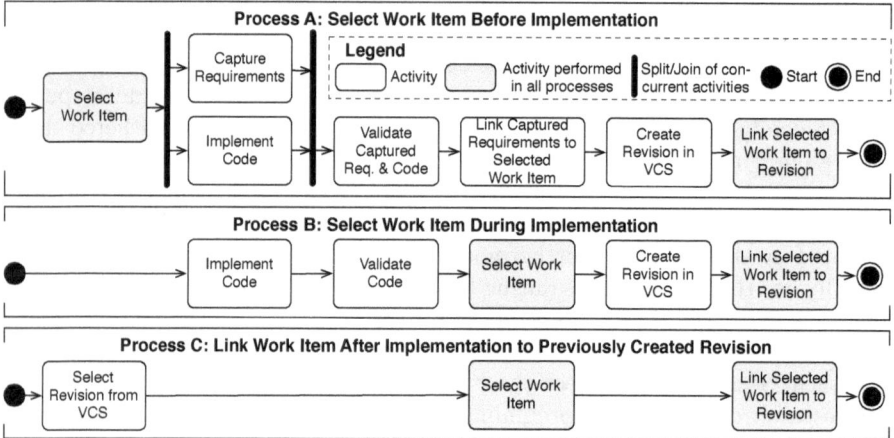

Fig. 1. Traceability Link Creation Processes A, B and C

Process A) Select Work Item Before Implementation: First, the developer selects a work item from his/her list of assigned work items. While working on the work item and implementing new code or changing existing code, all requirements the developer looks at during implementation are automatically captured. For example, s/he may look at requirements to know what to implement. When finishing the implementation of the work item, the developer is asked to validate all captured requirements and new/changed code, which means s/he confirms all related and removes all non-related requirements or code files. The validated requirements are linked to the work item and the validated code is stored in a new revision in the VCS, which is also linked to the work item.

Process B) Select Work Item During Implementation: In contrast to Process A, in Process B a developer does not need to select a work item before implementation. Instead, s/he starts directly with implementation. After the implementation of code and before creating a new revision stored in the VCS, the developer validates the new/changed code files and selects a work item from his/her list of assigned work items. A new revision with the validated code files is stored in the VCS and is automatically linked to the selected work item. In this process, no requirements are captured and need to be validated.

It is important to note that Processes A and B do not force developers to select a work item related to the current implementation. In case the developer implemented code that s/he does not want to be linked to a work item, s/he can omit the linking of a work item, which ends Processes A and B.

Process C) Link Work Item After Implementation to Previously Created Revision: In contrast to Processes A and B, Process C occurs after implementation and it represents an alternative way for the developer to link code to a work item. A VCS stores a history of all previously created revisions with information by whom and when each revision was created, as well as all changed code files. In case a developer has implemented code without selecting a work item before implementation (see Process A) or without selecting a work item during implementation (see Process B), s/he can manually select to link a previously created revision to a work item from his/her assigned work items list. Similar to Process B, no requirements are captured and validated.

A practitioner can perform a mixture of all three processes during the course of the project. However, one of the processes can only be applied once per revision. This means each revision in the VCS is either created (Process A,B) or linked (Process C) by only one of the three processes.

Inferring Traceability Links Between Requirements and Code: The created traceability links of Processes A, B and C are used to infer direct links between requirements and code based on the corresponding work items. In [3], we presented an algorithm for inferring links that is executed when the developer changes the completion status of a work item from *assigned* to *done*. The algorithm connects in a brute force manner all linked requirements of a work item with all the code files in the linked revisions of a work item. An in-depth description of the algorithm can be found in [3].

UNICASE Trace Client: We implemented our approach in the tool UNICASE Trace Client (UTC) [9]. It is an extension to the model-based CASE tool UNICASE [10], which is a plug-in for Eclipse developed in an open-source project. UTC integrates itself seamlessly in Eclipse and its supporting plug-ins, e.g. Subversion (a commonly used VCS). UTC implements the TIM and all its artifacts and traceability links as well as all three link creation processes.

3   Project Context

To evaluate our approach, we conduct a development project with undergraduate students. In the following, we describe the development project and provide information about the participants and the used development process.

Project Description: We are working together with a company from industry specialized on mobile business applications. The company integrates existing business applications into mobile applications for smartphones and tablet computers. For the company, a knowledge database is developed containing user-generated content as well as content retrieved from various Internet data sources (e.g., Google Maps, Wikipedia). The people of the company have a great interest in full traceability between requirements and code, because they want to maintain the developed application later on. Java and JavaScript were used as main programming languages. The entire project will last for five months from October 2012 until February 2013. In this paper, we report on preliminary results from the first phase (October 1st - November 8th, 2012) divided in two sprints.

Participants and Development Process: We recruited six undergraduate students for our development team, all having basic knowledge in software engineering. The team is applying agile software development techniques, e.g., they hold regular stand-up meetings discussing completed work, planned work and any problems preventing them to continue work. The development process is as follows: in the beginning, the team elicits and specifies a first draft of the requirements together with the company. In each sprint, the team details the requirements and breaks them down into work items describing their realization. They assign each work item to a developer and include it in a sprint. Thus, the situation we presume is present in the project (see Section 2). In the current state of the project, the team specified 3 features, 8 functional requirements and implemented 32 code files with 1.573 lines of code in 81 revisions.

4   Research Questions and Preliminary Results

Based on the gathered data in the project consisting of requirements, work items and code files stored as revisions in VCS, we are applying different analyses. Our research is driven by three research questions (RQ) and the preliminary results are presented in the following.

RQ1. What is the precision and recall of the inferred links? Precision and recall are two standard metrics used in information retrieval [4]. Precision is the fraction of retrieved instances that are relevant, while recall is the fraction of relevant instances that are retrieved. In our case, 'relevant' refers to a *correct traceability link*, which is as a link between a requirement and its code where the code is necessary to realize the requirement. The metrics are computed as:

$$P = \frac{RelevantLinks \cap RetrievedLinks}{RetrievedLinks} \quad (1) \qquad R = \frac{RelevantLinks \cap RetrievedLinks}{RelevantLinks} \quad (2)$$

We manually identified all correct traceability links based on the requirements and code. A total of 42 traceability links between requirements and code were created, while 37 were correct, 5 were wrong and 8 correct links were missing. Wrong traceability links are created when developers change and link code files that are not particularly related to a work item. Missing correct links are created where work items have been linked to the wrong requirement. Both situations are potential causes of errors in our approach. Our approach achieved precision of 0.881 and recall of 0.933. Results of this scale mean that our approach delivers high quality links, which is comparable to manually performed linkage [7].

RQ2. What traceability link creation process do developers use? This RQ is focusing on how often each process was used to link requirements, work items and code in the first place. The team executed all three processes a total of 81 times (Process A = 5, Process B = 23, Process C = 53). Thus, in 65% of the cases, the team implemented the code first and then linked it to work items (Process C). However, the students behaved differently during the development project. While some students mainly used Process B, others mostly used Process C. Since the requirements are not final and detailed in each sprint, the students only used Process A a few times to look at requirements during development.

RQ3. Do developers use the created links to navigate between requirements and code in the early phases of software development? Each inferred link between a requirement and a code file had a boolean attribute *used* (default value = false). When a developer clicked on the link and "used" it for navigation, the value was set to true. Although the project is still in an early phase, developers already used 9 links of the 42 created links for navigation between requirements and code, or vice versa. We think that the usage will increase in the later phases of the project.

5 Threats to Validity

From the very beginning of the project, we are striving to avoid external and internal threats to validity.

External Validity: In the development project, all undergraduate students had basic knowledge in software engineering. However, no undergraduate student had industrial experience. This does not allow us to draw conclusions for more experienced developers. In addition, Java and JavaScript were used as programming languages. Even though we do not expect this, effects might be different for other programming languages. The authors of this paper gave advice to the students during the project and made sure that they used UTC. The students might behaved differently if they did not have to use UTC.

Internal Validity: To decrease variability in knowledge across students regarding the tracing of requirements and code in UTC, we provided an introductory tutorial of UTC [9]. This ensured that all students knew how to use UTC.

6 Conclusion and Future Work

In this paper, we presented three traceability link creation processes linking requirements, work items and code. We presented preliminary results from applying our approach in practice in a development project conducted with undergraduate students. A finding of our results is that developers mainly link work items after implementation to previously created revisions. Our approach creates correct traceability links with high quality during development. In the current early project state, developers already used 9 of 42 created links to navigate between requirements and code.

Once the state of the project has further progressed, we want to deepen our analyses for the research questions in future work. Regarding RQ1, we will study the evolution of precision and recall of the traceability links, whether they increase or decrease over time. Furthermore, we want to apply existing approaches for automatically linking requirements and code and compare the results with respect to precision and recall to the links created by our approach in the project. To support comparison between the approaches and their results, we will consider the metrics F_2-Measure and MAP (Mean Average Precision), combining precision and recall into a single score. For RQ2, we will investigate how the usage of the three traceability link creation processes changes over the course of the project. With regard to RQ3, we will investigate whether developers use the traceability links in later phases of the project for navigation between requirements and code. Additionally, we want to perform more analyses on the gathered data, e.g., how many work items were assigned to each developer, or the minimum/maximum and average amount of lines of code traced per process.

Acknowledgment. The authors would like to thank the company for providing the opportunity for this project, the students for their participation as well as Ulrike Abelein and Florian Flatow for their help in organizing the project.

References

1. Asuncion, H., Taylor, R.: Automated techniques for capturing custom traceability links across heterogeneous artifacts. In: Cleland-Huang, J., Gotel, O., Zisman, A. (eds.) Software and Systems Traceability, pp. 129–146. Springer (2012)
2. Cleland-Huang, J.: Traceability in agile projects. In: Cleland-Huang, J., Gotel, O., Zisman, A. (eds.) Software and Systems Traceability, pp. 265–275. Springer (2012)
3. Delater, A., Narayan, N., Paech, B.: Tracing Requirements and Source Code during Software Development. In: Proceedings of the 7th International Conference on Software Engineering Advances, ICSEA 2012, pp. 274–282 (2012)
4. Frakes, W.B., Baeze-Yates, R. (eds.): Information Retrieval: Data Structures and Algorithms. Prentice-Hall (1992)
5. Maeder, P., Egyed, A.: Do software engineers benefit from source code navigation with traceability? - An experiment in software change management. In: Proceedings of the 26th International Conference on Automated Software Engineering, ASE 2011, pp. 444–447 (2011)
6. Maeder, P., Egyed, A.: Assessing the effect of requirements traceability for software maintenance. In: Proceedings of the 28th International Conference on Software Maintenance, ICSM 2012, pp. 171–180 (2012)
7. Maeder, P., Gotel, O.: Ready-to-use Traceability on Evolving Projects. In: Cleland-Huang, J., Gotel, O., Zisman, A. (eds.) Software and Systems Traceability, pp. 173–194. Springer (2012)
8. Omoronyia, I., Sindre, G., Roper, M., Ferguson, J., Wood, M.: Use case to source code traceability: The developer navigation viewpoint. In: Proceedings of the 17th International Requirements Engineering Conference, RE 2009, pp. 237–242 (2009)
9. UNICASE Trace Client, http://code.google.com/p/unicase/wiki/TraceClient
10. UNICASE, http://www.unicase.org/

Requirements Engineering Meets Physiotherapy: An Experience with Motion-Based Games

Liliana Pasquale[1], Paola Spoletini[2],
Dario Pometto[3], Francesco Blasi[4], and Tiziana Redaelli[3]

[1] Lero, University of Limerick, Ireland
liliana.pasquale@lero.ie
[2] DiSTA, Università dell'Insubria, Varese, Italy
paola.spoletini@uninsubria.it
[3] Unità Spinale, Ospedale Niguarda Ca'Granda, Milan, Italy
{dario.pometto,tiziana.redaelli}@ospedaleniguarda.it
[4] UO Broncopneumologia, Dipartimento di Fisiopatologia e dei Trapianti,
IRCCS Fonazione Ca'Granda Ospedale Maggiore Policlinico,
Università degli Studi di Milano, Italy
francesco.blasi@unimi.it

Abstract. [**Context and motivation**] In the last years motion-based games have achieved an increasing success. These games have great potential to support physiotherapeutic programs, as they can guide the patients in performing the right movements for their rehabilitation. [**Question/problem**] However, on the one hand, existing games performed on commercial systems (e.g., Wii, Kinect) are not suitable for people affected by motor pathologies. On the other hand, the design of games for physiotherapy is hard, as they should meet the "physiotherapy requirements" of the medical staff, provide an enjoyable experience to the patients, and overcome the technical limitations of the systems that support their execution. [**Principal ideas/results**] These limitations can be addressed by defining a standard process, independent from the considered pathology and that starts from the requirements collection and representation, to support the development of motion-based games for physiotherapy [**Contribution**] For this reason, this paper proposes RE-FIT, a methodology to elicit and model the RE-FIT extends existing requirements elicitation (brainstorming, surveys, and direct observation) and modeling techniques (FLAGS goal model). RE-FIT was developed in collaboration with the Spinal Unit of Niguarda Hospital and the Respiratory Medicine Section of Policlinico in Milan. Our experience demonstrated that RE-FIT is not only suitable to develop new physiotherapeutic games, but also to evaluate the adequacy of existing games for people affected by a specific pathology.

1 Introduction

In the last years motion-based games have achieved an increasing success. They provide a more enjoyable experience than standard games (based on traditional gamepads), as *"they are more interactive and give a better sense of being*

J. Doerr and A.L. Opdahl (Eds.): REFSQ 2013, LNCS 7830, pp. 315–330, 2013.
© Springer-Verlag Berlin Heidelberg 2013

there" [1]. Motion-based games are fully controlled by the players' movements that are captured through sensors (e.g., gyroscopes, infrared cameras, body scanners) provided by the game system (e.g., Wii, Kinect). Recently, motion-based games have been used to support physiotherapeutic programs [2], since they can guide patients to perform a set of controlled movements that are both suitable for their health status and beneficial for their rehabilitation. However, some of the existing solutions [3,4] directly use commercial games available on the market that might not be suitable for patients with limitations in motor capabilities. Furthermore, the absence of control on the correctness of movements in commercial games might even be dangerous for the patients' health. Other solutions in this direction are centered on a particular pathology [4,5,6] or rely on additional hardware (e.g., robots, electrical muscle stimulators) [7]. In the first case, the development of each game requires an ad-hoc process, which might not be adequate for other games that address different pathologies. In the second case, required hardware could be very expensive, making impossible to leverage the physiotherapeutic benefits of motion-based games outside the hospital.

Addressing these limitations can be crucial to facilitate the development and adoption of motion-based games for physiotherapy. However, the design of these games is hard, as they should meet the "physiotherapy requirements" of the medical staff, provide an enjoyable experience to the patients, and overcome the technical limitations of the game systems that support their execution. The cultural gap and the difference of vocabulary between medical staff and software designers makes the collection of physiotherapy requirements more prone to errors due to misunderstandings. Furthermore, existing requirements modeling techniques are not expressive enough to represent concepts that pertain to physiotherapy, such as movements and their impact on other requirements, aids (i.e., additional medical devices, such as decubitus cushions) necessary to help the patients to play, and controllers (i.e., the capabilities of the adopted game systems in detecting movements). Developed games must be able to signal wrong movements for physiotherapeutic purposes, but, at the same time, must tolerate small deviations to avoid unnecessary corrections.

This paper presents RE-FIT (Requirements Engineering For physIoTherapy), a novel methodology for eliciting and modeling the requirements of motion-based games used in physiotherapy. This methodology is the result of three years of experience on the field, in collaboration with the Spinal Unit of Niguarda Hospital and the Respiratory Medicine Section of Policlinico in Milan[1]. The elicitation process combines ad-hoc surveys, brainstorming, and direct observation. Surveys are the main technique through which the requirements of the game are identified. Brainstorming helps patients and medical staff understanding the questions that will be proposed in the survey. Direct observation allows software designers to visualize "on-the-field" how patients should perform the correct movements.

The requirements modeling process re-uses the FLAGS [8] goal model that expresses requirements as fuzzy temporal properties. This helped us developing

---

[1] A set of videos showing the validation of developed games with real patients can be found at http://www.dista.uninsubria.it/~paola.spoletini/REFIT.html

games that tolerate small deviations of the movements performed by the patients with respect to the correct ones. FLAGS was also extended to represent physiotherapy requirements, movements, aids, and controllers as first class entities during the requirements modeling phases. RE-FIT was successfully employed to evaluate and adapt a set of new games for patients affected by different spinal cord injuries. These games detect the correctness of the movements and provide an enjoyable experience to the patient. Finally, RE-FIT was also adopted to evaluate the degree of adequacy of existing games with respect to people affected by cystic fibrosis.

The reminder of the paper is organized as follows. Section 2 summarizes the research objectives, the evaluation technique, and the lessons learned from our experience in developing motion-based game for physiotherapy. Section 3 presents the RE-FIT methodology and Section 4 exemplifies it through a case study. Finally, Section 5 describes related work and Section 6 concludes the paper.

2   Our Preliminary Experience with Motion-Based Games

The overall objective of our research is to identify a requirements elicitation and modeling technique that is suitable to develop motion-based games for physiotherapy. This objective can be achieved by answering the following research questions:

- **RQ1:** What is a suitable requirements elicitation technique that can be adopted for stakeholders (physiotherapists, patients, software engineers) with different backgrounds and a partial view of the problem?
- **RQ2:** How to speedup the requirements elicitation process and avoid misunderstandings among stakeholders?
- **RQ3:** How to model requirements that represent concepts that pertain to physiotherapy, such as movements or aids?
- **RQ4:** How to provide a intuitive requirement model that can be understood by people who are not software engineers?
- **RQ5:** How to formalize requirements that can tolerate small violations?

To answer these questions, in our initial collaboration with Niguarda Hospital in Milan, we investigated different ad-hoc methodologies to develop motion-based games for physiotherapy. In particular, we considered the feasibility and effectiveness of different requirements elicitation techniques, such as interviews, brainstorming, scenarios, prototypes, direct observation, and joint application development. We also evaluated the expressiveness of existing goal models in representing physiotherapy requirements. We collected the data necessary for our evaluation by developing simple games based on striking a specific target (e.g., shooting gallery, drums) or avoiding obstacles (e.g., airplane and water craft games). Developed games targeted patients affected by spinal cord injuries at different cord segments. We assumed that patients have full motor functions of hands and different levels of control of their bust. Different teams of students from Politecnico di Milano (software designers) were trained for the particular pathology, through tutorials, brainstorming sessions, and interviews. All the training sessions were hosted by a doctor/physiotherapist and supervised by a requirements engineer. Each team of students developed a motion-based game without using any systematic methodology for eliciting and modeling the requirements. The motion-based games were tested with real patients, who were interviewed to collect their impressions.

However, the lack of a systematic requirements elicitation and modeling methodology caused delays in the final realization of the games. We also observed several mismatches between the expectations of the medical staff and the game prototype and this required to modify the prototype several times before its final release. Furthermore, the time to release the game prototype was completely dependent on the availability of the medical staff that had to spend a considerable amount of time to interact with software designers to explain the problems related to the considered pathology. The time to release of the game was also influenced by the background knowledge of software designers on the considered pathology.

For these reasons, after this experience, in the last year, we investigated the development of a general methodology to engineer requirements in physiotherapy (RE-FIT). To achieve this aim, we focused also on a different pathology, such as cystic fibrosis, and extended our collaboration with the Respiratory Medicine Section of Policlinico in Milan. During this experience we learned the following lessons.

Language Matters. Building a common vocabulary between medical staff and software engineers is fundamental, as these actors need to understand each other. This is challenging because doctors and physiotherapists think about games as a close reproduction of the physiotherapy programs and make the assumption that software designers have the background to understand the pathology. For example, when discussing about cystic fibrosis, they made the assumption that software designers knew about the possibility of infections, and, indeed, they did not clearly specify that playing in teams of patients should be forbidden in most of the cases. On the other hand, the medical staff often ignores technical features, such as the characteristics of developed games or the underlying sensors necessary to monitor the movements. This may be problematic for the software developers who need to associate physiotherapeutic movements with those that are permitted in the game.

Games Must Still Be Safe. Motion-based games for physiotherapy do not only require a direct mapping between physical movements prescribed in the physiotherapy program and game actions. They must also avoid situations when patients perform movements that can be harmful for their health. For example, for the watercraft game, the speed of the canoe movement should be carefully tuned to avoid the patients to incline their bust more than a maximum permitted angle.

Let Them Talk. Physiotherapists and doctors provide a clearer explanation of the pathology and the rehabilitation program when they are not interrupted. For this reason, interview is not the best elicitation technique at the beginning of requirements elicitation, when medical staff and software engineers have still not built a common vocabulary and a high degree of interaction is required. Conversely, we deem ad-hoc surveys more appropriate for requirements elicitation, after an initial brainstorming session, since the medical staff can answer questions independently, without being interrupted.

Avoid Training. Training is expensive, time consuming and the experience can be hardly transmitted to new engineers when the trained ones leave.

Understandable Requirements Are Worth It. Modeled requirements must be reviewed and validated iteratively by medical staff. To accelerate this phase, doctors and physiotherapists must easily recognize from the proposed requirements model the elements that pertain to the physiotherapy program, such as movements, aids and controllers.

Re-Use It before you Lose It. The effort employed for the development of motion-based games must not be wasted. The elements of the requirements model that can be re-used to develop games for other pathologies must be recognized. This would ultimately allow software engineers to build a library of patterns of physiotherapy requirements that can be reused in the elicitation and modeling of requirements for new/different motion-based games or to evaluate the adequacy of existing motion-based games to patients affected by a specific pathology.

3   The RE-FIT Methodology

Figure 1 represents the steps of the RE-FIT methodology to elicit and model the requirements of motion-based games in physiotherapy.

Requirements elicitation is performed through steps 1-3 and leverages two ad-hoc surveys (one for the medical staff and the other one for the patients). In order to model the requirements of the game, software designers use the answers collected through the surveys. Note that surveys are independent from the considered pathology and the kind of game to be designed. Before filling the survey, a brainstorming phase on the survey (step 1) must be performed by software designers and medical staff. On the one hand, this phase allows software designers to explain the questions to the medical staff. On the other hand, it allows the medical staff (mainly physiotherapists) to express their expectation and doubts. The brainstorming also helps building a common vocabulary between medical staff and software designers, and can reduce the time required to understand the answers and identify the requirements. A brief brainstorming is also performed by software designers and patients, even if, in this case, the vocabulary is not necessarily different.

In step 2, the medical staff and the patients fill two different surveys (one each), which differ for the language adopted in their questions. Then, the software designers re-elaborate the main objectives and operations involved in the physiotherapy programs, and recognize the patients' expectations from the game. In case software designers cannot associate a movement described in the answers given in the survey with the corresponding physical movement to be performed by the patient, the direct observation "on-the-field" is necessary (step 3). In this step, software designers observe the patients performing the movements indicated in the survey, under the supervision of a physiotherapist. This phase helps software designers understanding how a specific movement is executed and its possible negative side effects. Since the observation is limited to a subset of movements of the physiotherapy program, this step is not particularly time consuming.

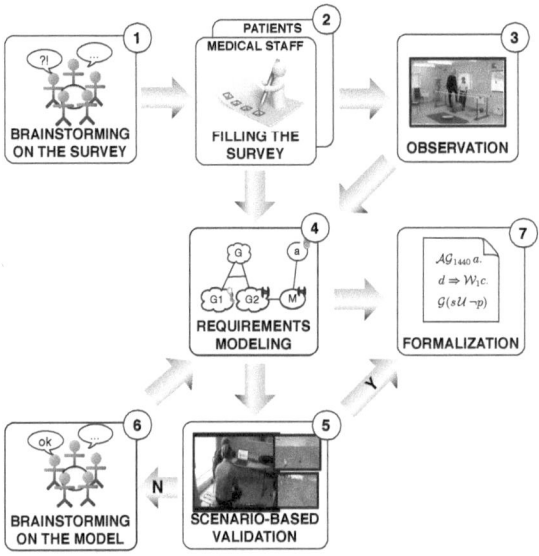

Fig. 1. The RE-FIT methodology

Requirements modeling and validation is performed through steps 4-7. The requirements collected in the first three steps are represented through an extended FLAGS model (step 4). FLAGS provide fuzzy goals that are necessary to add flexibility to the evaluation of the correctness and speed of movements. The FLAGS model is extended to distinguish the concepts that pertain to physiotherapy (physiotherapy requirements, movements, aids) and those associated with the game system (controllers). In this way, the model is more intuitive to physiotherapists and doctors that can easily identify the elements related to the physiotherapy program. In case software designers consider the requirements model appropriate (e.g., because it reuses already validated models), they can start to formalize some of its elements (goals, operations, controllers, aids) and then start the implementation. Otherwise, the requirements model must be validated "on-the-field" by patients and physiotherapists, who provide suggestions on mockups (e.g., screenshots, images, examples, prototypes) of the game (step 5). In case the medical staff does not agree on certain parts of the mockup, a brainstorming on the goal model must be performed (step 7). In this activity, software designers review (together with the medical staff) the parts of the requirements model that have been criticized during the previous step, and the model can be updated accordingly.

The rest of the section describes the ad-hoc surveys adopted and the extended FLAGS meta-model.

3.1 Ad-Hoc Surveys

As described above, the proposed elicitation technique leverages ad-hoc surveys[2] that include a set of open and multiple answer questions. The choice of the survey allows the medical staff to present the physiotherapy program without time constraints and interruptions. These surveys are the result of our experience in working with different medical departments and have been developed by a joint team of software designers and physiotherapists. In particular, we designed two types of surveys. The first one is adopted to collect physiotherapy requirements and must be filled by the medical staff. The second type of survey identifies the features that the game must provide to offer an enjoyable experience to its players, and, for this reason, it must be filled by the patients. The design of the surveys was not an easy task, since they must be complete to cover all the aspects of the physiotherapy program and the game. Furthermore, surveys should be not too long or detailed to maximize the probability to be filled in all their parts.

Before coming up with a final version of the surveys, a three months iterative review process was necessary. The surveys were validated and refined around 20 times in collaboration respectively with the medical staff having expertise on different pathologies and with patients having various age, sex, and pathology level. The validation of surveys was performed both by discussing the questions or by evaluating the degree or appropriateness of each answers with respect to its question. In addition, sample surveys have also been provided online to receive further feedback from a larger potential audience. Our surveys are independent from a specific kind of pathology, doctor's/physiotherapist's expertise, and patients' profile, and leverage a simple language that can be understood by different stakeholders. Moreover, since surveys can be re-used to develop different games, software designers do not have to attend long training sessions to acquire the medical vocabulary, as a brainstorming phase can be satisfactory.

The surveys are structured in several parts. The first part identifies the survey recipient and his/her main goals (including their priority). Sample of questions are: *"Who are you? (doctor, physiotherapist or patient)?"* or *"What are the main objectives that the game should satisfy? (List them from the most to the less important)"*. The second part is only present in the survey for the medical staff. It poses questions regarding the considered pathology and the caused physical

---

[2] The surveys for the medical staff and the patients are available at
www.dista.uninsubria.it/~paola.spoletini/REFIT.html

limitations. This is also necessary to identify the additional aids needed by the patients affected by the target pathology. Samples of questions are: *"Should the game target patients belonging to a specific age group?"*; *"Can patients with eyesight limitations use the game?"*; *"Does the patient need to use any aid to play (e.g., decubitus cushion, wrist weights)?"*. The third part contains questions regarding the environment in which the game should be performed and the type of required assistance. Note that in this case the medical staff and the patients can give contradictory answers to these questions. For example, this can happen when the doctors prefer to supervise the game in the hospital, while the patients want to have the freedom to play from home. Samples of questions are: *"In which environment the game should be played?"*, or *"Is it necessary that the patient is assisted/controlled during the use of the game? If so, indicate the minimum level of expertise required for the assistance."*.

The fourth part of the survey has questions that help identifying the required and forbidden movements that the patients must perform. Some of the questions in this part are included in all the surveys. Examples are: *"Which part of the body would you prefer to be exercised during the game?"*, or *"Which kind of movements would you prefer to be performed during the game?"*. While, more specific technical questions are only available on the survey for the medical staff. Examples are: *"For each movement listed at question 15, indicate which patient's parameters must be measured to detect the intensity/precision of the movement? (Examples can be speed and direction of the exercised parts of the body)."*

The fifth part includes questions necessary to understand the entertainment objectives that the game must achieve. In the survey for the patient, sample questions are: *"Would you like to play in team?"*, or *"Would you find interesting to visualize the score obtained by other players?"*. While, in the survey for the medical staff, questions are targeted to assess whether certain entertainment objectives should be forbidden. Sample questions are: *"Would you deem beneficial for the patients to play in team?"* or *"Is there any game configuration parameter that must only be tuned by doctors/physiotherapists (e.g., difficulty level, game duration)?"*.

The sixth part aims to understand which data can be stored for further use and how they can be manipulated. Sample of questions are: *"Which data do you want to be stored?"*, or *"Would you like the game to show statics about the overall scores of other patients?"*. Additional questions are also included to understand what can be the privacy concerns of the medical staff/patients regarding the data to disclose. Examples are: *"What are the privacy concerns regarding the data stored by the game? Which information do you want to disclose?"*.

3.2   The Extended FLAGS Meta-Model

As described above, identified requirements are represented through a goal model. Goals provide a very intuitive representation of the system, as they decompose high level goals into sub-goals, until a specific requirement of the system is identified. Furthermore, representing goals at different levels of abstraction makes easier to re-use its parts when similar requirements are common in different games and pathologies. We chose the FLAGS goal model that formalizes requirements in terms of fuzzy temporal propositions. This allows us to tolerate small requirements violations (c.g., when a movement is not perfectly executed) that are not harmful to the health of the patient and partially contribute to satisfy physiotherapy requirements.

However, the current version of FLAGS is not satisfactory to represent the main concepts used in physiotherapy programs (e.g., physiotherapy requirements, movements, aids, controllers) and their relationships. In this respect, the model is not even intuitive for the medical staff that cannot easily discriminate the physiotherapy concepts from the other functional and non-functional requirements of the system. For this reason, we extended the FLAGS meta-model, as shown in in Figure 2, to make it suitable to be used in physiotherapy.

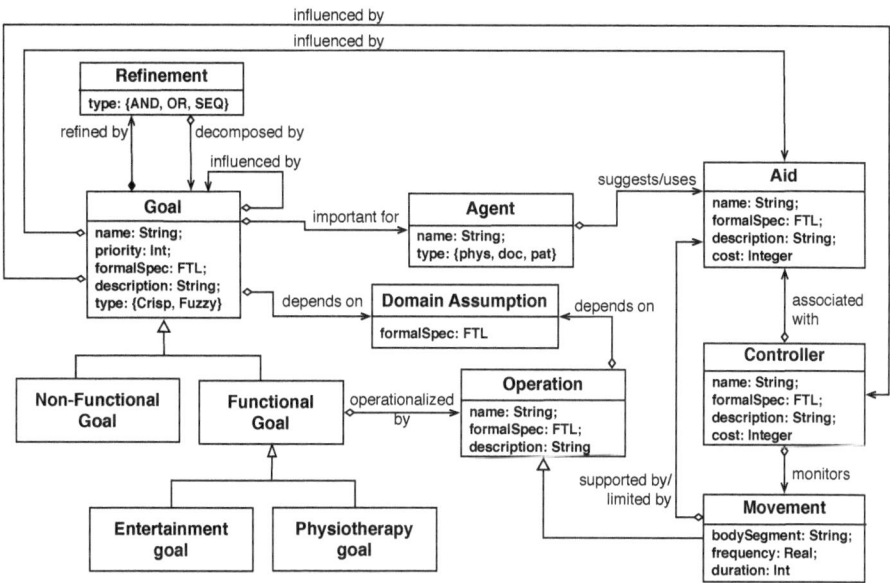

Fig. 2. The extended FLAGS meta-model

Agents represent physical persons who express a sub-set of the goals and the requirements of the game. An agent is identified by a *name* and can be a doctor, physiotherapist or a patient (*type*). In case an agent is a doctor/physiotherapist, it can *suggest* one or more aids to support the patient during the game. While, in case an agent is a patient, it can *use* suggested aids. *Aids* represent external devices that can facilitate the movements of the patients during the game. They are identified by a *name* and have a *cost*, as they can be more or less expensive. They are also characterized by a *description* and a specification (*formalSpec*). These describe how the aid must be used during the game (informally and formally, respectively).

Physiotherapy and *entertainment goals* explicitly extend functional goals. Each goal is identified by a *name*, has a *priority*, and is characterized by an informal *description* and a specification (*formalSpec*) that formalizes the property that measures the satisfaction of the goal. Goals may also be positively or negatively *influenced by* the satisfaction of other ones. Goals can also be valid when certain *domain assumptions* hold. In physiotherapy, these express a set of conditions on the environment where the game will be used. Goals can be *refined by* sub-goals necessary for their achievement. *Refinements* not only aggregate sub-goals through traditional *AND* and *OR* operators. For physiotherapy, we need to add the *SEQ* operator, to explicitly state that a goal can only be satisfied through a set of sub-goals, achieved in a specific order. This is fundamental to represent sequences of movements whose order can affect the success of the rehabilitation program of the patient. For example, if we consider a physiotherapy goal that concerns the maximization of the rotation speed of an arm. This goal will always require a warm up phase, the execution of specific movements (e.g., rotation of the chest), and a slow down phase.

Physiotherapy goals can be operationalized by *movements*. A movement extends an operation and is characterized by the part of body segment exercised (*bodySegment*), a target *frequency* and a *duration*. Each movement can be supported or even limited by an *aid* and this will also be reported in its formal and informal specification. Each *controller* (e.g., mote, board, and sensors) *monitors* one or more movements and may be used in *association with* an aid (in case an aid is adopted). The interaction of the controller with the aid must be informally described in its *description* and formally described in its specification (*formalSpec*). Finally, the satisfaction of any goal can also be influenced by the usage of aids and controllers and this must also be stated in its description and formal specification.

The language provided in FLAGS [8,9] to formally specify goals and operations is called FTL (Fuzzy-time Temporal Logic) and is obtained by extending the traditional linear temporal logic LTL with fuzzy constructs, embedding vagueness both at propositional and at the temporal level. The formalization of the requirements provides a detailed and mathematical formulation of the elements of the model. This specification can be used to derive part of the game logic, by combining , for example, the controller and the movement description. Moreover, using a formal specification could be very helpful at run-time [10] to monitor the current satisfaction level of goals and the correct usage of aids and controllers.

4   A Case Study

This section describes how RE-FIT can be applied to elicit and model the requirements of a water craft game aimed to improve the chest control in patients with spinal injuries in the lumbar region. We previously developed the game without applying RE-FIT. The requirements elicitation was time consuming due to several misunderstandings between software designers and the medical staff or the patients. The final prototype of the game, only partially satisfied the goals of doctors, physiotherapists, and patients. Using RE-FIT, it was necessary to perform a smaller number of iterations to validate collected requirements. This confirmed that the methodology can help software engineers to produce requirements models that better conform to the objectives of medical staff and patients.

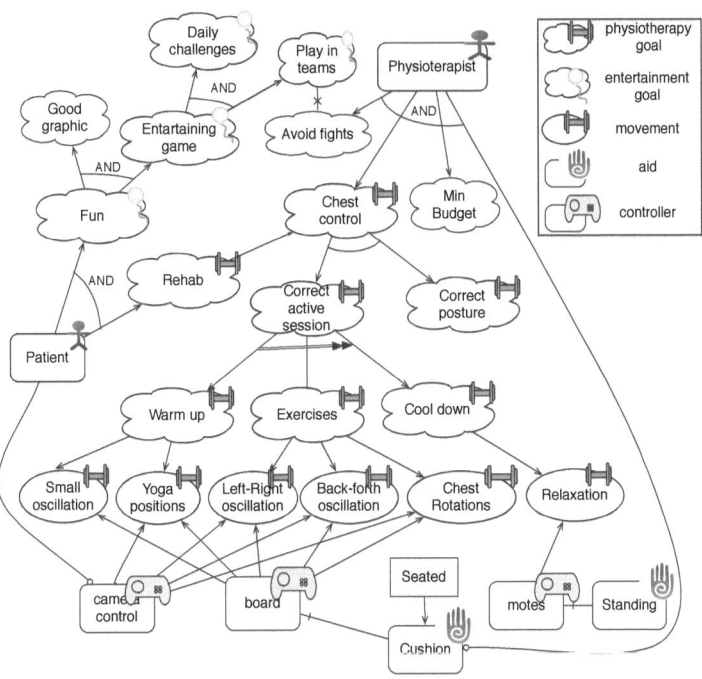

Fig. 3. A simplified version of the requirements model for the case study

As a first step, we collected the requirements from a few physiotherapists and around ten patients affected by the pathology under analysis. A brainstorming step was not really necessary with the patients, who only needed a brief explanation of some of the questions. Physiotherapists attended two brainstorming sessions of 2-3 hours. Then, both patients and physiotherapists received their survey and completed it within one week. From the analysis of the surveys, we identified two movements that were not clear for the designers: small and normal oscillation. To understand the difference of the impact of these two movements, we observed a session in the unit gym. This observation helped the designers to better understand the characteristics of the movements that were unclear and facilitated the choice of the controller to monitor the movements. For example, small oscillations can be tiny and difficult to be observed with a camera. Hence, this movement must be measured with a board on which the patient should sit. Note that the camera controller is not appropriate in this case, even if the majority of the patients identified it as the preferred controller. The overall elicitation of physiotherapy requirements took around three weeks and was highly dependent on the availability of the medical staff.

The requirements collected in the elicitation phase are modeled by using the extended version of FLAGS. A simplified version of the model is shown in Figure 3. To make the model more intuitive, we chose different symbols to differentiate entertainment goals (small balloon), physiotherapy goals, movements (weight), controllers (joystick), and aids (hand) from the other elements of the FLAGS model. The patient aims to complete part of the physiotherapy program (*rehab*) and have *fun*. The latter is achieved by providing a *good graphical interface* and by making it *entertaining*. Note that goal *fun* and its decomposition can even be re-used across different games for different pathologies. To make the game entertaining it is necessary to provide *daily challenges* for each gameplay and by allowing the patients to *play in teams*. This goal might be in conflict with another physiotherapist's goal, that requires to *avoid fights* between patients.

The main physiotherapy goal is aimed to improve the chest control, as required by the physiotherapists, who can also have budget constraints for buying possible aids and controllers. Moreover, the physiotherapists prefer that the patients use a decubitus cushion during the game. This aid can change the capability of sensing of the board. The chest control is achieved through goals *Correct active session* and *Correct posture*. To correct active session it is necessary to achieve a sorted sequence of subgoals: *Warm-up*, *Exercise* and *Cool-down*. Each subgoal is operationalized through movements (i.e., rotations and oscillations), that may be executed using different controllers (camera control, board, motes). For example, the left oscillation movement can be formalized as

$$\mathcal{AG}(\neg(\mathcal{L}_k(left\_oscillation))).$$

The evaluation of the formula is as higher as lower is the duration of the patient left oscillation (*left_oscillation*). In particular, temporal operator $\mathcal{AG}$ stands for almost always and evaluates a property by avoiding at most a fixed number of worse cases (i.e., where a property is minimally satisfied). A penalization will be assigned according to the number of avoided worse cases. If more worse cases are avoided, penalization will be more severe. $\mathcal{L}_t$, instead, stands for "lasts for k time units" and expresses that a property should last for k consecutive time units. In case the property does not hold from a certain time unit $n \in [0, k]$, a penalization is given depending on the difference between n and k. Notice that, we use the Zadeh's interpretation for connectives [11], since it is very intuitive and well known. In particular, we interpret $\wedge$ as the minimum value of operands, $\vee$ as the maximum value of their operands, $\neg$ as the complement of the value of its operand w.r.t. 1, and $\Rightarrow$ as the maximum between the negation of the antecedent and the consequent.

The following formula represents the behavior of the board

$$\mathcal{G}(move\_left(\alpha) \Rightarrow p\_move\_left(x)).$$

In case the patient moves the chest on the left of an angle α, then the player on the screen should move x mm to the left. This formula uses the temporal operator $\mathcal{G}$, that stands for "Always". The value of $\mathcal{G}$ at the current instant corresponds to the minimum of the values of its operand over the time.

The behavior of the board can also be influenced by the usage of the cushion, as indicated in the following

$$\mathcal{G}((move\_left(\alpha) \wedge cushion(t)) \Rightarrow p\_move\_left(x/2)).$$

In this case, the cushion reduces the movement of the player on the screen by half (i.e., the player on the screen will only move $x/2$ mm to the left).

Note that there is a mismatch between the controller suggested by the physiotherapist (board) and the one desired by patients (camera controls). All the aids and controllers influence the satisfiability level of the *Min Budget* goal, depending on their cost. However, these links are omitted in the figure for readability reasons.

The obtained goal model has also been used to evaluate the limitations of existing games in training patients with lumbar spinal injuries to better control the chest. As an example, we considered the watercraft game developed without applying RE-FIT. In this game, the patients have to control the navigation of a canoe in a river by moving their chest left and right to avoid obstacles or collect rewards, and back and forth to slow down and accelerate, respectively. The patient is sat on the board that measures the changes of weight to capture the player movements, independently on whether he/she is using a decubitus cushion. The game is single player and the bending angle of the oscillations can be customized depending on the players capabilities.

According to the model in Figure 3, the game does not completely satisfy the patients' and physiotherapists' goals. One of the main issue for patients is that the game does not include the possibility of playing with others. However, this goal is in conflicts with the one of the physiotherapist (no fights between patients), since competition in the game could be a source of tension. Alternative solutions can also be identified to satisfy the goals of both the agents, such as group navigation or meter relay. Furthermore, the water craft game does not consider a "Warm up" and a "Cool down" goals. While the "Warm-up" can partially be satisfied by incrementally increasing the difficulty of the game, the "Cool down" cannot be satisfied by using the current functionalities of the game. Finally, we can observe that the "Exercise" goal is identified and operationalized in terms of movements in the same way in both games. However, the formal description of the movements in the model must always be compared to the implementation of the movements in the game.

5   Related Work

Designing video games is an activity guided by market analyses and by the vision of the development team. In general, the direct interaction with the users, if present, is confined in the final phase of testing and validation. In [12], the video games production process is analyzed, by taking into account the emotional factors that can influence it. Similarly, Hunicke et al. ([13]) study the production process of games, trying to bridge the gap between design and development, game criticism, and technical game research. Unfortunately, none of these papers address the problems related to the elicitation of requirements of video games. Despite other approaches ([14,15]) have focused on the impact of the user's amusement on the requirements, they only consider general purpose games and neglect games for physiotherapy.

Requirements engineering has been widely applied in the health care domain, for the elicitation of medical requirements, to validate medical processes and analyze the behavior of medical devices. For example, in [16], classical requirements elicitation techniques are adapted to take into account the political and legal issues of the health care domain. Other work ([17]) applies requirements analysis to identify new constraints that must be satisfied by the medical devices to avoid violations of the medical process. In [18], instead, usability and user acceptance issues are considered in the early system development phases. To achieve this aim, the user satisfaction is explicitly considered in the requirements model. Finally, Garde et al. ([19]) start from the assumption that communication between different health care professionals of different institutions is unusual. For this reason, they provide an evolutionary prototyping approach that constantly develops and refines the generic domain model, depending on the interactions between different health care professionals.

In physiotherapy, similarly to the generic health care domain, the domain under analysis is complex and the interaction with the stakeholders cannot be frequent. Few attempts to use video games for physiotherapy ([20,21]) focus on their adaptation. They propose to continuously control the gameplays using a fuzzy system to avoid that patients assume wrong postures or perform wrong movements, which can be harmful for their health. However, despite this work is valuable, they did not investigated how to design motion-based games in a systematic way.

6   Conclusions

This paper introduces RE-FIT, a methodology to engineer the requirements of motion-based games for physiotherapy. This methodology is the result of a three-year collaboration with the Spinal Unit of Niguarda Hospital in Milan and a one-year collaboration with the Respiratory Medicine Section of Policlinico in Milan. Our experience allowed us to answer the research questions stated in Section 2 as follows.

- **RA1:** Requirements elicitation is mainly performed through a brainstorming session, the compilation of ad-hoc surveys and direct observation. The adoption of surveys is an effective choice as it minimized the interaction between software engineers and the medical staff.
- **RA2:** Long training sessions are avoided to speed-up the requirements elicitation. To avoid misunderstandings, requirements elicitation is conceived as

an iterative process, where requirements are constantly validated and refined through mockups and brainstorming sessions, respectively.

- **RA3-RA4:** After different interviews with the medical personel, we identified an intuitive way to embed physiotherapy requirements into existing goal models. The adoption of a goal model also allowed us to re-use the common subsets of requirements to develop games for different pathologies.
- **RQ5:** We employed a fuzzy language to represent requirements that can be partially satisfied and to tolerate small violations.

We were able to assess the external validity and the reliability of our results [22]. In particular, we generalize our findings by applying our methodology on a different set of pathologies, such as spinal injuries and respiratory pathologies. Furthermore, we assess the reliability of our procedure by testing it with a different set of students and medical personel. Despite our preliminary attempts to apply RE-FIT were very successful, it is still necessary to further validate it on other pathologies. Additional experience is also necessary to consolidate the methodology and gives it more respectability. As a future work, we will also investigate the applicability of the methodology in the elicitation and modeling of requirements of other health care domains.

Acknowledgement. We want to thank Prof. Alessandro Campi, who preliminarly collaborated with us on this idea. We also want to thank the students at Politecnico di Milano, in particular, Giacomo Rolli, Andrea Rusconi, and Laura Valsecchi, who designed and implemented the games prototypes necessary to develop RE-FIT.

References

1. Baylor News: Players Get More Pleasure from Motion-based Video Games, Baylor University Researchers Find (March 2012),
   http://www.baylor.edu/mediacommunications/
   news.php?action=story&story=110920
2. Griffiths, M.: Video Games and Health: Video Gaming is Safe for Most Players and Can Be Useful in Health Care. British Medical Journal 331(7509), 122–123 (2005)
3. Cameirão, M., Bermúdez i Badia, S., Duarte Oller, E., Verschure, P.F.M.J.: Neurorehabilitation Using the Virtual Reality Based Rehabilitation Gaming System: Methodology, Design, Psychometrics, Usability and Validation. Journal of Neuro-Engineering and Rehabilitation 7 (2010)
4. Burke, J., McNeill, M., Charles, D., Morrow, P., Crosbie, J., McDonough, S.: Serious Games for Upper Limb Rehabilitation Following Stroke. In: Proc. of the 1st Int. Conference on Serious Games and Virtual World, pp. 103–110 (2009)
5. Burke, J., McNeill, M., Charles, D., Morrow, P., Crosbie, J., McDonough, S.: Optimising Engagement for Stroke Rehabilitation Using Serious Games. The Visual Computer 25, 1085–1099 (2009)
6. Jannink, M., van der Wilden, G., Navis, D., Visser, G., Gussinklo, J., Ijzerman, M.: A Low-Cost Video Game Applied for Training of Upper Extremity Function in Children with Cerebral Palsy: A Pilot Study. Cyber Psychology & Behavior 11(1), 27–32 (2008)

7. Krebs, H., Hogan, N., Volpe, B., Aisen, M., Edelstein, L., Diels, C.: Overview of Clinical Trials With MIT-MANUS: A Robot-Aided Neuro-Rehabilitation Facility. Technology and Health Care 7(6), 419–423 (1999)
8. Baresi, L., Pasquale, L., Spoletini, P.: Fuzzy Goals for Requirements-Driven Adaptation. In: Proc. of the 18th International Requirements Engineering Conference, pp. 125–134 (2010)
9. Frigeri, A., Pasquale, L., Spoletini, P.: Fuzzy Time in LTL. CoRR abs/1203.6278 (2012)
10. Pasquale, L., Spoletini, P.: Monitoring Fuzzy Temporal Requirements for Service Compositions: Motivations, Challenges and Experimental Results. In: Proc. of the Workshop on Requirements Engineering for Systems, Services, and Systems of Systems (2011)
11. Zadeh, L.A.: Fuzzy sets. Information and Control 8(3), 338–353 (1965)
12. Callele, D., Neufeld, E., Schneider, K.: Requirements Engineering and the Creative Process in the Video Game Industry. In: Proc. of the 13th International Requirements Engineering Conference, pp. 240–252 (2005)
13. Hunicke, R., Leblanc, M., Zubek, R.: MDA: A Formal Approach to Game Design and Game Research. In: Proc. of the Challenges in Games AI Workshop, co-located with the National Conference of Artificial Intelligence, pp. 1–5 (2004)
14. Draper, S.W.: Analysing Fun as a Candidate Software Requirement. Personal and Ubiquitous Computing 3(3), 117–122 (1999)
15. Bentley, T., Johnston, L., von Baggo, K.: Putting some Emotion into Requirements Engineering. In: Proc. of the 7th Australian Workshop on Requirements Engineering, pp. 227–244 (2002)
16. Cysneiros, L.M.: Requirements Engineering in the Health Care Domain. In: Proc. of the 10th Anniversary IEEE Joint International Conference on Requirements Engineering, pp. 350–356 (2002)
17. Conboy, H.M., Avrunin, G.S., Clarke, L.A.: Process-Based Derivation of Requirements for Medical Devices. In: Proc. of the 1st International Health Informatics Symposium, pp. 656–665 (2010)
18. Doerr, J., Kerkow, D., Landmann, D., Graf, C., Denger, C., Hoffmann, A.: Supporting Requirements Engineering for Medical Products: Early Consideration of User-Perceived Quality. In: Proc. of the 30th International Conference on Software Engineering, pp. 639–648 (2008)
19. Garde, S., Knaup, P.: Requirements Engineering in Health Care: the Example of Chemotherapy Planning in Pediatric Oncology. Requir. Eng. 11(4), 265–278 (2006)
20. Borghese, N.A., Pirovano, M., Mainetti, R., Lanzi, P.L.: An Integrated Low-Cost System for At-Home Rehabilitation. In: Proc. of the 18th International Conference on Virtual Systems Multi Media (2012)
21. Pirovano, M., Mainetti, R., Baud-Bovy, G., Lanzi, P.L., Borghese, N.A.: Self-Adaptive Games for Rehabilitation at Home. In: Proc. of the 18th Interational Conference on Computational Intelligence in Games (2012)
22. Runeson, P., Höst, M.: Guidelines for Conducting and Reporting Case Study Research in Software Engineering. Empirical Softw. Engg. 14(2) (2009)

Use Case and Requirements Analysis in a Remote Rural Context in Mali

Anna Bon[1], Victor de Boer[2], Nana Baah Gyan[2], Chris van Aart[2],
Pieter De Leenheer[2], Wendelien Tuyp[1], Stephane Boyera[3], Max Froumentin[3],
Aman Grewal[3], Mary Allen[4], Amadou Tangara[4], and Hans Akkermans[2]

[1] Centre for International Cooperation, VU University, Amsterdam, The Netherlands
{a.bon,w.tuyp}@vu.nl
[2] Network Institute, VU University, Amsterdam, The Netherlands
{a.bon,v.de.boer,n.b.gyan,c.j.van.aart,pieter.de.leenheer}@vu.nl,
hans.akkermans@akmc.nl
[3] World Wide Web Foundation
{boyera,maxf,aman}@webfoundation.org
[4] Sahel Eco, ACI 200 Rue 402, 03 BP 259, Bamako, Mali
mary.saheleco@afribonemali.net, amtangs@yahoo.fr

Abstract. **[Context & motivation]** Few studies have reported on a systematic
use case and requirements analysis of low-tech, low-resource contexts such as
rural Africa. This, despite the widespread agreement on the importance of Information and Communication Technologies (ICT) for social and rural development, and despite the large number of ICT projects targeting underprivileged
communities. **[Question/problem]** Unfamiliarity with the local context and differences in cultural and educational backgrounds between end-users and software
engineers are the challenges for requirements engineering (RE) we encountered.
[Principal ideas/results] We describe a systematic approach to RE in developing areas, based on the Living Lab methodology. Our approach is supported by
extensive field research and based on co-creation within a multi-disciplinary and
multi-cultural team of developers and users. This approach creates a shared understanding of the problem and its local context, and optimizes communication.
[Contribution] We illustrate the approach using a case study of web- and voice-
based communication services, that we developed for a rural context in Mali.

Keywords: Use case analysis, African context, Living Lab methodology, market
information systems.

1 Introduction

ICT services are commonly regarded as an important tool in furthering social and rural development in developing economies. Economic growth, socio-economic development and poverty reduction have been attributed to the adoption of ICTs [1]. Information and Communication Technologies for (social) Development (ICT4D) have
therefore attracted the attention of international development organizations over the
past twenty years. At the United Nations World Summit on the Information Society,
goals were set for developing a *"people-centered, inclusive and development-oriented*

J. Doerr and A.L. Opdahl (Eds.): REFSQ 2013, LNCS 7830, pp. 331–346, 2013.
© Springer-Verlag Berlin Heidelberg 2013

Information Society so that people everywhere can create, access, utilize and share information and knowledge"[2].

In recent years the adoption of mobile telephony by rural communities has been extremely rapid. This has opened new opportunities for information and knowledge sharing and associated services in rural areas. Many ICT services have been developed and deployed over the past decade, of which a large number has been technology - rather than demand - driven, supported and financed by international donors. Many ICT4D projects have not survived after the end of the pilot phase [3]. Amongst the myriad of factors that make implementation of ICT services in low-tech, low-resource areas fail, we argue that the lack of a systematic use case and requirements analysis and a user centred approach is an important factor. Detailed descriptions of how use case and requirements analysis was actually done in rural contexts is necessary, especially since ICT4D projects are mainly initiated and led by technologically skilled teams that are usually unfamiliar with the local context.

We present a case study of a systematic use case and requirements analysis in a rural African context, by a multi-disciplinary and multi-cultural team, collaborating over an extended period of time. Given the initial unfamiliarity of the developers team with this local context, much time was spent on studying the environment, building trust relationships, and identifying the problem. Development was done in several phases, in which feedback led to new requirements, and new use cases. Every stage was characterized by extensive brainstorming, focus group discussions, demonstrations and co-creation sessions. In our approach we experienced that a typical use-case centric, incremental (spiral) development is only a starting point, when doing RE in low-tech low-resource settings. We start from the large generic problem, gradually narrowing down, towards specific use cases. By reducing the bigger issues to specific use cases, we avoid generic solutions that do not fit the context and the user's needs. This process takes several iterations, in which we are informed by field research, and several phases of requirements validation. Each step helps the further elicitation of the use case and brings new requirements, as soon as an intermediary mock-up, pilot or production system has been tested and evaluated in the local context. Experiences in sustainable land management projects in developing areas, by part of our multi-disciplinary research team, made us aware of the importance of openness, co-creation, ownership, sustainability and realism. This aligns well with key principles from the Living Lab methodology.

There are several variations in the definition of Living Lab (LL), but generally speaking, LL refers to a user-centred, open-innovation environment [4], [5], integrating concurrent research and innovation processes [6]. In the LL approach users are seen as co-creators and action research takes place in a real-life environment. Sustainability and value are often key principles in LL, as well as influence (co-creation), realism (real-life environments) and openness (open communication and innovation) [7].

Bergvall-Kreborn et al. give the following definition: *A Living Lab is a user-centric innovation milieu built on every-day practice and research, with an approach that facilitates user influence in open and distributed innovation processes engaging all relevant partners in real-life contexts, aiming to create sustainable values....*[8]

Many studies have reported Living Lab as a valuable approach for innovation. LL has been applied for innovations in less privileged communities. The Meraka Institute in South-Africa founded Living Lab South Africa (LLISA) and described in detail the approach of e-health development for rural communities [9]. Van der Welt et al. reported on the Soshanguwe Living Lab in a rural township in Tshwane, and the Venda Living Lab in Thohoyandou[10]. Both labs were set up for the co-development of ICTs, especially in the fields of health and agriculture. These two case studies were mentioned as part of an extensive framework description of the Living Lab approach. No description of the actual use case analysis is given in this paper, nor the specific services that were co-created in these labs. Hewlett Packard Corporation (HP), in India, has done a three year i-community programme aimed to bring access to ICTs and resulting benefits to rural citizens of Andhra Pradesh [11]. However, no reports of their detailed approach of use case analysis have been given. Despite the variety of papers that mention Living Lab as a valuable methodology in a development context, we could not find any literature describing a detailed approach.

The contributions of this paper are: (1) a pragmatic approach to requirements engineering, adapted to fit a low-tech, low-resource environment within a development context; and (2) a detailed description of two case studies of the development of mobile web-based information systems for an African rural context.

This paper is structured as follows: In section 2 our approach is described in a detailed case study. In section 3 the sustainable businesses and ecosystem are discussed. In the last section we discuss how the approach differs from traditional RE, and we sketch the road ahead for further work.

2   The Approach

The case study is located in a specific low-tech, low-resource rural context in Sub-Saharan Africa. It differs from a use case and requirements analysis in a traditional setting, in the sense that we start by studying and observing the generic, global scale problem, in the first stage of the project. Therefore, an important phase preceded the actual requirements elicitation, which consisted of a systematic context analysis.

The main challenge was to create a shared understanding of the context, especially because part of the team of (European) developers, was unfamiliar with the specific environment, whereas the envisaged users had low levels of (computer) literacy, and they had little idea in which way technology might support their local needs.

For this study extensive field research was done by a broad team. Borrowing from Living Lab, we especially aimed at co-creation in a real-life environment, where the problem was elicited and the (ICT) solution was developed in cooperation with the end-users. We held informal workshops, focus group discussions, brainstorm sessions and interviews, we showed storyboards and scenarios, involving all stakeholders. These stakeholders were local community radio journalists, ICT entrepreneurs, rural extension workers and small-holder farmers. Many field trips were organized to rural regions in Mali, Burkina Faso and Ghana. Small radio stations were visited and small-holder farmers were interviewed in their fields. This was all carried out locally by this multi-disciplinary, multi-cultural team.

Regreening in the Sahel	
Knowledge sharing for regreening	
Mobile phone-based knowledge sharing	
Voice-based system	
Market information system	M-event organizer
Radio Marché	Tabale

Fig. 1. The problems and solutions stack: from a generic problem to very specific use cases

Our approach is visualized in Fig. 1 as a problem stack, where we started from the big global problem, gradually narrowing down in several cycles of subsequent and re-curring problem and use case elicitation, user verification and validation, development, co-creation and adjustment. The iterations coincided with our several field trips, as summarized chronologically in Fig. 2. In the next sections, we will give detailed descriptions of these field trips and development cycles.

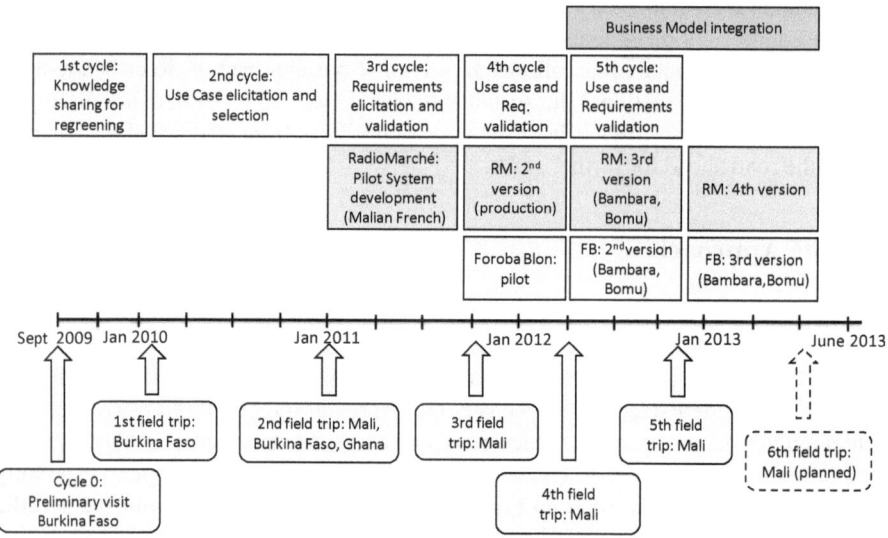

Fig. 2. Chronology of the different phases leading to Radio Marché and Foroba Blon

2.1 Cycle 0: Understanding the Context

The case study starts from a global scale problem of poverty and the need to fight desertification in the Sahel. The use case and requirements analysis in this paper targets people living in small rural communities in Mali. Mali is one of the poorest countries in the world[1] The main source of income in our target region is agriculture [12]. The

---

[1] The Worldbank, Africa Development Indicators.

production is mainly for subsistence, and the average income here is estimated to be between 1-2 dollars a day.

In the 1970s and 1980s, periods of drought severely deteriorated living conditions for many rural communities in this region. Twenty-five years later conditions have improved through farmer managed natural regeneration (FMNG) of trees. Using simple but effective farming techniques and inexpensive tools, farmers have managed to restore an area of over 5 million hectares of formerly degraded land. (see e.g. [13], [14]).

The success of the re-greening activities in Africa is mainly due to the rapid exchange and spread of local knowledge amongst large numbers of farmers. Word of mouth and farmer-to-farmer visits are traditional means of knowledge diffusion, but recently also mobile and community radio communications have become important. ICTs can enhance communication: combining existing radio and other spoken content with novel ways for voice-based access and mobile Web services may enable further increase of speed and spread of knowledge sharing among farmers.

2.2 Cycle 1: Knowledge Sharing for Regreening

Our first aim was creating an understanding of the actual generic problem, the local context and composing a general strategy for enhancing knowledge sharing in this context. This was done through a field trip to Burkina Faso in January 2010, and a two day workshop involving forty local stakeholders including representatives from farmer organizations, community radio stations, local NGOs in support of rural development, representatives from the local mobile telecommunication and internet providers, local ICT entrepreneurs and radio journalists. The European participants consisted of Web developers, information scientists, ICT4D experts, and experts in sustainable land management. The days before and after the workshop, the W4RA group visited several local villages and a number of small-holder farmers, and did several field visits to subsistence farms.

The main outcomes of the field trip to Burkina Faso were a better understanding of (i) the urgent need to improve knowledge-sharing in rural communities; (ii) the technical constraints such as no availability of internet connection or smart phones; (iii) the cultural conditions such as many different, under-resourced local African languages and low levels of literacy; (iv) the widespread availability and accessibility of (community) radio and mobile telephony in remote rural areas.

The core team, that worked together during three years, was composed of experts in different disciplines. Not only web developers, researchers in web, information science and business modelling, but also experts in agro-forestry. There latter are attached to Sahel Eco, a local Malian non-governmental organization in support of smallholder farmers and local rural communities. Sahel Eco's mission is to improve livelihoods through farmer-managed natural regeneration of trees, (FMNG). The team was temporarily joined, in several subsequent field trips, by experts from other disciplines, i.e. Living Lab experts, business experts, and computational linguists.

A formal (EU-funded) pilot project was set up, in which we focused on the development of knowledge sharing tools through voice-accessible ICTs, as to address the local contextual issues of low-literacy and low-infrastructure. The following technologies were applied in our study: (i) an open source voice platform named Emerginov[2], developed by Orange Labs, that enabled the deployment of voice-web services, and that integrated the GSM phone network and the Web, enabling the development and deployment of mobile web-based applications, and (ii) new language-packs for resourcing of under-resourced African languages, developed for this project by computational linguists from North-West University in South-Africa.

Fig. 3. Left to right: focus group discussion of developers and Malian farmers ; co-creation and validation and verification of the systems ; a journalist from local radio station Moutian in Tominian, Mali

2.3   Cycle 2: Sixteen Use Cases

A second visit to the region was organized in January 2011 as a two week road show through rural regions of Mali, Burkina Faso and northern Ghana, involving the core developers group and many local stakeholders (radio journalists, farmers), who joined the team. The objective of this trip was to collect use cases through demonstrations of pilot software and mock-ups. Focus group discussions were held with groups of smallholder farmers, community radio stations and local ICT practitioners. Qualitative data and usability feedback was collected at each demonstration site. This was pooled in during open brainstorming sessions to expand the list of possible mobile voice-based services, and to collect new ideas from the local stakeholders. An example of a voice-based demonstration during the road show of January 2011 went as follows:

– *Synopsis*: the demo is a portal that offers three services: 1) listening by mobile phone to a radio program which offers: (i) a song and (ii) information on agriculture, in Malian and French language; 2) recording a message to be broadcast; 3) retrieving the messages that have been recorded.
– *Goals*: the demo shows how voice services work using a simple phone. In the field we also showed an FM transmitter that demonstrated that a recorded message could be directly transmitted on the radio and received by people with their own radio-sets.

---

[2] Orange Labs Emerginov platform: `http://emerginov.org`

All key learnings from the road show were gathered and consolidated into a set of new services. At the end of this two week road show, a large number of interesting use case ideas had been collected. We used a semi-structured approach to describe the use cases in non-technical terms, to create a shared understanding of the problem at this stage. The sixteen use cases and their key stakeholders are shown in Table 1.

Table 1. Long list of use cases

Nr. Use case title	Main stakeholders
1 m-Milk ordering and delivery service of Tominian	Milk producers and NGO
2 m-Tree protection alert service Sahel Eco	Farmers and NGO
3 mobile-web Event organizer for vaccination of herds	Farmers
4 m-Farmer-expert directory service	Farmer organization
5 NGO info-line about legal issues in several languages	Sahel Eco
6 Leave announcement or select your favourite song	Radio
7 Shea butter and honey trading service	Radio and Sahel Eco
8 Access radio programs and announcements on your phone	Radio
9 Gourcy seed producers seed certification service	Farmer organization
10 Radio questions and answers about agricultural issues	Radio
11 m-collective purchase organizing service	Local buyers
12 m-GIS regreening service	Sahel Eco
13 m-Farmer social network	Sahel Eco
14 mobile-web regional market system	Farmer organization
15 Sahel Eco portal to Regreening and access to m-services	Sahel Eco
16 m-event organizer for re-greening events	Sahel Eco, farmers

Based on the priority given to each use case by the local partners, and the feasibility of the technical solutions, we selected two use cases to develop systems. (i) shea butter and honey trading service, to build a voice-based market information system, (ii) and m-event organizer, a voice-based mobile event organizer. The use cases are described in detail in the following section.

2.4   Cycle 3: A Voice-Based Market Information System

After the first round of use case elicitation, a pilot version of the shea butter and honey trading system was built, which was nicknamed Radio Marché. During the field visit in November 2011 this system was shown to the users in Mali, for requirements validation and verification. In the following section the use case and system is described, a UML model is shown (see Fig. 4a) and user feedback is given.

Radio Marché is a voice-based market information system, designed for farmers living and working in the area around the village Tominian, in Mali. Radio Marché is meant as a tool to improve communication between the farmers and their potential customers. It is designed according to the requirements of the following use case, based on existing procedures. The use case is shown in Fig. 4a. Radio Marché is described in detail in [15].

In 2010 Sahel Eco started the Village Tree Enterprise Project, to create a paper based Market Information System (MIS) involving nineteen small rural villages in the To-minian area, and four local community radio stations. This legacy system was dedicated to promoting sustainable use of forest resources, and developing small businesses based on non-timber tree products. The main product focus of the MIS is on shea nuts, shea butter, honey, wild fruits and nuts. The original MIS distributed up-to-date market information via community radio in the area. Our envisaged system thus started from this already functioning market information system (see Fig. 4b).

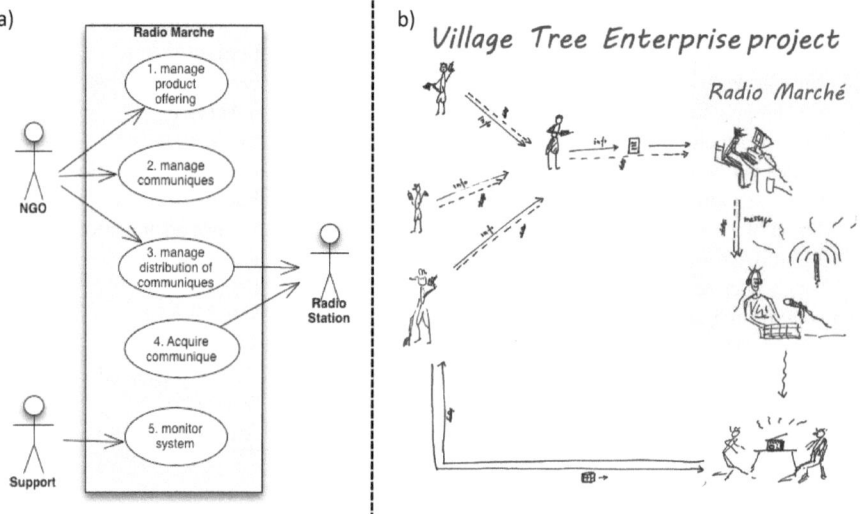

Fig. 4. The Radio Marché use case and systematic diagram

The original work flow was as such: An extension worker from Sahel Eco collects weekly market information from farmers in the villages near Tominian, about offerings of shea butter and honey. This information is communicated by the producers via sms or phone. The extension worker aggregates the data (product, quality, quantity, price, and contact phone number etc.) in an Excel sheet on his laptop. This document is then sent by email from a local community cyber-cafe to three community radio stations, whereas a hard copy of the information is physically brought to the radio that has no Internet. The radios broadcast the market offerings information including the phone numbers of the producers. Potential customers either phone Sahel Eco or phone the producer directly to negotiate a trade.

Summary of key requirements for Radio Marché The following requirements were collected in the first and second cycles of use case elicitation

- A web-based input-form for the extension worker to enter product offerings (honey, shea butter, nuts) received by phone or sms from producers;
- An automatically generated voice-based communiqué offering;

- Phone access to the voice communiqué for radio stations on a local phone line in Mali;
- The communiqué must be also accessible for radio station through web;
- The audio quality must be high enough for broadcasting over the radio;
- The service must be accessible through the internet, so that data can be entered remotely by the NGO extension worker;
- The voices in the message should sound familiar, i.e. local dialects or languages in the region of our project, the spoken languages are Malian French dialect, Bambara and Bomu;
- The voices of the radio journalists must be used to ensure trust and recognition of the system;

Radio Marché consists of several components: a web-form where the NGO extension worker enters the aggregated offerings which he receives from the farmers. This data, entered on the web-form is stored in a database. From this data a voice communiqué is automatically generated as an audio file. This audio file is accessible through mobile phone. The radio journalist calls a given phone number and hears the automated voice message. The voice message is generated using a local Malian voice. The language was one of the requirements collected during the early stages of use case analysis. In the pilot version we used a pre-recorded message spoken by one of our partners in French.

In our fourth cycle we did a new round of use case elicitation. This resulted in a use case for citizen journalism. The use case was a follow up of the Radio Marché system, and built on the experiences gained during the first three cycles. This use case will be described in section 2.8.

2.5   Cycle 4: Evaluation by the Users

The fourth cycle started again with a field trip to Mali in November 2011. During this trip, the pilot system was demonstrated and deployed in Mali. At the same time, the use case and its requirements were validated. Additional requirements were identified as the results of end-user involvement and feedback:

- Phone access has to be on a local phone line in Mali. The phone lines have to be local, to save costs for the end-users. This is an important requirement for the voice platform if it is to be deployed locally in a production environment;
- The web-form has to be more user-friendly. The original design has been adapted in several cycles to make it more intuitive. The message is accessible for a certain period through phone, by phoning a local number. The audio quality must be OK, the voice must sound natural;
- The created communiqué has to be issued through voice in multiple languages. The original communiqué is in a Malian French dialect. However, it is very important from the end-user's perspective to create voice communiqués in local languages such as Bomu and Bambara because many people, especially those targeted by the voice systems, do not speak French. There is need for a toolbox so that development of speech systems for under-resourced local languages becomes easier;
- Some radio stations do not have an Internet connection where others do. For the bigger stations a web interface where they can download the communiqué, is needed;

– User support, hardware and software maintenance are crucial. Local users will need training. Technical trainings are needed for local entrepreneurs of service providers who want to deploy voice systems.

The modified requirements were used to develop a second version of the Radio Marché system in this cycle. At the same time, the original pilot version remained deployed in its context.

2.6 Cycle 5: Enriching with Speech in Local Languages

Cycle five started with another trip to Mali, this time to test the new Malian language packs and to evaluate the French version. This trip provided insight into a number of technical and social reasons for why the system was not used as much as expected.

One issue was that Malian phone numbers were not available in the period November 2011- April 2012, due to communication issues with the Malian telecom operator. This flaw was only noticed when the technical team visited Mali in November 2012, and spoke to the radio journalist from the local radios.

Another issue were the seasonal fluctuations in production of non-timber forest products - which were unknown to the developers. In some months, no communiqués were issued due to absence of tree products. During the harvest season, the farmers restarted their trading efforts and send new offerings to Sahel Eco.

Automatic speech recognition for Bambara and Slot and Filler Text-to-Speech (TTS) for Bomu and Bambara were introduced. These were specifically developed for this project by partners from North-West University in South-Africa and recorded by our Malian partners from Sahel Eco and Radio Segou and Moutian, who provided their speech as input. The language packs were added to the second version of Radio Marché. This was an important requirement because many people in this region do not speak French, but only the local languages Bambara or Bomu.

2.7 Evaluating the Speech Systems

A field trip in November 2012 marked the deployment cycle of Radio Marché. During this field trip, the text-to-speech system for all three languages was evaluated. The Bambara and French Malian dialect speech were found to be highly intelligible, although a few grammatical issues were detected. These language problems are currently being addressed, as a next version of the text-to-speech system is being prepared.

In the next deployment step, scalability, sustainability and business models will be addressed, such as the possibility of using phone credit for automatic payments of communiqués, and voice-based entering of offerings, directly by the farmers.

2.8 Adding a New Use Case: A Radio Platform for Citizen Journalism

In Mali many community radio stations exist, some of them state funded and connected to the national broadcasting service ORTM (Office Radio Télévision du Mali), and others privately funded or completely self-supporting. According to their business, funding scheme, size and location some radio stations do have computers and the Internet, some have computers without an Internet connection and some do not have any computer facilities at all. All these radio stations are situated within the coverage area of mobile telephony. The wish of these radio stations is to have a system for citizen journalism, accessible through phone. Amongst the requirements are:

- User profiles, to control who is able to call the system;
- Voice menu prompts in local languages, where a citizen journalist (CJ) receives the menu in his or her language;
- Ability for CJs to retrieve, edit and delete messages;
- Ability for radio administrators to retrieve, edit, delete and broadcast messages through a Web interface;
- Ability for radio administrators to retrieve, edit, delete and broadcast messages through a Voice interface.

According to the use case, we proposed to build a radio platform, which was nicknamed Foroba Blon[3]. FB consists of a data store containing recorded voice messages and related meta-information.

The interface to the FB radio platform is the mobile phone, which is used for entering new voice-based content. Users of this interface are the listeners from the region entering letters-to-the-editor (LTE). These users only have mobile phones and no access to the Internet. Their calls are answered by the FB system with a pre-recorded welcome message in a local Malian voice inviting them to leave a message. For the sake of user-friendliness, the user interface and the dialogue for this category of users is kept as short and simple as possible, since the expected callers will be unfamiliar with interactive voice response systems and may not respond to a complex computer-generated dialogue asking to press buttons.

Another category of users of FB is that of registered village- reporters, calling from the field or from their village. They phone into FB and leave their spoken report for broadcasting. These users are previously registered, having their phone number, name, address and preferred language stored as a user profile in FB.

These users are trained to navigate the voice-menu, and use the interactive voice response system, asking to press a button on the phone to confirm or answer a question about their current location, subject of the message, etc. The FB system always answers the registered caller in his/her preferential language.

The voice messages are stored as audio files in the FB data store, together with meta-information being the date and time of the call, the length of phone calls in seconds, the phone number of the caller. Messages from registered, trusted users are linked to the owner, her address, and her preferred language.

In addition to the phone interface, the FB Radio Platform has a web interface, where internet-connected end-users/customers can access and upload a voice message. Depending on their customer relationship to the radio, they can log in to the radio-platform as (i) registered users such as well-known village reporters, or (ii) as unregistered users. There is an option to sign up and create a user account by registering the name, phone number, village and preferred language. Unregistered users can access former broadcasts, marked in the system as public information.

---

[3] Foroba Blon means a place where everyone may speak in front of the chief; the truth must be told respectfully, without insulting anyone.

For the radio administrator user, FB provides a web-based interface, enabling him to manage the data in the data store. It provides a file list where they can access, listen, broadcast, delete files, and add/update/delete meta-information. The radio station that has no computer nor internet, has only a very limited interface to the FB platform, since this is the constraint of a voice interface. He receives a welcome message asking if he wants to hear the last ten messages, or if he wants to hear/update/delete the welcome messages to the end-users.

The FB radio platform is hosted either locally, on a stand-alone computer or in the cloud. The FB platform consists of a voice platform running an open source web server and a local voice browser that handles the voice interaction. The local FB radio platform uses a GSM gateway to process the calls over the phone network. This device handles incoming and outbound calls and streams the voice messages to and from the phone.

In theory the FB radio platform could be physically hosted anywhere in the world, on any web server that is connected to the Internet. However, in the actual Malian case this is not possible. Firstly, the radio platform has to be accessible using an inexpensive local Malian phone number. Secondly, the web service accessed over the Internet must be accessible locally. The local connectivity is usually of low bandwidth and high latency, making voice web services hosted at datacenters in the US or Europe too slow for proper deployment in Mali. For these two reasons, the system has to be hosted locally in Mali. In the absence of good and reliable datacenters and hosting providers in Mali, the radios can opt to deploy the service locally at their premises.

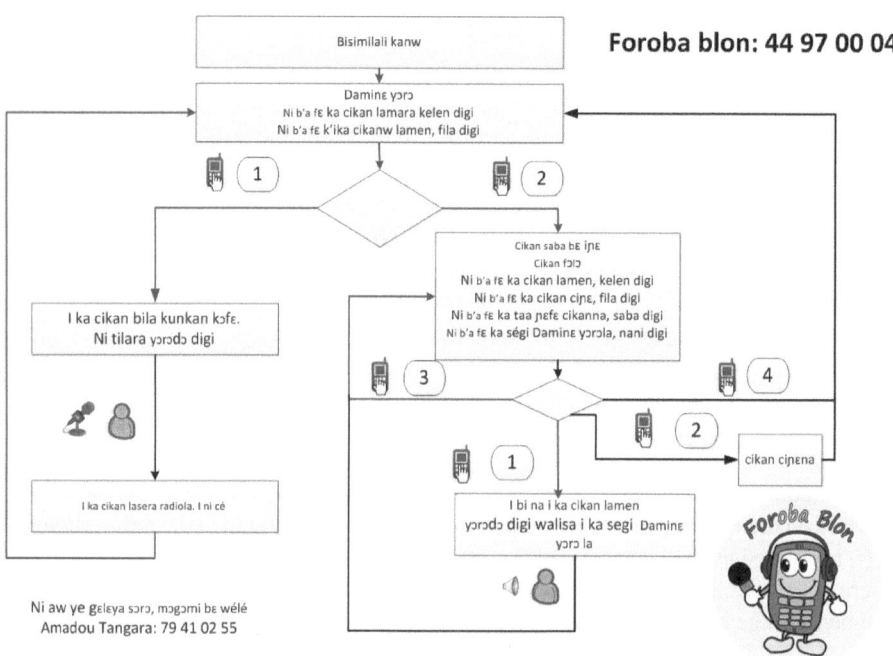

Fig. 5. Flow chart in the Bambara language for the Foroba Blon voice menu

2.9   The System Deployed Locally

In July 2012, the pilot version of the Foroba Blon system was shown to the end-users. They received a short training in how to use the interface. Their feedback was collected. They were asked to test the system in a production environment.

A third system, named Tabale, based on use case nr 16: m-event, was shown to users for the first time. In this paper we do not expand on this use case. The following feedback was given for FB. Visual representation of the call-flow and other usability aspects: We observed early on during the field testing with Radio ORTM Segou that a visual representation of the call flow was the need of the hour to adequately train both the radio staff and the correspondents on the field. We designed such a call flow menu card in French and Bambara and distributed hard copies liberally across the radio stations and correspondents. A snapshot of this call-flow is shown below.

3   Sustainable Business and Ecosystems

During our most recent field trip in November 2012, our systems were again tested and validated. We received more feedback, now based on real production tests. This feedback has not yet been processed at the time of writing this paper.

One of the key principles of the Living Lab approach and one of the conditions for successful deployment of ICT services in a low-resource environment is the emergence of new businesses to ensure sustainability beyond the pilot phase. The affordability of the service is critical, as well as the business models that have to sustain an ecosystem.

At the start of our use case and requirements analysis, we were aware of the importance of sustainability, and we tried to include elicitation of existing trading systems, and tried to model this. However, during the first 20 months this proved to be very difficult. The users were still not able to explain us how business would take place involving these newly developed services.

Only since the summer of 2012 the first systems were tested in a production environment. The radio stations started broadcasting market information and trade took off as a consequence of the radio broadcasts. The surprising outcome for Radio Marché was that the demand highly exceeded the supply of shea butter and honey, that was offered regularly over the radio. This showed us an unexpected flaw in Radio Marché from its business perspective. The ICT service was technically successful, but the underlying value chains were not yet in place. Our partners made suggestions and discussed how to better organize the sale of tree products. This was far beyond the scope of our project.

The surprising outcomes of the Radio Marché production test show how unexpected effects of technologies may occur after the kick-off of the production phase, through social uptake.

Next steps identified for this cycle are:

– Implementing the new speech TTS and ASR systems as voice prompts in Bambara and Bomu for the current voice services;
– Expanding the scale of Radio Marché across more villages, creating new instances of the service;
– Applying Linked Data principles to connect market information to other resources on the Web (of Data);

- Sustainability: Identifying business models for voice services that are feasible from a local business prospective;
- We are still using the voice-platform Emerginov, developed by Orange Labs and hosted by France Telecom in Senegal and Mali. We are working to find a more generic solution for this platform, to avoid dependency on one telecom provider, and to have other robust and inexpensive technical solutions, that can be deployed locally.

4   Conclusion

We have described a use case and requirements analysis in a low-tech, low-resource context in rural Mali. We did not find similar studies in the literature. Lack of a systematic use case and requirement analysis may explain the failure of certain ICT4D projects. The absence of voice-based systems in the majority of ICT4D projects in e.g. rural African contexts - voice interface being one of the most important requirements we found in our study - can be explained by a lack of proper requirements analysis. From the methodological and RE point of view, we argue that our approach, although starting from a typical use-case centric, incremental (spiral) development, has pragmatically included several elements from the Living Lab methodology [7] to fit this specific context:

Realism. Understanding the big picture and the real-life environment of e.g. African farmers is crucial to understand the context before identifying use cases. All development cycles must depart from the real-life environment.

Influence. The involvement of the users is more than just a user-centric approach. Examples of co-creation are e.g. the recording of Malian speech and voice-prompts in local dialects, by our Malian users. We argue that the only way to develop appropriate systems for this context is by engaging users and have them contribute to development, during all the cycles.

Value and Sustainability. Only by understanding the local business ecosystems, sustainable solutions can be sought to ensure local deployment.

Openness. This is the experience that open communication and trust relationships lead to better solutions. This key principle of Living Lab is built on the idea that requirements are not just hidden information, waiting to be elicited by RE experts, but rather social constructs [8]. We have seen use cases and requirements emerge through creative interaction amongst this multi-cultural and multi-disciplinary team of developers, extension workers, local radio journalists and farmers producing non-timber tree products such as honey and shea butter.

We are reporting about work in progress, so no final conclusions can be drawn on the sustainability of the systems. In 2013 we expect to continue the development of more innovative voice web-based services for rural communities in Mali. We will test and do more requirement validation and verification of Radio Marché with the users in their production environment. The following points are still open for further development:

- We want to transfer the experiences and methodology from this research project to a broad global community of ICT and Web developers, researchers and civil society, and local stakeholders.

– We want to support scaling up these innovations in the benefit of knowledge sharing for empowerment of the less privileged.

Acknowledgements. This research was supported by grants from the EU-FP7 funded VOICES project, and the International Press Institute. The language packs for Bomu and Bambara were developed by Etienne Barnard and his research team from North-West University in South-Africa.

The initiative for this research project in Sub-Saharan Africa was from a group named W4RA[4], Web alliance for Regreening in Africa, and was initiated and seed-funded by the Network Institute from VU University Amsterdam [16].

References

1. UNCTD Science and technology for development: the new paradigm of ICT. Information Economy Report 2007-2008, United Nations Conference on Trade and Development (2007)
2. WSIS Declaration of Principles. World Summit on the Information Society. United Nations, New York (2005), http://www.itu.int/wsis/tunis
3. Unwin, T. (ed.): ICT4D Information and Communication Technology for Development. Cambridge University Press (2009)
4. von Hippel, E.: Lead users: a source of novel product concepts. Management Science 32, 791–805 (1986)
5. Chesbrough, H.W.: Open Innovation: The new imperative for creating and profiting from technology. Harvard Business School Press, Boston (2003)
6. Bilgram, V., Brem, A., Voigt, K.-I.: User-Centric Innovations in New Product Development; Systematic Identification of Lead User Harnessing Interactive and Collaborative Online-Tools. International Journal of Innovation Management 12(3), 419–458 (2008)
7. Ståhlbröst, A.: Forming Future IT - The Living Lab Way of User Involvement. Doctoral Thesis Luleå University of Technology Department of Business Administration and Social Sciences. Division of Informatics (2008),
http://epubl.ltu.se/1402-1544/2008/62/LTU-DT-0862-SE.pdf
8. Bergvall-Kåreborn, B., Ihlström-Eriksson, C., Ståhlbröst, A., Svensson, J.: A milieu for innovation. In: 2nd ISPIM Innovation Symposium on Defining Living Labs (2009),
http://pure.ltu.se/portal/files/3517934/19706123_paper.pdf
9. Ruxwana, N.L., Herselman, M.E., Conradie, P.D.: ICT applications as e-health solutions in rural healthcare in the Eastern Cape Province of South Africa. Health Information Management Journal 39(1), 17–29 (2010)
10. van der Welt, J., Buitendag, A., Zaaiman, J., Jansen van Vuuren, J.C.: Community Living Lab as a Collaborative Innovation Environment. Issues of Information Science and Information Technology 6, 421–436 (2009)
11. Schwittay, A.: A Living Lab, Corporate Delivery of ICTs in Rural India. Science Technology Society 13-2, 175–209 (2008)
12. FAO: Financing agriculture and rural development in Africa: Issues, constraints and perspectives. In: Twenty-third Regional Conference for Africa, Johannesburg, South Africa, March 1-5 (2004)

---

[4] W4RA, Web Alliance for Regreening in Africa http://www.w4ra.org
http://w4ra.few.vu.nl

13. Reij, C., Tappan, G., Smale, M.: Agroenvironmental Transformation in the Sahel, Another kind of Green Revolution. IFPRI Discussion paper (2009)
14. Akkermans, N.: The Role of ICTS in Knowledge Sharing within Rural Communities in Ghana. Intership MA International Relations. University of Groningen,
    `ftp://akmc.biz/ShareSpace/W4RA-VOICES/Stageverslag`
15. de Boer, V., De Leenheer, P., Bon, A., Gyan, N.B., van Aart, C., Guéret, C., Tuyp, W., Boyera, S., Allen, M., Akkermans, H.: RadioMarché: Distributed voice- and web-interfaced market information systems under rural conditions. In: Ralyté, J., Franch, X., Brinkkemper, S., Wrycza, S. (eds.) CAiSE 2012. LNCS, vol. 7328, pp. 518–532. Springer, Heidelberg (2012)
16. Akkermans, H., Grewal, A., Bon, A., Tuyp, W., Allen, M., Gyan, N.B.: W4RA-VOICES field report. Tech. rep., Web Alliance for Regreening Africa (2011),
    `http://www.mvoices.eu/2011/03/25`
    `_Voices-W4RA_Public_Report.pdf`

Requirements Engineering in Practice: There Is No Requirements Engineer Position

Andrea Herrmann

Free Software Engineering Trainer and Researcher, Stuttgart, Germany
herrmann@herrmann-ehrlich.de

Abstract. **[Context and motivation]** For the requirements engineering (RE) community it is clear that requirements engineering is a specific activity and role within software development. **[Question/problem]** However: What about practice? Is RE seen there as a separate role? What qualifications do practitioners see as critical for this task? **[Principal ideas/results]** 141 job advertisements from 2009 and 67 from 2012 were analysed statistically in order to find out how practice perceives and staffs RE: Which official job title do those persons have who do RE? Which further responsibilities do these persons have? Which qualifications are demanded? **[Contribution]** The study´s main results are: The position "requirements engineer" hardly exists. RE instead is done by consultants, software engineers, architects, developers and project managers, who additionally have an average of 3 further tasks. RE is no task for job beginners: 73% of the job advertisements wish or demand previous job experience. Further important qualifications are: 94% soft skills (the Top 3 soft skills are: capacity for teamwork, English language and communication skills), 76% demand knowledge with respect to the technology used, while only 34% mention RE knowledge. RE is most often combined with solution design (77% respectively 61%).

Keywords: job advertisement, organisation, practice, requirements engineer, role.

1   Introduction and Motivation

For the requirements engineering (RE) community it is clear that requirements engineering is a specific activity and role within software development, which demands specific qualifications. However: What about practice? Is RE seen there as a separate role? What qualifications do practitioners see as critical for this task?

In this study, we define a person to be a natural person with an individual name. When a person is employed in an organisation, it is integrated into the hierarchical system which is modeled by the organisation´s organigram. The organigram´s basic elements are positions which have hierarchical relations with each other. Each position is identified by a job title, and usually specific expectations in terms of responsibilities, tasks and power (and salary) are linked to job titles. A position´s definition usually is organization-specific and is described in a job advertisement and

J. Doerr and A.L. Opdahl (Eds.): REFSQ 2013, LNCS 7830, pp. 347–361, 2013.

in the work contract. The concept of role describes a set of tasks and responsibilities and competencies, but is usually not identical with the position. While the position is attributed to a person permanently until change of position, e.g. promotion, project roles are attributed to persons dynamically, according to the current need. One person can work on several roles in parallel, but has only one position at a time.

In the present study, we analyse job advertisements which are an official model of how practitioners integrate RE in their organisations and which qualifications they believe to be critical for this task. Ideally, these job advertisements also reflect previous experience, i.e. they demand such qualifications which in the past had shown to be critical. Therefore, 141+67 job advertisements were analysed statistically in order to find out how practice perceives and treats RE.

The **research questions (RQ)** for this study are:

1. What is the job title of the person / position doing RE?
2. Which tasks are part of RE?
3. Which further tasks does this position include?
4. Which competencies are demanded?

These questions were chosen for three reasons:

a) Although theory offers proposals to all of them, it is little known whether practice shares this view or has developed its own Best Practices.
b) They reflect aspects of the way how practitioners choose and integrate the persons who are responsible for RE. For instance, if a person doing RE also must fill several more roles, then (s)he can put less focus on RE than a person for whom RE is a full-time task. The competencies demanded are potentially those which have been critical in previous projects.
c) They can be answered based on the information contained in published job advertisements.

This paper is structured as follows: Section 2 presents related work, Section 3 the study design and execution, Section 4 describes the study results. Section 5 discusses threats to validity. Section 6 concludes the paper with a summary.

2   Related Work

In this section, we review empirical studies which have investigated our four research questions in practice. It is not the intention of this section, to summarize the state of the art of theoretical work and the answers it proposes to the four research questions. We here focus on the perception of practitioners and how RE is executed in practice. Nevertheless, additionally to empirical studies, some few theoretical frameworks will be cited to show what answers to the four RQ we might find. There exist many case studies and field studies about different questions concerning RE. However, only few discuss job titles, multiple roles and the competencies which companies demand from the person who does RE. The remainder of this section is structured according to the four RQ.

2.1   RQ1: What Is the Job Title of the Person / Position Doing RE?

The Project Management Body of Knowledge PM BOK [11] sees RE as one of the knowledge areas (i.e., tasks) of the project manager. It foresees no specific job title or even person for doing RE.

In many organisations, the role of the requirements engineer is not defined clearly. The division of responsibilities and tasks varies depending on the organisational structure, project circumstances or personal capabilities [4].

Nikula et al. [10] investigated roles in software developing SME. They found, among 12 companies: "The most common specialist role for team members was designer for user interface, database, or alike that was present in seven companies. The next most common specialist groups were the technical writers and systems analysts, both found in six companies. Three companies had testers and five did not have any such specialists but called all employees developers." So, if five out of 12 SMEs do not define roles within their development team and the others have only few specialist roles, then we can expect that there is no specific requirements engineer role or position. As RE must be done by someone, we can expect that there might be developers and analysts who do RE.

Neill and Laplante [9] in their RE survey found the following positions to be involved in RE: executive, architect, consultant, project manager, system designer, analyst, and technical specialist.

Zowghi et al. [16] in their field study also found persons with many different job titles to be involved in RE: marketing, engineering and technical management, product development, support, customer support center, customers, product users.

We can expect that not only software development companies look for RE personnel, but also the customer side. An interview study in 25 German SMEs [15] investigated the participation of the business department in the RE process. This study found that business departments often have experience in process organisation, however no defined RE process or RE methods, partly caused by a lack of RE knowledge. None of the 25 organisations had established an explicit role of a requirements engineer. The interviewed persons, however, wish a more formalised and better qualified RE process for the future. The study found different scenarios of who is involved how in the RE: Sometimes, the developers already know the requirements (e.g. after a long cooperation), and business is not involved. Or business department defines the requirements for new information systems. Or top management decides about the introduction or upgrading of information systems with external technical and process consulting. This study shows some actors within the RE: business department (=user perspective), developers and external consultants.

2.2   RQ2 Which Tasks Are Part of RE?

We could not find any empirical study answering this question. RE is generally accepted to include elicitation, analysis, specification and validation [1], [13].

2.3   RQ3 Which Further Tasks Does This Position Include?

The fact that there is usually no separate RE role or position implies that those persons who do RE also have other tasks. But which are these? How many? This is not known, but previous studies found that the variety of tasks overstrains those who do RE [4] and recommend defining a separate RE role or position. Klendauer et al. [8] found in their case study: "In the interviews with software developers, we discovered that the formal introduction of the organisational role RA [Requirements Analyst] can facilitate the success of projects considerably. Through the clear task divisions that this introduces, the developers can focus on their primary job – the development of the software itself, while the analyst takes over all communication related tasks. However, to achieve this result, the RA must have the appropriate competencies in order to be effective. If not, they can be very obstructive. In two cases, the developers bypassed the analyst and directly contacted the customer for further inquiries."

2.4   RQ4 Which Competencies Are Demanded?

According to the study of Alenljung and Persson [2], the requirements engineer must cope with lack of communication, time pressure, cognitive load of his task and lack of resources. These authors emphasize the importance of knowledge about domain, product and RE, and the importance of communication. In the RE literature, it is consensus that additionally to RE knowledge, RE also demands communication and soft skills. However, there is no consensus on whether the person doing RE must have domain knowledge. Here again, we focus on the results of empirical research about RE practice and about needed competencies.

RE Knowledge (concepts, methods, tools)

Alexander, Robertson and Maiden [3] in a survey among 152 practitioners found that "respondees felt that training, own standards, tools, the regulator, first principles and experienced colleagues were the main influences on their requirements processes. Most of the other factors, which are mainly sources of process knowledge external to their organizations, had little influence."

In their case study in Sweden, Alenljung and Persson [2] found that requirements work has a low status within software development organisations. This means that "To become a requirements engineer is not viewed as a step upwards on the career ladder. Thus, experienced software engineers do not want to have that role. Instead, engineers fresh out of university are often recruited. Since there is a low understanding in the organisation in the difficulties of being a requirements engineer, education in RE is not, as far as we have seen in our case study, a requirement to become a requirements engineer. This results in requirements engineers having limited experience and limited knowledge about the product as such, the domain in which the product is to be used, and the RE task. The low status and lack of understanding also have other consequences. There are fewer possibilities to improvement of qualifications and fewer and less developed support tools. A couple of interviewees compare the support given to requirements engineers and the much more developed support a compiler gives to a programmer." And "There is not enough introduction to and education in RE for novice requirements engineers, which makes it difficult to carry out the RE tasks."

Nikula et al. [10] in their interviews with 12 SME found a significant lack of awareness in practice about what RE competencies even exist: "This paper presents the results of an empirical survey showing that the problem is not in the practitioners' lack of desire for improvement but in the management not knowing that many RE issues can be solved with standard practices that are well documented in literature. Raising the management awareness of RE practices would make it easier to start RE process improvement efforts in industry and thus eventually also raise the RE process maturity in companies." And: "No company had RM [requirements management] tools in use." The most frequently used RE tools were word processor and spreadsheets, and requirements are usually described in natural language.

Klendauer et al. [8] finds about RE tools: "Surprisingly, applying specific tools and advanced techniques did not seem to play a significant role from the interviewees' perspective."

Soft Skills (social and communication competencies)

Many empirical studies have found the importance of soft skills and communication skills especially in RE (see for instance [6], [7]), even more in distributed RE [12],[16]. Curtis, Krasner and Iscoe [6] in their 17 case studies found that the communication between requirements analysts and stakeholders, as well as between requirements analysts and developers, is of critical importance.

Klendauer et al. [8] conducted 64 interviews at eight major North American and European financial services companies in order to investigate the competencies of requirements analysts. The interviews use the critical incident technique. The competencies found are:

— need for power and control (deciding and initiating action; leading and supervising)
— agreeableness (working with people; adhering to principles and values)
— extraversion (relating and networking; presenting and communicating information; persuading and influencing)
— mental ability (writing and reporting; applying expertise and technology; analysing)
— openness (learning and researching; creating and innovating; forming strategies and concepts)
— Conscientiousness (planning and organising; delivering results and meeting customer expectations; following instructions and procedures)
— emotional stability (adapting and responding to change; coping with pressure and setbacks)
— need for achievement (achieving personal work goals and objectives; enterprising and commercial thinking)

Domain Knowledge

Berry [5] from several case studies concludes that ignorance (in the domain) of the person doing RE is useful. It helps to identify tacit assumptions. On the other hand, Curtis ct al. [6] emphasize that domain knowledge must be available.

3   Study Design and Execution

In order to answer the four RQ, job advertisements from an online job portal were analysed. The data selection and analysis proceeded like this:

1. First, IT-related job advertisements were read in the German job portal www.stepstone.de. Those job advertisements were selected for further analysis which include RE tasks.
2. The ad´s text was coded: job titles, tasks and demanded competencies were collected in a table and attributed to categories.
3. Quantitative analyses were executed on these data in order to answer the four RQ.

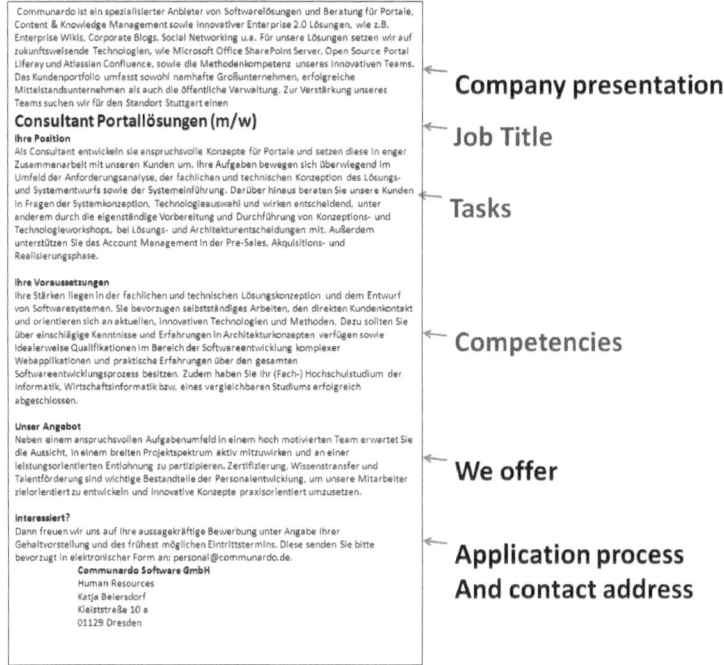

Fig. 1. Typical structure of a job advertisement

Step 1:

The search for relevant job advertisements was performed on two dates: on 17 July 2009 and on 29 October 2012. This allows us to also observe the changes within three years.

The jobs were searched under category "IT". The sub-categories which the portal offers were changed between the two searches. In 2009, the four sub-categories considered were Software Engineering, application analysis, IT consulting and IT systems analyst. In 2012, the sub-category considered was "Consulting, Engineering". The sub-categories from 2009 did no longer exist. It seems that these four were merged into this one. The search included the countries Germany, Switzerland and Austria, all application domains, and all types of jobs (permanent job, temporary appointment, etc; only internships were excluded).

In 2009, there were 16721 IT hits all together. Among these were: Software Engineering 709, Application analysis 124, IT consulting 458, and IT systems analyst 87. Out of these 1378, 141 advertisements described RE tasks.

In 2012, there were 10483 IT hits. Sub-category "Consulting, Engineering" included 2542 hits. Of these, the 589 most recent jobs advertisements from 25 to 29 October were analysed and 67 were found which contain RE tasks.

So, approximately 10% of the analysed job advertisements mentioned RE tasks.

We defined RE to be the elicitation, analysis, specification, validation and management of requirements [1], [13]. However, this task is usually not called RE, but can have many names. Therefore, the decision about relevance of an advertisement had to be done manually. No predefined key words were used, but instead the task sections were read and it was decided whether RE is included or not. The most frequent key words that were found to be an indicator of RE tasks were: customer requirements, problem analysis, functional specification, clarification of requirements with customers, analysis of business processes, communication of requirements to the development team. However, the following activities were considered to not be part of RE: making decisions about requirements, technical specification, solution design (e.g. security concepts, data base designs), solution development, software customizing, consulting in the meaning of selling the company's specific product, process improvement.

Step 2:
Job advertisements all have a similar structure, as shown in Fig. 1. For answering RQ1, the job titles were extracted. For RQ2 and RQ3, the task section was analysed, separating RE tasks and other tasks from each other. RQ4 refers to the competencies section which describes which competencies the applicant must have.

Job titles, tasks and competencies were coded in categories. These categories were not taken from literature, but were defined iteratively, as described by the Grounded Theory [14]. The categories did emerge from the data.

In what follows, the categories are listed and the original terms included in each category (mostly English translations of German terms) are given.

Job titles

— **Requirements Engineer[1]:** requirements engineer, requirements manager
— **Consultant:** consultant, analyst, business process manager, system planner, user experience specialist

---

[1] The term „Requirements Engineer" is also used in German.

— **Architect:** (solution) architect, design expert, IT infrastructure consultant
— **Developer:** (software) developer, project member, member of development team, programmer, technology associate
— **Sales Person:** engagement manager, lead engineer, sales support
— **Project Manager:** project manager, technical IT project leader, sub-project manager
— **Software Engineer:** software engineer, systems engineer, product manager

Non-RE Tasks we grouped along the following categories:

— **Feasibility analysis:** feasibility analysis, cost estimation,
— **Solution conception:** design, technical specification, solution design (e.g. security concepts, data base designs), architectural design, improvement / optimisation of business processes, analysis and assessment of IT architectures, specification of optimizations, specification of standardisations
— **Realisation:** implementation, development, programming, software customizing, system integration
— **Quality assurance:** testing, specification of test cases, reviews, quality management, integration testing, functional tests, load tests, usability tests
— **Documentation / training:** documentation, (user) training
— **Deployment:** installation, data migration, rollout
— **Maintenance / hotline:** (user) support, technical support, coaching, trouble-shooting, problem management
— **Project management:** project management, management of sub-project, deadline monitoring, risk management
— **Sales:** sales, sales support, identification of business opportunities, networking, bid proposal management, observation of market

The categories of competencies are RE competencies (with the sub-categories listed in Table 3) and further competencies as listed in Table 4, where soft skills have the sub-categories shown in Table 5.

4   Results

From the data gathered as described in Section 3, we derive the following answers to the RQ1 to RQ4.

4.1   Research Question RQ1 "What Is the Job Title of the Person / Position Doing RE?"

The job title „Requirements Engineer" does hardly exist. In 2009, only one such job title was found among 141 advertisement which described RE tasks, and in 2012, it was 3 among 67. RE is done by consultants, software engineers, developers, and many more. Table 1 shows the distribution of job titles of those persons who do RE, in 2009 and 2012. The largest group of persons doing RE have the job title of a consultant. There is a clear trend from 2009 to 2012 that there are more requirements engineers, more architects, a bit more software engineers and also more explicit double roles. Vice versa, in 2012 there are clearly less developers who also do RE. It is possible that this combination of developer position and RE tasks was not ideal in the past.

Table 1. Distribution of job titles of those persons who do RE, in 2009 and 2012

Job title	Number (%) in 2009	Number (%) in 2012
Requirements engineer	1 (0.7 %)	3 (4.5 %)
Consultant	72 (51 %)	29 (43.3 %)
Architect	12 (8.5 %)	11 (16.4 %)
Developer	36 (25.5 %)	5 (7.5 %)
Sales Person	2 (1.4 %)	0
Project manager	3 (2.1 %)	2 (3.0 %)
Software engineer	10 (7.1 %)	7 (10.4 %)
Double role	5 (3.5 %)	7 (10.4 %)
Others	0	3 (4.5 %)

4.2   Research Question RQ2 "Which Tasks Are Part of RE?"

The following categories of RE sub-tasks emerged from the data in the advertisements:

- elicitation of requirements
- analysis of processes
- documentation
- coordination of requirements with customers
- collaboration / coordination with development team
- management of requirements changes
- expectation management
- consulting in decision processes
- assessment of solutions
- consulting of customers with modelling, development of RE guidelines, doing RE trainings

These categories are more detailed than those found in literature (see Section 2).

4.3   Research Question RQ3 "Which Further Tasks Does This Position Include?"

RE is no full-time task. This is not only reflected by the fact that there are few positions with RE in the job title. Additionally, in the task list, many more tasks are listed. Those who do RE, additionally do several further tasks. Table 2 lists how many positions are described to do which non-RE task. While specifying the technical concept still is the most frequent non-RE task combined with RE, its frequency went down from 77.3% in 2009 to 61.2% in 2012. This is similarly the case for other tasks which demand technical knowledge like realisation, deployment, and feasibility analysis / cost estimation. For the non-technical tasks, the percentages stayed the same. In parallel to this development, the number of tasks which are done additionally to RE, went down from 3.23 in 2009 to 2.79 in 2012. This might reflect that RE is increasingly seen as a separate activity which cannot be done additionally to development and which demands a larger part of a person´s work day. As we see in Table 4, experience with a specific technology still is demanded at 76%. So, the discharge of RE-doing positions from technical tasks is not correlated to a discharge from technical knowledge.

Table 2. Tasks in 2009 and 2012

Task	Percentage in 2009	Percentage in 2012
solution design	77.3 %	61.2 %
realisation	53.9 %	44.8 %
deployment	41.1 %	23.9 %
quality assurance	37.6 %	38.8 %
project management	34.8 %	31.3 %
maintenance / hotline	24.8 %	23.9 %
documentation/ training	22.7 %	25.4 %
sales	19.1 %	19.4 %
feasibility analyses, cost estimation	12.1 %	10.4 %

4.4   Research Question RQ4 "Which Competencies Are Demanded?"

Only about one third of the job advertisements demand RE specific competencies: 37% (51) in 2009 respectively 34% (17) in 2012. Which RE competencies were demanded, is shown in Table 3.

Table 3. RE competencies demanded

RE competency	Number (%) in 2009	Number (%) in 2012
modelling methods	21/51 (41%)	10/23 (43%)
experience with RE	20/51 (39%)	4/23 (17%)
RE tools	16/51 (31%)	7/23 (30%)
experience process analysis	13/51 (25%)	7/23 (30%)
RE&M (requirements engineering & management) knowledge	10/51 (20%)	7/23 (30%)

The most remarkable fact about this is that so few specific RE knowledge or experience is demanded of those who do RE. The fact that those persons also have other tasks, is not sufficient as an explanation. Compared to the other tasks, RE competencies are demanded at a lower rate. Those advertisements which mention the solution conception, demand technical knowledge at 82% (in 2009) or 76% (in 2012), those who do development must have technical knowledge at 85.5% (in 2009) and 83.3% (in 2012). This can be interpreted as a lack of awareness that RE methods exist or are needed, or it is assumed that RE competencies are taught at universities and during apprenticeship anyway. Studies or apprenticeship are expected at 89% (in 2009) and 85% (in 2012). Remark: For the project management, it is even worse. Of those ads which mention project management tasks, only 26% demand project management knowledge (in 2009) or at 14.3% (in 2012).

However, RE is no tasks for job beginners: 72% (in 2009) respectively 73% (in 2012) of the advertisements wish or demand previous work experience.

Table 4 shows which further competencies are demanded. Soft skills and technical knowledge are most important, and also to have previous experience with the corresponding task. The importance of specific methods or tools has clearly diminished from 2009 to 2012, and the demand or wish for domain knowledge went down from 50% to 34%.

Table 4. Further competencies demanded

Competency	percentage (2009)	percentage (2012)
Technical knowledge	79 %	76 %
Experience with a method	31 %	13 %
Experience with a tool	27 %	12 %
Experience with a task	49 %	55 %
Project management knowledge	17 %	16 %
Soft skills	92 %	94 %
Domain knowledge	50 %	34 %

Table 5. Soft skills demanded. Given are percentage with respect to all ads

Competency	percentage (2009)	percentage (2012)
English language	57 %	72 %
Capacity for teamwork	57 %	52 %
Communication skills	55 %	60 %
Analytical skills	43 %	40 %
Sense of responsibility	43 %	33 %
Commitment	37 %	13 %
Self-confidence	35 %	30 %
Result orientation	30 %	18 %
Flexibility	29 %	28 %
Customer orientation	28 %	39 %
German language	28 %	33 %
Willingness to travel	27 %	45 %
Conceptual skills	26 %	18 %
Self-organisation	14 %	10 %

Table 5 shows which soft skills are explicitly demanded in detail. The soft skills often make up a long part of the ad's competencies section. The average number of soft skills per advertisement was 5.6 in 2009 and 7.8 in 2012 (counting only these ads where soft skills were mentioned). The most important soft skills in both 2009 and 2012 were English language skills, communication skills and capacity for teamwork. The major changes are observed in that English, willingness to travel and customer orientation are much more frequent now and result orientation and commitment has become less frequent.

5   Threats to Validity

This study might be affected by two major threats to validity: The job advertisements might not reflect real work conditions, and the results of their analysis depend on the coding procedure.

Do the job advertisements reflect real work? The job advertisements analysed are data material that has not been written for the purpose of this study but instead for the purpose of attracting competent job candidates. As such, this material might be afflicted with several threats to validity. One can imagine that job advertisements do not reflect the job reality in the following respects:

— The real tasks of an employee depend on the company's current demand and the future development of the organisation, but also on the person's real qualifications and availability. Therefore, it is possible that the job advertisement only names the main tasks without mentioning all or vice versa lists all potential tasks which finally will not all be done by the new colleague.

— Due to skills shortage on the German workforce market, especially in the software development field, job advertisements might either list only the main qualifications demanded in order not to be too restrictive or vice versa list all qualifications, knowing well that they would also accept a candidate who only fulfills 80% of them.

— Job advertisements in larger organisations might be written by the human resource department, using templates and previous versions, without consulting the future superior and without using experience from daily practice. The high demand of soft skills might even reflect a current "fashion".

Nevertheless, it can be assumed that job advertisements as official company publications are written and reviewed with high diligence by several experienced professionals in order to attract the right candidates. In fact, it seems that the job advertisements do not draw a too idealized picture of the RE job, as they often demand conflict handling skills, being able to do structured work under time pressure, and more than average commitment to work, and they list many qualifications as a must. They communicate that RE is a highly difficult task. As a researcher, I believe that job advertisements are empirical data material that is maybe even written with more diligence than answers to research questionnaires.

Finally, all data and conclusions from this study must be seen as statistical analysis results of job advertisements, not necessarily as reflection of the actual work practice. However, they reflect a model that practitioners, mainly human resource departments and managers, have of the work organisation and competencies demanded in daily work in RE.

Comparing our results to previous work (see Section 2), we find that our results are consistent with those of other researchers, who did case study research and surveys about the state of the practice. Our RQ1 finds a variety of job titles involved in RE, including analysts and developers as observed before. We cannot say how many customer-side positions mention RE because we did not include this criterion in the coding scheme and we expect that these end user positions would be published not in the IT section of the job portal. As can be seen in Section 2, other researchers also found that RE is done by persons with multiple roles and tasks and that soft skills are important, while RE knowledge often is not present, either because companies do not use RE methods or because they even do not know what specific RE competencies exist.

How do the answers to the RQs depend on the coding procedure? For answering RQ1 to RQ4, free text answers were coded in categories. The answers to the RQs therefore depend on the granularity and correctness of this coding. Other coders might have chosen different categories. In the answer to RQ1, for instance, we do not distinguish between roles on customer side and on contractor side, what other researchers do (see Section 2). In order to make the coding process transparent, in Section 3 it is documented which terms were attributed to which category. RQ2 led to an RE task list that does not correspond to task lists in the RE literature. It is what we read in the ads. In RQ3 and RQ4, quantitative analysis were done. The percentages, the number of tasks and the number of competencies, of course, directly depends on the granularity of the categories. More fine-grained categories would lead to higher numbers of tasks per position and competencies demanded. If other researchers would like to do a different coding on our data, we would share them.

6   Summary and Outlook

This study analyses 141 job advertisements from 2009 and 67 from 2012 with respect to the practice of RE. Which job titles do those have who do RE, which further tasks do they have and which competencies are demanded?

The job title "Requirements Engineer" hardly exists. RE tasks are done by persons who have different job titles and an average of 4.23 respectively 3.79 tasks. In few cases, the job title explicitly was a double role. RE is most often done by persons with the job title consultant. RE is most often combined with solution conception, realisation and quality assurance.

For doing RE, studies or apprenticeship are important preconditions, as well as work experience. However, specific RE knowledge is demanded explicitly only at 37% in 2009 and 34% in 2012. Further competencies demanded are soft skills, technical knowledge and previous experience with a specific task. The most important soft skills are English language, communication skills and capacity for teamwork.

Future studies could analyse similar data for other countries to compare internationally how RE is integrated into the organization. Furthermore, the study can be repeated in 2015 to observe trends for a longer period of time. Another approach could be to ask the four RQ in a questionnaire survey among practitioners or to analyse work conditions in case studies. Such studies can reveal differences between job advertisements and the reality of daily work.

References

[1] Abran, A., Moore, J.W.: SWEBOK: Guide to the Software Engineering Body of Knowledge. IEEE Computer Society, Los Alamitos (2004)

[2] Alenljung, B., Persson, A.: Factors that Affect Requirements Engineers in their Decision Situations: A Case Study. In: REFSQ Workshop 2005, pp. 25–39 (2005)

[3] Alexander, I., Robertson, S., Maiden, N.: What Influences the Requirements Process in Industry? – A Report on Industrial Practice. In: Proceedings of 13th International Requirements Engineering Conference, pp. 411–415 (2005)

[4] Aurum, A., Wohlin, C.: Requirements engineering: setting the context. In: Aurum, A., Wohlin, C. (eds.) Engineering and Managing Software Requirements, 1st edn., p. 478. Springer, Berlin

[5] Berry, D.M.: The Importance of Ignorance in Requirements Engineering. Journal of Systems and Software 28(1), 179–184 (1995)

[6] Curtis, B., Krasner, H., Iscoe, N.: A field study of the software design process for large systems. Communications of the ACM 31, 1268–1287 (1988)

[7] Jantunen, S.: The Benefit of Being Small: Exploring Market-Driven Requirements Engineering Practices in Five Organizations. In: 1st Workshop RE in Small Companies (RESC), 29th June 2010 at the REFSQ 2010 Conference in Essen (2010)

[8] Klendauer, R., Berkovich, M., Gelvin, R., Leimeister, J.M., Krcmar, H.: Towards a competency model for requirements analysts. Information Systems Journal 22(6), 475–503 (2012)

[9] Neill, C.J., Laplante, P.A.: Requirements Engineering: State of the Practice. IEEE Software 20(6), 40–45 (2003)

[10] Nikula, U., Sajaniemi, J., Kalviainen, H.: Management view on current requirements engineering practices in small and medium enterprises. In: Proc. Australian Workshop on Requirements Engineering (2000)

[11] PMI: A Guide to the Project Management Body of Knowledge - 3rd edn. PMI (2004)

[12] Prikladnicki, R., Audy, J.L.N., Evaristo, R.: An Empirical Study on Global Software Development: Offshore Insourcing of IT Projects. In: Proceedings of the International Workshop on Global Software Development, International Conference on Software Engineering (ICSE 2004), pp. 53–58. IEEE, Edinburgh (2004)

[13] Sommerville, I., Kotonya, G.: Requirements Engineering: Processes and Techniques. Wiley & Sons, Chichester (1998)

[14] Strauss, A.L., Corbin, J.M.: Basics of qualitative research grounded theory procedures and techniques, vol. 6. Sage, Newbury Park (1991)

[15] Weißbach, R.: Bridging the Communication Gap in Information System Projects – Enabling Non-IT Professionals for the Requirements Engineering Process. In: CARPE Networking Conference (2011),
http://julkaisut.turkuamk.fi/isbn9789522162519.pdf

[16] Zowghi, D., Damian, D., Offen, R.: Field Studies of Requirements Engineering in a Multi-Site Software Development Organization. In: Proc. Australian Workshop on Requirements Engineering. Univ. of New South Wales (2001)

Effective Requirements Elicitation in Product Line Application Engineering – An Experiment

Sebastian Adam[1] and Klaus Schmid[2]

[1] Fraunhofer IESE, Fraunhofer-Platz 1, 67663 Kaiserslautern
sebastian.adam@iese.fraunhofer.de
[2] University of Hildesheim, Hildesheim, Germany
schmid@sse.uni-hildesheim.de

Abstract. [**Context & Motivation**] Developing new software systems based on a software product line (SPL) is still a time-consuming task and the benefits of using such an approach are often smaller than expected. One important reason for this are difficulties in systematically mapping customer requirements to characteristics of the SPL. [**Question/problem**] Even though it has been recognized that the success of reuse strongly depends on how requirements are treated, it remains unclear how to perform this in an optimal way. [**Principal ideas/results**] In this paper, we present a controlled experiment performed with 26 students that compared two requirements elicitation approaches when instantiating a given SPL. [**Contribution**] Our findings indicate that a novel, problem-oriented requirements approach that explicitly integrates the reuse of SPL requirements into the elicitation of customer-specific requirements is more effective than a traditional SPL requirements approach, which distinguishes requirements reuse and additional elicitation customer-specific requirements.

1   Introduction

As a key concept for streamlining software development, software product lines (SPL) [1] have proven to be a promising strategy, especially when time to market is a crucial success factor. Basically, software product lines comprise *"a set of software-intensive systems that share a common, managed set of features satisfying the specific needs of a particular market segment and that are developed from a common set of core assets in a prescribed way"* [1]. Hence, the core idea of SPL-approaches is to engineer a set of reusable assets that can be composed and tailored according to pre-defined characteristics (so-called variabilities). The creation of these assets is called domain engineering (DE). Nevertheless, developing new systems based on an SPL (which is denoted as application engineering (AE)) is still a time-consuming task [3], and the benefits of using an SPL approach are often smaller than expected [4].

One important reason for the sub-optimal efficiency in AE is the non-systematic mapping of customer-specific requirements to SPL capabilities [6], even though it has been recognized that the success of AE mainly depends on how requirements are treated [18]. This is especially a problem in SPLs, in which the ideal prerequisite of a SPL does not hold, i.e., in which a significant number of customer-specific

J. Doerr and A.L. Opdahl (Eds.): REFSQ 2013, LNCS 7830, pp. 362–378, 2013.

requirements exist or often customer-specific variations are necessary. Due to the differences in customer-vocabulary and content of the requirements, it is very difficult to identify the best support the SPL can give to address the customer-demands. Thus, many companies have significant problems in requirements engineering during the AE phase, even though they still take advantage of the SPL approach in general, i.e., with regard to the common core features. The reason for this problem is that existing SPL methods just focus on the direct reuse of explicitly stated SPL requirements while neglecting the handling of "near-misses". Thus, it is very hard, if not impossible, to achieve effective alignment of actual customer needs with the available SPL capabilities [8, 9]. However, forcing requirements engineers to restrict elicitation to picking reusable requirements is not sufficient, if systems must take into account also several customer-specific requirements to maximize value. In order to identify those customer-specific requirements, traditional RE approaches are therefore additionally used. However, since using an SPL approach implies a certain set of constraints, not all these requirements can be realized as initially stated. Rather, trade-offs between ideal requirements and an optimized cost-benefit ratio must be made. So far, making this trade-off is challenging, as information about the feasibility of requirements is typically not explicitly available beyond the explicitly stated SPL variabilities.

Requirements elicitation in AE thus becomes an error-prone task and it relies on experts to predict the impact of requirements that can only be realized with additional development [6]. Hence, it is still hard to elicit requirements systematically in such a way that they are well aligned with a given SPL. In many cases, costly corrections are therefore needed in AE until a delivered system fulfills the customer's expectations.

In order to solve this problem, we need a requirements engineering (RE) approach for AE (called ARE) that is enriched with information about the possibilities of a given SPL beyond its explicitly anticipated features. This approach would offer precise elicitation guidelines, but also enough flexibility to enable the discussion of customer-specific requirements within the constraints of an SPL. However, as making requirements engineers aware of SPL characteristics is not easy, a scientific problem to be addressed deals with the question of how requirements engineers can be enabled to use sound product and process knowledge for guiding the elicitation more effectively.

While we have already discussed our ideas and solutions in this regard (see [2, 5, 7]) empirical evidence on corresponding benefits in comparison to state of the art ARE has not yet been sufficiently provided. In [2], we did show that an integrated ARE approach is suitable in its intended context, but we did not provide findings about concrete improvements. Thus, we present here an empirical study that was carried out to compare state of the art elicitation with an elicitation based on our approach.

In the next section, we introduce the approaches that were compared. In section 3, the controlled experiment is described. The paper closes with a conclusion in section 4.

2   Compared and Related Approaches

To the best of our knowledge, elicitation effectiveness has not been addressed in the context of AE so far. Thus, related work mostly consists of other approaches to ARE.

As this was already described exhaustively in [2], we will not duplicate it here and focus on a brief summary of the compared approaches. Basically, we introduce a state of the art approach for requirements engineering in AE, which we call "traditional ARE approach", and contrast it with our own approach [2, 22], which we call "integrated ARE approach" in this paper.

Basically, ARE is the requirements process in AE comprising the elicitation, analysis, specification, validation, and management of requirements for a system to be derived from a SPL. In contrast to single system RE, ARE must therefore be strongly aligned with the given SPL in order to assure that elicited requirements can be economically satisfied by exploiting the already existing SPL assets.

2.1   Traditional ARE Approach

Even if there is no common AE method, many traditional AE approaches share the ideas of Deelstra et al. [16] and distinguish an initial configuration phase (with direct reuse) and a phase of tuning iterations (with adaptations). Within the corresponding ARE, there is therefore an instantiation of an SPL's variable requirements that were explicitly anticipated and created during domain requirements engineering (DRE), and an elicitation of additional, customer-specific requirements from scratch [17]. For the first part, AE requirements engineers are typically provided with feature catalogues, variability models (VM), and/or reusable requirements that must be processed during elicitation [11]. This is also correspondingly implemented in tools [20] and supported by decision models' questionnaires [14]. Hence, for each explicitly anticipated variation point described in these models (e.g., "data base to be connected"), the foreseen variants (e.g., Oracle, IBM, MySQL) and their resulting implications are communicated to the stakeholder, who then makes a corresponding selection. For the second part, an additional requirements elicitation from scratch then takes place, ignoring the SPL context. This means that for all requirements not yet covered during DE, requirements approaches like those used in single system development are chosen (e.g., top-down approaches that starts with goals or tasks to be supported). Hence, in contrast to the discussion of explicit variants before, these approaches do not support an early assessment whether new requirements are feasible at which cost with the given SPL architecture.

2.2   Integrated ARE Approach

In our integrated ARE approach (see [2, 22]), there is no explicit distinction between the instantiation of variable requirements of an SPL and the elicitation of additional, customer-specific requirements. Rather, all customer requirements for a system to be derived from an SPL are elicited in an integrated top-down manner following a set of relevant requirements types to be discussed.

The main difference between this approach and the traditional approach is that customers are not explicitly asked which predefined SPL features they would like to have (solution-oriented requirements). Rather, their real needs and requirements are systematically analyzed in a problem-oriented manner, e.g., by considering goals,

Table 1. Analytic Comparison of Approaches

	Traditional ARE	Integrated ARE
Elicitation Phases	SPL instantiation + additional "from scratch" elicitation (if needed)	Integrated elicitation
Elicitation Drivers	Variation points + requirements types	Requirements types
Support for elicitation of already anticipated requirements	Predefined, enumerated variants and corresponding SPL requirements	Predefined, enumerated variants and corresponding SPL requirements
Support for elicitation of customer-specific requirements	Elicitation instructions without information about SPL capabilities	Elicitation instructions with declarative descriptions of SPL capabilities
Basis for ARE approach	SPL requirements created during DE + reference RE process	Actually implemented SPL + development strategy + reference RE process
Preparation of ARE material	During DRE (domain requirements engineering)	During an explicit ARE tailoring activity

tasks, business processes, etc. Thus, the elicitation of requirements that are already defined in the SPL and those, which are not, is not explicitly separated any more, which enables the usage of the same elicitation techniques and styles throughout ARE.

Nevertheless, the approach always enables requirements engineers to be aware of all the given SPL capabilities and limitations when a certain requirements type is discussed. First, if there are already existing requirements of a certain requirements type in the SPL, the corresponding SPL variants and their detailed requirements are provided to be discussed with the stakeholders. For instance, when a set of data base systems is supported by default in the SPL, these data base systems can be directly reused in elicitation instead of re-analyzing them anew.

Second, if stakeholders state requirements of a certain type that have not already been anticipated, declarative statements are provided that clearly explain under which conditions these requirements are economically feasible as new variants within the constraints of the given SPL. This means that the characteristics a new requirement / variant must fulfill in order to be feasible with the given SPL architecture are explicitly defined to make early feasibility assessments. For instance, instead of enumerating all possible data base systems that can be connected, a declarative statement such as "all data base systems that support SQL2008 or higher and that fulfill the following characteristics ... can be connected" could be provided. This enables requirements engineers to directly intervene when a requirement tends to lead to unexpected development problems.

To enable the provision of both the already anticipated requirements and the declarative statements, the idea is to represent them together with precise elicitation instructions in an integrated instructions document that defines a meaningful elicitation sequence by covering all relevant requirements types. Hence, the elicitation support for the ARE phase cannot just be derived from the results of the DRE phase, but must be explicitly tailored based on additional information about the SPL architecture, the intended development strategy for AE, best practice in requirements elicitation, etc.

The integrated ARE approach is therefore – in contrast to the traditional ARE approach – derived from the actually implemented SPL as achieved at the end of an entire DE iteration. Hence, more knowledge can be provided to requirements engineers enabling them to cover a more flexible spectrum of customer requirements. The differences between the two approaches are summarized in Table 1.

3   Controlled Experiment

Effectiveness is basically "the extent to which an activity fulfills its intended purpose or function" [10] and helps to measure the quality of its outcome. In the context of RE, effectiveness has therefore been recognized as being indispensable for assuring the overall success of an engineering project right from the start [19]. In this section, a controlled experiment for evaluating the effectiveness of the aforementioned elicitation approaches in AE is shown.

3.1   Goal, Questions, Hypotheses and Metrics

We use the GQM approach [12] as a basis for defining the measurements in our experiment. The evaluation goal was to *analyze two elicitation approaches for the purpose of comparison with regard to elicitation effectiveness from the viewpoint of requirements engineers in the context of a controlled experiment with students.* More precisely, our main research question RQ_M to be answered was whether requirements elicitation in ARE is more effective when using our integrated ARE approach than when using a traditional ARE approach (see section 2). As elicitation is basically the process of communicating with stakeholders by which requirements are determined [11], this research question was broken down into two sub-questions with related hypotheses, and metrics. In this regard, we consider a research question to be answered with "yes", if at least one related (improvement) hypothesis is confirmed, and there are no indicates for being worse in any other related metric.

RQ_1: *"Does the integrated ARE approach enable requirements engineers to communicate more effectively with stakeholders than the traditional ARE approach?"*

As communication includes basically the imparting or exchanging of information by speaking [21], we expect that using the integrated ARE approach requirements engineers...

- H_{11} ask for more relevant information (# asked relevant questions) [1]
- H_{12} ask for less irrelevant information (# asked irrelevant questions)
- H_{13} provide more correct information to stakeholders (# correctly answered stakeholder questions / # posed stakeholder questions)
- H_{14} need less expert involvement (# elicited requirements marked as "to be checked by experts")

...than requirements engineers using the instructions of the traditional ARE approach. In this context, relevant information is information that is needed to make a design

---

[1] For reasons of brevity, we omit the corresponding null hypotheses here.

decision during AE, while irrelevant information is information that do not affect a decision at all [5]. Thus, these hypotheses focus on eliciting and discussing requirements in a competent and streamlined way.

RQ₂: *"Does the integrated ARE approach enable requirements engineers to achieve better results (i.e., requirements that largely fit the SPL capabilities while being relevant for making decisions, and for satisfying customers too) than with the traditional ARE approach?"*

According to the taxonomy of AE requirements also described in [5], we expect that requirements engineers using instructions according to the integrated ARE approach...

- H_{21} elicit fewer unnecessary requirements (# accepted common requirements / # initially stated common requirements)
- H_{22} elicit fewer problematic requirements (# accepted problematic requirements / # initially stated problematic requirements)
- H_{23} achieve a higher satisfaction fit (# accepted feasible requirements / # initially stated requirements)
- H_{24} achieve a higher realization fit (# accepted feasible requirements / # accepted requirements)

...than requirements engineers using traditional ARE. According to [22], problematic requirements are requirements that are hard to realize within the constraints of a given SPL, as they conflict with the underlying architecture, while feasible requirements do not (even though they have not been anticipated explicitly). In our experiment, we determined in a sample solution (based on a fictitious SPL) whether a certain requirement used during the experiment is problematic, or feasible, respectively whether a certain question is relevant or irrelevant (see section 3.2.3).

3.2   Experimental Design and Setup

Based on the study goals, the hypotheses, and the related metrics, the experiment was carefully designed and prepared. Thus, we aimed to constructively avoid as many threats to validity as possible. Below, we describe the details of the experiment setup.

3.2.1 Participants (Subjects)

The participants in the experiment (see Table 2) were 26 computer science students (four female, 22 male) from the Technical University of Kaiserslautern, Germany enrolled in the RE lecture. Five of them were bachelor students, while the others were enrolled in the master course. The participants were 23.9 years old on average, and participated voluntarily and without compensation in the experiment. They were not informed about our hypotheses or study goal beforehand, and were also not informed about the experimental group to which they were assigned. Regarding their background, ten participants had gathered requirements engineering experience also outside the RE lecture. However, only four participants had made more than three interviews for the purpose of elicitation already; the average was 0.8 interviews. Their self-assessed English competency on a scale of 1 (very good) to 5 (very bad) was good (1.8) on average, and only six participants mentioned that their English knowledge was just medium (3). Regarding knowledge of SPL engineering, 15 participants mentioned that they were aware of the basic concepts. However, no participant had practical experience with SPLs so far. The threats to validity of using these students for the experiment are discussed in section 3.4.

3.2.2 Experimental Design

The experiment was designed as a control group study (see Figure 1). The method group (MG) used the integrated ARE instructions according to the template described in [2]. In contrast, the control group (CG) used traditional ARE instructions according to a VM-based ARE approach combined with a TORE [13] guideline. The SPL specification in which the main SPL features and the SPL architecture were described was given to all participants. Thus, the control group was equipped with state of the art material, while the method group was equipped with our novel approach.

During the experiment, both groups performed fictitious but controlled elicitation interviews in order to gather requirements. The participants' performance was measured using the aforementioned variables in order to enable statistical comparison.

Each participant was randomly assigned to exactly one group. As far as possible, we tried to assign the participants to the groups alternately. This was the preferred strategy, as we did not know the participants before and considered the order of their commitment as random. However, in order to assure equal distribution of RE-experienced and less experienced participants in both groups, their RE background was taken into consideration. Thus, the information about interview experience provided in the pre-questionnaires was used for balancing the groups. A statistical test showed that a significant difference regarding RE experience between the two groups could not be confirmed. However, additional balancing of the participants according to their awareness of basic SPL concepts was not possible, as only six participants had experience in RE and SPL engineering. We discuss in section 3.4. its influence on the results.

Table 2. Assignment of participants to groups

	MG	CG
# Subjects	13	13
# Subjects in master course	11	10
Average age	23.3	24.5
# Averagely performed interviews before	0.9	0.7
Average language competency	1.8	1.8
# more RE experienced subjects	6	4
# SPL-aware subjects	10	5

3.2.3 Material

For the execution of the experiment, as well as for data collection and analysis, different artifacts were used (http://www.iese.fraunhofer.de/download/Material.zip). Participants of both groups received a pre-questionnaire about their personal background, an SPL specification (ten pages long), study instructions, and a post-questionnaire, which were the same for both groups. The post-questionnaire contained "agreement" questions on a 5-point Likert scale and open questions. The participants of the method group additionally got ARE instructions according to [2] (seven pages long), while the participants of the control group received "traditional" elicitation instructions including a VM-based questionnaire (four pages long). In the context of this experiment, we apply elicitation instructions based on TORE [13], which proposes deriving requirements from stakeholder tasks in a stepwise manner "top-down".

It has to be noted that the entire material package provided to both groups artificially contained the same information about the underlying SPL. The material differed only in the place (i.e., concrete document) and way this information was represented and the strategy for the elicitation (see section 2). Here, "artificially" means that the SPL specification (handed out to both groups) was supplemented with information typically not contained in this material. For instance, state of the art SPL specifications describe predefined variants for a certain variation point, but no further (architectural) constraints on how a completely new variant must look. Hence, for making the evaluation results more comparable, the SPL specification was augmented by such information in order to provide both groups with the same knowledge. Furthermore, the elicitation instructions of the control group were also made very precise in order to provide proper guidance to the (less experienced) participants also there. The reason for artificially adjusting the material was again to increase the groups' comparability in order to minimize corresponding threats.

Besides the material for the participants, material was also needed for the fictitious stakeholder and the experiment observer (see description of the procedure below). Thus, an observer checklist with 64 check criteria (e.g., "does the participant ask for user roles (yes / no)"?, "does the participant gives the right answers to stakeholder questions regarding additional costs (yes / no)"?, etc.) was derived from a sample solution. This checklist was aligned with a list of 27 prepared requirements and 12 interrupting questions (e.g., about additional costs) with which the fictitious stakeholder was prepared in order to standardize her behavior. By using this prepared checklist it was then possible to precisely count the number of accepted, respectively rejected relevant, irrelevant, problematic, and unnecessary requirements.

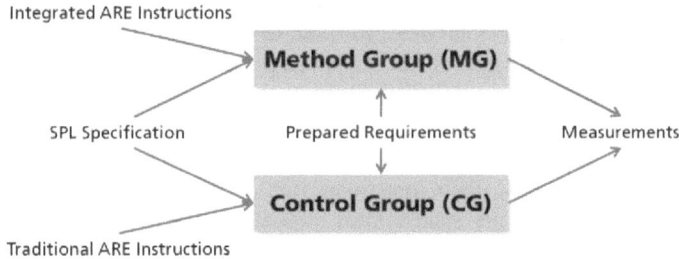

Fig. 1. Overall Setting of Experiment

3.2.4 Experiment Procedure and Data Collection

In order to assure the success of the experiment, the entire design and setup material was carefully analyzed by both RE experts and empirical research experts prior to experiment execution. After incorporating the received feedback, a student assistant was coached with the list of prepared requirements and interruption questions, as she had to play the role of a (fictitious) stakeholder who provides its requirements during the experiment. In order to check whether the material was understandable for the participants (who should play the role of a requirements engineer) and the fictitious stakeholder, and whether the scheduled timeframe was sufficient, we then performed a pilot run with two bachelor students. Thus, a pretest with the method group's material and one with the control group's material was carried out. The observations during this pretest were used to finally improve the material.

The experiment was split into 26 sessions of 90 minutes. The participants performed the experiment individually, as it was neither meaningful nor possible to let multiple participants perform elicitation interviews in parallel. In order to avoid the threat that one participant informs other participants about purpose, procedure, or material of the study, the participants had to sign a non-disclosure agreement that forbid them to disclose information until the end of the entire study. Further, before letting the participants perform the actual experiment, we used the pre-questionnaire for getting data about their experience, and for assigning them to a suitable group.

After group assignment, the participants received a package with the experiment material. Each participant could then use the first 35 minutes to become familiar with the material, before the actual experiment took place. This time was experienced as being sufficient because the students in the pretests needed less than 25 minutes both. In this experiment, the participants were asked to perform an elicitation role-play (in English) in which the fictitious stakeholder had to be interviewed using the provided material. The participants were asked to follow the provided elicitation instructions and to consider the SPL specification, if required (see Figure 2). The fictitious stakeholder stated the corresponding requirements that had been prepared during study planning and that were aligned with an observer checklist. To minimize threats due to differences in her behavior, we assured that she was not informed about which group a participant was assigned to. The fictitious stakeholder also posed questions to the participants; for instance, about the feasibility and costs of certain requirements. This was done in order to increase the representativeness of the study for elicitation sessions in the real world, as an interview in practice is never just a pure one-way communication. The purpose of these interruptions was to check whether the participants were able to provide sufficient information in order to make the elicitation more realistic.

An observer (played by the 1st author of this paper) tracked the interview questions asked by the participants, their reactions (i.e., acceptance or rejection) to the requirements of the fictitious stakeholder, as well as the answers to the fictitious stakeholder's interrupting questions using the aligned observer checklist. Hence, for each prepared requirement and interrupting question, there was a check item on the list in order to track whether the participants asked for this requirement, respectively how they reacted on it. The reason for using observations and not any specified results was that requirements elicitation and no specification was subject of our investigation. In particular, the likely heterogeneity in the quality of the participants' notes would probably have had a high impact on the evaluation so that no sound conclusion about elicitation performance could have been derived.

By using the filled observer checklists, the aforementioned metrics could be clearly determined by comparing it with the sample solution. In this regard, the usage of prepared requirements and a corresponding observer checklist aimed at making the results comparable, which would otherwise have been a significant threat to validity. Further, in order to avoid missing observations, the entire elicitation role-play was recorded using a voice recorder. The complete role-play took about 30 minutes on average in both groups. In a last step, the participants were asked to fill out a post-questionnaire in which they were asked to assess the helpfulness of the material.

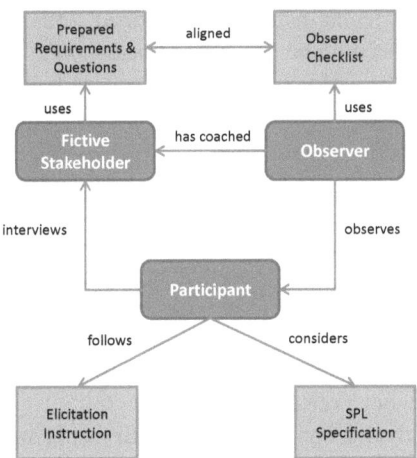

Fig. 2. Detailed Procedure and Data Collection

3.3   Experimental Analysis

3.3.1 Analysis Procedure

While data from the pre-questionnaire (e.g., age, interview experience, etc.) were directly entered into the statistical tool SPSS, the data gathered during observation (e.g., number of asked relevant questions, etc.) were recounted first in order to reduce the risk of measurement errors. The subjective ratings based on the Likert-scale in the post-questionnaire were collected in MS Excel. Additional qualitative comments were listed in MS Word. All data was processed anonymously and confidentially. For the quantitative observation data, descriptive statistics were then calculated. Further, the data distributions were analyzed using the Kolmogorov-Smirnov test. This was done to determine a suitable hypothesis test based on the different tests' assumptions regarding data distribution in an independent sample setting. For most hypotheses, we used the t-test for equality of means accordingly, except for those for which the Kolmogorov-Smirnov test had not confirmed equal distribution between the groups. As this was the case for H_{12}, H_{13}, H_{22}, we used the suitable independent samples median test instead. However, as the t-test is valid even under violation of its assumptions [15], we also used this test for non-parametric (but same) distributions. A cross-check with

Mann-Whitney U confirmed that the application of the t-test led to the same results. As all hypotheses were directional, we used one-tailed results with $\alpha=0.05$.

3.3.2 Observation Results

In this subsection, the observation results are shown (see Table 3) and explained.

Regarding the first hypothesis, which states that participants using the integrated ARE approach are able to ask more relevant questions, we found that there seems to be no significant difference (17.6 vs. 16.8). With a significance $p=0.166$, the corresponding null hypothesis "no difference or fewer" cannot be rejected. In contrast, the hypothesis that participants using the integrated ARE approach are able to ask fewer irrelevant questions could be confirmed ($mean_{MG}=0.77$ vs. $mean_{CG}=2.54$). Here, a significant difference between the method group and the control group could be observed. With $d=1.71$ and $p=0.002$, the corresponding null hypothesis "no difference or more" can be rejected.

Also the hypothesis that participants of the method group are able to provide more correct information about the SPL to the stakeholder could be confirmed ($mean_{MG}=0.77$ vs. $mean_{CG}=0.40$). With $d=1.49$ and $p=0.001$, the corresponding null hypothesis "no difference or fewer" can thus be rejected. However, even though the method group participants were able to provide more correct information on their own, there is no significant difference to the required expert involvement with $\alpha=0.05$ ($mean_{MG}=1.01$ vs. $mean_{CG}=1.62$). Thus, the corresponding null hypothesis "no difference or more" cannot be rejected.

However, as the method group was significantly better with regard to two metrics and not worse in the means of other two metrics (see Table 3), we consider *the integrated ARE approach to be better for enabling requirements engineers to communicate with stakeholders than when using the traditional approach.*

Table 3. Statistical Results of Experiment

		Mean	SD	t	p	reject H_0
H_{11}: #asked relevant questions*	MG	17.6	2.22	0.99	0.166	no
	CG	16.8	2.13			
H_{12}: #asked irrelevant questions	MG	0.77	0.93	-	0.002	yes
	CG	2.54	1.13			
H_{13}: # correctly answered stakeholder questions / # posed stakeholder questions	MG	0.77	0.20	-	0.001	yes
	CG	0.40	0.29			
H_{14}: # elicited requirements marked as „to be checked by experts"	MG	1.01	1.12	-	0.100	no
	CG	1.62	0.96	1.32		
H_{21}: # accepted common requirements / # initially stated common requirements	MG	0.62	0.36	1.42	0.084	no
	CG	0.81	0.33			
H_{22}: # accepted problematic requirements / # initially stated problematic requirements	MG	0.24	0.29	4.44	0.001	yes
	CG	0.70	0.25			
H_{23}: # accepted feasible requirements / # initially stated requirements	MG	0.64	0.06	1.52	0.071	no
	CG	0.59	0.08			
H_{24}: # accepted feasible requirements / # accepted requirements	MG	0.92	0.09	-	0.003	yes
	CG	0.83	0.07			

df=23, else df=24

Regarding the first hypothesis concerning "better results", which states that participants using the integrated ARE approach elicit fewer unnecessary requirements (i.e., requirements that are already implemented as commonalities with the SPL), we found that there seems to be no significant difference with $\alpha=0.05$ (mean$_{MG}$=0.62 vs. mean$_{CG}$=0.81). With $d=0.55$ and $p=0.084$, this hypothesis can therefore not be confirmed (i.e., the corresponding null hypothesis "no difference or higher" cannot be rejected). In contrast, the hypothesis that participants using the integrated ARE approach are able to elicit fewer problematic requirements could be confirmed (mean$_{MG}$=0.24 vs. mean$_{CG}$=0.70). With $d=1.73$ and $p=0.001$, the corresponding null hypothesis "no difference or more" can thus be rejected. However, with regard to the achievement of a higher satisfaction fit, which measures the degree to which a stakeholder's initially stated requirements are feasible and accepted, there seems to be no difference between the groups (mean$_{MG}$=0.64 vs. mean$_{CG}$=0.59). Thus, with $\alpha=0.05$, this difference is not significant, and the effect size d is only 0.56. The corresponding null hypothesis "no difference or lower" cannot be rejected. Finally, with regard to the practical problem that motivated our entire research, the last hypothesis could also be confirmed with $p=0.003$, and $d=1.12$. In particular, participants using the integrated ARE approach could achieve a 92% realization fit, while members of the control group only achieved 83% on average (+11%). This means that the degree of accepted requirements that are economically feasible with a given SPL is significantly higher when using the proposed approach than when using state of the art approaches. Thus, the corresponding null hypothesis "no difference or lower" can be rejected.

Again, as the method group is significantly better with regard to two metrics and not worse in the mean of the other metrics (see Table 3), we consider *the integrated ARE approach also more appropriate for achieving good results (i.e., requirements) than when using a traditional approach.* Thus, requirements elicitation in ARE seems to be more effective when using the integrated ARE approach.

3.3.3 Triangulation

During the interviews, the observer gathered several subjective impressions that were not tracked systematically, as we had not anticipated them before. In order to get an empirical explanation for these impressions, we established relationships (using statistical tests and qualitative analysis) between the objective observation data, the subjective assessment results, the qualitative comments, and the participants' backgrounds.

In the method group, only one participant objectively performed much worse than the other participants within this group. When considering the post-questionnaire of this participant, comprehension problems can be a potential explanation for this low performance. Interestingly, four further participants of the method group also mentioned comprehension problems with the instructions in their post-questionnaires. However, when considering the objective performance metrics, these participants did not perform significantly worse than the average in the method group. In line with their background, low English competency can thus be assumed as a possible explanation why they mentioned problems nevertheless. In the control group, five participants also mentioned handling problems or comprehension problems in their post-questionnaire, of which four participants actually performed worse than the average of their group. Interestingly, there were three other participants in the control group who also performed badly according to the defined measures, even though they did not mention any problems in their post-questionnaires. In order to get an answer to what the actual problems might be, we considered the background of all lower-performing participants. What most had in common was that they had already performed some interviews before. Thus, we hypothesize that they have had different expectations regarding what an elicitation session should look like and were therefore not willing to follow the precise guidelines described in the ARE instructions document.

This triangulation confirmed the subjective impression of the observer that the participants in the control group who claimed to have interview experience tended to invent their own questions and also gave their own answers to stakeholder questions. As a countermeasure when replicating the experiment, we recommend hindering participants to deviate too much from the ARE instructions document. However, when removing all RE-experienced participants from the sample, the confirmed hypotheses remain unchanged. Thus, we conclude that the non-compliant participants in the control group did not significantly affect the experimental results.

3.4   Threats to Validity

An important threat to *construction validity* is the mono-operation bias, as the study was performed based only on one fictitious SPL. Even though the detected improvement tendency is significantly valid within this setting, the actual improvements could differ when replicating the experiment in the context of other SPLs. Further, social threats to construct validity may also exist. Especially evaluation apprehension and experimenter expectancies may be issues. Even though the participants were explicitly informed that not their personal performance were being evaluated, most of them tried to look smart during the study. Thus, especially when they did not find sufficient information in the material fast, several participants tried to bring in their previous knowledge and experience, or to invent their own questions and answers (e.g., about security). Moreover, evaluation apprehension can be a reason why some participants only gave information about the feasibility of requirements when they were explicitly asked about this. When replicating the experiment, the participants should thus be instructed to adhere closer to the material. With regard to experimenter expectancies, there is the possible threat that the observer influenced the results unintentionally (e.g., by a certain look, comment, or interruption). When replicating the experiment, we thus recommend to not having an observer in the room again. Rather, the observer should sit behind a mirror glass or be replaced by video recording. However, this threat does not apply for the fictitious stakeholder, as she was not informed about the group assignments.

Concerning *internal validity*, the experiment was organized as single sessions, i.e., each participant did the study during a different timeslot. Thus, there is a risk that the concentration of the participants was different depending on which time of the day they participated, even though the distribution over a day was equal between the groups. There is also the risk that the intellectual capabilities and reading speed of the participants within the 35 minutes preparation slot may have an influence on the validity. However, as far as the experiment data can tell, this threat is of minor importance, as the participants of the method group, who had to read seven pages of instructions, performed better than the participants of the control group, who only had to read four pages. Further, as the experiment was a highly human-based process, there is a significant risk that also the fictitious stakeholder as well as the observer changed their behavior and attention within a day, and also within the course of sessions. In this regard, also learning effects can be assumed. However, in the measured data, we cannot detect any statistical difference between the participants at the beginning of the experiment and those at the end. In particular, as most participants were assigned alternately to the groups, all aforementioned threats are assumed to be rather low. With regard to material and instrumentation, further threats were also not detected. In particular, when running statistical tests without the participants, who mentioned comprehension or handing problems, the same hypotheses remain confirmed as when using the full set of participants. While we had an equal number of RE-experienced and less experienced people in both groups, there were twice as many people with SPL experience in the method group than in the control group, which may be a potential threat. However, when only comparing the SPL-experienced people in both groups, or only the SPL-inexperienced, we found that only hypothesis H_{12} (fewer irrelevant questions) does not hold anymore, while the other hypotheses remain unchanged.

The reliability of measures can be considered as a threat to *conclusion validity* as the performance metrics were just measured by one human observer using manual recording tools (e.g., pen and paper). This was especially a problem when the fictitious stakeholder interrupted a participant too early, as this made it sometimes hard to record whether a correct answer was given or whether a relevant question was posed. Further, the measured data could only be checked against a sample solution without having proven criteria for assessing the elicitation results. Thus, we recommend for replicating the experiment 1) more reliable instruments for observation, 2) clear rules for stakeholder's interruptions, 3) more precise assessment criteria for the requirements. While the statistical power was very high (up to ~1.00) and violation of statistical test assumptions avoided, another threat to conclusion validity could be the heterogeneity of the participants. Especially as students often differ significantly in their performance, the variance in each group would probably be lower with RE practitioners. Thus, while we had problems recruiting practitioners for our experiment, we recommend involving as many as possible when replicating the experiment.

Even though the elicitation interviews were made very realistic (e.g., by the interrupting questions, etc.), there are threats to *external validity*. An important threat in this regard is that all participants were students with less experience in RE or SPL engineering. However, it has to be noted that the approaches used in the experiment are, due to their precision, rather intended to be used by people (e.g., sales persons) without profound knowledge in requirements or product line engineering than by RE or SPL experts. Nevertheless, it makes sense to involve a group of such practitioners in order to increase the external validity of the results in future studies. The same threat holds true with regard to the fictitious SPL specification. Indeed, an external expert checked the SPL specification for realism. However, depending on the style and content of SPL specifications in industry, the effectiveness of the different ARE approaches may differ. Furthermore, elicitation sessions in practice are typically more complex and more interactive, involving a multitude of people, workshop techniques, etc. As such a setting cannot be replicated in a controlled environment, we recommend performing additional case studies in the future.

3.5   Interpretation and Possible Implications for Practice

Even though there were some threats to validity, the results of the controlled experiment have shown that our integrated ARE approach has the basic potential to let requirements engineers work more effectively in ARE. One significant result of the experiment is that participants of the method group asked fewer irrelevant questions than the participants of the control group. The reason for this improvement is that the elicitation instructions used in the method group were no generic "best practice" but tailored to the information needs of the fictitious SPL-context. However, it must also be noted that the time needed to perform the interviews was almost equal in both groups (~28 minutes). Thus, even though the higher effectiveness achieved in the same period indicates higher efficiency, no absolute time saving was achieved, because the time for irrelevant questions was spent on discussing other issues more thoroughly.

A second and third significant result of the experiment is that participants of the method group elicited fewer problematic requirements and achieved a higher realization fit than the control group participants. A likely reason for this improvement is that the existing constraints are explicitly mentioned in corresponding places in the method group's instructions. Apparently, such a direct representation of constraints in the elicitation instructions seems to be more suitable. As an implication for practice, better fitting requirements are therefore expected to be elicited, which could lead to less costly rework or late re-elicitations. Thus, it is expected that also the overall AE-efficiency may increase. Of course, this new hypothesis still has to be evaluated in industrial case studies. The final significant result is that participants of the method group could correctly answer more stakeholder questions than participants of the control group. The reason for this improvement is probably that process and product knowledge about a SPL is represented more appropriately in the instructions according to [2] than in the material given to the control group. A practical implication of this improvement could be that requirements engineers are enabled to discuss in a more competent way, which is indispensable when customer requirements are put into question or even rejected.

Finally, in our study, the method group did not perform worse in any metric than the control group. A likely explanation is that the integrated ARE approach enhances the state of the art and does not replace it. Thus, requirements engineers using this approach in practice should benefit without having any relevant drawbacks, at least in the context of SPLs where explicit requirements anticipation is limited.

4   Conclusion

Empirical evidence about elicitation effectiveness in ARE is rare, and there is still no best practice. This paper has therefore presented a controlled experiment in order to compare a state of the art ARE approach with a novel, integrated ARE approach [2].

The results of the study have shown that an approach, which incorporates product and process knowledge directly into top-down AE elicitation instructions, has the potential to enable requirements engineers to perform a significantly more effective elicitation than when focusing too much on the anticipated solution space. In particular, fewer irrelevant questions can be asked, more correct information can be provided to stakeholders, and fewer problematic requirements can be elicited when using an integrated ARE approach. This may finally lead to a higher realization fit in comparison to traditional ARE approaches.

For the future, it is interesting to see whether the effectiveness improvements could also lead to higher efficiency of AE as a whole. As it is difficult to investigate this in a controlled setting, we are going to transfer our approach to industry. In this context, it is – of course – important to see which investment is needed for this rollout. Our first experience with a medium-size SPL has shown that the integrated ARE approach can be introduced in about one person week, which seems to be an effort that should pay off, at least when rework during a project can be reduced by ~11% as in our study.

Acknowledgment. The work presented in this paper was performed in the context of the Software Cluster project EMERGENT (www.software-cluster.org). It was partially funded by the German Federal Ministry of Education and Research (BMBF) under grant no. "01IC10S01". The authors assume responsibility for the content. We thank all internal and external reviewers as well as the study participants for supporting us in preparing, executing, analyzing, and publishing the described experiment.

References

1. Clements, P., Northrop, L.: Software Product Lines: Patterns and Practice. Addison Wesley (2001)
2. Adam, S.: Providing software product line knowledge to requirements engineers – A template for elicitation instructions. In: Regnell, B., Damian, D. (eds.) REFSQ 2011. LNCS, vol. 7195, pp. 147–164. Springer, Heidelberg (2012)
3. Deelstra, S., Sinnema, M., Bosch, J.: Product derivation in software product families: a case study. The Journal of Systems and Software 74 (2005)
4. Rabiser, R., Grünbacher, P., Dhungana, D.: Supporting Product Derivation by Adapting and Augmenting Variability Models. In: SPLC. IEEE (2007)
5. Adam, S.: Towards Faster Application Engineering through Better Informed Elicitation – A Research Preview. In: REEW@RefSQ 2011, Essen (2011)
6. O'Leary, P., Rabiser, R., Richardson, I., Thiel, S.: Important Issues and Key Activities in Product Derivation: Experiences from Independent Research Projects. In: SPLC (2009)
7. Adam, S., Doerr, J., Ehresmann, M., Wenzel, P.: Incorporating SPL Knowledge into a Requirements Process for Information Systems. In: PLREQ @ REfSQ 2010. Essen (2010)
8. Djebbi, O., Salinesi, C.: RED-PL, a method for deriving product requirements from a product line requirements model. In: Krogstie, J., Opdahl, A.L., Sindre, G. (eds.) CAiSE 2007. LNCS, vol. 4495, pp. 279–293. Springer, Heidelberg (2007)

9. Guelfi, N., Perrouin, G.: A Flexible Requirements Analysis Approach for Software Product Lines. In: Sawyer, P., Heymans, P. (eds.) REFSQ 2007. LNCS, vol. 4542, pp. 78–92. Springer, Heidelberg (2007)

10. Analytic Quality Glossary: Effectiveness, http://www.qualityresearchinternational.com/glossary/effectiveness.htm (last visited: February 17, 2012)

11. Bühne, S., Halmans, G., Lauenroth, K., Pohl, K.: Scenario-Based Application Requirements Engineering. In: Software Product Lines. Springer (2006)

12. Basili, V.R., Caldiera, G., Rombach, H.D.: Goal Question Metric Paradigm. In: Encyclopedia of Software Engineering, vol. 1, pp. 528–532. John Wiley & Sons (1994)

13. Adam, S., Doerr, J., Eisenbarth, M., Gross, A.: Using Task-oriented Requirements Engineering in Different Domains – Experiences with Application in Research and Industry. In: Proceedings of RE 2009. IEEE (2009)

14. Bayer, J., Gacek, C., Muthig, D., Widen, T.: PuLSE-I: Deriving Instances from a Product Line Infrastructure. In: Proceedings of Conference and Workshop on the Engineering of Computer-based Systems. IEEE (2000)

15. Zimmermann, D.: Comparative Power of Student T Test and Mann-Whitney U Test for Unequal Sample Sizes and Variances. Journal of Experimental Education (1987)

16. Deelstra, S., Sinnema, M., Bosch, J.: Product derivation in software product families: a case study. The Journal of Systems and Software 74 (2005)

17. Eriksson, M., Börstler, J., Borg, K.: Managing requirements specifications for product lines – An approach and industry case study. Journal of Systems and Software (2009)

18. Laguna, M.A., López, O., Crespo, Y.: Reuse, Standardization, and Transformation of Requirements. In: Dannenberg, R.B., Krueger, C. (eds.) ICSR 2004. LNCS, vol. 3107, pp. 329–338. Springer, Heidelberg (2004)

19. The Standish Group International.: CHAOS Manifesto (2011), http://blog.standishgroup.com (last visited: January 18, 2012)

20. Schmid, K., Kennrich, K., Eisenbarth, M.: Requirements management for product lines: extending professional tools. In: Proceedings of Software Product Line Conference (2006)

21. Oxford Dictionary, http://oxforddictionaries.com/definition/english/communication

22. Adam, S.: Incorporating SPL Knowledge into Requirements Processes. PhD Theses in Experimental Software Engineering, vol. 44. Fraunhofer Verlag (to appear, 2013)

Monitoring System-of-Systems Requirements in Multi Product Lines

Thomas Klambauer[1], Gerald Holl[1], and Paul Grünbacher[2]

[1] Christian Doppler Laboratory for Automated Software Engineering
Johannes Kepler University Linz, Austria
{klambauer,holl}@ase.jku.at
[2] Institute for Systems Engineering and Automation
Johannes Kepler University Linz, Austria
paul.gruenbacher@jku.at

Abstract. [**Context and motivation**] Large-scale software-intensive systems are often considered as systems of systems comprising several interrelated product lines from which system variants are derived to meet the overall requirements. [**Question/problem**] If multiple teams and experts configure these individual systems, their individual configuration choices might conflict with the system-of-systems requirements. [**Principal ideas/results**] This research preview paper presents our ongoing work on a tool-supported approach for monitoring system-of-systems requirements formalized as constraints during distributed product derivation in multi product lines. [**Contribution**] The approach allows detecting violations of multi system requirements during the configuration of individual systems and provides immediate feedback to the involved configurers. Our approach is integrated in the product configuration tool DOPLER developed in cooperation with an industrial partner.

1 Introduction

Complex systems in the domains of industrial plants, transportation, or healthcare can often be considered as system of systems (SoS) integrating multiple independent and self-contained systems to satisfy the customer's requirements. Requirements engineering for systems of systems is challenging as it needs to address requirements at both the level of individual components and the overall system. For instance, SoS in the domain of metallurgical plants comprise multiple cooperating systems that need to work together to meet the contractual requirements. In such domains many of the customer requirements can be realized by configuring existing components rather than by adapting existing or developing new components. This means that the requirements are fairly stable and well-understood and development can benefit significantly from employing product line techniques to increase the degree of reuse and to accelerate the time-to-customer.

Frequently, the individual systems of an SoS are represented by separate product lines (PLs) which then together form a *multi product line* (MPL) [1]. The

J. Doerr and A.L. Opdahl (Eds.): REFSQ 2013, LNCS 7830, pp. 379–385, 2013.
© Springer-Verlag Berlin Heidelberg 2013

derivation of products in MPLs is usually performed in a distributed manner by multiple teams and experts [2]. Satisfying customer requirements is thus challenging as the configuration of the individual PLs needs to be coordinated. *Individual system requirements* (ISRs) in such a context restrain only single systems in an SoS while *multi-system requirements* (MSR) affect the entire SoS. For instance, the configurers might need to satisfy a throughput ISR of a processing system in an SoS and an energy consumption MSR. During product derivation it is thus essential to coordinate and adjust the configuration of the individual PLs to meet the MSRs. In a previously conducted case study [2] we showed that the situation is further aggravated as configurers of individual systems, while experts within that system, have only limited knowledge of the overall SoS which makes violations of MSRs more likely.

The development of SoS has been compared to the development of cities rather than the development of individual houses [3]. This means that requirements cannot be engineered in a top-down fashion. Rather, they need to be permanently *monitored* during configuration to immediately detect violations affecting the overall SoS. MSRs limit the realization options of configurers and can be seen as *constraints*. We aim at developing an approach that helps preventing the violation of MSRs in MPLs by checking these constraints.

Our work is related to existing research in requirements engineering and product line engineering (PLE). For instance, issues of refining and operationalizing requirements have been addressed in areas such as requirements-based monitoring [4, 5], architectural refinement of requirements [6], or the specification of quality requirements [7] to name but a few. In the PLE community, different approaches provide support for distributed configuration. For instance, Mendonca et al. [8] propose a collaborative and coordinated product configuration process which is guided by deriving a process model from an annotated feature model. Hubaux et al. [9] support configuration workflows based on multi-level staged configuration. In our own research we explored dependencies between individual PLs in MPLs [10] and investigated tool support for raising awareness of multi-system issues during distributed configuration [2].

This preview of our ongoing research presents highlights of our approach for monitoring MSRs formalized as constraints during the distributed configuration of MPLs. Our focus is on formalizing quantitative requirements which are frequent in the domain of our industrial partner. Our approach comprises a constraint specification system for MPLs using decision-oriented variability models [11] and an incremental consistency checking framework based on [12] checking the MSRs during the distributed configuration of an MPL. It provides tools informing configurers about deviations from requirements during distributed configuration.

2   Problem Illustration

Our industry partner Siemens VAI is developing and engineering large-scale systems in the domain of metallurgical plants comprising complex interdependent software-intensive systems sizing up to several million lines of code. Examples are continuous casting machines, furnaces, and rolling mills (cf. Fig. 1). The customers' requirements regarding such an SoS are manifold. MSRs affect the overall SoS and are thus particularly challenging to manage and realize. Frequent examples include requirements and constraints such as product costs, time to market, energy consumption, weight limitations, or CO_2 emissions. When a new metallurgical plant is erected, analysts formulate technical and economical requirements for the SoS to meet the customer's needs. Some will affect an individual system (Vacuum treatment in Fig. 1), while others affect multiple systems (Furnace, Caster, Rolling mill). For instance, there might be requirements regarding CO_2 emission affecting all systems of the metallurgical plant.

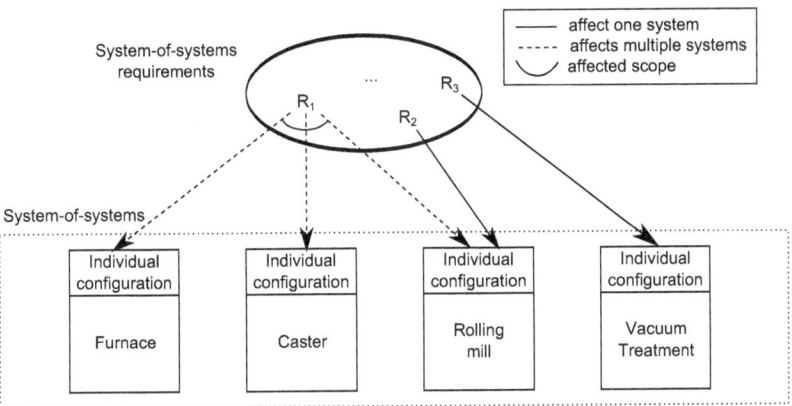

Fig. 1. MSRs affecting multiple systems in SoS need to be monitored during distributed configuration. ISRs can be met by configuring a single system.

In industrial practice suppliers define the variability of product lines to ease the derivation of a final product. For instance, variability models might exist for Furnace, Caster, Rolling mill, or Vacuum treatment. Experts can then configure the individual systems to comply with the requirements. However, there is a risk that experts lack the global perspective and are unaware of the configuration state of other systems which means that they might unintentionally violate requirements.

Examples of MSRs are resource constraints the PLs under configuration need to satisfy. For instance, a configurer in charge of a single system in an SoS may not be aware that his choices violate CO_2 restrictions. Another example are consistency constraints that need to be met to prevent contradictory configuration values between components. For instance, different configurers might choose conflicting locales or incompatible software interfaces.

In MPLs the MSRs cannot be engineered in a top-down manner. The systems constituting the SoS are PLs and the properties of the SoS thus emerge during product derivation. This means that requirements need to be *monitored* permanently to avoid deviations during the configuration process. This is challenging for MPLs comprising many PLs, a high number of contraints to be checked, and complex contraints involving business calculations and multiple PLs. Another challenge lies in providing immediate feedback to configurers in case of violations. Furthermore, requirements may be changed during the configuration process which requires a highly flexibly approach.

3   Monitoring Requirements during Configuration

In our ongoing research we are thus developing an approach that allows analysts formalizing SoS requirements, specifically MSRs, as constraints which are then monitored during the distributed product derivation in an MPL. This is reasonable as requirements in the investigated domain are stable and play a role in multiple systems developed over time. We use an incremental checking approach [12–14] which minimizes the need for re-evaluation by only considering changes of elements referenced by the constraint to provide instant feedback to configurers. Our framework allows adding and changing constraints at runtime to deal with updates of MSRs during configuration. The framework is integrated in the DOPLER product configuration tool [15] and uses an MPL model [2]. It constantly monitors the constraints and immediately notifies configurers in case constraints are violated. In contrast to related approaches that rely on satisfiability analysis (e.g., [16]), we do not aim at automatically suggesting fixes to conflicting configuration choices. Our discussion with industrial experts have shown that requirements conflicts need to be resolved by discussion to achieve consensus.

Fig. 2 shows the architecture and overall workflow. We will illustrate the approach using a simple example based on an earlier study [2]. We present two PLs of an MPL for a continuous steel casting machine: A *mold system*, which shapes the liquid steel into the desired width and thickness, and a *strand system* which bends the molded steel for further processing. However, the bend radius achievable by the strand is limited by its thickness. This represents an MSR which might be formulated as follows: *"The ratio of strand radius to mold thickness has to be within a 10% range of 30:1."*

The analyst formalizes this informal requirement as a constraint in the *Constraint Editor*. This is done using a subset of the Java language operating on provided PL model elements such as configuration choices (decisions values) and other attributes of the derived product [11]. We selected Java as host language due to the expressiveness required to formalize the constraints found in the domain.

The simple example constraint is shown in Listing 1.1. Depending on the current model configuration, the constraint evaluates to "Violated", "Fulfilled", or "Not applicable" (if the values determining the constraint state are not yet defined by the configurers). All constraints defined by the analyst are managed in a *Constraint Database* for the MPL.

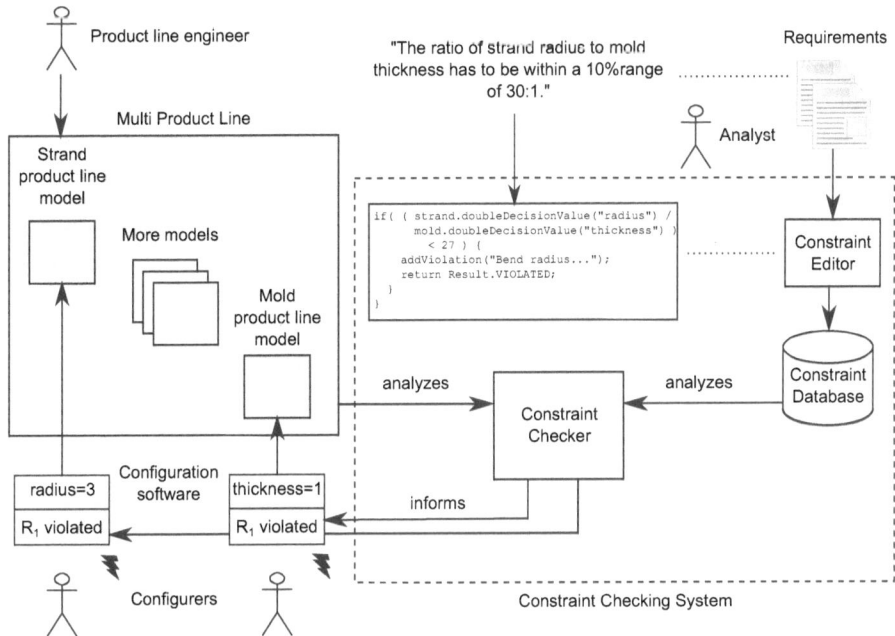

Fig. 2. Constraint specification and checking architecture

Listing 1.1. Example constraint code fragment

```
// models for tundish and ladle are already loaded
if( ( strand.doubleDecisionValue("radius") /
      mold.doubleDecisionValue("thickness") ) < 27 ) {
    addViolation("Bend radius too small for mold thickness");
    return Result.VIOLATED;
}
if( ( strand.doubleDecisionValue("radius") /
      mold.doubleDecisionValue("thickness") ) > 33 ) {
    addViolation("Bend radius bigger than necessary");
    return Result.VIOLATED;
}
return Result.OK;
```

During the distributed configuration of all PLs in the MPL the *Constraint Checker* monitors the changes made to the PL model to instantly determine violations of the MSRs. For instance, when an expert configures the mold or strand system, the checker evaluates the available constraints after each change and immediately informs the configurer in case of a violation to increase awareness about deviations from the MSRs. Our approach is iterative to allow adding, removing, or changing requirements even during configuration.

4   Summary and Outlook

Requirements Engineering for systems of systems is an emerging area of research. Based on our experience of developing MPL models for industrial plants we have been developing an approach for monitoring requirements compliance during product derivation in an MPL. Our goal is to ease the distributed configuration of systems of systems by providing instant feedback to configurers about deviations from requirements. Our approach assists analysts in specifying requirements as constraints and allows adding requirements at any time to ensure flexibility. The basic assumption that requirements are formalizable is met in the context as the requirements of our domain are generally well-understood and fairly stable. Furthermore, the approach does not require that all requirements are formalizable. Our current tool prototype provides the functionality to support the basic workflow. The approach is iterative meaning that changes can be made to requirements at any time. We plan to evaluate the approach with industrial users based on further MPL models.

References

1. Holl, G., Grünbacher, P., Rabiser, R.: A systematic review and an expert survey on capabilities supporting multi product lines. Information and Software Technology 54(8), 828–852 (2012)
2. Holl, G., Grünbacher, P., Elsner, C., Klambauer, T.: Supporting awareness during collaborative and distributed configuration of multi product lines. In: Proc. of the 19th Asia-Pacific Software Engineering Conference, Hong Kong (2012) (to appear)
3. Northrop, L., Feiler, P., Gabriel, R., Goodenough, J., Linger, R., Longstaff, T., Kazman, R., Klein, M., Schmidt, D., Sullivan, K., Wallnau, K.: Ultra-Large-Scale Systems – The Software Challenge of the Future. Software Engineering Institute, Carnegie Mellon (2006)
4. Robinson, W.N.: A requirements monitoring framework for enterprise systems. Requir. Eng. 11(1), 17–41 (2006)
5. Maiden, N.: Monitoring our requirements. IEEE Software 30(1), 16–17 (2013)
6. Vogl, H., Lehner, K., Grünbacher, P., Egyed, A.: Reconciling requirements and architectures with the CBSP approach in an iPhone app project. In: 19th IEEE International Requirements Engineering Conference, Trento, Italy, pp. 273–278 (2011)
7. Glinz, M.: A risk-based, value-oriented approach to quality requirements. IEEE Software 25(2), 34–41 (2008)
8. Mendonca, M., Cowan, D., Oliveira, T.: A process-centric approach for coordinating product configuration decisions. In: Proc. of the 40th Annual Hawaii Int'l Conference on System Sciences. IEEE Computer Society (2007)
9. Hubaux, A., Classen, A., Heymans, P.: Formal modelling of feature configuration workflows. In: Proc. of the 13th Int'l Software Product Line Conference, San Francisco, USA, pp. 221–230 (2009)
10. Holl, G., Thaller, D., Grünbacher, P., Elsner, C.: Managing emerging configuration dependencies in multi product lines. In: Proc. of the 6th Int'l Workshop on Variability Modeling of Software-Intensive Systems, pp. 3–10. ACM, Leipzig (2012)
11. Dhungana, D., Grünbacher, P., Rabiser, R.: The DOPLER meta-tool for decision-oriented variability modeling: a multiple case study. Automated Software Engineering 18(1), 77–114 (2011)
12. Egyed, A.: Instant consistency checking for the UML. In: Proc. of the 28th International Conference on Software Engineering, pp. 381–390 (2006)

13. Vierhauser, M., Grünbacher, P., Egyed, A., Rabiser, R., Heider, W.: Flexible and scalable consistency checking on product line variability models. In: Pecheur, C., Andrews, J., Nitto, E.D. (eds.) Proceedings 25th IEEE/ACM Int'l Conference on Automated Software Engineering, Antwerp, Belgium, September 20-24, pp. 63–72. ACM (2010)
14. Vierhauser, M., Grünbacher, P., Heider, W., Holl, G., Lettner, D.: Applying a consistency checking framework for heterogeneous models and artifacts in industrial product lines. In: Proc. of the 15th Int'l Conference on Model Driven Engineering Languages & Systems, Innsbruck, Austria (2012)
15. Rabiser, R., Grünbacher, P., Lehofer, M.: A qualitative study on user guidance capabilities in product configuration tools. In: Proc. of the 27th IEEE/ACM International Conference on Automated Software Engineering, Essen, Germany (2012)
16. Salinesi, C., Diaz, D., Djebbi, O., Mazo, R., Rolland, C.: Exploiting the versatility of constraint programming over finite domains to integrate product line models. In: 17th IEEE International Requirements Engineering Conference, RE 2009, pp. 375–376 (2009)

Adjusting to Increasing Product Management Problems: Challenges and Improvement Proposals in One Software Company

Sami Jantunen[1], Kati Hietaranta[2], and Donald C. Gause[3]

[1] Technology Business Research Center, Lappeenranta University of Technology,
FI-53851 Lappeenranta, Finland
[2] Maestro, Mannerheiminkatu 7, 53900 Lappeenranta, Finland
[3] Binghamton University and Savile Row, LLC, U.S.A.
sami.jantunen@lut.fi, kati.hietaranta@maestro.fi,
dgause@stny.rr.com

Abstract. **[Context and motivation]** This paper seeks to understand the essential product management challenges that one software product company has recently started to face. **[Question/problem]** The paper illustrates how the case company, Maestro, has been forced to adjust its management style due to the increasingly complex and turbulent business environment. The paper further illustrates how the evolving management style has affected the way product requirements are managed. **[Principal ideas/results]** The comparison of our results with existing product management literature suggests that traditional product management approaches are becoming increasingly inadequate to deal with growing amounts of interpretations, requirements interdependencies and market turbulence. **[Contribution]** The findings of this paper indicate a need for examining literature from management and organizational sciences in order to expand the traditional view of requirements models as static and purely design-time entities towards new kinds of approaches that are more effective in dealing with complexity and turbulence. The paper eventually results with an identification of research gaps and important topics for future research.

Keywords: Market driven requirements engineering, product management, organizing.

1   Introduction

The life of a company may be described as a series of developmental phases through which companies pass as they grow [1]. Each phase begins with a *period of evolution* and ends with a *revolutionary period* of substantial organizational turmoil and change [1]. Each evolutionary period is characterized by the dominant management style used to achieve growth. Management practices that work well in one phase may bring on a crisis in another. The critical task for managers in each revolutionary period is to find a new set of organizational practices that will become the basis for managing the next period of evolutionary growth [1].

J. Doerr and A.L. Opdahl (Eds.): REFSQ 2013, LNCS 7830, pp. 386–400, 2013.
© Springer-Verlag Berlin Heidelberg 2013

Many of the companies conducting software product business are growing companies. It is evident for such companies that their organizational practices do not remain stable [1]. We argue in this paper, that the changes in organizational practices influence strongly the way software product companies manage their product requirements. We further argue that existing requirements engineering approaches do not provide sufficient support for organizations that are increasingly facing challenges of requirements interdependencies, multiple interpretations and market turbulence. We illustrate our argument with an analysis of Maestro that has recently experienced a strong period of evolution and is now beginning to face a revolutionary period, with a need to adjust its current product management activities.

Our analysis seeks to find answers to two particular research questions: 1) what are the essential product management challenges that Maestro has recently faced, and 2) how would Maestro's personnel address these perceived challenges. The findings are then reflected on existing product management and organizational sciences literature in order to identify research gaps and important topics for future research.

The remainder of this paper is organized as follows. We first describe the case company, Maestro, with a brief historical analysis of how its business environment has changed in recent years (section 2). We then continue to describe the product management approach that Maestro is currently following (section 3). Section 4 then describes the research method of our study. Our findings, illustrating the perceived product management challenges and the gathered proposals to alleviate the experienced challenges, are then presented in section 5. Section 6 discusses our findings further, with a reflection to existing product management and organizational sciences literature and, finally, conclusions are drawn in section 7.

2   Description of the Case Company

Maestro is a software product company that provides extendable and comprehensive Enterprise Resource Planning (ERP) systems for small and medium sized enterprises and growth companies. Maestro started their business in 1986 by building software solutions to small accounting companies. At the time, software was developed in very close collaboration with customers. Collaborative software development style was positively experienced. People at Maestro understood deeply the details of customers' business processes and the means of supporting them the best possible way.

Since its establishment, Maestro has systematically extended its business. Product offering that once started from accounting and payroll software has been complemented with modules that support other business processes such as: finance management, material management, inventory management, electronic communications, sales and purchase, and reporting. In addition to the accounting companies, Maestro has extended its product offering to new customer segments including retail business, wholesale trade and chained commerce. Not only has the customer base become larger and more diverse, the size and complexity of existing customers' business has also increased. Consequently, Maestro's revenue has grown during the last five years approximately 25 percent per year.

Today, Maestro has evolved to be a company offering more than 90 software modules and over 30 products. The increased growth of Maestro's business has led to the increase of Maestro's personnel. Maestro currently employs 65 persons in the cities of Lappeenranta, Savonlinna and Helsinki. In addition, Maestro co-operates with domestic and international partners. These have been significant factors affecting the way products are managed and developed.

Over the years, increased complexity in business environment has caused challenges to the way Maestro manages and develops their software. Although, the gathered requirements across different customer segments and products have similarities with each other, they are not often entirely the same. The constraints and dependencies between customers' needs have become difficult to identify and manage. Due to customers' own growth, customers have become more specific and demanding regarding the functionality of Maestro's products. Consequently, the number of requirements and the pace they are gathered have continuously increased. Furthermore, the challenge of managing Maestro's products has become turbulent. Both technology and customers' processes are changing and developing rapidly. In order to keep supporting Maestro's customers' business processes, Maestro has been forced to implement increasingly complex and specific requirements at faster pace.

Rapid growth while offering wide range of products to a diverse set of customer segments has eventually made product management at Maestro increasingly difficult. Despite all the challenges, Maestro would still want to be close to its customers and genuinely listen to their business critical needs. In order to be able to keep accomplishing such objective, Maestro is forced to find new ways to deal with the challenge of managing its product development.

3   Product Management at Maestro

A simplified description of requirements management activities at Maestro is presented in Figure 1. All software development decisions at Maestro are influenced by the market needs. For such purpose, markets, technologies, customers, as well as the competitors, are continuously being tracked informally but actively. The primary result of the monitoring activities is increased knowledge that largely remains undocumented and is often tacit [2] by nature.

Another significant input for decision making is product-related ideas that may originate from anywhere in Maestro's organization or in the Maestro's value network. Typically, these ideas originate from customer specific systems development, sales, customer support, partner's organization or end users. All ideas and requests are submitted to the Events Management System (EMS) for which anyone has access, even the customer.

The management of the submitted proposals is visible to customers and includes several specific steps (Fig. 1).

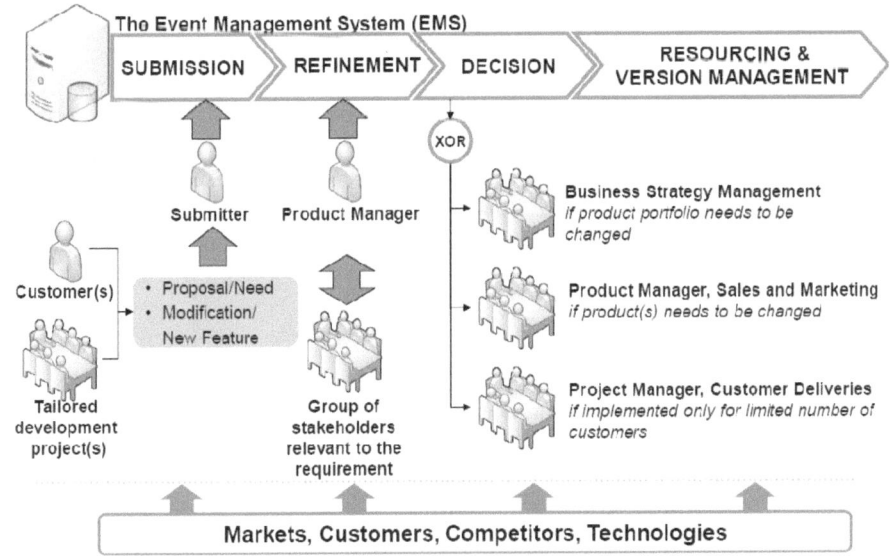

Fig. 1. Simplified description of requirements management activities at Maestro

At the time of *submission*, proposals are first linked to other proposals and/or customers. Each proposal is then always assigned to the product manager and to those specialists, who will be responsible on working the proposal further. Product manager is then responsible for further *refinement* of the requirement together with other relevant stakeholders such as project managers, partners, sales, customers, software developers.

The *decisions* related to the requirements are based on a number of different factors. Some of the questions decision makers need to consider include: Is the customer strategically important to Maestro? Is it a requirement that several customers need? Is there a significant financial impact? Did the requirement originate in conjunction of customer delivery project? Is the requirement mandatory? It should be noted that major customer deliveries also have significant impact on Maestro's product decisions.

Based on the diverse viewpoints to the proposal, the decisions of submitted proposals may occur in different parts of the organization. All strategic decisions are made by the management team that decides on significant changes to the existing product portfolio or existing products. Sales and marketing teams make general decisions of fitting the product and service offerings to the marketplace. If the submitted proposal will not be implemented to the core product, the proposal may still be implemented to a tailored customer delivery. In such case, the decision shall be made by the customer deliveries team.

4   Research Method

The study describes an exploratory case study with one revelatory case [3]. An overall objective for this research has been to understand better how Maestro can be more effective in managing its product development. This objective was initially proposed by Maestro's management for a master's thesis study conducted by one of Maestro's employees [4]. In this paper, the study was extended with an additional analysis by an external researcher. Overall, the research activities consisted of three steps (Fig. 2).

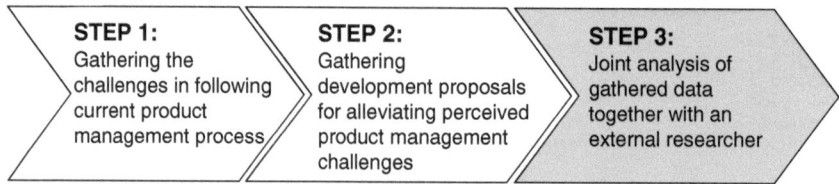

Steps 1 and 2 have been conducted internally by Maestro's employees

Fig. 2. Conducted research steps

The first two of the research steps have focused on gathering empirical data. These steps have been conducted internally within Maestro and are described in closer detail in Section 4.1. The third step, focusing on analyzing the data, is described in Section 4.2.

4.1   Data Gathering

The data gathering began by contacting eleven experts responsible on a diverse range of product related tasks in Maestro (Table 1). The experts were all employed by Maestro. Their work experience varied from 3 to 20 years. Each of the experts was sent Maestro's recently documented product management process description, along with a questionnaire questioning the essential challenges in following it. The responses for the questionnaire were either received via email or were written down during face to face meetings by one of the co-authors of this paper, as preferred by the interviewees.

In the second step, all gathered product management challenges were summarized and sent to the experts together with a new questionnaire asking for product management improvement proposals. Experts' responses were gathered in a similar manner as during the previous step.

As a result of the two first research steps, a total of 113 statements, each describing one perceived challenge or improvement proposal, were gathered from the expert group (Table 1). The method for analyzing these statements is described in the following section.

Table 1. Democraphics of data gathering

Source of statements	Respondents	Gathered statements
Software Developers	4	47
Customer Support	1	6
Sales	1	15
Project and Product Managers	3	28
Management	2	17
TOTAL:	*11*	*113*

4.2   Data Analysis

The gathered statements containing either challenges or improvement proposals were exported to an organization-specific network diagram. Each of the statements was represented as an individual text box. Each text box was color-coded in order to illustrate which part of the organization the statement originated from. Two of the authors then independently worked independently on copies of the diagram, adding associations between statements and moving similar statements closer to each other. This step of analysis resulted with two different interpretations of gathered data, each described as a map of interconnected clusters with similar statements next to each other (Fig. 3).

Fig. 3. Visual shapes of the knowledge maps created independently by two of the authors

The created network diagrams can be considered as knowledge maps, a visual display of captured information and relationships [5]. A knowledge map can serve as an inventory. It is a 'picture' of what exists in an organization or a 'network' of where it is located [6]. Knowledge maps have been reported to be an excellent way to capture and share explicit knowledge in organizational contexts [7], helping to support cognitive processing by reducing cognitive load and enhancing the representation of relationships among complex constructs [8]. Each way that one organizes information can create new knowledge and understanding.

The two different knowledge maps were then compared and discussed in order to find common interpretation of gathered data. The results of such dialogue are presented in section 5.

5   Results

Comparison of the two knowledge maps revealed three main themes (*requirements gathering, customer collaboration,* and *decision making*) in the gathered data along with several sub-themes (Fig. 4).

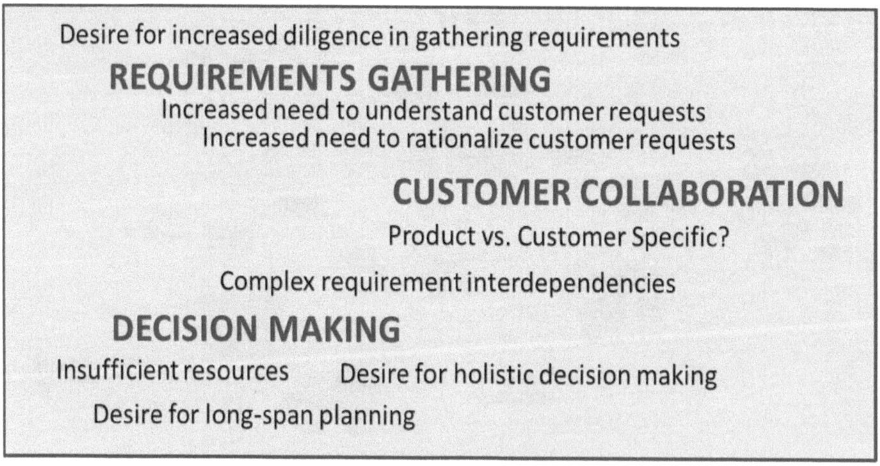

Desire for increased diligence in gathering requirements

REQUIREMENTS GATHERING
Increased need to understand customer requests
Increased need to rationalize customer requests

CUSTOMER COLLABORATION
Product vs. Customer Specific?

Complex requirement interdependencies

DECISION MAKING
Insufficient resources   Desire for holistic decision making
Desire for long-span planning

Fig. 4. Identified themes and sub-themes in gathered data

These themes are discussed below in the contexts of perceived product management challenges (section 5.1) and development proposals (section 5.2).

5.1   Perceived Product Management Challenges

Independently of this study, Maestro has recently responded to its increasing coordination challenges by introducing more rigorous product management processes. Along with the introduced processes, people have begun to specialize and share information more in explicit and documented form. As Maestro's culture has started to shift from flexible product management towards rigorous product management processes, old ways of working have begun to be a source of problems. Since the shift towards rigorous processes is still recent, the consequences of holding on to flexible working culture are not perhaps still fully understood.

Maestro's personnel have noticed that the way customers' wishes are elicited may have a significant impact on decision making. Currently, everyone seems to have their own way of submitting proposals.

"The same customer need is submitted multiple times from different viewpoints" –Sales

"There are already large amount of submitted requirements. Hence, determining the keywords for finding similar existing requirements is virtually impossible. The search for potentially similar requirements results with more than 200 requirements, none of which seems to be relevant. As a result, I submit a new requirement." –Product Manager

One typical challenge is that the customer need is often stated in terms of the customer's desired solution rather than the problem customer is facing.

"Submitted customer need may evolve to be something completely different. The one submitting the customer need should not be just a typist, who writes precisely what customer says." –Product Manager

When customers' wishes have been incompletely gathered, it has been difficult to determine what the customer really wanted and how the customer's wishes may be related to the other requirements. This challenge is made even more difficult with the fact that agreed ways of eliciting requirements are occasionally bypassed:

"Customers contact occasionally software developers directly." -Software Developer

"Small product related decisions are sometimes made informally. Unfortunately, quite often the impact of these decisions will turn out to be significant at later phases" –Software Developer

Gathering a diverse set of information about each of the customer's wishes would be important because making implementation decisions have turned out to be complex problem. There are always more requirements to implement than resources would allow. A commonly used approach to deal with this problem is to prioritize requirements. The design problem at Maestro, however, has proved to be much more complex in reality than existing prioritization methods can deal with. As an example, proposed requirement may have a significant impact to Maestro's other products. Before making final implementation decisions, one need to take a holistic view and determine how the proposed requirement would best serve Maestro's business purposes as a whole.

"Making implementation decisions are sometimes difficult, because the requested feature may be related to more than one application. Implementing the request into one product could potentially harm the functionality of other products. Hence, there are sometimes reluctance to process the request further for decision making" –Product Manager

Sometimes, the best option is to implement the requirements as a tailored delivery to a single customer. This may, in fact, be one significant factor making product management difficult at Maestro. Customer deliveries tend to have a higher priority compared to product development.

> "Sales case for a specific customer may override product decisions." -Software Developer

> "Product development suffers because of large customer delivery projects. If product development would have more resources, we would have the possibility to implement more of those requirements that would reduce the workload in customer support." – Product Manager

As Maestro's business has grown and become more diverse, current product management processes have turned out to be ineffective in coping with the complexity of the design problem. Maestro has currently nearly 1400 requirements waiting to be implemented in the requirements repository. Gathering customer requests hence seems not to be a problem. Requirements are gathered at greater pace than Maestro can digest.

> "The throughput of decision making process is currently slow. Some of the requests will never be processed. Some of the needs change over time. The impact of a requirement to other products and modules is not always fully understood" –Company Management

It is evident, that there is a need to adjust the product management practices in order to find more effective ways in dealing with the product management challenges.

5.2   Development Proposals

Maestro's employees have started to wish for increased discipline in following processes. Primary objective for following processes appears to be to gain a holistic understanding of the product related needs.

> "All requests should go through the same process, so that they their impact to the whole would be determined and understood. The challenge here is that processing information would be much more time and resource consuming than it currently is" -Company Management

> "We do not necessarily need to plan the product in the longer term than we currently do. However, we need to address the requests in a more holistic way. I mean, we would make decisions with more careful judgment rather than trying to gather short term wins from the customer delivery projects" -Company Management

In order to understand the elicited requirements better, people at Maestro want to pay more attention on the way requirements are elicited:

> "We need to have a standardized way of eliciting the requirements that guides to document clearly the underlying objective of the customer requirement. Furthermore, we currently do not keep track how the requirement has evolved over time. We need to be able to create a holistic understanding for the requests submitted into the Events Management System." –Product Manager

> "We need to gather at least following information for each customer request: Who is the customer? What is the context of the request? Why the request is needed? What problem the request is supposed to solve? Who can provide further information of the request? Who has been involved in the discussions?" –Software Developer

The Product Managers' role was considered important in developing deeper understanding of the requirements.

"We could have better guidance on how to follow processes. The use of Event Management System already guides us slightly towards more rigorous behaviour, but much more improvement could be gained through Product Managers' active and professional conduct. Product Managers have the ability to take a holistic view for the product. This would help them to make better decisions compared to project managers or software developers, who focus on one requirement at a time." –Software Developer

"The owner of the requirement should lead the problem solving. The preferred way would be to hold a meeting or perhaps use social media. The discussions related to the requirement should be decomposed to topics such as: what was discussed, what is the solution, what are the main issues ,so that the empty spots can be filled" –Software Developer

"It is good that customer can submit development proposals themselves, but the product manager should have enough time and resources to filter the requests, remove redundancy and further develop the proposals. The customer wishes should be pre-treated already at the beginning of the process so that time would not be wasted in enhancing and designing wishes that are not doable." –Company Management

The quest towards understanding the customer and the product-related needs as a whole appears to need a new kind of thinking at Maestro.

"We need to able to challenge the proposed requirement in a customer-driven way. Why the requirement is necessary? Can it be solved with existing functionality? Too often we just submit the requirement as customer has said it and leave the customer with an expectation that the elicited requirements shall be further processed." –Product Manager

"Product development should be more proactive. We too often react to customers needs hastily" -Sales

If the holistic understanding of the product related needs can be crystallized and communicated, it could turn out to be useful in guiding the product development activities.

"We should have a long term plan for products that would help to comprehend on a higher level what are we doing now and why. Some persons may currently have a holistic view for the product but the others may not necessarily know the rationale behind the requirements. We all should have clearly articulated goals to pursue." –Software Developer

6   Discussion

The findings of this study provide support to a claim that there is a strong correlation between the nature of the problem at hand and the management style that is effective to deal with the problem [1, 9]. Organizations are rarely established as ends in themselves. They are instruments created to achieve other ends [9].

Maestro initially organized their product development in a flexible and collaborative manner. Making product related decisions seemed to be easy at that time, because the same people were involved in eliciting requirements, making decisions and implementing them. Furthermore, continuous face-to-face communication allowed Maestro's employees to share information with much richer format than with documents. This form of organization has been found to work very well in entrepreneurial organizations where speedy decision making is at a premium, provided that tasks are not too complex [9, p. 51]. This has been the case also at Maestro. Collaborative product development was positively experienced until the product management challenge started to grow and become more complex.

After several years of growth, Maestro reached a point, where the old management style begun to be ineffective. Consequently, Maestro was forced to find new ways of coordinating the increasing number of its employees. A major challenge at this point of Maestro's development was to move towards a more disciplined approach in order to avoid unmanageable levels of informational chaos while concurrently maintaining the ability understand critical contextual information that is vital in the continued development of Maestro's increasingly complex products. Maestro has adjusted to this challenge by introducing more rigorous product management processes. Many of the changes are in line with the suggestions proposed in the Market-Driven Requirements Engineering (MDRE) literature. As some examples, Maestro has started to:

— emphasize the use of its *requirements repository* [10], the Event Management System (EVM);
— follow a process that guides the development of elicited customer requests and market trends towards product requirements and implementation decisions (Fig. 1). This process has similarities with the reference framework for software product management [11]; and
— strengthen the role of Product Manager as suggested in [12].

These changes have not, however, provided sufficient support for Maestro's product management challenges. Requirements have been submitted to the repository with a greater pace than Maestro can process them. The more requirements repository grew, the more difficult it has become to manage requirements. Increased number of submitted requirements has made it harder to merge similar requirements together or manage dependencies between the requirements. This, in turn, has increased the chances that new redundant requirements will be submitted to the repository.

Perhaps one reason for slow requirement throughput, causing the repository to grow, is the difficulties in making decisions. Practice has shown that existing prioritization methods do not match the complexity of real world problems. The real challenge is rarely a matter of selecting right set of requirements based on their priorities. Rather, the challenge is to determine the complex ways how the requirement candidate is related to Maestro's large number of interrelated products and to determine the consequences the requirement candidate may introduce if implemented. Furthermore, there are always many potential ways of implementing the requirement. The requirement candidate may, for example, be implemented as: 1) a core functionality that many products share, 2) within one product, or 3) as a tailored feature for a single customer. Whatever the decision is, the rationale for it is too often left undocumented. This reduces the possibilities for software developers to implement the requirements in way that decision makers wanted.

Interestingly, Maestro's experiences on following MDRE-processes have already been well described within organizational studies:

> Standardized procedures and channels of communication are often unable to deal effectively with new circumstances, necessitating numerous ad hoc meetings and committees, which, because they have to be planned to fit rather than disrupt the normal mode of operation, are often too slow or too late for dealing with issues. Problems of inaction and lack of coordination thus become rife. In such circumstances the organization frequently becomes clogged with backlogs of work because normal routine has been disrupted, and complex issues float up the organizational hierarchy as members at each level find in turn that they are unable to solve them [9, p. 29].

To make matters worse, recent product management changes has also introduced new kinds of challenges. Following the newly established product management processes has led to specialization of people. People who are involved in hearing the customer needs are less and less involved in making decisions and implementing the requests. Consequently, important opportunities to utilize one's tacit knowledge and to communicate with others have been inadvertently broken (Fig. 5).

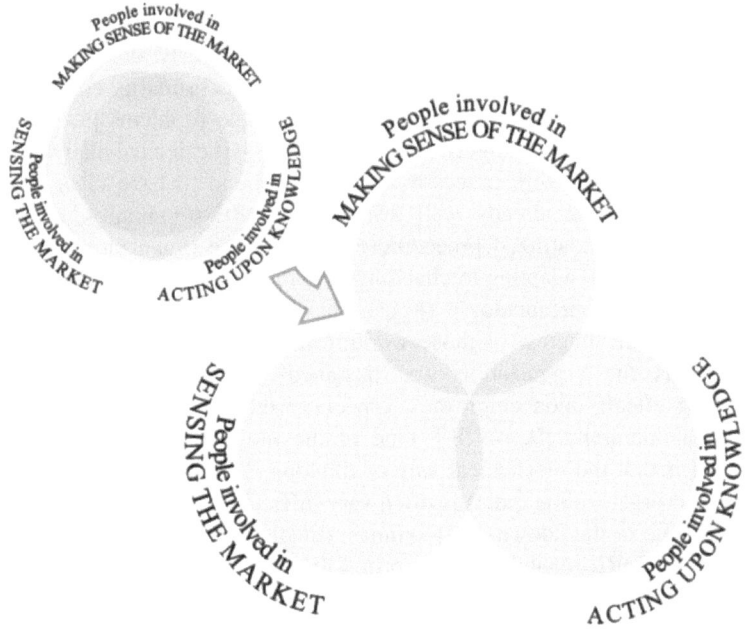

Fig. 5. Organizational change in Maestro as it has grown

Symptoms for these broken connections can be seen throughout the product management activities. As an example, products' strategic guidance has been weakened, because persons forming the corporate strategy are no longer actively involved in product management. As another example, software developers' understanding of requirements' rationale has started to degrade, because they see customers less frequently. It appears that, along with the more rigorous product management activities, Maestro has lost, to a certain degree, the benefits of intensive human collaboration that once helped them to deal with complex and turbulent situations.

Although people at Maestro wish for increased discipline when making product-related decisions, their underlying objective appears to differ, to a certain degree, from the majority of MDRE literature. Instead of relying on unjustified mathematical certainty in the search of the highest possible value with limited resources, Maestro wishes to increase the possibilities to understand the customer's challenges and needs more deeply and comprehensively. A common theme with the suggested product management improvements at Maestro was a desire to understand better the context of the proposed requirement.

7   Conclusions

The challenge of selecting requirements for product's future version is often dealt with processes that attempt to prepare gathered requirements one by one for rational decision making [13]. Organizations appear to be commonly seen as *machines* that are made up of interlocking parts, each playing a clearly defined role in the functioning of the whole [9]. This kind of organization is primarily coordinated with processes, that seek efficiency when dealing with stable problems [9, p. 46, 14, p. 127]. At times, this can prove highly effective; at others, it can have many unfortunate results [9]. Organizing with processes have been found to have clear limitations, many of which we are already well aware within RE-community. In particular, coordination with standardized procedures: a) can create organizational forms that have great difficulty in adapting to changing circumstances; b) can result in mindless and unquestioning bureaucracy; c) can have unanticipated and undesirable consequences as the interest of those working in the organization take precedence over the goals the organization was designed to achieve; and d) can have dehumanizing effects upon employees, especially those at the lower levels of the organizational hierarchy [9, p. 28.]. One of the most basic problems of modern management is that the mechanical way of thinking is so ingrained in our everyday conceptions of organization that it is often very difficult to organize in any other way [9, p. 6]. Despite of the known shortcomings, standardized procedures still appear to be the solution MDRE-related literature primarily offers [13].

The findings of this paper supports the argument, that organizations may also be seen as *organisms* that constantly try to adapt to changing circumstances, evolving to organizational forms of which mechanical organization is just one possibility [9]. The experiences learned from Maestro raises important questions for RE-research: Are we within RE community still locked too much in to the classical management theory suggesting that organizations can or should be rational systems that operate in as efficient a manner as possible? Managers today face a new set of problems, products of a volatile and unforgiving environment. How in an age of rapid change do you create organizations that are as adaptable and resilient as they are focused and efficient? [15]. Control is critical, but all too often it comes at the cost of initiative, creativity, and passion—the essential building blocks of organizational success [15]. Those on the front lines must be informed and empowered so they can do the right thing for customers without having to ask permission [15].

The fact that organizational studies were able to describe and explain Maestro's current product management challenges suggests that organizational studies form a fruitful discipline for seeking ideas for new kinds of product management approaches. In particular, we could learn from organizational studies:

— What types of currently useful organizational forms exist for application to RE's specific, and software engineering's in general, dilemma of accelerating complexity?
— In what kind of context a particular type of organization is effective?
— What are the key mechanisms needed to manage and coordinate particular types of organizations resulting in improved RE management?
— How does the choice of organizational form affect the way products are managed and the efficacy of their eventual products?

Finding answers for these questions may help the RE community to find new ideas to deal with design problems that are complicated, complex or even chaotic [16].

References

1. Greiner, L.E.: Evolution and revolution as organizations grow. Harvard Business Review (July-August 1972)
2. Polanyi, M.: Tacit Dimension. The University of Chicago Press, London (1966)
3. Yin, R.K.: Case Study Research: Design and Methods. Sage Publications (1994)
4. Hietaranta, K.: Tuotehallinnan tietoprosessin haasteet ja kehittäminen ohjelmistoyrityksessä. Lappeenranta University of Technology, Faculty of Technology Management, Industrial Management, vol. Master of Science, p. 102. Lappeenranta University of Technology, Lappeenranta (2011)
5. Vail, E.F.I.: Knowledge Mapping: Getting Strated With Knowledge Management. Information Systems Management 16, 16–23 (1999)
6. Egbu, C., Suresh, S.: Knowledge Mapping Techniques within The Construction Industry: An Exploratory Study. In: CIB 2008 Performance and Knowledge Management (2008)
7. Wexler, M.N.: The who, what and why of knowledge mapping. Journal of Knowledge Management 5, 249 (2001)
8. O'Donnell, A.M., Danserau, D.F., Hall, R.H.: Knowledge Maps as Scaffolds for Cognitive Processing. Educational Psychology Review 14, 71–86 (2002)
9. Morgan, G.: Images of Organization. Sage Publications, Thousand Oaks (1996)
10. Regnell, B., Brinkkemper, S.: Market-Driven Requirements Engineering for Software Products. In: Aurum, A., Wohlin, C. (eds.) Engineering and Managing Software Requirements. Springer (2005)
11. van de Weerd, I., Brinkkemper, S., Nieuwenhuis, R., Versendaal, J., Bijlsma, L.: Towards a Reference Framework for Software Product Management. In: 14th IEEE International Requirements Engineering Conference, pp. 319–322. IEEE Computer Society (2006)

12. Ebert, C.: The impacts of software product management. Journal of Systems and Software 80, 850–861 (2007)
13. Jantunen, S., Lehtola, L., Gause, D.C., Dumdum, U.R., Barnes, R.J.: The Challenge of Release Planning: Visible But Not Seen? In: 5th International Workshop on Software Product Management (IWSPM 2011) in Conjunction with 19th IEEE International Requirements Engineering Conference (2011)
14. Ståhle, P., Grönroos, M.: Dynamic Intellectual Capital. Tummavuoren kirjapaino Oy, Vantaa (2000)
15. Hamel, G.: Moon Shots for Management. Harvard Business Review (2009)
16. Snowden, D.J., Boone, M.E.: A Leader's Framework for Decision Making. Harvard Business Review (November 2007)

Author Index